SOUTH CAROLINA
A Documentary Profile of the Palmetto State

SOUTH CAROLINA
A Documentary Profile of the Palmetto State

Compiled and Edited by
ELMER D. JOHNSON *and* KATHLEEN LEWIS SLOAN

UNIVERSITY OF SOUTH CAROLINA PRESS
COLUMBIA, S. C.

For EUGENE B. SLOAN,
who would have reveled in it.

ACKNOWLEDGMENTS

Acknowledgment and appreciation are expressed to the following individuals and publishers for permission to quote from the following works:

David Kohn, *Internal Improvement in South Carolina, 1818–1828* (Washington, 1938); William W. Ball, Jr., *The State That Forgot: South Carolina's Surrender to Democracy*, by William Watts Ball (Indianapolis: Bobbs-Merrill Co., 1932); Robert Marsden Wallace, *The History of South Carolina*, by David Duncan Wallace, 4 vols. (New York: American Historical Society, Inc., 1935); The Graniteville Company, *Essays on Domestic Industry . . .* , by William Gregg (Graniteville, S.C.: Graniteville Co., 1945); J. Evans Eubanks, *Ben Tillman's Baby* (Augusta, Ga., 1950).

University of South Carolina Press: D.D. Wallace, *South Carolina: A Short History, 1520–1948* (Columbia, 1961); Robert L. Meriwether, ed., *The Papers of John C. Calhoun*, Vol. I (Columbia, 1959); Mary C. Simms Oliphant, et al., eds., *The Letters of William Gilmore Simms*, 5 vols. (Columbia, 1952–1956); Arney R. Childs, ed., *The Private Journal of Henry William Ravenel* (Columbia, 1947); Ben Robertson, *Red Hills and Cotton* (Columbia, 1960).

University of California Press, Frank J. Klingberg, *Carolina Chronicle: the Papers of Commissary Gideon Johnston, 1707–1716* (Berkeley, 1946); Oxford University Press, Allan Nevins, ed., *America Through British Eyes* (New York, 1948); Alfred A. Knopf, Inc., V.O. Key, *Southern Politics* (New York, 1949); University of Chicago Press, J.H. Easterby, ed., *The South Carolina Rice Plantation . . .* (Chicago, 1945); Garrett and Massie, Inc., A.G. Holmes, *Thomas Green Clemson* (Richmond, 1937); E.P. Dutton & Co., Inc., Richard Hakluyt, *The Principal Navigations, Voyages . . .* (London: Dent, 1926); Devin-Adair Co., William D. Workman, Jr., *The Case for the South* (New York, 1960); Harper & Row, Publishers, Inc., John Gunther, *Inside U.S.A.* (New York, 1951); Random House, Clyde T. Ellis, *A Giant Step* (New York, 1966).

University of North Carolina Press: Edgar W. Knight, ed., *A Documentary History of Education in the South Before 1860*, 3 vols. (Chapel

Hill, 1949–1952); Duncan Clinch Heyward, *Seed from Madagascar* (Chapel Hill, 1937); Ernest McPherson Lander, Jr., *A History of South Carolina, 1865–1960* (Chapel Hill, 1960).

The State Company, W.W. Boddie, *History of Williamsburg* (Columbia, 1923); The R.L. Bryan Company, James Henry Rice, Jr., *Glories of the Carolina Coast* (Columbia, 1925).

South Carolina Department of Archives and History: J.H. Wolfe, ed., *The Constitution of 1865* (Historical Commission of South Carolina, 1951); A.S. Salley, ed., *Commissions and Instructions from the Lords Proprietors* (Columbia, 1916), and A.S. Salley, ed., *Journal of the Commissioners of the Indian Trade* (Columbia, 1926).

Church Historical Society, *Historical Magazine of the Protestant Episcopal Church*, XIV (1954); *South Carolina Magazine* and the authors or next-of-kin, J. Roy Jones, III (Spring, 1940), Mrs. John A. Zeigler, VIII (March, 1945), Louise Jones DuBose, X (April, 1947), T.J. Tobias, XIII (March, 1950) and XVI (July, 1952); South Carolina Law Review, University of S.C., 3 *South Carolina Law Quarterly* 253 (1951).

Historical Society of South Carolina, *South Carolina Historical and Genealogical Magazine,* XLI (January, 1940), L (1949), LI (1950), LII (1951), LVIII (1957).

Newspapers: *The State,* Columbia, S.C.; *The News and Courier,* Charleston, S.C.; *The Anderson Independent,* Anderson, S.C.; Barnwell *People-Sentinel,* Barnwell, S.C.; *Charlotte Observer,* Charlotte, N.C.

PREFACE

This is an attempt to tell the South Carolina story in the words of the people who lived it.

The South Carolina story is an interesting one, covering a long period from the sixteenth century to the present. The story includes eras of peace and times of war, triumphs and troubles, progress and problems. Through its pages march the Indian and the Spaniard, the nobleman and the slave, the Yankee and the "Southron," the mill worker and the "boss." There were the "revolutions" of 1719, 1776, and 1876; the nullification of 1832; the secession of 1860; segregation and integration. When South Carolinians were not fighting the French or the Cherokees, the British or the Yankees, they were fighting among themselves, not always with guns, as in the Tory war of 1780–1783, but with words and laws, dividing the people of the state into Up Country and Low Country, Anglicans and Dissenters, Nullifiers and Unionists, Scalawags and Red Shirters, Reformers and Conservatives, Democrats, Republicans, and Independents. To South Carolinians and others, the story has been a long, proud, and glorious one.

Source materials for South Carolina history are plentiful. From the beginning there are firsthand accounts of major events, descriptions of most of the political leaders, accounts of wars, domestic wrangles, political troubles, and natural catastrophes. There are stories of life among the early settlers, too, which unfold the social, economic, educational, and religious history of the state. Government records, for the most part, are preserved, and many have been published. After 1732, an accurate and fairly complete history of the province and the state could be written from the information contained in the Charleston newspapers alone. Many travel accounts, by more or less objective outsiders, have been preserved, and from them a relatively unbiased description of life in South Carolina can be obtained.

In general, the problem has been not to find source material, but to select, condense, and arrange reports in order to tell a complete, connected story. Because of economic depression following the Civil War, the greatest dearth of material occurred in that period, until about 1914.

In the selections used, the original words of the sources are preserved, except in a few cases where paraphrasing has been noted. Some changes in form have been made in the interest of clarity for the modern reader. Punctuation, spelling, and capitalization, in most cases, have been made to conform to current usage. Paragraph structure has been changed occasionally, and some sentences have been rearranged. In one or two instances, information originally in tabular or statistical form has been converted into narrative. Omitted material has been noted by ellipses, again with a few exceptions, where several omissions in close conjunction would have created confusion. In all cases the purpose has been to present a continuous account, in clear and easy reading style, while retaining, as far as possible, the actual wording of the original.

Because of the controversy over the two subjects, contrasting accounts of the first shot at Fort Sumter and the Burning of Columbia have been included.

Newspapers, travel accounts, government documents and reports, yearbooks and handbooks, private letters, diaries and journals—all of these various sources have been employed in an attempt to present a complete picture of South Carolina. For every single item used, a dozen were available. Those selected were chosen for authenticity, for clarity of style and expression, for pertinence of the information contained, for interest, and for the objectivity—or lack of it, as the case may be—of the point of view of the writer. Most of the information is presented from the viewpoint of South Carolina. But, for contrast, a number of outsiders' accounts, both critical and laudatory, are included.

Use has also been made of the histories written about the state, especially those of D. D. Wallace, although he was not a "contemporary" of all the events about which he wrote. With some exceptions, all authors were contemporary, but it was necessary at times to use a few others to present certain times or events in the life of the state.

All in all, this is the South Carolina story. It is for South Carolinians and for all those who are interested in the state, one of the thirteen original colonies, and the part it has played in American life.

CONTENTS

SOUTH CAROLINA

A Documentary Profile of the Palmetto State

I
THE PERIOD OF EXPLORATION

South Carolina's history as an English colony began with the settlement of Charles Town in 1670, but that was almost a century and a half after the first Europeans set foot on Carolina soil. Long before, the French and the Spanish had explored the Atlantic coast, with the Spanish pushing as far as the mountains, both attempting settlements. Neither was successful, and their combined effect on South Carolina history was relatively insignificant.

Although some Europeans, including the two brothers John and Sebastian Cabot, had sailed along the Carolina coast before 1520, exploring for the English, it is believed that in that year the first Europeans landed in what is now South Carolina. This landing was by Spanish seamen from Santo Domingo, who sailed for the Carolina coast to find new lands and to obtain Indian slaves. Because of this exploration, Lucas Vasquez de Ayllón, an auditor from Santo Domingo, laid claim to the Carolina area, which he called "Chicora." He obtained a grant to the land from the king of Spain, basing his territorial claim on the discovery made by his pilot, Francis de Gordillo. De Allyón's was not a proprietary claim, but permission to foster settlement, which eventually gave him the status of governor. In 1526, de Allyón attempted to establish a settlement in the Winyaw Bay area, but he died in the attempt, along with many of his followers. Internal disruption and starvation among the survivors drove them back to Santo Domingo after the death of their leader.

In 1540, another Spanish explorer, Hernando De Soto, came overland from Florida, across Georgia, entered what is now South Carolina, and crossed the western part of the state into the North Carolina mountains. From there he continued southwestward, to his death and to eternal fame as the discoverer of the Mississippi River.

On May 27, 1561, a Spanish ship captained by Angel de Villafane sailed into Port Royal with a group of colonists who had survived the unsuccessful De Lund colonization attempt on the Gulf of Mexico. These colonists, exhausted from trying to settle North American territory, decided that the vague area of Santa Elena was unworthy of a colony.

The French also claimed Carolina, basing their right on a voyage made along the coast above the Cape Fear River by John Verrazzano in 1524. In 1562 this expedition was led by Jean Ribaut in an attempt to establish a French settlement in the Port Royal area. The colony was intended to provide a refuge for the persecuted French Huguenots, but it was unsuccessful. The few survivors of the ill-fated expedition determined to return to France. Weeks were spent in constructing a flimsy craft, the first ever built in the New World. But disaster struck soon after they had left American shores: the ocean was becalmed, and soon they had consumed all of their food and water. During the voyage, they turned cannibal when it was determined that one must be sacrificed if the others were to live. Finally, upon nearing the coast of France, the craft was sighted by an English vessel and towed to shore.

In 1566, the Spanish, having destroyed another French settlement the previous year, extended their claims northward along the coast in the form of forts and missionary stations. One presidio or fort was established in Santa Elena, located somewhere north of the Savannah River. Fort San Felipe, another of the forts built by the Spanish, was burned in 1577 after an Indian attack forced the soldiers and settlers to withdraw farther south along the coast. The Spanish returned to build another presidio the next year, probably on the same spot, called San Marcus.

In 1566, Captain Juan Pardo led his men from San Felipe into the back country in search of gold or a route to Mexico. The route Pardo followed is uncertain, but he did establish a fort somewhere on the edge of the Carolina mountains. After 1586, the Spanish withdrew from South Carolina, but they maintained their posts across the Savannah River in Georgia for another century and their permanent settlement at St. Augustine. Their supremacy in Florida was uncontested until 1761.

English interest in North America dates back to the voyage of John Cabot in 1497. No attempt was made at a settlement, however, before Sir Walter Raleigh's unfortunate "Lost Colony" on Roanoke Island, North Carolina, in 1584.

On October 30, 1629, Charles I of England granted the Carolina area to Sir Robert Heath, following successful settlements in Virginia and Massachusetts. No colony in Carolina resulted from this grant, however.

In 1663, Charles II decided that the Heath patent was in default and granted Carolina to eight wealthy Englishmen, friends and benefactors who had aided him in regaining his throne in 1660. The "Lords Proprietors of Carolina" sent out exploring expeditions, drew up a form of government for their proposed colony, and finally, in 1670, achieved a permanent settlement on the Ashley River.

The following excerpts are representative rather than inclusive, and are designed to give a general picture of the South Carolina region and its original inhabitants, as first seen by Europeans.

1. *Hernando De Soto's Visit to Cofitachiqui, 1540*

In the fall of 1539, Hernando De Soto, a Spanish explorer with a party of some 500 European and Indian followers, set out from Tampa Bay in Florida to explore the southern part of the present United States. He journeyed northeast across Georgia and early in 1540 reached the Indian town of Cofitachiqui, located, it is believed, at Silver Bluff, on the South Carolina side of the Savannah River, about 13 miles below Augusta, Georgia. After his visit there, De Soto took the Queen of Cofitachiqui as hostage and continued on his expedition, passing through the present counties of Edgefield, McCormick, Abbeville, Anderson, and Oconee before continuing into North Carolina. At least four accounts of his trip have been preserved. The following is taken from "The Narrative of the Expedition of Hernando de Soto, by the Gentleman of Elvas."

[The Gentleman of Elvas on De Soto's Expedition]

. . . He set out for Cofitachiqui, capturing three Indians in the road, who stated that the mistress of that country had already information of the Christians, and was waiting for them in a town. He sent to her by one of them, offering his friendship and announcing his approach. Directly as the Governor arrived, four canoes came towards him . . . . After a little time, the Cacica came out of the town, seated in a chair, which some principal men having borne to the bank, she entered a canoe. Over the stern was spread an awning, and in the bottom lay extended a mat where there were two cushions, one above the other,

Theodore H. Lewis, ed., "The Narratives of the Expedition of Hernando De Soto By the Gentleman of Elvas," *Spanish Explorers in the Southern United States, 1528–1543,* in the series *Original Narratives of Early American History,* gen. ed. J. Franklin Jameson (New York: Charles Scribner's Sons, 1907), 72–176. Original source materials for this and the other early periods of exploration are not plentiful, but they are adequate for most of the important events.

upon which she sat, and she was accompanied by her chief men, in other canoes . . . .

The Cacica presented [the Governor] much clothing of the country from the shawls and skins that came in the other boats; and drawing from over her head a large string of pearls, she threw them about his neck, exchanging with him many gracious words of friendship and courtesy. She directed that canoes should come to the spot, whence the Governor and his people passed to the opposite side of the river. So soon as he was lodged in the town, a great many turkeys were sent to him. The country was delightful and fertile, having good interval lands upon the streams; the forest was open, with abundance of walnut and mulberry trees. The sea was stated to be distant two days' travel . . . . The Cacica, observing that the Christians valued the pearls, told the Governor that, if he should order some sepulchres that were in the town to be searched, he would find many . . . . They examined those in the town, and found three hundred and fifty pounds weight of pearls, and figures of babies and birds made of them.

The inhabitants are brown of skin, well formed and proportioned. They are more civilized than any people seen in all the territories of Florida, wearing clothes and shoes . . . .

In the town were found a dirk and beads that had belonged to Christians, who, the Indians said, had many years before been in the port, distant two days' journey. He that had been there was the Governor-licentiate Ayllón, who came to conquer the land, and, on arriving at the port, died, when there followed divisions and murders among the chief personages, in quarrels as to who should command; and thence, without knowing anything of the country, they went back to Spain . . . .

The natives were asked if they had knowledge of any great lord farther on, to which they answered, that twelve days' travel thence was a province called Chiaha, subject to the chief of Cosa. The Governor then resolved at once to go in quest of that country, and being an inflexible man . . . there were none who would say a thing to him after it became known that he had made up his mind . . . .

On the third day of May, the Governor set out from Cofitachiqui; and, it being discovered that the wish of the Cacica was to leave the Christians, if she could, giving them no guides . . . because of the outrages committed upon the inhabitants, there never failing to be men of low degree among the many . . . the Governor ordered that she should be placed under guard, and took her with him. This treatment, which was not a proper return for the hospitable welcome he had received, makes true the adage: For well doing, etc.; and thus she was carried away on foot with her female slaves . . . . We traveled through her territories a hundred leagues, in which, according to what we saw, she was greatly obeyed; whatsoever she ordered being performed with diligence and efficacy.

2. *Laudonnière's Account of Ribaut's Settlement at Port Royal, 1562*

ADMIRAL COLIGNY, LEADER OF THE PROTESTANT FRENCH HUGUENOTS IN THEIR STRUGGLE FOR SURVIVAL AGAINST THE CATHOLIC MAJORITY OF SIXTEENTH-CENTURY FRANCE, LOOKED TO THE NEW WORLD FOR A REFUGE FOR HIS PEOPLE. AFTER THE FAILURE OF A COLONY IN BRAZIL, HE SENT JEAN RIBAUT WITH ABOUT 150 MEN TO FOUND A SETTLEMENT IN "FLORIDA." AFTER REACHING LAND NEAR ST. AUGUSTINE, RIBAUT'S PARTY CONTINUED NORTH ALONG THE COAST TO PORT ROYAL, WHERE A GROUP OF HIS MEN WERE LEFT TO HOLD THE POSITION WHILE HE RETURNED TO FRANCE FOR MORE SETTLERS AND SUPPLIES. WAR IN FRANCE PREVENTED RIBAUT'S IMMEDIATE RETURN; AFTER SEVERAL MONTHS, IN THE FACE OF STARVATION, THE SMALL BAND OF SETTLERS AT PORT ROYAL SET OUT ACROSS THE OCEAN IN AN OPEN BOAT. ONLY A FEW SURVIVED THE GRUESOME VOYAGE, IN WHICH THE MEN TURNED CANNIBAL; THESE FEW WERE PICKED UP BY AN ENGLISH VESSEL.

[Laudonnière]

Having cast anchor, the captain with his soldiers went on shore, and he himself went first on land; where he found the place as pleasant as was possible, for it was all covered with mighty, high oaks and infinite stores of cedars . . . smelling so sweetly, that the very fragrant odor made the place seem exceedingly pleasant. As we passed through these woods we saw nothing but turkey cocks flying through the forests; partridges, gray and red, little different from ours, but chiefly in bigness. We heard also within the woods the voices of stags, bears, lusernes, leopards and divers other sorts of beasts unknown to us. Being delighted with the place, we set ourselves to fishing with nets, and we caught such a number of fish that it was wonderful . . . .

From René Laudonnière, *A Notable Historie Containing Four Voyages Made by Certain French Captaines into Florida* . . . , reprinted in Richard Hakluyt, *The Principal Navigations, Voyages, Traffiques and Discoveries of the English Nation, 1589-1600*, 8 vols. (London: Dent, 1926) and (New York: E. P. Dutton & Co., Inc., and Everyman's Library), VIII, 461–86. Reprinted by permission of E.P. Dutton & Co.

A little while after . . . we perceived a troop of Indians, who . . . at our coming on shore . . . came to salute our general according to their barbarous fashion. Some of them gave him skins of chamois, others little baskets made of palm leaves, some presented him with pearls, but no great number. Afterward they went about to make an arbor to defend us in that place from the parching heat of the sun. But we would not stay as then. Wherefore the captain thanked them much for their good will, and gave presents to each of them, wherewith he pleased them so well before he went thence, that his sudden departure was nothing pleasant unto them . . . .

Notwithstanding, we returned to our ships, where after we had been but one night, the captain in the morning commanded to be put into the pinnace a pillar of hard stone fashioned like a column, wherein the arms of the King of France were engraven, to plant the same in the fairest place he could find. This done, we embarked ourselves, and sailed three leagues toward the West, where we discovered . . . a little island, separated from the firm land, where we went on shore; and by commandment of the captain, because it was exceedingly fair and pleasant, there we planted the pillar upon a hillock open round about to view, and environed with a lake half a fathom deep of very good and sweet water . . . .

Captain Ribaut therefore knowing the singular fairness of this river, desired by all means to encourage some of his men to dwell there, well foreseeing that this thing might be of great importance for the King's service, and the relief of the commonwealth of France . . . . Whereupon John Ribaut, being as glad as might be to see his men so well willing, determined the next day to search the most fit and convenient place to be inhabited . . . . Which done . . . he found a very open place . . . where he went on land, and seeing the place fit to build a fortress in, and commodious for them that were willing to plant there, he resolved . . . to cause the size of the fortification to be measured out. And considering that there stayed but six and twenty there, he caused the fort to be made in length about sixteen fathoms, and thirteen in breadth, with flanks according to the portion thereof . . . . We worked so diligently, that in a short space the fort was made in some sort defensible, in which meantime John Ribaut caused victuals and warlike ammunition to be brought for the defense of the place . . . . This being done, we sailed toward the North, and then we named this river Port Royal, because of the largeness and excellent fairness of the same . . . . [Following the departure of Ribaut, the 26 men left behind at first fared well, but later their supplies gave out. They were forced to beg food from their Indian neighbors, and a fire in the encampment destroyed much of their equipment.]

Behold therefore how our men behaved themselves very well hitherto, although they had endured many great mishaps. But misfortune or rather the last judgment of God would have it, that those which could not be overcome by fire nor water, should be undone by their ownselves . . . . They entered therefore into partialities and dissensions, which began about a soldier named Guernache, who was a drummer of the French bands; who, as it was told to me, was very cruelly hung by his own captain, and for a small fault which the captain also using to threaten the rest of his soldiers who stayed behind under his obedience . . . was the cause that they fell into a mutiny, because that many times he put his threatenings into execution; whereupon they so chased him, that at last they put him to death. . . . When they came home again they assembled themselves together to choose one to be governor over them whose name was Nicholas Barré, a man worthy of commendation, and one who knew so well to quit himself of his charge, that all rancour and dissension ceased among them . . . and they lived peaceably one with another.

During this time they began to build a small pinnance, with hope to return to France, if no succors came to them, as they expected from day to day. And though there was no man among them that had any skill, notwithstanding necessity, which is the master of all science, taught them the way to build it. After it was finished, they thought of nothing else saving how to furnish it with all things necessary to take their voyage . . . and used such speedy diligence that within a short time afterward they made it ready . . . . In the mean season the wind came so fit for their purpose that it seemed to invite them to put to sea; which they did without delay . . . . But being drunken with too excessive joy . . . they put themselves to sea . . . with so slender victuals, that the end of their enterprise became unlucky and unfortunate. . . .

After so long time and tedious travels, God in his goodness, using His accustomed favor, changed their sorrow into joy, and showed unto them the sight of land. . . . A small English bark boarded the vessel, in which there was a Frenchman who had been on the first voyage unto Florida, who easily knew them and spoke to them, and afterwards gave them meat and drink. . . . The Englishmen . . . resolved to put on land those that were most feeble, and to carry the rest unto the Queen of England, which purposed at that time to send into Florida. Thus you see in brief that which happened to them which Captain John Ribaut had left in Florida [South Carolina].

3. Robert Heath's Grant to Carolina, 1629

FRENCH HUGUENOTS REFUGEEING IN ENGLAND PROBABLY LED THE FIRST ENGLISH ATTEMPT TO COLONIZE CAROLINA. IN 1629, THE ATTORNEY GENERAL OF ENGLAND, SIR ROBERT HEATH, RECEIVED FROM KING CHARLES I A GRANT TO "CAROLANA," IDENTIFIED AS ALL THE LANDS IN AMERICA, FROM SEA TO SEA, BETWEEN NORTH LATITUDES 31 AND 36. ONE GROUP OF FRENCHMEN WAS SENT OUT IN 1630, BUT LANDED OFF COURSE AND REMAINED IN VIRGINIA. NO FURTHER SERIOUS EFFORT WAS MADE TO SETTLE "CAROLANA" UNDER THE HEATH GRANT.

[The Grant]

Whereas our beloved and faithful subject and servant Sir Robert Heath, Knight, our attorney general, kindled with a certain laudable and pious desire as well as of enlarging the Christian religion as our Empire and increasing the trade and commerce of this Kingdom: A certain region or territory to be hereinafter described, in our lands in the parts of America betwixt one and thirty and six and thirty degrees of northern latitude inclusively placed (yet hitherto untilled, neither inhabited by ours or the subjects of any other Christian king, prince or state, but in some parts of it inhabited by certain barbarous men who have not any knowledge of the Divine Deity), he being about to lead thither a colony of men large and plentiful, professing the true religion, sedulously and industriously applying themselves to the culture of the said lands and to merchandising to be performed by industry and at his own charges and others by his example. . . . Know therefore that we . . . do give, grant and confirm all that river of St. Matthew on the south side, and all that river . . . of the Great Pass on the north side, and all the lands . . . lying . . . in or between the said rivers . . . to the ocean upon the east side and so to the west and so far as the continent extends itself with all and every . . . islands . . . which lie inclusively within the degrees of 31 and 36 or northern latitude . . . to the foresaid Sir Robert Heath. . . .

William L. Saunders, ed., *The Colonial Records of North Carolina,* 10 vols. (Raleigh: P. M. Hale, State Printer, 1886–90), I, 20–33.

Know that we . . . do erect and incorporate them into a province and name the same Carolana, or the Province of Carolana . . . . Furthermore know ye that we . . . do give power to the said Sir Robert . . . to form, make and enact and publish . . . what laws soever may concern the public state of the said province, or the private profit of all according to the wholesome directions of and with the counsel, assent and approbation of the freeholders of the same province . . . .

Furthermore, lest the way to honours and dignities may seem to be shut and altogether barred up to men honestly born and who are willing to undertake this present expedition and are desirous in so remote and far distant a region to deserve well of us and of our Kingdom in peace and war, for that do we . . . give full and free power to the foresaid Sir Robert Heath . . . to confer favours, graces, and honors upon those well deserving citizens that inhabit within the foresaid province and the same with whatever titles and dignities (provided they be not the same as are now used in England) to adorn at his pleasure.

4. *The Second Charter of Carolina, June 30, 1665*

CHARLES II WAS RESTORED TO THE THRONE OF ENGLAND IN 1660, FOLLOWING THE PERIOD OF THE COMMONWEALTH, AND HIS RESTORATION WAS AIDED GREATLY BY MEMBERS OF THE ENGLISH NOBILITY. IN 1663, THE PROVINCE OF CAROLINA WAS GRANTED BY THE KING TO EIGHT OF THESE NOBLES, IN RETURN FOR THEIR FRIENDSHIP AND ASSISTANCE. SINCE THE FIRST CHARTER COVERED ROUGHLY THE SAME TERRITORY AS THE HEATH GRANT, WHICH WAS NOT ANNULLED UNTIL AFTER 1663, AND SINCE THE NOBLE "PROPRIETORS" DESIRED A LARGER GRANT, A SECOND CHARTER WAS ISSUED ON JUNE 30, 1665. WITH THE EXCEPTION OF THE BOUNDARIES, THIS CHARTER WAS VIRTUALLY IDENTICAL TO THE FIRST.

[The Second Charter]

Charles the Second, by the grace of God, of Great Britain, France and Ireland, King and Defender of the Faith, &c.

Whereas, by our letters patents, bearing date the four and twentieth day of March, in the fifteenth year of our reign, we were graciously pleased to grant unto our right trusty, and right well-beloved cousin and counsellor Edward, Earl of Clarendon, our high chancellor of England; our right trusty and right entirely beloved cousin and counsellor, George Duke of Albemarle, master of our horse; our right trusty and well-beloved William, now Earl of Craven; our right trusty and well-beloved counsellor, John Lord Berkeley; our right trusty and well-beloved counsellor, Anthony Lord Ashley, Chancellor of our Exchequer; our right trusty and well-beloved counsellor Sir George Carteret, Knight and baronet, Vice-Chancellor of our Household; our right trusty and well-beloved Sir John Colleton, Knight and baronet; and Sir William Berkeley, Knight, all that province . . . called Carolina, extending from the north end of the island, called Luke Island, which lyeth in the southern Virginia seas, and within six and thirty degrees of the northern latitude; and to the west, as far as the south seas; and so respectively as far as the river

B. R. Carroll, ed., *Historical Collections of South Carolina*, 2 vols. (New York: Harper, 1836), II, 38–57.

of Mathias, which bordereth upon the coast of Florida and within one and thirty degrees of the northern latitude, and so west in a direct line, as far as the south seas aforesaid.

Now, know ye that we, at the humble request of the said grantees, . . . and as a further mark of our especial favour towards them, we are graciously pleased to enlarge our said grant to them, according to the bounds and limits hereafter specified . . . all that province . . . extending north and eastward, as far as the north end of Carahtuke River, or inlet, upon a straight westerly line, to Wyonoake Creek, which lies within, or about the degrees of thirty-six and thirty minutes northern latitude, and so west, in a direct line as far as the south seas; and south and westward, as far as the degrees of twenty-nine inclusive northern latitude, and so west in a direct line as far as the south seas; together with all and singular ports, harbours, bays, rivers and islets, belonging unto the province or territory aforesaid. And also, all the soil, lands, fields, woods, mountains, ferms, lakes, rivers, bays and islets; . . . with the fishing of all sorts of fish, whales, sturgeons, and all other royal fishes in the sea . . . together with the royalty of the sea, upon the coast within the limits aforesaid. And moreover, all veins, mines, and quarries, as well discovered as not discovered, of gold, silver, gems and precious stones, and all other whatsoever; be it of stones, metal, or any other thing found or to be found within the province . . . aforesaid.

And furthermore, the patronage and avowsons of all the churches and chapels, which as Christian religion shall increase within the province . . . shall happen hereafter to be erected; together with license and power to build and found churches, chapels, and oratories in convenient and fit places . . . and to cause them to be dedicated and consecrated according to the ecclesiastical laws of our Kingdom of England . . . .

To have, hold, use, exercise and enjoy the same as amply, fully, and in as ample manner as any bishop of Durham in our Kingdom of England, ever heretofore had, held, used, or enjoyed . . . and them the said Edward Earl of Clarendon, George Duke of Albemarle, William Earl of Craven, John Lord Berkeley, Anthony Lord Ashley, Sir George Carteret, Sir John Colleton, and Sir William Berkeley, their heirs and assigns . . . . We do by these presents, for us, our heirs and successors for the same; to have, hold, possess and enjoy the said province . . . to them . . . for ever, to be holden of us, or our heirs and successors . . . .

Know ye therefore moreover, that we, reposing special trust and confidence in their fidelity, wisdom, justice and provident circumspection for us, our heirs and successors, do grant full and absolute power . . . to them the said Edward Earl of Clarendon [and others] . . . for the good and happy government of the said whole province or territory, full power and authority to erect, constitute and make several counties, baronies, and colonies, of and with the said province . . . and also to ordain, make and enact, and under their seals, to publish any laws and constitutions whatsoever, either appertaining to the public state of the said province or territory, or of any distinct or particular county, barony or colony . . . according to their best discretion, by and with the advice, assent and approbation of the freemen of the said province . . . or of the greater part of them, of their delegates or deputies, whom for enacting of the said laws, when and as often as need shall require, we will that the said Edward Earl of Clarendon [and others]. . . shall from time to time, assemble in such manner and form as to them shall seem best . . . . Which laws so passed as aforesaid, to be published . . . . Provided, nevertheless, that the said laws be consonant to reason, and as near as may be conveniently, agreeable to the laws and customs of this our realm of England.

And to the end the said province or territory, may be the more happily increased by the multitude of people resorting thither. . . . Therefore, we . . . do give and grant by these presents, full power . . . unto all the leige people of . . . England, or elsewhere within any other of our dominions . . . to transport themselves and families into the said province . . . and there to settle themselves, dwell and inhabit, any law, act, statute, ordinance, or other thing to the contrary notwithstanding. . . .

And further, of our especial grace. . . we have given, granted and confirmed . . . that . . . Edward, Earl of Clarendon [and others] . . . may assign, alien grant, demise or enfeoff the premises or any part or parcel thereof to him or them, that shall be willing to purchase the same; and to such person and persons, as they shall think fit, to have, and to hold to them the said person or persons, their heirs and assigns in fee simple or in fee tail, or for the term of life or lives . . . by such rents, services and customs, as shall seem fit to them . . . .

And because many persons born and inhabiting in the said province for their deserts and services may expect, and be capable of marks of honour and favour . . . we do by these presents, give and grant unto the said Edward Earl of Clarendon [and others]. . . full power and authority to give and confer unto, and upon such of the inhabitants of the said province . . . as they shall think, do, or shall merit the same, such marks of favour and titles of honour, as they shall think fit, so as their titles or honours be not the same as are enjoyed by, or conferred upon, any of the subjects of this our Kingdom of England . . . .

And further also, we do by these presents. . . give and grant, license to them, the said Edward Earl of Clarendon [and others] . . . full power, liberty and license, to erect, raise and build within the said province . . . such and so many forts, fortresses, castles, cities, burroughs, towns, villages, and other fortifications whatsoever . . . as shall be thought fit and convenient for the safety and welfare of the said province . . . .

And because that in so remote a country, and situate among so many barbarous nations, the invasions as well of savages as other enemies, pirates and robbers may probably be feared; therefore, we have given . . . unto the said Edward Earl of Clarendon [and others]. . . power by these presents to levy, muster, and train up all sorts of men, of what condition soever, or wheresoever born . . . and to make war and pursue the enemies aforesaid, as well by sea as by land, and by God's assistance, to vanquish and take them . . . .

Also . . . we do give and grant unto the said Edward Earl of Clarendon [and others] . . . full power and authority to exercise martial law against mutinous and seditious persons of those parts; such as shall refuse to submit themselves to their government, or shall refuse to serve in the war, or shall fly to the enemy . . . .

And because it may happen, that some of the people and inhabitants of the said province, cannot in their private opinions conform to the public exercise of religion according to the liturgy, forms and ceremonies of the church of England, or take or subscribe the oaths and articles made and established in that behalf . . . our will and pleasure there is, and we do . . . give and grant unto the said Edward Earl of Clarendon [and others] . . . liberty and authority, by such means and ways as they shall think fit, to give and grant unto such person or persons, . . . such indulgencies and dispensations, in that behalf . . . as they . . . shall in their discretion think fit and reasonable. And that no person or persons, unto whom such liberty shall be given, shall be any way molested, punished, disquieted or called in question for any differences in opinion or practice, in matters of religious concernment, who do not actually disturb the civil peace of the province . . . . But all and every such person and persons, may from time to time, and at all times, freely and quietly have and enjoy his and their judgments and consciences, in matters of religion, throughout all the said province . . . .

5. *The Role of the Barbadians in the Settlement of Carolina*

THE ISLAND OF BARBADOS IN THE WEST INDIES HAD BEEN SETTLED IN
THE EARLY SEVENTEENTH CENTURY BY THE ENGLISH. IN A FEW DECADES,
A RICH SUGAR-PLANTATION ECONOMY HAD DEVELOPED THERE. BY 1660,
HOWEVER, FOR ECONOMIC AND OTHER REASONS, SOME OF THE BAR-
BADIANS WERE INTERESTED IN MOVING ELSEWHERE. WHEN THEY HEARD
OF THE FIRST CHARTER OF CAROLINA, THEY SENT TO THE PROPRIETORS
THE "PROPOSALS OF SEVERAL GENTLEMEN OF BARBADOS," GIVEN IN THE
FIRST EXCERPT BELOW. THE REPLY WAS ENCOURAGING; FROM THE VERY
BEGINNING, ENGLISH PLANTERS FROM BARBADOS AND OTHER WEST IN-
DIAN ISLANDS PLAYED AN IMPORTANT ROLE IN THE SETTLEMENT OF
SOUTH CAROLINA.

[Proposal of August 12, 1663, signed by Tho:
Modyford and P. Colleton]

Several gentlemen and persons of good quality in this Island . . . do
earnestly with all humility desire and request that those Noble under-
takers who have lately obtained a charter of the Province of Carolina
from his Royal Majesty will be pleased . . . to send them an exemplifi-
cation of their said Charter . . . and together therewith and by virtue of
the said Charter to impower and authorize the aforesaid adventurers or
such of them as the said Grantees shall judge fit . . . to take up and
purchase of the natives such certain tract or tracts of land as they and
such as they shall send thither to settle may or shall find fit for the
accommodation of themselves and of their friends . . . in the form and
manner of a county or corporation, not exceeding or about the quantity of
thirty or thirty-two miles square, or one thousand square miles, which they
desire may be called the Corporation of the Barbados Adventurers . . . .
They also desire that a proclamation may be procured from the King
directed to all Governors in these his Majesty's plantations, requiring

Collections of the Historical Society of South Carolina (Richmond: William
Ellis Jones), V, 10–12.

them not to hinder any free and unengaged persons from going thither to settle . . . but rather to further the good and speedy settlement thereof . . . Barbados, Aug. 12, 1663 [.]

[Letter from the Lords Proprietors to the
"Gentlemen of Barbados," dated August 30, 1663]

Sirs, We find by a letter . . . from you . . . that several people of Barbados have inclinations to settle and plant in some part of the Province of Carolina, whom we desire by all ways and means to encourage, and that it may appear so, have inclosed sent you a declaration and proposals under the hands of all those concerned . . . which paper we desire you to communicate to all people that are disposed that way and to give what copies you please to such as shall desire them . . . .

We conceive it will be advantageous to the King, his people, and more particularly to your Islanders to go on with the settlement, where the air is, we are informed, wondrous healthy and temperate, the land proper to bear such commodities as are not yet produced in the other plantations and such as the nation spends in great quantities, as wine, oil, currants, raisins, silks, &c. . . . by means whereof the money of the nation that goes out for these things will be kept in the King's Dominions, and the planting part of the people will employ their time in planting those commodities that will not injure nor overthrow the other plantations which may very well happen if there be a very great increase of sugar works and more tobacco, ginger, cotton, and indigo made. . . . These reasons we conceive will convince the most concerned in your Islands to promote this work. . . .

Collections of the Historical Society of South Carolina (Richmond: William Ellis Jones), V, 13–14.

6. *William Hilton's View of the Carolina Coast, 1663*

The Barbadian planters followed up their interest in Carolina by sending Captain William Hilton in a ship to explore the coast. Hilton's account of his voyage, published in 1664 as "A True Relation of a Voyage Upon Discovery of Part of the Coast of Florida," was high in its praise of Carolina. The following excerpt gives Hilton's description of the plants and animals along the coast.

[Captain William Hilton]

Now our understanding of the land of Port Royal, River Jordan, and River Grandie, or Edisto, is as follows: The lands are laden with large tall oaks, walnut and bays, except facing on the sea, it is most pines tall and good. The land generally, except where the pines grow, is a good soil, covered with black mold, in some places a foot, in some places half a foot, deep; and in other places less, with clay underneath mixed with sand; and we think it may produce anything as well as most parts of the Indies that we have seen. The Indians plant in the worst land because they cannot cut down the timber on the best, and yet have plenty of corn, pompions, water-melons, and musk-melons. Although the land be overgrown with weeds through their laziness, yet they have two or three crops of corn a year as the Indians themselves inform us. The country abounds with grapes, large figs, and peaches; the woods with dear, conies, turkeys, quails, curlews, plovers, teal, herons; and as the Indians say, in winter with swans, geese, cranes, duck and mallard, and innumerable other waterfowls, whose names we know not, which lie in the rivers, marshes, and on the sands. There are oysters in abundance, with a great store of mussels; a sort of fair crabs, and a round shell-fish called horse-feet. The rivers are stored plentifully with fish that we saw leap and play. There are great marshes, but most as far as we saw of little worth, except for a root that grows in them the Indians make good bread of. The land we

Collections of the Historical Society of South Carolina (Richmond: William Ellis Jones), V, 24–25.

suppose is healthful, for the English that were castaway on that coast in July were there most part of that time of year that is sickly in Virginia; and not withstanding hard usage, and lying on the ground naked, yet had their perfect healths all the time. The natives are very healthful; we saw many very aged amongst them. The air is clear and sweet, the country very pleasant and delightful; and we could wish that all they that want a happy settlement, of our English nation, were well transported thither.

7. Robert Sandford's Port Royal Discovery, 1666

PARTLY AS A RESULT OF SIR WILLIAM HILTON'S EXPEDITION, THE BAR-
BADIAN PLANTERS DECIDED TO ESTABLISH A COLONY IN CAROLINA, AND
WITH THE PROPRIETORS' PERMISSION A SETTLEMENT WAS MADE IN MAY,
1664, AT THE MOUTH OF THE CAPE FEAR RIVER, IN WHAT IS NOW
NORTH CAROLINA. THIS COLONY LASTED ONLY TWO OR THREE YEARS,
BUT IN 1666 ROBERT SANDFORD, WHO WAS "SECRETARY AND REGISTER,"
LEFT AN INTERESTING ACCOUNT OF ITS PLANTING AND ALSO OF A VOYAGE
ALONG THE SOUTH CAROLINA COAST. THIS ACCOUNT WAS LAUDATORY,
AND THE "TESTIMONIAL" OF SIX OF HIS MEN, WHICH ACCOMPANIED
HIS REPORT, PICTURED CAROLINA AS AN ATTRACTIVE PLACE FOR FUTURE
SETTLEMENTS.

[Robert Sandford]

I spent the remainder of this day and the best part of the next in this
sound—went ashore on several islands, found them as good firm land as
any we had seen, exceedingly timbered principally with live oak and
large cedar and bay trees . . . . On one of them we entered a pleasant
grove of spruce, shading a very clear pasture of fine grass in which we
roused a brave herd of deer and thence called it the Discoverer's Park.
This island contains some hundreds of acres, both wood and marsh,
proper for planting, grazing and for feeding swine. And all the islands
that were in our view (some few small ones excepted that were only
marsh) are in all appearance alike good, proportionable to their bigness,
with high banks richly crowned with timber of the largest size. So that of
what we saw in this sound only, might be found habitation for thousands
of people with conveniences for their stock, of all kinds in such a way of
accommodation as is not common. And if the sound go through to such
a great river as the Indians talk of (which seems very probable) it will
put an additional value upon the settlements that shall be made in it. It
abounds besides with oyster banks and such heaps of shells as which no

Collections of the Historical Society of South Carolina (Richmond: William Ellis Jones), V, 77, 80, 82.

time can consume, but this benefit it has in common with all the rivers between this and Harv[e]y Haven which are stored with this necessary material for lime for many ages, and lying so conveniently that whatever near river or creek you can think fit to set a house on, there you may place your lime kiln also, and possibly in the bank just by, or very near, find clay for your brick tile, and the great and frequent schools of fish we met with gives us expectation of advantage and employment that way also. In sum, we could see of nothing here to be wished for but good store of English inhabitants, and that we heartily pray for. . . .

CHARLESTON HARBOR

The River lies in a bay between Harvey Haven and Cape St. Romain wherein we found 7 or 8 fathom of water very near the shore, and not the least appearance of shoals or dangers in any part of it. It shows with a very fair large opening clear of any flats or barring in the entrance only before the eastern points. We saw a breach but not far out. I persuade myself that it leads into an excellent country, both from the commendation the Indians gave it, and from what I saw in my ranging on the eastern part of Harv[e]y Haven the next neighboring land to this. Wherefore, in hopes that it may prove worthy of the dignity, I called it the River Ashley, from the right honorable Anthony Lord Ashley.

TESTIMONIAL BY SIX OF SANDFORD'S CREW

We whose names are hereunto subscribed having accompanied Lt. Col. Robert Sandford in a voyage of discovery on the coast and rivers of this province to the southward and westward of Cape St. Romain as far as the River Port Royal, and being all of us persons well experienced in the nature and quality of the several soils in these regions, and some of us by means of our travels thoroughly acquainted with most part of America, northern and southern continent, and islands, do hereby declare and testify to the whole world that the country which we did see from the River Grandy, now Harvey Haven, to Port Royal inclusive, doth for richness and fertility of soil, for excellence of rivers, havens, creeks, and sounds; for abundance of good timber of diverse sorts and many other requisites, both to land and sea building, and for sundry rare accommodations, both for navigation and plantation, exceed all places that we know in possession of our nation in the West Indies, and we do assure ourselves that a colony of English here planted with a moderate support in their infant tendency would in a very short time improve themselves to a perfect commonwealth enjoying a self-sufficiency of all the principal necessities to life, and abounding with a great variety of superfluity for the invitation of foreign commerce and trade, and which for its site and productions would be of more advantage to our native country, the Kingdom of England, and to the grandeur of our Sovereign Lord the King his Crown and dignity, than any (we may say all) his other dominions in America. And we do further avow that this country may be more securely settled and cheaply defended from any of the attempts of its native inhabitants than any of those other places which our countrymen have refined from the dross of Indian barbarism.

In witness whereof we have hereunto set our hands this 14th of July, 1666.

8. *Privileges Promised to the Carolina Settlers, 1666*

SEVERAL "PROMOTION PAMPHLETS" APPEARED IN THE LATE 1660s, AD-
VERTISING IN GLOWING TERMS THE ATTRACTIONS OF CAROLINA AS A PLACE
FOR SETTLEMENT. ONE OF THESE, ROBERT HORNE's *Brief Description
of Carolina*, CARRIES AS A SUPPLEMENT THE FOLLOWING LIST OF
"PRIVILEGES" PROMISED TO ANYONE WHO WOULD SETTLE IN CAROLINA.

[Robert Horne]

The chief of the privileges are as follows: First, there is full and free
liberty of conscience granted to all, so that no man is to be molested or
called in question for matters of religious concern; but every one to be
obedient to the civil government, worshipping God after their own way.

Secondly, there is freedom from custom, for all wine, silk, raisins, currants, oil, olives and almonds, that shall be raised in the Province for 7
years, after 4 tons of any of those commodities shall be imported in one
bottom. Thirdly, every freeman and freewoman that transport themselves
and servants by the 25 of March next, being 1667, shall have for himself,
wife, children and men-servants, for each 100 acres of land for him and
his heirs for ever, and for every woman-servant and slave 50 acres, paying at most ½ pence per acre per annum, in lieu of all demands, to the
Lords Proprietors. Provided, always, that every man to be armed with a
good musket full bore, 10 pounds of powder and 20 pounds of bullet, and
six months provisions for all, to serve them whilst they raise provision in
that country.

Fourthly, every man-servant at the expiration of their time, is to have
of the country 100 acres of land to him and his heirs forever, paying only
½ pence per acre, per annum, and the women 50 acres of land on the
same conditions; their masters also are to allow them two suits of apparel
and tools such as he is best able to work with, according to the custom of
the country. Fifthly, they are to have a Governor and Council appointed
from among themselves, to see the laws of the Assembly put in due exe-

A. S. Salley, ed., *Narratives of Early Carolina, 1650–1708* (New York: Charles
Scribner's Sons, 1911), 71–73.

cution; but the Governor is to rule but 3 years, and then learn to obey; also he has no power to lay any tax, or make or abrogate any law, without the consent of the Colony in their Assembly.

Sixthly, they are to choose annually from among themselves, a certain number of men, according to their divisions, which constitute the General Assembly with the Governor and his Council, and have the sole power of making laws, and laying taxes for the common good when need shall require. These are the chief and fundamental privileges, but the Right Honorable Lords Proprietors have promised (and it is their interest so to do) to be ready to grant what other privileges may be found advantageous for the good of the Colony.

[This list of privileges was followed by an appeal to skilled workmen to come to Carolina, and a bit of advice was added for the ladies.] If any maid or single woman have a desire to go over, they will think themselves in the golden age, when men paid a dowry for their wives; for, if they be but civil and under 50 years of age, some honest man or other will purchase them for their wives.

9. *The Proprietors' Instructions to Commander Joseph West, 1669*

WHEN THE FIRST GROUP OF SETTLERS WAS READY TO SAIL FOR CARO-
LINA, THE PROPRIETORS APPOINTED JOSEPH WEST COMMANDER OF THE
THREE VESSELS IN THE LITTLE FLEET AND TEMPORARY GOVERNOR
BETWEEN ENGLAND AND THE BERMUDA ISLANDS.

[Proprietors]

To our trusty and well-beloved Joseph West, Greeting—

We do hereby constitute and appoint you during our pleasure, Governor and commander in chief of our fleet and the persons embarked in it, bound for Carolina, or that shall embark in our said fleet before its arrival in Barbados . . . .

Mr. West, you are with all possible speed to sail with the fleet under your command for Kinsaile, in Ireland, where you are to endeavor to get twenty or twenty-five servants for our proper account and as soon as you have gotten them on board you are to sail directly to Barbados . . . .

Mr. West, God sending you safe to Barbados, you are there to furnish yourself with cotton seed, indigo seed, ginger roots; which roots you are to carry planted in a tub of earth, that they may not die before your arrival at Port Royal; also in another tub you may carry some canes . . . , also several sorts of vines of that island, and some olive sets . . . .

You are from time to time to give us accounts of your proceedings herein, how much land you have fallen, what you have planted, and how every specie thrives, also what cattle you have received from Virginia, how many calves you have every year, and what quantity of hogs, sheep, etc., and what you want . . . .

And you yourself, also are to observe and follow such orders and directions as from time to time you shall receive from us. And in all things to govern yourself as unto the duty and place of a governor and commander in chief doth belong, which place you are to execute till another governor

W. J. Rivers, *Sketch of the History of South Carolina* (Charleston: McCarter and Co., 1856), 342–45.

for that part of our Province that lies to the southward or westward of Cape Carteret shall appear with commission under our hands and the Great Seal of our Province, to whom you are then to submit, and this commission to become void to all intents and purposes. . . .

10. *Nicholas Carteret's Relation of the First English Landings in South Carolina, 1670*

GOVERNOR WEST'S INSTRUCTIONS WERE DATED JULY 27, 1669, BUT IT WAS NOT UNTIL MARCH, 1670, THAT THE CAROLINA COAST WAS REACHED. IN THE MONTHS BETWEEN THERE HAD BEEN STOPS IN IRE-LAND, BERMUDA, BARBADOS, AND THE BAHAMAS. TWO OF THE ORIGINAL THREE SHIPS WERE LOST TO STORMS, AND ONLY THE *Carolina* REACHED LAND. AFTER STOPPING AT THE PORT ROYAL AREA, THE SHIP CONTINUED TO ALBEMARLE POINT.

[Nicholas Carteret]

Sailing from Bermuda February 26th, we came up with the land between Cape Romana and Port Royal and in 17 days the weather being fair and the wind not friendly, the long boat went ashore the better to inform us as to the certainty of the place where we supposed we were. Upon its approach to the land a few of the natives who were upon the strand made fires and came towards us whooping in their own tongue and manner, making signs also where we should best land, and when we came ashore they stroked us on the shoulders with their hands, saying "Bony Conraro, Angles," knowing us to be English by our color (as we supposed). We gave them brass rings and tobacco at which they seemed well pleased. . . . A day or two after, the Governor, whom we took in at Bermuda with several others, went ashore to view the land . . . and as we drew to the shore a good number of Indians appeared clad with dear skins having with them their bows and arrows. . . . When we came up they gave us . . . some dear skins, some raw, some dressed, to trade with us for which we gave them knives, beads and tobacco, and glad they were of the market. By and by came their women clad in their moss robes, bringing their pots to boil a kind of thickening which they pound and make food of, and as they order it being dried makes a pretty sort of

Collections of the Historical Society of South Carolina (Richmond: William Ellis Jones), V, 165–68.

bread. They brought also plenty of hickory nuts, a walnut in shape and taste only differing in the thickness of the shell and the smallness of the kernel. The Governor and several others walking a little distance from the waterside, came to the hut palace of his majesty of the place, who meeting us took the Governor on his shoulders and carried him into the house in token of his cheerful entertainment. Here we had nuts and root cakes such as their women usually make as before, and water to drink, for they use no other liquor as I can learn. . . . While we were here his majesty's three daughters entered the palace, all in new robes of moss which they are never beholding to the tailor to trim up, with plenty of beads of divers colors about their necks. . . .

These Indians understanding our business to St. Helena told us that the Westoes, a ranging sort of people reputed to be man eaters, had ruinated that place, killed several of those Indians, destroyed and burned their habitations, and that they had come as far as Kiawah, doing the like there, the cassique of which place was within one sleep of us (which is 24 hours for they reckon after that way) with most of his people, whom in two days after came aboard us.

Leaving that place which is called Sowee [Modern-day Sewee], carrying the Cassique of Kiawah with us, a very ingenious Indian and a great linguist . . . we ran in between St. Helena and Combahee, where the distressed Indians sojourned, who were glad and crying "Hiddy doddy Comorado Angles, Westoe Skorrye" (which is as much as to say: English very good friends, Westoes are naught). They hoped by our arrival to be protected from the Westoes. . . . Many of us went ashore at St. Helena and brought back word that the land was good land, supplied with many peach trees, and a competence of timber, a few fig trees, and some cedar here and there, and that there was a mile and a half of clear land, fit ready to plant. . . .

The sloop which we have with us, bought at Bermuda, was dispatched to Kiawah, to view that land so much commended by the Cassique, brings back a report that the land was more fit to plant in than St. Helena, which begot a question, whether to remove from St. Helena thither, or stay. Some were of opinion it were more prudent forthwith to plant provisions where they were than betake themselves to a second voyage . . . [but] the Governor adhering for Kiawah, and most of us being of a temper to follow though we knew no reason for it. . . .

Thus we came to Kiawah. The land here and at St. Helena is much at one. The surface of the earth is a light blackish mold, under that is whiter, and about 3 or 4 feet is a clay . . . so is all the land I have seen.

11. *Indian Life and Customs*

MOST OF THE EARLY EXPLORERS AND VISITORS TO CAROLINA COMMENTED AT LENGTH ON THE NATIVES WHOM THEY SPOKE OF AS INDIANS. THOSE ALONG THE COAST, AND CONSEQUENTLY THOSE SEEN MOST AND DESCRIBED BY THE FIRST ENGLISHMEN, WERE OF THE MUSKHOGEAN FAMILY, LOOSELY ORGANIZED INTO SMALL TRIBES. MANY, OR MOST OF THE INDIANS, HAD ALREADY HAD SOME MEETINGS WITH WHITE MEN, USUALLY WITH THE SPANISH, AND THEREFORE WERE NOT ENTIRELY PRIMEVAL. THE FOLLOWING EXCERPTS GIVE SOME IDEA OF THE HOMES, DRESS, FOOD, AND TOWNS OF THE COASTAL INDIANS, AS THEY WERE FIRST OBSERVED. THE FIRST AUTHOR LISTED, "T.A.," DESCRIBED HIMSELF AS "GENTLEMAN," AND AS THE CLERK ON BOARD HM SHIP, THE *Richmond*. HE WAS THOUGHT TO HAVE BEEN EITHER THOMAS ASHE OR THOMAS AMY [AMORY?].

[T.A., Gentleman, Clerk on Board HM Ship,
the *Richmond,* in 1680]

The natives of the country are from time immemorial aboriginal Indians, of a deep chestnut color, their hair black and straight, tied various ways, sometimes oiled and painted, stuck through with feathers for ornament or gallantry, their eyes black and sparkling, little or no hair on their chins, well limbed and featured, painting their faces with different figures of a red or sanguine color, whether for beauty or to render themselves formidable to their enemies, I could not learn. They are excellent hunters, their weapons the bow and arrow, made of a reed, pointed with sharp stones, or fish bones; their clothing skins of the bear or deer, the skin dressed after their country fashion.

Manufactures, or arts amongst them I have heard of none, only little baskets made of painted reeds and leather dressed sometimes with black and red chequers colored. In medicine, or the nature of diseases, some

B. R. Carroll, ed., Historical Collections of South Carolina . . . , 2 vols. (New York: Harper, 1836), II, 80–81.

29

have an exquisite knowledge; and in the cure of scorbutic, venereal and malignant distempers are admirable; in all external diseases they suck the part affected with many incantations, philters and charms; in amorous intrigues they are excellent either to procure love or hatred; they are not very forward in discovery of their secrets, which by long experience are religiously transmitted and conveyed in a continued line from one generation to another, for which those skilled in this faculty are held in great veneration and esteem. Their religion chiefly consists in the adoration of the sun and moon; at the appearance of the new moon I have observed them with open extended arms then folded, with inclined bodies, to make their adorations with much ardency and passion; they are divided into many divisions or nations, governed by . . . petty princes, which our English call cassiques; their diet is of fish, flesh, and fowl, with Indian maize or corn; their drink, water; yet lovers of the spirits of wine and sugar. They have hitherto lived in good correspondence and amity with the English, who by their just and equitable carriage have extremely winned and obliged them; justice being exactly and impartially administered, prevents jealousies and maintains between them a good understanding, that the neighboring Indians are very kind and serviceable, doing our nation such civilities and good turns as lie in their power.

[Henry Woodward on a Westoe Voyage]

In the afternoon we met two Indians with their fowling pieces, sent by their chiefs to congratulate my arrival into their parts, who himself awaited my coming with divers others at the Westo River . . . . The two Indians we met had a canoe ready to pass us over, where so soon as we landed, I was carried to the captain's hut, who courteously entertained me with a good repast of those things they count rarities among them. . . . Having paddled about a league up, we came into sight of the Westo town . . . which stands upon a point of the river . . . . When we came within sight of the town I fired my fowling piece and pistol which was answered with a hollow and immediately thereupon they gave

A. S. Salley, ed., *Narratives of Early Carolina, 1650–1708* (New York: Charles Scribner's Sons, 1911), 132–33.

me a volley of fifty or sixty small arms. Here was a concourse of some hundreds of Indians, dressed up in their antique fighting garb . . . . The next day I viewed the town, which is built in a confused manner, consisting of many long houses whose sides and tops are both artificially done with bark, upon the tops of most whereof, fastened to the ends of long poles, hung the locks of hair of Indians they have slain. The inland side of the town being doubly palisadoed, and that part which fronts the river having only a single one . . . They had seldom less than one hundred fair canoes ready upon all occasions. They are well provided with arms, ammunition, trading cloth and other truck from the northward, for which at set times of the year they trade drest dear skins, furs and young Indian slaves.

[Robert Sandford]

Being entered the town we were conducted into a large house of circular form (their general house of State). Right against the entrance way a high seat of sufficient breadth for half a dozen persons, on which sat the Cassique himself, vouchsafing me that favor, with his wife on his right hand. . . . He was an old man of a large stature and bone. Round the house from each side the throne, quite to the entrance were lower benches filled with the whole rabble of men, women and children. In the center of this house is kept a constant fire, mounted on a great heap of ashes and surrounded with little low furrows. Capt. Cary and myself were placed on the higher seat on each side of the Cassique, and presented with skins, accompanied with their ceremonies of welcome and friendship (by stroking our shoulders with their palms and sucking in their breath the whilst). The town is situated on the side or rather in the skirts of a fair forest, in which at several distances are diverse fields of maize with many little houses straggling amongst them for the habitations of the particular families. On the east side and part of the south it hath a large prospect over meadows very spacious and delightful. Before the doors of their state house is a spacious walk rowed with trees on both sides, tall and full branched, not much unlike to elms, which serves for the exercise

A. S. Salley, ed., *Narratives of Early Carolina, 1650–1708* (New York: Charles Scribner's Sons, 1911), 91–92. Robert Sandford, "A Relation of a Voyage on the Coast of the Province of Carolina (1666)."

and recreation of the men, who by couple run after a marble bowl trolled out alternately by themselves, with six foot staves in their hands, which they toss after the bowl they contend for; an exercise approvable enough in the winter, but somewhat too violent (me thought) for that season and noontime of the day. From this walk is another less aside from the round house for the children to sport in.

READINGS

ADDITIONAL PRINTED SOURCE MATERIALS:

Carroll, B. R., ed. *Historical Collections of South Carolina, Embracing Many Rare and Valuable Pamphlets and Other Documents Relating to the History of That State from Its First Discovery to Its Independence in the Year 1776.* 2 vols.

Hodge, F. W., ed. *Spanish Explorers in the Southern United States, 1528–1543.*

Salley, Alexander, ed. *Narratives of Early Carolina, 1650–1708.*

South Carolina Historical Society. *Collections of the South Carolina Historical Society.* 5 vols.

CORRELATED TEXTS:

Snowden, Yates, ed. *History of South Carolina.* 2 vols. I, 3–65.

Wallace, David D. *History of South Carolina.* 4 vols. I, 3–81.

———. *South Carolina: A Short History,* 1–31.

II
THE PROPRIETARY PERIOD

The lords proprietors of Carolina retained their control of the province for over half a century, and during this period the settlement of the South Carolina coast was accomplished. Flattering reports of conditions in the new colony were published, and settlers were encouraged to come to Carolina from the British West Indies, England, Scotland, Ireland, and even from northern Europe. A provincial government was established in Charles Town, Negro slaves were imported by the thousands, and a plantation economy was firmly established by 1720. Most of the settlements remained within 25 miles of the coast and close to other waterways, although South Carolina Indian traders had pushed southward to the Gulf and westward to the Mississippi. By 1730 there were an estimated 8,000 whites and 12,000 slaves in South Carolina, and the latter were increasing faster than their masters.

It was a turbulent era, and the marvel is that the young colony survived. There was strife with the French, the Spanish, Indians, and pirates. There were difficulties between proprietors and colonists, governor and assembly, Anglicans and Dissenters, masters and slaves. The proprietors were responsible for the initial settlement, but once Carolina started growing they became neglectful and were less and less able to cope with its problems. The period of the Yamassee War, 1715–1718, showed plainly the weaknesses of the proprietary system and led in the end to the fall of the proprietary government. The "Revolution of 1719" was a bloodless one, but it was thorough. The proprietors were overthrown, and the king was asked to take over South Carolina as a royal colony. This he did officially in 1728, although the first royal governor did not arrive in Charles Town until 1730.

12. *The Fundamental Constitutions of March 1, 1670*

EVEN BEFORE THE FIRST SETTLERS HAD SAILED FOR CAROLINA, THE PROPRIETORS HAD PLANNED A "FORM OF GOVERNMENT" FOR THEIR COLONY. THESE FUNDAMENTAL CONSTITUTIONS WERE MORE THAN A FORM OF GOVERNMENT, FOR THEY VIRTUALLY CONTROLLED THE LIFE OF THE SETTLER, OR AT LEAST THEY WOULD HAVE, HAD THEY EVER BEEN ACCEPTED AND PUT INTO FULL EFFECT. ANTHONY ASHLEY-COOPER, ONE OF THE PROPRIETORS, AND HIS SECRETARY, JOHN LOCKE, WERE THE AUTHORS OF THE FUNDAMENTAL CONSTITUTIONS; LOCKE HAS USUALLY BEEN CONSIDERED MOST RESPONSIBLE. THE FEUDAL SYSTEM THAT WOULD HAVE EMERGED UNDER THESE CONSTITUTIONS WAS CONTRARY TO MUCH OF THE POLITICAL PHILOSOPHY THAT JOHN LOCKE LATER WROTE, BUT IT IS LIKELY THAT HE CONSIDERED SUCH A SYSTEM NECESSARY FOR A NEW GOVERNMENT IN A NEW WORLD. THERE WERE FIVE DIFFERENT SETS OF THE FUNDAMENTAL CONSTITUTIONS, ISSUED FROM 1669 TO 1698, VARYING IN LENGTH AND MINOR DETAILS. THEY AFFECTED SUCH MATTERS AS RELIGIOUS TOLERATION, GOVERNMENT, TRIAL BY JURY, AND REGISTRATION OF LAND TITLES, BIRTHS, MARRIAGES, AND DEATHS, BUT THEY WERE NEVER INSTITUTED IN THEIR FULL FORM. THE FOLLOWING EXCERPTS ARE TAKEN FROM THE SECOND SET, BECAUSE THIS WAS THE MOST COMPLETE VERSION AND THAT UNDER WHICH SETTLEMENT TOOK PLACE.

[From the Second Fundamental Constitutions]

Our sovereign Lord the King having, out of his royal grace and bounty, granted unto us the province of Carolina, with all the royalties, properties, jurisdictions and privileges of a county palatine, as large and ample as the county palatine of Durham, with other great privileges; for the better settlement of the government of the said place, and establishing the interest of the Lords Proprietors with equality and without confusion; and that the government of this province may be made most

B. R. Carroll, ed., *Historical Collections of South Carolina* . . . , 2 vols. (New York: Harper, 1836), II, 361–89.

agreeable to the monarchy under which we live, and of which this province is a part; and that we may avoid erecting a numerous democracy: we, the Lords and Proprietors of the province aforesaid, have agreed to this following form of government, to be perpetually established amongst us, unto which we do oblige ourselves, our heirs and successors, in the most binding ways that can be devised.

1. The eldest of the Lords Proprietors shall be Palatine . . . .

2. There shall be seven other chief offices erected, viz., the admirals, chamberlains, chancellors, constables, chief justices, high stewards, and treasurers; which places shall be enjoyed by none but the Lords Proprietors, to be assigned by lot . . . .

3. The whole province shall be divided into counties; each county shall consist of eight baronies, eight signiories, and four precincts; each precinct shall consist of six colonies.

4. Each signiory, barony, and colony shall consist of twelve thousand acres; the eight signiories being the share of the eight proprietors, and the eight baronies of the nobility; both which shares, being each of them one fifth part of the whole, are to be perpetually annexed, the one to the proprietors, the other to the hereditary nobility, leaving the colonies, being three fifths, amongst the people; that so in setting out, and planting the lands, the balance of the government may be preserved . . . .

9. There shall be just as many landgraves as there are counties, and twice as many cassiques, and no more. These shall be the hereditary nobility of the province, and by right of their dignity be members of parliament. Each landgrave shall have four baronies, and each cassique two baronies, hereditarily and unalterably annexed to, and settled upon, the said dignity . . . .

16. In every signiory, barony and manor, the respective lord shall have power, in his own name, to hold court-leet there; for trying of all causes both civil and criminal . . . .

17. Every manor shall consist of not less than three thousand acres, and not above twelve thousand acres, in one entire piece and colony; but any three thousand acres or more in one piece, and the possession of one man, shall not be a manor, unless it be constituted a manor by the grant of the palatine's court . . . .

21. Every lord of a manor, within his manor, shall have all the powers, jurisdictions and privileges, which a landgrave or cassique hath in his baronies.

22. In every signiory, barony, and manor, all the leet-men shall be under the jurisdiction of the respective lords . . . without appeal from

him. Nor shall any leet-man or leet-woman, have liberty to go off from the land of their particular lord, and live anywhere else, without licence obtained from their said lord, under hand and seal.

23. All the children of leet-men shall be leet-men, and so to all generations.

24. No man shall be capable of having a court-leet, or leet-men, but a proprietor, landgrave, cassique, or lord of a manor.

25. Whoever shall voluntarily enter himself a leet-man, in the registry of the county court, shall be leet-man . . . .

28. There shall be eight supreme courts. The first called the Palatine's Court, consisting of the Palatine and the other seven proprietors. The other seven courts, of the other seven great officers, shall consist each of them of a Proprietor, and six counsellors added to him . . . .

35. The chancellor's court, consisting of one of the proprietors, and his six counsellors . . . shall have the custody of the seal of the palatinate . . . and it shall not be lawful to put the seal of the palatinate to any writing, which is not signed by the Palatine or his deputy, and three other proprietors or their deputies . . . . To this court also belong all state matters, dispatches, and treaties with the neighboring Indians . . . .

37. The chief justice's court, consisting of one of the proprietors and his six counsellors . . . shall judge all appeals in cases both civil and criminal . . . .

38. The constable's court . . . shall order and determine of all military affairs . . . .

41. The admiral's court . . . shall have the care and inspection over all ports, moles and navigable rivers . . . and also all the public shipping of Carolina . . . and all maritime affairs. This court shall also have the power of the court of Admiralty . . . .

43. The treasurer's court . . . shall take care of all matters that concern the public revenue and treasury . . . .

44. The high-steward's court . . . shall have the care of all foreign and domestic trade, manufactures, public buildings, work-houses, highways . . . sewers . . . bridges . . . fairs, markets . . . and all things in order to the public commerce and health . . . also setting out and surveying of all lands . . . .

45. The chamberlain's court . . . shall have the care of all ceremonies, precedency, heraldry, reception of public messengers . . . the registry of all births, burials, and marriages . . . and shall also have power to regulate all fashions, habits, badges, games and sports . . . .

50. The grand council shall consist of the Palatine and seven proprietors, and the forty-two counsellors of the several proprietors' courts . . . .

51. The grand council shall prepare all matters to be proposed in parliament . . . .

55. The grand council shall meet the first Tuesday in every month . . . .

61. In every county there shall be a court, consisting of a sheriff, and four justices of the county . . . . These five shall be chosen and commissioned from time to time by the Palatine's court . . . .

64. No cause shall be twice tried in any one court, upon any reason . . . whatsoever.

66. The grand jury at the several assizes, shall, upon their oaths, and under their hands and seals, deliver in to the itinerant judges a presentment of such grievances, misdemeanors, exigencies or defects, which they think necessary for the public good of the county . . . .

68. In the precinct-court no man shall be a juryman under fifty acres of free-hold. In the county-court . . . no man shall be a grand jury man under three hundred acres of freehold . . . . In the Proprietors courts no man shall be a juryman under five hundred acres of freehold.

69. Every jury shall consist of twelve men; and it shall not be necessary that they should all agree, but the verdict shall be according to the consent of the majority.

70. It shall be a base and vile thing to plead for money or reward . . . .

71. There shall be a parliament, consisting of the proprietors or their deputies, the landgraves, cassiques, and one freeholder out of every precinct, to be chosen by the freeholders of the said precinct respectively . . . .

72. No man shall be chosen a member of parliament who hath less than five hundred acres of freehold . . . nor shall any have a vote in choosing the said member that hath less than fifty acres of freehold within the said precinct.

73. A new parliament shall be assembled the first Monday of the month of November every second year . . . . And if there shall be any occasion of a parliament in these intervals, it shall be in the power of the Palatine's court to assemble them in forty days notice, and at such time as the said court shall think fit; and the Palatine's court shall have power to dissolve the said parliament when they shall think fit . . . .

76. No act or order of parliament shall be of any force, unless it be ratified in open parliament during the same session, by the Palatine or his deputy, and three more of the Lords Proprietors or their deputies . . . .

78. The quorum of the parliament shall be one half of those who are members . . . .

81. There shall be a registry in every precinct, wherein shall be enrolled all deeds, leases, judgments, mortgages, and other conveyances, which may concern any of the land within the said precinct . . . .

84. There shall be a registry in every signiory, barony and colony, wherein shall be recorded all the births, marriages and deaths, that shall happen . . . .

92. All towns incorporate shall be governed by a mayor, twelve aldermen, and twenty-four of the common council . . . . The said common council shall be chosen by present householders of the said town . . . .

95. No man shall be permitted to be a freeman of Carolina, or to have any estate or habitation within it, that doth not acknowledge a God; and that God is publicly and solemnly to be worshipped.

97. But since those . . . who remove from other parts to plant there, will unavoidably be of different opinions concerning matters of religion, the liberty whereof they will expect to have allowed them, and it will not be reasonable for us on this account to keep them out . . . therefore any seven or more persons agreeing in any religion, shall constitute a church or profession, to which they shall give some name, to distinguish it from others . . .

101. No person above seventeen years of age shall have any benefit or protection of the law . . . who is not a member of some church or profession . . . .

102. No person of any other church or profession shall disturb or molest any religious assembly . . . .

107. . . . It shall be lawful for slaves, as well as others, to enter themselves and be of what church or profession any of them shall think best . . . but yet no slave shall hereby be exempted from that civil dominion his master has over him . . . .

110. Every freeman of Carolina shall have absolute power and authority over his negro slaves . . . .

111. No cause, whether civil or criminal, of any freeman, shall be tried in any court of judicature, without a jury of his peers . . . .

113. Whosoever shall possess any freehold in Carolina . . . shall . . . pay yearly unto the Lords Proprietors for each acre of land . . . one English penny, or the value thereof, to be as a chief rent . . . .

116. All inhabitants and freemen of Carolina above 17 years of age and under 60, shall be bound to bear arms, and serve as soldiers whenever the grand council shall find it necessary . . . .

117. A true copy of these Fundamental Constitutions shall be kept in a great book by the register of every precinct, to be subscribed before the said register. Nor shall any person . . . have any estate or possession in Carolina . . . who hath not before a precinct register subscribed these Fundamental Constitutions . . . .

118. Whosoever alien shall . . . subscribe these Fundamental Constitutions, shall be thereby naturalized.

119. In the same manner shall every person, at his admittance into any office, subscribe these Fundamental Constitutions.

120. These Fundamental Constitutions, in number a hundred and twenty, and every part thereof, shall be and remain the sacred and unalterable form and rule of Government of Carolina for ever. Witness our hands and seals, the first day of March, 1670.

13. *First Instructions for the Governor and Council, July 27, 1669*

THE LORDS PROPRIETORS HAD PREPARED, IN ADDITION TO THE FUNDA-
MENTAL CONSTITUTIONS, ORDERS AND INSTRUCTIONS FOR THE IMMEDIATE
GOVERNMENT OF THE FIRST SETTLEMENT. JOSEPH WEST WAS TO BE
COMMANDER OF THE THREE SHIPS AND THE FIRST GROUP OF SETTLERS
UNTIL THEY REACHED BARBADOS. THERE SIR JOHN YEAMANS, THE
LEADER OF THE BARBADIAN PLANTERS WHO WANTED TO SETTLE IN
CAROLINA, WAS TO APPOINT THE FIRST GOVERNOR. WILLIAM SAYLE WAS
YEAMAN'S CHOICE, AND UNDER HIS DIRECTION THE EXPEDITION REACHED
THE SOUTH CAROLINA COAST ON MARCH 15, 1670. PORT ROYAL WAS
THE ORIGINAL SITE SELECTED FOR THE FIRST SETTLEMENT IN CAROLINA.

[Proprietors and their Instructions]

In regard the number of people which will at first be set down at
Port Royal will be so small, together with want of landgraves and
cassiques, that it will not be possible to put our Grand Model of Government in practice at first, and that notwithstanding we may come as
nigh the aforesaid Model as is practicable:

1. As soon as you arrive at Port Royal you are to summon all the
freemen that are in the colony, and require them to elect five persons
who being joined to the five deputed by the respective Proprietors, are to
be the Council, with whose advice and consent, or at least six of them,
all being summoned, you are to govern according to the Limitations and
Instructions following, observing what can at present be put in practice of
our Fundamental Constitutions and Form of Government.

2. You are to cause all the persons so chosen to swear allegiance to our
Sovereign Lord the King, and subscribe fidelity and submission to the
Proprietors and the form of government by them established . . . .

3. You and your Council are to choose some fitting place whereon to
build a Fort under the protection of which is to be your first town, placing
your houses so as the guns of your Fort may command all your
streets . . . .

Collections of the Historical Society of South Carolina (Richmond: William
Ellis Jones), V, 119–23.

6. You are not to suffer anyone to take up lands within two miles and a half of any Indian town . . . we hoping in time to draw the Indians into our government.

7. You are by and with the consent of your Council, to establish such courts, and so many as you shall for the present think fit for the administration of justice till our Grand Model of Government can come to be put in execution.

8. You are to summon the freeholders of the Colony and require them in our names to elect twenty persons, which together with our deputies for the present are to be your Parliament, by and with whose consent, or the major part of them, you are to make such laws as you shall from time to time find necessary; which laws being ratified by you and any three of our five deputies, shall be in force as in that case provided in the 12th and other articles of our Fundamental Constitutions and Form of Government . . . .

12. You are to cause the land to be laid out in squares containing 12,000 acres, every of which squares that shall be taken up by a Proprietor is to be a Signiory. And each square that shall be taken up by a Landgrave or Cassique is to be a Barony; and each of those squares which shall be taken up or planted on by any of the people shall be a Colony, and reserved wholly for the use of the people as they come to settle, keeping the proportion of twenty-four Colonies to eight Signiories and eight Baronies.

13. You are to order the people to plant in Town, and one Town at least in the Colony . . . .

15. We have Sent a stock of victuals, clothes and tools for the supply of those people, who through poverty have not been able to supply themselves sufficiently for such an enterprise, to prevent abuses in the distribution whereby one may come to want, and another have too much, you and the major part of our deputies by direction in writing are to order our storekeeper how much of each sort shall be delivered weekly to the respective persons, wherein you are to have special regard to those that are not able to furnish themselves.

16. You and the major part of our deputies, are by our order in writing to direct our storekeeper how much of the Indian trade sent shall be delivered to any of the Indian cassiques to purchase their friendship and alliance, wherein we desire you to be as good husbands as may be, that there may be left a considerable store to answer all emergencies, and never let the Indians know what quantity you have, it having been observed to be prejudicial to those that have suffered them to see all their stores.

14. *An Early Report from the Council to the Proprietors, September 9, 1670*

GOVERNOR SAYLE AND HIS ADVISORS FOUND PORT ROYAL AN UNSATIS-
FACTORY SITE FOR A FIRST SETTLEMENT, AND ON THE ADVICE OF A
FRIENDLY INDIAN, THE "CASSIQUE OF KIAWAH," THEY MOVED NORTHWARD
TO THE ASHLEY RIVER; JUST ABOVE TOWN CREEK THEY ESTABLISHED
THEIR FIRST "CHARLES TOWN." ABOUT 150 PEOPLE COMPOSED THIS FIRST
SETTLEMENT. A KNOWLEDGE OF THEIR EARLY TRIALS AND TROUBLES CAN
BE GAINED FROM THE FOLLOWING REPORT OF THE GOVERNOR'S COUNCIL.

[The Governor's Council]

The *Carolina's* safe arrival has very much encouraged our people, the
more for that she had brought us provisions of Indian corn, pease and
meal for eight months, so as we make no question but (by God's
assistance) thoroughly to defend and maintain your Honor's interests
and our rights in this place till we receive a further aid which we very
much stand need of, that so plantations may be managed and your
Honors find what we endeavor to persuade that this country will not
deceive your Honors and others expectations, for which purpose we have
dispatched the *Carolina* to Barbadoes where we understand are a considerable number of people ready to be shipped for this place . . . .
Blessed be to God, we have not lost above four of our people who died
upon distempers usual in other parts, so far may your Honors further
be convinced of the healthfulness of the place.

The stores of all sorts we very much want a supply, especially clothing,
being all disposed of all ready and many of the people unsatisfied, and
the winter is like to prove pretty sharp. The powder was all damnified
especially when the stern of the ship broke in, so as there is a great
necessity of ten barrels of powder more.

We have received some cows and hogs from Virginia, but at an
immoderate rate, considering the smallness of their growth; 30 shillings

Collections of the Historical Society of South Carolina (Richmond: William
Ellis Jones), V, 179–80.

for a hog, a better than which may be brought in England for 10 shillings. If your Honors had a small stock in Bermuda from thence may be transported to this place a very good breed of large cows, hogs and sheep at far easier rates . . . .

We are in great want of an able minister by whose means corrupted youth might be very much reclaimed, and the people instructed in the true religion, and that the Sabbath and service of Almighty God be not neglected . . . .

Council at Ashley River, dated at Albemarle Point, September 9, 1670.

15. *First Indian Troubles, 1671*

AT FIRST THE INDIAN NEIGHBORS OF THE ASHLEY RIVER SETTLEMENT WERE FRIENDLY AND GREETED THE ENGLISH AS ALLIES AGAINST THE MORE WARLIKE INDIANS TO THE SOUTH AND WEST. BUT THE SETTLERS SOON FOUND THAT THE LOCAL INDIANS, PARTICULARLY THE COOSAS (KUSSOES), WERE NOT TO BE TRUSTED. ALONG WITH THEIR OTHER TROUBLES, THE "COUNCIL AT ASHLEY RIVER" HAD TO CONSIDER MEANS OF PROTECTING THE SETTLEMENT, TO KEEP THE INDIANS FROM DESTROYING THEIR CROPS AND STORES. THE FOLLOWING EXCERPTS ARE FROM THE COUNCIL JOURNALS.

[From Council Journals]

The Governor and Council taking into their serious consideration the languishing condition that this Colony is brought into, by reason of the great quantity of corn from time to time taken out of the plantations by the Kussoe and other Southward Indians. And for as much as the said Indians will not comply with any fair entreaties to live peaceably and quietly, but instead thereof upon every light occasion, have and do threaten the lives of all or any of our people whom they will suppose unfriendly to them, and do daily persist and increase in their insolencies so as to disturb and invade some of our plantations in the night time, but that the evil of their intentions have hitherto been prevented by diligent watchings. And for as much as the said Indians have given out that they intend for and with the Spaniards to cut off the English people in this place, and have been observed to make more than an ordinary preparation for some such purpose, and have altogether withdrawn themselves from that familiar correspondence with our people which formerly they used, whereby the more friendly sort of Indians are very much discouraged and retarded from entertaining any amity or trading with our people by all which and many other evident conse-

Council Journals, Sept. 27, 1671, and Oct. 26, 1671, reprinted in W. J. Rivers, *Sketch of the History of South Carolina* (Charleston: McCarter and Co., 1856), 372–74.

quences and hostile postures of the said Indians, it is adjudged by the Governor and Council aforesaid, that the said Indians are endeavoring and contriving the destruction of this settlement and his Majesty's subjects therein, for the prevention of which, it is advised and resolved and thereupon ordered and ordained by the said Governor and Council, that an open war shall be forthwith prosecuted against the said Kussoe Indians and their coadjutors, and for the better effecting thereof, that Commissions be granted to Capt. John Godfrey and Capt. Thomas Gray, to prosecute the same effectually . . . .

Upon serious consideration this day had, of the better safeguard, and defense of this Colony, it is ordered, ordained and declared by the Grand Council that all and every person, and persons, now in this Colony, except such as are members of the Grand Council, or officers attending the same, shall appear in arms, ready fitted in their several companies, according to the list now given in, at the time and place appointed by their several Commanders, for the better informing them in the use of their arms, and the other exercises of military discipline, in order to a due preparation against any sudden invasion, in case any such should happen.

16. *The Appointment of Joseph West as Governor, May, 1674*

AFTER THE DEATH OF GOVERNOR WILLIAM SAYLE IN MARCH, 1671, JOSEPH WEST SERVED AS GOVERNOR FOR ABOUT A YEAR. THEN SIR JOHN YEAMANS CAME TO THE PROVINCE AND ASSUMED THE GOVERNORSHIP AS A PROPRIETOR'S DEPUTY. YEAMAN'S ADMINISTRATION WAS A TROUBLED ONE, AND IN 1674, AS THE FOLLOWING EXCERPT FROM THE PROPRIETORS' INSTRUCTIONS TO THE "GOVERNOR AND COUNCIL AT ASHLEY" REVEALS, JOSEPH WEST WAS AGAIN MADE GOVERNOR.

[Proprietors]

We have herewith sent a patent to Mr. West to be landgrave, and a commission to be governor, who has all along, by his care, fidelity and prudence in the management of our affairs to our general satisfaction, recommended himself to us as the fittest man there for this trust. This we cannot forbear plainly to say, though we have a great regard to Sir John Yeamans, as a considerable man that hath come and settled amongst us. When Mr. West had formerly the management of affairs . . . we had some encouragement to send supplies to men who took into consideration how we might be reimbursed as well as they could, which was all we expected. But immediately with Sir John Yeamans' assuming the government the fact of things altered. The first news was of several proposals for the increasing of our charge; the same hath ever since continued on, and in our very last dispatches a scheme sent to us of ways of supplying you, which would presently require the disbursement of several thousand pounds, and all this without the least mention of any thought how we might be repaid either our past debts, which already amount to several thousand pounds, or be better answered for the future. But, instead thereof, complaints made and reproaches insinuated, as if we had dealt ill or unjustly by you, because we would not continue to feed and clothe you without expectation or demand of any return. This, we must let [you] know, put a stop to your supplies

W. J. Rivers, *Sketch of the History of South Carolina* (Charleston: McCarter and Co., 1856), 332–34.

more than the Dutch war; for we thought it time to give over a charge which was like to have no end, and the country was not worth the having at that rate; for it must be a bad soil that will not maintain industrious people, or we must be very silly that would maintain the idle . . . . That Sir John Yeamans' management has brought things to this state, we are well satisfied . . . . And therefore, if you intend to have supplies for the future, you will do well to consider how you are to pay us, in what commodities you can best do it, and how the trade of those commodities you can produce may be so managed as to turn to account . . . .

17. The Founding of Charleston, 1680–1682

THE ORIGINAL CAROLINA SETTLEMENT NEAR TOWN CREEK PROVED
BOTH UNHEALTHY AND DIFFICULT TO DEFEND AGAINST THE INDIANS. BY
1680 THERE WERE ALREADY SOME SETTLERS ON OYSTER POINT, BETWEEN
THE ASHLEY AND COOPER RIVERS, AND IN THAT YEAR THE MAIN SETTLE-
MENT WAS MOVED OFFICIALLY TO THAT LOCATION. THE FIRST EXCERPT
HERE IS TAKEN FROM THE INSTRUCTIONS OF THE LORDS PROPRIETORS TO
THE GOVERNOR AND COUNCIL, DATED MAY 17, 1680. THE SECOND IS A
DESCRIPTION OF CHARLES TOWN IN 1682, TAKEN FROM "CAROLINA, OR
A DESCRIPTION OF THE PRESENT STATE OF THAT COUNTRY," BY "T. A.,"
PUBLISHED IN 1682.

[Proprietors]

We again desire you to take note that the Oyster Point is the place
that we do appoint for the Port Town, which you are to call Charles
Town, and to take care that all ships that come into Ashley or Cooper
Rivers do there load and unload . . . .

["T. A."]

The principal place where the English are now settled lies situated on
a point of land about two leagues from the sea, between Ashley and
Cooper Rivers, so named in honor of the Right Honorable the Earl of
Shaftsbury, a great patron to the affairs of Carolina. The place called

Council Journals, Sept. 27, 1671, and Oct. 26, 1671, reprinted in W. J. Rivers,
Sketch of the History of South Carolina (Charleston: McCarter and Co., 1856),
393.

B. R. Carroll, ed., *Historical Collections of South Carolina* . . . , 2 vols. (New
York: Harper, 1836), II, 81–83.

Charles Town, by an express order from the Lords Proprietors of Carolina in the year 1680, their ordnance and ammunition being removed
thither from Old Charles Town, which lay about a league higher up
Ashley River, both for its strength and commerce. It is very commodi-
ously situated from many other navigable rivers that lie near it on
which the planters are seated; by the advantage of creeks, which have a
communication from one great river to another at the tide or ebb; the
planters may bring their commodities to the town as to the common
market and magazine both for trade and shipping. The town is
regularly laid out into large and capacious streets, which to buildings is
a great ornament and beauty. In it they have reserved convenient places
for building a church, town-house, and other public structures, an
artillery ground for the exercise of their militia, and wharves for the
convenience of their trade and shipping. At our being there, there was
judged in the country a 1000 or 1200 souls, but the great numbers of
families from England, Ireland, Barbadoes, Jamaica, and the Caribees,
which daily transport themselves thither, have more than doubled that
number. The commodities of the country as yet proper for England
are furs and cedar; for Barbadoes, Jamaica and the Caribee Islands,
provisions, pitch, tar and clapboard; for which they have in exchange
sugar, rum, molasses and ginger, etc. Such things which are proper and
requisite for the planter to be stored with before he leaves England for
his better settlement there at his arrival are, chiefly servants, all kinds of
iron work for the cleaning of land, pruning of vines, for the kitchen and
for building. Commodities proper for the merchant to transport thither
for his advantage: clothing of all kinds, both linen and woolen, hats,
stockings, shoes; all kinds of ammunition, guns, fowling-pieces, powder,
matches, bullet, nails, locks and knives; all haberdashers ware; cordage,
and sails for shipping; spirits and spices, viz., cloves, nutmegs and
cinnamon. Finally, to encourage people to transport themselves thither,
the Lords Proprietors give unto all masters and mistresses of families, to
their children, menservants and maid-servants, if above sixteen years of
age, fifty acres of land to be held forever, annually paying a penny an
acre to the Lords Proprietors to commence in 2 years after it is surveyed.

18. The Troubles of an Early Settler, 1684

JUDITH MANIGAULT, WIFE OF PETER MANIGAULT AND MOTHER OF
GABRIEL MANIGAULT, ONE OF SOUTH CAROLINA'S PROMINENT COLONIAL
CITIZENS, WROTE THE LETTER BELOW. SHE WAS ONE OF MANY FRENCH
HUGUENOTS WHO, PERSECUTED IN FRANCE, ESCAPED AFTER MUCH SUF-
FERING AND MADE A NEW LIFE IN SOUTH CAROLINA. WHETHER THIS
IS TYPICAL OF THE CONDITIONS OF ALL OF THE EARLY SETTLERS IS DIFFI-
CULT TO SAY, BUT THE VOYAGE OVER WAS A DANGEROUS ONE, AND THE
EARLY DAYS IN THE NEW PROVINCE PRESENTED MANY PROBLEMS.

[Judith Manigault]

Since you desire it, I will give you an account of our quitting France,
and of our arrival in Carolina. During eight months we had suffered
from the contributions and the quartering of soldiers, with many other
inconveniences. We therefore resolved on quitting France by night,
leaving the soldiers in their beds, and abandoning the house with its
furniture . . . . We remained in London three months, waiting for a
passage to Carolina. Having embarked, we were sadly off; the spotted
fever made its appearance on board our vessel, of which disease many
died, and among them our aged mother. Nine months elapsed before our
arrival in Carolina. We touched at two ports—one a Portuguese, and
the other an island called Bermuda, belonging to the English, to refit our
vessel, which had been much injured in a storm. Our captain having
committed some misdemeanor, was put in prison, and the vessel seized.
Our money was all spent, and it was with great difficulty we procured
a passage in another vessel. After our arrival in Carolina, we suffered
every kind of evil. In about eighteen months our eldest brother, unac-
customed to the hard labor we were obliged to undergo, died of a fever.
Since leaving France we have experienced every kind of affliction—

David Ramsay, *History of South Carolina* . . . , 2 vols. (Charleston: David
Longworth for the author, 1809), I, 6–8.

disease, pestilence, famine, poverty, hard labor. I have been for six months together without tasting bread, working the ground like a slave; and I have even passed three or four years without always having bread when I wanted it. God has done great things for us, in enabling us to bear up under so many trials.

19. The Spanish Raid of 1686

THE SPANISH IN FLORIDA HAD AGREED TO AN ENGLISH SETTLEMENT
AT CHARLES TOWN BUT OPPOSED ANY SETTLEMENT FARTHER SOUTH.
IN 1684, A GROUP OF SCOTTISH DISSENTERS, UNDER THE LEADERSHIP OF
LORD CARDROSS, HAD BEGUN A SETTLEMENT NEAR PORT ROYAL, BUT
BEFORE IT BECAME FIRMLY ESTABLISHED IT WAS VIRTUALLY WIPED OUT
IN A RAID BY THE SPANISH. THE FOLLOWING REPORT IS TAKEN FROM
EDWARD RANDOLPH'S "LETTER TO THE BOARD OF TRADE," WRITTEN IN
1699, BUT COMPILED FROM CONTEMPORARY ACCOUNTS.

[Edward Randolph]

In the year 1686, one hundred Spaniards, with Negroes and Indians,
landed at Edisto, (50 miles to the southward of Charles Town), and
broke open the house of Mr. Joseph Morton, then Governor of the
Province, and carried away Mr. Bowell, his Brother-in-law, prisoner,
who was found murdered 2 or 3 days after; they carried away all his
money and plate, and 13 slaves to the value of £1500 sterling, and their
plunder to St. Augustine. Two of the slaves made their escape from
thence, and returned to their master. Some time after, Governor Morton
sent to demand his slaves, but the Governor of St. Augustine answered
it was done without his orders, but to this day keeps them, and says he
can't deliver them up without an order from the King of Spain. About
the same time they robbed Mr. Grimball's House, the secretary of the
Province, whilst he attended the Council at Charles Town, and carried
away plunder to the value of over £1500 sterling. They also fell upon a
settlement of Scotchmen at Port Royal, where there was not above 25
men in health to oppose them. The Spaniards burnt down their houses,
destroyed and carried away all that they had, because (as the Spaniards
pretended) they were settled upon their land, and had they at any time
a superior force, they would also destroy this town built upon Ashley
and Cooper Rivers. This whole bay . . . they likewise lay claim to.

A. S. Salley, ed., *Narratives of Early Carolina, 1650–1708* (New York: Charles
Scribner's Sons, 1911), 205–206.

20. *Edward Randolph's Report on South Carolina, 1699*

EDWARD RANDOLPH, COLLECTOR OF CUSTOMS FOR THE ENGLISH
COLONIES IN AMERICA, VISITED SOUTH CAROLINA IN 1699 AND WROTE
AN EXTENSIVE REPORT ON ITS HISTORY AND ECONOMIC CONDITIONS. THE
FOLLOWING EXCERPTS ARE TAKEN FROM HIS REPORT.

[Edward Randolph]

There are but few settled inhabitants in this Province; the Lords
have taken up vast tracts of land for their own use, as in Colleton
county and other places, where the land is most commodious for settlement, which prevents peopling the place, and makes them less capable
to preserve themselves. As to their civil government, 'tis different from
what I have met with in the other Proprietaries. Their militia is not
above 1500 soldiers, white men, but they have thro' the Province generally 4 Negroes to 1 white man, and not above 1100 families, English
and French . . . .

Their chief town is Charles Town, and the seat of government in this
Province, where the Governor, Council and Triennial Parliament set, and
their courts are holden, being above a league distance from the entrance
to their harbor mouth, which is barred, and not above 17 foot of water
at the highest tide, but very difficult to come in . . . .

The great improvement made in this Province is wholly owing to the
industry and labor of the inhabitants. They have applied themselves to
make such commodities as might increase the revenue of the Crown, as
cotton, wool, ginger, indigo, etc. But finding them not to answer the
end, they are set upon making pitch, tar and turpentine, and planting
rice, and can send over great quantities yearly, if they had encouragement
from England to make it, having about 5000 slaves to be employed in
that service, upon occasion, but they have lost most of their vessels,
which were but small, by war with the French and Spaniards, so that

A. S. Salley, ed., *Narratives of Early Carolina, 1650–1708* (New York: Charles
Scribner's Sons, 1911), 204–205, 207–209.

they are not able to send those commodities to England for a market, neither are sailors here to be had to man their vessels.

I humbly propose that if his Majesty will for a time suspend the duties upon commodities, and that upon rice also, it will encourage the planter to fall vigilantly upon making pitch and tar, etc., which the Lords Proprietors ought to make their principle care to obtain from his Majesty, being the only way to draw people to settle in their Province . . . . Some persons have offered to deliver in Charles Town Bay upon their own account 1000 barrels of pitch and as much tar . . . , tar at 8 shillings a barrel, and very good pitch at 12 shillings per barrel, and much cheaper if it once became a trade. The season for making those commodities in this Province being two months longer than in Virginia and more northern plantations, a planter can make more tar in any one year here with 50 slaves than they can do with double the number in those places, their slaves here living at very easy rates and with few clothes . . . .

If this place were duly encouraged it would be the most useful to the Crown of all the plantations upon the continent of America.

21. *The Carolina Expedition Against St. Augustine, 1702*

IN 1702, ENGLAND BEGAN A LONG WAR WITH FRANCE AND SPAIN
KNOWN AS "QUEEN ANNE'S WAR." BECAUSE THE SPANISH WERE IN
FLORIDA AND THE FRENCH IN THE MISSISSIPPI VALLEY, SOUTH CARO-
LINA BECAME A FRONTIER IN THE WAR AND WAS OPEN TO ATTACK FROM
THREE SIDES. IN 1702, FOLLOWING SKIRMISHES BETWEEN SOUTH CARO-
LINA TRADERS AND THE FRENCH AND SPANISH, GOVERNOR JAMES MOORE
TOOK THE OFFENSIVE, LEADING AN EXPEDITION OF CAROLINIANS AGAINST
ST. AUGUSTINE, THE SPANISH POST IN FLORIDA. THIS WAS AN ABORTIVE
ATTEMPT, BUT IN 1704 MOORE LED A SUCCESSFUL RAID AGAINST THE
SPANISH POSTS IN WEST FLORIDA. IN 1706, THE FRENCH AND SPANISH
RETALIATED WITH A NAVAL ATTACK ON CHARLES TOWN, BUT THE
ATTACKERS WERE DRIVEN OFF WITH GREAT LOSSES TO THEMSELVES.
THE FOLLOWING EXCERPTS FROM JOHN OLDMIXON'S *British Empire in
America* (1708) DESCRIBES MOORE'S EXPEDITION AGAINST ST. AUGUSTINE.

[John Oldmixon]

The next thing that comes in our way is the War of Augustino.

Two thousand pounds were raised by an act of Assembly, to defray
the charge of this expedition. The governor pressed as many merchant
ships as were necessary to transport the troops he intended to embark;
who were ordered to rendezvous at Port-Royal. The number of men
were listed for this enterprise were 1200, 600 English, and 600 Indians.
Col. Moore took the command on himself, as general of all the forces
that should be raised within the limits of his government. Col. Robert
Daniel, a very brave man, commanded a party who were to go up the
river in periagas, and come upon Augustino on the land side, while the
Governor sailed thither and attacked it by sea. They both set out in
August, 1702. Col. Daniel in his way took St. John's, a small Spanish
settlement; as also St. Mary's, another little village belonging to the

B. R. Carroll, ed., *Historical Collections of South Carolina* . . . , 2 vols. (New
York: Harper, 1836), II, 422–24. The Carolinians also fostered an Indian
attack (Talapoosas), unsuccessfully, in 1707 against Fort San Carlos at Pensacola.

Spaniards. After which he proceeded to Augustino, came before the town, entered and took it; Col. Moore not yet being arrived with the fleet.

The inhabitants having notice of the approach of the English had packed up their best effects, and retired with them into the castle, which was surrounded by a very deep and broad moat. They had laid up provisions there for 4 months, and resolved to defend themselves to the last extremity. However, Col. Daniel found a considerable booty in the town. The next day, the Governor arrived, and a Council of War was immediately called, in which 'twas resolved to land. Accordingly the Governor came ashore, and his troops following him, the entrenched, posted their guards in the church, and blocked up the castle. The English held the possession of the town a whole month, but finding they could do nothing for want of mortars and bombs, they dispatched a sloop for Jamaica; but the commander of the sloop, instead of going thither, came to Carolina, out of fear or treachery. Finding others offered to go in his stead, he proceeded in the voyage himself, after he had lain sometime at Charles-Town.

The Governor all this while lay before the Castle of Augustino, in expectation of the return of the sloop. Which hearing nothing of, he sent Col. Daniel, who was the life of the action, to Jamaica, on the same errand. This gentleman being hearty in the design, procured a supply of bombs, and returned towards Augustino. But in the meantime two ships appeared in the offing, which, being taken to be two very large men of war, the Governor thought fit to raise the siege, and abandon his ships, with a great quantity of stores, ammunition, and provisions, to the enemy. Upon which the two men of war entered the port of Augustino, took the Governor's ships. Some say he burnt them himself. Certain it is, they were lost to the Spanish, and that he returned to Charles-Town overland, 300 miles from Augustino. The two men of war that were thought to be so large, proved to be two small frigates, one of 18, and the other of 16 guns.

When Col. Daniel came back to Augustino, he was chased, but got away, and Col. Moore retreated with no great honor homewards. The periagas lay at St. John's, whither the Governor retired, and so to Charles-Town, having lost but two men in the whole expedition.

22. *The Petition of the Carolina Dissenters in 1705*

RELIGIOUS DISTINCTIONS HAD BEEN APPARENT IN SOUTH CAROLINA
ALMOST FROM THE BEGINNING, AND SOON AFTER 1700 THE DIFFERENCES
BETWEEN THE ANGLICANS AND THE DISSENTERS (AS ALL NON-ANGLI-
CANS WERE CALLED) HAD BECOME PARTICULARLY STRONG. IN 1703, SIR
NATHANIEL JOHNSON BECAME GOVERNOR. TAKING A STRONG ANGLICAN
STAND, HE PUSHED THROUGH THE ASSEMBLY EARLY IN 1704 AN ACT THAT
PREVENTED ALL DISSENTERS FROM HOLDING OFFICE IN THE PROVINCE.
THIS WAS FOLLOWED IN THE FALL OF 1706 WITH ANOTHER ACT ESTAB-
LISHING THE CHURCH OF ENGLAND AS THE OFFICIAL, TAX-SUPPORTED
BODY. THESE ACTS AROUSED OPPOSITION, AND THE DISSENTERS SENT
A PETITION TO ENGLAND BY JOSEPH BOONE. THERE, AFTER LONG CONSID-
ERATION, THE HOUSE OF LORDS AND THE ATTORNEY GENERAL CONDEMNED
BOTH ACTS, AND QUEEN ANNE ORDERED THE PROPRIETORS TO DECLARE
THEM VOID.

[Joseph Boone]

To the Right Honourable the Lords Spiritual and Temporal in
Parliament Assembled,

The Humble Petition of Joseph Boone, Merchant, on behalf of himself
and many other inhabitants of the Province of Carolina, and also of
several merchants of London, trading to Carolina, and the neighbouring
colonies of Her Majesty in America,

Sheweth to your Lordships, That the late King Charles the Second,
by his Charter under the Great Seal of England, bearing Date the
Twenty fourth of March, 1663, did grant to Edward, Earl of Clarendon
. . . and others, their heirs and assigns, all that tract of land in North
America, commonly called Carolina, to be held of the Crown of England,

*The humble address of . . . Lords Spiritual and Temporal . . . presented to
Her Majesty on Wednesday the Thirteenth day of March, 1705, relating to the
Province of Carolina . . .* (London: Printed by Charles Bill, 1705), 3 pp. The
1704 Church Act attempted to establish the Church of England as the official
church. The only difference between this act and the 1706 act was that the latter
was more carefully drawn.

as a County-Palatine, with power to them, their heirs and assigns, to make laws for the good government of the said colony, with the advice, assent, and approbation of the freemen of the said Colony, and the greatest part of them, so as the said laws may be consonant to reason, and as near as conveniently can be, agreeable to the laws and customs of England . . . .

That for the better peopling the said Colony, express provision is made in the said Charter, for a toleration and indulgence to all Christians in the free exercise of their religion.

That in the year 1669, the Lords Proprietors of the said Colony, settled the method of the government of the said colony in several articles, which were called . . . the Fundamental Constitutions . . . .

That in the said Fundamental Constitutions, there is an express provision, that no person should be disturbed for any speculative opinion in religion, and that no person should on the account of religion be excluded from being a member of the General Assembly, or from any other office of the Civil Administration . . . .

That the said Charter being made soon after the time of the happy restoration of King Charles the Second, and the re-establishment of the Church of England by the Act of Uniformity, many of the subjects of this Kingdom, who were so unhappy as to have some scruples about conforming to the rites of the said Church, did transplant themselves and families into the said Colony; by means whereof the greatest part of the inhabitants there were Protestant Dissenters from the Church of England, and through the equality and freedom of the said Fundamental Constitutions of the said Colony, all the inhabitants there lived in great peace, and even the Ministry of the Church of England had support from Protestant Dissenters; and the number of the inhabitants, and the trade of the said Colony daily increased to the great improvement of Her Majesties customs, and the manifest advantage of the merchants and manufacture of this Kingdom.

That in the year 1703, when a new General Assembly was to be chosen, which by the Constitution is to be chosen once in two years [,] the election was managed with very great partiality and injustice, and all sorts of people, even servants, Negroes, aliens, Jews and common sailors were admitted to vote in elections.

That the ecclesiastical government of the said Colony is under the jurisdiction of the Lord Bishop of London, but the Governor, and his adherents, have at last, which the said adherents had often threatened, totally abolished it; for the said Assembly hath lately passed an Act, whereby twenty lay persons therein named are made a Corporation for the exercise of several exorbitant powers, to the great injury and oppression of the people in general, and for the exercise of all ecclesiastical jurisdiction, with absolute power to deprive any minister of the Church of England of his benefice, not only for his immorality, but even for his imprudence or incurable prejudices or animosities between such minister and his parish; and the only Church of England minister that is established in the said Colony, the Reverend Mr. Edward Marston, hath already been cited before their Board; which the inhabitants of that Province take to be a High Ecclesiastical Commission Court, destructive to the very being and essence of the Church of England, and to be had in the utmost detestation and abhorrence by every man that is not an enemy to our Constitutions in church and state.

That in the said General Assembly another Act was passed, to incapacitate every person from being a member of any General Assembly that should be chosen for the time to come, unless he had taken the Sacrament of the Lords Supper according to the rites of the Church of England, whereby all Protestant Dissenters are made uncapable of being of the said Assembly. And yet, by the said Act, all persons who will take an oath, that they have not received the sacrament in any dissenting congregation for one year past, tho' they have not received it in the Church of England, are made capable of being of the said Assembly. And we take the liberty humbly to inform your Lordships, that in the Preamble to the said Act it is asserted, that by the laws and usage of England, all members of Parliament are obliged to conform to the Church of England, by receiving the sacrament of the Lords Supper according to the rites of the said Church, which assertion is notoriously and manifestly false.

That this Act was passed in an illegal manner by the Governors calling the Assembly to meet the 26th of April, when it then stood prorogued to the 10th of May following, and yet this Act hath been ratified by the Lords Proprietors here in England, who refused to hear what could be offered against it, and contrary to the petition of above one hundred and seventy of the chief inhabitants of the said Colony, and of several eminent merchants trading thither, and though the Commons of the same Assembly quickly after passed another bill to repeal it, which the Governor rejected.

That the said grievances daily encreasing, your petitioner Joseph Boone is now sent by many principal inhabitants and traders of the said Colony to represent the languishing and dangerous condition of the said Colony, to the Lords Proprietors thereof; but his humble applications to them have hitherto had no effect.

That the ruin of the said Colony would be to the great disadvantage of the trade of this Kingdom, to the apparent prejudice of Her Majesties customs, and the great benefit of the French, who watch all opportunities to improve their own settlements in those parts of America.

[The House of Lords approved the petition and presented it to the Queen, recommending that the law in question be disallowed. The Queen replied:]

I thank the House for laying these matters so plainly before me; I am very sensible of what great consequences the plantations are to England, and will do all that is in my power to relieve my subjects in Carolina, and to protect them in their just rights.

23. The Church Act of November 30, 1706

THE SUCCESS OF THE DISSENTERS WAS SHORT-LIVED. IN 1706 THE CAROLINA ASSEMBLY PASSED A SECOND ACT ESTABLISHING THE CHURCH OF ENGLAND IN THE PROVINCE, AND THIS TIME IT WAS APPROVED BY THE PROPRIETORS. THE CHIEF SIGNIFICANCE OF THIS ACT WAS TO COMBINE THE CIVIL AND ECCLESIASTICAL FUNCTIONS OF THE PROVINCE. THE CHURCH OF ENGLAND REMAINED THE ESTABLISHED CHURCH IN SOUTH CAROLINA UNTIL THE REVOLUTION. THE ACT OF 1706 ITSELF IS RATHER LONG; THE EXCERPT BELOW IS A BRIEF SUMMARY.

An Act for the Establishment of Religious Worship in this Province According to the Church of England, and for the Erecting Churches for the Public Worship of God, and also for the Maintenance of Ministers and the Building of Convenient Houses for Them.

[Brief Summary of Church Act]

The Act prescribed that the Book of Common Prayer and the Psalter should be used, and that the administration of the sacraments and other rites and ceremonies of the Church of England should be performed by every minister or reader established by law. All churches, or congregations, for the maintenance of whose ministers any certain income or revenue was provided by law, were to be of the Church of England, and were to be considered established churches. The expense of building churches, parsonages, etc., could come from subscriptions for that purpose, with the balance to be paid out of the public treasury. Supervisors for building these churches and parsonages were appointed. Each established minister was to draw £50 from the public treasury

Code of South Carolina Laws, from its Founding through 1838, 10 vols., ed. Thomas Cooper, I–V; ed. David T. McCord, VI–X. Summarized from *Code, South Carolina Statutes at Large* (Columbia: A. S. Johnston, printer, 1837), II, 282–87. Bounds of the several parishes were not defined in the November act but were included in the Act of December 18, 1708.

annually, and was to be chosen by the majority of the parish communicants who were freeholders or paid taxes. Church government was to be in the hands of seven vestrymen and two churchwardens, who were to be elected on Easter Monday of each year by the qualified voters of the Parish who were members of the Church of England.

The province was divided into ten parishes: St. Philip's in Charles Town; Christ Church, southeast of Wando River; St. Thomas, between Wando and Cooper rivers; St. John, west of Cooper River; St. James, on Goose Creek; St. Andrew, on the Ashley River; St. Dennis, in Orange Quarter, for the French there; St. Paul, in the south of Colleton County; St. Bartholomew, in the north of Colleton County; and St. James, Santee, in Jamestown, another French colony on the Santee River.

24. The Council's Report on Conditions in the Province, September 17, 1708

THE FOLLOWING PARAGRAPHS ARE TAKEN FROM A REPORT ON ECONOMIC CONDITIONS IN SOUTH CAROLINA MADE BY GOVERNOR NATHANIEL JOHNSON AND HIS COUNCIL FOR THE USE OF THE LORDS PROPRIETORS AND THE BOARD OF TRADE.

[Governor Nathaniel Johnson and Council]

We, the governor and council, in obedience to her sacred Majesty's command and your lordships' Instructions, have carefully inquired into the present circumstances of this Province . . . .

The number of inhabitants in this Province of all sorts, are computed to be 9580 souls; of which there are 1360 freemen, 900 free women, 60 white servant men, 60 white servant women, 1700 white free children, 1800 negro men slaves, 1100 negro women slaves, 1200 negro children slaves, 600 Indian men slaves, 500 Indian women slaves, and 300 Indian children slaves.

The freemen of this Province by reason of the late sickness brought hither from other parts, though now very healthy . . . are within the five years last past decreased about 100, free women about 40; white servants, from the aforesaid reasons, and having completed their servitude, are decreased 50; white servant women, for the same reasons, are decreased 30; white children are increased 500; negro men slaves, by importation, 300; negro women slaves, 200; Indian men slaves, by reason of our late conquest over the French and Spanish . . . and other Indian engagements, are within these five years increased to the number of 400, and the Indian women slaves to 450; negro children to 600, and Indian children to 200.

The whole number of the militia of this Province, 950 white men, fit to bear arms . . . to which might be added a like number of negro men slaves, the captain of each company being obliged by an act of Assembly,

W. J. Rivers, *Sketch of the History of South Carolina* (Charleston: McCarter and Co., 1856), 231–38.

to enlist, train up, and bring into the field for each white, one able slave armed with a gun or lance . . . .

The commodities exported from this Province to England, are rice, pitch, tar, buck and doeskins in the hair and Indian dressed; also some few furs, as beaver, otter, wildcat, raccoon, a little silk, white oak pipe staves, and sometimes some other sorts. We are sufficiently provided with timber fit for masts and yards of several sizes, both pine and cypress, which may be exported very reasonable, and supplied at all times of the year . . . .

From this Province are exported to several of the American islands, as Jamaica, Barbados . . . and the Bahama Islands—staves, hoops and shingles, beef, pork, rice, pitch, tar, green wax, candles made of myrtle berries, tallow and tallow candles, butter, English and Indian peas, and sometimes a small quantity of tanned leather. Goods imported from the foregoing islands are—rum, sugar, molasses, cotton . . , salt, and pimiento . . . . We are also furnished with negroes from the American islands . . . , from which also comes a considerable quantity of English manufactures, and some prize goods, viz. claret, brandy, etc., taken from the French and Spaniards.

We have also commerce with Boston, Rhode Island, Pennsylvania, New York, and Virginia; to which places we export Indian slaves, light deerskins, dressed, some tanned leather, pitch, tar, and a small quantity of rice. From thence we receive beer, cider, flour, dry codfish and mackerel, and from Virginia some European commodities. Further, we have a trade to the Madeiras, from which we receive most of our wines . . . and to which place we send the same commodities as to the other islands . . . .

The trade of this Province is certainly increased of late years . . . and the inhabitants, by a yearly addition of slaves, are made the more capable of improving the produce of the Colony. Notwithstanding it is our opinion that the value of our import is greater (if we include our negroes) than our export, by which means it comes to pass that we are very near drained of all our silver and gold coin, nor is there any remedy to prevent this, but by a number of honest laborious people to come among us, that would . . . in time make our exportation equalize if not exceed our importation . . . .

There are not above ten or twelve sail of ships belonging to this Province . . . neither are there above twenty seafaring men who may be properly accounted settlers . . . in the Province. There are not as yet any manufacturers settled in the Province, saving some particular planters who, for their own use only, make a few stuffs of silk and cotton, and a sort of cloth of cotton and wool of their own growth to clothe their slaves . . . .

The Indians under the protection of his Majesty's government are numerous and may be of great use in time of invasion . . . . From the aforesaid Indians . . . are bought and shipped for England, one year with another, at least 50,000 skins; to purchase which requires at least £2500 or £3000 first cost of goods in England. The goods proper for a trade with the Indians are English cottons, broadcloth of several colors, duffels, red and blue, beads of several sorts and sizes, and axes, hoes, falchions, small guns, powder, bullets, and small shot.

25. John Oldmixon's Description of South Carolina in 1708

JOHN OLDMIXON'S *British Empire in America*, WHICH WAS PUBLISHED IN 1708, WAS BOTH A HISTORY AND A GEOGRAPHICAL DESCRIPTION. ALTHOUGH OLDMIXON NEVER VISITED SOUTH CAROLINA, HIS FACTS WERE TAKEN FROM CONTEMPORARY SOURCES, PROBABLY DIRECTLY FROM THE OFFICE OF THE SECRETARY TO THE LORDS PROPRIETORS. THE PROVINCE WAS DIVIDED INTO FOUR COUNTIES AT THIS TIME.

[John Oldmixon]

Craven County . . . is pretty well inhabited by English and French; of the latter there is a settlement on Santee River . . . . The next river to Santee is Sewee river, where some families from New England settled, and in the year 1706, the French landing there, they were vigorously opposed by this little colony, who beat off the invaders, having forced them to leave many of their companions dead behind them. This county sends 10 members to the Assembly . . . .

Berkeley County . . . the northern parts of this shire are not planted, but the southern are thick of plantations, on account of the two great rivers, Cooper and Ashley . . . . Charles Town, the capital of this Province, is built on a neck of land between Ashley and Cooper rivers, but lying most on Cooper river . . . . This is the only free port in the Province, which is a great discouragement to it, and a vast injury to trade . . . . It has 6 bastions, and a line all around it . . . . If all these works are well made and can be well manned, we see no reason why they should not defend as well as beautify the town, which is a market town, and thither the whole product of the Province is brought for sale. Neither is its trade inconsiderable, for it deals near 1000 miles into the continent. However, it is unhappy in a bar, that admits no ships above 200 tons. Its situation is very inviting, and the country about it agreeable and fruitful. The highways are extremely delightful, especially that called Broadway, which for three or four miles makes a road and walk so

B. R. Carroll, ed., *Historical Collections of South Carolina* . . . , 2 vols. (New York: Harper, 1836), II, 446–61.

pleasantly green that . . . no prince in Europe, by all his art, can make so pleasant a sight for the whole year. There are several fair streets in the town, and some very handsome buildings . . . . As for public edifices, the church is the most remarkable; it is large and stately enough; but the number of the professors of the Anglican worship increasing daily, the auditory begin to want room, and another church . . . .

There is a public library in this town, and a free-school has been long talked of . . . . The library is kept by the minister for the time being. It owes its rise to Dr. Thomas Bray; as do most of the American libraries, for which he zealously solicited contributions in England. Not far off, by Cartaret Bastion, is the Presbyterian meeting house . . . . Between Colleton and Ashley Bastions is the Anabaptist meeting house . . . . The French church is in the chief street, besides which there is a Quaker meeting house in the suburbs . . . . We may see by this description that the town is full of Dissenters . . . . There are at least 250 families in this town . . . , in the whole amounting to about 3000 souls. In Charles Town the Governor generally resides, the Assembly sits, the courts of judicature are held, the public offices are kept, and the business of the province is transacted . . . .

Dorchester is in this shire, bordering on Colleton County. It is a small town, containing about 350 souls. There is a meeting-house belonging to the [Congregationalists] Independents here . . . . Berkeley county sends ten members to the Assembly.

The same does Colleton county, which Stono river waters . . . . The northeast part of this division of the Province is full of Indian settlements, and the Stono and other rivers form an island called Boone's Island, a little below Charles Town, which is well planted and inhabited . . . . Two miles higher is Wilton, by some called New London, a little town, consisting of about 80 houses . . . . This county has 200 freeholders, that vote in the election for Parliament . . . . There is an orthodox church in this precinct . . . .

Carteret County is not yet inhabited, but is generally esteemed to be the most fruitful and pleasant part of the Province . . . . All along Port Royal river, and in all this part of Carolina, the air is so temperate, and the seasons of the year so regular, that there is no excess of heat or cold, nor any troublesome variety of weather . . . .

This country is in a very flourishing condition . . . . It is a pity this people should not be easy in their government; for all their industry, all the advantages of the climate, soil and situation for trade, will be useless to them, if they live under oppression . . . .

We shall conclude this . . . account of Carolina, with a list of the present Proprietors, and chief officers of the Colony:

Proprietors: William Lord Craven; Henry Duke of Beaufort; The Honorable Maurice Ashley, Esq., brother to the Earl of Shaftesbury; John Lord Cartaret; Sir John Colleton, Baronet; Joseph Blake, Esquire; John Archdale, Esquire; and Nicholas Trott, Esquire.

Sir Nathaniel Johnson, Governor, salary £200 a year; Col. James Moore, Col. Thomas Broughton, Col. Robert Gibbs, Mr. Nicholas Trott, Mr. Ward, Mr. Henry Noble, Counsellors; William Rhett, Esq., Speaker of the Assembly; Mr. Trott, Chief Justice; Mr. Ward, Secretary; Col. James Moore, Judge of the Admiralty Court; Mr. How, Surveyor-General; Col. James Moore, Attorney General and Receiver General; Mr. Trott, Naval Officer; Col. Thomas Broughton, Collector of the Customs; and Mr. Joseph Boone, Agent for the Colony in England.

26. *The Proprietors' Instructions for Governor Craven, 1712*

As each new governor took office, he was given a Commission as proof of office, a general statement of his powers and duties, and a set of Instructions defining specific duties and problems to be met and solved. The following for Governor Charles Craven, at his appointment in 1712, illustrate the nature of proprietary Instructions and also point out some of the major problems which South Carolina faced in that year.

[Instructions to Governor Craven]

You are with our Council to consider how the trade of that part of our Province which is committed to your care may be by the most proper and legal means promoted and advanced and how the several useful and profitable manufacturers already settled in that part of our said Province may be further improved, and how and in what manner new and profitable manufactures may be introduced, and you are also to consider of the best and most effectual means to establish the fishery of our said Province, and what encouragement is proper for us to give to increase the same.

You are from time to time to make representations touching the premises to us as the nature of the business shall require, which said representations are to be in writing and to be signed by you and the major part of the Council.

You are to take care that all Acts of Assemblies that have been confirmed by us, or our predecessors be fairly wrote out and transmitted to us by the first opportunity; and you are to examine into and weigh such Acts of the Assemblies as shall from time to time be sent or transmitted hither for our approbation, and to set down and represent as aforesaid the usefullness or mischief thereof to Her Majesty's imperial crown of Great

A. S. Salley, ed., *Commissions and Instructions from the Lords Proprietors of Carolina to Public Officials of South Carolina, 1685–1715*, for the South Carolina Historical Commission (Columbia: The State Co., 1916), 243–46. Reprinted by permission of the South Carolina Department of Archives and History.

Britain, to our Province, itself, or to our jurisdiction and power granted to us by the Royal Charter in case such law should be confirmed and established by us, and to consider what matters may be recommended as fit to be passed in the Assemblies there.

You are to enquire into and transmit to us an account of all monies that have been given for public uses by the Assemblies in our Province, and how the same are and have been expended or laid out, and what persons do, and how and by whom they are impowered to receive the same.

You are by and with the advice and consent of any four or more of our deputies to adjourn, prorogue and dissolve the General Assembly as often as you shall think requisite so to do . . . .

You are to take great care that the Indians be not abused, and that justice be duly administered to them in our courts, and that you endeavor your utmost to create a firm friendship with them, and to bring them over to your part for your better protection and defense against the enemy—the neighboring French and Spaniards against whom you are to protect our said Province and we assure you of our utmost assistance for your security.

You are to transmit to us as soon as you can conveniently get it handsomely transcribed a full and exact account of our yearly rents; what they amount to in the whole, and the particular men from whom due, and what from each man; also what has been received, by whom, and how applied and what land, to whom and for what sold.

You are to take care that all persons may be admitted to peruse the public record of our Province, provided they make such perusal at the place where the same are constantly kept and pay the customary and usual fees.

You shall immediately upon recept of these present issue out your warrant to eight such persons as you shall deem most proper, viz., to four of the inhabitants of Colleton County and to four of the inhabitants of Granville County, to sound the river of Port Royal and to examine which is the fittest place to fix a town upon, and return the same into the notaries office which return you are to transmit to us as soon as you shall receive the same.

Whereas it was agreed at our Board that the office of Surveyor General of South Carolina would be better executed by the several surveyors of the respective counties, you are therefore to direct such persons to be the several surveyors of each county as you shall deem most proper and that each of them shall make such returns of the land they shall survey and set out, and the quit rents reserved for the same into our secretary's office according to the usual custom of our Province.

And lastly we do require you, our said Governor, to execute and perform all other things necessary and proper for answering our intentions in the premises, and which shall or may tend to the good government of our Province aforesaid.

27. *The Yamassee War, 1715–1716*

THE PROPRIETORS' HOPES OF FRIENDSHIP WITH THE CAROLINA INDIANS WERE NOT FULFILLED. IN 1715 A WAR BROKE OUT BETWEEN THE COLONIES AND THE YAMASSEE INDIANS, A TRIBE FROM THE SAVANNAH RIVER AREA, IN WHICH THE YAMASSEES WERE DEFEATED AND DRIVEN FROM SOUTH CAROLINA. THE YAMASSEES LATER JOINED WITH THE SEMINOLE INDIANS IN FLORIDA. THE CAROLINIANS WERE ALSO HAVING TROUBLE WITH COASTAL PIRATES; AND THE COMBINATION OF INDIAN AND PIRATE PROBLEMS, ADDED TO THE DIFFERENCES BETWEEN COLONISTS AND PROPRIETORS, HASTENED THE END OF THE PROPRIETORSHIP.

[Francis Yonge to John Lord Carteret]

After some years intercourse and dealing between the inhabitants and several nations of Indians, with whom they traded, . . . for several thousand pounds a year, the said Indians, unanimously agreed to destroy the whole settlement, by murdering and cutting to pieces all the inhabitants, on a day they had agreed on; and although some private intimations were given the people of their design, it was totally disbelieved, so that on a certain day, in the year 1715, they killed all, or most, of the traders that were with them in their town; and going among the plantations, murdered all who could not fly from their cruelty, and burned their houses. The occasion of this conspiracy, which was so universal, that all the Indians were concerned in it, except a small clan or two that lived amongst the settlements, insomuch that they amounted to between eight and ten thousand men, was attributed to some ill usage they had received from the traders, who are not (generally) men of the best morals; and that no doubt of it might give some cause to their discontents; to which may be added the great debts they owed the inhabitants, which it is said amounted to near 10,000 pounds sterling, with the goods then amongst them; all which they seized and made their

B. R. Carroll, ed., *Historical Collections of South Carolina* . . . , 2 vols. (New York: Harper, 1836), II, 144–46.

own, and never paid their debts, but cancelled them, by murdering their creditors.

In this war near 400 of the inhabitants were destroyed, with many houses and slaves, and great numbers of cattle, especially to the southward near Port Royal, from whence the inhabitants were entirely driven, and forced into the settlements near Charles-Town.

This town being fortified, they there had time to think what to do; and not mustering above 1200 men, they sent to Virginia and the neighboring colonies for assistance; and for want of money, of which they have very little in the country, they formed bills of credit to pass current in all payments . . . . This, their necessary defense brought the public in debt near £80,000, and entailed great annual charges upon them, to maintain garrisons, which they were forced to erect and keep at great expense.

In this very great extremity, they sent agents to England with an account of their deplorable state, and to beg assistance from their Proprietors; but not having very great expectations from them, as very rightly imagining they would not be brought to expend their English estates to support much more precarious ones in America, their agents were directed to lay a state of their circumstances before Her Majesty, Queen Anne, and to beg the assistance of the Crown.

Their agents soon sent them an account that they found a disposition in Her Majesty to send them relief, and to protect them, but that the objection was they were a Proprietary government; and it was the opinion of the then Lords Commissioners of Trade and Plantations, that if the Queen was at the expense of protecting and relieving the Province, the Government thereof should be in the Crown . . . .

28. *The Clergy in Carolina*

BEARING THE HARDSHIPS OF THE NEW WORLD ALONG WITH THE EARLY SETTLERS WERE MEMBERS OF THE CLERGY. MOST IMPORTANT OF THESE WERE THE REPRESENTATIVES OF THE SOCIETY FOR THE PROPAGATION OF THE GOSPEL IN FOREIGN PARTS. IN CHARLESTON, COMMISSARY GIDEON JOHNSTON REPORTED REGULARLY AND FAITHFULLY TO HIS SPONSORS IN ENGLAND, AND FOR THE PERIOD OF HIS SERVICE (1707–1716) A GLIMPSE IS AFFORDED INTO THE LIFE OF THAT TIME. GIDEON, HUSBAND OF HENRIETTA JOHNSTON, AMERICA'S FIRST PASTELLIST, SUFFERED FROM ILL HEALTH AND POVERTY, AND CONFESSED THAT THE SMALL INCOME FROM HIS WIFE'S PAINTING SOMETIMES SUPPLIED THEM WITH FOOD. HIS COMMENTARY COVERS MANY SUBJECTS, AS WITNESS THE LETTER OF NOVEMBER 16, 1711, FOLLOWING:

[Commissary Gideon Johnston]

I am so much taken up with the Duties of my place, that you must not expect I should write all this Lre [letter] at once. N[e]ver was there a more sickly or fatall season than this for the small Pox, Pestilential ffevers, Pleurises, and fflex's have destroyed great numbers here of all Sorts, both Whites, Blacks and Indians,—and these distempers still rage to an uncommon degree. Three Funeralls of a day, and sometimes four are now very usual; and all that I gett by these is a few rotten Glov's [the custom of the day], and an abundance of trouble day & night; for I do solemnly protest that I have not recd a penny this way these 9 months past.—

The Town looks miserably thin, and disconsolate, and there is not one house in twenty [and] I speak modestly that has not Considerably suffer'd and still labours under this generall Calamity. . . . Tis true in

Frank J. Klingberg, ed., *Carolina Chronicle. The Papers of Commissary Gideon Johnston, 1707–1716.* University of California Publications in History, L. K. Koontz, D. K. Bjork, C. N. Howard, eds., Los Angeles (Berkeley and Los Angeles: University of California Press, 1946) and (London: Cambridge University Press), vol. 35, 99, 101, 103. Reprinted by permission of University of California Press.

the time of the great sickness here . . . vast numbers P[er]ished But then in two Months time, upon the approach of Winter all was over. But the distempers now rageing are so farr from decreasing, the winter began very early, and is very sharp, that, on the Contrary they gather fresh strength and vigour by it, some attribute this mortality to one thing, and some to another. But I verily think, it is a Sort of Plague, a kind of Judgemt upon the Place (ffor they are a sinfull People) . . . .

Decemb: 26. Instead of the usual Joy & ffestivity of this Season and the continual ffluttering of People up and down the streets, very few are seen to walk abroad, and there is scarce any thing to be heard but Sighs and Complaints, and sad accents of Sorrow at every corner; unless it be among Sailers, and Such hardned Wretches, as are Impenetrable to anything of this kind . . . . Bless God I am afraid of noe Distemper; and I am so well used to all its smells that they are now growen ffamiliar and easy to me . . . .

I do not doubt but you have heard, if not from me, yet from Mr Urmston and other hands of the missace [sic] of many of our friends in North Carolina by the Tuscororo Indians . . . . Our Government here has ordered a Body of 1200 Indians and some white men to march to the Assistance of that distressed People under the Com[mand] of Col Barnevrett [Colonel John Barnwell?] and they have advanced the sume of 4000£ for that Expedicon. This with the sume of 3000£ more raised a very little time before, has greatly Increased the Publick debts; so that the Country is now in debt 23000£ deep . . . .

29. The Elections Act of 1716

THE ELECTIONS ACT OF 1716 WAS THE FIRST TO DESIGNATE THE PARISHES AS ELECTION UNITS AND THE CHURCH WARDENS AS ELECTION OFFICIALS. THIS LAW WAS REPEALED IN 1718 BUT WAS LARGELY RE-ENACTED IN THE ELECTIONS LAW OF 1721, AND THE PARISH REMAINED THE ELECTION UNIT FOR THE ASSEMBLY DOWN TO THE REVOLUTION.

[Elections Act]

An Act to keep inviolate and preserve the freedom of elections, and appoint who shall be deemed and adjudged capable of choosing or being chosen members of the Commons House of Assembly.

Forasmuch as the far greatest part of the inhabitants in their respective counties of this Province, are at a considerable distance from the stated places of election, whereby they are at great expense of time and money, besides all other hazards, in coming to choose members of the Commons House of Assembly: and whereas the several counties of this Province are divided into distinct parishes, so that in them elections from members of the Commons House of Assembly may be managed so as in a great measure to prevent the bad effects of the present manner of electing the said members, which being duly considered by several Grand Juries of this Province, they have presented the same to be a great grievance, and have desired that it might be redressed.

I. Be it therefore enacted, by his Excellency John Lord Cartaret, Palatine, and the rest of the true and absolute Lords and Proprietors of this Province, by and with the advice and concent of the rest of the members of the General Assembly, now met in Charlestown, for the South and West part of this Province, and by the authority of the same, that from and after the dissolution of this present Assembly, the persons to serve as members in any succeeding Commons House of Assembly, shall be elected and chosen after the manner and at the places appointed by this Act.

South Carolina Statutes at Large, II, 683–91.

II. And be it further enacted . . . that the elections for members of the Commons . . . in the distinct parishes hereafter named, shall not continue longer than two days . . . and that in each parish the church-warden or church-wardens, (who are hereby authorized and appointed to make publication of the writs for and to manage such elections), upon the closing of the poll . . . shall put all the votes then delivered in and rolled up by the electors, into some box, glass or paper, sealed up with the seals of any two or more of the electors that are then present, and upon the opening of the poll, shall unseal the said box, in order to proceed in the said election.

III. And for the preventing of frauds in all elections, as much as possible, it is hereby enacted . . . that the names of the electors for members of the Commons . . . shall be fairly entered in a book or roll for that purpose . . . .

IV. And be it further enacted . . . that the said church-warden . . . shall within seven days after the scrutiny is made, give public notice . . . to every person or persons so elected . . . .

V. . . . The inhabitants of the parish of St. Philips, Charlestown, qualified to vote for members of Assembly . . , shall . . . proceed to elect four persons to represent the inhabitants of the said parish . . . .

VI. . . . The inhabitants of . . . the parish of Christ Church [shall vote] for two persons; those of the parish of St. Johns for three persons; those of the parish of St. Andrews for four persons; and those of the Parish of St. James Goose Creek for three persons, to serve in the Commons House of Assembly . . . .

VIII. . . . The inhabitants of the Parish of St. Paul [shall vote] for four persons, and those of the parish of St. Bartholomew for three persons, to serve in the said Commons House of Assembly . . . .

IX. . . . The inhabitants of the parish of St. Helena in Granville County [shall vote] for three persons, to serve in the said Commons House of Assembly . . . .

X. . . . The inhabitants of the parish of St. James, on Santee river, in Craven County [shall elect] one person to serve in the said Commons House of Assembly . . . .

XIV. . . . It is hereby enacted . . . that within two months after the ratification of this Act, surveyors shall be appointed by the Governour . . . to run out the bounds and limits of the said several parishes . . . with all convenient speed . . . .

XVI. . . . In case there should be wanting church-wardens in any parish, to manage the said elections, then . . . the Governour and Council . . . shall have power . . . to nominate and appoint two proper persons in their stead, to manage the said elections . . . .

XX. . . . Every white man, and no other, professing the Christian religion, who hath attained to the age of one-and-twenty years, and hath been in this Province for the space of six months . . . and upon his oath . . . . be proved to be worth thirty pounds current money of this Province, shall be deemed a person qualified to vote for . . . members of the Commons House of Assembly for the parish wherein he actually is resident . . . and that every person qualified to be elected for . . . the said Commons House of Assembly, shall . . . take his corporal oath on the holy evangelists, that he is, in his own proper person, worth five hundred pounds current money of this Province . . . or that he is possessed of five hundred acres of land in the parish . . . .

XXIV. . . . No person may, for any reason whatsoever, be discouraged from giving in his vote at any election of a member . . . of the Commons House of Assembly, at such time and place as shall be duly appointed for that purpose. . . .

XXVI. . . . In every succeeding Commons House of Assembly no less than sixteen members duely met, shall make an house to transact the business of this house; and in passing any law there shall not be less than nine affirmatory . . . .

Read three times and ratified in open Assembly, the 15th day of December, 1716.

30. *The Petition of the Carolina Assemblymen, March, 1717*

THE FAILURE OF THE PROPRIETORS TO COME TO THE AID OF THE CARO-
LINA COLONISTS DURING THE YAMASSEE WAR ADDED TO THE ACCUMU-
LATED DIFFERENCES BETWEEN THE PROVINCE AND ITS OWNERS AND LED
TO A GENERAL FEELING THAT THE ONLY SALVATION FOR SOUTH CAROLINA
LAY IN ROYAL OWNERSHIP. ACCORDINGLY, IN MARCH, 1717, THE COM-
MONS HOUSE OF ASSEMBLY, SITTING IN CHARLES TOWN, ADDRESSED
THE FOLLOWING PETITION TO KING GEORGE I.

[Commons House of Assembly]

To the King's Most Excellent Majesty, the humble address of the
representatives and inhabitants of South Carolina:

We, your Majesty's most dutiful and loyal subjects, the representatives
and inhabitants of the Province of South Carolina in America, out of the
extreme grief we are under to see our country still harassed, and our fellow subjects killed and carried away by our savage Indian enemies, with
the utmost submission, are obliged again to intrude on your Majesty's
more weighty affairs, and presume . . . to lay before your Majesty the
state of this, your afflicted Colony . . . .

Our troubles, instead of coming to a period, daily increase upon us,
and we now see ourselves reduced by these, our misfortunes, to such a
dismal extremity, that nothing but your Majesty's most royal and gracious
protection (under God) can preserve us from ruin. Our Indians continue
committing so many hostilities, and infesting our settlements and plantations to such a degree, that not only those estates which were deserted at
the breaking out of the war cannot be resettled, but others are daily likewise thrown up to the mercy of the enemy, to the impoverishment of
several numerous families.

We further take the liberty to inform your Majesty that notwithstanding all these our miseries, the Lords Proprietors of this Province, instead

W. J. Rivers, *Sketch of the History of South Carolina* (Charleston: McCarter
and Co., 1856), 464–65.

of using any endeavors for our relief and assistance, are pleased to term all our endeavors to . . . procure protection, the business of a faction and party. We most humbly assure your Majesty that it is so far from anything of that nature that all the inhabitants of this Province in general are not only convinced that no human power but that of your Majesty can protect them, but earnestly and fervently desire, that this once flourishing Province may be added to those under your happy protection . . . .

We wish your Majesty a long and happy reign, and that there may never be wanting one of your royal line to fill the British throne . . . .

31. *The Revolution of 1719*

THE DIFFICULTIES BETWEEN THE SOUTH CAROLINIANS AND THE PRO-
PRIETORS RESULTED IN 1719 IN THE FINAL OVERTHROW OF THE PROPRIE-
TORSHIP. IT WAS A BLOODLESS "REVOLUTION," BUT AN EFFECTIVE ONE.
ROBERT JOHNSON, SON OF FORMER GOVERNOR NATHANIEL JOHNSON,
WAS THE PROPRIETARY GOVERNOR AT THE TIME. HE WAS WELL LIKED, BUT
HIS PERSONAL POPULARITY COULD NOT MAKE UP FOR THE DISLIKE OF THE
PROPRIETORS. THE FOLLOWING ACCOUNT IS TAKEN FROM FRANCIS
YONGE'S *Narrative of the Proceedings of the People of South Carolina
in the Year 1719* . . . .

[Francis Yonge]

. . . Being furnished with proper materials, the original papers, and
an eye-witness to most that then passed in the Province, I can answer for
the truth of the facts hereafter related . . . .

The Lords Proprietors who lived in England, although most of them
men of quality, whether they left it to an under-officer who they trusted
with their dispatches and who abused his trust . . . or whatever was
the cause . . . gave no manner of credit to what was told and desired
of them by the whole body of the people . . . but to show they were
resolved to be despotic and absolute, they acted just contrary to what
they were requested . . . to do . . . .

Before and after this, the gentlemen that were chosen to be of the
Assembly had many private meetings in the country; their Association
was formed . . . and almost every body in the whole Province did
sign it, except some few who more immediately belonged to the Proprietors. In it, they promised and agreed to stand by and support
whatsoever should be done by their Representatives then newly chosen,
in disengaging the country from the yoke and burden they labored
under from the Proprietors, and putting the Province under the government of his Majesty . . . . The Convention (as they now called them-

B. R. Carroll, ed., *Historical Collections of South Carolina* . . . , 2 vols. (New
York: Harper, 1836), II, 143–92.

selves) issued a proclamation in their own names, which was in substance, to order and direct all officers civil and military to hold their offices and employments until further orders from them; and finding Mr. Johnson [Governor Robert] would not come into their schemes, they resolved to have a Governor of their own choosing. And accordingly they chose Colonel [James] Moore, who was commander in chief of the militia, under and next to the Governor, but had been removed from his command some small time before, on account of his being very warm in opposing the authority of the Proprietors . . . .

On Monday, the 21st of December, 1719, Mr. Johnson came to town from his plantation . . . and wrote circular letters to his Council to meet him, but they did not come; he had talked to Colonel [Alexander Parris] Paris, the commanding officer of the militia of the town, and engaged him in his interest, as he thought...Notwithstanding which, when he came early on the Monday morning, he found the militia drawn up in the market-place, with colors flying at the forts, and on-board all the ships in the harbor, and great solemnity preparing for their proclaiming their Governor. It would be tedious to the reader to enumerate all that he did at this juncture to oppose their proceedings; some he menaced, and handled more roughly, and some spoke fair to, to persuade them from what they were doing; and going to the commanding officer, he asked him, how he dared appear in arms contrary to his orders, and commanded him in the King's name to disperse his men. But he answered he was obeying the orders of the Convention. And the Governor approaching him, he commanded his men to present their muskets at him, and bid him stand off at his peril. Mr. Johnson was in hopes some gentlemen and others might have joined him; but the defection was so general, that hardly a man but was in arms . . . . Surely, after this, no one will say but Mr. Johnson did all that was possible to prevent the defection of the people . . . .

The people having thus overcome all the little opposition could be made, proceeded to choose a council of twelve, after the manner of the King's governments; of these, Sir Hovendine Walker was chosen President; so they now had their Governor, Council and Convention (as they called themselves) ; but they soon after voted themselves an Assembly, and as such made laws, appointed officers, especially a new chief justice . . . , a secretary, and a provost-marshall . . . .

Soon after this, the new government sent home Col. Barnwell, their agent, to lay their grievances before his Majesty, to beg his protection, and that he would be pleased to take them under his own immediate government . . . . The country's agents procured a hearing before the then Lords of the Regency in Council, his Majesty being in Germany; when their Excellencies were of opinion, the Lords Proprietors had forfeited their Charter, and ordered the Attorney General to take out a *scire facias* against it. They also appointed General Francis Nicholson Provisional Governor, with his Majesty's Commission. And this put an end to any further attempts on the part of Mr. Johnson, and was a good reason to persuade any of his friends from joining with, or assisting him any further, now that what was done had a sort of sanction from the Government of England.

And thus the government became the King's, to the great joy of the people of the Province, who, if they have acted (as it cannot be denied they have) in a manner not the most legal, the necessities of their affairs must plead their excuse. . . . And I believe it will be thought that the Lords Proprietors gave them no small provocations, but made it almost absolutely necessary for them to do what they did, since they found there was no other way of getting rid of their Chief Justice [Nicholas] Trott, who had tyrannized over them for many years, and though often complained of, they could never get removed. Which, together with the right of the Lords Proprietors insisted on, of repealing their laws, the absolute necessity they lay under of the more immediate assistance of the Crown together with their refusing to part with their lands, all these concurring, made them resolved to run all hazards, to have them remedied . . . .

They therefore pray for the continuance of his Majesty's government, who, ever since he has been pleased to take it upon him, has protected their trade by his ships of war, and their country by his forces, and who is always ready to hear the complaints of his subjects, though, never so remote, and is the only power (under God) that is able to defend them . . . .

32. *Agriculture*

THE EARLY ECONOMY OF SOUTH CAROLINA WAS BASED ON AGRI-
CULTURE AND TRADE, WITH THE FORMER GRADUALLY ASSUMING PRIMARY
IMPORTANCE. IT HAD BEEN HOPED THAT CAROLINA WOULD PRODUCE SUCH
SUBTROPICAL CROPS AS OLIVES, SILK, GINGER, AND WINES, BUT NONE OF
THESE PROVED COMMERCIALLY PROFITABLE, AND NOT UNTIL AFTER 1690
WAS RICE DEVELOPED AS A STAPLE CROP. COTTON AND TOBACCO WERE
BOTH GROWN TO A SMALL EXTENT, BUT NOT COMMERCIALLY. OF THE
FOLLOWING EXCERPTS, THE FIRST WAS WRITTEN IN 1682, THE SECOND
IN 1708.

[Thomas Ashe]

The peach tree in incredible numbers grows wild. Of the fruit
expressed, the planters compose a pleasant refreshing liquor; the remainder of the fruit serves the hog and cattle for provision. The
mulberry tree everywhere amidst the woods grows wild. The planters
near their plantations, in rows and walks, plant them for use, ornament
and pleasure. What I observed of this fruit was admirable . . . . A
manufactory of silk well encouraged might soon be accomplished, considering the numerousness of the leaf for provision, the clemency and the
moderateness of the climate to indulge and nourish the silkworm. To
make trial of its success, was the intention of those French Protestant
passengers transported thither in his Majesty's frigate the Richmond
. . . but their design was too early anticipated; the eggs which they
brought with them being hatched at sea, before we could reach the
land, the worms for want of provision were untimely lost and destroyed.
The olive tree thrives there very well . . . ; if the olive be well improved, there may be expected from thence perhaps as good oil as any
the world yields.

A. S. Salley, ed., *Narratives of Early Carolina, 1650–1708* (New York: Charles
Scribner's Sons, 1911), 139–56.

Vines of divers sorts, bearing both black and gray grapes, grow, climbing their highest trees, running and over-spreading their lower bushes. Five kinds they have already distinguished, three of which by replantation, and if well cultivated, they own, will make very good wine . . . .

Gardens as yet they have not much improved or minded, their designs having otherwise more profitably engaged them in settling and cultivating their plantations with good provisions and numerous stocks of cattle; which two things by planters are esteemed the basis and props of all new plantations and settlements . . . . But now their gardens begin to be supplied with such European plants and herbs as are necessary for the kitchen, viz., potatoes, lettuce, coleworts, parsnips, turnips, carrots and radishes; their gardens also begin to be beautified and adorned with such herbs and flowers which to the smell or eye are pleasing and agreeable, viz., the rose, tulip, carnation, lily, etc. Their provision which grows in the field is chiefly Indian corn, which produces a vast increase, yearly, yielding two plentiful harvests, of which they make wholesome bread and good biscuit, which gives a strong, sound and nourishing diet; with milk I have eaten it dressed various ways. Of the juice of the corn when green, the Spaniards with chocolate, aromatized with spices, make a rare drink of an excellent delicacy. I have seen the English amongst the Caribees roast the green ear on the coals, and eat it with a great deal of pleasure. The Indians of Carolina parch the ripe corn, then pound it to a powder, putting it in a leathern bag. When they use it they take a little quantity of powder in the palms of their hands, mixing it with water, and sup it off; with this they will travel several days. In short, it is a grain of general use to man and beast . . . , many thousands of both having from it the greater part of their subsistence. At Carolina they have lately invented a way of making with it a good sound beer; but it is strong and heady. By maceration, when duly fermented, a strong spirit like brandy may be drown off from it . . . .

Pulse they have of great variety, not only of what Europe yields, viz., beans, pease , . . etc., but many other kinds proper to the place, and to us unknown . . . ; strawberries, raspberries, billberries, and blackberries grow frequently up and down the woods. Hemp and flax thrives exceedingly well . . . . What they have planted has been rather for experiment and observation, whether it would be agreeable to the soil and climate . . . . What they have sown, the planters assured us, grew exceedingly well, as also barley . . . . Tobacco grows very well; and they have an excellent sort . . . but finding a great deal of trouble in the planting and curing of it, and the great quantities which Virginia, and the other of his Majesty's plantations make, rending it a drug over all Europe, they do not much regard or encourage its planting . . . .

Tar made of the resinous juice of the pine (which boiled to a thicker consistency is pitch) they make great quantities yearly, transporting several tons to Barbados, Jamaica, and the Caribee Islands. Indigo they have made and that good; the reason why they have desisted I cannot learn . . . . Sponges growing on the sandy shores I have gathered good and large . . . .

The great increase of their cattle is rather to be admired than be believed. Not more than six or seven years past the country was almost destitute of cows, hogs and sheep, now they have many thousand head. The planter in winter takes no care for their provision, which is a great advantage . . . . The cows the year round browse on the sweet leaves growing on the trees and bushes, or on the wholesome herbage growing underneath. They usually call them home in the evening for their milk, and to keep them from running wild. Hogs find more than enough of fruits in the summer, and roots and nuts in the winter. From the abundance of their feeding, when the stock increases and grows strong, great numbers forsake their own plantations, running wild in the woods . . . ; the older surround the younger, and boldly oppose, and oftentimes attack their invaders. Their sheep bears good wool; the ewes at a time often have two or three lambs; they thrive very well, the country being so friendly to their natures . . . .

Of beasts bearing furs, they have a great story of variety, whose skins serve the Indians for clothing and bedding, and the English for many uses, besides the great advantage made of them by their being sent to England . . . . There are also great stocks of tame fowl, viz., geese, ducks, cocks, hens, pigeons, and turkeys . . . .

Metals or minerals I know not of any, yet it is supposed and generally believed that the Appalachian mountains, which lie far up within the land, yields ore both of gold and silver . . . .

[John Archdale]

Carolina . . . produces rice, the best of the known world, being a commodity for sending home, as also pitch, tar, buckskins . . . and furs . . . ; and it hath already such plenty of provisions, as beef, pork, etc., that it furnishes in a great measure Barbados and Jamaica . . . . I understand that silk is come into great improvement, some families making 40 or 50 pounds a year and the plantation work not neglected, little Negro children being serviceable in feeding the silk-worms, etc. And I must give Sir Nathaniel Johnson the reputation of being the principal promoter thereof, and of a considerable vineyard also. I further understand that the inhabitants work up the silk into druggets, mixed with wool, which is an excellent wear for that country . . . .

B. R. Carroll, ed., *Historical Collections of South Carolina* . . . , 2 vols. (New York: Harper, 1836), II, 93–118.

33. Education

ALTHOUGH THERE WERE PRIVATE TUTORS AND TEACHERS IN CHARLES
TOWN BEFORE 1712 AND MINISTERS INSTRUCTED THE CHILDREN OF THEIR
CONGREGATIONS, THE FIRST ATTEMPT AT PUBLIC EDUCATION CAME WITH
THE FREE SCHOOL ACT OF 1712. THE "FREE SCHOOLS" WERE LARGELY
FOR THE POOR; THAT SET UP IN CHARLES TOWN HAD ONLY A SMALL
ATTENDANCE. ST. HELENA'S PARISH ALSO SET UP A FREE SCHOOL, BUT
ASIDE FROM THESE TWO VENTURES LITTLE CAME FROM THE ACT.

An Act for Founding and Erecting of a Free School in Charleston,
for the Use of the Inhabitants of this Province of South Carolina.

Whereas, it is necessary that a free school be erected for the instruction
of the youth of this Province in grammar and the other arts and sciences
and useful learning, and also in the principles of Christian religion; and
whereas several charitable and well disposed Christians, by their last will
and testaments, have given several sums of money for the founding of
a free school, but no person yet is authorized to take the charge and care
of erecting a free school . . . .

I. Be it therefore enacted . . . that the Honorable Charles Craven,
Esq., Governor, and 15 other men shall forever hereafter be one body
politic and corporate in deed and in name, by the name of the Commissioners for Founding Erecting, Governing, Ordering and Visiting a
School for the Use of the Inhabitants of South Carolina . . . and that
they . . . be persons able and capable in law to purchase lands , . . .
tenements . . . and all other manner of goods, chattels and things
whatsoever . . . for the better support and maintenance of masters or
teachers for the said school, and also for the erecting of school houses,
and convenient dwelling houses for the accomodation of the said several
school masters and teachers . . . .

VIII. And be it further enacted . . . that all gifts or legacies formerly
given for the use of the free school of this Province, by any person or
persons whatsoever, are hereby appropriated for the school intended to

South Carolina Statutes at Large, II, 389–96.

be founded and erected, pursuant to the several powers granted to the said commissioners, . . and the monies so received . . . shall be disposed of by order of the said commissioners . . . towards the purchasing of lands, and the erecting of a school house . . . .

IX. And be it further enacted . . . that the said Commissioners . . . are hereby authorized to take up grant from the Lords Proprietors, or purchase . . . so much land as they shall think necessary and convenient for the several masters, teachers and professors, and shall also direct the building of a school house upon the same, and such dwelling houses . . . for the accomodation of the . . . teachers, and shall also appoint one or more persons to be supervisor or supervisors of said buildings . . . .

X. And be it further enacted . . . that Mr. John Douglas shall be master . . . of the said school . . . .

XI. And be it further enacted . . . that upon the death, departure . . . resignation or removal of the said John Douglas, that the said commissioners . . . shall have full power . . . to nominate and appoint another fit person to be master of the said school . . .

XII. And be it further enacted . . . that the person to be master of the said school shall be of the religion of the Church of England, and conform to the same, and shall be capable to teach the learned languages, that is to say, Latin and Greek . . . and to catechize and instruct the youth in the principles of the Christian religion, as professed in the Church of England.

XIII. And be it further enacted . . . that the said Commissioners . . . shall have power . . . to set down and prescribe such orders, rules, statutes, and ordinances for the order, rule and good government of the said school . . . .

XIV. And be it further enacted . . . that any person or persons that within seven years after the ratification of this Act, will contribute twenty pounds . . . towards the erecting and founding of the said school . . . shall have power to nominate any one person to be taught free in the said school for the space of five years . . . .

XV. And be it further enacted . . . that the school-master shall . . . occupy, possess and enjoy to him . . . all such land as shall . . . be taken up, purchased, had or received for the use . . . of the said school . . . and also . . . shall have and receive out of the public treasury of this Province, the full sum of one hundred pounds per annum, to be paid him half-yearly.

XVI. And be it further enacted . . . that . . . the said school-master . . . shall teach freely and without any manner of fee or reward whatsoever . . . any number of scholars, not exceeding twelve . . . to be nominated . . . by the . . . Commissioners . . . .

XVII. And be it further enacted . . . that for every scholar the said master shall teach, besides those . . . to be taught free, he shall be allowed at the rate of four pounds per annum . . . to be paid him by the parent or guardian of such scholar.

XVIII. And be it further enacted . . . that in case the said school master shall have more scholars . . . than one man can well manage . . . then the said Commissioners . . . shall order and appoint a fit person to be usher of the said school . . . and for his encouragement shall be allowed not exceeding fifty pounds per annum . . . .

XIX. Be it further enacted . . . that a fit person shall be nominated and appointed by the said Commissioners, to teach writing, arithmetic, and merchants' accounts, and also the arts of navigation and surveying . . . and for his encouragement shall be allowed . . . not exceeding fifty pounds per annum . . . .

XXI. Be it enacted . . . that as soon as a schoolmaster is settled in any other, or all the rest of the parishes of this Province, and approved by the vestry of such parish or parishes, such school master so approved . . . shall receive the sum of ten pounds per annum out of the public treasury . . . .

XXII. And be it further enacted . . . that the vestry of each parish . . . shall have the power to appoint a place where the parish school shall be built, and shall draw upon the public receiver towards the building the same, the sum of twelve pounds . . . .

34. *The Society for the Propagation of the Gospel*

THE SOCIETY FOR THE PROPAGATION OF THE GOSPEL IN FOREIGN PARTS WAS NOT ONLY VERY ACTIVE IN PROMOTING THE RELIGIOUS LIFE OF THE PROVINCE BUT WAS ALSO PARTICULARLY CONCERNED WITH EDUCATION. THIS MISSIONARY AGENCY ORGANIZED BY THE CHURCH OF ENGLAND ENCOURAGED ITS MINISTERS TO DO MISSIONARY WORK AMONG THE INDIANS AND NEGROES AND TO TEACH THEM THE RUDIMENTS OF LEARNING. QUITE FREQUENTLY THE MINISTERS WERE THE ONLY PEOPLE IN A NEIGHBORHOOD WITH A LIBRARY, AND THEIR BOOKS WERE EAGERLY BORROWED. NOTABLE AMONG THE MINISTERS SENT, IN ADDITION TO GIDEON JOHNSTON, WAS DR. FRANCIS LE JAU. DR. LE JAU CONTRIBUTED MUCH TO THE EDUCATIONAL ADVANTAGES OF THE PROVINCE AND ALSO MADE A STUDY OF THE INDIANS, COMPILING RECORDS OF THEIR SPEECH. JOHNSTON'S WIFE, HENRIETTA, AN EDUCATED WOMAN, OPENED A SCHOOL IN CHARLESTON IN ORDER TO SUPPORT HER FAMILY AFTER THE ACCIDENTAL DROWNING OF HER HUSBAND. THE FOLLOWING EXCERPT ON EDUCATION IN EARLY CAROLINA IS TAKEN FROM DAVID HUMPHREY'S ACCOUNT, WITH INFORMATION COMPILED FROM LETTERS AND REPORTS SENT IN TO THE LONDON OFFICES OF THE SOCIETY BY ITS MINISTERS IN SOUTH CAROLINA.

[David Humphrey]

The missionaries represent frequently to the Society the great want of schools in this Province, for the instruction of the children in the principles of religion and teaching convenient learning. Dr. Le Jau, at Goose Creek, did very earnestly press the Society to allow a salary for a schoolmaster in his parish, and they appointed Mr. Dennis schoolmaster in the year 1710; he had a good number of scholars for several years till the Indian war broke out, which dispersed the people and all

B. R. Carroll, ed., *Historical Collections of South Carolina* . . . , 2 vols. (New York: Harper, 1836), II, 565–61. Humphrey's account was published in 1729 and was entitled *Historical Account of the Incorporated Society for the Propagation of the Gospel in Foreign Parts* . . . .

his scholars. The Society appointed also the Rev. Mr. Guy to be school-master in Charlestown . . . . There is now a handsome school-house built by act of Assembly, and the schoolmaster allowed a salary of £100 proclamation money. Upon Mr. Guy's being removed . . . Mr. Morrit was fixed school-master here; but being lately chosen minister of a parish, and leaving the school, the Society have appointed the Rev. Mr. Lambert, schoolmaster and catechist, or afternoon preacher there; and accounts have been transmitted to the Society, that he discharges his duty with diligence, and hath been very useful in training up the youth.

The people of the whole country are thoroughly sensible of the neces-sity of schools, for the Christian education of their children, and have in several places taken measurers for founding of schools. An act of Assembly was passed in the year 1724 for establishing of a free school in the town of Dorchester, in the parish of St. George. Upon this occasion some of the most considerable gentlemen of this colony, wrote to the Society, "The chief source of irreligion and immorality here, is the want of schools; and we may justly be apprehensive, that if our children continue longer to be deprived of opportunities of being instructed, Christianity will of course decay insensibly, and we shall have a genera-tion of our own, as ignorant as the native Indians . . . ." The people also of St. Paul's parish have lately raised a sum of money by voluntary subscriptions, for founding a free school; and Mr. Whitmarsh of this parish, lately deceased, hath left £500 for this purpose; they have now good hopes of raising a sufficient fund for building and endowing one. The Rev. Mr. Ludlam, late the Society's missionary at Goose Creek, bequeathed all his estate, which hath been computed to be about £2000 Carolina, for building and endowing a school at Goose Creek . . . . The late Richard Beresford, Esq., of St. Thomas's parish, in this Colony, has been a great promoter of the founding of schools. He died in March, 1722, and by his will bequeathed the annual profits of his estate, which was very considerable . . . to apply one third . . . for the support of one or more schoolmasters who should teach reading, accounts, mathe-matics, and other liberal learning; and the remaining two-thirds, towards the support and maintenance of the children of the poor of that parish, who should be sent to this school . . . . It is now to be hoped this necessary work, of the education of the youth, will be carried on with success . . . .

35. *The Indian Trade*

NEXT TO AGRICULTURE, THE TRADE WITH THE INDIANS IN HIDES AND FURS WAS THE MOST IMPORTANT VENTURE OF THE EARLY SOUTH CAROLINIANS. THIS TRADE HAD GROWN RATHER HAPHAZARDLY PRIOR TO 1710, AND THE UNFAIR METHODS USED BY THE TRADERS WERE IN LARGE PART RESPONSIBLE FOR THE YAMASSEE WAR (1715–1717). HOWEVER, IN 1710, TO CONTROL THE INDIAN TRADE, COMMISSIONERS OF THE INDIAN TRADE OF SOUTH CAROLINA WERE APPOINTED BY THE GOVERNOR. THE FOLLOWING LIST OF "INSTRUCTIONS FOR THE SOUTH CAROLINA INDIAN TRADERS" WAS ISSUED IN 1711:

[Instructions to Indian Traders]

1. That your behavior be such towards the Indians that they may have no reason or grounds of complaint either of your severity towards them, or your unreasonable proceedings in letting your horses and hogs destroy their crops which is their general complaint, nor give them any offence on any account whatsoever.

2. That you neither directly nor indirectly carry up, give, sell or any other way dispose of, to or among the Indians any rum or other spirits . . . .

3. And whereas all debts contracted for rum or any other spirits whatever are contrary to law, we do declare all such bargains, sales and agreements void and of no effect and do strictly charge and command you that you do not on any pretence whatsoever demand any pay or satisfaction for any debts so contracted.

4. That you compel no Indian or Indians to pay their relations'

A. S. Salley, ed., *Journal of the Commissioners of the Indian Trade of South Carolina, 1710–1715,* for the South Carolina Historical Commission (Columbia: The State Co., 1926), 18–20. Reprinted by permission of the South Carolina Department of Archives and History. *See also,* W. L. McDowell, Jr., ed., *Journals of the Commissioners of the Indian Trade, Sept. 20, 1710–Aug. 29, 1718,* and *Documents Relating to Indian Affairs, 1750–1754,* and *Documents Relating to Indian Affairs, 1754–1765,* Nos. 1, 2, and 3 in the Series: *The Colonial Records of South Carolina* [The Indian Books] (Columbia: S.C. Archives Dept., 1956 and 1958; and University of South Carolina Press, 1970).

debts, any farther than they are possessed of the effects of the person deceased, unless they have promised and engaged to pay the same in a public manner before the King or chief man of the town. Neither shall you compel any town to pay any private debts unless they are or have been contracted by the consent and approbation of the King and chief men on any account or pretense whatsoever.

5. You shall not bargain, agree for, buy or purchase any slave or slaves, skins or furs, from any Indian or Indians but in their respective towns and until such goods and slaves have been three days in the said towns in their owners' possession . . . .

6. And if any person or persons shall bring any goods or merchandizes whatsoever into any Indian town or settlement to traffic or trade with any Indian or Indians for any slaves, skins or furs, without being qualified by a license as the Act directs, you are hereby impowered to seize such goods or any slave or slaves, skins or furs purchased by the said persons . . . .

7. That you from time to time and at all times in your journeys amongst the Indians advise and acquaint the Commissioners and the agent of what shall come to your knowledge of all matters relating to the safety of the government and trade.

8. No Indian shall be deemed a slave and bought at such unless taken in war, and even those taken in war and made free by their respective masters when they have in them a right and property so to do, shall be deemed free men and citizens of the said nation.

9. You shall not permit or allow any of your slaves to go to war on any pretense whatsoever.

10. If you are a person thought worthy by the Governor to bear his commission in any post you shall not abuse it by making use thereof to promote your particular interests with the Indians.

11. You shall not export or convey out of this Province any skins or furs or any Indian slave or slaves before you pay the duty for the same as the Act directs, and if you intend to export any Indian slave or slaves, skins, or furs by land to Virginia or elsewhere out of this Province, you shall then come down to Charles Town to enter the same and pay the duty as the Act directs.

12. You are carefully to observe to carry yourself civilly and respectively to the Agent.

13. And that you perform and keep all and singular the instructions given you by John Wright, Esq., Agent, or the Agent for the time being, provided that they be not repugnant to the Law for that purpose.

Given at a Board of Commissioners meeting, August 3, 1711.

36. Slavery

THE INCREASING NUMBER OF NEGRO SLAVES IN THE PROVINCE LED TO
THE PASSING, IN 1690, OF THE FIRST SLAVE CODE, AN ADAPTATION OF
THE SLAVE LAWS IN FORCE IN THE ISLAND OF BARBADOS. THE CODE WAS
QUITE HARSH AND AFFORDED THE SLAVE LITTLE PROTECTION. ANOTHER
PROBLEM IN CONNECTION WITH SLAVERY WAS THAT OF CONVERTING THE
NEGROES TO CHRISTIANITY. IT WAS GENERALLY ASSUMED THAT THE
SLAVE WOULD BE CONVERTED, BUT MUCH OPPOSITION TO THIS CAME
FROM THE OWNERS, AS THE SECOND EXCERPT BELOW INDICATES. THE
FIRST SELECTION IS A PARAPHRASE OF THE SLAVE CODE OF 1690; THE
SECOND IS THE REPORT BY AN EARLY MINISTER ON THE TROUBLES
ATTENDANT UPON CONVERTING THE SLAVES.

[Paraphrased Slave Code, 1690]

All slaves should have convenient clothes, and no slave should be
freed by becoming a Christian. Slaves should not be sold in the first
instance to satisfy a debt, but only when other goods and chattels of the
debtor were not sufficient to satisfy the demands of the creditors. The
slave should be restricted to the limits of his master's plantation or
premises, except when accompanied by the master, or with his ticket of
leave in writing upon each occasion of his going abroad. For striking a
white man, a slave could be branded, mutilated, or even put to death,
for repeated offenses. Runaways were to be arrested and committed to
prison until called for by their owners. Slave houses should be regularly
searched for arms and stolen goods. For crimes, the slave was to be
tried by a court of two justices and three freeholders rather than by a
jury. An owner was not liable for any injury or even death to a slave,
if such was the result of punishment for an actual offense, but any one
else killing a slave, except in self-defense, was liable to three months'
imprisonment and the payment of £50 to the owner. If a white servant

Paraphrased from *South Carolina Statutes at Large*, VII, 343–47.

killed a slave, he was to be given 39 lashes and forced to serve the slave's owner up to four years.

[Commissary Gideon Johnston]

It is true that an odd slave here and there may be converted when a minister has leisure, and opportunity for so doing, but this seldom happens . . . . But alas, as the opportunities are neither great nor frequent for carrying on so good a work so the success must be little and inconsiderable in comparison of what might be expected because there are so many rubs and impediments that lie in the way.

First, the slaves have no time to be instructed by the minister, but on the Lord's day; and then he has work enough with the white folks on his hands . . . . Secondly, the plantations are so many and so remote and distant from one another that the slaves cannot be well assembled together for their instruction . . . . Thirdly, the masters of slaves are generally of opinion that a slave grows worse by being a Christian . . . . Fourthly, the legislature does not countenance or encourage work of this importance as much as it should and could . . . . Fifthly, there are many planters who to free themselves from the trouble of feeding and clothing their slaves, allow them one day in the week to clear ground, and plant for themselves as much as will clothe and subsist them and their families. In order to do this, some masters give their slaves Saturday, some half that day, and others Sunday only . . . .

Thus I have given a short account of those more obvious impediments that lie in the way of the slaves' conversion, nor indeed do I see any likelihood humanely speaking, how this necessary work, so shamefully and scandalously neglected hitherto can be carried on with any great hope of success, if the Legislature does not promote and encourage it by proper laws to be enacted for that purpose . . . . The ignorance, therefore, of these poor slaves in the principles of Christianity, in a Christian country and under a Christian government, is not so much their fault as their unhappiness in falling into the hands of such ill masters who not only neglect to instruct them, but scoff at those that attempt it . . . .

Frank J. Klingberg, ed., *Carolina Chronicle. The Papers of Commissary Gideon Johnston, 1707–1716.* University of California Publications in History, L. K. Koontz, D.K. Bjork, C.N. Howard, eds., Los Angeles (Berkeley and Los Angeles: University of California Press, 1946) and (London: Cambridge University Press), vol. 35, 123–34. Reprinted by permission of University of California Press.

37. Early Epidemics

BESIDES MIASMA—WHICH THE PEOPLE WROTE ABOUT AND SPOKE OF
AT GREAT LENGTH—THE CONSTANT THREAT OF MALARIA, ECONOMIC AND
POLITICAL TROUBLES, WARS WITH THE SPANISH AND INDIANS, SOUTH
CAROLINIANS WERE FACED WITH MANY OTHER TROUBLES, PARTICULARLY
EPIDEMICS OF YELLOW FEVER AND SMALLPOX. THE FIRST SELECTION
BELOW IS TAKEN FROM A LETTER OF THE GOVERNOR AND COUNCIL TO THE
LORDS PROPRIETORS, DATED JANUARY 17, 1700; THE SECOND IS FROM A
PERSONAL LETTER WRITTEN BY MRS. AFFRA COMING OF CHARLES TOWN,
DATED MARCH 6, 1699, TO HER SISTER IN ENGLAND.

[Governor James Moore and Council]

A most infectious pestilential and mortal distemper (the same which
hath always been in one or more of his Majesty's American plantations
for eight or nine years past) was from Barbados or Providence brought
in among us in Charles Town about the 28th or 29th of August last,
and much decay of trade and mutations of your Lordships' public
officers has been occasioned thereby. This distemper from the time of
its beginning aforesaid to the first day of November killed in Charles
Town at least 160 persons. Among them were Mr. Ely, Receiver general; Mr. Amory, Receiver for the public treasury; Edward Rowlins,
Deputy marshall; and Edmund Bohun, Chief Justice. Amongst a great
many other good and capital merchants and housekeepers in Charles
Town, the Rev. Mr. Marshall, our minister, was taken away by the
said distemper. Besides those that have died in Charles Town, 10 or 11
have died in the country, all of whom got the distemper and were
infected in Charles Town, went home to their families and died; and
what is notable, not one of their families was infected by them.

Frederick Dalcho, *An Historical Account of the Protestant Episcopal Church in South Carolina* . . . (Charleston: E. Thayer, 1820), 35–36.

[Mrs. Affra Coming]

I am sorry that I should be the messenger of so sad tidings as to desire you not to come to me till you can hear better times than here is now, for the whole country is full of trouble and sickness; it is the small pox which has been mortal to all sorts of the inhabitants and especially the Indians who it is said to have swept away a whole neighboring nation, all but 5 or 6 who ran away and left their dead unburied . . . . Besides, the want of shipping this fall, winter and spring is the cause of another trouble, and has been followed by an earthquake and burning of the town, or one third of it, which they say was of equal value with what remains, besides the great loss of cattle which I know by what has been found dead of mine . . . . All these things put together makes the place look with a terrible aspect, and none knows what will be the end of it.

Edward McCrady, *The History of South Carolina Under the Proprietary Government, 1670–1719* (New York: Macmillan Co., 1897), 307.

READINGS

ADDITIONAL PRINTED SOURCE MATERIALS:

Carroll, B. R., *Historical Collections of South Carolina.* 2 vols.

Johnston, Gideon, *Carolina Chronicle: the Papers of Commissary Gideon Johnston, 1707–1716,* ed. Frank J. Klingberg.

Lejau, Francis. *Carolina Chronicle, 1706–1717,* ed. Frank J. Klingberg.

Salley, A. S. *Narratives of Early Carolina.*

South Carolina Historical Commission. *Commissions and Instructions from the Lords Proprietors of Carolina to Public Officials of South Carolina, 1685–1715,* ed. A. S. Salley.

The Statutes at Large of South Carolina, ed. Thomas Cooper and David J. McCord. 10 vols.

South Carolina Historical Society. *Collections.* (Especially Vol. V, *The Shaftesbury Papers*).

CORRELATED TEXTS:

Crane, Verner W. *The Southern Frontier, 1670–1732.*

McCrady, Edward. *The History of South Carolina Under the Proprietary Government, 1670–1719.*

Rivers, W. J. *A Sketch of the History of South Carolina to the Close of the Proprietary Government by the Revolution of 1719, with an Appendix Containing Many Valuable Records Hitherto Unpublished.*

Sirmans, M. Eugene. *Colonial South Carolina: A Political History, 1663–1763.*

Snowden, Yates, ed. *History of South Carolina.* I, 66–187.

Wallace, D. D. *The History of South Carolina.* I, 82–254.

———. *South Carolina: A Short History,* 32–105.

III
THE ROYAL PERIOD

During the period from 1720 to 1775, South Carolina experienced an era of slow but steady growth. This was owing, in part, to Governor Robert Johnson's "Township Scheme," which helped to people the province. From a scattered settlement of about 15,000 white people and nearly twice that many Negroes, clustered along the coast, by the time of the American Revolution the province had grown to approximately 75,000 white people and 100,000 Negroes. The population was spread throughout the present area of the state except for the westernmost tip, which remained in Cherokee Indian hands, and the region of the Catawba Indians who were settled in their Nation near what is now Fort Mill. Even these lands, however, notably that of the Catawbas, were invaded by the white man, who pushed in to make settlements.

The royal government was at first a distinct improvement over that of the proprietors', but many of the problems of the earlier era remained. Such royal governors as Francis Nicholson, Robert Johnson, and James Glen proved to be excellent administrators, but there still remained external difficulties with Indians, Spanish, and French, who ranged along the Carolina borders, and internal fears of slave insurrection from the large numbers of Negroes. There were the problems of inducing new settlers to come to the colony, of settling them in the interior, and of eventually providing them with local government. There were economic problems, particularly in commerce, where imports continued to exceed exports. Paper money had to be issued to provide a medium of exchange and to pay debts. There was the continuing struggle between assembly and governor, with the assembly gradually gaining the upper hand, especially in financial control of the province.

Indigo was reintroduced successfully by Eliza Lucas and other planters as a staple crop and rapidly became an important economic factor. A newspaper was begun in Charles Town in 1732, and that port town, by the middle of the eighteenth century, had grown to be a social and

101

cultural center equal in importance to New York and Boston. The new settlers—Swiss, French, German, Welsh, Irish, and Scotch-Irish— brought with them new ideas and different talents and soon challenged the older inhabitants for the leadership of the province. The increase in the number of churches and in church membership was noticeable, and, despite the establishment of the Anglican Church, other Protestants, particularly the Presbyterians, Baptists, and Lutherans, grew in numbers and importance. Indeed, the church was often the center of the new settlements, with the minister combining his church duties with those of teacher and community leader. Education lagged, however, and although Charles Town had schools of various kinds there were few elsewhere in the province. A few planters' sons were sent to England, Europe, or the northern provinces for their higher education, but other children were fortunate if they learned their "reading and writing" from their parents, a minister, or perhaps a wandering tutor.

On the whole, despite epidemics, wars, and economic troubles, the royal period was one of comparative prosperity for South Carolina. Relationship with the British parliament was generally good, but there was some opposition to British rule apparent by the 1760's. As the Revolution approached, South Carolina, along with Virginia and Massachusetts, took the lead in guiding the other colonies toward independence.

38. The Proprietors' Surrender of Carolina to the King

ALTHOUGH AN EARLY REBELLION AGAINST THE LORDS PROPRIETORS WAS STAGED BY SOUTH CAROLINA IN 1719, AND A ROYAL GOVERNOR HAD BEEN APPOINTED IN 1721, THE OFFICIAL PROCEEDINGS IN THE TRANSFER OF OWNERSHIP TO THE CROWN WAS A LENGTHY AFFAIR, AND IT WAS NOT UNTIL 1729 THAT THE FOLLOWING ACT WAS PASSED, MAKING SOUTH CAROLINA LEGALLY A ROYAL COLONY. SIX PROPRIETORS OWNED OR CONTROLLED SEVEN OF THE SHARES. THE EIGHTH SHARE WAS OWNED BY LORD GRANVILLE, WHO RELINQUISHED GOVERNMENTAL RIGHTS TO HIS SHARE BUT RETAINED LAND RIGHTS TO A STRIP OF ACREAGE IN THE NORTHERN PART OF NORTH CAROLINA.

An Act for Establishing an Agreement with Seven of the Lords Proprietors of Carolina, for the Surrender of Their Title and Interest in That Province to His Majesty.

And whereas, the said Henry, now Duke of Beaufort; William, Lord Craven; James Bertie, Henry Bertie, Sir John Colleton, and Archibald Hutcheson . . . being six of the present Lords Proprietors of the Province and territory (of Carolina) . . . , have by their humble petition, to his Majesty in Council, offered and proposed to surrender to his Majesty, their said respective shares and interests, not only of and in the said government, franchises and royalties . . . but also all the right and property they have in and to the soil in the aforesaid Provinces or territories . . . . That in consideration of such surrender his Majesty would be pleased to direct, and to cause to be paid to each of them . . . the sum of two thousand five hundred pounds a piece . . . that from and after the payment of the said sum of seventeen thousand five hundred pounds . . . his Majesty . . . shall have, hold and enjoy all and singular the said seven eights parts or share . . . .

William L. Saunders, ed., *The Colonial Records of North Carolina*, 10 vols. (Raleigh: P. M. Hale, State Printer, 1886–90), II, 32–47.

39. *Alexander Cuming's Treaty with the Cherokees, 1730*

AFTER THE END OF THE YAMASSEE WAR, THE INDIANS IN THE LOWER PART OF THE PROVINCE CEASED TO BE A PROBLEM TO THE CAROLINIANS, BUT, AS THE INTERIOR BECAME FREQUENTED BY ENGLISH TRADERS, CONTACT WAS MADE WITH THE MORE POWERFUL CHEROKEES. NEW PROBLEMS AROSE. THE CHEROKEES WERE IMPORTANT TO ENGLISH IMPERIAL DESIGNS, NOT ONLY AS POTENTIAL ENEMIES OR FRIENDS BUT ALSO TO PROVIDE A BUFFER BETWEEN CAROLINA AND FRENCH LOUISIANA AS SOURCES OF SUPPLY IN THE IMPORTANT TRADE IN SKINS AND HIDES. FOR THIS REASON, SIR ALEXANDER CUMING, A RATHER ODD CHARACTER WHO HAD JUST COME OVER FROM ENGLAND, WAS SENT ON A MISSION TO THE CHEROKEES. HE WON FROM THEM THE FOLLOWING TREATY OF TRADE AND FRIENDSHIP:

[Cherokee Treaty]

Whereas the six chiefs, with the consent of the whole nation of Cherokees, at a general meeting of their nation at Nequassee, were deputed by Moytoy, their chief warrior, to attend Sir Alexander Cumming to Great Britain, where they had seen the Great King George; and Sir Alexander by authority from Moytoy and all the Cherokees had laid the crown of their nation, with the scalps of their enemies and feathers of glory at his Majesty's feet, as a pledge of their loyalty. And whereas the great King had commanded the Lords Commissioners of Trade and Plantations, to inform the Indians that the English on all sides of the mountains and lakes were his people, their friends his friends, and their enemies his enemies—that he took it kindly that the great nation of Cherokees had sent them so far to brighten the chain of friendship between him and them and between his people and their people . . . . It is agreed that his children in Carolina do trade with the Indians, and furnish them with all manner of goods they want, and

David Ramsay, *History of South Carolina* . . . , 2 vols. (Charleston: David Longworth for the author, 1809), I, 101–103.

to make haste to build houses and plant corn from Charleston towards the towns of the Cherokees behind the great mountains; that he desires the English and the Indians to live together as children of one family; that the Cherokees be always ready to fight against any nation, whether white men or Indians, who shall dare molest or hurt the English; that the nation of Cherokees on their part shall take care to keep the trading path clean; that there be no blood on the path where the English tread . . . ; that the Cherokees shall not suffer their people to trade with white men of any other nation but the English, nor permit white men of any other nation to build any forts or cabins, or plant any corn among them upon lands which belong to the great King; and if any such attempt shall be made, the Cherokees must acquaint the English governor therewith, and do whatever he directs in order to maintain and defend the great King's right to the country of Carolina; that if any Negroes shall run into the woods from their English masters, the Cherokees shall endeavor to apprehend them and bring them to the plantation from whence they run away or to the governor, and for every slave so apprehended and brought back, the Indians that bring him shall receive a gun and a watchcoat; that if by any accident it shall happen that an Englishman shall kill a Cherokee, the king or chief of the nation shall first complain to the English governor, and the man who did the harm shall be punished by the English laws as if he had killed an Englishman; and in like manner if any Indian happens to kill an Englishman, the Indian shall be delivered up to the governor to be punished by the same English laws as if he were an Englishman.

40. *Governor Robert Johnson's Township Plan, 1731*

ALTHOUGH ROBERT JOHNSTON, PROPRIETARY GOVERNOR, WAS DEPOSED
IN 1719, HE RETURNED TO THE POSITION OF ROYAL GOVERNOR IN 1730.
ONE OF HIS MAJOR PROJECTS WAS THE SETTLEMENT OF THE INTERIOR,
AND TO THIS END HIS "TOWNSHIP PLAN" WAS EVOLVED. THE SETTLE-
MENT OF THE BACK COUNTRY WITH EUROPEANS WAS INTENDED TO
OFFSET THE LARGE NUMBERS OF SLAVES, TO FORM A BUFFER AREA
BETWEEN CHARLESTON AND THE INDIANS, AND TO INCREASE THE
STRENGTH OF THE PROVINCE AGAINST THE FRENCH AND SPANISH.

[Peter Purry]

The King of Great Britain having about three years ago purchased this
Province of the Lords Proprietors thereof, has since studied to make
agriculture, commerce and navigation flourish in it. His Majesty imme-
diately nominated Col. [Robert] Johnson, a worthy gentleman, to be
Governor thereof; who, at his departure for Carolina, received orders and
Instructions, but in particular was directed instantly to mark out places
in a proper situation for building eleven towns, viz.: Two on the river
Altamaha; two on the river Savannah, one at the head of the river
Ponpon, two on the river Santee, one at the river Wateree, one at the
river Waccamaw, and one at the river Pedee.

The district of each of these towns is to contain the extent of 20,000
acres of land, formed into a square, bordering on the river, and divided
into shares of fifty acres for each man, woman or child of one family;
which may be augmented as the planters shall be in a condition to
cultivate a larger quantity of ground, and every one of them shall have
an equal share of the better and worse lands, and also the same right
on the river.

Each town shall be formed into a parish, the extent whereof shall be
about six miles round the town on the same side of the river; and as

Peter Purry, *A Description of the Province of Carolina*, in B. R. Carroll, *Historical
Collections of South Carolina . . .* , 2 vols. (New York: Harper, 1836), II,
124–25.

soon as a parish shall contain one hundred masters of families, they may send two members to the Assembly of the Province, and enjoy the same privileges as the other parishes of the Province . . . .

The rent shall be four shillings per annum for every hundred acres, except that for the first ten years the lands shall be entirely free, and all those that shall settle in the said towns shall enjoy the same advantages.

His Majesty further grants to every European servant, whether man or woman, fifty acres of land free of all rents for ten years, which shall be distributed to them after having served their master for the time agreed on . . . .

[Hewat on Settling Townships]

The plan of settling townships, especially as it came accompanied with the royal bounty, has proven beneficial in many respects. It encouraged multitudes of poor oppressed people in Ireland, Holland and Germany to emigrate, by which means the Province received a number of frugal and industrious settlers. As many of them came from manufacturing towns in Europe, it might have been expected that they would naturally have pursued those occupations to which they had been bred, and in which their chief skill consisted. But this was by no means the case, for, excepting a few of them that took up their residence in Charleston, they procured lands, applied to pasturage and agriculture, and by raising hemp, wheat and maize in the interior parts of the country, and curing hams, bacon and beef, they supplied the market with abundance of provisions, while at the same time they found that they had taken the shortest way of arriving at easy and independent circumstances.

Alexander Hewat, *An Historical Account of the Rise and Progress of the Colonies of South Carolina and Georgia*, in B. R. Carroll, *Historical Collections of South Carolina* . . . , 2 vols. (New York: Harper, 1836), I, 376.

41. Governor Robert Johnson's Death, May 3, 1735

DURING HIS TERM AS ROYAL GOVERNOR, ROBERT JOHNSON WAS BOTH AN EFFICIENT ADMINISTRATOR AND A POPULAR LEADER, EARNING THE TITLE IN SOUTH CAROLINA HISTORY OF "GOOD GOVERNOR JOHNSON." THE FOLLOWING OBITUARY NOTE INDICATES THE ESTEEM IN WHICH HE WAS HELD BY HIS COUNTRYMEN.

[Newspaper Account of Gov. Robert Johnson's Death and Funeral]

On Saturday last between twelve and one o'clock died, after a long and lingering illness, his Excellency, Robert Johnson, Esquire, Captain General, Governor and Commander in Chief in and over this, his Majesty's Province, and was decently interred on Monday last in a vault near the altar in Charles Town Church. His pall was supported by the gentlemen of his Council and his corpse was attended to the grave by the Lower House of Assembly preceded by the Speaker and a numerous body of Gentlemen and Ladies, who came from all parts of the Province, where timely notice could be had of his death, to pay the last respects to one whom they might justly look upon as their common father.

The troop and two companies of the Charles Town Fort appeared on the melancholy occasion to add to the solemnity of the procession. The principal mourners were his Excellency's two sons and two daughters, his brother-in-law, Thomas Broughton, Esq., the present governor, and his family. His Excellency died in the 59th year of his age and the fifth of his government. He had on his advancement disposed of his patrimony in England, so that his interest might concur with his inclination in promoting the welfare of that country his Majesty had done him the honor to intrust him with the care of, and accordingly always kept up a good correspondence with the Assembly, as they were all fully convinced by the whole tenor of his conduct that the interest of the Province lay principally at his heart. But it is needless to enlarge upon a life and character so well known, and which has rendered his death so universally and deservedly lamented over the whole Province.

South Carolina Gazette, 1732–1775 (Charleston, S.C.), May 10, 1735.

42. *Inducement to Settlers, 1739*

THE ATTEMPTS TO ENTICE ADDITIONAL EUROPEAN SETTLERS TO SOUTH
CAROLINA CONTINUED THROUGHOUT MOST OF THE ROYAL PERIOD. THE
FOLLOWING SELECTION GIVES THE INDUCEMENTS OFFERED TO POTENTIAL
SETTLERS IN THE WELSH TRACT AREA ON THE PEE DEE.

[From Newspaper Report]

In Council, the 7th day of July, 1739: There being great reason to
believe that many poor people of the Principality of Wales would
remove into this Province, provided they could be sure of having the
same bounty (over and above the land) as other poor Protestants have
heretofore had who have become settlers in his Majesty's townships,
Resolved that the sum of six thousand pounds shall be reserved out of
the Township Fund, to be appropriated as a bounty to the first two
hundred people above twelve years of age (two under twelve years of
age to be deemed as one) who shall arrive here from the Principality of
Wales, and become settlers upon the Welch Tract upon Pedee, within
the space of two years from hence, the said bounty to be proportioned as
follows, viz.:
To each above twelve years of age, twelve bushels of corn, one barrel
of beef, fifty weight of pork, one hundred weight of rice, one bushel of
salt. To each male above twelve years of age, also, one axe, one broad
hoe, one cow and calf, and one young sow. And the charge of measuring
out, and the fifty acres of land per head allowed by his Majesty.

South Carolina Gazette, 1732–1775 (Charleston, S.C.), July 7–14, 1739.

43. The Stono Slave Insurrection, 1739

IN A COLONY IN WHICH SLAVES OUTNUMBERED THEIR MASTERS ALMOST
TWO TO ONE, THE DANGER OF A SLAVE REBELLION WAS ALWAYS PRESENT.
IN SOUTH CAROLINA THIS DANGER WAS ENHANCED BY THE PRESENCE IN
FLORIDA OF THE SPANISH, WHO ENCOURAGED RUNAWAYS. THE RUN-
AWAY SLAVE WAS ABLE TO FIND REFUGE WITH THE SPANISH, AND IN
TIMES OF WAR, THERE WAS ALWAYS THE POSSIBILITY OF THE SLAVES
BEING INCITED TO INSURRECTION BY THE ENEMY. THE FOLLOWING
CONCERNS AN INSURRECTION AT STONO.

[Report on the Stono Insurrection]

In September, 1739, our slaves made an insurrection at Stono, in the
heart of our settlements, not twenty miles from Charles Town, in which
they massacred twenty-three whites, after the most cruel and barbarous
manner to be conceived; and having got arms and ammunition out of a
store, they bent their course to the southward, burning all the houses
on the road. But they marched so slow, in full confidence of their own
strength from their first success, that they gave time to a party of our
militia to come up with them. The number was in a manner equal on
both sides, and an engagement ensued, such as may be supposed in such
a case. But by the blessing of God, the Negroes were defeated, the
greatest part being killed on the spot, or taken; and those that then
escaped were so closely pursued, and hunted day after day, that in the
end all but two or three were killed or taken and executed. That the
Negroes would not have made this insurrection had they not depended
on St. Augustine for a place of reception afterwards, was very certain;

South Carolina Commons House of Assembly, Committee to Inquire into the
Causes of the Failure of the Expedition Against St. Augustine: Report, in B. R.
Carroll, *Historical Collections of South Carolina* . . . , 2 vols., (New York:
Harper, 1836), II, 357–59.

and that the Spaniards had a hand in prompting them to this particular action, there was but little room to doubt . . . .

With indignation we looked at St. Augustine . . . . That den of thieves and ruffians! Receptacle of debtors, servants and slaves! Bane of industry and society! and revolved in our minds all the injuries this Province had received from thence ever since its first settlement . . . .

44. The Slave Code of 1740

THE SLAVE CODE OF 1690 WAS REVISED IN 1722 AND AGAIN IN 1735, BUT THE STONO INSURRECTION OF 1739 LED TO THE PASSAGE OF NEW AND MORE RESTRICTIVE SLAVE LAWS. THIS SLAVE CODE OF 1740 WAS HARSH IN SOME RESPECTS BUT IT ADDED MANY PROVISIONS FOR THE BENEFIT OF THE SLAVE. CHANGED SLIGHTLY FROM TIME TO TIME, IT REMAINED THE BASIC SLAVE LAW OF SOUTH CAROLINA AS LONG AS THAT INSTITUTION EXISTED. THE FOLLOWING IS A SUMMARY AND PARAPHRASE OF THE ORIGINAL ACT.

[Paraphrased Slave Code, 1740]

All Negroes and mulattoes were to be considered slaves unless they could prove that they were born free or had been manumitted. Children of slave mothers were to be slaves; of free mothers, free. No slave could leave his master's property without a pass, and any slave caught off his master's property could be challenged by any white man. If the slave resisted capture, he could legally be killed. No slave was to be allowed to carry firearms except in company with his master or some other white man. A slave attempting to leave the province without permission was subject to the death penalty. For striking a white person, a slave could be punished at the discretion of the local magistrate; and for a third offense, he could be executed. Slaves executed for crimes were to be paid for out of the provincial treasury. A person taking up a runaway slave was to be paid for his keep until he could be returned to his owner or turned over to the police. Lists of runaway slaves were to be published regularly by the provost marshal. Slaves in prison were not to be worked, but were to be given twenty lashes every Monday. At least one white man was to be present on any plantation where ten or more slaves were working. Slaves were not allowed to own horses, cattle or hogs, or boats or canoes; nor were they permitted to carry on trade for their own profit. No slave could be given his freedom without the

Paraphrased from *South Carolina Statutes at Large*, VII, 397–99.

permission of the General Assembly of the province. In case of threatened insurrection, any militia commander could call out his troops for action.

On the other hand, no slave could be punished by anyone taking his life or permanently crippling him without a trial before a magistrate. All slaves were to be provided with sufficient clothing for the season, housing, and food, and, in case any owner or person in charge of slaves neglected to provide such, the local magistrate was authorized to inquire into the matter and to order such relief for the slave as he thought fit. No strong liquors were to be sold to slaves. An owner could be fined for working a slave on Sunday, except in absolute necessity. Cruelty to a slave by the agent of an owner was made the responsibility of the owner, even if he were not present. Owners were prohibited from working their slaves more than 15 hours per day in the spring and summer and 14 hours per day in fall and winter. However, a slave could not give evidence against a white man in court, and for want of other evidence a white man upon oath could clear himself from any charge by a slave.

45. The Expedition Against St. Augustine, 1740

SOUTH CAROLINIANS HAD LONG CONSIDERED THE SPANISH IN FLORIDA
AS THEIR MAJOR ENEMY, AND THE KNOWLEDGE THAT THEY WERE BEHIND
THE STONO SLAVE REBELLION OF 1739 MADE IT IMPERATIVE THAT
SOMETHING BE DONE TO PUNISH THEM. IN 1740, ENGLAND WAS AT
WAR WITH SPAIN IN WHAT WAS KNOWN AS THE "WAR OF THE SPANISH
SUCCESSION" IN EUROPE AND AS "KING GEORGE'S WAR" IN AMERICA.
THE TIME FOR REVENGE SEEMED AT HAND. GENERAL EDWARD OGLE-
THORPE, ONE OF THE FOUNDERS OF GEORGIA, WAS IN THE COLONY AND
OFFERED TO LEAD AN EXPEDITION AGAINST THE SPANISH AT ST. AUGUS-
TINE. THE SOUTH CAROLINA ASSEMBLY PROVIDED THE FUNDS, BUT THE
ATTEMPT WAS A FAILURE. IN RETALIATION, THE SPANISH ATTACKED
GEORGIA IN 1742, BUT THEY WERE DRIVEN OFF BY A COMBINED FORCE OF
GEORGIANS, SOUTH CAROLINIANS, AND FRIENDLY INDIANS.

[Hewat Writing of Oglethorpe and the Expedition Against St. Augustine]

On the 9th day of May, the General passed over to Florida with four
hundred select men of his regiment, and a considerable party of
Indians . . . .

A few days afterward, the General marched with his whole force,
consisting of above two thousand men, regulars, provincials, and Indians,
to Fort Moosa, situated within two miles of Augustine, which on his
approach the Spanish garrison evacuated, and retired into the town
. . . . Notwithstanding the despatch of the British army, the Spaniards
. . . had collected all the cattle in the woods around them, and drove
them into the town; and the General found, both from a view of the
works, and the intelligence he had received from prisoners, that more
difficulty would attend this enterprise than he at first expected . . . .
The castle was built of soft stone, with four bastions; the curtain was

Alexander Hewat, *An Historical Account of the Rise and Progress of the Colonies
of South Carolina and Georgia*, in B. R. Carroll, *Historical Collections of South
Carolina* . . . , 2 vols. (New York: Harper, 1836), I, 336–40.

sixty yards in length, the parapet nine feet thick; the rampart twenty feet high . . . and newly made bombproof. Fifty pieces of cannon were mounted, several of which were twenty-four pounders . . . . The garrison consisted of seven hundred regulars, two troops of horse, four companies of armed Negroes, besides the militia of the Province, and Indians.

The General now plainly perceived that an attack by land upon the town, and an attempt to take the castle by storm would cost him dear before he could reduce the place, and therefore changed his plan of operations. With the assistance of the ships of war, which were now lying at anchor off St. Augustine bar, he resolved to turn the siege into a blockade, and try to shut up every channel by which provisions could be conveyed to the garrison . . . . Then he sent Colonel Vanderdussen, with the Carolina regiment, over a small creek, to take possession of a neck of land called Point Quartel, above a mile distant from the castle, with orders to erect a battery upon it; while he himself, with his regiment, and the greatest part of the Indians, embarked on boats, and landed on the island of Anastatia . . . . Batteries were soon erected, and several cannon mounted with the assistance of the active and enterprising sailors. Having made these dispositions, General Oglethorpe then summoned the Spanish governor to a surrender; but the haughty Don, secure in his stronghold, sent him for answer that he would be glad to shake hands with him in his castle.

This insulting answer excited the highest degree of wrath and indignation in the General's mind; and made him resolve to exert himself to the utmost for humbling his pride. The opportunity of surprising the place now being lost, he had no other secure method left but to attack it at the distance in which he then stood. For this purpose he opened his batteries against the castle, and at the same time threw a number of shells into the town. The fire was returned with equal spirit both from the Spanish fort and from six half galleys in the harbor, but so great was the distance, that though they continued the cannonade for several days, little damage was done on either side . . . . About the same time . . . some small ships from Havana with provisions and a reinforcement of men, got into Augustine, by the narrow channel, to the relief of the garrison . . . . Then, all prospects of starving the enemy being lost, the army began to despair of forcing the place to surrender. The Carolina troops, enfeebled by the heat, dispirited by sickness, and fatigued by fruitless efforts, marched away in large bodies. The navy being short of provisions, and the usual season of hurricanes approaching, the commander judged it imprudent to hazard his Majesty's ships by remaining longer on that coast. Last of all, the General himself, sick of a fever, and his regiment worn out with fatigue . . . with sorrow and regret followed, and reached Frederica about the 10th of July, 1740.

Thus ended the unsuccessful expedition against Augustine, to the great disappointment of both Georgia and Carolina. Many heavy reflections were afterward thrown out against General Oglethorpe for his conduct during the whole enterprise . . . . He, on the other hand, declared that he had no confidence in the firmness and courage of the Carolinians; for that they refused obedience and at last abandoned his camp, and retreated to Carolina. The truth was, so strongly fortified was the place, both by nature and art, that probably the attempt must have failed, though it had been conducted by the ablest officer, and executed by the best disciplined troops. The miscarriage, however, was particularly ruinous to Carolina, having not only subjected the Province to a great expense, but also left it in a worse situation than it was before the attempt.

46. The Hurricane of September, 1752

NATURAL DISASTERS WERE NO EASIER FOR THE SOUTH CAROLINIANS TO
BEAR THAN ECONOMIC AND POLITICAL TROUBLES, FIRES, AND EPIDEMICS.
THE HURRICANE OF SEPTEMBER, 1752, BROUGHT HAVOC UPON THE CITY
OF CHARLESTON AND NEIGHBORING PLANTATIONS. THE FOLLOWING
DESCRIBES THE EFFECT OF THE HURRICANE.

[George Milligen-Johnston]

There are three remarkable hurricanes remembered by the inhabitants;
the last happened on the 15th of September, 1752. The summer preceding
was uncommonly hot and dry . . . . Very little rain fell between July
and September 14, when the wind in the afternoon began to blow with
great violence from the north-east and continued increasing until the
morning of the 15th, when its force was irresistible; it stopped the course
of the Gulf Stream, which poured in upon us like a torrent, filling the
harbour in a few minutes. Before eleven o'clock, A.M., all the vessels
in the harbour were on shore, except the Hornet, man-of-war, who rode
it out by cutting away her masts. All the wharfs and bridges were
ruined, and every house and store, etc., upon them were beaten down,
as were also many houses in the town, with abundance of damaged roofs,
chimneys, etc. Almost all the tiled or slated houses were uncovered,
and great quantities of merchandise, etc., in the stores of the Bay Street
were damaged by their doors being burst open. The town was likewise
overflowed, the water having risen ten feet above high water mark at
spring-tides, and nothing was to be seen but ruins of houses, canoes,
wrecks of boats, masts, yards, barrels, staves, etc., floating and driving
with great violence through the streets and around the town. The
inhabitants, finding themselves in the midst of a tempestuous sea . . .
began to despair of life, but . . . they were soon delivered from their
apprehensions, for, about ten minutes after eleven o'clock the wind

George Milligen-Johnston, *A Short Description of the Province of South Carolina,*
in B. R. Carroll, *Historical Collections of South Carolina* . . . , 2 vols. (New
York: Harper, 1836), II, 474–76.

veered to east southeast, south and southwest very quick, and then . . .
the waters fell about five feet in the space of ten minutes. Without that
sudden and unsuspected fall, every house and inhabitant of this town
must, in all probability, have perished. The shifting of the wind left the
stream of the Gulf of Florida to follow its own wonted course, and
before three o'clock P.M., the hurricane was entirely over. Many people
were drowned, and others much hurt by the fall of houses. For about
forty miles round Charles-town, there was hardly a plantation that did
not lose every outhouse on it, and the roads, for years afterward, were
encumbered with trees blown and broken down.

47. The Cherokee Treaty of July 2, 1755

FOLLOWING ALEXANDER CUMING'S TREATY WITH THE CHEROKEES IN 1730, THAT POWERFUL GROUP OF INDIANS REMAINED MORE OR LESS FRIENDLY WITH THE SOUTH CAROLINIANS FOR NEARLY THREE DECADES. HOWEVER, IN THE LATE 1740s AND IN THE EARLY 1750s, FRENCH INTRIGUES ALMOST WON THE CHEROKEES TO THEIR SIDE. IN 1747 AND IN 1753, GOVERNOR JAMES GLEN MADE TREATIES WITH THE CHEROKEES, OBTAINING CESSIONS OF LAND FROM THEM AND AT THE SAME TIME PROMISING THEM FORTS FOR PROTECTION AGAINST THEIR ENEMIES. BUT ILL WILL CONTINUED TO EXIST, AND GLEN HOPED BY THE TREATY TO TIE THE CHEROKEES FINALLY AND EFFECTIVELY TO THE BRITISH AND TO SOUTH CAROLINA IN PARTICULAR. DESPITE HIS EFFORTS, THE CHEROKEES WAGED WAR FROM 1759 TO 1761. WHEN IT CAME TO AN END, THERE WAS RELIEF FOR BOTH THE ENGLISH AND THE INDIANS. IT HAD BEEN WAGED BETWEEN ONLY ONE TRIBE AND THE ENGLISH NATION AND HAD NOT SPREAD TO OTHER TRIBES, SUCH AS THE CATAWBAS AND THE CHOCTAWS. THE CHIEF REASON FOR THIS WAS THE INDIANS' DEPENDENCE ON THE ENGLISH FOR THEIR SUPPLIES AND GROWING NEEDS. THE FOLLOWING CONCERNS GOVERNOR GLEN AND THE INDIANS.

[Governor Glen Arranging a Treaty with the Cherokees]

In 1755, Governor Glen met the Cherokee warriors in their own country, with a view to purchase some lands from them; and, after the usual ceremonies previous to such solemn treaties were over, the Governor sat down under a spreading tree and Chulochcullah, being chosen speaker for the Cherokee nation, came and took a seat beside him. Then the Governor arose, and made a speech in the name of the King, representing his great power, wealth and goodness, and his particular regard for his children the Cherokees. He reminded them of

Alexander Hewat, *An Historical Account of the Rise and Progress of the Colonies of South Carolina and Georgia*, in B. R. Carroll, *Historical Collections of South Carolina . . .* , 2 vols. (New York: Harper, 1836), I, 433–35.

the happiness they had long enjoyed by living under his protection; and added that he had many presents to make them, and expected they would surrender a share of their territories in return for them. He acquainted them of the great poverty and wicked designs of the French, and hoped they would permit none of them to enter their towns. He demanded lands to build two forts in their country, to protect them against their enemies, and to be a retreat to their friends and allies, who furnished them with arms, ammunition, hatchets, clothes and everything that they wanted.

When the Governor had finished his speech, Chulochcullah arose, and holding his bow in one hand, his shaft of arrows and other symbols used by them on such occasions, in the other, in answer spoke . . . :

"We, our wives and our children, are all children of the great King George—I have brought this child, that when he grows up he may remember our agreement on this day and tell it to the next generation, that it may be known forever . . . . We freely surrender a part of our lands to the great King . . . . We hope the King will pity his children the Cherokees, and send us guns and ammunition. We fear the French— give us arms and we will go to war against the enemies of the great King . . . . My speech is at an end. It is the voice of the Cherokee nation . . . ."

At this Congress, a territory of prodigious extent was ceded and surrendered to the King. Deeds of conveyance were drawn up, and formally executed by their head men in the name of the whole people. It contained not only much rich land, but there the air was more serene, and the climate more healthy, than in the maritime parts. It exhibited many pleasant and romantic scenes, formed by an intermixture of beautiful hills, fruitful valleys, rugged rocks, clear streams and gentle water falls . . . . The acquisition at that time was so far of importance to Carolina as it removed the savages at a greater distance from the settlements, and allowed the inhabitants liberty to extend backwards, in proportion as their number increased. Soon after the cession of these lands, Governor Glen built a fort about three hundred miles from Charlestown, afterward called Fort Prince George, which was situated on the banks of the River Savannah, and within gun-shot of an Indian town called Keowee . . . .

About a hundred and seventy miles further down there was another strong-hold, called Fort Moore, in a beautiful commanding situation on the banks of the same river. In the year following another fort was erected, called Fort Loudoun, among the Upper Cherokees, situated on Tennessee River, upwards of five hundred miles distant from Charlestown . . . . These strong-holds . . . were garrisoned by his Majesty's independent companies of foot, stationed there for the protection of the two Provinces . . . .

48. *Charleston in 1763*

THERE ARE SEVERAL GOOD DESCRIPTIONS OF CHARLESTON IN THE MID-EIGHTEENTH CENTURY, BUT THE FOLLOWING IS ONE OF THE BEST. IT IS TAKEN FROM GEORGE MILLIGEN-JOHNSTON's *A Short Description of the Province of South Carolina.* ON THE OTHER HAND, THERE IS RELATIVELY LITTLE INFORMATION ON THE EARLY BEGINNINGS OF OTHER SOUTH CAROLINA TOWNS. THE SECOND SELECTION, A BRIEF NOTE FROM *An Historical Account of the Rise and Progress of the Colonies of South Carolina and Georgia,* GIVES ALEXANDER HEWAT's OPINION OF OTHER TOWNS IN THE 1760s.

[George Milligen-Johnston]

The Province is divided into four counties and nineteen parishes. Charles-town is the metropolis . . . . The streets are broad, straight, and uniform, intersecting one another at right angles. Those that run east and west extend from one river to the other. Bay Street, which fronts Cooper River and the ocean, is really handsome and must delight the stranger who approaches it from the sea.

There are about eleven hundred dwelling-houses in the town, built with wood or brick; many of them have a genteel appearance, though generally incumbered with balconies or piazzas; and are always decently, and often elegantly, furnished; the apartments are contrived for coolness, a very necessary consideration.

The white inhabitants are about four thousand, and the Negro servants near the same number. I have examined a pretty exact register of the births and burials for fifteen years, excepting when the small-pox prevailed, nearly equal . . . .

The town is divided into two parishes, St. Philip's and St. Michael's. St. Philip's church is one of the handsomest buildings in America. It is

B. R. Carroll, *Historical Collections of South Carolina* . . . , 2 vols. (New York: Harper, 1836), II, 483–85.

of brick, plastered, and well enlightened on the inside. The roof is arched except over the galleries; and two rows of Tuscan pillars support the galleries and arch that extend over the body of the church . . . . The west end of the church is adorned with four Tuscan columns, supporting a double pediment, which has an agreeable effect. The two side doors, which enter into the belfry, are ornamented with round columns of the same order . . . . The steeple rises octagonal, with windows on every other face, till it is terminated by a dome, upon which stands a lanthorn for the bells, and from which rises a vane in the form of a cock.

St. Michael's church is built of brick; it is not yet finished. It consists of a lofty and well-proportioned steeple, formed of a tower and spire. The tower is square from the ground, and in this form rises to a considerable height . . . . The body of the steeple is carried up octangular within the pillars, on whose intablature the spire rises, and is terminated by a gilt globe, from which rises a vane in the form of a dragon. This steeple is one hundred and ninety-two feet in height, and is very useful to the shipping, who see it long before they make any other part of land . . . . The church is eighty feet in length, without including the tower . . . and fifty-eight feet wide.

Besides the churches, there are meeting houses for the members of the Church of Scotland, for those called Independents, two for Baptists, one for French, and one for German Protestants. Though all of them are neat, large and convenient, they are too plain to merit particular descriptions.

Near the center of the Town is the State-House, a large, commodious brick building, with the south frontis decorated with four columns . . . . It consists of two stories besides the roof; on the lower are the court-room, the secretary's office, and apartments for the house-keeper; on the upper story are two large, handsome rooms: one is for the Governor and Council, the other for the Representatives of the people, with lobbies and rooms for their clerks. The room, called the Council Chamber, appears rather crowded and disgusting, than ornamental and pleasing, by the great profusion of carved work in it; in the upper part of the house or roof is a large room for the Provincial armory. Near the State House is a very neat market place, well-regulated and plentifully supplied with provisions.

[Alexander Hewat]

With respect to the towns in Carolina, none of them, excepting Charleston, merit the smallest notice. Beaufort, Purysburgh, Jackson-burgh, Dorchester, Camden and Georgetown, are all inconsiderable villages, having in each no more than twenty, thirty, or at most, forty dwelling houses. But Charleston, the capital of the Province, may be ranked with the first cities of British America, and yearly advances in size, riches and population.

B. R. Carroll, *Historical Collections of South Carolina* . . . , 2 vols. (New York: Harper, 1836), I, 501.

49. The Regulator Troubles of 1767–1768

THE ONLY POLICE OFFICIALS, AND THE ONLY COURTS, EXCEPT FOR A FEW MAGISTRATES, WERE LOCATED IN CHARLESTON. AS THE INTERIOR PARTS OF THE PROVINCE WERE SETTLED, AT A DISTANCE FROM 75 TO 200 MILES FROM THE CAPITAL, THE OUTLYING SETTLEMENTS WERE WITHOUT LAW AND ORDER. CRIMINALS WERE PLENTIFUL, MANY OF THEM COMING FROM CHARLESTON OR FROM NORTH CAROLINA; AND THE LAW-ABIDING CITIZENS IN THE BACK COUNTRY WERE FORCED TO TAKE THE LAW INTO THEIR OWN HANDS BY FORMING VIGILANTE BODIES CALLED "REGULATORS." THE ACTIONS OF THE REGULATORS WERE, OF COURSE, ILLEGAL, AND THE LOW COUNTRY OFFICIALS FELT THAT THE GROUPS WERE ALMOST AS MUCH IN NEED OF PUNISHMENT AS THE CRIMINALS. THE FOLLOWING SELECTIONS CONCERN BOTH SIDES OF THE PROBLEM.

[Newspaper Report on Activities of Villains]

The gang of villains from Virginia and North Carolina who have for some years past in small parties, under particular leaders, infested the back parts of the Southern Provinces, stealing horses from one and selling them to the next, notwithstanding the late public examples made of several of them, we hear are more formidable than ever as to numbers, and more audacious and cruel in their thefts and outrages. 'Tis reported that they consist of more than 200, form a chain of communication with each other, and have places of general meeting; where (in imitation of Councils of War) they form plans of operation and defense, and (alluding to their secrecy and fidelity to each other) call their places Free Mason Lodges. Instances of their cruelty to the people in the back settlements where they rob or otherwise abuse, are so numerous and shocking that a narrative of them would fill a whole *Gazette,* and every reader with horror. They at present range in the Forks between Broad,

South Carolina Gazette, July 27–Aug. 3, 1767.

Saluda and Savannah Rivers. Two of the gang were hanged last week in Savannah . . . . Two others . . . were killed when these were taken.

[Activities of the Regulators]

[At a meeting of the Council] . . . His Excellency informed the Board that he had received information that a considerable number of the inhabitants between Santee and Wateree rivers had assembled, and in a riotous manner gone up and down the country, committing riots and disturbances, and that they had burnt the houses of some persons who were reported to be harborers of horse thieves, and talk of coming to Charles-Town to make complaints. The Board gave it as their opinion to his Excellency that to prevent the mischief such commotions would be attended with, it would be proper for his Excellency to issue a Proclamation, commanding them to disperse, and enjoining all officers to take care to preserve the public peace.

[Extract of a Letter from a Gentleman at Pedee to his friend in Town]

I wish you would inform me what is generally thought in town of the Regulators, who now reign uncontrolled in all the remote parts of the Province. In June, they held a Congress at the Congarees, where a vast number of people assembled; several of the principal settlers on this River, men of property, among them. When these returned, they requested the most respectable people in these parts to meet on a certain day; they did so, and, upon the report made to them, they unanimously adopted the Plan of Regulation, and are now executing it with indefatigable ardor. Their resolution is, in general, effectually to deny the Jurisdiction

Council Journal, Oct. 5, 1767, in Alexander Gregg, History of the Old Cheraws (New York: Richardson and Co., 1867), 135.

South Carolina Gazette, Sept. 2, 1768.

of the Courts holden in Charles-town over those parts of the Province that ought by right to be out of it; to purge, by methods of their own, the country of all idle persons, all that have not a visible way of getting an honest living, all that are suspected or known to be guilty of mal-practices, and also to prevent the service of any writ or warrant from Charles-town; so that a Deputy Marshal would be handled by them with severity. Against those they breathe high indignation. They are every day, excepting Sundays, employed in this Regulation work, as they term it. They have brought many under the lash, and are scourging and banishing the baser sort of people, such as the above, with universal diligence.

Such as they think reclaimable, they are a little tender of; and those they task, giving them so many acres to tend in so many days, on pain of flagellation, that they may not be reduced to poverty, and by that be led to steal from their industrious neighbors. This course, they say, they are determined to pursue, with every other effectual measure, that will answer their purpose; and that they will defend themselves in it to the last extremity. They hold correspondence with others in the same plan, and are engaged to abide by and support each other whenever they may be called upon for that purpose. This it seems, they are to continue till County Courts, as well as Circuit Courts, shall be rightly established, that they may enjoy, by that means, the rights and privileges of British subjects, which they think themselves now deprived of. They imagine that, as the jurisdiction of the Courts in Charles-town extends all over the Province, Government is not a protection, but an oppression; that they are not tried there by their peers; and that the accumulated expenses of a law-suit, or prosecution, puts justice out of their power; by which means the honest man is not secure in his property, and villainy becomes rampant with impunity.

Indeed, the grievances they complain of are many, and the spirit of Regulation rises higher and spreads wider every day. What this is to end in, I know not; but thus matters are situated; an account of which, I imagine, is not unacceptable, though perhaps disagreeable to hear.

50. *The Circuit Court Act of 1769*

THE DEMANDS OF THE REGULATORS WERE FINALLY MET IN PART BY
THE PASSAGE OF THE CIRCUIT COURT ACT OF 1769. THE FOLLOWING
SELECTION GIVES THE BACKGROUND AND RESULTS OF THE ACT.

[David Ramsay]

For the first 99 years of Provincial Carolina, Charlestown was the
source and center of all judicial proceedings. No courts were held beyond
its limits, and one provost marshall was charged with the service of
processes over the whole Province. For the first 70 or 80 years, when the
population rarely extended beyond an equal number of miles, this was
patiently borne; but in the course of the next 20 years it became intolerable. The distance and expense of attending courts in Charlestown
were so inconvenient, that people in the back country were induced
occasionally to inflict punishments in their own way, and by their own
authority, on knaves and villains. Associations were formed under the
name of Regulators, who enforced justice in a summary way. For the
accommodation of these remote settlers, and to remove all apology for
these irregular proceedings, incompatible with orderly government, an
act was passed in 1769 called the Circuit Court Act; by which new
district courts were established at Beaufort, Georgetown, Cheraws,
Camden, Orangeburgh and Ninety-Six . . . . One difficulty stood in the
way, the removal of which was necessary before the projected reform
could go into operation. The important and lucrative office of Provost
Marshal for the whole Province was held by patent from the Crown by
Richard Cumberland, well known in the literary world for his talents
and writings. The proposed Circuit Court Act contemplated the abolition of the office of Provost Marshal of the Province, and the appoint-

David Ramsay, *History of South Carolina* . . . , 2 vols. (Charleston: David
Longworth for the author, 1809), II, 125–26.

ment of seven Sheriffs; one for Charlestown and one for each of the six new districts. To reconcile private right with public convenience, the Province paid £5000 sterling to Mr. Cumberland as a compensation for his resigning the office of Provost Marshal. The new arrangement went into operation soon afterwards.

51. *Agriculture*

THE MID-EIGHTEENTH CENTURY SAW AGRICULTURE SURPASS TRADE ABROAD AS THE MOST IMPORTANT ECONOMIC FACTOR IN SOUTH CAROLINA WITH THE DEVELOPMENT OF TWO STAPLE CROPS—RICE AND INDIGO. INDIGO WAS ENCOURAGED BY THE BRITISH GOVERNMENT, A SMALL SUBSIDY BEING PAID ON EACH POUND SHIPPED TO ENGLAND. BUT IT WAS THE CULTURE OF RICE WHICH CHARACTERIZED THE LOW COUNTRY PLANTATIONS. OF THE FOLLOWING SELECTIONS, THE FIRST IS GOVERNOR JAMES GLEN'S *Description of South Carolina;* THE SECOND IS FROM MRS. ELIZA PINCKNEY'S JOURNAL; AND THE THIRD COMES FROM GEORGE MILLIGEN-JOHNSTON'S *A Short Description of the Province of South Carolina.*

[Governor James Glen]

The land of South Carolina . . . is remarkable for the diversity of its soil; that near the coast is generally sandy, but not therefore unfruitful; in other parts there is clay, loam and marl . . . . The best land for rice is a wet, deep, miry soil, such as is generally to be found in cypress swamps; or a black greasy mould with a clay foundation . . . . Good crops are produced even the first year . . . . The proper months for sowing are March, April and May; the method is to plant it in trenches or rows made with a hoe, about three inches deep; the land must be kept pretty clear from weeds; and at the latter end of August or the beginning of September, it will be fit to be reaped . . . . Afterward it is threshed with a flail, and then winnowed; which was formerly a very tedious operation, but it is now performed with greater ease by a very simple machine, a wind fan, but lately used here . . . .

The next part of the process is grinding, which is done in small mills made of wood, about two feet in diameter; it is then winnowed again and afterwards put into a mortar made of wood, sufficient to contain

B. R. Carroll, *Historical Collections of South Carolina* . . . , 2 vols. (New York: Harper, 1836), II, 200, 204, 209.

from half a bushel to a bushel, when it is beat with a pestle of a size suitable to the mortar and to the strength of the person who is to pound it; this is done to free the rice from a thick skin, and is the most laborious part of the work. It is then sifted from the flour and dust, made by the pounding; and afterwards by a wire-sieve . . . it is separated from the broken and small rice, which fits it for the barrels in which it is carried to market. They reckon thirty slaves a proper number for a rice plantation, and to be tended with one overseer . . . . Rice last year bore a good price, being at a medium about forty-five shillings our currency per hundred weight; and all this year it hath been fifty-five shillings . . . .

Indian corn delights in high loose land; it does not agree with clay, and is killed by much wet; it is generally planted in ridges, made by the plow or hoe, and in holes about six or eight feet from each other; it requires to be kept free from weeds, and will produce, according to the goodness of the land, from fifteen to fifty bushels an acre . . . . The common computation is that a Negro will tend six acres, and that each acre will produce from ten to thirty-five bushels; it sells generally for about ten shillings currency a bushel, but is at present fifteen.

Indigo is of several sorts; what we have gone mostly upon, is the sort generally cultivated in the Sugar Islands, which requires a high, loose soil, intolerably rich, and is an annual plant . . . . An acre of land may produce about eighty pounds weight of good indigo; and one slave may manage two acres and upwards, and raise provisions besides . . . . As much of the land hitherto used for indigo is improper, not above thirty pounds weight of good indigo per acre can be expected from the land at present cultivated . . . .

South Carolina abounds with black cattle, to a degree much beyond any other English colony, which is chiefly owing to the mildness of the winter, whereby the planters are freed from the charge and trouble of providing for their cattle, suffering them to feed all the winter in the woods. These creatures have mightily increased since the first settlement of the Colony . . . It was then reckoned a great matter for a planter to have three or four cows; but now some people have a thousand head of cattle, and for one man to have two hundred is very common. They likewise have hogs in abundance, which go daily to feed in the woods, and come home at night, also some sheep and goats.

[Eliza Lucas Pinckney]

Out of a small patch of indigo growing at Wappoo [Plantation] . . . the brother of Nicholass Cromwell besides saving a quantity of seed, made us 17 pounds of very good indigo . . . . Mr. Deveaux has made some likewise, and the people in general are very sanguine about it. Mr. [Charles] Pinckney sent to England by the last man of war 6 pounds to try how it is approved of there. If it is, I hope we shall have a bounty from home; we already have a bounty of 5 shillings currency from this Province upon it. We please ourselves with the prospect of exporting in a few years a good quantity from hence, and supplying our mother country with a manufacture for which she has so great a demand, and which she is now supplied with from the French colonies, and many thousand pounds per annum thereby lost to the nation, when she might as well be supplied here, if the matter was applied to in earnest.

[George Milligen-Johnston]

The soil, in many parts of the Province, is very proper for the cultivation of olive trees and vines, articles that have hitherto almost [been] totally neglected; a little attention to them would save much money expended on oil and wine, which we now import. The cotton-tree likewise grows naturally in this Province, and might be of great use in clothing the poorer sort of white inhabitants and the Negroes, if any pains were taken to cultivate it . . . .

Harriott Horry (Rutledge) Ravenel, *Eliza Pinckney* (New York: Charles Scribner's Sons, 1902), 104–105.

B. R. Carroll, *Historical Collections of South Carolina* . . . , 2 vols. (New York: Harper, 1836), II, 483.

52. Education

PUBLIC EDUCATION MADE LITTLE PROGRESS DURING THE ROYAL PERIOD, BUT THERE WAS SOME PROGRESS IN PRIVATE EDUCATION, PARTICULARLY IN SCHOOLS SPONSORED BY BENEVOLENT SOCIETIES. THE FIRST SELECTION DESCRIBES THE TEACHING PROGRAM IN THE CHARLESTON FREE SCHOOL IN 1723; THE SECOND IS AN ACT FOR ESTABLISHING A FREE SCHOOL IN DORCHESTER, 1734; THE THIRD, A PRIVATE SCHOOL ADVERTISEMENT, 1744; AND THE FOURTH, THE CHARTER OF THE WINYAH INDIGO SOCIETY, WHICH OPERATED A SCHOOL IN GEORGETOWN AFTER 1755.

[The Rev. Thomas Morritt]

The Latin tongue is the intent of my mission, and for that method I shall observe no other than what is usually practiced in other grammar schools in England. I shall chiefly use Lilly for the rudimental part and then I shall proceed to . . . Erasmus, Ovid, Virgil, Horace, Lucius, Justine, Tacitus, Suetonius . . . and Claudian, and as for the Greek authors, I shall teach such parts of Isocrates and Lucian's Dialog as are usually published for the use of schools; the minor poets, Homer and Euripedes; and in order to give the boys a taste of classic geography, I shall cause to be read Dionysious Periegetes and Cluver Geographia and these I shall be somewhat particular upon to compare them with the modern geography . . . . Juston and others I shall cause to be frequently read and perused to give the boys a taste of chronology . . . . Kennet's Goodwin, and Potter's Antiquity shall also be read in order to be acquainted with the rights, customs and ceremonies of the ancients, these at spare times or at home. I shall endeavor to oblige the boys to read over together . . . the History of the Heathen Gods, Pantheon, etc., but as for the boys which I shall have constantly in the house with

The Reverend Thomas Morritt, to the Society for the Propagation of the Gospel, in *Historical Magazine of the Protestant Episcopal Church*, Vol. XIV (1945), 158–59, 163–64. Reprinted by permission of The Church Historical Society, Austin, Texas.

me and such as are boarders, I do intend besides these books already mentioned to make them read 3 times a week at least if not every night, classic history, especially such historians as we have translated into our own language. Those books I shall cause to be read an hour at nights between 8 and 9 and I shall not omit at that time to instruct them in chronology and geography and teach them the use of the globes.

I have 10 boys sent me out of the country, besides one that came from Philadelphia and another that came from the Bahama Islands which are boarders, in all 52, of which I daily expect an augmentation rather than a decrease.

An Act for Establishment of A Free School in the Town of Dorchester, April 9, 1734:

Whereas, by the blessing of Almighty God, the youth of this Province are very numerous, and their parents so well inclined to have them instructed in grammar, and other liberal arts and sciences, and other useful learning, and also in the principles of the Christian religion, that the free school erected . . . in Charlestown for this purpose is not sufficient fully to answer the good intent of such an undertaking . . . .

1. Be it enacted . . . that the honorable Alexander Skene [and others] . . . be . . . commissioners for founding, erecting, governing, ordering and visiting a free school at the town of Dorchester, in the Parish of St. George, in Berkeley County, for the use of the inhabitants of South Carolina. . . .

10. And be it further enacted . . . that the said commissioners and their successors shall have power . . . to purchase, have, take and receive . . . so much land as they shall think necessary and convenient for the masters and teachers of the school hereby intended to be established, and shall direct the building of such houses as may be necessary to be erected thereon for their accommodation. . . .

11. And be it further enacted . . . that the master of the said school shall be capable to teach the learned languages, Latin and Greek, and to catechise and instruct the youth in the principles of the Christian religion. . . .

[Stephen Hartley]

On Monday, being the 25th instant, the subscriber intends, God willing, to open school in the Parish of St. Thomas, at the place where Mr. Robert How formerly taught, being about a half a mile from the Brick Church, and twelve from Charles-Town. The house erected for that purpose is a fine spacious building, wherein an hundred children may be genteely accommodated. Those inclinable for boarding their children with me, may depend on the utmost care and diligence, by teaching them exactly and expeditiously, reading, writing in all the usual hands, arithmetic in all its parts, merchant's accounts, or, the Italian method of bookkeeping, etc. Stephen Hartley, June 4, 1744.

The Charter of the Winyaw Indigo Society, 1755

Whereas several inhabitants of the Parish of Prince George Winyaw, and others, taking into consideration the great disadvantage the said inhabitants labored under for want of a school for the education of children, did, on or about the seventh day of March, 1755, enter into a voluntary society for founding and erecting a free school at George-town, in the parish aforesaid, and have, at a considerable expense,

South Carolina Gazette, June 4, 1744.

Edgar W. Knight, ed., *A Documentary History of Education in the South Before 1860,* 3 vols. (Chapel Hill: University of North Carolina Press, 1949–1952), II, 277–78. Copyright, 1950, By The University of North Carolina Press. Reprinted by permission of The University of North Carolina Press.

employed masters of the said school, who already have a great number of children under their care and tuition, which undertaking they hope will in time, if duly encouraged and properly established, be of great advantage to the religious as well as the civil concerns of this Province, and are desirous of having the Society incorporated thereby to put them upon a more solid and lasting foundation than they can be by their voluntary subscriptions only; for promoting, therefore, so good a work, we humbly pray his most sacred Majesty that it may be enacted.

1. And be it enacted . . . that Thomas Lynch, Esquire, President . . . and the rest of the present members of the said Winyaw Indigo Society . . . shall forever hereafter be one body corporate and politic, in deed and in name, by the name of the Winyaw Indigo Society . . . .

4. And be it also enacted . . . that it shall and may be lawful for the said corporation or society to found, erect, endow, maintain and support such school or schools, for the maintenance and education of such poor and helpless orphans or indigent children, and for binding them apprentices, as they shall judge proper objects of charity, and to appoint and choose, and at their pleasure displace, remove and supply such officers, school-masters, servants, and other persons to be employed for the use of the said school or schools . . . and to appoint such salaries, perquisites, or other rewards for their labor or service therein, as they shall from time to time approve of and think fit. . . .

53. Government

James Glen, the chief executive of South Carolina from 1743 to 1756, was sincerely interested in his duties and became known as the "energetic governor." His effectiveness in dealing with the Indians and his encouragement of agriculture and trade within the colony made him one of the best colonial governors. During his administration he compiled an extensive report on South Carolina, including its history, geography, and economic and social conditions, which was published in 1763 as *A Description of the Province of South Carolina* . . . . The following description of the government and public finances of the colony are taken from this work.

[Governor James Glen]

The government of South Carolina is one of those called Royal governments, to distinguish it, I presume, from the charter governments, such as Massachusetts-Bay, Connecticut, and Rhode Island; and from the Proprietary governments, such as Pennsylvania and Maryland. Its constitution is formed after the model of our Mother Country; the Governor, Council, and Assembly constitute the three branches of the legislature, and have power to make such laws as may be thought necessary for the better government of the Province, not repugnant to the laws of Great Britain . . . .

The Governor is appointed by patent, by the title of Governor in Chief and Captain-General in and over the Province; he receives also a Vice Admiral's commission, but alas, these high sounding titles convey very little power . . . and I have often wished the Governor had more . . . . The members of the Council are appointed by the King . . . and are twelve in number, to which number the Surveyor-General of the Customs must be added . . . . The Assembly consists of forty-four mem-

B.R. Carroll, *Historical Collections of South Carolina* . . . , 2 vols. (New York: Harper, 1836), II, 219–23.

bers elected every third year by the freeholders of sixteen different parishes, but the representation seems to be unequal, some parishes returning five, others four, three, two or only one, and some towns which, by the King's Instructions have a right to be erected into parishes, and to send two members, are not allowed to send any.

There is a Court of Chancery, composed of the Governor and Council, and there is a Master in Chancery, and a Register belonging to the Court. The Court of King's Bench consists of a Chief Justice appointed by his Majesty, and some assistant justices. The same persons constitute the Court of Common Pleas; there is a Clerk of the Crown who is also Clerk of the Pleas; an Attorney General, and a Provost-Marshal. There is a Secretary of the Province, who is also Register, and pretends a right to be the Clerk of the Council; there is also a Clerk of the Assembly, a Surveyor-General of the land, a Receiver-General of the quit-rents, a Vendue-Master and Naval Officer, all of which officers are appointed by the Crown.

There is a Court of Vice-Admiralty; the Judge, Register and Marshal thereof are appointed by the Lords Commissioners of the Admiralty. There is a Comptroller of the Customs; three collectors, one at each port, viz., Charles-Town, Port Royal, and Winyaw; there are likewise two searchers at Charles-Town; all these are appointed by the Commissioners of the Customs, or by the Lords Commissioners of the Treasury. The Public Treasurer, the Country Comptroller, the Commissioners of Indian Affairs, and several other officers are appointed by the General Assembly. The clergy are elected by the people. The Governor appoints Justices of the Peace, and officers in the militia, which are offices of no profit, and some trouble, and therefore few will accept of them unless they are much courted. . . .

The public revenues within the Province of South Carolina arise partly from goods imported, imposed by a law called the general duty-law; and partly from taxes upon real and personal estates, wherein are comprehended lands, houses, money at interest, stock in trade, etc. The species of goods liable to duties are sugar, rum, madeira wine, and a few other sorts of commodities; but not one commodity of the produce or manufacture of Great Britain is charged with any duty in this Province. The monies raised as aforesaid are appropriated to defray the ordinary and extraordinary expenses of the Province government—excepting some particular expenses which are provided for by other funds; and the after-mentioned heads of appropriation will best show in what manner those public revenues are applied:

Province debts, such as were contracted by the expedition to St. Augustine and for the relief of Georgia; the salaries of such officers as have not appointments upon quit-rents; the stipends of our clergy; the salaries of schoolmasters and ushers; the salary, etc., of our agent in Great Britain; the pay of gunners at our several forts; the settling of foreign Protestants in this Province; the additional pay allowed to the three independent companies of regular troops serving here; the keeping in repair of our fortifications and public buildings; presents to the chiefs of the Indian nations, but his Majesty has been graciously pleased to relieve us from this article of expense; troops of rangers, casually taken into pay upon any alarm, for which I hope there will not hereafter be much occasion; and two galleys equipped and kept in pay for the defense of our island passages . . . .

54. *Indians*

ALSO CONTAINED IN GOVERNOR GLEN'S REPORT ON SOUTH CAROLINA
WAS AN EXTENSIVE ACCOUNT OF THE NEIGHBORING INDIAN TRIBES AND
THE TRADE WITH THEM. THE FOLLOWING SELECTION LISTS THE MORE
IMPORTANT TRIBES AND THEIR RELATIONSHIP WITH SOUTH CAROLINA.

[Governor James Glen Reports on Strength of Indian Tribes]

The concerns of this country are so closely connected and interwoven
with Indian affairs, and not only a great branch of our trade, but even
the safety of this Province, do so much depend upon our continuing in
friendship with the Indians, that I thought it highly necessary to gain
all the knowledge I could of them, and . . . I think it expedient upon
the present occasion to give a general account of the several tribes and
nations of Indians with whom the inhabitants of this Province are or may
be connected in interest . . . .

There are among our settlements several small tribes of Indians consisting of some few families each; but those tribes of Indians which we,
on account of their being numerous and having lands of their own, call
nations, are all of them situated on the western side of this Province
. . . . The Catawba nation of Indians has about three hundred fighting
men; brave fellows as any on the continent of America, and our firm
friends; their country is about two hundred miles from Charles Town.
The Cherokees live at the distance of about three hundred miles from
Charles Town, though indeed their hunting grounds stretch much
nearer to us. They have about three thousand gun men, and are in
alliance with this government. . . . The Creek Indians are situated
about five hundred miles from Charles Town; their number of fighting
men is about two thousand five hundred, and they are in friendship
with us.

The Chickasaws live at the distance of near eight hundred miles
from Charles Town; they have bravely stood their ground against the

B. R. Carroll, *Historical Collections of South Carolina* . . . , 2 vols. (New York:
Harper, 1836), II, 242–47.

repeated attacks of the French and their Indians; but are now reduced to two or three hundred men. The Choctaw nation of Indians is situated at a somewhat greater distance from us, and till within this year or two have been in the interest of the French by whom they were reckoned to be the most numerous of any nation of Indians in America, and said to consist of many thousand men. . . .

There are also a few Yemassees, about twenty men, near St. Augustine; and these are all the Indians in this part of the world that are in the interest of the Crown of Spain. . . .

The tranquillity of South Carolina will depend upon preserving our interest with the Indians, which it will be very difficult to do, unless the presents are continued to them, and those forts built which I have formerly proposed, or at least, one of them, and that to be in the country of the Cherokees. . . .

55. Religion

THE ROYAL PERIOD SAW A GRADUAL INCREASE IN THE NUMBER OF CHURCHES AND MINISTERS IN SOUTH CAROLINA. IN ADDITION TO ANGLICANS AND BAPTISTS, WHO BY 1751 HAD FORMED THE CHARLESTON BAPTIST ASSOCIATION, THERE WERE PRESBYTERIANS AND LUTHERANS IN LARGE NUMBERS AMONG THE NEWCOMERS. THE SOCIETY FOR THE PROPAGATION OF THE GOSPEL CONTINUED ITS EFFORTS IN THE COLONY, AND THE FIRST SELECTION IS A REPORT FROM ONE *Society* MINISTER ON HIS PARISH IN 1736. THE SECOND SELECTION IS TAKEN FROM THE JOURNAL OF GEORGE WHITEFIELD, AN EVANGELIST WHO VISITED SOUTH CAROLINA IN THE EARLY 1740s.

Thomas Thompson, St. Bartholomews in
South Carolina, May 1, 1736, to
the Rev. Dr. Humphreys, Secretary of the Society in London:

Reverend Sir: In the parish of St. Bartholomew there are one hundred and twenty families of white people, and twelve hundred Negroes. Two thirds of the white inhabitants have been educated in one or other of the ways of the separation, and are generally ignorant and uncharitable. My endeavors to convince and reclaim them with a spirit of meekness and gentleness are not altogether in vain, for they often make the greater part of my congregation. Those of the Church through the want of education, and of a fixed Minister for some years past know but little of the nature of true religion, or of the constitution of the Church. There are only nine of them actual communicants. I wish I may be able to give a more comfortable and satisfactory account concerning the spiritual state of this parish; for the predominant vice here, as far as I can observe, is . . . excessive love and eager pursuit of the things of this world, as makes men wholly unmindful of the concerns of Another, and indifferent about all the means of religious instruction. I have baptized upwards of a hundred children since I first came into

South Carolina Historical and Genealogical Magazine, Vol. 50 (1949), 178.
Reprinted by permission of The Historical Society of South Carolina.

this parish, and sixteen since I entered upon my mission. This parish being of large extent, I officiate once a month at Chihaw, the remotest part of it, where a convenient building has been lately erected for that purpose.

[George Whitefield]

Sunday, January 6, 1740. We went to public service in the morning, but did not preach, because the curate had not a commission to lend the pulpit, unless the Commissary (Rev. Alexander Garden) then out of town, were present. Most of the town, however, being eager to hear me, I preached in the afternoon in one of the dissenting meeting houses, but was grieved to find so little concern in the congregation. The auditory was large, but very polite. I question whether the Court-End of London could exceed them in affected finery, gaity of dress and a deportment ill becoming persons who have had such divine judgments lately sent amongst them. I reminded them of this in my sermon, but I seemed to them as one that mocked.

Monday, January 7. Finding the inhabitants desirous to hear me a second time, I preached in the morning in the French church. The audience was so great that many stood without the door . . . . One of the men of the town, most remarkably gay, was observed to weep. Many were melted into tears. Instead of the people going out, as they did yesterday, in a light, unthinking manner, a visible concern was in most of their faces. After sermon, I and my friends dined at a merchant's and as I was passing along, a letter was put into my hands wherein were these words: "Remember me in your prayers, for Christ's sake, who died for me, a sinner." Many of the inhabitants, with full hearts, entreated me to give them one more sermon, and though I was just about to take the boat, I thought it my duty to comply with their request. Notice was immediately given, and in about half an hour a large congregation assembled in the Dissenting meeting house. In the evening I supped at another merchant's house and had an opportunity for nearly two hours to converse of the things of God with a large company.

George Whitefield's *Journal,* in Yates Snowden, ed., *History of South Carolina,* 5 vols. (Chicago: The Lewis Publishing Co., 1920), I, 242–43.

56. *Slavery*

DURING THE ROYAL PERIOD, THE NUMBER OF SLAVES INCREASED CON-
SIDERABLY, BEING ALWAYS FAR LARGER THAN THE NUMBER OF WHITE
PERSONS IN THE PROVINCE. THE PLANTATION OWNERS WERE CONCERNED
ABOUT THE WELFARE OF THEIR SLAVES, BUT THERE WAS A CONSTANT
FEAR OF INSURRECTIONS, AND STRONG LAWS WERE PASSED TO REGULATE
SLAVERY AS AN ECONOMIC AND SOCIAL INSTITUTION. THESE EXCERPTS
INCLUDE HENRY LAURENS'S INSTRUCTIONS FOR THE CARE OF HIS SLAVES,
GEORGE MILLIGEN-JOHNSTON ON THE RELATIONS OF THE SLAVES AND
THE INDIANS, AND A LAW PROHIBITING TEACHING SLAVES TO WRITE.

Henry Laurens to His Overseer, May 30, 1765:

I have now to recommend to you the care of my Negroes in general, but
particularly the sick ones. Let them be well attended night and day, and
if one wench is not sufficient, add another to nurse them. With the well
ones use gentle means mixed with easy authority first—if that does not
succeed, make choice of the most stubborn one or two and chastise them
severly but properly and with mercy, that they may be convinced that the
end of correction is to be amendment . . . .

[George Milligen-Johnston]

The Negro slaves are about seventy thousand; they, with a few exceptions do all the labor or hard work in the country, and are a considerable

D. D. Wallace, *The Life of Henry Laurens* (New York: G. P. Putnam's Sons,
1915), 133.

B. R. Carroll, *Historical Collections of South Carolina* . . . , 2 vols. (New York:
Harper, 1836), II, 413.

part of the riches of the Province; they are supposedly worth, upon an average about forty pounds sterling each. And the annual labor of the working slaves, who may be about forty thousand, is valued at ten pounds sterling each. They are in this climate necessary, but very dangerous domestics, their number so much exceeding the whites, a natural dislike and antipathy, that subsists between them and our Indian neighbors is a very likely circumstance, and for this reason: In our quarrels with the Indians, however proper and necessary it may be to extirpate them, or to force them from their lands; their ground would soon be taken up by runaway Negroes from our settlements, whose numbers would daily increase, and quickly become more formidable enemies than Indians can ever be, as they speak our language, and would never be at a loss for intelligence.

Prohibition against Teaching Slaves to Write, 1740:

And whereas, the having of slaves taught to write, or suffering them to be employed in writing, may be attended with great inconvenience; be it therefore enacted . . . that all and every person or persons whatsoever, who shall hereafter teach, or cause any slave or slaves to be taught, to write . . . shall for every such offense forfeit the sum of one hundred pounds current money.

South Carolina Statutes at Large, VII, 413.

57. Trade

A MOST IMPORTANT FEATURE OF SOUTH CAROLINA'S ECONOMY IN THE ROYAL PERIOD WAS ITS TRADE WITH THE INDIANS, OTHER COLONIES, AND ENGLAND. CHARLES TOWN WAS BECOMING THE MOST IMPORTANT PORT IN THE SOUTHERN COLONIES, AND A RELATIVELY WEALTHY MERCHANT CLASS WAS DEVELOPING THERE. THE FOLLOWING SELECTIONS GIVE THE CONDITION OF THE CAROLINA TRADE AS SEEN BY PETER PURRY IN 1731 AND BY GOVERNOR GLEN AROUND 1750.

[Peter Purry]

The trade of Carolina is now so considerable, that of late years there has sailed from thence annually over 200 ships, laden with merchandizes of the growth of the country, besides three ships of war, which they commonly have for the security of the commerce, and last winter they had constantly five, the least of which had above 100 men on board. It appears by the custom house entries from March, 1730, to March, 1731, that there sailed within that time from Charles-Town 207 ships, most of them for England, which carried among other goods 41,957 barrels of rice, about 500 pound weight per barrel; 10,754 barrels of pitch, 2063 of tar; and 1159 of turpentine; of deer skins 300 casks, containing 8 or 900 each; besides a vast quantity of Indian corn, pease, beans, etc., beef, pork, and other salted flesh; beams, planks and timber for building, most part of cedar, cypress, sassafras, oak, walnut and pine.

They carry on a great trade with the Indians, from whom they get these great quantities of deer skins, and those of other wild beasts, in exchange for which they give them only lead, powder, coarse cloth, vermillion, iron ware, and some other goods, by which they have a very considerable profit.

There are between 4 and 600 houses in Charles Town, the most of which are very costly; besides five handsome churches . . . . If you travel

B. R. Carroll, *Historical Collections of South Carolina* . . . , 2 vols. (New York: Harper, 1836), II, 128–29.

into the country, you will see stately buildings, noble castles, and an infinite number of all sorts of cattle. If it be asked, what has produced all this? the answer is, it is only the rich land of Carolina.

[Governor James Glen]

The trade between South Carolina and Great Britain, one year with another, employs twenty-two sail of ships. Those ships bring from Great Britain to South Carolina all sorts of woolen cloths, stuffs and drugges, linens, . . . silks and muslins; nails of all sizes, hoes, hatchets, and all kinds of iron-wares; bedticks, strong beer, bottled cider, raisins, fine earthen wares, pipes, paper, rugs, blankets, quilts, hats . . . , stockings . . . , gloves; pewter dishes and plates; brass and copper wares; guns, powder, bullets, flints, glass beads, cordage, woolen and cotton cards, steel hand mills, grind-stones, looking and drinking glasses, lace; thread, coarse and fine; mohair, and all kinds of trimmings for clothes; pins, needles, etc.

In return for these commodities and manufactures there are sent from South Carolina to Great Britain about seventy thousand deerskins a year; some furs, rosin, pitch, tar, raw silk, rice, and . . . indigo; but all these are not sufficient to pay for European goods, and Negro slaves with which the English merchants are continually supplying the South Carolina people. . . .

Besides the twenty-two sail of ships which trade between South Carolina and Great Britain, as before mentioned, there enter and clear annually at the Port of Charles Town, about sixty sail of ships, sloops, and brigantines, which are employed in carrying on the after named branches of trade between South Carolina and other countries.

The trade between South Carolina and Jamaica, Barbadoes, the British Leeward Island, the Island of St. Thomas (a Danish sugar colony), and Curacao (a Dutch sugar colony) . . . are beef, pork, butter, candles, soap, tallow, myrtle wax candles, rice, some pitch and tar, cedar and pine boards, shingles, hoop staves, and heads for barrels. The commodities sent

B. R. Carroll, *Historical Collections of South Carolina* . . . , 2 vols. (New York: Harper, 1836), II, 254–56, 269–70.

in return from those places to South Carolina are sugar, rum, molasses, cotton, chocolate made up, cocoa nuts, Negro slaves, and money. . . .

The commodities sent from South Carolina to other northern colonies are tanned hides, small deer skins, gloves, rice, slaves taken from the Indians in war, some tar and pitch. The commodities sent in return from those other northern colonies (New England, New York and Pennsylvania) are wheat, flour, biscuit, strong beer, salted fish, onions, apples and hops.

The commodities sent from South Carolina to Madeira and the other western islands belonging to Portugal are beef, pork, butter, rice, casks, staves, heading for barrels, etc. The commodities sent in return from those islands to South Carolina are wines.

The salt used in South Carolina is brought from the Bahama Islands. From Guinea and other parts of the coast of Africa, Negro slaves are imported into South Carolina, but the ships which bring them there, being sent from England . . . , the Carolina returns for the same are sent thither. . . .

An account of the quantities of rice which have been exported from the Province of South Carolina within 10 years from 1730 to 1739: To Portugal, in all, 83,379 barrels; to Gibraltar, 958 barrels; to Spain, 3,570 barrels; to France, only the last two years, 9,500 barrels; to Great Britain, Ireland and the British plantations, approximately 30,000 barrels; to Holland, Hamburg and Bremen, including Sweden and Denmark, 372,118 barrels; the total . . . 499,525 barrels.

58. *General Social Conditions During the Royal Period*

BY THE MIDDLE OF THE EIGHTEENTH CENTURY, THE PEOPLE OF SOUTH
CAROLINA WERE DEVELOPING INTO AMERICANS, WITH A DIFFERENT WAY
OF LIFE AND A DIFFERENT CULTURE FROM THAT IN ENGLAND. THIS WAS
NOTICED BY MISS ELIZA LUCAS (LATER MRS. CHARLES PINCKNEY)
WHEN SHE FIRST CAME TO CHARLESTON FROM HER FATHER'S SUGAR
PLANTATION IN THE WEST INDIES; AND ALSO BY THE REVEREND ALEXAN-
DER HEWAT, FRESH FROM SCOTLAND. THE FIRST SELECTION GIVES MR.
HEWAT'S IMPRESSIONS OF THE CAROLINIANS; THE SECOND, THOSE OF
MISS LUCAS AND ALSO HER DESCRIPTION OF A PLANTATION AND THE 1759
SMALLPOX. THE LAST SELECTION, FROM DAVID RAMSAY, DESCRIBES THE
LIFE OF A SETTLER ON THE SOUTH CAROLINA FRONTIER IN THE 1750s
AND 1760s.

[Alexander Hewat]

In stature, the natives of Carolina are about middle size; for in Europe
we meet with men both taller and shorter. They are, generally speaking,
more forward and quick in growth than the natives of cold climates.
Indeed we may say, there are no boys or girls in the Province, for from
childhood they are introduced into company, and assume the air and
behavior of men and women . . . . They commonly marry early in life,
and of course are involved in domestic cares and concerns before their
minds have had time to ripen in knowledge and judgment. In the progress of society they have not advanced beyond that period in which men
are distinguished more by their external than internal accomplishments.
Hence, it happens that beauty, figure, agility and strength form the principal distinctions among them, especially in the country. Among English
people, they are chiefly known by the number of their slaves, the value of
their annual produce, or the extent of their landed estate. For the most
part they are lively and gay, adapting their dress to the nature of the

B. R. Carroll, *Historical Collections of South Carolina* . . . , 2 vols. (New York:
Harper, 1836), I, 504–505.

climate in which they live, and discover no small taste and neatness in their outward appearance. Their intercourse and communication with Britain being easy and frequent, all novelites in fashion, dress and ornament are quickly introduced; and even the spirit of luxury and extravagance, too common in England, is beginning to creep into Carolina. Almost every family keep their chaises for a single horse, and some of the principal planters of late years have imported fine horses and splendid carriages from Britain. They discover no bad taste for the polite arts, such as music, drawing, fencing and dancing; and it is acknowledged by all, but especially by strangers, that the ladies in the Province considerably outshine the men. They are not only sensible, discreet and virtuous, but also adorned with most of those polite and elegant accomplishments becoming their sex. The Carolinians in general are affable and easy in their manners and exceedingly kind and hospitable to all strangers.

[Miss Eliza Lucas's Impressions of South Carolinians in 1741:]

The people are in general hospitable and honest, and the better sort add to these a polite, gentile behavior. The poorer sort are the most indolent people in the world or they could never be wretched in so plentiful a country as this. The winters here are very fine and pleasant, but four months in the year is extremely disagreeable, excessively hot, [with] much thunder and lightning and mosquitoes and sand flies in abundance.

Charles Town, the metropolis, is a neat pretty place. The inhabitants are polite and live in a very gentile manner. The streets and houses [are] regularly built—the ladies and gentlemen gay in their dress, [and] upon the whole you will find as many agreeable people of both sexes for the size of the place as almost anywhere. St. Philip's Church in Charles Town is a very elegant one, and much frequented. There are several more places of public worship in this town, and the generality of people are of a religious turn of mind . . . .

Harriott Horry (Rutledge) Ravenel, *Eliza Pinckney* (New York: Charles Scribner's Sons, 1902), 18–19.

[A Description of William Middleton's Estate "Crowfield":]

The house stands a mile from, but in sight of, the road, and makes a very handsome appearance; as you draw near it, new beauties uncover themselves; first the fruitful vine mantling the wall, loaded with delicious clusters. Next a spacious basin in the midst of a large green presents itself as you enter the gate that leads to the house which is neatly finished, the rooms well contrived and elegantly furnished.

From the back door is a spacious walk a thousand feet long; each side of which nearest the house is a grass plot ornamented in a serpentine manner with flowers; next to that on the right hand is what immediately struck my rural taste, a thicket of young, tall live oaks . . . . Opposite on the left hand is a large square bowling green, sunk a little below the rest of the garden, with a walk quite round composed of a double row of fine, large flowering laurel and catalpas which afford both shade and beauty . . . the bottom of this charming spot . . . is a large fish pond with an island rising out of the middle . . . and upon it is a Roman temple . . . . Beyond this are the smiling fields dressed in vivid green.

[Mrs. Eliza Pinckney Describes the Smallpox Epidemic of 1760:]

A great cloud seems at present to hang over this Province. We are continually insulted by the Indians on our back settlements, and a violent kind of small-pox that rages in Charles Town almost puts a stop to all business. Several of those I have to transact business with are fled into the country, but by the Divine blessing, I hope a month or two will change the prospect. We expect shortly troops from General Jeffrey Amherst

Harriott Horry (Rutledge) Ravenel, *Eliza Pinckney* (New York: Charles Scribner's Sons, 1902), 53–54.

Harriott Horry (Rutledge) Ravenel, *Eliza Pinckney* (New York: Charles Scribner's Sons, 1902), 197–98.

which I trust will be able to manage these savage enemies; and the small–pox as it does not spread into the country, must be soon over for want of subjects.

I am now at Belmont [Plantation of Charles Pinckney] to keep my people out of the way of the violent distemper, for the poor blacks have died very fast, even by inoculation; but the people in Charles Town were inoculation mad, I think I may call it, and rushed into it with such precipitation that I think it impossible they could have had either a proper preparation or attendance, had there been ten doctors in town to one. The doctors could not help it; the people would not be said nay . . . . I am just . . . finishing my superintendence over a little small–pox hospital, a very small one indeed, as it did not contain more than fifteen patients. I lost only one, who took it in the natural way.

[David Ramsay Describes the Method of Settlement on the Frontier]

There have always been in Carolina single men and sometimes families migrating from the earlier settlements and breaking ground on bare creation. The difficulties of such undertakings have been constantly lessening, but are always considerable. The time of commencing them is in March, or about the breaking up of the winter. The parties go with family and plantation utensils, a few bushels of corn, and some domestic animals. After fixing on a site, they build in two or three days a cabin with logs cut down and piled one upon another in the form of a square or a parallelogram. The floor is of earth, the roof is sometimes of bark, but oftener of split logs. The light is received through the door and in some instances through a window of greased paper, or the bottom of a broken glass bottle. Experience, without the aid of philosophy, teaches them that fresh air is harmless; and they are therefore not anxious to exclude it by stopping crevices between the logs. Though sometimes they attempt it by introducing clay between them, especially on the lower parts, or as high as their heads. Shelter being provided their next care is to provide food.

David Ramsay, *History of South Carolina* . . . , 2 vols. (Charleston: David Longworth for the author, 1809), II, 246–50.

This is frequently accomplished before the few bushels of corn brought with them are expended. To expedite vegetation, the large trees are deprived of their power to shade the ground by cutting a circle around their trunks. This deadens them by preventing the sap from ascending. The under wood is destroyed. The ground, thus exposed to the action of the sun, is roughly prepared for planting by ploughing or hoeing. To its virgin soil is committed seed corn in March, or early in April. In 90 or 100 days it is so far advanced as to afford a great deal of nourishment in the form of roasting ears. In six weeks more it is ripe. The increase on this new land is often great, and the grain will keep from one crop to another. Till it is so far grown as to be fit for eating, the settler is supported by corn brought with him, or bought or borrowed from his neighbors; and with such fresh fish as he can catch . . . . Thus in the short space of one summer, the settler is possessed of a fixed residence, and has shelter and provisions from his own resources. His axe and his gun in the meantime furnish him with the means of defense against Indians, wild beasts, and robbers. Lightwood, or the heart of dry pine logs, affords a cheap substitute for candles. . . . The surplus of his crop may be bartered for homespun garments; or, if he is happily married, he may convert the wool of his sheep, the flax or cotton of his field into coarse clothing for domestic use. . . . From such humble beginnings hundreds of families in Carolina have been gradually raised to easy circumstances. . . . Settlers of the latter description are not long content with their cabins and lightwood torches. In a few years they construct either a frame house or one made of hewn logs. In either case it is floored with boards, and covered with oak, pine, or cypress shingles; and for the most part consists of two stories or floors, one above the other, and is divided into two apartments. A distinction takes place between the dwelling house and the kitchen. Other grains besides corn are cultivated. Potatoes, cabbages, turnips, and garden vegetables are raised, and the table is supplied with wholesome and agreeable food. Apple or peach trees are planted, and from them cider is obtained and whiskey distilled. . . . He purchases one or two slaves. He builds a barn and other out-houses. His children are put in school. He becomes a member of a church. Tea, coffee and sugar are found on his table; his house is glazed and decently furnished . . . . Proceeding in this manner in the course of a moderate life, the industrious settler becomes an independent in easy, and often comfortable circumstances.

READINGS

ADDITIONAL PRINTED SOURCE MATERIALS:

Carroll, B. R., *Historical Collections of South Carolina.*

Hewat, Alexander. *Historical Account of the Rise and Progress of the Colonies of South Carolina and Georgia.*

Milling, Chapman J., ed. *Colonial South Carolina; Two Contemporary Descriptions by Governor James Glen and Doctor George Milligen-Johnston.*

McDowell, W. L., Jr., ed. *Journals of the Commissioners of the Indian Trade, Sept. 20, 1710–Aug. 29, 1718.*

————. *Documents Relating to Indian Affairs, 1750–1754, 1754–1765,* 2 vols.

Salley, A. S., ed. *Documents Relating to Indian Affairs.*

Woodmason, Charles. *The Carolina Back-Country on the Eve of the Revolution.*

CORRELATED TEXTS:

Brown, Richard M. *The South Carolina Regulators.*

McCrady, Edward. *South Carolina Under the Royal Government, 1719–1776.*

Meriwether, R. L. *The Expansion of South Carolina, 1729–1765.*

Sirmans, M. Eugene. *Colonial South Carolina: A Political History, 1663–1763.*

Smith, W. Roy. *South Carolina as a Royal Province, 1719–1776.*

Snowden, Yates, ed. *History of South Carolina.* I, 191–313.

Wallace, D. D. *History of South Carolina.* I, 298–462; II, 1–65.

————. *South Carolina: A Short History,* 106–230.

IV
THE REVOLUTIONARY PERIOD

In the decade following the French and Indian War, the American colonies developed a unity of purpose and action that led them toward a rebellion against Great Britain, and the eventual winning of independence. In this movement, South Carolina played a major role, and the Low Country planters and merchants provided a leadership equal to any in the thirteen American colonies. From the first opposition to the Stamp Act in 1765 until the end of the war with the Treaty of Paris in 1783, South Carolinians were in the forefront of the resistance to the British.

Through years of struggling with the proprietary and royal governors for control of the provincial government, the South Carolina Assembly developed much experience in self-government. When it was prorogued by the last royal governor, William Campbell, assembly leaders moved to form first a general committee, then a constitutional convention, and finally a permanent legislature for a sovereign state. Similarly, the local militia became regiments for defense, and preparations were made for war. Many of their officers had gained military experience against the Cherokees in 1760–1761. Not all South Carolinians wanted separation from Great Britain. There were many "tories" who remained loyal to their king, and some were ready to fight for him instead of for the "rebel" colony of South Carolina. These loyalists constituted a major problem for the young state for a decade and at times, particularly after the fall of Charles Town, seemed to outnumber the patriots.

Aside from skirmishes with the tories, the first military engagement of the war came in June, 1776, when the British attempted to take Charles Town by a naval attack. They were defeated, and for the next three years South Carolina was spared the rigors of actual warfare. In 1779, the British again attacked Charles Town and were repulsed, but in May, 1780, the city fell, and soon much of the state was overrun. With its governor, John Rutledge, a refugee in North Carolina and most of its leaders captured, South Carolina's future looked dark in the summer of 1780, but

155

the state fought on. In August, 1780, there was another setback when American forces under General Horatio Gates were defeated at Camden. But in October of the same year, victory against the British at King's Mountain brought hope to the South Carolinians. Early the next year, another victory came at Cowpens. In the meantime, the partisan leaders, Thomas Sumter, Francis Marion, and Andrew Pickens—also known as the guerrilla fighters—were keeping the British occupied over much of the state. Later, with the aid of General Nathanael Greene and his Continental troops, they cleared most of the state of British and tory resistance, although Charles Town was not evacuated by the enemy until December 14, 1782. Independence came with the Treaty of Paris in 1783, but economic and political troubles continued. Agriculture and trade had been virtually destroyed, and the war had left strong feelings of difference between ex-whigs and ex-tories, between Low Country and Up Country. Not until the 1790s, with a new capital at Columbia, a new state constitution, and cotton as a staple crop, was South Carolina able to find relative security and prosperity.

59. *South Carolina and the Stamp Act, 1765*

After long neglecting to enforce the Navigation Acts, the British parliament in 1765, under the leadership of George Grenville, passed a revenue act raising the stamp tax on papers and documents. This act was opposed by the American colonies on the ground that they were being taxed without representation. When the stamps reached Charles Town, an aroused citizenry refused to allow them to go on sale. Moreover, South Carolina sent delegates to a convention in New York to join with the other colonies in urging the repeal of the Stamp Act.

[A Newspaper Account of South Carolinians'
Protests over the Stamp Act]

Saturday, October 19th: Early this morning, in the middle of Broad Street and Church Street, near Mr. Dillon's . . . appeared suspended on a gallows twenty feet high, an effigy designed to represent a distributor of stamp paper, with a figure of the devil on its right hand, on his left a boat, with a head stuck upon it, distinguished by a blue bonnet; to each of which were affixed labels expressive of the sense of a people unshaken in their loyalty, but tenacious of just liberty, who had conceived "that all internal duties imposed upon them without the consent of their immediate or even virtual representatives, was grievous, oppressive and unconstitutional; and that an extension of the powers and jurisdiction of Admiralty Courts in America would subvert one of their most darling legal rights and privileges, that of trial by juries." On the gallows, in very conspicuous characters, was written, "Liberty and No Stamp Act" and on the back of the principal figure these words, viz., "Whoever shall dare attempt to pull down these effigies, had better been born with a millstone about his neck and cast into the sea." In this situation, the effigies continued the whole day without one person offering to disturb or take them down . . . .

South Carolina Gazette, 1732–1775 (Charleston, S.C.), Oct. 19–31, 1765.

In the evening the figures were taken down, and received in a cart or wagon, drawn by eight or ten horses, when a procession commenced down Broad Street to the Bay, attended at least by two thousand souls, continuing from thence to the Exchange, and up Tradd Street, halting at the door of a house belonging to George Saxby (the then supposed distributor of stamps) occupied by Capt. William Coats.

Some small injuries to the windows of which it was impossible to prevent from so great a number (whom it required great prudence and no less exertion of influence in many to restrain from levelling it to the ground), not owing, however to any personal dislike to Mr. Saxby, but their detestation of the office . . . . Upon the doors being at length opened, and no such papers found, the cart and its contents proceeded to the green, back of the brick barracks, when the effigies were committed to the flames, amidst the loud and repeated shouts of an increasing multitude. The bells of St. Michael's rang muffled all day and during the procession there was a most solemn knell for the burial of a coffin on which was inscribed "American Liberty."

No outrages whatever were committed during the whole procession, except a rifling damage done to Mr. Saxby's house . . . . But after the procession and funeral, diligent search was made for another gentleman, upon a report prevailing in the evening that he was appointed distributor of the stamps, and not Mr. Saxby, in order to be informed "whether he intended to execute the act." This gentleman not being found that night, had like to have produced some commotion, but the next day being Sunday, a solemn declaration, signed by him, was stuck up at the Exchange, imputing "that he neither had received a commission, knew of his appointment, or that the stamps were consigned to him", which in some measure appeased the people. . . .

Friday evening, October 25th: Arrived the *Carolina Packet,* Captain Robson, from London, upon which there was some slight appearance of a tumult, but it subsided as soon as it was shown that no stamp officer was on board, and that Mr. Saxby had taken his passage, and was on board the *Heart of Oak,* Captain Gunn.

Saturday afternoon, October 26th: The *Heart of Oak* arrived, also Mr. Saxby, and upon having information of what had passed here, instead of coming up to town in the ship, he went ashore at Fort Johnson, and it being then certainly known that Mr. Caleb Lloyd was actually to be distributor of the stamps for the Province, numbers of people again assembled, and seemed very uneasy; but Mr. Saxby, being made acquainted at the Fort, of the commotions which had arisen throughout

America on account of the Stamp Act, and that it was as little relished here as elsewhere, he expressed great concern that his acceptance of an office under it (that of inspector of the duties) had proved so odious and disagreeable to the people, and in order to restore the public peace (which there was too much reason otherwise to fear might be disturbed), made a voluntary offer to suspend the execution of his office (which was all that seemed to be desired) till the determination of the King and Parliament of Great Britain should be known, upon a united application to be made from his Majesty's colonies for a repeal of an act that had created so much confusion. Mr. Lloyd, who was then also at Fort Johnson, made a like voluntary declaration in regard to his office of distributor, and on Sunday evening, October 27th, these declarations in writing were publicly read on the Bay to the general joy of the inhabitants, which was shown by loud and repeated acclamations, and the ringing of St. Michael's bell unmuffled.

[The South Carolina Assembly]

Friday, July 26th, 1765: Captain Christopher Gadsden reported, from the committee appointed to consider the letter sent from the Speaker of the House of Representatives of the Province of Massachusetts-Bay, to the Speaker of this House, and to report their opinion thereupon of the expediency and utility of the measures therein proposed, and the best means of effecting the relief therein mentioned:

That they are of the opinion the measure therein proposed is prudent and necessary, and therefore recommend to the House to send a committee to meet the committees from the House of Representatives or Burgesses of the several British colonies on the Continent at New York, on the first of October next.

That the said committee be ordered to consult there with those other committies, on the present circumstances of the colonies, and the difficulties which they are and must be reduced to, by the operation of the acts of Parliament for levying duties and taxes on the colonies; and to con-

Journal of the South Carolina Assembly, in Hezekiah Niles, ed., *Principles and Acts of the Revolution in America* (Baltimore: n.p., 1822), 455–56.

sider of a general and united, loyal and humble representation of their condition to His Majesty and Parliament, and to implore relief; that the result of their consultation shall, at their return, be immediately laid before the House, to be confirmed or not, as the House shall think proper.

And the said report being delivered in at the clerk's table and read a second time, the question was severally put, that the House do agree to the first, second and third paragraphs of this report. It was resolved in the affirmative.

Friday, August 2nd, 1765: Motion being made, Resolved, that this House will provide a sum sufficient to defray the charges and expenses of a committee of three gentlemen on account of their going to, convening at, and returning from the meeting of the several committees proposed to assemble at New York on the 1st Tuesday in October next, to consult there with those other committees on the present circumstances of the colonies, and the difficulties which they are and must be reduced to by the operation of the acts of Parliament for levying duties and taxes on the colonies . . . .

Ordered, that the public treasurer do advance out of any monies in his hands, to the said committee, a sum not exceeding six hundred pounds sterling, for the purpose aforesaid . . . .

Ordered, That the following gentlemen be appointed a committee for the purpose aforesaid, viz., Mr. Thomas Lynch, Mr. Christopher Gadsden, and Mr. John Rutledge . . . .

[Alexander Hewat on Repeal of Stamp Act]

When the news of the repeal of this Act reached America, it afforded the colonists, as might have been expected, matter of great triumph. The most extravagant demonstrations of joy, by bonfires, illuminations, and ringing of bells, were exhibited. . . . The Carolinians sent to England for a marble statue of Mr. [William] Pitt, and erected it in the middle of

Alexander Hewat, *An Historical Account of the Rise and Progress of the Colonies of South Carolina and Georgia,* in B. R. Carroll, *Historical Collections of South Carolina* . . . , 2 vols. (New York: Harper, 1836), I, 532.

Charleston, in grateful remembrance of the noble stand he had made in defense of their rights and liberties. Addresses were sent home to the King, acknowledging the wisdom and justice of his government in the repeal of the grievous act, and expressing their happiness that their former harmony and commercial intercourse, so beneficial to both countries were restored.

60. *The Reception of the Tea Act, 1773*

FOLLOWING THE REPEAL OF THE STAMP ACT IN 1766, TENSIONS BE-
TWEEN THE COLONISTS AND THE BRITISH RELAXED FOR A SHORT TIME,
BUT IN 1767 PARLIAMENT PASSED THE TOWNSHEND REVENUE ACTS, PLAC-
ING A TAX OR DUTY ON SUCH IMPORTED ITEMS AS WINE, PAPER, GLASS,
LEAD, TEA, AND PAINTERS' COLORS. REACTION TO THESE ACTS TOOK THE
FORM OF NONIMPORTATION AGREEMENTS, AND SOUTH CAROLINIANS
JOINED THE OTHER COLONISTS IN REFUSING TO PURCHASE THE TAXED
ITEMS. AGAIN PARLIAMENT GAVE IN, TO THE EXTENT OF REPEALING ALL
THE DUTIES EXCEPT THAT ON TEA. THIS WAS FOLLOWED IN 1773 BY THE
TEA ACT, WHICH IS DISCUSSED IN THE FOLLOWING EXCERPTS FROM
DAVID RAMSAY AND HENRY LAURENS.

[David Ramsay]

The experiment of taxation was renewed in the year 1767, but in a
more artful manner. Small duties were imposed on glass, paper, tea and
painter's colors. The colonists again petitioned and associated to import
no more British manufactures. In consequence of which, all the duties
were taken off excepting three pence a pound on tea. Unwilling to contend with the mother country about paper claims, and at the same time
determined to pay no taxes but such as were imposed by their own legis-
latures, the colonists associated to import no more tea; but relaxed in all
their other resolutions, and renewed their commercial intercourse with
Great Britain.

The tax on tea was in a great measure rendered a barren branch of
revenue, by the American resolution of importing none on which the
Parliamentary duty was charged. In the year 1773, a scheme was adopted
by the East-India Company, to export large quantities of that commodity
to be sold on their account in the several capitals of the British colonies.
This measure tended directly to contravene the American resolutions.

David Ramsay, *History of South Carolina* . . . , 2 vols. (Charleston: David
Longworth for the author, 1809), I, 223–24.

The colonists reasoned with themselves, that as the duty and the price of the commodity were inseparably blended if the tea was sold, every purchaser would pay a tax imposed by the British Parliament as part of the purchase money. Jealous of the designs of the mother country, and determined never to submit to British taxation, they everywhere entered into combinations to obstruct the sales of the tea sent out by the East India Company. The cargoes sent to South Carolina were stored, the consignees being restrained from offering it to sale. In other Provinces the landing of it being forbidden, the captains were obliged to return without discharging their cargoes. In Boston, a few men in disguise threw into the river all that had been exported to that city by the East India Company.

A Letter from Henry Laurens to George Appleby, February 15, 1774:

I won't say the people have proceeded too far in drowning and enforcing back the tea; possibly it may prove to have been the most effectual and therefore wisest method; but at present I commend the proceeding at Charleston in preference to all the rest: the consignees refuse the commissions; the people will not purchase the commodity; it must remain in store and perish or be returned at the expense of those who sent it. There is a constitutional stubbornness in such conduct which must be approved of by every true Englishman, and open the understanding of those whose stubborn attempts to ensnare America are supported by no other plea than power.

D. D. Wallace, *The Life of Henry Laurens* (New York: G. P. Putnam's Sons, 1915), 194.

61. Resolutions of the General Committee, July 6, 1774

AFTER KING GEORGE III INSISTED ON RETAINING THE TAX ON TEA AND PRESSURE WAS BROUGHT TO BEAR UPON THE AMERICAN COLONIES TO INCREASE THEIR TRADE WITH THE EAST INDIA COMPANY—WHICH WAS IN GRAVE FINANCIAL DIFFICULTY—OPPOSITION AROSE IN SOUTH CAROLINA AND ELSEWHERE. ON DECEMBER 3, 1773, AFTER A PUBLIC MEETING HAD BEEN CALLED, A MASS OF PEOPLE, CHIEFLY LANDOWNERS, MET IN THE HALL OVER THE EXCHANGE BUILDING IN CHARLESTON TO PROTEST THE SALE OF TEA. TWO HUNDRED AND FIFTY-SEVEN CHESTS, CONSIGNED BY THE EAST INDIA TEA COMPANY, HAD ARRIVED TWO DAYS BEFORE. DURING THE MEETING IT WAS RESOLVED THAT NO MORE TEA WOULD BE IMPORTED, LANDED, OR VENDED, AND CHRISTOPHER GADSDEN WAS APPOINTED CHAIRMAN OF A COMMITTEE TO SEEK SIGNATURES THROUGHOUT THE COLONY TO SUPPORT THE RESOLUTION. FROM THIS MEETING THE "GENERAL COMMITTEE" BECAME ORGANIZED BY THE LATE SUMMER OF 1774. AN EXTRALEGAL BODY, THE COMMITTEE GRADUALLY BECAME THE RULING POWER OF SOUTH CAROLINA. THE RESOLUTIONS OF JULY 6, 1774, FOLLOWING, WERE IN ANSWER TO THE PARLIAMENTARY ACTS PUNISHING MASSACHUSETTS FOR THE BOSTON TEA PARTY. SPECIFICALLY CALLED FOR WERE REPRESENTATIVES TO BE SENT TO THE FIRST CONTINENTAL CONGRESS.

[Resolutions Passed by the General Committee]

Resolved, that his Majesty's subjects in North America owe the same allegiance to the Crown of Great Britain that is due from his subjects born in Great Britain.

Resolved, that his Majesty's subjects in North America are entitled to all the inherent rights and liberties of his natural born subjects within the Kingdom . . . .

David Ramsay, *History of the Revolution in South Carolina*, 2 vols. (Trenton: Isaac Collins, 1785), I, 18–22.

Resolved, that it is repugnant to the rights of the people, that any taxes should be imposed on them, unless with their own consent given personally or by their representatives.

Resolved, that it is a fundamental right, which his Majesty's liege subjects are entitled unto, that no man should suffer in his person or property without a fair trial, and judgment given by his peers or by the law of the land.

Resolved, that all trials of treason, or for any felony or crime whatever, committed and done in this his Majesty's Colony, by any person or persons residing therein, ought of right to be had and conducted in and before his Majesty's courts held within the said Colony according to the fixed and known course of proceedings . . . .

Resolved, that the late act for shutting up the port of Boston, and the two bills relative to Boston, which . . . are of the most alarming nature to all his Majesty's subjects in America . . . are calculated to deprive many thousand Americans of their rights, properties and privileges, in a most cruel, oppressive and unconstitutional manner, and are the most dangerous precedents . . . .

Resolved, therefore, that not only the dictates of humanity, but the soundest principles of true policy and self-preservation, make it absolutely necessary for the inhabitants of all the colonies to support the people of Boston, by all lawful ways in their power, and especially to leave no justifiable means untried to procure a repeal of those acts immediately relative to them, and also all others affecting the constitutional rights and liberties of America in general. And as the best means to effect this desirable end, it is

Resolved, that Henry Middleton, John Rutledge, Christopher Gadsden, Thomas Lynch, and Edward Rutledge, Esquires, be, and they are hereby appointed, deputies, on the part and behalf of this Colony, to meet the deputies of the several colonies in North America in general Congress, on the first Monday in September next, in Philadelphia . . . to consider the act lately passed, and bills depending in Parliament, with regard to the Port of Boston . . . also the grievances under which America labors, by reason of the several acts of Parliament that impose taxes or duties for raising a revenue, and lay unnecessary restrictions and burdens on trade, and of the statutes, Parliamentary acts, and Royal instructions, which make an invidious distinction between his Majesty's subjects in Great Britain and America, with full power and authority in behalf of us and our constituents, to concert, agree to, and effectually to prosecute such legal measures (by which we for ourselves and them most

solemnly engage to abide) as in the opinion of the said deputies . . .
shall be most likely to obtain a repeal of the said acts and a redress of
these grievances.

Resolved, that while the oppressive acts relative to Boston are enforced,
we will cheerfully from time to time contribute towards the relief of such
poor persons there whose unfortunate circumstances may be thought to
stand in need of most assistance.

Resolved, that a Committee of ninety-nine persons be now appointed
to act as a General Committee, to correspond with the committees of the
other colonies, and to do all matters and things necessary to carry out
these resolutions into execution; and that any twenty-one of them, met
together, may proceed on business, their power to continue till the next
general meeting.

62. *The Association of June 2, 1775*

THE NONIMPORTATION AGREEMENTS WITH WHICH THE COLONISTS
HAD MET THE EARLIER TAX LAWS HAD TAKEN THE FORM OF "ASSOCIA-
TIONS," OR GENERAL STATEMENTS ENFORCED BY PUBLIC OPINION. AFTER
THE BRITISH HAD FIRED ON AMERICANS AT THE BATTLES OF LEXINGTON
AND CONCORD, THE SOUTH CAROLINA ASSOCIATION OF JUNE 2, 1775,
WAS ADOPTED, GOING BEYOND MERE ECONOMIC BOYCOTTS AND PLEDGING
THEIR LIVES IN THE DEFENSE OF THEIR RIGHTS.

[David Ramsay on the Beginning
of the Revolutionary War]

The actual commencement of hostilities against this continent by the
British troops in the bloody scene on the 19th of April last near Boston—
the increase of arbitrary impositions from a wicked and despotic ministry
—and the dread of insurrections in the colonies—are causes sufficient to
drive an oppressed people to the use of arms. We, therefore, the sub-
scribers, inhabitants of South Carolina, holding ourselves bound by that
most sacred of all obligations—the duty of good citizens toward an
injured country, and thoroughly convinced that, under our present distressed circumstances, we shall be justified before God and man in resisting force by force—do unite ourselves under every tie of religion and
honor, and associate as a band in her defense against every foe—hereby
solemnly engaging that, whenever our Continental or Provincial councils
shall decree it necessary, we will go forth, and be ready to sacrifice our
lives and fortunes to secure her freedom and safety. This obligation to
continue in full force until a reconciliation shall take place between
Great Britain and America, upon constitutional principles—an event
which we most ardently desire. And we will hold all those persons
inimical to the liberty of the colonies who shall refuse to subscribe this
Association.

David Ramsay, *History of the Revolution in South Carolina*, 2 vols. (Trenton:
Isaac Collins, 1785), I, 33–34.

167

63. *Charleston Sons of Liberty and the Liberty Tree*

THE SONS OF LIBERTY BECAME ACTIVE IN SOUTH CAROLINA AS THE ORGANIZATION SPREAD UP AND DOWN THE ATLANTIC SEABOARD. CHARLESTON, LIKE BOSTON, HAD ITS "LIBERTY TREE." THE SYMBOL WAS A LIVE OAK WHICH STOOD IN MAZYCK'S PASTURE OUTSIDE THE CITY LIMITS. THE SITE OF THE TREE WAS IN THE SQUARE BOUNDED BY CHARLOTTE, WASHINGTON, CALHOUN, AND ALEXANDER STREETS. HERE CHRISTOPHER GADSDEN ADDRESSED THE CHARLESTON MECHANICS, URGING THEM TO STAND FIRM FOR THEIR RIGHTS. THE NON-IMPORTATION ASSOCIATION LIKEWISE HELD ITS MEETINGS UNDER THE LIBERTY TREE, AND, BENEATH ITS BRANCHES THE DECLARATION OF INDEPENDENCE WAS PROCLAIMED IN IMPOSING CEREMONIES UPON ITS SIGNING. WHEN THE BRITISH CAPTURED CHARLESTON, THEY CUT DOWN THE TREE AND BURNED IT, LEAVING ONLY A BLACKENED STUMP. THE LEADER OF THE CHARLESTON MECHANICS WAS WILLIAM JOHNSON, A BLACKSMITH OF MEANS WHO HAD COME TO CHARLESTON FROM NEW YORK. THE FIRST SELECTION IS A LIST OF THE MEN WHO MET UNDER THE TREE; THE SECOND IS A POEM PUBLISHED BY "PHILO PATRIAE," PRINTED BY THE ARDENT PATRIOT, PETER TIMOTHY IN HIS SOUTH CAROLINA GAZETTE. "PHILO PATRIAE" IS BELIEVED TO HAVE BEEN CHRISTOPHER GADSDEN.

[List of Men Who Gathered under the Liberty Tree]

Christopher Gadsden, Merchant, then 42 years old.
William Johnson, Blacksmith.
Joseph Veree, Carpenter.
John Fullerton, Carpenter.
James Brown, Carpenter.
Nath'l. Libby, Ship Carpenter.
George Flagg, Painter and Glazier.
Thos. Coleman, Upholsterer.
John Hall, Coachmaker.
Wm. Field, Carver.
Robert Jones, Sadler.
John Loughton, Coachmaker.
W. Rodgers, Wheelwright.

John Calvert, Clerk in some office.
H. Y. Bookless, Wheelwright.
J. Barlow, Sadler.
Tunis Teabout, Blacksmith.
Peter Munclean, Clerk.
Wm. Trusler, Butcher.
Robert Howard, Carpenter.
Alex. Alexander, Schoolmaster.
Ed. Weyman, Clerk of St. Philip's Church, and glass grinder.
Thos. Swarle, Painter.
Wm. Laughton, Tailor.
Daniel Cannon, Carpenter.
Benjamin Hawes, Painter.

South Carolina Historical and Genealogical Magazine, vols. 40–41 (Jan., 1940), 117–22. Reprinted by permission of The South Carolina Historical Society.

[Poem by "Philo Patriae"]

ON LIBERTY-TREE

Honos erit huic quoque Arbori
Quereus [sic] Libertati Sacra.

As Druid Bards, in Times of old,
E'er Temples were enshrin'd with Gold,
Beneath the Umbrage of a Wood,
Perform'd their Homage to their God;
So let the Muse expatiate free,
Under thy Shade, delightful Tree!
Its humble Tribute while it pays
To LIBERTY in votive Lays.

Some on the Laurel fix their Love,
Some on the Myrtle do approve
While others on the Olive's Bough,
With lavish Song their Praise bestow;
But me, nor Laurel does delight,
Nor Cytherea's Grove invite,
Nor shall Minerva's Tree proclaim
As the LIVE-OAK so high a Fame.

No Region boasts so firm a Wood,
So fit to cut the Crystal Flood
And Trade's wide blessings to convey,
From Land to Land, from Sea to Sea.
No Soil e'er grew a Tree so fair,
Whose Beauty can with thine compare.
Unmatch'd thy awful Trunk appears,
The Product of an Hundred Years.
Thy graceful Head's bent gently down,
Which ever-verdant Branches crown.
Thro' thy twinn'd Foliage Zephyrs play,
And feather'd Warblers tune their Lay.

R. W. Gibbes, *Documentary History of the American Revolution,* Rev. ed. 3 vols. (New York: D. Appleton & Co., 1855), I, 10.

Here LIBERTY divinely bright,
Beneath thy Shade, enthron'd in Light,
Her beaming Glory does impart
Around, and gladdens ev'ry Heart.

Hail! O Heav'n-born Goddess hail!
Each Bosom warm, each Breast assail,
With Flame, like that which Greece inspir'd,
When with thy living Lyre fir'd:
Or, such, as late by thee imprest
Glow'd in a Pym's and Hambden's [sic] Breast,
Those fav'rite Sons, whose gen'rous Soul,
No Threat cou'd awe, no Bribe controul,
Who nobly brave, did dare arraign
A worthless Stuart's tyrant Reign.
Propitious still, thy Vot'ries aid,
Beneath this TREE, Celestial Maid!

Hither to Thee thy SONS repair,
On thee, repose each anxious Care;
Bravely resolv'd to live or die,
As thou shalt guide their Destiny.

No secret Schemes, no sly Intrigues,
No Measures dark, no private Leagues
(Such as in Courts are daily found)
Do e'er approach thy sacred Ground:
But hither in the Face of Day
Thy gentle SONS their Duty pay.

Hither resort the Friends of Man
His common Rights and Claims to scan;
United, firmly to maintain
Those RIGHTS, which God and Nature mean.
RIGHTS! which when truly understood,
Are Cause of universal Good.
Rights! which declare, "That all are free,
"In Person and in Property.
"That Pow'r supreme, when giv'n in Trust,
"Belongs but to the Wise and Just
"That Kings are Kings for this sole Cause,
"To be the Guardians of the Laws.

"That Subjects only should obey,
"Only submit to sov'reign Sway,
"When Sov'reigns make those Laws their Choice
"To which the People give their Voice.
"That in free States, 'tis ever meant
"No Laws should bind, without Consent;
"And that, when other Laws take Place,
"Not to resist, wou'd be Disgrace;
"Not to resist, wou'd treach'rous be,
"Treach'rous to Society."

These, these are Rights, most just and true
Which FREEDOM'S SONS proclaim their Due.
SONS! not unworthy of their Sires;
Whom ev'ry Spark of Glory fires;
Whom Violence shall ne'er controul,
Nor check the Vigour of their Soul:
Determin'd, to their latest Hour,
T' oppose and check despotic Power.
Sworn Foes to Tyrants lawless Sway,
They'll to Posterity convey
That gen'rous Plan, so dearly bought
For which their fam'd Forefathers fought:
That Plan! which formed in NASSAU'S Days,
Will ever gain a Briton's Praise.

Be these your Arts, be these your Laws,
Ye SONS, engaged in FREEDOM'S Cause;
With zealous Heart, undaunted Breast,
It's [sic] sacred Guardians stand confest.

Wide and more wide, may thy Domain,
O LIBERTY! its Power maintain,
Parent of Life! true Bond of Law!
From whence alone our Bliss we draw
Thou! who dids't once in ancient Rome,
E'er fell Corruption caus'd its Doom,
Reign in a Cato's godlike Soul,
And Brutus in each Thought controul;
Here, here prolong thy wish'd for Stay,
To bless and cheer each passing Day,
Tho' with no pompous Piles erect,

Nor sculptur'd Stones, thy shrine is deckt;
Yet here, beneath thy fav'rite Oak,
Thy Aid will all thy SONS invoke.
Oh! if thou deign to bless this Land,
And guide it by thy gentle Hand,
Then shall AMERICA become
Rival, to once high-favour'd Rome [.]

Philo Patriae
[Christopher Gadsden]

Sept. 18, 1769

64. *William Henry Drayton's Declaration to the Tories, September 13, 1775*

WHEREAS MANY LOW COUNTRY MEN WERE STRONGLY BEHIND THE GENERAL COMMITTEE IN ITS OPPOSITION TO BRITISH MISRULE, THE MAJORITY OF THE UP COUNTRY CITIZENS REMAINED LOYAL TO THE KING. SECTIONAL DIFFERENCES WERE STRONG, AND MOST UP COUNTRY SETTLERS FELT LITTLE IN COMMON WITH CHARLESTON. IN ORDER TO WIN OVER SOME OF THE "UNAFFECTED" TO THE AMERICAN CAUSE, JUDGE WILLIAM HENRY DRAYTON AND THE REVEREND WILLIAM TENNENT WERE SENT INTO THE INTERIOR—OR BACK COUNTRY—TO EXPLAIN THE SITUATION TO THE PEOPLE THERE AND TO INDUCE THEM TO JOIN THE LOW COUNTRY LEADERS IN ACCEPTING THE CONTROL OF THE GENERAL COMMITTEE AND THE PROVINCIAL CONGRESS. THE FOLLOWING IS TAKEN FROM DRAYTON'S ADDRESS TO THE TORIES AT NINETY-SIX.

[Drayton Addresses the Tories at Ninety-Six]

Whereas the tools of administration have encouraged certain inhabitants of this Colony to attempt, by every practicable measure to oppose and to counteract the virtuous efforts of America; these inhabitants, men of low degree among us, though of eminence in this country; men totally illiterate, though of common natural parts; men endeavoring, at this calamitous time, to rise in the world, by misleading their honest neighbors; men who are by his Excellency the Governor promised to be amply rewarded for such an infamous conduct; these men knowingly deceiving their neighbors, and wickedly selling their country, have practised every art, fraud and misrepresentation, to raise in this Province an opposition to the voice of America. To oppose this hellish plan, the honorable the Council of Safety for this Colony commissioned the Reverend William Tennent and myself to make a progress through the

David Ramsay, *History of the Revolution in South Carolina*, 2 vols. Trenton: Isaac Collins, 1785), I, 303–307.

disturbed parts of this Colony "to explain to the people at large the nature of the unhappy disputes between Great Britain and the American colonies"; thousands heard and believed us; they owned their full conviction; they expressed their concern that they had been misled; and they most sincerely acceded to the association formed by the authority of our late Congress. Such a proceeding did not accord with the designs of these men, betrayers of their country, or the wishes of his Excellency the Governor, who by letters instigated them to strengthen their party. To prevent a further defection, the leaders of the party resolved, by the din of arms, to drown the voice of reason. For such an infernal purpose, by the instigation of Moses Kirkland, on or about the 29th of August last, men did actually assemble in arms, and with hostile intentions. My immediately assembling, and marching with a part of the militia, caused these men to disperse; but now, other leaders, of the same malignant party, correspondents of his Excellency the Governor, have assembled men in arms, on the north side of Saluda river, who are now actually encamped at a charge and expense which his Excellency the Governor has promised to repay; and these men threaten to attack the troops under my orders. Wherefore, to prevent the effusion of civil bloodshed, I think it my duty to issue this declaration, in order that I may leave no moderate step untried to recover a few of our unhappy countrymen from these delusions, by which they have been drawn on to lift their arms against their injured country, gloriously struggling to enjoy the rights of mankind. . . .

And whereas the leaders of our unhappy and deceived countrymen, now assembled in arms against the liberties of America, have drawn them into this dangerous and disgraceful situation, by filling their minds with fears and apprehensions that their lives and properties are in danger from the designs of the Congress, the Honorable Council of Safety, the General Committee, and the troops under my orders, because they, our said countrymen, have not acceded to our Association: wherefore, to remove all such ill-founded apprehensions, in the name of and by the authority vested in me by the honorable the Council of Safety, I solemnly declare, that all such apprehensions are actually groundless; and I also declare, in the name of the Council of Safety, that our said unhappy and deceived countrymen may, in perfect safety of their lives, persons and property, repair to, and continue to dwell and abide at home, so long as they shall choose to behave peaceably. We shudder even at the idea of distressing them in any shape; we abhor the idea of compelling any person to associate with us; we only with sorrow declare that any person who will not associate with, and aid and comfort us in this arduous struggle for our liberties, cannot by us be considered as friendly to us; and, therefore, that we cannot aid and comfort such person, by holding that intercourse and communication with such person as is usually held between friends.

And thus having, in the name of this Colony, declared the terms upon which peace and safety may be had and enjoyed by our unfortunate countrymen as aforesaid, it is my duty also to declare, that I shall march and attack, as public enemies, all and every person in arms, or to be in arms, in this part of the Colony, in opposition to the measurers of Congress; and having, with the utmost patience and industry, gently endeavored to persuade men to a peaceable conduct, I now shall, with equal patience and industry, prosecute military measures with the utmost rigor; and I make no doubt but that, with the assistance of the Almighty—witness our endeavors to avert the calamities of war—we shall speedily obtain the wish of every virtuous American: peace, safety, and security to our rights. Given under my hand, this 13th day of September, 1775, at camp, near Ninety-Six.

65. *The Withdrawal of the Last Royal Governor, 1775*

PRO-BRITISH SOUTH CAROLINIANS SIGNED A TREATY IN WHICH THEY
AGREED TO REMAIN NEUTRAL IN RETURN FOR PEACE, BUT SOME OF THE
TORY LEADERS STILL CONTINUED TO CORRESPOND WITH GOVERNOR
WILLIAM CAMPBELL. THIS SUB ROSA EFFORT WAS TO LEARN THE
GOVERNOR'S DESIRES TO HELP MAINTAIN THEIR RESISTANCE TO THE
PATRIOTS. FINALLY, AS HOSTILITIES FLARED, GOVERNOR CAMPBELL
DISSOLVED THE LAST ROYAL ASSEMBLY ON SEPTEMBER 15, 1775, AND
WITHDREW FROM THE CITY OF CHARLESTON TO THE PROTECTION OF A
BRITISH WARSHIP IN THE HARBOR. FROM THE *Tamar* HE CONTINUED
HIS CORRESPONDENCE. THE EXCERPTS PRINTED HERE ARE AN EXCHANGE
OF LETTERS BETWEEN CAMPBELL AND THE GENERAL COMMITTEE.

[The General Committee's Address
to Governor William Campbell, September 29, 1775]

It is with great concern we find that, for some days past, your
Excellency has been pleased to withdraw yourself from Charleston, the
seat of your government, and have retired on board the King's ship.
The inconveniences which must unavoidably arise to the people deprived, by this step, of that access to your Excellency, which is absolutely
necessary for transacting public affairs, is apparent; and we submit to
your Excellency's consideration, whether the retirement of our Governor
to a King's ship, in this time of general disquietude, when the minds
of the people are filled with the greatest apprehensions for their safety,
may not increase their alarm, and excite jealousies of some premeditated
design against them. We therefore entreat, that your Excellency will
return to Charleston, the usual place of residence of the Governor of
South Carolina; and your Excellency may be assured, that whilst, agreeable to your repeated and solemn declarations, your Excellency shall
take no active part against the good people of this colony, in the present

David Ramsay, *History of the Revolution in South Carolina*, 2 vols. (Trenton:
Isaac Collins, 1785), 300–301.

arduous struggle for the preservation of their civil liberties, we will, to the utmost of our power, secure to your Excellency that safety and respect for your person and character, which the inhabitants of Carolina have ever wished to show to the representative of their Sovereign.

By order of the General Committee, Henry Laurens, Chairman.

[Governor William Campbell's Reply, September 30, 1775]

I have received a message, signed by you, from a set of people who style themselves a General Committee. The presumption of such an address from a body assembled by no legal authority, and whom I must consider as in actual and open rebellion against their Sovereign, can only be equaled by the outrages which obliged me to take refuge on board the King's ship in the harbor. It deserves no answer, nor should I have given it any, but to mark the hardiness with which you have advanced, that I could so far forget my duty to my Sovereign and my country, as to promise I would take no active part in bringing the subverters of our glorious constitution, and the real liberties of the people, to a sense of their duty. The unmanly arts that have already been used to prejudice me in the general opinion, may still be employed by that Commitee. But I never will return to Charleston till I can support the King's authority, and protect his faithful and loyal subjects. Whenever the people of this Province will put it in my power to render them essential service, I will, with pleasure, embrace the opportunity, and think it a very happy one.

I am, Sir, your most humble servant,

To Henry Laurens, Esq.   WILLIAM CAMPBELL

David Ramsay, *History of the Revolution in South Carolina,* 2 vols. (Trenton: Isaac Collins, 1785), I, 301–302.

66. *The Constitution of 1776*

ON NOVEMBER 19, 1775, THE FIRST SOUTH CAROLINA CASUALTIES OF
THE REVOLUTION WERE SUFFERED DURING A CLASH BETWEEN WHIG AND
TORY FORCES AT NINETY-SIX. FOLLOWING THIS ENCOUNTER, COLONEL
RICHARD RICHARDSON LED A LARGE FORCE OF WHIGS THROUGH THE
UP COUNTRY TO PACIFY THE UPRISINGS THERE. THE GENERAL COM-
MITTEE WAS IN COMPLETE CONTROL IN THE COLONY, AND, AT THE
ADVICE OF THE CONTINENTAL CONGRESS, THE PROVINCIAL CONGRESS
WAS CALLED INTO MEETING IN MARCH, 1776, TO DRAW UP A CONSTITU-
TION TO FORMALIZE THE REVOLUTIONARY GOVERNMENT. THE FIRST
SELECTION IS THE RESOLUTION ADOPTED BY THE CONTINENTAL CON-
GRESS, AND THE SECOND CONTAINS SIGNIFICANT EXCERPTS FROM THE
CONSTITUTION OF 1776.

Resolution of the Continental Congress, February 8, 1776

Resolved, that if the Convention of South Carolina find it necessary
to establish a form of government in that Colony, it be recommended to
said Convention to call a full and free representation of the people;
and that the said representatives, if they think it necessary, establish
such form of government as, in their judgment will best promote the
happiness of the people, and most effectually secure peace and good
order in the Colony, during the continuance of the present dispute
between Great Britain and the colonies.

John Drayton, *Memoirs of the American Revolution,* 2 vols. (Charleston: A. E.
Miller, 1821), II, 171.

A Constitution, or Form of Government, Agreed to and Resolved upon by the Representatives of South Carolina:

Whereas, the British Parliament, claiming of late years a right to bind the North American colonies by law, in all cases whatsoever, have enacted statutes for raising a revenue in those colonies, and disposing of such revenue as they thought proper, without the consent and against the will of the colonists. And whereas, it appearing to them that (they not being represented in Parliament) such claim was altogether unconstitutional, and if admitted, would at once reduce them, from the rank of freemen to a state of the most abject slavery; . . . and whereas the judges of courts of law here, have refused to exercise their respective functions, so that it is become indispensably necessary that during the present situation of American affairs, and until an accommodation of the unhappy differences between Great Britain and America can be obtained, (an event which, though traduced and treated as rebels, we still earnestly desire) some mode should be established by common consent, and for the good of the people the origin and end of all governments, for regulating the internal policy of this Colony. The Congress being vested with powers competent for the purpose and having fully deliberated touching the premises do therefore resolve:

I. That this Congress, being a full and free representation of the people of this Colony, shall henceforth be deemed and called the General Assembly of South Carolina, and as such shall continue until the twenty-first day of October next . . . .

II. That the General Assembly shall, out of their own body, elect by ballot a Legislative Council, to consist of thirteen members (seven of whom shall be a quorum), and to continue for the same time as the General Assembly.

III. That the General Assembly and the said Legislative Council shall jointly choose by ballot from among themselves, or from the people at large, a President and Commander-in-Chief, and a Vice President of the Colony. . . .

V. That there be a Privy Council, whereof the Vice President of the Colony shall of course be a member . . . and that six other members be chosen by ballot, three of the General Assembly, and three of the

South Carolina Statutes at Large, I, 128–34.

Legislative Council; . . . The Privy Council (of which four to be a quorum) to advise the President and Commander-in-Chief when required . . . .

VII. That the legislative authority be vested in the President and . . . the General Assembly and Legislative Council. All money bills for the support of government shall originate in the General Assembly . . . . All other bills and ordinances may arise in the General Assembly or Legislative Council, and may be altered, amended or rejected by either. Bills having passed the General Assembly and Legislative Council may be assented to or rejected by the President . . . . Having received his assent, they shall have all the force and validity of an act . . . .

VIII. That the General Assembly and Legislative Council may adjourn themselves respectively, and the President and Commander-in-Chief shall have no power to adjourn, prorogue or dissolve them, but may, if necessary, call them before the time to which they shall stand adjourned. And where a bill has been rejected, it may, on a meeting after an adjournment of not less than three days of the General Assembly and Legislative Council, be brought in again . . . .

XI. That on the last Monday in October next, and the day following, and on the same days of every second year thereafter, members of the General Assembly shall be chosen, to meet on the first Monday in December then next, and continue for two years from the said last Monday in October. The General Assembly to consist of the same number of members as this Congress does, each parish and district having the same representation as at present, viz.; the parish of St. Philip and St. Michael, Charlestown, 30 members; the parish of Christ Church, 6 members; the parish of St. John in Berkeley County, 6 members; the parish of St. Andrew, 6 members; the parish of St. George, Dorchester, 6 members; the parish of St. James, Goose Creek, 6 members; the parish of St. Thomas and St. Denis, 6 members; the parish of St. Paul, 6 members; the parish of St. Bartholomew, 6 members; the parish of St. Helena, 6 members; the parish of St. James, Santee, 6 members; the parish of Prince George, Winyaw, 6 members; the parish of Prince Frederick, 6 members; the parish of St. John, in Colleton County, 6 members; the parish of St. Peter, 6 members; the parish of Prince William, 6 members; the parish of St. Stephen, 6 members; the district to the eastward of Wateree river, 10 members; the district of Ninety-Six, 10 members; the district of Saxe-Gotha, 6 members; the district between Broad and Saluda rivers, in three divisions, viz.: the lower district, 4 members; the Little river district, 4 members; the upper or Spartan district, 4 members; the district between Broad and Catawba rivers,

10 members; the district called the New Acquisition, 10 members; the parish of St. Matthew, 6 members; the parish of St. David, 6 members; the district between Savannah river and the north fork of Edisto, 6 members . . . .

XV. That the delegates of this Colony in the Continental Congress be chosen by the General Assembly and Legislative Council, jointly by ballot . . . .

XVI. That the Vice President . . . and the Privy Council . . . shall exercise the powers of a Court of Chancery . . . .

XIX. That justices of the peace shall be nominated by the General Assembly and commissioned by the President . . . during pleasure . . . .

XX. That all other judicial officers shall be chosen by ballot, jointly by the General Assembly and Legislative Council . . . .

XXI. That Sheriffs qualified as by law directed, shall be chosen in like manner by the General Assembly and Legislative Council, and commissioned by the President . . . for two years only.

XXII. That the Commissioners of the Treasury, the Secretary of the Colony, Register of mesne conveyances, Attorney general, and Powder receiver, be chosen by the General Assembly and Legislative Council, jointly by ballot, and commissioned by the President . . . during good behavior . . . .

XXVI. That the President . . . shall have no power to make war or peace, or enter into any final treaty, without the consent of the General Assembly and Legislative Council . . . .

XXVIII. That the resolutions of the Continental Congress, now of force in this Colony, shall so continue until altered or revoked by them.

XXIX. That the resolutions of this or any former Congress of this Colony, and all laws now of force here (and not hereby altered) shall continue, until altered or repealed by the Legislature of this Colony . . . .

XXX. That the executive authority be vested in the President . . . limited and restrained as aforesaid. . . .

XXXIII. That all persons who shall be chosen and appointed to any office or to any place of trust, before entering upon the execution of office, shall take the following oath: "I, A. B., do swear that I will, to the utmost of my power, support, maintain and defend the Constitution of South Carolina, as established by Congress on the twenty-sixth day of March, one thousand seven hundred and seventy-six, until an accommodation of the differences between Great Britain and America shall take place, or I shall be released from this oath by the legislative authority of the said Colony—So help me God". And all such persons shall also take the oath of office. . . .

67. The Address of the Assembly to
President John Rutledge, April 3, 1776

UNDER THE CONSTITUTION OF 1776, JOHN RUTLEDGE WAS ELECTED
PRESIDENT OF SOUTH CAROLINA, AND HENRY LAURENS VICE-PRESIDENT.
THE SAME BODY THAT HAD DRAWN UP THE CONSTITUTION, NOW CALLING
ITSELF THE ASSEMBLY, DREW UP THE FOLLOWING ADDRESS TO RUTLEDGE:

[The Assembly to President Rutledge]

May it please your Excellency: We, the Legislative Council and
General Assembly of South Carolina, convened under the authority of
the equitable Constitution of Government established by a free people,
in Congress, on the 26th ult., beg leave most respectfully, to address
your Excellency. Nothing is better known to your Excellency than the
unavoidable necessity which induced us, as members of Congress, on
the part of the people, to resume the powers of Government; and to
establish some mode for regulating the internal policy of this Colony;
and, as members of the Legislative Council and General Assembly,
to vest you, for a time limited, with the executive authority. Such
constitutional proceedings on our own part we make no doubt will be
misconstrued into acts of the greatest criminality by that despotism which,
lost to all sense of justice and humanity, has already pretended that we
are in actual rebellion. But, Sir, when we reflect upon the unprovoked,
cruel, and accumulated oppressions under which America in general and
this country in particular, has long continued; oppressions, which
gradually increasing in injustice and violence, are now by an inexorable
tyranny perpetuated against the United Colonies, under the various
forms of robbery, conflagration, massacre, breach of the public faith,
and open war—conscious of our natural and inalienable rights, and
determined to make every effort in our power to retain them; we see
your Excellency's elevation from the midst of us, to govern this country,
as the natural consequences of such outrages.

John Drayton, *Memoirs of the American Revolution,* 2 vols. (Charleston: A. E.
Miller, 1821), II, 264.

By the suffrages of a free people, you, Sir, have been chosen to hold the reins of government; an event, as honorable to yourself, as it is beneficial to the public.

We firmly trust, that you will make the Constitution the great rule of your conduct, and, in the most solemn manner, we do assure your Excellency that, in the discharge of your duties under that Constitution, which looks forward to an accommodation with Great Britain (an event which, though traduced and treated as rebels, we still earnestly desire), we will support you with our lives and fortunes.

68. *The Battle of Sullivans Island, June 28, 1776*

GOVERNOR WILLIAM CAMPBELL HAD PLEAD WITH THE BRITISH GOV-
ERNMENT FOR SOME TIME TO SEND A MILITARY FORCE TO WIN SOUTH
CAROLINA BACK TO THE KING. FINALLY, IN JUNE, 1776, A NAVAL FORCE
WITH A LARGE NUMBER OF TROOPS ON BOARD, COMMANDED BY SIR
HENRY CLINTON, ENTERED CHARLESTON HARBOR AND PREPARED TO LAY
SIEGE TO THE TOWN. THE GALLANT DEFENSE BY THE MEN IN THE
PALMETTO-LOG FORT AT THE ENTRANCE OF THE BAY, UNDER THE COM-
MAND OF COLONEL WILLIAM MOULTRIE, SAVED THE TOWN. INCLUDED
HERE ARE A REPORT FROM GENERAL CHARLES LEE TO GENERAL GEORGE
WASHINGTON, A "CIRCUMSTANTIAL ACCOUNT OF THE PROCEEDINGS OF
THE BRITISH FLEET AND ARMY," AND RAMSAY'S ACCOUNT. THE HIS-
TORIAN GIVES THE NAMES OF THE VESSELS INVOLVED.

[General Lee to General Washington]

Charlestown, July 1, 1776.

My Dear General: I have the happiness to congratulate you on a very
signal success (if I may not call it a victory) which we have gained
over the mercenary instruments of the British tyrant. . . . Having lost
an opportunity (such as I hope will never again present itself) of taking
the town, which, on my arrival, was utterly defenseless, the Commodore
thought proper, on Friday last, with his whole squadron, consisting of
two fifties, six frigates, and a bomb . . . to attack our fort on Sullivans
Island. They dropped their anchors about eleven in the forenoon, at
the distance of three or four hundred yards, before the front battery
. . . . They immediately commenced the most furious fire that I ever
heard or saw. I confess I was in pain from the little confidence I
reposed in our troops, the officers being all boys, and the men raw
recruits. What augmented my anxiety was, that we had no bridge
finished of retreat or communication, and the creek or cove which

Peter Force, comp., *American Archives* . . . , Fourth Series, 6 vols. (Washington:
M. St. Clarke and Peter Force, 1837–1853), VI, 1183–84.

separated it from the continent is near a mile wide. I had received, likewise, intelligence that their land troops intended at the same time to land and assault. I never in my life felt myself so uneasy; and what added to my uneasyness was, that I knew our stock of ammunition was miserably low. I had once thoughts of ordering the commanding officer to spike his guns, and when his ammunition was spent, to retreat with as little loss as possible. However . . . I then determined to maintain the post at all risks, and passed the creek or cove in a small boat, in order to animate the garrison *in propria persona;* but I found they had no occasion for such encouragement. They were pleased with my visit, and assured me they never would abandon the post but with their lives. The cool courage they displayed astonished and enraptured me; for I do assure you, my dear General, I never experienced a hotter fire—twelve full hours of it was continued without intermission. The noble fellows who were mortally wounded conjured their brethren never to abandon the standard of liberty. Those who lost their limbs deserted not their posts. Upon the whole, they acted like Romans in the third century. However, our works was so good and solid, that we lost but few—only ten killed on the spot, and twenty-two wounded; seven of whom lost their legs or arms. The loss of the enemy . . . was very great . . . .

Colonel [William] Moultrie, who commanded the garrison, deserves the highest honours. The manifest intention of the enemy was to land, at the same time the ships began to fire, their whole regulars on the east end of the Island. Twice they attempted it, and twice they were repulsed . . . by the South-Carolina Rangers, in conjunction with a body of North-Carolina Regulars . . . .

For God's sake, my dear General, urge the Congress to furnish me with a thousand cavalry. With a thousand cavalry, I could insure the safety of these Southern Provinces, and without cavalry, I can answer for nothing . . . .

God bless you, my dear General, and crown you with success, as I am most entirely and affectionately yours,

CHARLES LEE.

Circumstantial Account of the proceedings of the British Fleet and Army, both before and after their defeat at Sullivans Island, on the 28th of June, 1776:

. . . General Lee was at Haddrell's Point at the beginning of the action, and went in a boat, through a thick fire, to the fort, where he staid some time. He says, in the whole course of his military service, he never knew men behave better; and cannot sufficiently praise both officers and soldiers for their coolness and intrepidity. The behavior of two Sergeants deserves to be remembered. In the beginning of the action, the flag-staff was shot away; which being observed by Sergeant [William] Jasper, of the Grenadiers, he immediately jumped from one of the embrasures upon the beach, took up the flag, and fixed it on a spunge-staff; with it in his hand, he mounted the merlon, and notwithstanding the shot flew as thick as hail around him, he leisurely fixed it. Sergeant McDonald, of Captain Huger's company, while exerting himself in a very distinguished manner, was cruelly shattered by a cannon-ball; in a few minutes, he expired, after having uttered these remarkable words: "My friends, I am dying; but don't let the cause of liberty expire with me." . . .

We hear that the fort on Sullivans Island will be in the future called Fort Moultrie, in honour of the gallant officer who commanded there on the memorable 28th of June, 1776.

[Ramsay's Report on the Battle of Sullivans Island]

On the 28th the fort on the island was briskly attacked by the two fifty-gun ships, *Bristol* and *Experiment;* four frigates, the *Active, Acteon,*

Peter Force, comp., *American Archives* . . . , Fifth Series (unfinished), 3 vols. (Washington: M. St. Clair Clarke and Peter Force, 1848–1853), I, 435–36.

David Ramsay, *History of the Revolution in South Carolina,* 2 vols. (Trenton: Isaac Collins, 1785), I, 144–48.

Solebay, and *Syren,* each of twenty-eight guns; the *Sphynx* of twenty guns; the *Friendship,* armed vessel of twenty-two guns; *Ranger,* sloop, and *Thunder-Bomb,* each of eight guns. Between 10 and 11 o'clock in the forenoon, the *Thunder-Bomb* began to throw shells. The *Active, Bristol, Experiment* and *Solebay* came boldly on to the attack. A little before 11 o'clock the garrison fired four or five shots at the *Active* while under sail. When she came near the fort she dropped anchor, and poured in a broad-side. Her example was followed by three other vessels, and a most tremendous cannonade ensued. The *Thunder-Bomb,* after having thrown about sixty shells, was so damaged as to be incapacitated from firing. Colonel Moultrie, with three hundred and forty-four regulars, and a few volunteer militia, made a defense that would have done honor to experienced veterans. The unanimous thanks of Congress were given to General Charles Lee, and Colonels Moultrie and Thomson for their good conduct on this memorable day. In compliment to the commanding officer, the fort from that time was called Fort Moultrie. During the engagement the inhabitants stood with their hands at their respective posts, prepared to receive the British wherever they might land. Impressed with high ideas of British bravery, and dissident of the maiden courage of their own new troops, they were apprehensive that the forts would either be silenced or passed, and that they should be called to immediate action. The various passions of the mind assumed alternate sway, and marked the countenances with anxious fears or cheerful hopes. Their resolution was fixed to meet the invaders at the water's edge, and dispute every inch of ground, trusting the event to Heaven, and preferring death to slavery.

General Clinton was to have passed over to Sullivan's Island with the troops under his command on Long Island, but the extreme danger to which he must unavoidably have exposed his men, induced him to decline the perilous attempt. Colonel William Thomson, with three hundred riflemen of his regiment, Colonel Clark, with two hundred regulars of the North Carolina line, Colonel Horry, with two hundred South Carolina militia, and the Raccoon company of militia riflemen with an eighteen pounder and a field-piece, were stationed at the east end of Sullivan's Island, to oppose their crossing, but no serious attempt to land on Sullivan's Island was made, either from the fleet or by the detachment on Long Island. The *Sphynx, Acteon* and *Syren* were sent round to attack the western extremity of the fort. This was so unfinished as to afford very imperfect cover to the men at the guns in that part, and also so situated as to expose the men in the other parts of the fort to a very dangerous cross-fire. Providence on this occasion remarkably interposed in behalf of the garrison, and saved them from a fate that, in all probability, would otherwise have been inevitable. About 12 o'clock, as the three last-mentioned ships were advancing to attack the western wing of the fort, they all got entangled with a shoal called the Middle Ground; two of them ran foul of each other. The *Acteon* stuck fast. The *Sphynx,* before she cleared herself, lost her bowsprit; but the *Syren* got off without much injury. The ships, in front of the fort, kept up their fire till near 7 o'clock in the evening with intermissions; after that time it slackened. At half past nine the firing on both sides ceased; and at eleven the ships slipped their cables. Next morning all the men of war except the *Acteon* had retired about two miles from the island. The garrison fired several shots at the *Acteon;* she at first returned them, but soon after the crew set her on fire, and abandoned her, leaving her colors flying, guns loaded, and all her ammunition and stores. She was in a short time boarded by a party of Americans, commanded by Captain Jacob Milligan, which brought off her colors, the ship's bell, and as many sails and stores as three boats could contain. The Americans on board the *Acteon,* while flames were bursting out on all sides, fired three of her guns at the Commodore, and then quitted her. In less than half an hour after their departure, she blew up. The *Bristol* had forty men killed and seventy-one wounded. Captain Morris, who commanded her, lost his arm. Every man, who was stationed in the beginning of the action on her quarter deck, was either killed or wounded. The *Experiment* had twenty-three killed and seventy-six wounded. Captain Scott, who commanded her, lost his arm. Lord William Campbell, the late governor of the Province, who, as a volunteer, had exposed himself in a post of danger, received a wound in his side, which ultimately proved mortal. Commodore Sir Peter Parker suffered a slight contusion. The fire of the fort was principally directed against the *Bristol* and the *Experiment,* and they suffered very much in their hulls, masts and rigging. Not less than seventy balls went through the former. The *Acteon* had Lieutenant Pike killed, and six men wounded. The *Solebay* had eight men wounded. After some days the troops were all re-embarked and the whole fleet sailed for New York.

The loss of the garrison was ten men killed and twenty-two wounded. Lieutenants Hall and Gray were among the latter. Though there were many thousand shot fired from the shipping, yet the works were little damaged; those which struck the fort were ineffectually buried in its soft wood. Hardly a hut or a tree on the island escaped.

69. *The South Carolina Resolutions on the Declaration of Independence*

THE NEWS OF THE DECLARATION OF INDEPENDENCE REACHED CHARLESTON ON AUGUST 5, 1776. ALTHOUGH THE SOUTH CAROLINA DELEGATION, THEN COMPOSED OF EDWARD RUTLEDGE, THOMAS HEYWARD, JR., THOMAS LYNCH, JR., AND ARTHUR MIDDLETON, HAD SIGNED WITHOUT SPECIFIC AUTHORIZATION FROM THE GENERAL COMMITTEE, THE PEOPLE WERE ALMOST UNANIMOUS IN THEIR APPROVAL OF THE ACTION. FIRST SELECTION IS A BRIEF DESCRIPTION OF THE RECEPTION OF THE NEWS IN CHARLESTON, AND THE OTHER TWO ARE RESOLUTIONS ADOPTED BY THE LEGISLATIVE COUNCIL AND THE GENERAL ASSEMBLY ON SEPTEMBER 20.

[David Ramsay]

The Declaration of Independence arrived in Charleston at a most favorable juncture. It found the people of South Carolina exasperated against Great Britain for her late hostile attack, and elevated with their successful defense of Fort Moultrie. It was welcomed by a great majority of the inhabitants . . . with the firing of guns, ringing of bells, . . . and all the usual parade of a public rejoicing. . . . In private it is probable that some condemned the measure, as rashly adventurous beyond the ability of the state; but these private murmurs never produced to the public ear a single expression of disapprobation.

David Ramsay, *History of the Revolution in South Carolina,* 2 vols. (Trenton: Isaac Collins, 1785), I, 174.

The Resolution of the Legislative Council:

The declaration of the Continental Congress that the United Colonies are, and of right ought to be, free and independent states; that they are absolved from all allegiance to the British crown; and that all political connection between them and the state of Great Britain is and ought to be totally dissolved, calls forth all our attention. It is an event which necessity had rendered not only justifiable, but absolutely unavoidable. It is a decree now worthy of America. We thankfully receive the notification of, and rejoice at it; and we are determined at every hazard to endeavor to maintain it, that so, after we have departed, our children and their latest posterity may have cause to bless our memory.

The Resolution of the General Assembly:

It is with the most unspeakable pleasure we embrace this opportunity of expressing our joy and satisfaction in the declaration of the Continental Congress, declaring the United Colonies free and independent states, absolved from allegiance to the British Crown, and totally dissolving all political union between them and Great Britain—an event unsought for, and now produced by unavoidable necessity, and which every friend to justice and humanity must not only hold justifiable as the natural effect of unmerited persecution, but equally rejoice in, as the only effectual security against injuries and oppressions, and the most promising source of future liberty and safety.

David Ramsay, *History of the Revolution in South Carolina*, 2 vols. (Trenton: Isaac Collins, 1785), I, 175.

David Ramsay, *History of the Revolution in South Carolina*, 2 vols. (Trenton: Isaac Collins, 1785), I, 176.

70. *The Cherokee Treaty of May 20, 1777*

IN THE SUMMER OF 1776 THE CHEROKEES, AT THE INSTIGATION OF THE BRITISH, BEGAN TO ATTACK THE FRONTIER SETTLEMENTS OF NORTH AND SOUTH CAROLINA. IN RETALIATION, BOTH STATES COMBINED TO SEND A LARGE EXPEDITION AGAINST THE INDIANS. COLONEL ANDREW WILLIAMSON LED THE SOUTH CAROLINIANS IN THIS "SNOW CAMPAIGN" DURING THE WINTER OF 1776–1777, AND THE CHEROKEES WERE SEVERELY DEFEATED. FOLLOWING A PERIOD OF NEGOTIATION, THE TREATY WAS SIGNED MAY 20, 1777, WITH THE CHEROKEES GIVING UP ALL CLAIM TO THEIR LANDS IN ANY PART OF WHAT IS NOW SOUTH CAROLINA.

[The Cherokee Treaty]

Article I. The Cherokee nations acknowledge that the troops, during last summer, repeatedly defeated their forces, victoriously penetrated through their lower towns, middle settlements and valleys, and quietly and unopposed built, held, and continue to occupy, the fort at Seneca, thereby did effect and maintain the conquest of all Cherokee lands eastward of the Unacaye mountain; and, to and for their people, did acquire, possess and yet continue to hold, in and over the said lands, all and singular the rights incidental to conquest; and the Cherokee nation, in consequence thereof do cede the said lands to the said people, the people of South Carolina.

Article II. South Carolina will immediately send a supply of goods into the Cherokee nation and settlements for sale, and permit the Cherokees, during their good behavior, to inhabit the middle settlements and valleys westward of the highest part of the Oconee mountain; but they shall not, beyond a line extended southwest and northeast across the highest part of the Oconee mountain, proceed or advance . . . .

Article III. The government of South Carolina will endeavor that the Cherokees be furnished with supplies of goods as usual; and that the trade shall be put under the best regulations . . . .

David Ramsay, *History of the Revolution in South Carolina,* 2 vols. (Trenton: Isaac Collins, 1785), I, 350–54.

Article VI. All white and Indian persons shall be set at liberty as soon as possible; all Negroes taken during the late war, and who now are, or hereafter may be, in the power of the Cherokees, shall, as soon as possible be delivered to the Commanding officer at Fort Rutledge....

Article VIII. The hatchet shall be forever buried, and there shall be an universal peace and friendship re-established between South Carolina, including the Catawba nation and Georgia on the one part, and the Cherokee nation on the other; there shall be a general oblivion of injuries; the contracting parties shall use their utmost endeavors to maintain the peace and friendship now re-established, and the Cherokees shall at all times, apprehend and deliver to the commanding officer at Fort Rutledge, every person, white or red, who, in their nation or settlements, shall by any means endeavor to instigate a war by the Cherokee nation or hostility or robbery, by any of their people, against or upon any of the American states, or subjects thereof.

71. *Palmetto Day Celebration in Charleston, June 28, 1777*

FOR SOME THREE YEARS AFTER THE DEFEAT OF THE BRITISH FLEET AT CHARLESTON, SOUTH CAROLINA WAS FREE FROM HOSTILITIES. ON THE FIRST ANNIVERSARY OF THE BATTLE OF FORT MOULTRIE, CHARLESTONIANS CELEBRATED "PALMETTO DAY." THE FOLLOWING IS TAKEN FROM THE JOURNAL OF AN ANONYMOUS FRENCH VISITOR.

[Charleston's Celebration as Viewed by An Unidentified Frenchman]

At the break of dawn the Palmetto Day celebration began with numerous discharges of artillery, beginning at Fort Moultrie, since it is to that fort that the glory of the day belongs. Next came the firing . . . at Fort Johnson, then those of the other emplacements in the city and along the shore, next the guns of the men of war in the harbor, then . . . the privateers, and finally even the guns of foreign ships joined in as an expression of good will for the Americans.

At midday the Congress assembled at the State House and reviewed the militia of the Province, with the volunteers and the artillery corps. The forts and all the vessels in the harbor responded with a second artillery discharge, and then the two companies of volunteers, the heroes of the 28th of June, lined up and took again the oath of allegiance to the cause of Independence. All the townspeople cheered them, and after firing three rounds of musketry in the air, the volunteers disbanded and went home.

At two o'clock, the Congress, along with the commanders of the forts and some of the militia officers, returned to the State House to a grand dinner. The food here was served in abundance, and even in profusion, but without pomp and without much etiquette. At the end of the dinner, all the guests present drank toasts to the health of the President

"A Frenchman Visits Charleston in 1777," in *South Carolina Historical and Genealogical Magazine*, LII (1951), 90–91. Reprinted by permission of The South Carolina Historical Society.

of the Province, Mr. Rutledge; of the President of the Continental Congress, Mr. John Hancock; of General Washington; of General Moultrie; of all those loyal to the common cause, and also to the prosperity of Carolina and of all the thirteen provinces; to their constant union and amity; to the Liberty Tree, and finally to the firm and faithful resolution to defeat the British.

At the central square, at the foot of the Statue of Pitt, a detachment of artillery volunteers, gave thirteen tremendous cheers, each one accompanied by a round of cannon fire, and all applauded by the surrounding people from the streets, the balconies and the windows.

About sundown, the forts and the artillery on the ships fired a last round, and this served to mark the end of the celebration for them, but in the center of the town another portion of the celebration was still well attended. This was a dinner, given out in the open under the palmettoes, for the militia and volunteers, their families and friends. Although these public feasts seem to affect the natural taciturnity of these Americans, their expressions of joy in their liberty usually took the form of toasts cheered by everyone, to Congress, to General Moultrie, to the men and officers who were killed on the 28th of June, and above all to one of their brave sergeants, who, seated among them, received with apparent pleasure the homage they paid to him . . . .

A fine display of fireworks, illuminating almost the whole town, brought an end to the festivities which had allowed the people to forget for a while their present troubles, but in more happy times such a celebration would undoubtedly have been followed with gay parties, balls and dances. . . .

72. *The Constitution of 1778*

THE DECLARATION OF INDEPENDENCE, CREATING THE SOVEREIGN STATE OF SOUTH CAROLINA, MADE IT NECESSARY TO REVISE THE TEMPORARY CONSTITUTION OF 1776. IN 1777, A NEW CONSTITUTION WAS DRAWN UP, PRINTED, AND CONSIDERED FOR NEARLY A YEAR, PUBLICLY AND IN THE LEGISLATIVE HALLS, BEFORE IT WAS FINALLY ADOPTED ON MARCH 19, 1778. SOME NOTABLE CHANGES WERE MADE, PRINCIPALLY THAT THE CHIEF EXECUTIVE OR "PRESIDENT" WOULD ASSUME THE TITLE OF GOVERNOR AND THAT THE LEGISLATIVE COUNCIL WOULD BECOME A POPULARLY ELECTED SENATE. IN MANY WAYS THE NEW GOVERNMENT WAS SIMILAR TO THE OLD.

The Constitution:

Whereas, the Constitution or Form of government agreed to and resolved upon by the freemen of this country, met in Congress the twenty-sixth day of March, 1776, was temporary only and suited to the situation of their public affairs at that period, looking forward to an accommodation with Great Britain, an event then desired. And whereas, the United Colonies of America have been since constituted independent states, and the political connection heretofore subsisting between them and Great Britain entirely dissolved . . . it therefore becomes absolutely necessary to frame a Constitution suitable to that great event. Be it therefore constituted and enacted . . . that the following articles agreed upon by the freemen of this State, now met in General Assembly, be deemed and held the Constitution and Form of government of the said State . . . .

I. That the style of this country be hereafter, the State of South Carolina.

II. That the legislative authority be vested in a General Assembly, to consist of two distinct bodies, a Senate and a House of Representatives . . . .

South Carolina Statutes at Large, I, 137–46.

III. That as soon as may be, after the first meeting . . . they shall jointly in the House of Representatives, choose by ballot from among themselves, or from the people at large, a Governor and Commander in Chief, a Lieutenant-Governor, both to continue for two years, and a Privy Council, all of the Protestant religion . . . .

V. That every person who shall be elected Governor . . . or Lieutenant-Governor or a member of the Privy Council, shall be qualified as follows: the Governor and Lieutenant Governor shall have been residents in this State for ten years, and the members of the Privy Council, five years, preceding their election, and shall have in this state a settled plantation or freehold in their . . . own right, of the value of at least ten thousand pounds currency, clear of debt . . . .

IX. That the Privy Council shall consist of the Lieutenant Governor . . . and eight other members, five of whom shall be a quorum . . . . The Privy Council is to advise the Governor . . . when required, but he shall not be bound to consult them unless directed by law . . . .

XI. That the executive authority be vested in the Governor . . . in manner herein mentioned.

XII. That each parish and district throughout this State shall, on the last Monday in November next and the day following, and on the same days of every succeeding year thereafter, elect by ballot one member of the Senate, except the District of St. Philip and St. Michael's parishes, Charleston, which shall elect two members . . . ; and that no person shall be eligible to a seat in the said Senate unless he be of the Protestant religion, and hath attained the age of thirty years, and hath been a resident in this State at least five years. Not less than thirteen members shall be a quorum to do business . . . . No person . . . shall take his seat in the Senate, unless he possess a settled estate and free hold in his own right in the said parish or district, of the value of two thousand pounds currency at least, clear of debt . . . .

[The numbers of representatives to be chosen from the various parishes and districts are the same as those in the Constitution of 1776, except the parish of Prince George, Winyaw, four members; the parish of all Saints, two members; the parish of St. Matthew, three members, and the parish of Orange, three members.]

XIII. The qualifications of electors shall be that every free white man, and no other person, who acknowledges the being of a God . . . and who has attained to the age of twenty-one years, and hath been a resident and an inhabitant in this State for . . . one whole year before the day appointed for the election . . . and hath a freehold at least of fifty acres of land, or a town lot . . . or hath paid a tax . . . in a sum equal to the tax on fifty acres of land, to the support of this government, shall be deemed a person qualified to vote for, and shall be capable of electing a representative, or representatives to serve as a member or members in the Senate and House of Representatives, for the parish or district where he actually is a resident, or in any other parish or district in this State where he hath the like freehold . . . . No person shall be eligible to sit in the House of Representatives unless he be of the Protestant religion, and hath been a resident in this State for three years . . . . The qualification of the elected, if residents in the Parish or District for which they shall be returned, shall be the same as mentioned in the election act, and construed to mean clear of debt . . . .

XV. That at the expiration of seven years after the passing of this Constitution, and at the end of every fourteen years thereafter, the representation of the whole State shall be proportioned in the most equal and just manner according . . . to the number of white inhabitants and . . . taxable property.

XVI. That all money bills for the support of government shall originate in the House of Representatives . . . . All other bills and ordinances may take rise in the Senate or House . . . . Acts and ordinances having passed the General Assembly shall have the great seal affixed to them by a joint committee of both Houses, who shall then be signed by the President of the Senate and Speaker of the House . . . and shall thenceforth have all the force and validity of a law . . . .

XVII. The Governor . . . shall have no power to adjourn, prorogue or dissolve them, but may, if necessary, by and with the advice of the Privy Council, convene them before the time to which they shall stand adjourned. And where a bill hath been rejected by either House, it shall not be brought in again that session without leave of the House, and a notice of six days being previously given. . . .

XXI. And whereas the ministers of the gospel are by their profession dedicated to the service of God and . . . ought not to be diverted from the great duties of their function—therefore no minister of the gospel . . . shall be eligible either as Governor, Lieutenant Governor, a member of the Senate, House of Representatives, or Privy Council in this State.

XXII. That the delegates to represent this State in the Congress of the United States, be chosen annually by the Senate and House . . . jointly, by ballot . . . .

XXIV. That the Lieutenant Governor of the State and a majority of the Privy Council . . . shall . . . exercise the powers of a Court of

Chancery; and there shall be ordinaries appointed in the several districts of this State, to be chosen by the Senate and House . . . jointly by ballot . . . .

XXVI. That justices of the peace shall be nominated by the Senate and House . . . jointly, and commissioned by the Governor . . . during pleasure . . . .

XXVII. That all other judicial officers shall be chosen by ballot, jointly, by the Senate and House of Representatives . . . .

XXVIII. That the sheriffs, qualified as by law directed, shall be chosen in like manner . . . and commissioned by the Governor . . . for two years . . . .

XXIX. That two Commissioners of the Treasury, the Secretary of the State, the Register of Mesne Conveyances in each district, Attorney General, Surveyor General, Powder Receiver, Collectors and Comptrollers of the Customs . . . be chosen in like manner . . . and commissioned by the Governor . . . for two years . . . . Provided . . . that the present and all future Commissioners of the Treasury, and Powder Receivers, shall each give bond with approved security agreeable to law . . . .

XXXIII. That the Governor . . . shall have no power to commence war, or conclude peace, or enter into any final treaty, without the consent of the Senate and House . . . .

XXXIV. That the resolutions of the late Congress of this State, and all laws now of force here (and not thereby altered) shall so continue until altered or repealed by the Legislature of this State . . . .

XXXVI. That all persons who shall be chosen and appointed to any office, or to any place of trust, civil or military, before entering upon the execution of office, shall take the following oath:

"I, A.B., do acknowledge the State of South Carolina to be a free, sovereign and independent State, and that the people thereof owe no allegiance or obedience to George the Third, King of Great Britain, and I do renounce, refuse, and abjure any allegiance or obedience to him. And I do swear (or affirm, as the case may be) that I will, to the utmost of my power, support, maintain and defend the said State against the said King George the Third . . . and will serve the said State in the office of ——— with fidelity and honor, and according to the best of my skill and understanding. So help me God."

XXXVIII. That all persons and religious societies who acknowledge that there is one God, and a future state of rewards and punishments, and that God is publicly to be worshipped, shall be freely tolerated . . . . That all denominations of Christian Protestants in this State, demeaning themselves peaceably and faithfully, shall enjoy equal religious and civil privileges. . . . No person shall disturb or molest any religious assembly. . . . No person shall by law, be obliged to pay towards the maintenance and support of a religious worship. . . . But the churches, chapels, parsonages, glebes, and all other property now belonging to any societies of the Church of England, or any other religious societies, shall remain and be secured to them forever. The poor shall be supported, and elections managed in the accustomed manner, until laws shall be provided to adjust those matters in the most equitable way.

XXXIX. That the whole State shall, as soon as proper laws can be passed for these purposes, be divided into districts and counties, and county courts established.

XL. That the penal laws, as heretofore used, shall be reformed, and punishments made in some cases less sanguinary, and in general more proportionate to the crime.

XLI. That no freeman of this State be taken or imprisoned, or disseized of his freehold, liberties or privileges, or outlawed, exiled, or in any manner destroyed or deprived of his life, liberty or property, but by the judgment of his peers, or by the law of the land.

XLII. That the military be subordinate to the civil power of the State.

XLIII. That the liberty of the press be inviolably preserved . . . .

XLV. That the Senate and House . . . shall not proceed to the election of a Governor or Lieutenant Governor, until there be a majority of both Houses present.

In the Council Chamber, the 19th day of March, 1778, assented to.

73. Thomas Pinckney Reports a British Raid on His Plantation, May, 1779

IN MAY, 1779, THE BRITISH, HAVING ALREADY CAPTURED SAVANNAH, SENT GENERAL AUGUSTINE PREVOST OVERLAND TOWARD CHARLESTON IN AN ATTEMPT TO CAPTURE THAT CITY. HE PROBABLY WOULD HAVE SUCCEEDED, HAD IT NOT BEEN FOR THE TIMELY APPEARANCE OF GENERAL BENJAMIN LINCOLN, WHO WITH A STRONG FORCE CAME TO THE AID OF GENERAL WILLIAM MOULTRIE IN DEFENDING THE PORT. HOWEVER, THE BRITISH DID SUCCEED IN OVERRUNNING MOST OF THE COASTAL AREA BETWEEN SAVANNAH AND CHARLESTON AND IN RAIDING PLANTATIONS EVEN FARTHER INLAND. THE FOLLOWING IS AN ACCOUNT OF SUCH A RAID ON THOMAS PINCKNEY'S PLANTATION, AS HE REPORTED IT IN A LETTER TO HIS MOTHER, MAY 17, 1779.

[Thomas Pinckney Writing to His Mother]

A North Carolina soldier was five days sick at my house at Ashepoo, and was there when the enemy came. He reports that they took with them 19 Negroes, among whom were Betty, Prince, Chance, and all the hardy boys. They left the sick women, and the young children, and about five fellows who are now perfectly free and live on the best produce of the plantation. They took with them all the best horses they could find, burnt the dwelling house and books, destroyed all the furniture, china, etc., killed the sheep and poultry and drank the liquors.

The overseer concealed himself in the swamp and afterwards returned. I hope he will be able to keep the remaining property in some order, though the Negroes pay no attention to his orders. As however our Light Horse has scoured that country, and we still have some small parties out, I am hopeful all will not be lost.

Harriott Horry (Rutledge) Ravenel, *Eliza Pinckney* (New York: Charles Scribner's Sons, 1902), 276–77.

74. *The Siege of Charleston, March–May, 1780*

IN MARCH, 1780, THE BRITISH RETURNED TO CHARLESTON BY LAND AND SEA AND LAID SIEGE TO THE CITY. FOR ABOUT TWO MONTHS THE SURROUNDED GARRISON HELD OUT, BUT FINALLY, WITH LITTLE HOPE OF AID, IT SURRENDERED ON MAY 12, 1780. THE FOLLOWING NOTES ARE TAKEN FROM GENERAL WILLIAM MOULTRIE'S DIARY OF THE SIEGE.

[From General William Moultrie's Diary]

Tuesday, March 28, 1780: The enemy crossed Ashley River, in force, above the ferry.

Wednesday, 29th: The enemy advanced on the Neck. The Light Infantry were this evening reinforced with two companies, and the command given to Col. John Laurens.

Thursday, 30th: The enemy came on as far as Gibbes', where they continued skirmishing throughout the day with our Light Infantry . . . . Capt. Bowman of the North Carolina Brigade killed; Major Hyrne and seven privates wounded. The enemy were all this day transporting troops from Old Town, on Wappoo Creek, to Gibbes'.

Sunday, April 2nd: Last night the enemy broke ground, and this morning appeared two redoubts: one nearly opposite the nine gun battery . . . the other a little to the left of the same . . . .

Monday, 3rd: The enemy employed in completing their two redoubts, and erecting one on our left an equal distance from the road.

Wednesday, 5th: Last night the enemy continued his approaches to Hampstead Hill, on which they erected a battery for twelve cannon . . . . The battery from Wappoo and the galleys have thrown several shot into town, by which one of the inhabitants of King Street was killed. . . .

Friday, 7th: This afternoon twelve sail of the enemy's vessels passed Fort Moultrie, under a very heavy fire.

Sunday, 9th: The enemy last night continued their approaches from their redoubt on the left, and threw up a battery for ten cannon . . . .

General William Moultrie's Diary, in *Charleston Yearbook* (1884), 291–307.

Monday, 10th: Sir Henry Clinton and Admiral Arbuthnot summoned the town. General [Benjamin] Lincoln refused to surrender. . . .

Thursday, 13th: Between 9 and 10 o'clock this morning, the enemy opened their cannon and mortar batteries. The cannonade and bombardment continued, with short intermissions, until midnight; the galleys and battery at Wappoo also fired. Some women and children were killed in town . . . ; two houses were burnt.

Friday, 14th: The enemy began an approach on the right, and kept up a fire of small arms.

Saturday, 15th: The enemy continued approaching on the right. A continual fire of small arms, cannon and mortars. A battery of two guns opened by the enemy on James Island . . . .

Saturday, 22nd: Approaches continued on our left in front of the advance redoubt.

Monday, 24th: A party composed of 300 men . . . under the command of Lt. Col. Henderson, made a sortie upon the enemy's approaches . . . at daylight; they were completely surprised. . . .

Wednesday, 26th: The enemy were very quiet all day and last night; we suppose they are bringing cannon into their third parallel . . . . Brig. Gen. Du Portail arrived from Philadelphia . . . . On Gen. Du Portail declaring that the works were not tenable, a Council was again called upon for an evacuation, and to withdraw privately with the Continental troops; when the citizens were informed upon what the Council were deliberating, some of them came into Council, and expressed themselves very warmly, and declared to Gen. Lincoln that if he attempted to withdraw the troops and leave the citizens, that they would put an end to all thoughts of an evacuation of the troops; cut up his boats and open the gates to the enemy; this and nothing was left for us but to make the best terms we could. . . .

Friday, 28th: The enemy busy in throwing up their third parallel, within a few yards of the canal . . . .

Saturday 29th: A deserter from them says they are preparing a bridge to throw over the canal . . . .

Tuesday, May 2nd: Last night the enemy was making a ditch on the right to drain the canal . . . .

Thursday, 4th: Our rations of meat reduced to six ounces; coffee and sugar allowed only to the soldiers . . . .

Saturday, 6th: Fort Moultrie is in the hands of the enemy.

Monday, 8th: A second summons from Sir Henry Clinton informing us of the fall of Fort Moultrie, and that the remains of our cavalry were cut to pieces the day before yesterday. Our meat quite out; rice, sugar and coffee served out.

Friday, 12th: (On the evening of the 9th) followed a tremendous cannonade, about 180 or 200 pieces of heavy cannon fired off at the same moment, and the mortars from both sides threw out an immense number of shells; it was a glorious sight to see them like meteors crossing each other and bursting in the air; it appeared as if the stars were tumbling down. The fire was incessant almost the whole night; cannon balls whizzing and shells hissing continually amongst us; ammunition chests and temporary magazines blowing up; great guns bursting, and wounded men groaning along the lines. It was a dreadful night. It was our last great effort but it availed us nothing. After this our military ardor was much abated; we began to cool, and we cooled gradually, and on the 11th of May we capitulated, and on the morning of the 12th we marched out and gave up the town. . . .

75. *South Carolina under the British*

THE FALL OF CHARLESTON BROUGHT GLOOM TO THE AMERICAN CAUSE. THIS WAS NOT TRUE OF THE SOUTH CAROLINA LOYALISTS, HOWEVER, WHO STILL WANTED AN ACCOMMODATION WITH THE MOTHER COUNTRY. BUT FOR OTHERS THERE WAS NO REASON FOR REJOICING—THEY HAD LOST THEIR CAPITAL, THEIR GOVERNOR WAS IN FLIGHT, THEIR ARMY WAS PITIFUL IN NUMBERS, AND THERE WAS INDICATION THAT THE BRITISH WOULD CONQUER THE WHOLE STATE. INCLUDED HERE ARE GENERAL CLINTON'S REPORT ON THE SUBMISSION OF SOUTH CAROLINA, THE OATH OF ALLEGIANCE TO THE KING REQUIRED OF THE CONQUERED CITIZENS, COLONEL ISAAC HAYNE'S REASON FOR TAKING THE BRITISH OATH OF ALLEGIANCE, DAVID RAMSAY'S ACCOUNT OF CONDITIONS IN CHARLESTON AFTER ITS SUBMISSION, AND MRS. ELIZA LUCAS PINCKNEY'S STORY OF THE TRIALS SHE EXPERIENCED WHILE LIVING UNDER THE BRITISH.

[General Henry Clinton on the Submission
of South Carolina, June 4, 1780]

With the greatest pleasure I further report . . . that the inhabitants from every quarter repair to the detachments of the army, and to this garrison (Charles-town) to declare their allegiance to the King, and to offer their services in arms for the support of the Government. In many instances they have brought in as prisoners their former oppressors or leaders; and I may venture to assert, that there are few men in South Carolina who are not either our prisoners or in arms with us.

Banastre Tarleton, *History of the Campaigns of 1780–1781* . . . (London: T. Cadell, 1787), 80.

[The Oath of Allegiance to the King,
Forced upon South Carolinians in 1780]

I, A. B., do hereby acknowledge and declare myself to be a true and
faithful subject of his Majesty, the King of Great Britain, and that I
will at all times hereafter be obedient to his government; and that
whenever I shall be thereunto required, I will be ready to maintain and
defend the same against all persons whatsoever.

[Col. Isaac Hayne's Reasons for Taking the
British Oath of Allegiance]

If the British would grant me the indulgence, which we in the day of
our power gave to their adherents, of removing my family and property,
I would seek an asylum in the remotest corner of the United States
rather than submit to their government; but as they allow no other
alternative than submission or confinement in the capital at a distance
from my wife and family at a time when they are in the most pressing
need of my presence and support, I must for the present yield to the
demands of the conquerors. I request you to bear in mind, that previous
to my taking this step, I declare that it is contrary to my inclination and
forced upon me by hard necessity. I will never bear arms against my
country. My new masters require no service of me but what is enjoined
by the old militia law of the Province, which substitutes a fine in lieu of
personal service. That I will pay as the price of my protection. If my
conduct should be censured by my countrymen, I beg that you would
remember this conversation and bear witness for me, that I do not mean
to desert the cause of America.

Alexander Gregg, *History of the Old Cheraws* (New York: Richardson and Co.,
1867), 304.

David Ramsay, *History of South Carolina* . . . , 2 vols. (Charleston: David
Longworth for the author, 1809), I, 454–55.

[David Ramsay on the British Occupation of Charleston, 1780]

Every ungenerous construction was put on an ambiguous capitulation, to the disadvantage of the citizens; and their rights founded thereon were, in several instances most injuriously violated. Continental officers were stripped of their property, on the pretense that they were soldiers and had no right to claim under the character of citizens. The conquerors deprived the inhabitants of their canoes by an illiberal construction of the article which gave them the shipping in the harbor. Many slaves, and a great deal of property, though secured by the capitulation, were carried off by Sir Henry Clinton's army in June, 1780. Immediately after the surrender, five hundred Negroes were ordered to be put on board the ships for pioneers to the Royal forces in New York. These were taken wherever they could be found, and no satisfaction was made to their owners. The common soldiers, from their sufferings and services during the siege, conceived themselves entitled to a licensed plunder of the town. That their murmurings might be soothed, the officers connived at their reimbursing themselves for their fatigues and dangers at the expense of the citizens. Almost every private house had one or more of the officers, or privates, of the Royal army quartered upon them. In providing for their accommodation very little attention was paid to the convenience of families. The insolence and disorderly conduct of persons thus forced upon the citizens were in many instances intolerable to freemen heretofore accustomed to be masters in their own houses. . . . The officers, privates, and followers of the Royal army, were generally more intent on amassing fortunes by plunder and rapine than on promoting a reunion of the dissevered members of the Empire. . . . The Royal officers, instead of soothing the inhabitants into good humor, often aggravated intolerable injuries by more intolerable insults; they did more to re-establish the independence of the State than could have been effected by the armies of Congress . . . .

David Ramsay, *History of South Carolina* . . . , 2 vols. (Charleston: David Longworth for the author, 1809), II, 356–58.

[Mrs. Eliza Pinckney's Troubles in Occupied Charleston]

It may seem strange that a single woman, accused of no crime, who had a fortune to live genteely in any part of the world, that fortune too in different kinds of property and in four or five different parts of the country, should in so short a time be so entirely deprived of it as to be unable to pay a debt under sixty pound sterling, but such is my singular case. After the many losses I have met with, for the last three or four desolating years from fire and plunder, both in country and town, I still had something to subsist upon, but alas the hand of power has deprived me of the greatest part of that, and accident the rest. Permit me to particularize in part . . . .

The labor of the slaves I had working at my son Charles' [Charles Cotesworth] sequestrated estate, by Mr. Cruden's permission, has not produced one farthing since the fall of Charles Town. Between thirty and forty head of tame cattle, which I had on the same plantation, with the same permission, was taken last November by Major Yarborough, and his party for the use of the army, for which I received nothing.

My house in Ellory Street, which Capt. McMahon put me in possession of soon after I came to town, and which I immediately rented at one hundred per annum sterling, was in a short time after filled with Hessians, to the great detriment of the house and annoyance of the tenant, who would pay me no more for the time he was in it, than twelve guineas. I applied to a Board of Field Officers which was appointed to regulate those matters; they gave it as their opinion that I ought to be paid for the time it had been, and the time it should be, in the service of Government, which it is to this day. I applied as directed for payment, but received nothing. Even a little hovel, which I built to please one of my Negroes and which in the late great demand for houses would have been of service to me, was taken from me, and all my endeavors to get it again proved fruitless.

My plantation up the path which I hired to Mr. Simpson for fifty guineas the last year, and had agreed with him for eighty guineas for

Harriott Horry (Rutledge) Ravenel, *Eliza Pinckney* (New York: Charles Scribner's Sons, 1902), 301–302.

the present year, was taken out of his possession and I am told Major Frayser now has it for the use of the Cavalry, and Mr. Simpson does not seem inclined to pay me for the last half year . . . .

To my regret and to the great prejudice of the place, the wood has also been all cut down for the use of the garrison, for which I have not got a penny. The Negroes I had in town are sometimes impressed on the public works and make fear of being so a pretense for doing nothing. Two men and two women bring me small wages but part of that was stolen before it reached me.

76. *The Battle of Camden, August 16, 1780*

Upon receiving the intelligence of the fall of Charleston, General Washington sent General Horatio Gates, who was in command of a small army of Maryland, Virginia, and North Carolina troops, to the aid of South Carolina. General Gates and his force advanced resolutely into South Carolina but were engaged at Camden by a British Army under the command of Lord Cornwallis. Gates was defeated. Following this defeat, there were no organized American troops left in the state except those partisans fighting under Thomas Sumter, Francis Marion, and other guerrilla leaders. The following concerns the Battle of Camden.

[The Battle, as Reported by David Ramsay]

The arrival of this force [General Gates] being quite unexpected, Lord Cornwallis was distant from the scene of action. No sooner was he informed of the approach of General Gates than he prepared to join his army at Camden. He arrived and superseded Lord Rawdon in command on the 14th. His inferior force, consisting of about 1700 infantry and 500 cavalry, would have justified a retreat; but considering that no probable event of an action could be more injurious to the Royal interest than that measure, he chose to stake his fortune in a contest with the conqueror of Burgoyne. On the night of the fifteenth he marched out with his whole force to attack the Americans; and at the same hour General Gates put his army in motion, with a determination to take an eligible position between Sanders' creek and Green Swamp about eight miles from Camden. The advanced parties of both met about midnight, and a firing commenced. . . . After some time both parties retreated to their main bodies, and the whole lay on their arms. In the morning a severe and general engagement took place. The American army was formed in the following manner: the Second Maryland Brigade, commanded by Brig.

David Ramsay, *History of South Carolina* . . . , 2 vols. (Charleston: David Longworth for the author, 1809), I, 360–63.

Gen. Gist, on the right of the line, flanked by a morass; the North Carolina militia, commanded by Maj. Gen. Caswell, in the center; and the
Virginia militia, commanded by Brig. Gen. Stevens, on the left, flanked
by the North Carolina militia's light infantry, and a morass. The artillery
was posted in the interstices of brigades, and on the most advantageous
grounds. Maj. Gen. Baron de Kalb commanded on the right of the line,
and Brig. Gen. Smallwood commanded the First Maryland Brigade,
which was posted as a corps-de-reserve two or three hundred yards in the
rear. In this position the troops remained till dawn of day. As soon as the
British appeared about two hundred yards in front of the North Carolina
troops, the artillery was ordered to fire, and Brig. Gen. Stevens to attack
the column which was displayed to the right. That gallant officer advanced with his brigade of militia in excellent order within fifty paces of
the enemy, who were also advancing, and then called out to his men,
"My brave fellows, you have bayonets as well as they, we'll charge them."
At that moment the British infantry charged with a cheer, and the Vir-
ginians, throwing down their arms, retreated with the utmost precipitation. The militia of North Carolina followed the unworthy example,
except a few of Gen. Gregory's brigade, who paused a very little longer.
A part of Col. Dixon's regiment fired two or three rounds, but the greater
part of the whole militia fled without firing a single shot. The whole left
wing and center being gone, the Continentals who formed the right wing,
and the corps-de-reserve, engaged about the same time, and gave the
British an unexpected check. The Second Brigade, consisting of Maryland and Delaware troops, gained ground, and had taken no less than
fifty prisoners. The First Brigade being considerably out-flanked, were
obliged to retire; but they rallied again, and with great spirit renewed the
battle. This expedient was repeated two or three times. The British
directed their whole force against these two devoted corps, and a tremendous fire of musketry was continued on both sides with great steadiness.
At length, Lord Cornwallis observing that there was no cavalry opposed
to him, poured in his dragoons and ended the contest. Never did men
behave better than the Continentals in the whole of this action; but all
attempts to rally the militia were ineffectual. Lt. Col. Tarleton's legion
charged them as they broke, and pursued them as they were fleeing.
Without having it in their power to defend themselves, they fell in great
numbers under the legionary sabers. Maj. Gen. Baron de Kalb, an illus-
trious German in the service of France, who had generously engaged in
the support of American independence, and who exerted himself with

great bravery to prevent the defeat of the day, received eleven wounds, of which . . . he in a short time expired . . . .

The Americans lost eight field-pieces, the whole of their artillery, upwards of 200 wagons and the greatest part of their 209 baggage. The loss of the British, in killed and wounded, was about 300.

77. The Battle of Kings Mountain, South Carolina, October 7, 1780

WITH THE LOW COUNTRY FIRM IN THEIR CONTROL, THE BRITISH, IN
AUGUST, 1780, DISPATCHED MAJOR PATRICK FERGUSON INTO THE UP
COUNTRY TO ACCEPT THE ALLEGIANCE OF THE INHABITANTS, RECRUIT
NEW TROOPS, AND FORAGE FOR SUPPLIES. HIS TRIP AROUSED THE IRE OF
THE BACK COUNTRYMEN WHO GATHERED TO OPPOSE HIM. THESE TROOPS
WERE JOINED BY THE GREAT INDIAN FIGHTER, GENERAL JAMES WILLIAMS,
MORE NORTH CAROLINIANS, AND SOME SOUTH CAROLINIANS. AMONG THE
SOUTH CAROLINIANS WAS THE GUERRILLA FIGHTER, ANDREW PICKENS.
FERGUSON, THE ONLY NATIVE AMONG THE BRITISH FORCES (AS OTHERS
HAD BEEN RECRUITED IN NORTHERN AND SOUTHERN PARTS OF THE COUN-
TRY), RETREATED TOWARD A REUNION WITH CORNWALLIS, BUT HE WAS
CAUGHT AND DEFEATED AT HIS ENCAMPMENT AT KINGS MOUNTAIN. THIS
WAS THE FIRST MAJOR VICTORY FOR THE AMERICANS IN THE SOUTH, AND
IT WAS IMPORTANT BOTH PSYCHOLOGICALLY AND MILITARILY, AS A TURN-
ING POINT IN THE AMERICAN REVOLUTION. THE FIRST EXCERPT IS TAKEN
FROM COLONEL WILLIAM CAMPBELL'S OFFICIAL REPORT TO THE CON-
TINENTAL CONGRESS; THE SECOND IS A TORY'S ACCOUNT OF THE BATTLE.

[Colonel William Campbell's Official Report]

On receiving intelligence that Maj. Ferguson had advanced as high up
as Gilbert Town, in Rutherford County, and threatened to cross the
mountains to the western waters, Col. William Campbell, with four hundred men from Washington County, Virginia; Col. Isaac Shelby, with
two hundred and forty from Sullivan County, North Carolina; and Lt.
Col. John Sevier, with two hundred and forty men, of Washington
County, North Carolina, assembled at Watauga, on the 25th of September, where they were joined by Col. Charles McDowell, with one hundred and sixty men from the counties of Burke and Rutherford, who had
fled before the enemy to the western waters.

Virginia Gazette, Nov. 18, 1780, in Lyman C. Draper, *Kings Mountain and Its
Heroes* (Cincinnati: P. G. Thompson, 1881), 522–24.

We began our march on the 26th of September, and on the 30th we were joined by Col. Cleveland on the Catawba River, with three hundred and fifty men, from the counties of Wilkes and Surry. No one officer having properly a right to command in chief, on the 1st of October, we dispatched an express to Maj. Gen. Gates, informing him of our situation, and requesting him to send a general officer to take command of the whole. In the meantime Col. Campbell was chosen to act as commander till such a general officer should arrive. We marched to the Cowpens, on Broad River, in South Carolina, where we were joined by Col. James Williams, with four hundred men, on the evening of the 6th of October, who informed us that the enemy lay encamped somewhere near the Cherokee Ford, of Broad River, about thirty miles distant from us.

By a council of the principal officers, it was then thought advisable to pursue the enemy that night with nine hundred of the best horsemen, and leave the weak horses and footmen to follow as fast as possible. We began our march with nine hundred of the best men, about eight o'clock the same evening; and, marching all night, came up with the enemy about three o'clock p.m. of the 7th, who lay encamped on the top of Kings Mountain [South Carolina], twelve miles north of the Cherokee Ford, in the confidence that they could not be forced from so advantageous a post. . . . We advanced, and got within a quarter of a mile of the enemy before we were discovered.

Col. Shelby's and Col. Campbell's regiments began the attack, and kept up a fire on the enemy, while the right and left wings were advancing to surround them, which was done in about five minutes, and the fire became general all around. The engagement lasted an hour and five minutes, the greater part of which time a heavy and incessant fire was kept up on both sides. Our men in some parts, where the regulars fought, were obliged to give way a small distance, two or three times; but rallied and returned with additional ardor to the attack. The troops upon the right having gained the summit of the eminence, obliged the enemy to retreat along the top of the ridge to where Col. Cleveland commanded, and were there stopped by his brave men. A flag was immediately hoisted by Capt. De Peyster, the commanding officer (Maj. Ferguson having been killed a little before) for a surrender. Our fire immediately ceased, and the enemy laid down their arms, the greatest part of them charged, and surrendered themselves to us prisoners at discretion.

It appears from their own provision returns for that day, found in their camp, that their whole force consisted of eleven hundred and twenty-five men; out of which they sustained the following loss: Of the regulars, one Major, one Captain, two Sergeants, and fifteen privates killed; thirty-five privates wounded, left on the ground, not able to march: two captains, four Lieutenants, three Ensigns, one Surgeon, five Sergeants, three corporals, one Drummer, and forty-nine privates taken prisoners. Loss of the Tories—two Colonels, three Captains, and two hundred and one privates killed; one Major, and one hundred and twenty-seven privates wounded, and left on the ground, not able to march; one Colonel, twelve Captains, eleven Lieutenants, two Ensigns, one quarter-master, one adjutant, two commissaries, eighteen sergeants, and six hundred privates taken prisoners. Total loss of the enemy, eleven hundred and five men at King's Mountain.

The losses on our side were—one Colonel, one Major, one Captain, two Lieutenants, four Ensigns, nineteen privates killed—total twenty-eight killed; one Major, three Captains, three Lieutenants, and fifty-five privates wounded—total, sixty-two wounded.

[Lt. Allaire's "Tory" Account of the
Battle of Kings Mountain]

About two o'clock in the afternoon twenty-five hundred rebels, under the command of Brig. Gen. Williams, and ten colonels, attacked us. Maj. Ferguson had eight hundred men. The action continued an hour and five minutes; but their numbers enabled them to surround us. The North Carolina regiment seeing this, and numbers being out of ammunition, gave way, which naturally threw the rest of the militia into confusion. Our poor little detachment, which consisted of only seventy men when we marched to the field of action, were all killed and wounded but twenty; and those brave fellows were soon crowded as close as possible by the militia. Capt. De Peyster, on whom the command devolved, saw it impossible to form six men together; thought it necessary to surrender to save the lives of the brave men who were left. We lost in this action Maj. Ferguson, of the 71st Regiment, a man much attached to his King and country . . . . I have every reason to regret his unhappy fate. We

Lyman C. Draper, *Kings Mountain and Its Heroes* (Cincinnati: P. G. Thompson, 1881), 510, quoting Lt. Anthony Allaire's Diary.

had eighteen men killed on the spot; Capt. Ryerson and thirty-two privates wounded of Maj. Ferguson's detachment; Lt. McGinnis, of Allen's regiment of Skinner's brigade, killed. Taken prisoners, two captains, four lieutenants, three ensigns, one surgeon, and fifty-four sergeants rank and file, including the mounted men under the command of Lt. Taylor. Of the militia, one hundred were killed, including officers; wounded, ninety; taken prisoners, about six hundred. Our baggage all taken, of course. Rebels lost Brig. Gen. Williams, one hundred and thirty-five, including officers, killed; wounded, equal to ours.

78. The Battle of Cowpens, January 17, 1781

Following the Battle of Kings Mountain, Lord Cornwallis sent Lt. Col. Banastre Tarleton into the South Carolina Up Country to win the area back to the king. To counteract Colonel Tarleton's activities, Gen. Daniel Morgan was sent by Gen. Nathanael Greene to command the American forces in that vicinity. The almost inevitable clash between the two forces came on January 17, 1781, at the Cowpens, in what is now Cherokee County. Coming as it did after the American victory at Kings Mountain, the battle of Cowpens further weakened the British forces in the South and hastened the final defeat of General Cornwallis at Yorktown. At Cowpens, the odds favored the British, but immediately upon the arrival of Gen. Andrew Pickens at the camp a council of war was called. When Pickens learned that further retreat was contemplated, he urged General Morgan to make a stand. Sensing that his words were falling on deaf ears, he declared that he would make a stand alone if it became necessary. Morgan then suggested that they cross the river. Because of Pickens's protest over that move, the battle was fought as he had originally suggested. This account is from General Morgan's official report to General Greene, dated January 19, 1781.

[General Morgan's Report]

The troops I have the honor to command have been so fortunate as to obtain a complete victory over a detachment from the British army, commanded by Lt. Col. Tarleton. The action happened on the 17th inst., about sunrise, at the Cow pens . . . . To give you a just idea of our

James Graham, *Life of General Daniel Morgan* (New York: Derby and Jackson, 1858), 466–70. Includes Morgan's account of the Battle of the Cowpens. *See also* Alice Noble Waring, *The Fighting Elder: Andrew Pickens 1739–1817,* for the heroic actions of South Carolinians in the battle (Columbia: University of South Carolina Press, 1962).

operations, it will be necessary to inform you that on the 14th inst., having received certain intelligence that Lord Cornwallis and Lt. Col. Tarleton were both in motion, and that their movements clearly indicated their intentions of dislodging me, I abandoned my encampment on Grindall's Ford on the Pacolet, and on the 16th, in the evening, took possession of a post about seven miles from the Cherokee Ford on Broad river. . . . My situation at the Cowpens enabled me to improve any advantages I might gain, and to provide better for my own security should I be unfortunate. These reasons induced me to take this post, at the risk of its wearing the face of a retreat.

I received regular intelligence of the enemy's movements from the time they were first in motion. On the evening of the 16th inst., they took possession of the ground I had removed from in the morning, distant from the scene of action about twelve miles. An hour before daylight one of my scouts returned and informed me that Lt. Col. Tarleton had advanced within five miles of our camp. On this information, I hastened to form as good a disposition as circumstances would admit, and from the alacrity of the troops, we were soon prepared to receive him. The light infantry, commanded by Lt. Col. Howard, and the Virginia militia under the command of Maj. Tripplett, were formed on a rising ground, and extended a line in front. The third regiment of dragoons, under Lt. Col. Washington, were posted at such a distance in their rear, as not to be subjected to the line of fire directed at them, and to be so near as to be able to charge the enemy should they be broken. The volunteers of North Carolina, South Carolina and Georgia, under the command of the brave and valuable Col. [Andrew] Pickens, were situated to guard the flanks. Maj. McDowell, of the North Carolina volunteers, was posted on the right flank in front of the line, one hundred and fifty yards; and Maj. Cunningham, of the Georgia volunteers, on the left, at the same distance in front. Cols. Brannon and Thomas, of the South Carolinians, posted on the right of Maj. McDowell, and Cols. Hays and McCall of the same corps, on the left of Maj. Cunningham. Capts. Tate and Buchanan, with the Augusta riflemen, supported the right of the line.

The enemy drew up in single line of battle, four hundred yards in front of our advanced corps. The first battalion of the 71st Regiment was opposed to our right; the 7th Regiment to our left, the infantry of the legion to our centre, the light companies on their flanks. In front moved two pieces of artillery. Lt. Col. Tarleton, with his cavalry, was posted in the rear of his line.

The disposition of battle being thus formed, small parties of riflemen were detached to skirmish with the enemy, upon which their whole line moved on with the greatest impetuosity, shouting as they advanced. McDowell and Cunningham gave them a heavy and galling fire, and retreated to the regiments intended for their support. The whole of Col. Pickens' command then kept up a fire by regiments, retreating agreeably to their orders. When the enemy advanced to our line, they received a well-directed and incessant fire. But their numbers being superior to ours, they gained our flanks, which obliged us to change our position. We retired in good order about fifty paces, formed, advanced on the enemy, and gave them a fortunate volley, which threw them into disorder. Lt. Col. Howard, observing this, gave orders for the line to charge bayonets, which was done with such address, that they fled with the utmost precipitation, leaving their fieldpieces in our possession. We pushed our advantages so effectually, that they never had an opportunity of rallying, had their intentions been ever so good.

Lt. Col. [William] Washington having been informed that Tarleton was cutting down our riflemen on the left, pushed forward, and charged them with such firmness, that instead of attempting to recover the fate of the day, which one would have expected from an officer [Tarleton] of his splendid character, broke and fled.

The enemy's whole force were now bent solely in providing for their safety in flight—the list of their killed, wounded, and prisoners, will inform you with what effect. Tarleton, with the small remains of his cavalry, and a few scattering infantry, he had mounted on his wagon-horses, made their escape. He was pursued twenty-four miles, but owing to our having taken a wrong trail at first, we never could overtake him.

. . . There were one hundred non-commissioned officers and privates, and ten commissioned officers killed, and two hundred rank and file wounded. We have now in our possession five hundred and two non-commissioned officers and privates prisoners, independent of the wounded, and the militia are taking up stragglers continually. Twenty-nine commissioned officers have fell into our hands. . . .

The officers I have paroled; the privates I am conveying by the safest route to Salisbury. Two standards, two fieldpieces, thirty-five wagons, a traveling forge, and all their music are ours. Their baggage, which was immense, they have in a great measure destroyed. . . . From our force being composed of such a variety of corps, a wrong judgment may be formed of our numbers. We fought only eight hundred men, two-thirds of which were militia. The British, with their baggage-guard, were not less than one thousand one hundred and fifty, and these veteran troops. Their own officers confess that they fought one thousand and thirty-seven. . . .

Our loss was very inconsiderable, not having more than twelve killed and about sixty wounded . . . . Such was the inferiority of our numbers, that our success must be attributed to the justice of our cause and the bravery of our troops. . . .

79. *Activities of Marion's Brigade, March, 1781*

WHILE THE LOW COUNTRY WAS IN THE HANDS OF THE BRITISH, MANY
SOUTH CAROLINIANS UNDER THE LEADERSHIP OF FRANCIS MARION,
THOMAS SUMTER, AND OTHERS CONTINUED THEIR GUERRILLA WARFARE
AGAINST THE CONQUERORS. "FARMING BY DAY AND FIGHTING BY NIGHT"
WAS THEIR PROCEDURE, WHILE THEY CONTINUALLY HARASSED THE BRIT-
ISH FORCES. WITH THE AID OF GEN. NATHANAEL GREENE AND HIS CON-
TINENTAL TROOPS, WHICH ARRIVED IN THE STATE IN THE SUMMER OF
1781, THEY WERE ABLE TO DRIVE THE BRITISH GRADUALLY TO CHARLES-
TON. THE FOLLOWING ACCOUNT, WRITTEN BY COL. PETER HORRY, A
MEMBER OF MARION'S BRIGADE, COVERS MARION'S ACTIVITIES FOR A SHORT
TIME AND SHOWS THE COMMANDER'S HIT-AND-RUN TACTICS.

[Peter Horry]

Marion so effectually thwarted the schemes of the British against South
Carolina that to drive him out of the country was with them a favorite
object. The house burnings and devastations perpetrated by Weyms and
the Tories under his direction had not produced that intimidation and
disposition to submit which had been vainly expected from men who
disregarded property when put in competition with liberty. A new and
well concerted attempt to destroy, or disperse, the Brigade which had
given so much trouble to the late conquerors was made early in 1781.

Colonel Watson moved down from Camden along the Santee, and
Colonel Doyle crossing Lynch's creek, marched down on the east side of
it. The point of their intended junction was supposed to be at Snow's
Island. General Marion heard first of the approach of Watson, and
marched from Snow's Island with almost the whole of his force to meet
him. At Tawcaw Swamp, . . . he laid the first ambuscade for Watson.
General Marion had then but very little ammunition, nor more than
twenty rounds to each man. His orders were to give two fires and retreat;

David Ramsay, *History of South Carolina* . . . , 2 vols. (Charleston: David
Longworth for the author, 1809) I, 411–15.

and they were executed by Colonel Peter Horry with great effect. Watson made good the passage of the swamp, and sent Major Harrison with a corps of Tory cavalry and some British in pursuit of Horry. This had been foreseen by the cautious Marion; and Captain Daniel Conyers, at the head of a party of cavalry, was placed in a second ambuscade. As soon as the Tories and British came up, Conyers in a spirited and well directed charge killed with his own hands the officer who led on the opposite charge. Conyer's men followed his gallant example. Many of Harrison's party were killed, and the remainder made their escape to the main body of the British. Such work required little powder and ball. General Marion continued to harass Watson on his march, by pulling up bridges and opposing him in like manner at every difficult pass until they had reached near the lower bridge on Black river, seven miles below Kingstree. Here Watson made a feint of marching down the road to Georgetown. Marion being too weak to detach a party to the bridge, had taken an advantageous post on that road, when Watson, wheeling suddenly about, gained possession of the bridge on the west side. This was an important pass on the road leading into the heart of Williamsburg and to Snow's Island . . . . General Marion, informed of Watson's movements, without delay approached the river, plunged into it on horseback and called to his men to follow. They did so. The whole party reached the opposite shore in safety, and marched forward to occupy the east end of the bridge. Marion detached Major James with forty musqueteers and thirty riflemen under McCottry to burn the bridge . . . . Watson opened the fire of his artillery on them, but it was unavailing. In the meantime, Major James' party had fired the bridge. Thus were Marion's friends saved from similar plunderings and conflagrations with those they had suffered under Weyms. The practice of Watson was to burn all the houses of Marion's men that were in the line of his march.

Watson was so much intimidated by this affair, that he immediately quitted the lower bridge and proceeded by forced marches for Georgetown. General Marion repassed Black river and hung alternately on the rear, the flanks, or the front of the enemy, until they had reached Sampit bridge nine miles from Georgetown. There McCottry gave them a parting fire from his riflemen. During these transactions Watson commanded five hundred men, and Marion not half that number. The loss of the British is unknown; that of Marion but one man.

The three officers and all the men employed by the General at the lower bridge were inhabitants whose plantations and families would have been exposed to the enemy had they made good their passage. From

Sampit bridge Marion marched directly for Snow's Island. There he heard of the approach of Doyle, who had driven Colonel Erwin from the Island and taken possession of the pass of Lynch's creek at Witherspoon's Ferry. When McCottry, advancing in front, arrived at Witherspoon's on the south bank, the British on the north were scuttling the ferry boat. A short conflict took place . . . and Doyle fell back to Camden. . . . With a party of militia Marion marched to Georgetown and began regular approaches against the British post in that place. On the first night after his men had broken ground, their adversaries evacuated their works and retreated to Charlestown.

80. *The Battle of Eutaw Springs, September 9, 1781*

ALTHOUGH SKIRMISHES BETWEEN BRITISH FORAGING PARTIES AND THE
WHIGS, OR BETWEEN WHIGS AND TORIES, CONTINUED THROUGHOUT MOST
OF 1782, THE LAST MAJOR BATTLE OF THE REVOLUTION IN SOUTH CARO-
LINA WAS FOUGHT AT EUTAW SPRINGS ON SEPTEMBER 9, 1781. AFTER
THIS BATTLE, THE BRITISH RETIRED TO THE VICINITY OF CHARLESTON,
WHERE THEY HELD ON FOR ANOTHER YEAR, BUT THE MAJORITY OF THE
STATE WAS RETURNED TO AMERICAN CONTROL.

[David Ramsay on Eutaw Springs]

The whole American force proceeded . . . to attack the British Army
commanded by Lt. Col. Stewart. On the approach of the Americans the
British had retired from the Congarees about forty miles nearer Charles-
town, and taken post at the Eutaw Springs. Greene drew up his force,
consisting of about two thousand men, in two lines. The front consisted
of the militia from North and South Carolina, and was commanded by
Generals Marion and [Andrew] Pickens, and by Col. De Malmedy. The
second consisted of the Continental troops from North Carolina, Virginia
and Maryland, and was led on by General Sumner, Lt. Col. Campbell,
and Col. Williams. Lt. Col. Lee, with his legion, covered the right flank;
Lt. Col. Henderson, with the state troops, covered the left. Lt. Col. [Wil-
liam] Washington, with his cavalry, and Capt. Kirkwood with the Delaware troops, formed a corps of reserve. As the Americans advanced to the
attack, they fell in with two advanced parties of the British, three or
four miles ahead of their main army. These, being briskly charged by the
legion and state troops, soon retired. The front line continued to fire and
advance on the British till the action became general, and till they, in
their turn, were obliged to give way. They were well supported by Gen.
Sumner's North Carolina brigade of Continentals, though they had been
under discipline only for a few weeks, and were chiefly composed of

David Ramsay, *History of South Carolina* . . . , 2 vols. (Charleston: David
Longworth for the author, 1809), I, 432–35.

militia-men who had been transferred to the Continental service to make reparation for their precipitate flight in former actions. In the hottest of the engagement, when great execution was doing on both sides, Col. Williams and Lt. Col. Campbell, with the Maryland and Virginia Continentals, were ordered by Gen. Greene to charge with trailed arms. Nothing could surpass the intrepidity of both officers and men on this occasion —they rushed on, in good order, through a heavy cannonade and a shower of musketry, with such unshaken resolution that they bore down all before them.

The state troops of South Carolina were deprived of their gallant leader, Lt. Col. Henderson, who was wounded very early in the action; but they were nevertheless boldly led by Lt. Col. [Wade] Hampton, second in command, to a very spirited and successful charge, in which they took upwards of a hundred prisoners. Lt. Col. Washington brought up the corps of reserve on the left, and charged so briskly with his cavalry and Capt. Kirkwood's light infantry, as gave them no time to rally or form. The British were closely pursued and upwards of five hundred prisoners were taken. On their retreat they took their posts in a strong brick house and in impenetrable shrubs and a picketted garden. From these advantageous positions they renewed the action. Lt. Col. Washington made every possible exertion to dislodge them from the thickets, but failed in the attempt; had his horse shot under him, was wounded and taken prisoner. Four six-pounders were ordered up before the house from which the British were firing under cover. These pieces finally fell into their hands, and the Americans retired out of the reach of their fire. They left a strong picket on the field of battle, and retreated to the nearest water in their rear. In the evening of the next day, Lt. Col. Stewart destroyed a great quantity of his stores, abandoned the Eutaw, and moved toward Charlestown, leaving upwards of seventy of his wounded, and a thousand stand of arms. He was pursued for several miles but without effect. The loss of the British amounted to upwards of eleven hundred men. That of the Americans was about five hundred, in which number were sixty officers.

81. *The Evacuation of Charleston by the British, December 13–14, 1782*

THE BATTLE OF YORKTOWN WAS FOUGHT IN OCTOBER, 1781, BUT THE PEACE NEGOTIATIONS DRAGGED THROUGH 1782 AND INTO 1783. DURING THESE NEGOTIATIONS THE BRITISH CONTINUED TO OCCUPY POSTS IN THE UNITED STATES. CHARLESTON WAS OCCUPIED UNTIL DECEMBER 14, 1782, AND SMALL SKIRMISHES CONTINUED TO TAKE PLACE AROUND IT. THE FOLLOWING ACCOUNT OF THE FINAL BRITISH EVACUATION IS TAKEN FROM COL. PETER HORRY'S *Life of Marion*; THE STATISTICS ARE FROM A MANUSCRIPT CONTAINED IN THE MASSACHUSETTS HISTORICAL SOCIETY AND PRINTED IN THE *Charleston Yearbook* (1883).

[Peter Horry]

On the memorable 14th of December, 1782, we entered and took possession of our capital, after it had been two years, seven months and two days in the hands of the enemy. The style of our entry was quite novel and romantic. On condition of not being molested while embarking, the British offered to leave the town unhurt. Accordingly, at the firing of a signal gun in the morning, as agreed on, they quitted their advance works near the town gate, while the Americans, moving on close in the rear, followed them all along through the city down to the water's edge, where they embarked on board their three hundred ships, which, moored out in the bay in the shape of an immense half-moon, presented a most magnificent appearance. The morning was as lovely as pure wintry air and cloudless sunbeams could render it, but rendered far lovelier still by our procession if I may so call it, which was well calculated to awaken the most pleasurable feelings. In front were the humble remains of that proud army, which one and thirty months ago, captured our city, and thence, in the drunkenness of victory, had hurled menaces and cruelties disgraceful to the British name. And close in the rear, was our band of

Peter Horry, *The Life of General Francis Marion* (Philadelphia: Joseph Allen, 1852), 284–85.

Patriots, bending forward with martial music and flying colors, to play
the last joyful act of the drama of their country's deliverance, to proclaim
liberty to the captive, to recall the smile on the cheek of sorrow, and to
make the heart of the widow leap for joy. Oh! it was a day of jubilee
indeed; a day of rejoicing never to be forgotten. Smiles and tears were
on every face.

[Charleston Yearbook (1883), 416.]

Return of people embarked from South Carolina, December 14, 1782:

To What Place	Men	Women	Children	Blacks	Total
Jamaica	600	300	378	2613	3891
East Florida	796	363	456	2211	3826
England	137	74	63	56	330
Halifax	163	133	121	53	470
New York	100	40	50	50	240
St. Lucia	20			350	370
Totals	1816	910	1068	5333	9127

82. *The Founding of Columbia, 1785*

WITH THE SETTLING OF THE UP COUNTRY, MUCH OF THE STATE'S
POPULATION WAS IN FAVOR OF REMOVING THE SEAT OF GOVERNMENT
FROM THE COLONIAL CAPITAL AT CHARLESTON. FOLLOWING THE AMERI-
CAN REVOLUTION, THEREFORE, A MOVEMENT WAS BEGUN TO ERECT A NEW
CAPITAL NEARER THE CENTER OF SOUTH CAROLINA. AFTER SEVERAL SITES
HAD BEEN CONSIDERED, THAT NEAR THE JUNCTION OF THE BROAD AND
SALUDA RIVERS, NEAR THEIR CONFLUENCE WITH THE CONGAREE, WAS
DECIDED UPON. THE FIRST SELECTION APPEARED IN A CHARLESTON
NEWSPAPER, AND THE SECOND IS RAMSAY'S REPORT.

[Newspaper Report on Progress of Columbia]

A gentlemen lately arrived from the neighborhood of Friday's Ferry
informs that the new town called Columbia is in a very forward way of
being soon erected; saw mills are building on every stream within its
vicinity, and such an opinion is entertained of the utility of this new
undertaking that land thereabouts has risen 150 per cent in value.

[David Ramsay]

The extension of settlements far to the west loudly demanded on
republican principles a removal of the seat of government from the
vicinity of the Atlantic Ocean. The general principle being resolved
upon, no private views could control the sovereign people from estab-

Charleston *Morning Post* (Charleston, S.C.), May 1, 1786.

David Ramsay, *History of South Carolina* . . . , 2 vols. (Charleston: David
Longworth for the author, 1809), II, 103–104.

lishing their government where they pleased; and wherever they fixed it a town would of course be speedily formed.

A high and commanding situation about 120 miles from Charleston, and about three miles from the junction of the Broad and Saluda Rivers, commonly known by the name of the plane of Taylor's Hill, was selected. In many respects this choice was judicious; perhaps a much better place could not have been made to the east of the mountains. There was sufficient elevation to carry off with management all superfluous water. Some of the defects in the original plan of Charleston were obviated. No lots were to be less than half an acre. The two main streets crossing each other at right angles were to be each 150 feet wide, and none were to be less than sixty. . . . The place is sufficiently high to have in it no other than running water; and the streets are wide enough to admit without inconvenience three rows of trees to be planted in each of them. These advantages, with the surrounding woods and vegetation, especially when drained of every drop of stagnant water, may keep the town healthy till the rising value of its lots paves the way for the destruction of pure air by a crowded population. . . . The natural advantages of Columbia and its scattered settlements, together with the improved plan of the town, bid fair, under the direction of a well regulated police, to preserve it healthy for several years; but from its greater heat it will be more exposed to diseases than Charleston when population, compact settlement, and consequent filth, shall be equal in both.

83. *South Carolina and the Federal Constitution of 1787*

DURING THE REVOLUTION, THE UNITED COLONIES, INCLUDING SOUTH CAROLINA, HAD FORMED THEMSELVES INTO THE UNITED STATES UNDER THE ARTICLES OF CONFEDERATION. FROM 1776 TO 1789 SOUTH CAROLINA WAS A SOVEREIGN STATE, PART OF A CONFEDERATION OF SOVEREIGN STATES. THIS ARRANGEMENT PROVED UNSATISFACTORY, AND IN 1787 SOUTH CAROLINA SENT DELEGATES TO A CONSTITUTIONAL CONVENTION TO HELP DRAW UP THE CONSTITUTION OF THE UNITED STATES. THIS DISTINGUISHED GROUP, ALL ABLE MEN, INCLUDED JOHN RUTLEDGE, CHARLES COTESWORTH PINCKNEY, CHARLES PINCKNEY, AND PIERCE BUTLER. CHARLES PINCKNEY, THE NEXT TO THE YOUNGEST MAN THERE, EARNED FAME FOR HIS PART IN THE FRAMING OF THE CONSTITUTION BY PRESENTING A COMPLETE OUTLINE. THIS PRESENTATION, ON MAY 29, 1787, CONTAINED OVER THIRTY OF THE PROVISIONS OF THE CONSTITUTION OF THE UNITED STATES AS FINALLY ADOPTED, INCLUDING SOME OF THE MOST FUNDAMENTAL. THE NEW CONSTITUTION SET UP THE RELATION BETWEEN THE STATES AND THE UNION, A FEDERAL JUDICIARY, AND OTHERS; AND PINCKNEY'S CONTRIBUTION SPELLED OUT WHAT POWERS THE FEDERAL GOVERNMENT MIGHT EXERCISE. PINCKNEY WAS ALSO THE DELEGATE WHO CHAMPIONED THE FREEDOM OF THE PRESS. SUBSTANTIAL CONTRIBUTION WAS ALSO MADE BY JOHN RUTLEDGE. SOUTH CAROLINA RATIFIED THE CONSTITUTION ON MAY 23, 1788. THE REACTION TO THE CONSTITUTION FOLLOWS IN THE EXCERPT BELOW, AND THE STATE'S PART IN THE CONFEDERATION IS SUMMARIZED.

[David Ramsay]

The eight years of war in Carolina were followed by eight years of disorganization, which produced such an amount of civil distress as diminished with some their respect for liberty and independence. . . . Peace and liberty were found inadequate to promote public happiness without the aid of energetic government. . . . A constitution to form a more perfect union, establish justice, ensure domestic tranquillity, provide for the common defense, promote the general welfare, and secure the blessings of liberty, were wanting. To obtain such a one, Carolina concurred with the other states to meet in a general convention, and appointed Henry Laurens, John Rutledge, Charles Cotesworth Pinckney, Pierce Butler, and Charles Pinckney to attend and act in her behalf. They agreed upon and submitted to the people a plan of general government; by which every legislative power necessary for national purposes was vested in a Congress, consisting of two branches, a Senate and House of Representatives . . . . And a supreme executive officer with the name of President was charged with the execution of the national laws and the care of the national interests. And a supreme judiciary was also organized to decide all questions to the decision of which state judiciaries were improper. Thirteen independent states were formed into one nation as far as their common interests were concerned; and one uniform legislative, executive and judicial power pervaded the whole. The individual states were left in full possession of every power for their interior government, but restrained from coining money, emitting bills of credit, making any thing but gold and silver a tender in payment of debts, passing any bill of attainder, ex post facto law, or law impairing the obligation of con-

David Ramsay, *History of South Carolina* . . . , 2 vols. (Charleston: David Longworth for the author, 1809), II, 430–32. *See also* Edwin Emery, *The Press and America*, 2nd ed. (Englewood Cliffs, N.J.: Prentice-Hall, Inc., 1962), 130, for information on Charles Pinckney and the "freedom of the press," and Vernon L. Parrington, *The Romantic Revolution in America: 1800–1860*, in *Main Currents in American Thought*, 2 vols. (New York: Harcourt, Brace & World, Inc., Harvest Book, 1927), II, 104–105. Chapter IV, "Adventures in Belles Lettres," Part I, is devoted to "Old Charleston," and Parrington writes of Federalism and Charles Cotesworth Pinckney; and discusses other South Carolina figures.

tracts. This constitution was submitted to a convention of the people of South Carolina consisting of 224 members, by which it was accepted and ratified on behalf of the state on the 23rd day of May, 1788. Their acceptance of a constitution which, among other clauses, contained the restraining one which has been just recited was an act of great self-denial. To resign power in possession is rarely done by individuals, but more rarely by collective bodies of men. The power thus given up by South Carolina, was one she thought essential to her welfare, and had freely exercised for several preceding years. . . .

This acceptance and ratification was not without opposition. In addition to the common objections which had been urged against the constitution, South Carolina had some local reasons for refusing or at least delaying a final vote on the question. Doubts were entertained of the acceptance of the Constitution by Virginia. To gain time until the determination of that leading state was known, a motion for postponement was brought forward. This, after an animated debate, was overruled by a majority of 46. The rejection of it was considered as decisive in favor of the Constitution. When the result of the vote was announced, an event unexampled in the annals of Carolina took place. Strong and involuntary expressions of applause and joy burst forth from the numerous transported spectators. . . . The Constitution went into operation with general consent, and has ever since been strictly observed.

84. *The Constitution of 1790*

FOLLOWING THE RATIFICATION OF THE UNITED STATES CONSTITUTION, THE STATE OF SOUTH CAROLINA WAS ONCE AGAIN IN NEED OF A NEW STATE CONSTITUTION. THIS WAS ADOPTED IN JUNE, 1790, FOLLOWING A CONSTITUTIONAL CONVENTION MARKED BY A STRUGGLE FOR POWER BETWEEN LOW COUNTRY LEADERS AND THOSE OF THE UP COUNTRY. THE RESULTING DOCUMENT SERVED THE STATE UNTIL 1865.

THE CONSTITUTION

We, the delegates of the people of The State of South Carolina, in general convention met, do ordain and establish this Constitution for its government.

ARTICLE I

Section 1. The legislative authority of this state shall be vested in a general assembly, which shall consist of a Senate and House of Representatives.

Section 2. The House of Representatives shall be composed of members, chosen by ballot, every second year, by the citizens of this State, qualified as in this Constitution provided.

Section 3. The several election districts in this State shall elect the following number for Representatives, viz., Charleston, 15 members; Christ Church, 3; St. John, Berkeley, 3; St. Andrew, 3; St. George, Dorchester, 3; St. James, Goose Creek, 3; St. Thomas and St. Dennis, 3; St. Paul, 3; St. Bartholomew, 3; St. James, Santee, 3; St. John, Colleton, 3; St. Stephen, 3; St. Helena, 3; St. Luke, 3; Prince William, 3; St. Peter, 3; All Saints, 1; Winyaw, 3; Kingston, 2; Williamsburg, 2; Liberty, 2; Marlborough, 2; Chesterfield, 2; Darlington, 2; York, 3; Chester, 2; Fairfield, 2; Richland, 2; Lancaster, 2; Kershaw, 2; Claremont, 2; Clarendon, 2; Abbeville, 3; Edgefield, 3; Newberry, 3; Laurens, 3; Union, 2;

South Carolina Statutes at Large, I, 184–97.

Spartan, 2; Greenville, 2; Pendleton, 3; St. Matthew, 2; Orange, 2; Winton, 3; Saxegotha, 3. . . .

Section 4. Every free white man, of the age of twenty-one years, being a citizen of this State, and having resided therein two years previous to the day of election, and who hath a freehold of fifty acres of land, or a town lot, or . . . hath paid a tax the preceding year of three shillings sterling . . . shall have a right to vote for a member or members to serve in either branch of the legislature, for the election district in which he holds such property, or is so resident. . . .

Section 6. No person shall be eligible to a seat in the House of Representatives unless he is a free white man, of the age of twenty one years, and hath been a citizen and resident in this State three years previous to his election . . . and possessed, in his own right, of a settled freehold estate of five hundred acres of land, and ten Negroes; or of a real estate of the value of one hundred and fifty pounds sterling, clear of debt. . . .

Section 7. The Senate shall be composed of members to be chosen for four years in the following proportions, by the citizens of this State, qualified to elect members to the House of Representatives, at the same time, in the same manner, and at the same places, where they shall vote for Representatives, viz., Charleston, 2 members; Christ Church, 1; St. John, Berkeley, 1; St. Andrew, 1; St. George, 1; St. James, Goose Creek, 1; St. Thomas and St. Dennis, 1; St. Paul, 1; St. Bartholomew, 1; St. James, Santee, 1; St. John, Colleton, 1; St. Stephen, 1; St. Helena, 1; St. Luke, 1; Prince William, 1; St. Peter, 1; All Saints, 1; Winyaw and Williamsburg, 1; Liberty and Kingston, 1; Marlborough, Chesterfield, and Darlington, 2; York, 1; Fairfield, Richland, and Chester, 1; Lancaster and Kershaw, 1; Claremont and Clarendon, 1; Abbeville, 1; Edgefield, 1; Newberry, 1; Laurens, 1; Union, 1; Spartan, 1; Greenville, 1; Pendleton, 1; St. Matthew and Orange, 1; Winton, 1; Saxegotha, 1.

Section 8. No person shall be eligible to a seat in the Senate, unless he is a free white man, of the age of thirty years, and hath been a citizen and resident in this State, five years . . . legally seized and possessed, in his own right, of a settled freehold estate, of the value of three hundred pounds sterling . . . clear of debt. . . .

Section 10. Senators and members of the House of Representatives shall be chosen on the second Monday in October next, and the day following, and on the same days in every second year thereafter . . . and shall meet on the fourth Monday in November, annually, at Columbia . . . .

Section 11. Each House shall judge of the elections, returns and qualifications of its own members, and a majority of each House shall constitute a quorum to do business . . . .

Section 15. Bills for raising a revenue shall originate in the House of Representatives, but may be altered, amended, or rejected by the Senate. All other bills may originate in either House . . . .

Section 17. No money shall be drawn out of the public treasury, but by the legislative authority of the State.

Section 18. The members of the Legislature . . . shall be entitled to receive out of the public treasury . . . a sum not exceeding seven shillings sterling a day, during their attendance on, going to, and returning from the Legislature . . . .

Section 21. No person shall be eligible to a seat in the Legislature whilst he holds any office of profit or trust under this State, the United States, or either of them . . . .

Section 23. And whereas the ministers of the gospel are, by their profession, dedicated to the service of God, and the cure of souls, and ought not to be diverted from the great duties of their function; therefore, no minister . . . shall be eligible to the office of Governor, Lieutenant-Governor, or to a seat in the Senate or House of Representatives.

ARTICLE II

Section 1. The executive authority of this State shall be vested in a Governor to be chosen in manner following: As soon as may be, after the first meeting of the Senate and House of Representatives . . . when a majority of both Houses shall be present, the Senate and House of Representatives shall jointly, in the House of Representatives, choose, by ballot, a Governor, to continue for two years, and until a new election shall be made.

Section 2. No person shall be eligible to the office of Governor, until he hath attained the age of thirty years, and hath resided within this state, and been a citizen thereof ten years, and unless he be seized and possessed of a settled estate . . . in his own right, of the value of fifteen hundred pounds sterling, clear of debt. No person having served two years as Governor, shall be re-eligible to that office till after the expiration of four years . . . .

Section 3. A Lieutenant Governor shall be chosen at the same time, in the same manner, continue in office for the same period, and be possessed of the same qualifications as the Governor . . . .

Section 5. In case of the impeachment of the Governor, or his removal from office, death, resignation, or absence from the State, the Lieutenant Governor shall succeed to his office . . . .

Section 6. The Governor shall be commander in chief of the army and navy of this State, and of the militia, except when they shall be called into the actual service of the United States.

Section 7. He shall have power to grant reprieves and pardons . . . .

Section 8. He shall take care that the laws be faithfully executed in mercy . . . .

Section 11. All officers in the executive department, when required by the Governor, shall give him information in writing, upon any subject relating to the duties of their respective offices.

Section 12. The Governor shall from time to time give to the General Assembly information on the condition of the State, and recommend to their consideration such measures as he shall judge necessary and expedient. . . .

ARTICLE III

Section 1. The judicial power shall be vested in such superior and inferior courts of law, and equity, as the Legislature shall, from time to time direct and establish. . . .

ARTICLE IV

Section 1. All persons who shall be chosen or appointed to any office of profit or trust, before entering on the execution thereof, shall take the following oath:

"I do swear (or affirm) that I am duly qualified according to the Constitution of this State, to exercise the office to which I have been appointed, and will, to the best of my abilities, discharge the duties thereof, and preserve, protect, and defend the Constitution of this State and of the United States".

ARTICLE V

Section 1. The House of Representatives shall have the sole power of impeaching . . . .

Section 2. All impeachments shall be tried by the Senate . . . .

Section 3. The Governor, Lieutenant Governor, and all the civil officers, shall be liable to impeachment, for any misdemeanor in office . . . .

ARTICLE VI

Section 1. The judges of the Superior Courts, commissioners of the treasury, Secretary of the State, and Surveyor-General, shall be elected by the joint ballot of both Houses, in the House of Representatives. The commissioners of the treasury, Secretary of this State, and Surveyor-General, shall hold their offices for four years; but shall not be eligible again for four years after the expiration of the time for which they shall have been elected.

Section 2. All other officers shall be appointed as they hitherto have been, until otherwise directed by law. . . .

ARTICLE VII

Section 1. All laws of force in this State at the passing of this Constitution shall so continue, until altered or repealed by the Legislature . . . .

ARTICLE VIII

Section 1. The free exercise and enjoyment of religious profession and worship without discrimination or preference, shall, for ever hereafter, be allowed within this State to all mankind . . . .

Section 2. The rights, privileges, immunities and estates of both civil and religious societies, and of corporate bodies, shall remain as if the Constitution of this State had not been altered or amended.

ARTICLE IX

Section 1. All power is originally vested in the people; and all free governments are founded on their authority, and are instituted for their peace, safety, and happiness.

Section 2. No freeman of this State shall be taken or imprisoned, or disseized of his freehold, liberties, or privileges, or outlawed, or exiled, or in any manner destroyed or deprived of his life, liberty, or property, but by the judgment of his peers, or by the law of the land; nor shall any bill of attainder, ex post facto law, or law impairing the obligation of contracts, ever be passed by the Legislature of this State.

Section 3. The military shall be subordinate to the civil power.

Section 4. Excessive bail shall not be required, nor excessive fines imposed, nor cruel punishments inflicted.

Section 5. The legislature shall not grant any title of nobility or hereditary distinction . . . .

Section 6. The trial by jury, as heretofore used in this State, and the liberty of the press, shall be forever inviolably preserved.

ARTICLE X

The business of the treasury shall be, in future, conducted by two treasurers, one of whom shall hold his office and reside at Columbia; the other shall hold his office and reside in Charleston.

Section 2. The Secretary of State and Surveyor-General, shall hold their offices both in Columbia and in Charleston. They shall reside at one place and their deputies at the other . . . .

Section 4. The Governor shall always reside, during the sitting of the Legislature, at the place where their session may be held, and at all other times, wherever in his opinion, the public good may require.

Section 5. The Legislature shall, as soon as may be convenient, pass laws for the abolition of the rights of primogeniture, and for giving an equitable distribution of the real estate of intestates.

ARTICLE XI

Section 1. No convention of the people shall be called, unless by the concurrence of two thirds of both branches of the whole representation.

Section 2. No part of this Constitution shall be altered, unless . . . agreed to by two thirds of both branches of the whole representation . . . .

85. Economic and Social Conditions Near
the End of the Century

SOUTH CAROLINA'S CONDITION WAS CHAOTIC—POLITICALLY, ECONOMI-
CALLY, AND SOCIALLY. THE FOLLOWING EXCERPTS FROM DAVID RAMSAY
WILL GIVE SOME IDEA OF THE SERIOUSNESS OF THE SITUATION; AND
NOTES FROM BISHOP FRANCIS ASBURY'S TRAVEL JOURNAL INDICATE THE
TRAVEL, RELIGIOUS, AND SOCIAL CONDITIONS AS HE FOUND THEM IN 1786.

[David Ramsay]

In consequence of these civil wars between the Whigs and Tories—
the incursions of the savages—and the other calamities resulting from
the operations of the British and American armies, South Carolina
exhibited scenes of distress which were shocking to humanity. The single
district of Ninety-Six has been computed by well-informed persons
residing therein, to contain within its limits fourteen hundred widows
and orphans, made so by the war. . . .

The possessions of the planters were laid waste, their laborers were
carried off or greatly reduced by deaths and desertion. . . . The demand
for the Carolina indigo having greatly decreased, the prices became
so reduced as to render it no longer expedient to plant it as an object
of agricultural pursuit. . . . In the course of the Revolution, the small
crops of rice were consumed in the country, and . . . the crop of
1783, the first after the evacuation of Charleston, amounted only to
61,974 barrels. With the return of peace, the cultivation of rice was
resumed, and continued to increase until the year 1792, when the crop
exported amounted to 106,419 barrels. About this time cotton began to
employ so much of the agricultural force of the State, that the crops of
rice since that period have rarely exceeded what they were about the
middle of the eighteenth century.

The manufacture of flour was suspended by the Revolutionary War.
In the course of it, Mr. Broome, one of Col. Lee's cavalry, passed over

David Ramsay, *History of South Carolina* . . . , 2 vols. (Charleston: David
Longworth for the author, 1809), I, 452; II, 205, 216–17, 445–49, 540.

the foundation of Mr. Kershaw's mills [at Camden]. Struck with the advantages of the situation there he returned when peace took place, and erected as complete a set of mills as any in the United States. And in the year 1801, 40,000 bushels of wheat were manufactured at two or three flour mills, all of which were within one mile of Camden . . . . Excellent merchant mills were erected in Laurens District on the waters of Little River, by Thomas Wadsworth; and at Greenville on the waters of the Reedy River, by Alston; and in different parts of the state by others. . . .

Since the termination of the Revolution, ship building has been resumed and prosecuted with spirit in South Carolina. In the year 1798, the frigate *John Adams,* carrying thirty-two guns, was built at Cochran's ship-yard by Paul Pritchard. . . .

The morality of the inhabitants had been prostrated by laws violating private rights in the plea of political necessity—by the suspension of the courts of justice—by the disregard for the institutions of religion which is a never-failing attendant on military operations—by the destruction or dilapidation of churches and the consequent omission of public worship addressed to the Deity. All this time, the education of the rising generation was neglected, and the youth of the country had little other training than what they got in camps amidst the din of arms.

In such a condition of public affairs, to reproduce a state of things favorable to social happiness, required all the energies of the well disposed inhabitants. They immediately set about the God-like work. Assemblies were called—the best practicable laws were passed—courts were re-established—and from them impartial justice was dispensed— churches were rebuilt—the public worship of the Deity was resumed— the people were taught their duty by public instructors—schools were instituted and encouraged—the education of youth recommenced. By degrees the wounds inflicted by war on the morality and religion of the inhabitants began to heal. Their losses of property were made up from the returns of a fruitful soil, amply rewarding the labors of its cultivators. . . .

The cultivation of the former great staples, particularly rice and indigo, required large capitals. They could not be raised to any considerable purpose but by Negroes. In this state of things poor white men were of little account otherwise than as overseers. There were comparatively few of that intermediate and generally most virtuous class which is neither poor nor rich. By the introduction of the new staple the poor became of value, for they generally were or at least might be elevated to this middle grade of society. Land suitable for cotton was easily attained, and in tracts of every size either to purchase or rent. The culture of it entailed no diseases; might be carried on profitably by individuals or white families without slaves, and afforded employment for children whose labor was of little or no account on rice or indigo plantations. The poor having the means of acquiring property without the degradation of working with slaves, had new and strong incitements to industry . . . . As they became more easy in their circumstances, they became more orderly in their conduct. The vices which grew out of poverty and idleness were diminished. In estimating the value of cotton, its capacity to excite industry among the lower classes of people, and to fill the country with an independent industrious yeomanry, is of high importance.

Bishop Asbury's South Carolina Visit, 1786:

January 4, 1786: We crossed Great Pedee and Lynch's Creek, and wet my books. Coming to Black Mingo, we lodged at a tavern, and were well used. Sleeping upstairs, I was afraid the shingles, if not the roof of the house, would be taken away with the wind.

Saturday, 7th: I preached at Georgetown twice to about eighty people each time. This is a poor place for religion. Here I was met by Brother Henry Willis.

Tuesday, 10th: Rode to Wappetaw. It was no small comfort to me to see a very good frame prepared for the erection of a meeting-house for us, on that very road along which, last year, we had gone pensive and distressed, without a friend to entertain us.

Wednesday, 11th: Preached at St. Clair Caper's. We had a good time and many hearers, considering that neither place nor weather was favorable. My soul enjoyed great peace, and I was much engaged with God that my labors might not be in vain. From Caper's I came to Cainhoy by water.

Friday, 13th: I came to Charleston; being unwell, Brother Willis supplied my place.

Albert M. Shipp, ed., *History of Methodism in South Carolina* (Nashville: Southern Methodist Publishing House, 1883), 159–66.

Sunday, 15th: We had a solemn time in the day, and a full house and a good time in the evening. Our congregations here are large, and our people are encouraged to undertake the building of a meeting house this year. Charleston has suffered much—a fire about 1700, another in November, 1740, and lastly the damage sustained by the late war. The city is now in a flourishing condition.

Friday, 20th: I left the city, and found the road so bad that I was thankful I had left my carriage, and had a saddle and a good pair of boots. We were waterbound at Wasmassaw, where I found a few who had been awakened by the instrumentality of our preachers.

Monday, 23rd: The Wasmassaw being still impassable, we directed our course up the lowlands through the wild woods, until we came to Mr. Winter's, an able planter who would have us to dine with him and stay the night. His wife's mother being ill, and desiring the sacrament, we went to her apartment and there had a solemn time. In this worthy family we had prayer night and morning.

Tuesday, 24th: We made an early start. We stopped at a tavern for breakfast. The landlord had seen and heard me preach three years before in Virginia, and would receive no pay. We rode to the Congaree, and lodged where there was a set of gamblers. I neither ate bread nor drank water with them. We left early next morning, and after riding nine miles, came to a fire, where, stopping and broiling our bacon, we had a high breakfast. At Weaver's Ferry, we crossed the Saluda. . . .

Friday, 27th: I had near four hundred hearers at Parrott's log church, near Broad river. We had ridden about two hundred miles in the last eight days. . . .

March 26th: Crossed Pacolet river . . . . My body is weak, and so is my faith for this part of the vineyard. God is my portion, saith my soul. This country improves in cultivation, wickedness, mills and stills: a prophet of strong drink would be acceptable to many of these people . . . . I crossed Lawson's Fork at the high shoals, a little below the Beauty Spot. I could not but admire the curiosity of the people— my wig was as great a subject of speculation as some wonderful animal from Africa or India would have been. I had about one hundred people at the meeting house, some come to look at, and others to hear me. After Brother W. and myself had preached, we passed the Cow Pens, where Morgan and Tarleton had their fray. . . .

86. *Agriculture*

ASIDE FROM THE DESTRUCTION OF PLANTATIONS DURING THE WAR, THE MOST SIGNIFICANT EFFECT OF THE REVOLUTION ON SOUTH CAROLINA AGRICULTURE WAS THE LOSS OF THE INDIGO BOUNTY. THIS, WITH THE DECLINE IN THE PRICE OF THAT PRODUCT, PUT AN END TO COMMERCIAL GROWING OF INDIGO IN THE STATE AND MADE ROOM FOR THE INTRODUCTION OF COTTON, BOTH THE SHORT STAPLE AND SEA ISLAND VARIETIES, AFTER THE DEVELOPMENT OF THE COTTON GIN IN THE 1790s. IN 1785 A STATE AGRICULTURAL SOCIETY WAS FORMED TO IMPROVE FARMING METHODS, BUT IT HAD LITTLE SUCCESS. EXCERPTS FROM RAMSAY GIVE THE AIMS OF THE SOCIETY AND AGRICULTURAL CONDITIONS IN THE 1780s AND 1790s.

[David Ramsay]

In 1785, a society was incorporated to promote the interests of agriculture. The object was to institute a farm for agricultural experiments—to import and circulate foreign articles that were suitable to the climate of Carolina, and to direct the attention of the agriculturalists of the State to useful objects, and to reward such as improved the art. They imported and distributed some cuttings of vines and olives. The latter answered well, but the vicinity of Charlestown proved too moist for the former . . . .

Their efforts hitherto have been crippled from the want of funds. This defect has been lately done away from the successful issue of a lottery, instituted for the benefit of the institution. It is now clear of debt and possessed of forty-two acres of land in the vicinity of Charlestown, in which agricultural experiments are occasionally made. The society consist of forty members, whose annual subscription of twenty-five dollars each, added to the proceeds of the late lottery, will enable them to proceed with vigor in their original pursuits. . . .

In addition, they have resolved to offer medals—

David Ramsay, *History of South Carolina* . . . , 2 vols. (Charleston: David Longworth for the author, 1809), II, 224–25.

For an efficacious and practical method of destroying the caterpillars which infest the cotton plant, or preventing their ravages;

For the best and most practicable method of discharging stains from cotton and rendering it perfectly white;

For the greatest quantity of sweet oil made from olives raised in the State;

For the greatest quantity of oil obtained from ground nuts, and from the seed . . . of cotton, and of sunflowers;

Also for the greatest quantities of the levant senna, cassia senna, raised, cured and brought to market in the State; and the greatest quantity of rhubarb, rheum palmatum, castor oil, hops, and madder, all to be raised in the State;

And, to the person who shall first, within the State, establish and keep a flock of sheep of the true marino breed;

And for the greatest quantity of figs, the produce of the State, dried and brought to market.

The society have also resolved to establish a nursery of the most useful and ornamental trees, shrubs, and plants, and to offer them for sale at moderate prices.

[David Ramsay]

The first Provincial Congress in South Carolina held in January 1775, recommended to the inhabitants "to raise cotton," yet very little practical attention was paid to their recommendation. A small quantity only was raised for domestic manufactures. This neglect cannot solely be referred to the confusion of the times, for agriculture had been successfully prosecuted for ten years after the termination of the Revolutionary war before the Carolinians began to cultivate it to any considerable extent. In this culture the Georgians took the lead. They began to raise it as an article of export soon after the peace of 1783. Their success recommended it to their neighbors. The whole quantity exported from Carolina in any one year prior to 1795 was inconsiderable, but in

David Ramsay, *History of South Carolina* . . . , 2 vols. (Charleston: David Longworth for the author, 1809), II, 213–214, 219.

that year it amounted to 1,109,653 pounds. The cultivation of it has been ever since increasing, and on the first year of the nineteenth century, eight million pounds were exported from South Carolina. The uncertainty of this crop has disgusted a few planters, and brought them back to the less hazardous culture of rice. These two staples have so monopolized the agricultural force of the State, that for several years past other articles of export and even provisions have been greatly neglected. . . .

The soil of Carolina produces also hemp and flax. They are noted as articles of export in the year 1784, but only in the small quantity of three tons of the former and 171 casks of the latter . . . . Barley has been successfully cultivated, also, and some exported.

87. *Education*

THE REVOLUTIONARY WAR CLOSED THE SCHOOLS OF THE STATE FOR VARYING PERIODS OF TIME AND PREVENTED THE ESTABLISHMENT OF OTHERS. ONCE CONDITIONS WERE MORE SETTLED, THOUGHTS AGAIN TURNED TO THE EDUCATION OF THE YOUTH. THERE WAS A CONSENSUS THAT SONS WOULD NO LONGER BE SENT ABROAD, AS HAD BEEN CUSTOMARY, AND THAT GIRLS, TOO, SHOULD RECEIVE A CERTAIN AMOUNT OF TRAINING. THE IMPETUS OF EDUCATION FEVER WAS FELT PARTICULARLY IN THE FIELD OF ADVANCED STUDIES. THE STATE-CHARTERED SCHOOLS AND THE "COLLEGE ACT OF 1785" POINTED IN THIS DIRECTION. IN 1785 THE LEGISLATURE CHARTERED THREE COLLEGES: MOUNT SION [ZION] AT WINNSBORO, CAMBRIDGE (NEAR NINETY-SIX), AND THE COLLEGE OF CHARLESTON. CAMBRIDGE DID NOT SURVIVE; MT. ZION, A LEADER IN THE SOUTH FOR GENERATIONS, IS MAINTAINED AS AN ELEMENTARY SCHOOL; AND THE COLLEGE OF CHARLESTON IS NOW STATE-SUPPORTED. EXCERPTS CONCERN SOCIETIES FORMED AND THE COLLEGE ACT.

[David Ramsay]

Since the Revolution, societies and academies have been formed and incorporated at different periods in almost every part of the State, primarily for the encouragement and support of schools. To these generally have been given by the Assembly the escheated and unsold confiscated property in their respective districts.

The names of these as far as can be recollected are the Mount Zion Society, incorporated in 1777; St. David's in 1778; the Minerva Academy, fourteen miles below Columbia, in which about fifty-six scholars are educated; the Camden Orphan Society, in which a few children are educated on charity and about sixty pay for their education. The trustees of this institution have purchased the large elegant mansion house of the late Col. Joseph Kershaw for the use of the school and its

David Ramsay, *History of South Carolina* . . . , 2 vols. (Charleston: David Longworth for the author, 1809) II, 360–66.

245

teachers. The Clarendon Orphan Society, incorporated in 1798; the trustees for establishing public schools in the district of Orangeburgh, incorporated also in 1798; the Mount Bethel Academy; the Clermont Society for the purpose of endowing a seminary of learning at States-burgh, and the friendly Cambridge Society . . . .

In the year 1795 the citizens of Beaufort preferred a claim to have a charter granted for a college to be erected in their vicinity. The advocates of the measure urged the uncommon healthiness of the place, the great number of their youth, and the danger of sending them from the wholesome air and pure morals of their native spot either to the capital or distant parts of the country. They prevailed so far as to obtain a charter and such funds as they could collect from the sale of escheated and confiscated property in the District, and also from the sales of vacant lots in the town of Beaufort . . . . Suitable buildings for the accommodation of the students were begun, and schools set on foot preparatory to the college. The seminary blossomed well, but little fruit has been yet gathered, though there is reason to believe that when its funds are productive, and the world is composed to peace, it will realize the hopes of its friends. It has many natural advantages favorable to the proper education of youth.

The South Carolina College Act of 1785:

Whereas, the proper education of youth is essential to the happiness and prosperity of every community, and is therefore an object well worthy of the attention of this Legislature; and whereas, the incorporated Mount Sion [Zion] Society have petitioned this House that a college may be erected and established by law at the Village of Winnsborough, in this State, for the instruction of youth in the learned languages and the liberal arts and sciences, and that the said college may be committed to the management, direction, and government of trustees to be chosen and appointed by the said Society out of their number:

South Carolina Statutes at Large, IV, 674–78.

I. Be it therefore enacted . . . that there be erected and established . . . at the Village of Winnsborough, in the district of Camden, in this State, a college for the education of youth in the learned and foreign languages, and in the liberal arts and sciences, under the style, name, and title of the Mount Sion College.

II. And whereas it is much desired by many well disposed persons that a public seminary of learning for the education of youth should be established in or near Charleston, and it is not doubted but that many persons will contribute largely towards the same, if a proper piece of ground was appropriated for that purpose, and a law passed for empowering commissioners to receive such donations, and for erecting a college as soon as a sufficient sum shall be raised for that purpose, Be it therefore enacted . . . that his Excellency the Governor [and 22 others] . . . shall forever be one body politic and corporate, in deed and in name, by the style of the "Trustees of the College of Charleston", and that . . . they . . . be able and capable in law to have, receive, take and enjoy . . . all sums of money, goods, chattels and things whatsoever . . . for building, erecting, and supporting the said college in or near Charleston . . . and that the land heretofore given and appropriated for a free school in Charleston, shall be . . . reserved for the use of the said college or seminary of learning in Charleston, and that the same shall not be applied to any other use or purpose.

III. And whereas, by the liberal subscriptions which have been made towards the erecting and maintaining a seminary of learning at Ninety-Six, and the exertions of the trustees appointed by an Act of the General Assembly, passed the thirteenth day of August in the eighth year of the Independence of the United States of America, to whom the government of the public school was committed, a very considerable fund hath already accumulated, and a prospect of still greater additions; and whereas it is just and proper to give all possible encouragement to, and enlarge the foundations of the said public school, in common with the others by this act to be established; Be it therefore enacted . . . that the Honorable Benjamin Guerard . . . [and 12 others] . . . together with the trustees of the public school established at Ninety-Six . . . are hereby appointed trustees of a college to be erected at or near the town of Ninety-Six, which shall be called and known by the name of the "College of Cambridge" . . . .

V. The head or principal of the said college shall be called and styled "The President" and the masters thereof shall be called and styled

"Professors" . . . . The trustees appointed as aforesaid shall have regular and stated meetings for the dispatch of business, at such times and at such places as they, or a quorum of them shall appoint. The said trustees . . . being regularly convened, shall be capable of doing and transacting all the business and concerns of the said colleges respectively and particularly of electing and appointing the President and professors, of appointing a treasurer, secretary, stewards, managers, and all other necessary and customary officers . . . ; of fixing and ascertaining their several salaries and stipends, and removing or displacing any or all of them for misconduct or malversation in office; of prescribing the course of studies to be pursued, and in general of framing, establishing, and enacting all such orders, rules, statutes, and ordinances, as shall appear to them necessary for the good government of the said colleges, not repugnant to the laws of this State. The Presidents and professors, or a majority of them, shall be styled and called the "Faculty of the Colleges," which faculty shall have the power of enforcing the rules and regulations adopted by the trustees for the government of the pupils, by rewarding or censuring them, and finally by suspending such of them as after repeated admonitions shall continue disobedient and refractory, until the determination of a quorum of trustees can be had. No person shall be eligible as a trustee of the said colleges unless he shall profess the Christian Protestant religion . . . .

VI. And be it further enacted . . . that the said trustees . . . shall have full power, by the presidents of the said colleges respectively . . . to grant and confer such degree or degrees in the liberal arts and sciences, to any of the students . . . thought worthy thereof, as are usually granted and conferred in other colleges in Europe and America, and to give diplomas or certificates thereof, signed by them, and sealed with the common seal of the society, to authenticate and perpetuate the memory of such graduation. . . .

88. *The Negro and Conditions of Life*

BECAUSE THE BRITISH TREATMENT OF THE NEGRO SLAVES WAS SO CRUEL, THE SLAVES HAD FARED MUCH WORSE THAN THEIR OWNERS DURING THE REVOLUTION. THEY WERE CONSIDERED "PROPERTY" AND, AS THE SPOILS OF WAR, WERE TAKEN IN LARGE NUMBERS BY THE ENEMY AND SENT TO THE WEST INDIES, TO FLORIDA, OR TO BRITISH POSTS IN THE NORTH, WHERE THEY WERE FORCED TO WORK AT BUILDING FORTIFICATIONS. THOSE WHO WERE LEFT BEHIND SUFFERED THE RAVAGES OF WAR ALONG WITH THEIR MASTERS. TO SOME MEN OF THE TIMES, SLAVERY WAS AN EVIL DEVICE, AND THEREFORE, WHEN THE CONSTITUTIONAL CONVENTION MET SHORTLY AFTER THE WAR, THEY CALLED FOR AN END TO THE SLAVE TRADE. HENRY LAURENS, THE GREAT DIPLOMAT AND STATESMAN— WHO HAD BEEN EXCHANGED AS A PRISONER OF WAR FOR LORD CORNWALLIS AFTER HAVING BEEN HELD IN THE TOWER OF LONDON—WAS ONE OF THOSE OPPOSED TO SLAVERY. FOLLOWING ARE EXCHANGES OF LETTERS BETWEEN LAURENS AND HIS SON, INDICATING THEIR VIEWS. WHAT A FRENCH TRAVELER HAS TO SAY IS ALSO OF INTEREST; IN THE EXCERPT BELOW HE SPEAKS OF THE SELF-PRIDE SHOWN BY THE NEGROES IN SOUTH CAROLINA AND CONTRASTS THEIR FAVORABLE POSITION WITH THAT OF NEGROES ELSEWHERE.

Letter of Henry Laurens to his son,
John Laurens, August 14, 1776:

My Negroes there, all to a man, are strongly attached to me—so are all of mine in this country; hitherto not one of them has attempted to desert; on the contrary, those that are more exposed hold themselves ready to fly from the enemy in case of a sudden descent. Many hundreds of that color have been stolen and decoyed by the servants of King George the Third. Captains of British ships of war and noble lords have busied themselves in such inglorious pilferage, to the disgrace of their

Edwin Anderson Alderman et al., eds., *Library of Southern Literature,* 16 vols. (New Orleans: The Martin and Hoyt Co., 1908–1913), VII, 3084–88.

master and the disgrace of their cause. These Negroes were first enslaved by the English; acts of Parliament have established the slave trade in favor of the home-residing English . . . . Negroes are brought by Englishmen and sold as slaves to Americans. Bristol, Liverpool, Manchester, Birmingham, etc, live upon the slave trade . . . .

You know, my dear son, I abhor slavery. I was born in a country where slavery had been established by British Kings and Parliaments, as well as by the laws of that country ages before my existence. I found the Christian religion and slavery growing under the same authority and cultivation. I nevertheless disliked it. In former days there was no combating the prejudices of men supported by interest; the day I hope is approaching when, from principles of gratitude as well as justice, every man will strive to be foremost in showing his readiness to comply with the golden rule. Not less than twenty thousand pounds sterling would all my Negroes produce if sold at public auction tomorrow. I am not the man who enslaved them . . . nevertheless I am devising means for manumitting many of them, and for cutting off the entail of slavery. Great powers oppose me—the laws and customs of my country, my own and the avarice of my countrymen. What will my children say, if I deprive them of so much estate? These are difficulties, but not insuperable. I will do as much as I can in my time, and leave the rest to a better hand.

John Laurens to His Father, Henry Laurens, October 26, 1776:

The equitable conduct which you have resolved upon with respect to your Negroes will undoubtedly meet with great opposition from interested men. I have often conversed upon the subject, and I have scarcely ever met with a native of the Southern provinces or the West Indies who did not obstinately recur to the most absurd arguments in support of slavery . . . .

Edwin Anderson Alderman et al., eds., Library of Southern Literature, 16 vols. (New Orleans: The Martin and Hoyt Co., 1908–1913), VII, 3088.

[A Frenchman Comments on South Carolina Slaves, 1777:]

Without wishing to draw a parallel here between the type of Negroes that one finds in the English colonies and those in the French colonies, I cannot help mentioning that there is a very noticeable difference. Although the Negroes here are under the yoke of slavery, one does not hear them complain as much as ours and one does not see them cringe or appear afraid of every white man as they do in our colonies, where every one of them seems to think that every white man has a whip or club ready to mistreat them at any moment.

Without affecting the foolish pride of our free Negroes, the Anglo-American Negro slaves have an air of self-respect about them that does not appear to be arrogance, and yet shows that they look upon white men other than their masters as human beings and not as tyrants. On Santo Domingo, on the other hand, every slave expects to be ordered around by every white man he meets, and beaten if he does not obey without a murmur.

These conditions, which so much offend the Frenchmen who come to the Islands, prove without a doubt that it is the training which the slaves receive while they are becoming civilized that makes them troublesome or not. Here, under the protection of the law, the despotism of the master is restrained, and the treatment of the slave is relatively good, while in our islands, where there are few laws in favor of the Negroes, one sees the ferocity and severity of their treatment by the whites increase rather than diminish. Here the self-respect and serenity of the slave in the presence of white people shows the manner in which they are treated by their masters, and just as the agriculture here shows an improvement over that in our islands, so the conditions of the slaves here shows up our colonies at a disadvantage when compared to the Anglo-American way of life.

"A Frenchman Visits Charleston in 1777," in *South Carolina Historical and Genealogical Magazine,* LII (1951), 92. Reprinted by permission of The South Carolina Historical Society.

READINGS

ADDITIONAL PRINTED SOURCE MATERIALS:

Drayton, John. *Memoirs of the American Revolution, From Its Commencement to the Year 1776 Inclusive* . . . . 2 vols. (This is based largely on William Henry Drayton's papers).

Lee, Richard Henry. *Memoirs of the War in the Southern Department of the United States* . . . . 2 vols. (Later editions in 1827 and 1870, the latter edited by Robert E. Lee).

Moultrie, William. *Memoirs of the American Revolution, So Far as Related to the States of North Carolina, South Carolina and Georgia* . . . . 2 vols.

Ramsay, David. *The History of the Revolution of South Carolina from a British Colony to an Independent State* . . . . 2 vols.

Walsh, Richard, ed. *The Writings of Christopher Gadsden, 1746–1805.*

CORRELATED TEXTS:

Draper, Lyman C. *King's Mountain and Its Heroes: A History of the Battle of King's Mountain, October 7, 1780, and the Events Which Led to It.*

McCrady, Edward. *The History of South Carolina in the Revolution, 1775–1780.*

———. *The History of South Carolina in the Revolution, 1780–1783.*

Singer, Charles G. *South Carolina in the Confederation.*

Snowden, Yates, ed. *History of South Carolina.* I, 335–536.

Wallace, D. D. *History of South Carolina.* II, 66–359.

———. *South Carolina: A Short History,* 231–345.

V
THE ANTEBELLUM PERIOD

The period of South Carolina history from 1800 to 1860 was one of steady growth, of relatively little change in basic political and social structure, and of a gradual involvement in sectional differences that was to lead to civil war. The state doubled its population from about 350,000 to about 700,000, while the nation as a whole increased from five million to 31 million. In the same years, the Negro population in South Carolina increased from 42 percent to 58 percent. Cotton production became the economic mainstay of the state, both on the Low Country plantation and on the Up Country farm. Few immigrants came from Europe to the state; thousands of South Carolinians migrated west and southwest to new cotton regions. In the state government the power of the Low Country was contested, but the general economic-political philosophy of that area—based on cotton exports, low tariffs, and the protection of the institution of slavery—spread throughout most of the state and the South.

For the first twenty years of the nineteenth century, the path of South Carolina, economically and politically, headed in the same direction as that of the nation as a whole. John C. Calhoun, Langdon Cheves, and William Lowndes, among others, were strong nationalists, while David R. Williams foresaw an industrial South Carolina that would rival New England. The growth of the textile industry in New England and old England was strongly dependent upon the growth of cotton production in the South, and cotton growing was profitable. But the price of cotton fluctuated according to international supply and demand, while the price of manufactured goods purchased by the cotton producer tended to rise as the United States tariff rates rose. South Carolina and, to a lesser extent, other cotton producing states, opposed the higher tariff rates demanded by the more industrialized North. John C. Calhoun, for example, favored the higher tariff voted by Congress in 1816, but by 1828 he had come to oppose adamantly such "protective tariffs" entirely. As a result, Calhoun led South Carolina to the point of the Nullification

Convention of 1832, when the state attempted to prevent the collection of federal tariffs but was prevented by the forceful action of President Andrew Jackson, another South Carolinian, and the Congress.

Slavery underwent a tremendous change during the 1820s, as it became more institutionalized from the expansion of cotton production. The advent and development of the cotton gin changed the master-slave relationship from the "kinder task system" to a higher incidence of absentee ownership. The rigorous "gang system," in which overseers ran the plantations, was instituted. Harsh treatment of the slaves was not the rule, however; the system devolved on the "mean" and more toward humane treatment.

Although the slavery issue and the sectionalism that accompanied it were gradually moving the state and the South toward secession, South Carolina continued to be represented in Washington by a series of outstanding men. From the Federalists Thomas and Charles C. Pinckney of the early 1800s, through the 40-year national political career of John C. Calhoun, to James L. Orr and J. H. Hammond in the 1850s, the state was provided with able leadership in Congress. No major issue was debated without a South Carolinian taking a prominent part. It was said, and not entirely without truth, that Charleston ruled the state, the state ruled the South, and the South ruled the nation from 1820 to 1860. If the antebellum period in South Carolina was not all moonlight and roses, it was nevertheless a golden era—with the white gold of cotton. Coming as this period did between a turbulent revolution and a disastrous civil war, it was remembered as "the good old days."

89. *The Constitutional Amendments of 1808 and 1810*

THE CONSTITUTION OF 1790 PLACED THE LOW COUNTRY IN CONTROL OF BOTH HOUSES OF THE LEGISLATURE, ALTHOUGH THIS SECTION OF SOUTH CAROLINA CONTAINED ONLY ABOUT ONE-THIRD OF THE STATE'S WHITE POPULATION. THERE WAS STILL IN EFFECT A PROPERTY REQUIRE-MENT FOR VOTING AND HOLDING OFFICE. THESE CONSTITUTIONAL RE-QUIREMENTS SEEMED OUT OF PLACE IN A "DEMOCRACY" AND AROUSED MUCH OPPOSITION, ESPECIALLY IN THE UP COUNTRY. IN THE AMEND-MENTS OF 1808 AND 1810, THESE PROVISIONS WERE REVISED BY MAKING REPRESENTATION MORE EQUAL AND BY GIVING THE VOTE TO ALL ADULT WHITE MALES. ELECTION DISTRICTS IN MOST OF THE STATE WERE COUNTIES, BUT IN THE COASTAL AREA THEY WERE THE SMALLER PARISHES. THE TWO AMENDMENTS ARE GIVEN HERE.

The Constitutional Amendment Ratified December 17, 1808:

The House of Representatives shall consist of one hundred and twenty-four members; to be apportioned among the several election districts of the state, according to the number of white inhabitants contained, and the amount of all taxes raised by the legislature, whether direct or indi-rect, or of whatever species, paid in each, deducting therefrom all taxes paid on account of property held in any other district, and adding thereto all taxes elsewhere paid on account of property held in such district; and enumeration of the white inhabitants for this purpose shall be made in the year one thousand eight hundred and nine, and in the course of every tenth year thereafter, in such manner as shall by law be directed; and representatives shall be assigned to the different districts in the above mentioned proportion, by act of the Legislature at the session immediately succeeding the above enumeration. . . .

In assigning representatives to the several districts of the State, the Legislature shall allow one representative for every sixty-second part of the whole number of white inhabitants in the State; and one representa-

South Carolina Statutes at Large, I, 193–95.

tive also for every sixty-second part of the whole taxes raised by the Legislature of the State. . . .

The Senate shall be composed of one member from each election district, as now established for the election of members of the House of Representatives, except the district formed by the Parishes of St. Philip and St. Michael, to which shall be allowed two senators as heretobefore.

The Constitutional Amendment Ratified December 19, 1810:

Every free white man of the age of twenty-one years, paupers and non-commissioned officers and private soldiers of the army of the United States excepted, being a citizen of this state, and having resided therein two years previous to the day of election, and who hath a freehold of fifty acres of land or a town lot, of which he hath been legally seized and possessed at least six months before such election, or not having such freehold or town lot, hath been a resident in the election district in which he offers to give his vote, six months before the said election, shall have a right to vote for a member or members to serve in either branch of the Legislature, for the election in which he holds such property, or is so resident.

South Carolina Statutes at Large, I, 193–95.

90. *John C. Calhoun and the War of 1812*

FOREMOST OF THE NEW LEADERS OF SOUTH CAROLINA AFTER REVOLU-
TIONARY TIMES WAS THE BRILLIANT JOHN CALDWELL CALHOUN. A
"BACKCOUNTRYMAN," CALHOUN MARRIED A LOW COUNTRY WOMAN OF
WEALTH, HIS COUSIN FLORIDE COLHOUN. CALHOUN HAD GRADUATED
FROM YALE COLLEGE IN 1804 AND THEN PRACTICED LAW IN HIS NATIVE
STATE. AFTER SERVING IN THE SOUTH CAROLINA LEGISLATURE, CALHOUN
WAS ELECTED TO CONGRESS IN 1810. THERE HE WAS APPOINTED TO THE
FOREIGN RELATIONS COMMITTEE, AND HE WAS THE FIRST PERSON TO
ADVOCATE THAT AMERICA MUST RETAIN THE INDEPENDENCE IT HAD WON
FROM ENGLAND. CALHOUN HAD GONE TO CONGRESS IMBUED WITH A
SPIRIT OF NATIONALISM, AND IT WAS HIS ADDRESS OF DECEMBER 12, 1811,
IN DEFENSE OF HIS COMMITTEE'S REPORT RECOMMENDING THAT THE
UNITED STATES ARM ITSELF IN PREPARATION FOR WAR THAT BROUGHT
HIM TO THE NATION'S ATTENTION. DURING HIS SERVICE TO HIS COUNTRY,
CALHOUN SERVED AS VICE-PRESIDENT, AS SECRETARY OF WAR WHEN HE
SET UP THE DEPARTMENT, AS ACTING SECRETARY OF THE NAVY, AND VIR-
TUALLY AS ACTING PRESIDENT OF THE UNITED STATES DURING A MONTH
OF CRISES. CALHOUN'S PORTRAIT HANGS IN THE "HALL OF FAME" IN
WASHINGTON AS ONE OF THE FIVE "ALL-TIME GREAT SENATORS," AND HIS
STATUE STANDS IN THE ROTUNDA OF THE CAPITOL. THE FIRST SELEC-
TION IS EXCERPTED FROM HIS "REPORT ON THE CAUSES AND REA-
SONS FOR WAR," AND THE SECOND DESCRIBES CHARLESTON'S STATE OF
PREPAREDNESS WHEN THE WAR OF 1812 APPEARED IMMINENT.

[John C. Calhoun's Causes and Reasons for War]

July 3, 1812

The period has now arrived, when the United States must support
their character and station among the Nations of the Earth, or submit to

Robert L. Meriwether, ed., *The Papers of John C. Calhoun* (Columbia: University of South Carolina Press, 1959), I, 110–22. Copyright, 1959, by the
South Carolina Archives Department. Reprinted by permission of the University of South Carolina Press.

the most shameful degradation. Forebearance has ceased to be a virtue. War on the one side, and peace on the other, is a situation as ruinous as it is disgraceful. The mad ambition, the lust of power, and commercial avarice of Great Britain, arrogating to herself the complete dominion of the Ocean, and exercising over it an unbounded and lawless tyranny, have left to the Neutral Nations—an alternative only, between the base surrender of their rights, and a manly vindication of them. Happily for the United States, their destiny, under the aid of Heaven, is in their own hands. . . . They have suffered no wrongs, they have received no insult, however great, for which they cannot obtain redress. . . .

From this period [1793] the British Government has gone on in a continued encroachment on the rights and interests of the United States, disregarding . . . obligations which have heretofore been held sacred by civilized Nations. . . .

From this review of the multiplied wrongs of the British Government since the commencement of the present War, it must be evident to the Impartial world, that the contest which is now forced on the United States, is radically a contest for their sovereignty and Independence.

Your Committee, believing, that the freeborn sons of America are worthy to enjoy the liberty which their Fathers purchased at the price of so much blood and treasure . . . feel no hesitation in advising resistance by force—In which the Americans of the present day will prove . . . that we have not only inherited that liberty which our Fathers gave us, but also the will & power to maintain it . . . . your Committee recommend an immediate appeal to Arms.

[Charleston's Fortification during the War of 1812]

It was determined to fortify the city [Charleston] on the land side by a line of works across the Neck, from Ashley to Cooper rivers, thus completely cutting off the city from the country. The engineer was immediately set to work to lay out the plan, which was soon done, and the citizens determined to carry it into execution with a ditch in front, ten

Harvey T. Cook, *The Life and Legacy of David Rogerson Williams* (New York: n.p., 1916), 115–16.

feet deep and twenty feet wide, so that it was twenty feet from the bottom of the ditch to the top of the battlement. In the construction of the wall every shovel full of earth was pounded down, until it was as solid as it was possible to make it. It was then handsomely sodded. There were zigzags equidistant, along the whole line, in which the heaviest guns were mounted to rake the ditch. The guns were all mounted in barbet at first, but it was soon discovered that that plan would expose the men too much. Embrasures were then cut which greatly disfigured the work, but would have been a great safeguard to the men, had there been an attack. The men of small arms were completely sheltered, except at the moment of firing, and then only their heads would have been exposed. There were 78 pieces of cannon on the wall, and the lines were manned by seven thousand men, to which three thousand men could have been added in an hour. This great piece of work was the production of the citizens and their slaves. A large sum was subscribed to pay laborers. All took their turn at the work—even the ladies, to the number of several hundreds, marched out and carried sods all one day. It was a glorious sight to see the patriotic enthusiasm which prevailed. The British officers who came to Charleston immediately after the peace pronounced it the handsomest and best put together piece of field work they ever saw.

91. *Charleston in 1817*

In the summer of 1817 a Frenchman, the Baron de Montlezun, visited Charleston. His impressions of the city at that time were recorded as follows:

[Baron de Montlezun]

Although the cities of the United States generally resemble each other to a large extent, yet one perceives a certain difference at Charleston. Its lay-out is not so strictly traced; no public building is remarkable for its architectural taste. The streets are wide and furnished with sidewalks, which however, are not paved. The dust is a great annoyance in summer. The houses are for the most part of wood, with some of brick. Many are flush with the street. Churches are numerous and as in the north, have adjacent cemeteries strewn with funeral stones. . . .

The shops and stores appear to be abundantly supplied with the finest European merchandise. There is a rather large number of private carriages. One sees some which are really elegant, as well as some cabriolets. The breed of horses is fine and plentiful . . . .

Offhand I should say that the city has a length of two miles and a breadth of one. Its greatest ornaments are Broad Street, running east and west, and Meeting Street, north and south. Their intersection, marked by the new church [St. Michael's] is rather impressive. The houses which have the best appearance, not because of their architecture, but because of the pleasing nature of the long covered galleries on each floor and their very pretty gardens, are situated on the outskirts of the city. These gardens present a very pleasing effect, particularly at this time when the foliage is in all its freshness. Some are planted in grass and others in vegetables, but they are all generally adorned with rose bushes decked out in their triumphant colors, with fig trees, with native lilacs and with peach trees blossoming in all their brilliance.

South Carolina Historical and Genealogical Magazine, XLIX (1948), 139–51.
Reprinted by permission of The South Carolina Historical Society.

It is very charming, on coming from Havana, to know while you are going through any section of the city after nightfall that you are in perfect safety and do not have to worry about the dagger of the individual that you may hear behind you. Negroes and people of color, free or slave, are obliged by law to be in their houses by ten o'clock in the evening; those who disobey are arrested. . . .

The farms around Charleston grow scarcely anything but truck; it is only at some distance away that they can cultivate rice, corn and cotton, typical products of the country. . . .

Charleston is the chief port of the two Carolinas and of all the southern part of the United States from Chesapeake Bay as far as the frontiers of Florida. The population of Charleston is estimated at 40,000. This city has a theatre; they are building one also at Savannah. The same troupe will play six months in each of these cities. They are undertaking to establish a museum at Charleston, after the example of the northern cities. . . .

There are entire streets here where one sees only French shops, among others, King Street, which is very long; nevertheless nearly all the French who inhabit Charleston are unhappy and wish to return to their country. Several families are to embark shortly to return to France. . . .

The planters of Carolina emigrate to the north during the summer in order to avoid the fevers and other diseases which invariably occur in that season. In the same period the rich merchants also leave Charleston for Philadelphia or New York. Others take refuge at Sullivan's Island to enjoy the sea breeze. . . .

Charleston's theatre on the outside looks like the unattractive home of a middle class citizen. Its interior is small and badly arranged. Its breadth is not more than eighteen feet. It is composed of a pit with benches, with galleries round about, and two rows of boxes, which are more than sufficient for the resident or visiting connoisseurs. It is located on Broad Street . . . .

On the same street, a short distance away, is the Vauxhall, the pompous name given to an enclosure of half an acre which comprises a cafe, baths and several square fathoms of grass plots forming the public garden. Likewise on Broad Street there is the Court House, where the law courts sit. The second story of this building has been set aside as a public library. It contains several rooms . . . . This library is open every day from ten in the morning until two. It contains perhaps twenty or twenty-five thousand volumes. . . .

The bank of the State of South Carolina is just opposite. The building which houses it and which bears its name is unnoteworthy. The jingle of dollars resounds all about . . . .

The Carolinians are no less addicted to spirituous liquors than the inhabitants of the other parts of America. As a result, quarrels are frequent and duels arise from them. . . .

At Charleston, as everywhere else, beautiful women are rare, but you see some very pretty girls. Hardly twenty years old, these roses wither with astonishing rapidity, like northern flowers transplanted beneath the tropic sun. . . .

92. *Need for Transportation in the 1820s*

DESPITE THE FALL IN THE PRICE OF COTTON SOON AFTER THE TURN OF THE NINETEENTH CENTURY, MORE ACREAGE WAS ALLOTED TO ITS GROWTH. LEADERS OF THE STATE, URGING BETTER WATER TRANSPORTATION TO THE PORTS ON THE COAST, ALSO DEMANDED BETTER ROADS TO CROSS SOUTH CAROLINA. IN 1818, SOUTH CAROLINA APPROPRIATED $1,000,000 TO BE EXPENDED WITHIN FOUR YEARS FOR DREDGING RIVERS, CUTTING CANALS, AND IMPROVING OR LAYING OUT NEW TURNPIKES. AMONG THE ROADS WAS THE "STATE ROAD" WHICH CONNECTED CHARLESTON WITH THE UPPER PART OF GREENVILLE, ONE OF THE BRIDGES OF WHICH IS STILL IN EXISTENCE TODAY [POINSETT]. THESE WERE "TOLL" ROADS; A ROUND TRIP FROM COLUMBIA TO CHARLESTON FOR A FOUR-HORSE WAGON WAS $9.00. A REPORT ON THE TIMES FOLLOWS:

[Report by Civil and Military Engineer
of State of South Carolina]

The road system of South Carolina is oppressive and ineffectual. More than eighty thousand laborers are called out to work upon the roads during twelve days of the year. This is not indeed a tax, but it is a loss equivalent to a very heavy tax on the community. Not less than $480,000, at the moderate rate of fifty cents per diem for each laborer, are annually expended on the roads . . . .

I beg leave however respectfully to recommend that a good road be made, extending from Charleston in a northwardly direction about fifty miles; thence to branch off through Camden, Columbia and the head of of the Edisto. The northern branch will enter North-Carolina by Lancaster district. The middle branch ought to pass from Columbia along the ridge between the Tyger and Enoree rivers to the Saluda Gap. A

Report of Civil and Military Engineer of the State of South Carolina, 1818, in David Kohn, comp., *Internal Improvement in South Carolina, 1817–1828* (Washington: n.p., 1938), A–1–22. Copyright 1938, David Kohn. Reprinted by permission of David Kohn.

263

good road over this passage of the Blue Ridge would doubtless attract a great portion of the trade of East Tennessee to this state. The most southern branch might unite with the central road at the passage of the mountains. A road ought to be made leading from Columbia through Winnsborough, Chester and York. . .

In order to promote the establishment of these roads, it would be adviseable to grant conditional charters which should go into operation when stock to a certain amount has been subscribed for this purpose; the legislature taking such a portion of the stock as may be deemed expedient. The causeways over the sections are generally in bad order . . . . That which connects north and south Santee on the mail road to Charleston is divided into portions, and allotted by agreement to the different individuals, who are liable to work on the whole causeway. Many of these sections are in tolerable order, but some . . . are almost impassable. The labor of keeping the causeway in repair is so very burthensome, that it would be better to grant a toll to some individual who would undertake to put and keep it in good order. This is the less objectionable as no produce is transported by this road, which is used only by the mail stages and by traveling carriages.

The principal causeways on the mail stage road to Savannah are Rantole's, the Horseshoe, Pocataligo and Coosawhatchie. On the first a toll is levied, but they are all equally bad. In order to make these causeways good, fascines should be prepared as long as the causeway is wide, firmly bound, and at least one foot in diameter. They ought to be laid across the road in three or four layers, strongly pinned down and covered with mud and sand. A causeway constructed in this manner, from the elasticity of the fascines, is less liable to be cut through by the narrow rimmed wheels of our waggons, than if made in the common method with logs and poles. . . .

The heavy burthen of the tedious and expensive carriage by our present routes, is felt by all who reside in the interior of the state. . . . The expense of labor in this state is great, and the difficulty of procuring workmen has already occasioned a delay in the works contemplated by the last legislature.

[Robert Mills]

South Carolina Canals in 1826:

The Santee river enters the ocean by two mouths. There is a good steam-boat navigation on this stream to the junction of the Congaree and Wateree, and up both these rivers to Camden and Columbia. The Wateree above Camden, to the North Carolina line, is interrupted by four principal falls, around which canals have been cut, except at Rocky Mount, where the work is now going on. The first fall is at the Wateree Canal, which is five miles long, of fifty-two feet, and having six locks; the second is at Rocky Mount, where there is a fall of 121 feet, requiring thirteen locks. . . . The third fall is at the Catawba Canal, where there is a fall of fifty-six feet in three miles. The canal and seven locks here are finished. The fourth fall is at Landsford, where a canal two miles long with five locks completes the navigation. . . . The Congaree is formed by the confluence of the Broad and Saluda rivers, where there is a fall of thirty-four feet, which is overcome by a canal three miles long, and five locks. On the Broad river, the navigation for small boats extends to King's Creek, with the aid of Lockart's Canal, which overcomes a fall of fifty-one feet by seven locks in two miles. . . . Green river, a main branch of the Broad river, extends to a point in the Blue Ridge where this mountain is very low and narrow; on the opposite side of the mountain rises the French Broad, a large branch of the Tennessee. It is confidently presumed that the Atlantic and western waters may be united here by a navigable canal with great comparative ease.

The Saluda river is navigable 120 miles above Columbia. There are three canals on it: First, the Saluda Canal, two miles and a half long, with five locks overcoming a fall of thirty-four feet. Second, Dreher's Canal, one mile long, and with four locks, overcoming a fall of twenty-one feet. Third, Louck's Canal, which has a single lock of six feet lift. . . .

From Winyaw bay to Santee river, the Winyaw Canal, six miles long, has been partly executed, and from the Santee to the head of Owendaw,

Robert Mills, *Statistics of South Carolina* . . . (Charleston: Hurlburt and Lloyd, 1826), 157–60. Mills, the great visionary, pushed the movement to interlink South Carolina by canals and locks to the waters of the Mississippi.

there is good schooner navigation. From the head of Owendaw to schooner navigation on the Wando, the distance is about eight miles; a canal here would require only eight feet depth of digging to be fed with tide water. Wando river enters Charleston Harbor. From Charleston to Savannah, there is a steam boat navigation between the islands and the mainland, with the exception of about half a mile between the Broad and Savannah rivers, where a canal is now cutting. Hence it will be seen, that with fourteen miles of canaling, a good steamboat navigation entirely inland and parallel to the coast, may be effected from the North Carolina to the Georgia lines. . . .

The Cooper river is a good navigable stream to the entrance of Biggin Creek, 34 miles by land from Charleston. From this point to the Santee river, the Santee Canal, 22 miles long, has been constructed, passing a summit 69 feet above the tide waters in Cooper river, and 34 feet above the Santee. There are on this canal thirteen locks. A great part of the produce from the upper Santee, Congaree, Broad, Saluda, Wateree, and Catawba rivers pass this canal in boats carrying 120 bales of cotton, or 25 tons of merchandise.

93. *Slaves and Insurrections*

FROM ITS BEGINNING THE PROVINCE OF SOUTH CAROLINA HAD BEEN CONCERNED WITH SURVIVAL. TO CONTEND WITH THE NUMEROUS ENEMIES, IN TIMES OF NECESSITY SLAVES WERE ARMED DESPITE THE CONTINUING FEAR THAT THE NEGROES WOULD RISE AGAINST THE WHITE POPULATION. SLAVE IMPORTATION, FORBIDDEN BY A LAW WHICH WAS LATER REPEALED, CONTINUED, AND NEGROES POURED IN FROM NORTHERN STATES, WHERE SLAVERY HAD BEEN REJECTED BECAUSE IT HAD PROVED ECONOMICALLY UNFEASIBLE DUE TO THE RIGOROUS WINTER CLIMATE. WHAT WAS PROBABLY THE MOST SERIOUS THREAT TO SOUTH CAROLINA WAS A PLOT HATCHED BY A GROUP OF NEGROES LED BY DENMARK VESEY. VESEY, KNOWN AS A "REMARKABLE MAN," HAD PURCHASED HIS FREEDOM IN 1800 WITH MONEY RECEIVED AS A LOTTERY PRIZE. VESEY WAS A PROSPEROUS CARPENTER AND HAD BUILT UP A FOLLOWING AMONG THE NEGROES. THE FOLLOWING ARE PARTS OF THE TRIAL TESTIMONY.

[Testimony of Jesse, A Slave, Given During
the Trial in July, 1822]

I was invited to Denmark Vesey's house, and when I went, I found several men met together, among whom was Ned Bennett, Peter Poyas, and others whom I did not know. Denmark opened the meeting by saying he had an important secret to communicate to us, which we must not disclose to any one, and if we did, we should be put to instant death.

An Official Report of the Trials of Sundry Negroes Charged with an Attempt to Raise An Insurrection in the State of South Carolina . . . Prepared and Published at the request of the Court. By Lionel H. Kennedy and Thomas Parker (Charleston: James R. Schenck, Printer, 1822), 61, 66–67. Rolla, a slave of Governor Thomas Bennett, was a principal witness.

[Rolla]

The voluntary confession of Rolla to the Court, made after all the evidence had been heard but before his conviction—

I know Denmark Vesey—

On one occasion he asked me what news, I told him none; he replied we are free but the white people here won't let us be so, and the only way is to rise up and fight the whites. I went to his house one night to learn where the meetings were held. I never conversed on the subject with Batteau or Ned.

Vesey told me he was the leader in this plot. I never conversed either with Peter or Mingo. Vesey induced me to join; when I went to Vesey's house there was a meeting there, the room was full of people, but none of them white. That night at Vesey's we determined to have arms made, and each man put in 12½ cents toward that purpose. Though Vesey's room was full I did not know one individual there. At this meeting Vesey said we were to take the Guard-House and Magazine to get arms; that we ought to rise up and fight against the whites for our liberties; he was the first to rise and speak, and he *read to us from the Bible, how the Children of Egypt were delivered out of Egypt from bondage.*

94. Some South Carolina Towns in 1826

In 1826, Robert Mills published his *Statistics of South Carolina*, a combination history, geography, and chamber-of-commerce report for the whole state. The following are some of his descriptions of the towns of the state.

[Robert Mills describes the towns of South Carolina]

GREENVILLE

The village of Greenville is the seat of justice of the District of the same name, and is beautifully situated on a plain, gently undulating. The Reedy river placidly leaves its southern borders previous to precipitating itself in a beautiful cascade, over an immense body of rocks.

The village itself is regularly laid out in squares, and is rapidly improving. It is the resort of much company in the summer, and several respectable and wealthy families have located themselves here on account of the salubrity of the climate. These have induced a degree of improvement which promises to make Greenville one of the most considerable villages in the State. It has been preferred for a residence to Pendleton, perhaps on account of its not being affected so immediately by the cold damps of the mountains, though equally distant from them. Paris Mountain presents a fine relief to the eye, looking north from the village, being only seven miles distant from it . . . .

The public buildings are: A handsome brick courthouse, lately erected; a jail; a Baptist meeting house; and Episcopal church; and two neat buildings for the male and female academy. Of public houses there are three which will vie in accommodation and appearance with any in the State. The private houses are neat; some large and handsome. Two of the former governors of the State had summer retreats here: Governors Allston and Middleton. Judge Thompson's house commands a beautiful

Robert Mills, *Statistics of South Carolina* . . . (Charleston: Hurlburt and Lloyd, 1826), 572–73, 725–26, 498, 559–60, 590–91, 742, 772–73, 523.

view of the village. The number of houses is about 70; the population about 500.

SPARTANBURG

The village of Spartanburg is the seat of the courts of the District. It contains 26 houses, including three law offices, one physician's, one saddler's, one tailor's, and three blacksmith's shops. The population amounts to 300. A handsome and substantial jail, built of granite and soapstone, has been just erected. The court house looks very shabby alongside of it; but an appropriation is made for the erection of a new one, which will correspond to the demands and increasing improvement of the District. There are but three houses of public entertainment in the village . . . .

CEDAR SPRING, SPARTANBURG COUNTY

Cedar Spring is a village that is growing into some importance. It has derived its name from a large cedar tree, that formerly ornamented the banks of the spring; and at present consists of a large Baptist meeting house, nine small but decent dwelling houses, laid out with regularity and facing the spring, 200 yards distant, surrounded by a beautiful grove of oak and hickory trees, which afford most delightful shade. A very select society is formed here, consisting of several respectable families. The census gives 35 whites. An academy is established here, which promises well. In it are taught the Latin and Greek languages, and mathematics, besides the usual course of English studies. During the summer much company resort here to enjoy the salubrity of the place, and to drink of the fine waters of the spring. This spring is about 50 feet in circumference, and has three principal sources, which force their contents to the surface, and form a basin three feet deep. This water contains a small portion of lime. It forms a most delightful cold bath, and experience has proved it beneficial in cases of rheumatism, agues and fevers, ulcers, etc. The known efficacy of the water, the beauty of the site, and of the surrounding landscape, offer powerful attractions to those who are seeking health and pleasure to visit it.

CHERAW

Cheraw is . . . the market for all the produce raised in the country round. It was the first settlement for business made in this section of the state. Old Col. [Joseph] Kershaw established a store here about the same time he did in Camden and Granby. Though much business in a private way was then done, yet the place did not grow into a town until within the last six years; since this period it has progressed with singular rapidity, and now contains about 150 dwelling houses, and 12 or 1300 inhabitants. It is situated on the west side of Pedee river, on a plain which rises 100 feet above the river . . . . Its trade with the back country of North Carolina is becoming extensive. Its cotton trade alone is about 20,000 bales per annum; mostly drawn from that quarter. A steam boat navigation extends up to the town, and two of these vessels (sometimes three) besides a number of bay-boats, are regularly employed in the trade to Charleston and Georgetown. . . . The great western post road now passes through Cheraw; and a line of stages runs each way three times a week, and one to Georgetown once a week. Two weekly papers are printed here, and great promise is held out that this town will become as eminent for the encouragement of literature and the useful arts, as for commerce. Several societies are in embryo, and much intelligence concentrated here.

GEORGETOWN

Georgetown is situated on the north side of Sampit river, near its junction with Winyaw bay, and in a straight line 8½ miles from the sea. . . . The best way to get a proper idea of Georgetown is to view it from the top of some high building. It then appears to be a considerable place. The number of houses is estimated to exceed 300. The white population is between 6 and 700; and the black about 12 or 1400. The public buildings are a court house and jail, and three places of religious worship, one for Episcopalians, one for Baptists, and one for Methodists. The courthouse has been lately erected of brick, and is a great ornament to the town. The jail is well kept, great attention being paid to the comfort and convenience of the prisoners. There is also a public library here, and an institution called the Winyaw Indigo Society, incorporated in 1756. The original design of the founders of this institution was of a patriotic and charitable nature. It had in view the improvement of the culture and manufacture of indigo and the endowment of a free school. The object of the society is now wholly confined to the education of orphan children. . . . The markets are not well supplied with meats; but this is of the less importance as the sea furnishes abundance of fish and oysters. . . . The inhabitants of Georgetown, and its vicinity, have a delightful and salubrious retreat in the sickly season, on North Island, and the adjacent sea islands. . . . Three hours bring the citizens from the town to the sea. The good things of this life are here really enjoyed by the inhabitants in abundance; for the land and the ocean lay their treasures at their feet.

CAMDEN

Camden . . . is the oldest inland town in the State, being settled in 1750, and laid out into regular squares and streets in 1760. It is handsomely situated on a plain, elevated from 70 to 100 feet above the Wateree river, on the east bank of the same, and about a mile from the river. . . . The limits of the town embrace one mile in breadth, from east to west, and one and three-quarters in length, from south to north. . . . The town was much injured during its occupation by the British army in 1780. Since the Revolution it has flourished considerably, and now has about 300 dwelling and other houses; and more than 2000 inhabitants. It possesses a considerable back country trade. The cotton purchased in this place the last year exceeded 20,000 bales. Camden carries on a considerable trade with Charleston; all the cotton being sent there, and in return large quantities of dry goods and groceries are received. The geographical position of this town gives it great advantages for trade; and fully warrants every exertion to be made to improve its facilities of communication with the river. A navigable canal appears to be perfectly practicable . . . . By examining the map of the two states it will be easily seen that wealth and prosperity await this town at no very distant day. Its citizens should therefore prepare for these advantages, by inviting permanent capital and population to the place. . . . The town council have built a large and substantial town-hall, under which is the market place. Adjoining to the town-hall is a handsome subscription library, containing a choice selection of the best authors, particularly in history. In front of this building rises a high tower, containing the staircase, crowned by a cupola, ornamented with a clock, and surmounted by a spire. This spire is a very conspicuous object, enlivens the town, and gives an air of importance to the place.

SUMTER

Sumterville is properly the district town, from the circumstance of its being the seat of justice. . . . Besides a handsome court house and jail, the village contains twelve or thirteen houses, two churches, two or three stores, and a tavern. It was founded in 1800, and lies very central to the district, though not convenient for trade, as there is no navigable water within fifteen miles. Should it be required, there is very little doubt but that the waters of Black river might be rendered navigable, within a short distance of Sumterville.

YORK

The district town is called Yorkville . . . . It is situated centrally to the district, on the dividing ridge between the waters of the Broad and Catawba rivers. The village is regularly laid out in squares; and contains, by the census taken in 1823, 292 whites and 159 blacks; total 451. Of these there are 52 mechanics, 8 lawyers, 2 physicians, and 1 clergyman. There are 8 stores, 5 taverns, a male and female academy, post office, and a printing office, which issues 2 papers weekly; one devoted to agricultural subjects. The number of houses is about 80. . . . There are several neat private houses in and near the village; one formerly belonging to Judge Smith, now the female academy, has a handsome appearance. The academies are in a flourishing state. . . . The increasing prosperity of this village, its salubrious site, interesting scenery, continuity to the mountains, and cheapness of living, will have a tendency to give it a preference in the minds of those who are seeking residence in the upper country.

HAMBURG

Edgefield District contains the new and rapidly rising town of Hamburg, situated on the northeast bank of the Savannah river, opposite to Augusta, in Georgia, and possessing, in every point of view the same advantages for commerce. Hamburg owes its existence to the industry and enterprise of Henry Shultz, and now contains 200 houses and about 1200 inhabitants, although previous to the 1st of July, 1821, not a single house had been erected. There are at present between fifty and sixty stores, which do a vast deal of business. There were received here, in the season of 1821, about 17,000 bales of cotton; and in the fall and winter of 1822, about 26,000; besides tobacco, flour, and other productions, engrossing nearly all the Carolina produce, which before was carried to Augusta. Its rapid and increasing commerce is principally assisted, and indeed produced, by the steamboat navigation between Charleston and this place, first reduced to successful experiment by the indefatigable industry of Mr. Schultz. The steam boats are fitted for the accommodation of passengers, as well as for freight; they carry from 600 to 1000 bales of cotton each, and ply regularly between Hamburg and Charleston, returning with proportionable cargoes of goods.

95. *The Anti-Tariff Resolutions of 1828*

SINCE SOUTH CAROLINA'S COTTON WAS SOLD ON A RELATIVELY FREE WORLD MARKET, WHILE ITS CITIZENS PURCHASED MANUFACTURED GOODS THAT WERE MADE COSTLY BY PROTECTIVE TARIFFS, THE STATE FELT IT- SELF CAUGHT BETWEEN ECONOMIC FORCES THAT IT COULD NOT CONTROL. FOR THIS REASON THE HIGH TARIFFS PASSED BY CONGRESS IN 1824 AND IN 1828 WERE PARTICULARLY DISLIKED BY LEADING SOUTH CAROLINIANS, AND THERE WAS MUCH TALK OF THE STATE'S RIGHT TO "NULLIFY" A FEDERAL LAW. THE "EXPOSITION AND PROTEST" WAS ADOPTED AS A RESO- LUTION BY WHICH THE SOUTH CAROLINA LEGISLATURE IN THE FALL OF 1828 VOICED THIS IDEA OF NULLIFICATION; THE FOLLOWING SELECTION GIVES THE REASONING BEHIND IT.

[Legislature of South Carolina]

Exposition and Protest Resolution:

1st. Because the good people of this Commonwealth believe that the powers of Congress were delegated to it, in trust for the accomplishment of certain specified objects which limit and control them, and that every exercise of them for any other purposes is a violation of the Consti- tution as unwarrantable as the undisguised assumption of substantive, independent powers not granted, or expressly withheld.

2nd. Because the power to lay duties on imports is and, in its very nature, can be, only a means of effecting objects specified by the Con- stitution; since no free government and, least of all, a government of enumerated powers, can of right impose any tax, any more than a penalty which is not at once justified by public necessity, and clearly within the scope and purview of the social compact; and since the right of confining appropriations of the public money to such legitimate and constitutional objects is as essential to the liberties of the people as their unquestionable privilege to be taxed only by their own consent.

South Carolina Statutes at Large, I, 244–45.

275

3rd. Because they believe that the tariff law passed by Congress at its last session, and all other acts of which the principal object is the protection of manufactures, or any other branch of domestic industry, if they be considered as the exercise of a supposed power in Congress to tax the people at its own good will and pleasure, and to apply the money raised to objects not specified in the Constitution, is a violation of these fundamental principles, a breach of a well-defined trust and a perversion of the high powers vested in the Federal Government for federal purposes only.

4th. Because such acts, considered in the light of a regulation of commerce, are equally liable to objection; since, although the power to regulate commerce may, like other powers be exercised so as to protect domestic manufactures, yet is clearly distinguishable from a power to do so both in the nature of the thing and in the common acceptation of the terms, and because the confounding of them would lead to the most extravagant results, since the encouragement of domestic industry implies an absolute control over all the interests, resources and pursuits of a people, and is inconsistent with the idea of any other than a simple, consolidated government.

5th. Because, from the contemporaneous exposition of the Constitution in the numbers of the Federalist (which is cited only because the Supreme Court has recognized its authority), it is clear that the power to regulate commerce was considered by the Convention as only incidentally connected with the encouragement of agriculture and manufactures; and because the power of laying imposts and duties on imports was not understood to justify, in any case, a prohibition of foreign commodities, except as a means of extending commerce by coercing foreign nations to a fair reciprocity in their intercourse with us, or for some other bona fide commercial purpose.

6th. Because, whilst the power to protect manufactures is nowhere expressly granted to Congress, nor can be considered as necessary and proper to carry into effect any specified power, it seems to be expressly reserved to the States by the tenth section of the first article of the Constitution.

7th. Because, even admitting Congress to have a constitutional right to protect manufactures by the imposition of duties or by regulations of commerce, designed principally for that purpose, yet a tariff of which the operation is grossly unequal and oppressive is such an abuse of power as is incompatible with the principles of a free government and the great ends of civil society—justice and equality of rights and protection.

8th. Finally, because South Carolina, from her climate, situation and peculiar institutions is, and must ever continue to be, wholly dependent upon agriculture and commerce not only for her prosperity, but for her very existence as a State; because the valuable products of her soil—the blessings by which Divine Providence seems to have designed to compensate for the great disadvantages under which she suffers in other respects—are among the very few that can be cultivated with any profit by slave labor; and if, by the loss of her foreign commerce, these products should be confined to an inadequate market, the fate of this fertile State would be poverty and utter desolation; her citizens, in despair, would emigrate to more fortunate regions, and the whole frame and constitution of her civil polity, be impaired and deranged, if not dissolved entirely.

Deeply impressed with these considerations, the representatives of the good people of this Commonwealth, anxiously desiring to live in peace with their fellow citizens, and to do all that in them lies to preserve and perpetuate the Union of the States and the liberties of which it is the surest pledge—but feeling it to be their bounden duty to expose and resist all encroachments upon the true spirit of the Constitution, lest an apparent acquiescence in the system of protecting duties should be drawn into precedent—do, in the name of the Commonwealth of South Carolina, claim to enter upon the Journals of the Senate their protest against it as unconstitutional, oppressive and unjust.

96. *The Nullification Controversy, 1832–1833*

THE PROTEST OF 1828 WAS IGNORED BY CONGRESS, AND IN 1832
ANOTHER HIGH TARIFF WAS PASSED. THIS TIME SOUTH CAROLINA
CALLED A FORMAL CONVENTION OF THE PEOPLE, FOR THE PURPOSE OF
NULLIFYING THE FEDERAL TARIFF. THIS BEGAN A SERIES OF EVENTS:
THE PASSAGE OF THE FEDERAL FORCE BILL AND THE COMPROMISE TARIFF
OF 1833; THE ADOPTION OF A SPECIAL TEST OATH FOR ALL SOUTH
CAROLINA OFFICIALS; THE REPEAL OF THE NULLIFICATION ORDINANCE;
AND THE NULLIFICATION OF THE FORCE BILL BY THE SOUTH CAROLINA
CONVENTION, BEFORE ITS ADJOURNMENT. THE STATE WAS SHARPLY
DIVIDED INTO "UNIONISTS" AND "NULLIFICATION LEADERS." NULLIFIERS
ASSUMED THAT, IF THE ONE "RIGHT" FOR WHICH THEY WERE CON-
TENDING WAS SURRENDERED, "THE WHOLE FABRIC OF GOVERNMENT WAS
WORTHLESS." THEY DECLARED THAT THE SUPREME COURT WAS A
"WILLING TOOL." AND THAT THE STATES OF THE UNION WOULD BE
TRAMPLED BY A CONGRESS THAT HAD NO CHECKS AND BALANCES.
FRANCIS W. PICKENS (WHOM MANY HAVE TERMED THE MAN MOST
RESPONSIBLE FOR THE CIVIL WAR), DECLARED: "I AM FOR ANY EXTREME,
EVEN 'WAR UP TO THE HILT,' RATHER THAN GO DOWN IN INFAMY AND
SLAVERY 'WITH A GOVERNMENT OF UNLIMITED POWERS'." OTHER
LEADING NULLIFIERS WERE CHANCELLOR WILLIAM HARPER, ROBERT
BARNWELL RHETT, EDITOR OF THE *Charleston Mercury*, WILLIAM C.
PRESTON, WADDY THOMPSON, ARMISTEAD BURT (IN WHOSE HOME IN
ABBEVILLE THE LAST MEETING OF THE CONFEDERATE CABINET WAS
HELD), NATHANIEL HEYWARD, ROBERT J. TURNBULL, JUDGE COLCOCK,
ELDRED SIMKINS, A. P. BUTLER, JAMES HAMILTON, JR., H. L. PINCKNEY,
AND, OF COURSE, JOHN C. CALHOUN. UNIONISTS INCLUDED JOEL R.
POINSETT, JAMES L. PETIGRU, WILLIAM DRAYTON, HENRY MIDDLETON;
JUDGES DAVID JOHNSON, WILLIAM JOHNSON, J. B. O'NEALL, THOMAS
LEE, AND J. S. RICHARDSON; GOVERNORS RICHARD I. MANNING, JOHN
TAYLOR, AND THOMAS BENNETT; CHANCELLOR DESAUSSURE, AND
OTHERS. ONE OF THE MOST OUTSPOKEN UNIONISTS WAS BENJAMIN F.
PERRY, WHOSE REACTION TO THE TEST OATH IS RECORDED HERE AMONG
THE EXCERPTS.

The South Carolina Nullification Ordinance,
November 24, 1832:

An ordinance to nullify certain acts of the Congress of the United States, purporting to be laws laying duties and imposts on the importation of foreign commodities.

Whereas the Congress of the United States, by various acts, purporting to be acts laying duties and imposts on foreign imports, but in reality intended for the protection of domestic manufactures, and the giving of bounties to classes and individuals engaged in particular employments, at the expense and to the injury and oppression of other classes and individuals . . . hath exceeded its just powers under the Constitution, which confers on it no authority to afford such protection, and hath violated the true meaning and intent of the Constitution, which provides for equality in imposing the burdens of taxation upon the several states and portions of the confederacy: And whereas the said Congress exceeding its just power to impose taxes and collect revenue for the purpose of effecting and accomplishing the specific objects and purposes which the Constitution of the United States authorizes it to effect and accomplish, hath raised and collected unnecessary revenue for objects unauthorized by the Constitution:

We, therefore, the people of the State of South Carolina in convention assembled, do declare and ordain, and it is hereby declared and ordained, that the several acts and parts of acts of the Congress of the United States, purporting to be laws for the imposing of duties and imposts on the importation of foreign commodities, and now having actual operation and effect within the United States, and more especially, an act entitled "An Act to alter and amend the several acts imposing duties on imports," approved on the nineteenth day of May, 1828, and also an act entitled "An Act in alteration of the several acts imposing duties on imports," approved on the fourteenth day of July, 1832, are unauthorized by the Constitution of the United States, and violate the true meaning and intent thereof, and are null, void, and no law, nor binding upon this State, its officers or citizens; and all promises, contracts, and obligations, made or entered into, or to be made or entered into, with purpose to

South Carolina Statutes at Large, I, 201–203.

secure the duties imposed by the said Acts, and all judicial proceedings which shall be hereafter had in affirmance thereof, are and shall be held utterly null and void. . . .

And we, the people of South Carolina, to the end that it may be fully understood by the government of the United States, and the people of the co-States, that we are determined to maintain this, our ordinance and declaration, at every hazard, do further declare that we will not submit to the application of force, on the part of the Federal Government, to reduce this State to obedience; but that we will consider the passage, by Congress, of any act authorizing the employment of a military or naval force against the State of South Carolina, her constituted authorities or citizens; or any act abolishing or closing the ports of this State, or any of them, or otherwise obstructing the free ingress and egress of vessels to and from the said ports, or any other act on the part of the Federal Government, to coerce the State, shut up her ports, destroy or harrass her commerce, or to enforce the acts hereby declared to be null and void, otherwise than through the civil tribunals of the country, as inconsistent with the longer continuance of South Carolina in the Union; and that the people of this State will thenceforth hold themselves absolved from all further obligation to maintain or preserve their political connection with the people of the other States, and will forthwith proceed to organize a separate government, and do all other acts and things which sovereign and independent States may of right to do.

The Federal Force Bill of 1833:

Be it enacted by the Senate and House of Representatives of the United States of America, in Congress assembled, That whenever, by reason of unlawful obstructions, combinations, or assemblages of persons, it shall become impracticable, in the judgment of the President, to execute the revenue laws, and collect the duties on imports in the ordinary way . . . it shall and may be lawful for the President to direct that the custom house . . . be . . . kept in any secure place within some port . . . either upon land or on board any vessel; and, in that case, it shall be the duty of the collector to reside at such place, and there

Public Statutes at Large of the United States, IV, 632–35.

to detain all vessels and cargoes . . . until the duties imposed on said cargoes, by law, be paid in cash . . . and in such cases it shall be unlawful to take the vessel or cargo from the custody of the proper officer . . . unless by process from some court of the United States; and in case of any attention, or assemblage of persons too great to be overcome by the officers of the customs, it shall . . . be lawful for the President of the United States . . . to employ such part of the land or naval forces, or militia of the United States, as may be deemed necessary for the purpose of preventing the removal of such vessel or cargo, and protecting the officers of the customs in retaining the custody thereof.

The Test Oath, Passed by the South Carolina Legislature, 1833:

I do solemnly swear or affirm that I will be faithful and true allegiance bear to the State of South Carolina so long as I may continue a citizen thereof; and that I am duly qualified, according to the Constitution of this State, to exercise the office to which I have been appointed; and that I will, to the best of my abilities, discharge the duties thereof, and preserve, protect and defend the Constitution of this State and of the United States. So help me God.

The Repeal of the Nullification Ordinance,
March 15, 1833:

Whereas the Congress of the United States, by an Act recently passed, has provided for such a reduction and modification of the duties upon foreign imports, as will ultimately reduce them to the Revenue Standard —and provides that no more revenue shall be raised than may be necessary to defray the economical expenses of the Government:

Yates Snowden, ed., *History of South Carolina*, 5 vols. (Chicago: The Lewis Publishing Co., 1920), II, 600.

South Carolina Statutes at Large, I, 380.

It is therefore ordained and declared, that the Ordinance adopted by
this Convention on the 24th day of November last, entitled "An Ordinance to Nullify Certain Acts of the Congress of the United States,
. . . ," and all acts passed by the General Assembly of this State, in
pursuance thereof, be henceforth deemed and held to have no force or
effect . . . .

The Nullification of the Force Bill, March 18, 1833:

An ordinance to nullify an act of Congress of the United States,
entitled "An Act further to provide for the collection of duties on
imports," commonly called the Force Bill:

We, the people of the State of South Carolina in Convention assembled, do declare and ordain, that the Act of the Congress of the
United States, entitled "An Act further to provide for the collection of
duties on imports," approved the 2nd day of March, 1833, is unauthorized by the Constitution of the United States, subversive of that
Constitution, and destructive of public liberty; and that the same is, and
shall be deemed, null and void, within the limits of this State; and it
shall be the duty of the Legislature, at such time as they may be necessary to prevent the enforcement thereof, and to inflict proper penalties
on any person who shall do any act in execution or enforcement of the
same within the limits of this State.

We do further ordain and declare, that the allegiance of the citizens
of this State, while they continue such, is due to the said State; and
that obedience only, and not allegiance, is due by them to any other
power or authority, to whom a control over them has been or may be
delegated by the State; and the General Assembly of the said State is
hereby empowered, from time to time, when they may deem it proper,
to provide for the administration to citizens and officers of the State or
such of the said officers as they may think fit, of suitable oaths or
affirmations, binding them to the observance of such allegiance, and
abjuring all other allegiance; and, also, to define what shall amount

South Carolina Statutes at Large, I, 400–401.

to a violation of their allegiance, and to provide the proper punishment for such violation.

[Benjamin F. Perry on the Test Oath:]

By the magic of this same spirit of Nullification we have had invented new Oaths of Allegiance, and new Bills of Treason, for the purpose of entrapping the consciences and crushing the spirit of Freemen! Although we have lived happily and prospered for the last fifty years under the old constitutional oath, a new one is now to be required, in order to prevent our patriotism extending itself beyond the Savannah river on the one side, and the western mountains and eastern swamps of Carolina on the other. For what was this oath of allegiance intended, if it was not for the purpose of weakening the bonds of this Union, and confining to a single spot that patriotism which should be as broad as our country? I ask if this amendment was not made avowedly to teach us—yes, swear us—that our first and highest duty is to South Carolina? This principle established, the Sovereignty of the State must follow, and a rapid stride has been made towards the dissolution of the Union.

Benjamin F. Perry, *Biographical Sketches of Eminent American Statesmen* (Philadelphia: The Ferree Press, 1887), 79–80.

97. Coming of the Railroads

IN THE 1800s THE FASCINATING NEW IDEA OF RAILROADS CROSSING THE STATE EXCITED THE PEOPLE. THERE WAS MUCH TALK OF THE "BLUE RIDGE RAILROAD," WHICH WOULD CONNECT THE PORT CITY OF CHARLESTON WITH KNOXVILLE, TENNESSEE, ACROSS THE MOUNTAINS. THE RAILROAD NEVER BECAME AN ACTUALITY, BUT, BEFORE THE VENTURE ENDED, THE STATE OF SOUTH CAROLINA HAD BEEN BILKED OF ABOUT 16 MILLION DOLLARS. THE DEMISE OF THE RAILROAD WAS LAID CHIEFLY AT THE DOOR OF ITS MOST FORMIDABLE OPPONENT, STATE SENATOR E. G. PALMER OF RIDGEWAY. AT FIRST, HOWEVER, THE IDEA WAS ENTHUSIASTICALLY RECEIVED, AND JOHN C. CALHOUN WROTE A LETTER TO THE *Messenger* CONCERNING AN EXPLORATORY VISIT WHICH HE, THE INDIAN AGENT JAMES MCKINNEY, COLONEL JAMES GADSDEN, AND W. SLOAN MADE TO THE VICINITY OF THE KEOWEE RIVER. THE SECOND EXCERPT IS PRESIDENT ELIAS HORRY'S REPORT ON THE FOUNDING OF THE CHARLESTON AND HAMBURG RAILROAD; THE NEXT IS A DESCRIPTION OF A "SULKY RIDE"; AND THE LAST IS A REPORT BY A BRITISH TRAVELER, ALEXANDER MCKAY.

[From John C. Calhoun]

To the Editor of the Messenger: Fort Hill, Sept. 22, 1836
Dear Sir,—Believing it to be the duty of every citizen to lay before the public such facts as may come to his knowledge and which may contribute to the selection of the route for the contemplated Rail Road from Charleston to Louisville, Lexington and Cincinnati, I have selected the Messenger as the medium of communicating some information that may not be unimportant which I acquired in a recent visit in company with Col. Gadsden, to the portion of the Alleghany chain lying along the head waters of the Keowee River.

Concluding, as well from what I had heard as from the peculiar formation of the mountains in that quarter that there was a favourable prospect of a gap, I determined to visit the region personally, in order

The Messenger (Pendleton, S.C.), September 22, 1836.

to ascertain how firm my impression might be correct. Knowing from a conversation with Col. Gadsden last fall, that he had similar impressions, I requested him by letter to join me, if his duties and convenience would permit, with which he readily complied, as well to test the truth of his own, as my impression. Mr. W. Sloan, my neighbor at my request, accompanied us; and we were joined near the mountains, by Mr. James M'Kinney, whose thorough knowledge of that section of the mountains was of the greatest service. We commenced our examination near his residence, and extended it to the gap in the mountain, from which the White Water, one of the Western branches of the Keowee, takes its source, and thence down the Tuckasiege, which rises on the Western side of the same gap, to where it joins Little Tennessee; the distance about 45 miles by estimation. On our return, we examined the parts of the route that required further attention, and extended the examination from where we first commenced, across the Keowee River just below the old Fort along the old Indian path to Mr. Perry's. From thence to where the route would strike the dividing ridge between the waters of Saluda and Savannah, about 8 or 10 miles below Pickensville, there can be no difficulty, as there can be none from that point to Charleston.

Our entire examination, then extends from Mr. Perry's to the mouth of the Tuckasiege; a line of about 84 miles, to which we devoted eight days of incessant labour, examining on foot the most difficult and inaccessible points.

The result was satisfactory beyond expectation. I can only speak for myself. Col. Gadsden will of course reserve his opinion till it is his duty to speak officially.

In order to give anything like a satisfactory view of the route, over which we passed, it will be necessary to divide it into sections, and to present the facts connected with each, separately. The first section proceeding west, extends from Mr. Perry's to the point near Mr. M'Kinney's at which we commenced our examination on our way out. Its length is about 10 miles. It is cut by the Keowee River, which as its banks are high in places and the river small, may be passed at a great elevation and moderate cost. The rise towards the mountain from the commencement to the termination of the section can be conveniently overcome by gradually ascending eastern slope of the river ridge till it strikes some convenient point for crossing, and then ascending in like manner to the point where the section terminates, on the summit of the dividing ridge between Little River and Keowee. The rise, it is believed, will not any where exceed 25 feet in the mile. The next section, extends from the point where the last terminated to the top of the Alleghany. It terminates just at the point where the Chatuga mountain joins the Alleghany. At this point, the White Water, one of the branches of the Keowee, which rises on the summit of the Mountain, (a stream about the size of the 18 mile) after cutting down and turning the Chatuga mountain, leaps from the top of the Alleghany in two perpendicular falls near to each other about 45 or 50 feet, and then continues its rapid descent to the Valley below. The length of the section is about 29 miles; and from the best information we can obtain, the elevation to be overcome will not exceed 30 feet to the mile. The line of ascent may be conveniently lengthened or shortened to a considerable extent to suit the grading so as to diminish the rise probably below what I have estimated, or if it should be thought advisable to reduce it to the lowest rate, it may be effected with little expense or delay, and without a stationary Engine, but using the power which the waters of the White Water afford, & which is more than sufficient to elevate the heaviest train.

The next section is on the top of the Alleghany, and extends from the termination of the last, where the White Water leaps from the top of the mountain to the east to the point where the Tuckasiege makes a similar leap but to the West. The length of the line is about 16 or 17 miles. It passes through two Vallies of nearly equal length and extent, divided by a low narrow ridge of about 150 feet high. The two vallies are nearly on the same level. The one on the east of the ridge is called Cashier's and that on the west Yellow Valley, from the brownish yellow which the decayed fern gives to it. The eastern extends from South-east to northwest from the fall of the White Water where the valley opens, about 8 miles; and from northest to southwest from the Chimney Top to the Whiteside mountains—two elevated peaks rising a thousand feet, or more, above the Valley. The White Water collects its waters in the Eastern and the Tuckasiege in the Western Valley. The sources of both are on the top of the low ridge that separates them, and but a few feet apart. The two Vallies form the gap, which we named the Carolina Gap, to distinguish from the Raburn or Georgia Gap, which is 35 or 40 miles to the Southwest of it.

The low ridge or the crest of the Alleghany, as it may be called, that separates the Vallies, may be easily passed at a low angle by gradually ascending on the slopes on the Southwest side of Cashier's to its summit and descending in like manner on the opposite side, on the Southwestern slope of the Yellow Valley; but it would be both shorter and cheaper in the long run to pierce the ridge with a tunnel which would give a beautiful and nearly level run for 16 miles on the summit of the Allegahany, from fall to fall.

The next section extends from the termination of the last, at the head of the falls of the Tuckasiege to some point down the River sufficiently distant to afford a gradual descent along the sides of the mountains through which it flows.

President Elias Horry's Report on the
Founding of the Charleston-Hamburg Railroad, October, 1833:

In South Carolina, particularly in Charleston, a respectable portion of our citizens wisely determined that railroads would be eminently beneficial to the State; that they would revive the diminishing commerce of our city and tend to bring back the depreciated value of property to its former standard. . . . Industry and talent had lost encouragement and met not their merited rewards. These evils had commenced and accumulated within a few years and were still progressing; and during this same period the Northern and Eastern States and cities had attained to great and increasing affluence and prosperity, while those of the South were gradually falling into decay. To improve, therefore, the welfare of Charleston and forward as much as possible her prosperity and that of the State, our best merchants and most intelligent men decided in favor of adopting the railroad system. The plan was that a railroad be located from Charleston to Hamburg, on the Savannah river, and that a branch be extended from the main line when completed to Columbia, and afterward another branch to Camden. A petition was accordingly presented to the Legislature on this important subject, for the establishment of a company, and granting to it a charter. . . . The present charter of the South Carolina Canal and Railroad Company was granted on the 30th of January, 1828. . . .

To forward this desirable purpose, the Chamber of Commerce met on the 4th of February, 1828, and appointed a committee of ten to inquire into the effects likely to result to the trade and general interest of the city of Charleston by the establishment of a railroad communication

Yates Snowden, ed., *History of South Carolina,* 5 vols. (Chicago: The Lewis Publishing Co., 1920), II, 596–98.

between the city and the town of Hamburg; and they were authorized to collect and report every information on the subject of railroads which they may deem necessary to form an opinion on the probable cost of and the revenue likely to be derived from the enterprise. . . .

A number of our citizens were also desirous of ascertaining the levels and the situation of the lands through which the location of a railroad could be made between Charleston and Hamburg. To obtain this information, two respectable surveyors were employed, and Col. Abraham Blanding, of Columbia, gave to them his friendly assistance and experience . . . . The report of the committee was published and that of the surveyors was, on the 15th of March, laid before the citizens who caused the survey, and before the commissioners . . . . The commissioners opened the subscription books on the 17th of March. Three thousand five hundred and one shares were subscribed for in Charleston; at Columbia, Camden and Hamburg, none. . . .

The stockholders were organized as a company on the 12th of May, 1828, by the commissioners, at the City Hall in Charleston. They elected the late William Aiken, Esq., president, and twelve other gentlemen directors who, together, formed the Direction . . . .

The Direction entered promptly on the discharge of their duties. Correspondences were formed in England and at the North. Surveyors and civil engineers were employed and other officers were appointed. Surveys for information were made and a line with a view to location was nearly completed. The railroad had been commenced agreeably to the stipulations of the charter. The number of stockholders had increased, various contracts had been made and most in full progress, when [President William Aiken] died on the 5th of March, 1831, in the midst of his usefulness . . . .

The compass of this address will not permit me to detail the proceedings of the Direction in the prosecution of this great work . . . . Numerous have been the duties of the Direction, and sometimes they have been arduous. They now have the satisfaction to announce to the public the completion of the road from the Depository, at Lines Street, to Hamburg.

How delightful, fellow citizens, it is to the mind of an individual when he can reflect that he has contributed by his exertions to the welfare of his fellowmen and to that of his country. The fact must be acknowledged, and the stockholders of the South Carolina Canal and Railroad Company, especially those who engaged early in the enterprise, must feel that delight in a very eminent degree, when they reflect on the public good they have rendered to this State and to a large portion of their country, by constructing a railroad from the vicinity of Charleston to Hamburg, a distance of 136 miles; and this, too, through opposition, as well as encouragement, and through all the difficulties, labors and expenditures attendant on the execution of so great a work.

[W. H. Wills]

A sulky ride through South Carolina in 1837:

. . . The village of Bennettsville, or Marlboro Court House . . . is comparatively a new and really a nice little place. It has several large and handsome dwellings; a stone Courthouse; a tavern; six or seven stores; a grogshop and two pretty churches, one a Methodist and the other a Baptist. Ten miles further, I saw the first good land and the first corn up that have presented themselves since leaving Edgecombe county. The spring has been so late and cold that corn could not come up. Vegetation too, has scarcely begun to spring . . . ; if it were not for the plowed fields and occasionally a budding tree one would scarcely suppose it the 10th of April. Half an hour more brought me to Pedee River, which I crossed on a ferry boat. . . . Two miles from Big Bluff, where I crossed the river, is Society Hill, at which place I arrived between 11 and 12 o'clock and where I got my dinner at the only public house in the place. It derives its name from the circumstance of several families removing from Long Bluff and settling here some years ago, and once was not only a pretty place, but select society resided here. But like all the towns and villages which I have yet seen (Bennettsville excepted) it is on the decline. About two o'clock I departed and took the road to Camden, distance 51 miles. Four miles below Society Hill I took a left hand road said to be four or five miles further but much better. At about sunset I reached a Mr. Parrot's, to where I was recommended, having rode today 35 miles.

Tuesday, April 11. I had my horse fed and got my breakfast, but on offering to pay, the good man would not receive anything, but insisted

W. H. Wills, "A Sulky Ride in 1837," in Southern History Association, *Publications*, VI (November, 1902), 476–82.

on my calling on him again if I passed that way. 6½ o'clock I started for Camden. . . . 1½ o'clock I stopped at a Mr. J. Peebles', where I got my dinner and horse fed, and 3½ o'clock left for and arrived at Camden at 6½ o'clock. I have thus passed over 35 miles today, the last twenty the most dreary I have ever seen—nought save pine trees and sand hills to be seen. Not a bird was heard, nor even a frog dared raise his croaking voice in that drear land. I felt thankful and glad when I arrived at a place of rest. In Camden I put up at McAdams' Hotel, where I was very well attended to. . . . The streets looked clean, as if attention was paid to them. No shade trees, however, and I must think it is very warm in the summer.

Wednesday, April 12. After getting an early breakfast at the Hotel, and paying for it pretty well, too, at 6 o'clock I bid adieu to Camden and took the road to Columbia. . . . Two miles from Camden I came to the Wateree river which I crossed on a ferry-boat and paid higher than I have ever paid ferriage before—50¢. There was formerly a bridge at this place, but it has decayed and not much standing. I understand it is contemplated to rebuild it. I soon found that the road was as bad as had been represented. Long hills of sand up which I must slowly toil and then a level equally heavy. In almost every part of the road are large turn-outs to avoid the main track. . . . A ride of 17 miles brought me at 11½ o'clock to Mr. Rabbs, the stage house, where my horse was fed and I got dinner. Ham and eggs again. . . . A little before night I entered the city of Columbia and put up at Clarke's Hotel, now kept by Roach and Thompson. This is a handsome house, appears to be well regulated, accommodations are good, and I was treated very politely . . . . I have often heard that Columbia was one of the handsomest towns in the Southern states, and I prepared myself not to expect too much. But I was not at all disappointed. It is indeed a lovely place. The town stands upon a commanding eminence, regularly laid off. The streets are wide and straight and very clean, and the houses all neat and apparently recently painted. This is the seat of government for South Carolina. . . . The population numbers about 6000 inhabitants.

Thursday morning, 13th, at 6 o'clock I was again on the road. One mile's ride brought me to the Congaree River, which I crossed on a good bridge, just below where that River and the Saluda come together . . . . Eleven miles from this river stands the village of Lexington which I passed through. I saw nothing here to attract my attention or elicit a remark, only that the notions of the inhabitants in regard to building run in the same stream. There are fifteen to twenty-five houses in the village and almost every dwelling I saw is built with a shed in front and one in the rear of the building. Thinks I to myself, these folks like sheds better than I do, and if I was to build here I should choose to be singular. 8 miles farther brought me to Mr. Poindexter's where I got a good dinner. Yes, a real good dinner, for in addition to ham and eggs we had boiled meat, greens, etc., and best of all, sweet potatoes and milk. O, what luxury! Milk!—the first I have seen since leaving Tarboro. . . . At 2 o'clock I started and at dark reached the house of Mr. Watson, this day riding 40 miles. After having my horse well provided for, I partook with a good appetite of a nice supper. The coffee was really first rate. These people make a good appearance and I presume are wealthy. The house is neat and well furnished, at least the drawing room. A good carpet, handsome chairs, mantel, glass, etc. The country for the last thirty miles has somewhat improved. . . . The farms are more neat, the houses better and show much more comfort. I passed one or two gardens quite tasteful in their arrangements and a fine collection of flowers . . . .

Friday morning, 14th. I got breakfast and at 7 o'clock took a left hand road at Watson's for Augusta. . . . Hungry, hot and tired I stopped at 12 o'clock at the house of a Mr. Wise, 18 miles from Watson's . . . . I was somewhat surprised to find the road over which I had just travelled rocky and hilly . . . , more undulating than any country I have seen as low down as this. In the afternoon I renewed my journey and arrived at Augusta after night and put up at the "Eagle and Phoenix Hotel." 3 miles opposite to Augusta is the little village of Hamburg in South Carolina. I saw nothing about it remarkable and I believe it is only known as the depot of the "Hamburg and Charleston Railroad."

[Alexander McKay on Railroad Travel in the 1840s:]

From Columbia I proceeded by railway towards Augusta. For the first half of the way the country was very uninteresting, being com-

Allan Nevins, ed., *America Through British Eyes* (New York: Oxford University Press, 1948), 249–50. Copyright 1948 by Oxford University Press, Inc. New edition revised and enlarged. First edition 1923 *(American Social History as Recorded by British Travellers)*, copyright by Allan Nevins. Reprinted by permission of Oxford University Press.

paratively flat and sandy, and covered, for the most part, with the interminable pitchpine. Indeed, the pine barrens extend, with but little interruption, almost the entire way between the two places, the distance between them being from eighty to ninety miles. Here and there are some long stretches of marshy ground, over which the railway is carried, not by embankments, but upon piles, which impart to it a dangerous and shaky appearance. I was not surprised at the anxiety which almost every passenger manifested to get over these portions of the line without accident, especially when I learnt that there was danger in being detained upon them after-nightfall. It was not simply therefore, by the dread of a breakneck accident that they were animated, their fears being divided between such a possibility and any contingency which might expose them to the nocturnal miasmas of the marshes.

98. *Columbia in 1848*

The following is a description of Columbia as seen by Alexander McKay in 1848.

[Alexander McKay]

Columbia, the seat of government in South Carolina, is situated on the banks of a river called the Congaree, a stream of petty dimensions in America, but one which would cut a very respectable figure in the geography of a European kingdom. . . . One would think that in selecting a site for their capital, fertility in the circumjacent region would be a sine qua non with any people. But not so with the Carolinians, who, in order to have it in as central a position as possible, have placed it in the midst of one of the most barren districts of the State. Luckily, its limited population renders it easy of supply, for it is difficult to see how a large community could subsist on such a spot, unless they could accommodate themselves to pine cones as their chief edible. But Palmyra managed to subsist in the desert, and so may Columbia in the wilderness, which is the only appellation which can properly be bestowed upon the dreary and almost unbroken expanse of pine forest which surrounds it.

Notwithstanding all its disadvantages in point of position, Columbia is, on the whole, rather an interesting little town. There is about it an air of neatness and elegance, which betokens it to be the residence of a superior class of people—many of the planters whose estates are in the neighborhood making it the place of their abode; as well as the governor, the chief functionaries of the State subordinate to him, and some of the judges. There is little or nothing connected with the government buildings worthy of attention, their dimensions being very limited, and

Allan Nevins, ed., *America Through British Eyes* (New York: Oxford University Press, 1948), 248–49. Copyright 1948 by Oxford University Press, Inc. New edition revised and enlarged. First edition 1923 *(American Social History as Recorded by British Travellers)*, copyright by Allan Nevins. Reprinted by permission of Oxford University Press.

their style of a simple and altogether unambitious description. The streets, as in the majority of the southern towns of more recent origin, are long, straight, and broad, and are lined, for the most part with trees . . . . Here in this small, quiet, and unimposing-looking town are conducted the affairs of a sovereign state at a cost of under £50,000, including not only the salaries of all its functionaries political, judicial, and municipal, but also the payments of the members of the legislature during their attendance at its annual sitting.

99. *Slavery versus Emancipation*

THE MOST IMPORTANT QUESTION BETWEEN THE EARLY AND THE MID-1850's WAS THAT OF SLAVERY VERSUS ABOLITIONISM. EVERY SECTION OF AMERICA WAS CONCERNED WITH IT, AND EVERYONE HAD AN OPINION ON THE GREAT SOCIAL CONTROVERSY. THE SOUTH, ESPECIALLY, DEFENDED SLAVERY ON THE BASIS OF "STATE'S RIGHTS." THE THREE EXCERPTS HERE SHOW THE FEELINGS OF THE TIMES.

[Captain Basil Hall on South Carolina Slavery, 1828]

It appears that when the Negroes go to the field in the morning, it is the custom to leave such children behind as are too young to work. Accordingly, we found a sober old matron in charge of three dozen shining urchins, collected together in a house near the centre of the village. Over the fire hung a large pot of hominy, a preparation of Indian corn, making ready for the little folks' supper, and a very merry, happy looking party they seemed. The parents and such children as are old enough to be useful go out to work at daybreak, taking their dinner with them to eat on the ground. They have another meal towards the close of day after coming home. Generally, also, they manage to cook up a breakfast, but this must be provided by themselves out of their own earnings, during those hours which it is the custom, in all plantations, to allow the Negroes to work on their own account . . . .

A special task for each slave is . . . pointed out daily by the overseer; and as soon as this is completed in a proper manner, the laborer may go home to work at his own piece of ground, or to tend his pigs and poultry, or play with his children—in a word, to do as he pleases. The assigned task is sometimes got over by two o'clock in the day, though this is rare, as the work generally lasts till four or five o'clock. I often saw gangs of Negroes at work till sunset.

Allan Nevins, ed., *America Through British Eyes* (New York: Oxford University Press, 1948), 117–18. Copyright 1948 by Oxford University Press, Inc. New edition revised and enlarged. First edition 1923 *(American Social History as Recorded by British Travellers)*, copyright by Allan Nevins.

295

We went into several of the cottages, which were uncommonly neat and comfortable and might have shamed those of many countries I have seen. Each hut was divided into small rooms or compartments fitted with regular bed places; besides which, they all had chimneys and doors, and some, though only a few of them, possessed the luxury of windows. I counted twenty-eight huts, occupied by one hundred and forty souls, or about five in each. This number included sixty children. . . .

It will be easily understood, indeed, that one of the greatest practical evils of slavery arises from persons who have no command over themselves being placed, without any control, in command of others. Hence passion without system must very often take the place of patience and method; and the lash—that prompt but terrible instrument of power, and one so dangerous in irresponsible hands—cuts all the Gordian knots of this difficulty, and, right or wrong, forces obedience by the stern agony of fear, the lowest of all motives to action. The consequence, I believe, invariably is that where service is thus, as it were, beaten out of men, the very minimum of work, in the long run, is obtained. Judicious slave holders, therefore, whether they be humane persons or not, generally discover, sooner or later, that the best policy by far is to treat these unfortunate dependents with as much kindness as the nature of the discipline will allow.

[William John Grayson on Slavery, 1850s]

The question of Negro slavery in the United States has been discussed for many years. . . . In a broad view of the transfer of the African to America, it may be regarded not merely as an act of commercial enterprise or avarice, but as an emigration of the blacks to a new country. It was an emigration hardly more forced than that of the starving Irish peasantry and not attended perhaps with greater suffering. The Negro was brought to a country where he could be trained to those habits of industry which alone constitute the foundation of civilization and make it possible for a people to improve. The advancement of the

"Autobiography of William John Grayson," *South Carolina Historical and Genealogical Magazine*, LI (1950), 29–30. Reprinted by permission of The South Carolina Historical Society.

black in all relations, civil, social or religious, must come from the white race. The Negro has never been able to originate a civilization. The white man cannot live in the Negro's country. The Negro must therefore be brought to the home of the white. This has been accomplished by slavery only. The benefits bestowed on the Negro are obvious. The slaves of North America are the most civilized of the African race. In Africa there is no black tribe comparable to the four millions of slaves in the American States. They have reached this point of improvement under the master's care. No matter what the motive, such is the fact. Nor has the motive been merely selfish. Instead of the libels lavished on the masters of North America, the eulogies of the Christian world are due to them as the only practical friends of the Negro race. In the various aspects to the Negro's life, in his church, his cabin, his field, his amusements and occupations, there is room for poetic description. If the peasant's life anywhere admits this, why not the slave's? Strip the subject of cant and the Negro slave is the peasant of the Southern States, as comfortable, as joyous, as picturesque as any other.

[John C. Calhoun on Abolitionism, 1850]

This hostile feeling on the part of the North toward the social organ-ization of the South long lay dormant; but it only required some cause, which would make the impression on those who felt most intensely that they were responsible for its continuance, to call it into action. The increasing power of this government, and of the control of the Northern section over all of it, furnished the cause. It was they who made an impression on the minds of many that there was little or no restraint to prevent the government to do whatever it might choose to do. This was sufficient to itself to put the most fanatical portion of the North in action, for the purpose of destroying the existing relation between the two races in the South.

The first organized movement toward it commenced in 1835. Then, for the first time, societies were organized, presses established, lecturers

Edwin Anderson Alderman et al., eds., *Library of Southern Literature*, 16 vols. (New Orleans: The Martin and Hoyt Co., 1908–1913), II, 704–706.

sent forth to excite the people of the North, and incendiary publications scattered over the whole South through the mail. The South was thoroughly aroused; meetings were held everywhere, and resolutions adopted, calling upon the North to apply a remedy to arrest the threatened evil, and pledging themselves to adopt measures for their own protection, if it was not arrested. At the meeting of Congress, petitions poured in from the North, calling upon Congress to abolish slavery in the District of Columbia, and to prohibit what they called the internal slave trade between the states, avowing at the same time, that their ultimate object was to abolish slavery, not only in the District of Columbia, but in the states and throughout the Union. At this period the number engaged in the agitation was small, and it possessed little or no personal influence.

Neither party in Congress had, at that time, any sympathy for them or their cause; the members of each party presented their petitions with great reluctance. Nevertheless, as small and as contemptible as the party then was, both of the great parties of the North dreaded them. They felt that, though small, they were organized in reference to a subject which had a great and commanding influence over the Northern mind. Each party, on that account, feared to oppose their petitions, lest the opposite party should take advantage of the one who opposed favoring them. The effect was that both united in insisting that the petitions should be received, and Congress take jurisdiction of the subject for which they prayed; and, to justify their course, took the extraordinary ground that Congress was bound to receive petitions on every subject, however objectionable it might be, and whether they had, or had not jurisdiction over the subject. These views prevailed in the House of Representatives, and partially in the Senate, and thus the party succeeded in their first movement in gaining what they proposed—a position in Congress, from which the agitation could be extended over the whole Union. This was the commencement of the agitation, which has ever since continued, and which, as it is now acknowledged, has endangered the Union itself. As to myself, I believed, at that early period, that, if the party who got up the petitions should succeed in getting Congress to take jurisdiction, that agitation would follow, and that it would, in the end, if not arrested, destroy the Union.

[B. F. Perry on Emancipation, 1850]

It is doubtful which would be most injured by emancipation, the slave himself, the Southern master, or the Northern abolitionists, engaged in commerce or manufacturing. No change could better the condition of the slave. He is happier and better provided for than he ever would be in a state of freedom and self-reliance. There are not in the world the same number of Africans so happy and so civilized as our slaves are in the Southern States. Freedom to them would be a great evil.

It is now almost universally admitted in England that emancipation in the West India Islands has been a curse to the slave, as well as an act of gross injustice to the master. This spirit of fanaticism, which first made its appearance in England, has pretty well run out. It must do so in the United States. It is not in the nature of fanaticism to continue. It must die away and burn out. Truth alone continues, and not madness. This abolition question has doubtless had its best days in the North. The equal division of the Northern people into Whigs and Democrats gave the abolition party the balance of power, and an importance which they never otherwise could have obtained.

B. F. Perry, *Biographical Sketches of Eminent American Statesmen* (Philadelphia: The Ferree Press, 1887), 136–37.

100. *John C. Calhoun's Last Speech, March 4, 1850*

THROUGHOUT HIS 40 YEARS IN STATE AND NATIONAL POLITICS, JOHN C. CALHOUN HAD REPRESENTED THE MAJORITY OPINION IN SOUTH CAROLINA AS THE STATE'S POSITION AND HIS OWN CHANGED FROM NATIONALISM THROUGH NULLIFICATION TO SECTIONALISM AND THE THREAT OF SECESSION. WITH THE ACQUISITION OF NEW WESTERN TERRITORY AFTER THE MEXICAN WAR, THE QUESTION OF THE EXTENSION OF SLAVERY CAME TO THE FOREFRONT, AND CALHOUN SAW THAT, IF IT WERE NOT SETTLED, IT WOULD LEAD EVENTUALLY EITHER TO SECESSION BY SOME OF THE STATES OR TO CIVIL WAR. THIS, HIS LAST SPEECH, WAS DELIVERED BY A COLLEAGUE, SENATOR JAMES M. MASON OF VIRGINIA, WHEN CALHOUN HIMSELF WAS TOO ILL TO GIVE IT. CALHOUN DIED SHORTLY THEREAFTER, ON MARCH 31, 1850, AND WAS BURIED IN CHARLESTON.

[Calhoun's Last Speech, Delivered in the Senate by Senator Mason]

I have, Senators, believed from the first that the agitation of the subject of slavery would, if not prevented by some timely and effective measure, end in disunion. Entertaining this opinion, I have, on all proper occasions, endeavored to call the attention of each of the two great parties which divide the country to adopt some measures to prevent so great a disaster, but without success. The agitation has been permitted to proceed, with almost no attempt to resist it, until it has reached a period when it can no longer be disguised or denied that the Union is in danger. You have thus forced upon you the greatest and the gravest question that can ever come under your consideration: How can the Union be preserved? . . .

What is it that has endangered the Union? To this question there can be but one answer: that the immediate cause is the almost universal discontent which pervades all the States composing the southern section

Congressional Globe, XIX (1850), Part I, 451–55.

of the Union . . . . The next question, going one step further back, is: What has caused this widely-diffused and almost universal discontent?

It is a great mistake to suppose, as is by some, that it originated with demagogues, who excited the discontent with the intention of aiding their personal advancement . . . . No, some cause, far deeper and more powerful than the one supposed, must exist, to account for discontent so wide and deep . . . . It will be found in the belief of the people of the southern States, as prevalent as the discontent itself, that they cannot remain, as things now are, consistently with honor and safety, in the Union. The next question to be considered is: What has caused this belief?

One of the causes is, undoubtedly, to be traced to the long-continued agitation of the slave question on the part of the North . . . . There is another, lying back of it, with which this is intimately connected, that may be regarded as the great and primary cause. That is to be found in the fact that the equilibrium between the two sections in the Government, as it stood when the constitution was ratified and the Government put in action, has been destroyed. . . . The loss of the equilibrium is to be attributed to the action of this Government . . . .

That the Government claims, and practically maintains, the right to decide in the last resort as to the extent of its powers, will scarcely be denied by any one conversant with the political history of the country. That it also claims the right to resort to force to maintain whatever power she claims, against all opposition, is equally certain . . . . It also follows that the character of the Government has been changed, in consequence, from a Federal Republic, as it originally came from the hands of its framers, and that it has been changed into a great national consolidated Democracy. It has indeed, at present, all the characteristics of the latter, and not one of the former, although it still retains its outward form.

The result of the whole of these causes combined is that the North has acquired a decided ascendency over every department of this Government, and through it a control over all the powers of the system . . . . There is a question of vital importance to the southern section, in reference to which the view and feelings of the two sections are as opposite and hostile as they can possibly be.

I refer to the relation between the two races in the southern section, which constitutes a vital portion of her social organization. Every portion of the North entertains views and feelings more or less hostile to it. Those most opposed and hostile regard it as a sin, and consider themselves under the most sacred obligation to use every effort to destroy it. . . . Those less opposed and hostile, regard it as a crime— an offense against humanity, as they call it; and although not so fanatical, feel themselves bound to use all efforts to effect the same object; while those who are least opposed and hostile, regard it as a blot and a stain on the character of what they call the nation, and feel themselves accordingly bound to give it no countenance or support. On the contrary, the southern section regards the relation as one which cannot be destroyed without subjecting the two races to the greatest calamity, and the section to poverty, desolation, and wretchedness; and accordingly they feel bound by every consideration of interest and safety, to defend it. . . .

The responsibility of saving the Union rests on the North, and not the South. The South cannot save it by any act of hers, and the North may save it without any sacrifice whatever, unless to do justice, and to perform her duties under the Constitution, should be regarded by her as a sacrifice. . . .

I have now, Senators, done my duty in expressing my opinions fully, freely, and candidly, on this solemn occasion. In doing so, I have been governed by the motives which have governed me in all the stages of the agitation of the slavery question since its commencement. I have exerted myself, during the whole period, to arrest it with the intention of saving the Union, if it could be done; and, if it could not, to save the section where it has pleased Providence to cast my lot, and which I sincerely believe has justice and the Constitution on its side. Having faithfully done my duty to the best of my ability, both to the Union and my section, throughout this agitation, I shall have the consolation, let what will come, that I am free from all responsibility.

101. Benjamin F. Perry's Speech Against Secession, December 11, 1850

ALTHOUGH JOHN C. CALHOUN SPOKE FOR A MAJORITY OF SOUTH CAROLINIANS, A SMALL MINORITY LED BY SUCH MEN AS BENJAMIN F. PERRY OF GREENVILLE FELT THAT THE UNION WAS WORTH PRESERVING. IN MANY WAYS THE SPEECH DELIVERED BY PERRY TO THE SOUTH CAROLINA HOUSE OF REPRESENTATIVES WAS A REPLY TO THE PHILOSOPHY OF CALHOUN.

[Benjamin F. Perry on Secession]

Whilst I differ, sir, with those around me in regard to the true policy of South Carolina, I yield to none of her sons in my readiness and willingness to defend her interests and her honor. There is no tie which binds a man to his native State that I do not feel for Carolina. . . .

I am not ignorant of, or insensible to, the wrongs and injuries inflicted by the Federal Government on the Southern States . . . . They commenced many years since with a high and onerous tariff of protection for the benefit of one section of the country at the expense of another. Then came a grand and stupendous system of internal improvements, to spend the money raised by these high duties and enrich the North and West. A National Bank was a part of the same scheme for making the South dependent, in all her commercial arrangements with the North. But this whole American system has been broken down. The Bank went overboard under the administration of General Jackson, and so did internal improvements. The downfall of the tariff and the triumph of free trade were the crowning glory of Mr. Polk's brilliant administration. The prodigal distribution of the public lands, and the odious and revolting principles of the Wilmot Proviso were next attempted. . . .

B. F. Perry, *Biographical Sketches of Eminent American Statesmen* (Philadelphia: The Ferree Press, 1887), 112–13, 134–36, 142–43.

Nor am I unmindful, Mr. Chairman, of the indignities and insults of the Northern people, and their utter disregard of constitutional guarantees. And I am ready, sir, and ever have been, to defend, at any and every hazard, the rights of the South. But I am disposed to defend them prudently, wisely, and successfully. I am unwilling to see South Carolina pursue a course which must inevitably prove disastrous to her, and ruinous to the cause of the South. Whilst I shall defend, at any and every hazard, the rights of the South, and the honor of Carolina, I am also disposed, if possible, to preserve the Union of the States. . . .

If any one supposes the Federal Government will stand aloof and permit South Carolina peaceably to secede from the Union, he is certainly a most sanguine and hopeful patriot, and must think that a great change has come over the nation since the days of Andrew Jackson . . . .

Nothing can be more mistaken than the policy pursued by the South in regard to their dependence on the North for almost everything consumed in the Southern States. It should be our pride and our ambition to be independent of the North in every respect. We should import our own goods and manufacture for ourselves. We should live at home, and spend our money at home, encourage our own mechanics, and refuse to trade with the North. In this way, we can show our resentment and self-denial, and retaliate most effectually, without dissolving the Union, or incurring the horrors of a civil war and revolution . . . .

I am willing, Mr. Chairman, to unite in any constitutional mode of resenting and redressing our wrongs. I am in favor of taxing Northern goods, which has been proposed in North Carolina and Virginia, and which may be done constitutionally in the hands of our own merchants. I will go for non-intercourse with those cities where this abolition agitation is kept up, and I think true patriotism would dictate such a course on the part of our merchants. I am willing for the State to give proper encouragement to manufacturing and the direct importation of goods. These measures if steadily pursued, and enforced with proper spirit and patriotism, may bring the Northern people to their senses. . . .

I never have, I never can, advise a tame submission to wrong; but I am for a rational and successful defense by the union of the South, which will redress our wrongs, secure our rights, and preserve the Union of the States.

102. *The Right of Secession Ordinance, April, 1852*

SOUTH CAROLINA FOLLOWED THE PHILOSOPHY OF JOHN C. CALHOUN RATHER THAN THAT OF BENJAMIN F. PERRY—AT LEAST TO THE POINT OF CALLING A CONVENTION TO CONSIDER SECESSION. THE CONVENTION MEMBERS WERE ELECTED IN FEBRUARY, 1851, BUT THE MEETING WAS POSTPONED BECAUSE OTHER SOUTHERN STATES WERE AT THAT TIME UNWILLING TO JOIN SOUTH CAROLINA IN SECESSION. WHEN THE CONVENTION FINALLY MET, IN APRIL, 1852, SECESSION DID NOT TAKE PLACE, BUT THE CONVENTION ADOPTED A RESOLUTION DECLARING THE RIGHT TO SECEDE. THE RESOLUTION FOLLOWS.

[Resolution on the Right to Secede]

We the people of the State of South Carolina, in Convention assembled, do declare and ordain, and it is hereby declared and ordained, that South Carolina, in the exercise of her sovereign will as an independent State, acceded to the Federal Union, known as the United States of America, and that in the exercise of the same sovereign will, it is her right, without let, hindrance, or molestation from any power whatsoever to secede from the Federal Union; and for the sufficiency of the causes which may impel her to such separation, she is responsible alone under God, to the tribunal of public opinion among the nations of the earth.

Yates Snowden, ed., *History of South Carolina*, 5 vols. (Chicago: The Lewis Publishing Co., 1920), II, 643.

103. *South Carolina and the Kansas Question, 1854–1856*

THE KANSAS-NEBRASKA ACT OF 1854 OPENED THOSE TERRITORIES TO SETTLEMENT BOTH BY SLAVE-OWNERS AND NON-SLAVE-OWNERS, WITH THE UNDERSTANDING THAT THE FUTURE STATES CREATED FROM THE TERRITORIES COULD BE EITHER SLAVE OR FREE, AS THEIR CITIZENS CHOSE. IN RESPONSE TO THIS ACT, BOTH SLAVE-OWNERS AND ABOLITIONISTS RUSHED SETTLERS TO KANSAS, AND THE RESULT WAS SEVERAL YEARS OF VIRTUAL CIVIL WAR IN THE TERRITORY BEFORE IT BECAME A FREE STATE IN 1861. SOUTH CAROLINIANS WANTED TO AID KANSAS IN BECOMING A SLAVE STATE, AND A MOVE WAS UNDERWAY IN 1855 TO INDUCE SETTLERS TO GO THERE AND TAKE THEIR SLAVES WITH THEM. THE FIRST SELECTION IS A COPY OF A NEWSPAPER NOTICE SENT TO SOUTH CAROLINA CONGRESSMAN PRESTON S. BROOKS; THE SECOND IS HIS REPLY.

Letter from Captain E. B. Ball

At the solicitation of many friends, I will proceed to organize a company of one hundred men, to proceed to Kansas, about the last of March. This pioneer band needs the aid of moneyed citizens. They go to a far off country for the purpose of securing homes and at the same time to defend Southern institutions. They appeal to their native State for aid with the hope that their appeal will not be in vain.

It is impossible that the people of South Carolina can hear without emotion the news which daily comes to us from Kansas. The long and bitter animosities have at last ripened, and slavery and abolition, the North and the South, confront each other in armed and deadly war. The issue has come, and to the people of the South, and of this State, to each and every slave-holder, the question addresses itself: What shall we do for Kansas? Shall we look listlessly, tamely on, while our friends, surrounded by the hosts of Abolition, are risking their fortunes, perhaps

J. H. Easterby, ed., *The South Carolina Rice Plantation As Revealed in the Papers of Robert F.W. Allston* (Chicago: University of Chicago Press, 1945), 130–31. Copyright 1945 by The University of Chicago. Reprinted by permission of The University of Chicago Press.

shedding their blood in our behalf? Can we do nothing, give nothing of our abundance in such a cause?

We trust that these questions may be answered in a worthy and liberal manner. Let Patriotism and State pride, and Southern spirit, be expressed in some suitable, practical form of aid for Kansas.

Preston S. Brooks's Reply to Captain Ball, December 31, 1855:

In reply to your letter of the 28th, I must first repeat my proposition. The pledge was to give a hundred dollars to each company of one hundred men that might go to Kansas under pledge to remain two years. Whenever you organize a company of a hundred men and start for Kansas, I will pay to your Treasurer the amount pledged. If my colleagues are not called upon to contribute to companies which may be raised in their own districts, they authorize me to say that each will contribute handsomely to the aid of your company.

Your intention of appealing through the press to the spirit and patriotism of the people of the State, is admirable. There are men scattered all over the State also who are willing to go, but not in sufficient numbers to form a separate company in each district. Come out with your publication, and when you get one hundred men, solemnly pledged to go to Kansas, I feel authorized to pledge the South Carolina Delegation for two hundred and fifty dollars.

You will certainly have the hundred dollars from me, whenever you are ready to move with a hundred men, or should you fail in getting the full number of a hundred men, then you may call me on the day that you start for as many dollars as you have men under pledge to go and to remain two years in Kansas.

J.H. Easterby, ed., *The South Carolina Rice Plantation As Revealed in the Papers of Robert F.W. Allston* (Chicago: University of Chicago Press, 1945), 130–31. Copyright 1945 by The University of Chicago. Reprinted by permission of The University of Chicago Press.

104. *Representative Brooks's Explanation*
of His Caning of Senator Sumner, May 22, 1856

SENATOR CHARLES SUMNER OF MASSACHUSETTS, NEVER A FRIEND OF
THE SOUTH EITHER BEFORE OR AFTER THE CIVIL WAR, WAS ONE OF THE
BITTEREST OPPONENTS OF SLAVERY. IN A SPEECH IN THE UNITED STATES
SENATE, HE SEVERELY RIDICULED SENATOR A. P. BUTLER OF SOUTH CAR-
OLINA, WHO AT THAT TIME WAS ILL AND NOT PRESENT. REPRESENTATIVE
PRESTON S. BROOKS, NEPHEW OF SENATOR BUTLER, FELT IT HIS DUTY TO
AVENGE HIS UNCLE, WITH THE RESULTS DESCRIBED IN THE LETTER FOL-
LOWING. FOR HIS ACT, BROOKS WAS DETESTED BY THE NORTH, BUT HE
WAS HONORED BY THE SOUTH, PARTICULARLY SOUTH CAROLINA. BROOKS
RESIGNED FROM HIS OFFICE, BUT HE WAS RE-ELECTED BY THE PEOPLE.
ABOUT A YEAR LATER HE DIED. A DELEGATION FROM SOUTH CAROLINA
WAS SENT TO ACCOMPANY HIS BODY HOME, AND IT WAS SAID THAT
MOURNERS LINED THE ROADWAY FROM AUGUSTA TO EDGEFIELD AS THE
ESCORT MOVED THAT WAY AFTER HAVING BROUGHT THE HERO ACROSS
THE BORDER TO THE TOWN.

Preston Brooks to his Brother, J. H. Brooks:

As you will learn by telegraph that I have given Senator Sumner a
caning, and lest Mother should feel unnecessary alarm, I write to give a
detailed statement of the occurrence. Sumner made a violent speech in
which he insulted South Carolina and Judge Butler grossly. The Judge
was and is absent and his friends all concurred in the opinion that the
Judge would be compelled to flog him. This Butler is unable to do as
Sumner is a very powerful man and weighs 30 pounds more than myself.
Under the circumstances I felt it to be my duty to relieve Butler and
avenge the insult to my State. I waited an hour and a half in the grounds
on the day before yesterday for Sumner, when he escaped me by taking
a carriage. Did the same thing yesterday with the same result.

South Carolina Historical and Genealogical Magazine, LII (1951), 1–4. Reprinted
by permission of The South Carolina Historical Society.

I then went to the Senate and waited until it adjourned. There were some ladies in the Hall, and I had to wait a full hour until they left. I then went to Sumner's seat and said, "Mr. Sumner, I have read your speech with care and as much impartiality as was possible and I feel it my duty to tell you that you have libeled my State and slandered a relative who is aged and absent and I am come to punish you for it." At the concluding words I struck him with my cane and gave him about 30 first rate stripes with a gutta percha cane which had been given me a few months before . . . . Every lick went where I intended. For about the first five or six licks he offered to make fight, but I plied him so rapidly that he did not touch me. Towards the last he bellowed like a calf. I wore my cane out completely but saved the head which is gold. The fragments of the stick are begged for as sacred relics. Every Southern man is delighted and the Abolitionists are like a hive of disturbed bees. They are making all sorts of threats. It would not take much to have the throats of every Abolitionist cut. I have been arrested, of course, and there is now a resolution before the House, the object of which is to result in my expulsion. This they can't do, it requiring two thirds to do it, and they can't get a half. Every Southern man sustains me. The debate is now very animated on the subject. Don't be alarmed; it will all work right. The only danger that I am in is from assassination, but this you must not intimate to Mother.

105. *Agriculture and a Footnote to Cotton*

DURING THE ANTEBELLUM PERIOD COTTON BECAME THE MAIN STAPLE CROP, DOMINATING THE AGRICULTURE OF SOUTH CAROLINA EXCEPT IN THE COASTAL, RICE AREA. THERE WAS CONSTANT EFFORT ON THE PART OF THE STATE'S AGRICULTURAL LEADERS TO IMPROVE FARM LANDS, FIND NEW KINDS OF FERTILIZERS, DEVELOP NEW FARM PRODUCTS, AND ENCOURAGE THE RAISING OF STOCK. THE RAILROADS ADDED GREATLY TO THE FEASIBILITY OF COTTON-RAISING. IN THE FOLLOWING SELECTIONS DAVID RAMSAY DESCRIBES EARLY COTTON PRODUCTION, AROUND 1800; ROBERT MILLS DEPLORES THE CONDITION OF AGRICULTURE IN THE STATE IN 1826; AND W. J. GRAYSON DESCRIBES THE DEPENDENCE ON COTTON IN THE 1850s.

[David Ramsay on Early Cotton Culture]

So much cotton is now made in Carolina and Georgia that, if the whole was manufactured in the United States, it would go far in clothing a great proportion of the inhabitants of the Union; for one laborer can raise as much of this commodity in one season as will afford the raw materials for 1500 yards of common cloth, or a sufficiency for covering 150 persons. . . . This staple is of immense value to the public and still more so to individuals. It has trebled the price of land suitable to its growth, and when the crop succeeds and the market is favorable the annual income of those who plant it is doubled to what it was before the introduction of cotton.

The cotton chiefly cultivated on the sea coast is denominated the black seed or long staple cotton, which is of the best quality and admirably adapted to the finest manufactures. The wool is easily separated from the seed by roller-gins which do not injure the staple. A pair of rollers worked by one laborer gives about 25 pounds of clean cotton daily. The cotton universally cultivated in the middle and upper country is called the green seed kind. It is less silky and more wooley, and adheres so tenaciously to

David Ramsay, *History of South Carolina* . . . , 2 vols. (Charleston: David Longworth for the author, 1809), II, 214–15.

the seed that it requires the action of a saw-gin to separate the wool from the seed. This cuts the staple exceedingly; but as the staple of this kind of cotton is not fit for the finer fabrics it is not considered injurious. The quality of these two kinds is very different. The wool of the green seed is considerably the cheapest; but that species is much more productive than the other. An acre of good cotton land will usually produce 150 pounds of clean wool of the long staple kind. An acre of land of equal quality will usually produce 200 pounds of the green seed or short staple kind. Besides these, yellow or nankeen cotton is also cultivated in the upper country for domestic use. Two ingenious artists, Miller and Whitney of Connecticut, invented a saw-gin for the separation of the wool from the seed, which has facilitated that operation in the highest degree. The Legislature of South Carolina purchased their patent right for $50,000, and then munificently threw open its use and benefits to all its citizens. . . .

[Robert Mills on South Carolina Agriculture in 1826]

The agriculture of South Carolina, though flourishing, is far short of perfection. The art of manuring is little understood, and less practiced. The bulk of the planters, relying on the fertility of the soil, seldom plant any land but what is good, and change the same when it begins to fail for that which is fresh, giving themselves little trouble to keep their fields in heart. This system of cultivation is highly to be deplored and deprecated, as it tends to ruin the agricultural interests of the country; we should husband our natural resources, not waste and destroy them; we owe it to posterity, to the State, to ourselves, to improve the soil, and not to impoverish it. The agricultural system can to a certain degree as well be practiced in this as in any other state, and with more success, for the country abounds in manure, arising from rich bottoms, oyster shell beds, marls, salt marshes, and even from the products of the land itself, the cotton seed, etc. System, industry and perseverance only are requisite to insure permanencey to the best planting interests of the State.

Robert Mills, *Statistics of South Carolina* . . . (Charleston: Hurlburt and Lloyd, 1826), 155–56.

The country (though too slowly) is approximating to this desirable state of things; agricultural societies are forming in different sections of the state. As early as 1785 such a society was incorporated in Charleston. It is now doing well, and promises great usefulness; offering and awarding premiums to successful candidates in agricultural improvements, by which means the capacities of the soil are developed, and confidence given to others to put the same into practice. In Pendleton, Columbia, Abbeville, Edgefield, Cheraw, and other places, societies for the promotion of agriculture are established, all which will have their influence, and by persevering, eventually induce our planters and farmers to attend to their best interests in the cultivation of the soil.

[W. J. Grayson on the Cotton Economy in the 1850s]

The cultivation of a great staple like cotton or tobacco starves everything else. The farmer curtails and neglects all other crops. He buys from distant places, not only the simplest manufactured articles, his brooms and buckets, but farm products, grain, meat, hay, butter, all of which he could make at home. What is obtained in this way is sparingly consumed. If grain and hay are bought, horses, mules and cattle suffer from short supplies. Success or failure in the crop for market makes little difference in the supply of food. If the crop is short, everything is put on half rations; if it succeeds, the planter seeks an additional enjoyment, a jaunt to the North, or a voyage to Europe, and mules, pigs and cattle fare little better than before. This is true in a greater or less degree of the whole cotton growing region. It is especially true of the low country planters in Georgia and Carolina. They devote themselves to their cotton fields. They buy their corn from North Carolina, their meat from Kentucky, their hay from New York, their butter from farmers a thousand miles away in a climate that makes it necessary to house and feed everything six months in the year. Under this system the country that might be the most abundant in the world is the least plentiful. The beef is lean,

"Autobiography of William John Grayson," *South Carolina Historical and Genealogical Magazine*, XLVIII (1957), 131–32. Reprinted by permission of The South Carolina Historical Society.

the poultry poor, the hogs a peculiar breed with long snouts and gaunt bodies, toiling all summer to keep themselves alive with partial success, and in the winter making a slender and uncertain return for the damage they have wrought to fields and fences. The planter buys salt butter from the North when he might enjoy home made fresh butter all the year round. It is said he has no grasses. He may have green pastures of rye or oats, through the winter and in summer make ample supplies of roots and hay. He neglects them all. With a hundred head of cattle he is without milk for his coffee. The practice is to turn the cattle out in November that they may take care of themselves among the woods and swamps. They are driven up in May, the calves marked, the cows milked and butter made for a few months of summer. Twenty cows will then produce what a good dairy cow yields in England. It never occurs to the planter to keep up a few cows and feed them. He goes on year after year, buying salt butter and drinking his coffee without milk. . . .

106. *Education*

ALTHOUGH A STATEWIDE PUBLIC SCHOOL LAW HAD BEEN PASSED IN 1811, IT PROVIDED ONLY FOR A WEAK SYSTEM OF PUBLIC EDUCATION AND WAS INADEQUATELY SUPPORTED THROUGH THE ANTEBELLUM PERIOD, DESPITE FREQUENT ATTEMPTS TO IMPROVE IT. IN THE FIELD OF HIGHER EDUCATION, SEVERAL PRIVATE COLLEGES WERE OPENED, AND THE STATE UNIVERSITY, THEN SOUTH CAROLINA COLLEGE, WAS FOUNDED. MOST OF THE TOWNS AND DISTRICTS HAD ONE OR MORE "ACADEMIES," EITHER MALE OR FEMALE. THE FIRST SELECTION GIVES THE CHARTER OF SOUTH CAROLINA COLLEGE; THE SECOND, A DESCRIPTION OF A PRIVATE ACADEMY; THE THIRD, THE PUBLIC SCHOOL LAW OF 1811; THE FOURTH, AN ADVERTISEMENT FOR AN UP COUNTRY FEMALE ACADEMY IN THE 1840s; AND THE FIFTH, AN ACCOUNT OF A COLLEGE DUEL IN THE 1830s.

The Charter of South Carolina College, 1801:

Whereas the proper education of youth contributes greatly to the prosperity of society, and ought always to be an object of legislative attention; and whereas, the establishment of a college in a central part of the State, where all its youth may be educated, will highly promote the instruction, the good order and the harmony of the whole community:

I. Be it therefore enacted . . . that his Excellency the Governor [and others] . . . be trustees . . . by the name of "The Trustees of the South Carolina College" and that by the said name they and their successors shall and may have perpetual succession and be able and capable in law to have, receive and enjoy . . . lands, tenements and hereditaments, of any kind or value . . . and personal property of any kind whatsoever, which may be granted or bequeathed to them for the purpose of building, erecting, endowing and supporting the said college in the town of Columbia.

II. And be it enacted . . . that . . . the said trustees, or a quorum of them, being regularly convened, shall be capable of doing or transacting

South Carolina Statutes at Large, V, 403–405.

all the business of the college aforesaid; but more particularly of electing all the customary and necessary officers of the said institution, of fixing their several salaries, of removing any of them for neglect or misconduct in office, of prescribing the course of studies to be pursued by the students; and in general of framing and enacting all such ordinances and by-laws as shall appear to them necessary for the good government of the said college . . . .

III. And be it enacted . . . that the head of the said college shall be styled "The President", and the masters thereof shall be styled "The Professors" . . . and the President and professors or a majority of them shall be styled "The Faculty of the College" which faculty shall have the power of enforcing the ordinances and by-laws adopted by the trustees for the government of the pupils . . . .

V. And be it further enacted . . . that the trustees of the said college are hereby authorized and empowered to draw out of the treasury of this State the sum of fifty thousand dollars, to be appropriated to the purpose of erecting a building of brick or stone, and covered with tile or slate, suitable to the accommodation of the students of the said college, and suitable for fully carrying on the education of the said students, and for the erection of such other buildings as may be necessary for the use of said college; and . . . the sum of six thousand dollars yearly and every year, to be appropriated for the purpose of paying the salaries of the faculty of the said college, and for the further support of the same . . . .

VII. And be it further enacted . . . that the said trustees with the concurrence of the commissioners of Columbia, shall be empowered to make choice of any square or squares, yet unsold, in the town of Columbia, for the purpose of erecting said college, and the buildings attached thereto, having strict reference to every advantage and convenience necessary for such institution . . . .

[David Ramsay]

Dr. Moses Waddell's academy, in the early 1800s.

There are several private schools, both in Charlestown and the country for teaching classical and mathematical learning. Among these, one under

David Ramsay, *History of South Carolina* . . . , 2 vols. (Charleston: David Longworth for the author, 1809), II, 369–71.

the care of the Rev. Dr. Waddell of Abbeville District deserves particular notice. In it from seventy to eighty students are instructed in the Latin, Greek, and French languages; and such of the arts and sciences as are necessary to prepare a candidate for admission into the higher classes at the northern colleges. The school house is a plain log building, in the midst of the woods in a hilly and healthy country, and too small to accommodate all the scholars in the hours of study. To obviate this inconvenience they are permitted and encouraged to build huts in the vicinity. These are the rough carpentry of the pupils, or constructed by workmen for about four dollars. In these, when the weather is cold, and under the trees when it is warm, the different classes study. To the common school or recitation room they instantly repair when called for by the name of the Homer, the Zenophon, the Cicero, the Horace or Virgil class, or by the name of the author whose writings they are reading. In a moment they appear before their preceptor, and with order and decorum recite their lessons—are critically examined in grammar and syntax—the construction of sentences—the formation of verbs—the antiquities of Greece and Rome—the history and geography of the ancients, illustrative of the author whose works they recite; and are taught to relish his beauties, and enter into his spirit. Thus class succeeds class without the formality of definite hours for study or recreation till all have recited. In the presence of the students assembled, a solemn and appropriate prayer imploring the Eternal in their behalf, begins and ends the exercises of each day. In this manner the classics are taught 190 miles from the sea-coast. The glowing periods of Cicero are read and admired. The melody and majesty of Homer delight the ear and charm the understanding in the very spot, and under the identical trees, which sixty years ago resounded with the war-whoop and horrid yellings of savage Indians. Of the large number that attend this school, nine in ten are as studious as their friends could wish . . . . The sagacious preceptor . . . by patience in teaching and minutely explaining what is difficult . . . secures the affections of his pupils and smoothes their labors; while at the same time judicious praise rouses ambition, and kindles in their breasts an ardent love for improvement and an eagerness to deserve and gain applause.

South Carolina's First Statewide Public School Law, 1811:

I. Be it enacted . . . that immediately after the passing of this Act there shall be established in each election district within this State, a number of free schools, equal to the number of members which such district is entitled to send to the House of Representatives in the Legislature of this State.

II. And be it further enacted . . . that in each of these schools the primary elements of learning, reading, writing and arithmetic, shall always be taught, and such other branches of education as the commissioners to be hereinafter appointed may from time to time direct.

III. And be it further enacted . . . that every citizen of this State shall be entitled to send his . . . children . . . to any free school in the district where . . . he may reside, free from any expense whatsoever on account of tuition; and where more children shall apply for admission at any one school than can be conveniently educated therein, a preference shall always be given to poor orphans and the children of indigent and necessitous parents.

IV. And be it further enacted . . . that for the support and maintenance of the said free schools, the sum of three hundred dollars per annum for each school, is hereby, and for ever appropriated, to be paid out of the treasury of this State, in the manner hereinafter directed until other sufficient funds may by law be provided.

V. And be it further enacted . . . that for the purpose of carrying this act into effect, there shall be appointed a number of commissioners in each election district, which number shall not be less than three nor more than thirteen.

VI. And be it further enacted . . . that the said commissioners shall be appointed by the Legislature, by nomination, and shall continue in office for three years from the time of their appointment, and until a new appointment shall be made.

VII. And be it further enacted . . . that the said commissioners of the free schools shall have power to determine the situation of the schools in each district, to appoint masters for each school, and to remove them at pleasure, to arrange the system of instruction until some general system be organized, to decide on the admission of scholars . . . and to superintend generally the management of the schools in their respective districts, and shall have power to draw on the comptroller for the sums appropriated for the schools in their respective districts . . . .

X. And be it further enacted . . . that the secretary of each board of commissioners shall keep a regular journal of the transactions of the said board, which shall be always open to the inspection of the Legislature.

XI. And be it further enacted . . . that in all cases where the sum of money allotted by this Act for the support of each school shall be found insufficient to maintain a master for the whole year, that then the commissioners shall be authorized to employ a master for the greatest length of time for which sum a competent person can be engaged . . . .

XIV. And be it further enacted . . . that until the number of schools established by the State shall be sufficient to educate the children in every part of each district, the commissioners shall be authorized and required, if they think it expedient or necessary, to remove the schools, annually, into different parts of their respective districts, provided, nevertheless, that no school shall be established in any part of any district, unless the inhabitants shall, at their own expense, provide a sufficient school house for the accommodation of the scholars.

XV. And be it further enacted . . . that in all districts where a school or schools are already or may hereafter be established by private funds or individual subscription, it shall be lawful for the commissioners of the free schools, at their discretion, to unite such part of the funds provided by this Act for such districts with such school or schools, in such manner as may appear to them best calculated to promote the objects of this Act. . . .

[Newspaper Report]

A female academy in the 1840s:

Limestone Springs Female High School, Spartanburg District; Rev. Thomas Curtis, D.D., late of Charleston, and Rev. William Curtis, late of Columbia, Principals.

Southern Chronicle (Columbia, S.C.), Oct. 15, 1845.

The attention of the public will be directed to this school by the well known salubrity of its location, and the purity and valuable qualities of the Springs. Centrally situated in the north of the State, the elevation of the country secures to it a cool atmosphere in the summer as in winter the neighboring mountainous region protects it from the cold . . . . The Principals have purchased this property as the most eligible location for a school of high order which they could anywhere procure.

The establishment will be strictly literary, and in no respect denominational or sectarian. It is called a Female High School, to indicate a determination on the part of the principals to afford their pupils every branch of a solid, finished and moral education. They have had personal experience in the schools of Europe, and aim to combine the advantage of Northern and Southern instruction. On the part of the pupils, estrangement from home, its duties and associations—will thus be prevented. Parents may consult health, climate and a wise economy, which the Principals, themselves students and parents, can honestly engage for a family guidance and comfort to pervade the whole of this Southern School.

There will be five departments, including the primary, embracing all the pursuits of the best schools from early to mature years, as detailed in the prospectus. Lectures on prominent subjects will be delivered throughout the year. For instruction in the French language, in music and in painting, arrangements have been . . . completed with the best teachers, native and foreign . . . .

[J. Marion Sims]

A college duel in the 1830s:

There was a real duel in South Carolina College just after I graduated. It was between Roach, of Colleton, and Adams, of Richland District. Roach was a young man about six feet high and a physical beauty. Adams was no less so, though not so tall. Both men were of fine families, and Adams was supposed to be a young man of talent and promise. It

Harry Marion Sims, ed., *The Story of My Life, by J. Marion Sims (1813–1883),* (New York: D. Appleton & Co., 1889), 88–91.

occurred this way. They were very intimate friends; they sat opposite to each other in the Stewards' Hall, at table. . . . Both caught hold of a dish of trout at the same moment. Adams did not let go; Roach held on to the dish. Presently Roach let go of the dish and glared fiercely in Adams' face, and said: "Sir, I will see you after supper." They sat there all through the supper, both looking like mad bulls . . . . Roach left the supper-room first, and Adams immediately followed him. Roach waited outside the door for Adams. There were no hard words and no fisticuffs —all was dignity and solemnity. "Sir," said Roach, "What can I do to insult you?" Adams replied, "This is enough, sir, and you will hear from me." Adams immediately went to his room and sent a challenge to Roach. It was promptly accepted, and each went up town and selected seconds and advisers. . . .

They fought at Lightwood Knot Springs, ten miles from Columbia. They were both men of coolest courage. . . . They were fighting at ten paces distant. They were to fire at the word "one," raising their pistols. . . . When the word "Fire!" was given, each started to raise his pistol; but each had on a frock coat, and the flag of Roach's coat caught on his arm, and prevented his pistol from rising. When Adams saw that, he lowered his pistol to the ground. The word was then given a second time: "Are you ready? Fire! One!". They both shot simultaneously . . . .

Adams was shot through the pelvis, and he lingered a few hours and died in great agony. Roach was shot through the right hip-joint, two or three inches below where his ball entered Adams' body. He lingered for a long time, and came near dying of blood-poisoning; but after weeks and months of suffering, he was able to get up, but was lame for life . . . . He studied medicine and went to Philadelphia, to the Jefferson Medical College, and there he gave himself up entirely to dissipation. He had delirium tremens and died in Philadelphia, in an attack of it; I think it was in the month of January, 1836.

107. *Manufacturing up to the 1840s*

ALTHOUGH THE 1840S WAS A PREMATURE TIME TO TALK ABOUT COM-
MERCIAL MANUFACTURING IN SOUTH CAROLINA, THE IDEA HAD BEEN CIR-
CULATING AS EARLY AS THE DAYS FOLLOWING THE WAR OF 1812, WHEN
FEEBLE ATTEMPTS WERE MADE TO DEVELOP A TEXTILE INDUSTRY IN SOUTH
CAROLINA. AROUND 1820, SOME GOODS WERE BEING PRODUCED. WHEN
THE PRICE OF COTTON FELL, THE CONSENSUS WAS THAT COTTON GOODS
SHOULD BE MANUFACTURED AS AN ALTERNATIVE TO A SURPLUS AND THAT
THIS WOULD BRING DIVERSIFICATION TO SOUTH CAROLINA. ONE EARLY
MILL WAS ESTABLISHED AT SOCIETY HILL BY GOVERNOR D. R. WILLIAMS;
IN THE LATE 1820S, THIS MILL WAS PRODUCING YARN, COTTON CORDAGE,
AND COARSE COTTON CLOTH. COTTON FACTORIES AND OTHER TYPES OF
MILLS WERE BEGUN IN THE 1830S, AND BY 1839 THERE WERE 15 OPERAT-
ING, WITH A TOTAL CAPITAL OF $617,450. PRIOR TO THE 1860S—CHIEFLY
IN THE 1840S—MANUFACTURING HAD GROWN TO BE SIGNIFICANT. AMONG
THE PRINTING AND BINDING PLANTS THERE WERE 12 NEWSPAPERS. THERE
WERE DISTILLERIES, SUGAR REFINERIES, GRIST MILLS, AND SAWMILLS.
OTHER FACTORIES PRODUCED BRICKS AND LIME, CARRIAGES AND WAGONS,
DRUGS AND MEDICINES, EARTHENWARE, FURNITURE, HARDWARE AND CUT-
LERY, HATS, LEATHER AND SADDLES, MACHINERY, FLOUR, PAPER, PRECIOUS
METALS, SHIPS, SOAP AND CANDLES, TOBACCO, WOOL, AND COTTON. A
FIRM STILL FAMILIAR TO SOUTH CAROLINIANS WAS ESTABLISHED DURING
THIS PERIOD. WILLIAM GREGG OPENED THE FIRST COTTON MILL AS THE
ADVENT OF THE TEXTILE INDUSTRY WHICH CAME INTO FULL FLOWER
AFTER THE CIVIL WAR. THE FIRST SELECTION DESCRIBES GOVERNOR WIL-
LIAMS'S EARLY ENTERPRISE; THIS IS FOLLOWED BY A DESCRIPTION OF AN
OIL MILL, AN ASSESSMENT OF INDUSTRY IN SOUTH CAROLINA IN 1826,
AND GREGG'S IDEAS ON MANUFACTURING IN THE 1840S.

[H. T. Cook]

David R. Williams's early industrial enterprises:

His excellency, Governor Williams, in company with Mr. Matthews, has erected in the vicinity of Society Hill a manufactory for spinning cotton yarn. The number of spindles at present employed is three or four hundred; but the works are now enlarging and it is expected a thousand spindles or upwards will be in motion in the course of the present year. This establishment so honorable to the founders, promises, we are glad to hear, a handsome remuneration of profit. . . .

[David R. Williams]

I have not replied earlier, because our oil mill was so nearly fin-ished . . . . Our oil mill is after the Dutch mode, of pestles and wedges. Our grinding stones are not quite four feet in diameter and twelve inches thick. The cotton seed kernels are so much easier to grind than flax seed, these stones as small as they are, may easily grind for two pair of pestles and wedges. That the whole process is simple and not difficult to under-stand, you will infer when I tell you, no person concerned about ours, except myself, has ever seen an oil mill before. . . . Without resorting to any of the patented methods of refining oil, I have succeeded by a very simple and cheap process to refine our oil so as to answer all the purposes of the best sperm oil, in our cotton factory. . . . In its present state we find it burns very well with a little attention to the wick. By other means than those I have used as yet, I am satisfied it will be much superior to the best animal oil lamps, it being entirely inodorous, a circumstance of great importance in establishments requiring many lights.

Columbia Telescope, March 16, 1816, quoted in H. T. Cook, *The Life and Legacy of David Rogerson Williams* (New York: n.p., 1916), 203–204.

Harvey T. Cook, *The Life and Legacy of David Rogerson Williams* (New York: n.p., 1916), 203–204.

[Robert Mills on South Carolina Industry in 1826]

Coarse cottons and woolens, for common clothing, are manufactured in Spartanburg district to some extent, and some for sale. Two cotton factories are established on Tyger river, which do very good business. Bar iron is made at Nesbit's forge, on Tyger river, and at the furnace, north of the Court-house. Immense quantities of hollow ware, cannon balls, screws for cotton packing, etc., have been cast at these places.

The two species of iron ore are the magnetic, or gray ore, and the hydrate, or brown ore. The only furnace in the upper country now in operation which uses the brown ore is the one belonging to Col. Nesbit in Spartanburg District. Two furnaces make use of the gray ore; they are in the districts of York and Spartanburg. It is also carried from York to North Carolina, where it is reduced to iron. The gray ore makes the best iron, either for bar iron, or castings.

There is a cotton factory, owned by Mr. Garrison, in Pendleton district, which manufactures for sale, on a small scale. A rifle gun factory is established on the Chatuga creek. In Richland district there are several excellent merchant mills, capable of manufacturing the finest flour, and numerous saw and cotton gin mills. Within a mile and a half of Edgefield Court-house there is a village of sixteen or seventeen houses, and as many families, called the Pottery or Pottersville . . . . This village is altogether supported by the manufacture of stoneware, . . . better and cheaper than any European or American ware of the same kind. In Abbeville district, Mr. Gilbert established some years ago a cotton factory on Little river, and had the whole work, castings, turnings, etc., executed on the spot; an instance of considerable ingenuity and enterprise. Domestic cottons and woolens are the only articles manufactured . . . . Formerly an armory was established in Greenville district, on the waters of Reedy river, but since the peace it has declined . . . .

Robert Mills, *Statistics of South Carolina* . . . (Charleston: Hurlburt and Lloyd, 1826), 25, 353–54, 523, 575, 677, 721, 730.

[William Gregg on Manufacturing in the 1840s]

A change in our habits and industrial pursuits is a far greater desideratum than any change in the laws of our Government which the most clamorous opponents of the tariff could devise. He who has possessed himself of the notion that we have the industry, and are wronged out of our hard earnings by a lazy set of scheming Yankees, to get rid of this delusion, needs only seat himself on the Charleston wharves for a few days, and behold ship after ship arrive, laden down with the various articles produced by Yankee industry. Let him behold these vessels discharging their cargoes and count the cost to South Carolina. From the month of September till May, our wharves are crowded, not only with the articles manufactured by the handicraftsmen of the North, but with vast quantities of dairy articles, and all kinds of culinary vegetables, which are far better adapted to the soil of South Carolina, than to those places where they are grown. . . .

Let South Carolina be true to herself, let her go to work with a determination to resist the Northern tariffites, by resolving not to purchase or use their articles of manufacture. This will cure the evil, and bring us to the point we desire to arrive at, by an easier and much shorter road than legislative action. Limited as our manufactures are in South Carolina, we can now more than supply the State with coarse cotton fabrics. Many of the fabrics now manufactured here are exported to New York, and, for aught I know, find their way to the East Indies. We can most assuredly make our own axe handles, raise our own cabbages, beets, potatoes, and onions; our boys, as in older times, may be taught to make their own toy wagons and wheel-barrows, our wives and sisters can hem our handkerchiefs and bake our bread. If we continue in our present habits, it would not be unreasonable to predict, that when the Raleigh Rail-road is extended to Columbia, our members of the Legislature will be fed on Yankee baker's bread. . . .

William Gregg, *Essays on Domestic Industry, Or, An Enquiry into the Expediency of Establishing Cotton Manufacturing in South Carolina* (Graniteville, S.C.: The Graniteville Co., 1941), 19, 21–22, 26, 48–49. Reprinted by permission of The Graniteville Company.

No man can doubt the fact, that any large cotton planter would be a far more useful citizen, were his plantation converted into a provision farm, and he engaged . . . with half his force in cotton spinning . . . instead of producing the same—thus lightening instead of increasing the burden of the country. . . .

Shall we pass unnoticed the thousands of poor, ignorant, degraded white people among us, who, in this land of plenty, live in comparative nakedness and starvation? Many a one is reared in proud South Carolina, from birth to manhood, who has never passed a month, in which he has not some part of the time, been stinted for meat. Many a mother is there, who will tell you that her children are but scantily supplied with bread, and much more scantily with meat, and if they be clad with comfortable raiment, it is at the expense of their scanty allowance of food. These may be startling statements, but they are nevertheless true, and if not believed in Charleston, the members of our Legislature, who have traversed the State, in electioneering campaigns, can attest their truth.

It is only necessary to build a manufacturing village of shanties, in a healthy location in any part of the State, to have crowds of these poor people around you, seeking employment at half the compensation given to operatives at the North. It is indeed painful to be brought in contact with such ignorance and degradation; but on the other hand, it is pleasant to witness the change, which soon takes place in the condition of those who obtain employment. The emancipated, pale-faced children soon assume the appearance of robust health, and their tattered garments are exchanged for those suited to a better condition; if you visit their dwellings, you will find their tables supplied with wholesome food; and on the Sabbath, when the females turn out in their gay colored gowns, you will imagine yourself surounded by groups of city belles.

108. *Public Welfare in the 1820s*

DURING THE COLONIAL PERIOD, THE IDEA WAS ESTABLISHED IN SOUTH CAROLINA THAT PARISHES HAD SOME RESPONSIBILITY FOR THE CARE OF THE ORPHANED, THE POOR, THE CRIPPLED, THE INSANE, AND THE AGED. BY THE 1820s SOME FACILITIES FOR THESE DEPENDENT GROUPS WERE AVAILABLE IN CHARLESTON, AND TO A LESSER EXTENT ELSEWHERE. FOR THE MOST PART, THE FAMILY WAS STILL RESPONSIBLE FOR ITS UNFORTU-NATES. ROBERT MILLS WRITES ON WELFARE FACILITIES AND SERVICES IN THE STATE, AND NOTES THAT THE NEW INSANE ASYLUM IS JUST BEING COMPLETED IN COLUMBIA.

[Robert Mills]

The orphan house (in Charleston) . . . is a spacious brick building raised three stories above the basement offices. The length of the house is 180 feet, and breadth 30 feet. This valuable institution . . . went into operation in 1794. It is well endowed, supported chiefly by the . . . city, aided by private donations. The annual expenses for fuel, diet, clothing, officers' salaries, etc., is $14,000.00. It is under the superintendence and direction of twelve commissioners, annually elected by the city council, who are assisted in the female department by several ladies. From 180 to 200 destitute orphans and children of indigent parents are here educated and supported. . . .

The public prison is situated on Magazine Street, corner of Back Street. It is a large three story brick building, with very roomy and comfortable accommodations for those whose unfortunate lot it is to be there confined . . . . It is divided into solitary cells, one for each criminal, and the whole made fire-proof. A spacious court is attached to the prison, and every attention to cleanliness is paid throughout, which is highly creditable to those who have charge of the institution. . . .

The work house, adjoining the jail, is appropriated entirely to the confinement and punishment of slaves. These were formerly compelled

Robert Mills, *Statistics of South Carolina* . . . (Charleston: Hurlburt and Lloyd, 1826), 419–20.

only occasionally to work; no means then existing of employing them regularly and effectually. The last year the city council ordered the erection of a tread-mill; this has proved a valuable appendage to the prison, and will probably supersede every other species of punishment there. . . .

The poor-house, and asylum for lunatic persons, situated near the corner of Queen on Mazyck Street . . . is a spacious building, neat in its appearance, and commodious in its internal arrangements. It was founded at a very early period; is built of brick, three stories high, and crowned with a large cupola, which serves also to ventilate the house. The interior accommodations are roomy and airy. Great attention is paid to cleanliness and order. The number of paupers and out-door pensioners provided for by this institution averages 983 in the year; of these, twenty are lunatic persons who are placed in an out-building by themselves. It is expected that as soon as the Lunatic Asylum in Columbia goes into operation, most of these insane persons will be removed there. The annual expense of supporting these poor amounts to near $17,000. which is provided for by the city council. The fund appropriated by the State for the poor here is called the "transient poor fund," and comprises strangers or non-residents of the city; it has, for some years amounted to about $12,000 annually.

The Marine Hospital is located in the rear of the Medical College, where the sick stranger or poor mariner is taken care of. The expenses of this institution exceed annually $5700. The number admitted: 296. . . .

In addition to the above . . . there are several associations for relieving distress and furthering religious objects, composed entirely of females, whose kind and indefatigable attentions to the wants of the poor, claim for them the highest meed of praise . . . . This city possesses a greater number of charitable institutions, in proportion to its population, than any other in the Union . . . .

[Robert Mills]

The poor of Edgefield district are put to work under a superintendant. The tax to support them, formerly amounting to thirty per cent on the

Robert Mills, *Statistics of South Carolina* . . . , (Charleston: Hurlburt and Lloyd, 1826), 420.

general tax, has been considerably reduced under the present regulation. This is a subject of deep interest to the community. It is very evident that the old system (still existing in some of the districts) is deplorably deficient. The manner in which alms were formerly dispensed, have tended rather to increase than decrease pauperism; nay, it offered a premium to idleness, as nothing was required of the pauper but to receive alms. Though it is disgraceful for any one to receive alms who is able to work, (if only to pick the specks, or the seed, out of the cotton) yet that he should have no excuse, the mendicant ought to be provided with work. The money that was formerly laid out (amounting to upwards of three hundred dollars annually) for the idle support of the poor, is now so disbursed as to produce a far different effect. It should be a fixed rule, in giving alms, never to bestow money, except under very particular exigencies; such as sickness, or to pay house rent, etc. Every person having the use of his hands, if not in bodily pain, is capable of earning ten or twelve cents a day, which is sufficient to support life. . . .

The number of poor in Fairfield district does not exceed 30, and the expense of keeping them, about $200. The *poor fund* is raised by adding a certain percentage upon the general tax of the district, which is not to exceed thirty per cent upon our general tax. . . .

[Robert Mills]

There are few paupers in Newberry district at this time. The expense of supporting them amounts to from $60 to $100 a year; they are let to the lowest bidder by the commissioners. . . .

A poor house and farm are provided for the poor of Pendleton district, where they are furnished with such work as they are capable of performing. The only expense attending this establishment is paying the salary of the keeper or superintendent. . . .

The Asylum for lunatic persons at Columbia . . . is now nearly finished and probably will soon go into operation. The design of it is both novel and convenient. It combines elegance with permanence, economy

Robert Mills, *Statistics of South Carolina* . . . , (Charleston: Hurlburt and Lloyd, 1826), 421.

and security from fire. The rooms are vaulted with brick, and the roof covered with copper. The building is large enough to accommodate upwards of 120 patients, besides furnishing spacious corridors, hospitals, refectories, a medical hall, several parlors, keepers apartments, kitchens and sundry offices. The whole is surrounded by a lofty enclosure. The cost of the whole is considerably within $100,000.

109. *Religion*

COMPARED WITH THE COLONIAL PERIOD, THE ANTEBELLUM ERA WAS A
RELIGIOUS ONE, AT LEAST AS FAR AS CHURCHES, CHURCH ASSOCIATIONS,
AND CHURCH-SPONSORED SCHOOLS WERE CONCERNED. THE FIRST SELEC-
TION DESCRIBES THE CONDITION OF CHURCHES IN THE STATE IN THE
EARLY NINETEENTH CENTURY; THE SECOND IS A DESCRIPTION OF A CAMP
MEETING IN THE LOW COUNTRY.

[David Ramsay]

South Carolina religious groups in the early nineteenth century:

The Episcopal Church languished in South Carolina for several years
after the Revolution. Though it maintained a respectable standing in
their two ancient houses of worship in Charleston, it made for some time
but little progress in the country. Better prospects are now before its
members. . . . Their long neglected places of worship in the country are
repairing, and new ones are building. Divine service according to the
Book of Common Prayer is now regularly performed in Beaufort by the
Rev. Mr. Hicks; in St. Andrews by the Rev. Mr. Mills; in St. Bartholomews, by the Rev. Mr. Fowler; in St. Johns, by the Rev. Mr. Gadsden;
in St. Thomas by the Rev. Mr. Nankeville; at the High Hills of Santee
by the Rev. Mr. Ischudy; and at St. James, Santee, by the Rev. Mr.
Mathews. In most of the other parishes where the establishment operated
before the Revolution, there are Episcopal churches, but at present no
settled ministers. . . .

The Presbyterians . . . have a numerous and wealthy congregation in
the capital, and the Presbytery of Charleston consists of five ministers. To
them seven Congregations look up for religious instruction. The Presbytery at present consists of the following congregations and ministers:
Stoney Creek, Prince Williams, Rev. R. Montgomery Adams; Edisto

David Ramsay, *History of South Carolina* . . . , 2 vols. (Charleston: David
Longworth for the author, 1809), II, 23–32.

Island, Rev. Donald M'Leod; John and Wadmalaw Islands, Rev. Dr. Clarkson. . . . Of the numerous emigrants to the western parts of Carolina, in the last fifty years of the 18th century, a great majority were Presbyterians. They had little regular preaching among them until about the year 1770, when missionaries from the northward formed them into churches. These were revived and increased after the Revolution, and . . . are now formed into two Presbyteries consisting of more than 20 ministers and . . . 60 congregations. There is also a Presbytery of seceders in South Carolina consisting of nine ministers, who have under their care 22 congregations . . . .

The Baptists . . . anterior to the Revolution . . . had increased to about thirty churches. Since the establishment of equal religious rights they have increased so that they now have five associations consisting of 100 ministers, 130 churches, 10,500 communicants, and about 73,500 adherents. . . .

The Independents or Congregationalists . . . kept possession of their ancient house of worship, long known by the name of White Meeting. They erected an additional house of worship in Archdale Street, in which divine service was first performed in 1787. These two houses form one church, and have common interests and ministers, with equal salaries and privileges. The Independents also have a church, near Dorchester, supplied by the Rev. Mr. McKelhenney; in Christ Church under the pastoral care of the Rev. Dr. McCalla; on James Island under that of Mr. Price; in Beaufort under Mr. Palmer, and in St. Bartholomews at present vacant.

The Methodists made their first appearance as a religious society in South Carolina in the year 1785. For the last ten or fifteen years they have increased beyond any former example. . . . Their society in South Carolina is divided into twelve circuits and stations, in which there are twenty-six traveling preachers who continue to ride daily . . . . They commonly ride around a circuit in five or six weeks. Exclusive of the twenty-six travelling preachers there are in the State of South Carolina about ninety-three local preachers, generally married men, who labor all the week and preach at an average each two sermons in each Sunday . . . . They have in South Carolina about two hundred churches or stations for preaching, which are constructed in so plain a style as to cost on an average about one hundred and thirty-five dollars each . . . . There are four Methodist churches in Charleston . . . . To these belong forty heads of families, or about one hundred and seventy white persons, and fifteen hundred and twenty persons of color.

[David Ramsay]

A description of a Low Country camp meeting:

Camp meetings which began in Kentucky, and parts adjacent, found their way into South Carolina about the year 1800. These were held in different places and different seasons, but oftenest in the autumn. They were attended by several thousands, many of whom came from considerable distances; and they usually kept together on the same ground from the Thursday of one week till the Tuesday of the next. The Holy Sacrament was always administered on the intervening Sunday, and to persons of different sects; who, forgetting all differences on minor subjects, chose to commune together. The bagging provided for the envelopement of their cotton was easily formed into tents for their temporary lodging. Huts made in a few hours and covered wagons answered the same purpose. The farmers brought their families, provisions, and bedding, in wagons from their respective homes. They took their station where wood and water were of easy attainment, and in general fared well. From their stores they hospitably entertained strangers who came as visitors. Two, three, or four tents or stands for preaching were erected at such distances that divine service could be performed in each of them at the same time without any interference. From five to twelve or fifteen ministers of different denominations attended and with short intervals for refreshment and repose, kept up in different places a constant succession of religious exercises by night as well as by day. Besides the performance of divine service by the ministers in their respective tents, there were frequently subdivisions of the people at convenient distances, where praying, exhorting, and singing of psalms was carried on by lay persons, and the whole so managed that they did not disturb each other. The auditors whose motive was curiosity, freely passed from one scene to another, and could in the space of a few minutes and the circuit of a few acres, indulge their taste for variety. Others were more stationary and hung on the lips of their favorite preachers. . . . That the camp meetings were intended for good, and that they frequently issued in the reformation of several who attended them, was the general opinion of the candid, liberal, and virtuous.

David Ramsay, *History of South Carolina* . . . , 2 vols. (Charleston: David Longworth for the author, 1809), II, 33–35.

110. *Industry and Utilities Between 1826 and 1866*

Up to 1860, South Carolina's staple crop, cotton, was the glory of agricultural expertise, and the railroads had made it possible to transport the commodity far and wide with ease. Robert Mills describes industry during the 1820s. This is followed by a story, written after the Civil War, which tells how the railroads affected the internal portion of South Carolina.

[Robert Mills]

The commerce of South Carolina [is] greater with England than with any other foreign country. Most of her staple commodity, cotton, is shipped there; if not directly, yet indirectly, through other ports; and large quantities of her manufactured articles are received in turn.

A considerable trade is also kept up with the West Indies and France, some little with Spain, United Netherlands, Russia, Germany, Madeira, and lately, South America. But much of the direct trade with Europe is taken from South Carolina by the cities of New York, Boston, and Philadelphia; which, while it lessens the amount of our domestic exports, in the Custom House returns, goes to swell those of the States of New York, Massachusetts, and Pennsylvania. . . .

The amount of domestic exports directly shipped from Charleston to foreign ports, is now only $7,475,747, and the amount of duties collected only $736,020, whilst in 1815, the revenue amounted to $1,408,863, and the exports in 1816 . . . to near $11,000,000.

The value of our direct imports from foreign ports for the last year amounted only to $2,030,916. The residue, which may be estimated at five times this amount, demanded by the exigencies of the State, is all derived from the Northern cities, particularly New York.

South Carolina owns but little shipping; the most of the produce being exported in vessels belonging to Northern merchants. The domestic ton-

Robert Mills, *Statistics of South Carolina* . . . (Charleston: Hurlburt and Lloyd, 1826), 161–62.

nage would scarcely exceed thirty thousand. The amount of tonnage which cleared for foreign ports from Charleston in the year 1824 was:

In vessels of the United States   67,941 tons.
In foreign vessels   18,211 tons.
                          Total   86,152 tons.

The value of the several articles exported to foreign ports in 1824 was as follows:

Rice $1,114,297
Cotton   5,605,948
Other   208,570

SOUTH CAROLINA RAILROADS

Charleston, June 27, 1866
[Unidentified writer]

Our railroad system has been a gradual accretion from a small commencement. It has not sprung into existence with all those applications of capital and appliances of science and skill which have marked the more recent works of this character. It had its source simply in the attempt to remedy a defect of nature. The South Carolina Railroad had its origin in the fact that the occasionally low state of the Savannah river prevented the great staple of the South from reaching the Charleston market at reasonable periods. One of the earliest projectors of this road was Alexander Black, a man of indomitable energy and perseverance, who had emigrated from Ireland young, self-educated, and self-reliant, with strong, practical sense. This early effort to bring Charleston into connection with the Interior was made by constructing an experimental road of only one hundred and fifty feet in extent, by the use of horse power, running diagonally, on the ground now occupied by Mr. Memminger's house in Wentworth street.

Mr. Black was aided by Tristam Tupper, a man of equal energy of purpose, and by combined exertions completed a road one hundred and

Daily News and Herald (Savannah, Ga.), June 27, 1866.

thirty-six miles in length, the longest then in existence. When it is recollected that steam power applied to railroads was then in its infancy, this is one of the most striking examples of successful enterprise on record. It was completed in October, 1833, having been commenced in 1828. At the commencement of the enterprise the design was to plank the road and use horse-power. Before it was completed the application of steam to railroads was discovered, and thus rendered railroads more effective than was ever imagined at the inception of the idea of Railroads as a means of transportation.

THE SOUTH CAROLINA RAILROAD

It is not, perhaps, generally known, that the first extensive Railroad built in this country was the one which connects Charleston and Hamburg.

The enterprise of our Charleston merchants set in motion the iron horse which now travels his useful and unremitting course over the thousands of Railroads which cover this country like a net work.

The South Carolina Canal and Railroad Company was chartered in 1827, and the work commenced in this city in 1831. It was finished to Hamburg in 1833. The first locomotive made in England for this road, was soon succeeded by the "Miller," of American construction, bearing the name of a citizen of Charleston. In 1835, the first project for connecting this city with the Ohio river was abandoned, because a continuous charter through all the intermediate States could not be obtained.

In 1842, the branch from Branchville to Columbia, sixty-eight miles, was completed, and in 1848, the Camden Branch, thirty-seven miles, was finished.

This road, with its connections by means of the Charlotte and South Carolina Railroad, and the Greenville and Columbia Railroad, has done much towards developing the internal resources of this and neighboring States. In times past, the flour, wheat, corn, turpentine and cotton, within the reach of the South Carolina Railroad and its connections, were brought to Charleston, thence to be exported to Northern or foreign markets. In exchange for these productions, our merchants did a thriving business in supplying the interior of this State, Georgia, North Carolina, Alabama, Tennessee, and even Mississippi.

As the different connecting Railroads were opened, especially the Georgia Railroad and its branches, the business of the South Carolina

Railroad increased, and the receipts which in 1834 only amounted to $166,000, in ten years reached $533,000, and continued to increase in amount until the breaking out of the late war. Through freights as well as local rates were then apportioned with liberality and judgment. Just after the close of the war, when the South Carolina Railroad found themselves greatly embarrassed for want of money wherewith to repair the serious injuries inflicted by the Federal troops, and the folly of our own generals, our merchants bore patiently the high charges for freights on this Road. The Company could not borrow money, and the Road had to pay for its repairs out of its earnings. This state of things has passed away, the Road has been put in complete running order to Columbia and Augusta.

Great credit is due to the managers of this Road, for the energy displayed in rebuilding the tracks on both branches, together with the extensive bridges which had been destroyed by military orders from both parties in the recent revolution and war. We may now look with confidence for a gradual reduction of freights, whereby the trade and commerce of Charleston may be restored, and the receipts of the Company, at the same time, be so greatly increased as to warrant further improvements.

THE NORTH-EASTERN RAILROAD

The North-Eastern Railroad, although not so far a profitable investment for the stockholders, is an important connection in the great chain of travel along the seaboard. Bringing to Charleston the valuable products of the rich Pee Dee valley, and affording the nearest mail and passenger route to the North, this enterprise must, in time, prove exceedingly profitable. The various interests which are dependent for their proper development upon this road, render its prospects and management matters of serious consideration to the people of Charleston. Commencing with the coal fields of North Carolina, we must, at once perceive how important to this city it is, that this useful mineral fuel, which lies in abundance in our sister State, should be transported over the Coal Fields Railroad to Cheraw, thence by the Cheraw and Darlington Railroad to Florence, and thence by the North-Eastern Railroad to Charleston.

Next is the junction of this road with the Wilmington and Manchester Railroad at Florence, giving the shortest route from Charleston to New York, and affording to the citizens of lower Georgia, by way of the

Savannah Railroad, and of Florida, by the steamers connecting with Charleston, the advantages of cheap and rapid travel to the northern cities.

At the same point, Florence, the Cheraw and Darlington Railroad pours into the North-Eastern cars the valuable productions of the Pee Dee valley. The seaport of Georgetown must also, at an early day, connect with this road by a short line, which has been in agitation for some time past.

Looking now to the management of the road we find much to admire.

Chartered in 1851, the North-Eastern Railroad had to contend with many difficulties and obstacles from its inception. The bridge over the Santee is a monument to the energy of the officers of the Company, and to the genius of the inventor, Dr. Potts. This remarkable structure received serious injury during the war, having lost all the wood work by the folly of our own military leaders, and one of the iron cylindrical piers by the action of the Union gun boats. The whole is now completely restored. Under the conduct of Presidents Huger, McKay, MacFarlan, and its present head, Mr. A. F. Ravenel, assisted by that able and indefatigable superintendent, Mr. S. S. Solomons, this road has always been managed with remarkable success. The regularity with which the trains were run—the almost entire exemption from accidents, and the quantity of work accomplished—speak well for the energy and ability of its managers. We trust the revival of trade will soon enable this company to recover from its losses, and compensate its stockholders for their patience and confidence in its ultimate success.

THE CHARLESTON AND SAVANNAH RAILROAD

The Charleston and Savannah Railroad Company was chartered by the State of South Carolina in December, 1853, and by Georgia, in February, 1854. The projectors of this enterprise entertained high hopes of its profitable character, and beneficial influence upon the trade and travel of both cities. This short line of one hundred miles would complete the sea-board route between New York and the Gulf; would open a lucrative business with South-western Georgia, Florida and Alabama; would greatly increase the commercial operations between Charleston and Savannah, and would derive much profit from the local trade and travel of the wealthy country through which it passed. In view of the great political crisis then looming up in the distance, it was thought important to form a close connection between States having common interests and institutions. The wisdom of this view was fully proven during our recent troubles, when this Road did such good service in conveying troops and munitions of war, as well as various products and merchandise, between the two cities, and the various military posts from the Ashley to the Savannah rivers.

The first President was Thos. F. Drayton. On the 29th March, 1858, the first locomotive on this Road, the "Ashley," commenced work in conveying rails and cross ties to the track layers. Drane & Singletary, soon after that time, commenced operations as contractors, and soon showed such energy and rapidity of movement, as to astonish our usually slow people. On the 15th of November, 1858, freight and passenger trains ran to the Edisto river, and on the 20th of November, 1860, the entire Road was completed. On the 26th May, 1860, the last rail was put in position. Just a month before the Ordinance of Secession was issued, this Road, destined to play so important a part in the revolution, was completed. A few months afterwards, the appearance of the Federal fleet on our coast brought into play all the energy of the newly elected President, W. J. Magrath, and taxed to the utmost the carrying capacity of the road. In 1862, Mr. B. D. Hasell became President, and the business of the road continued to improve and yielded a net income of nearly $160,000. The year 1863, under the management of Mr. R. L. Singletary, the present President, the net income reached $393,000. The want of a bridge across the Ashley river, which had been severely felt by the managers for years past, prevented the road from doing even a larger business. But this favorable state of things was soon to be changed by the military reverses of the South. In December, 1864, General Sherman's army approached Savannah. The Federals at Hilton Head soon took up a position near the line of the road, and from that time the trains were run at the imminent risk of life and property. Disaster followed disaster, until finally the failure of our cause involved this road in a common ruin.

The directors of the road are, however, using every exertion to recover from the present depressed condition. The road has been rebuilt to Saltkehatchie, about half the entire length of the line, and we may hope by next fall to see the entire line in operation. The rich lands through which the road passes are now either deserted, or at best but partially cultivated. But the common sense of the nation must in time be felt, and this valuable portion of our State must share in the return of former prosperity and wealth.

111. *Life and Culture in the 1800s*

AN AFFLUENT SOCIETY, MADE WEALTHY BY THE PRODUCTION OF RICE AND THEN OF COTTON BEFORE THE CIVIL WAR, TURNED ITS THOUGHTS TO CULTURE. WITH THE INSTALLATION OF "DEMOCRACY" AND THE RISE OF THE COMMON MAN, STORIES BEGAN TO EMPLOY AN AMERICAN THEME. SOUTH CAROLINA WAS WELL REPRESENTED IN THE TWO "NATIONAL PERIODS" OF LITERATURE WHICH DIVIDED THE NINETEENTH CENTURY. IN THE FIRST PERIOD, HEROES LIKE FRANCIS MARION WERE IMMORTALIZED. IMAGINARY TALES AND POETRY CHARACTERIZE THE MIDDLE OF THE CENTURY, AND TOWARD THE END OF THE CENTURY SAD STORIES AND POEMS ABOUT THE WAR CAME TO THE FOREFRONT. AMONG SOUTH CAROLINA'S BEST KNOWN WRITERS AND POETS WERE HENRY TIMROD, PAUL HAMILTON HAYNE, WILLIAM GILMORE SIMMS, ROBERT GIBBES, WILLIAM MAXWELL MARTIN, AND J. GORDON COOGLER. EXCERPTS HERE INCLUDE THE PROSE OF AN ABLE WRITER, DUNCAN CLINCH HEYWARD, WHO TELLS OF LIFE ON HIS FATHER'S PLANTATION; POE'S CRITICISM OF SIMMS; AND J. GORDON COOGLER'S FAMOUS COUPLET, WHICH IS FREQUENTLY MIS-ATTRIBUTED TO H. L. MENCKEN. COOGLER WAS A COLUMBIAN AND ACHIEVED FAME IN LITERARY CIRCLES IN THE PERIOD FOLLOWING THE CIVIL WAR.

[Life on the Plantation Described by Duncan Clinch Heyward]

Early in the morning, except when the weather would not permit, the driver, standing in his door at the head of the street, would awaken the field hands by blowing a horn, though on some plantations a bell was rung. They were awakened early enough to give them time to cook their breakfasts. . . .

Duncan Clinch Heyward, *Seed from Madagascar* (Chapel Hill: University of North Carolina Press, 1937), 179–82, 185. Copyright, 1937, By the University of North Carolina Press. Reprinted by permission of The University of North Carolina Press.

In the spring and summer the men and sometimes the women went to the fields without shoes, the latter usually wearing cotton leggings fitting closely and coming nearly to their knees. Their dresses came just below their knees and were tied just below the waist with a cord, thus forming a roll. When the dews were heavy, the men rolled up their pants to keep them dry . . . . The women with few exceptions wore colored handkerchiefs on their heads.

The field hands were classed as half hands or full hands, and the work of each, in both character and amount, was what long experience had shown could be done and done thoroughly, for in slavery days great stress was laid on the quality of the work.

It was always the custom during the spring and summer months to allow the field hands to finish their work early enough to give them at least two hours by the sun in order that they might work for themselves, or if they did not care to work, they were allowed to do as they pleased. During the winter months opportunity was given them to gather firewood and to grind corn. To all full field hands who would make use of it, high land was allotted, and they were encouraged to plant crops for themselves; and this many of them did. In fact, on rice plantations probably more Negroes planted their own crops on a small scale when they were slaves than they did after they became free. Negroes who did plant for themselves after freedom usually wanted to plant more land than they could cultivate, thinking that by so doing they would become more independent and could work or not, as they chose. The result was that many of them were continually in debt and at the end of the year had nothing.

Each year during November or December woolen cloth was distributed to the Negroes, and in May or June cloth of a lighter material . . . . Every field hand was given five and a half yards of gray cloth and a smaller quantity for each of his or her children. For a baby a mother received one and a half yards. The drivers, carpenters, and other head men, to distinguish them from the rest, were allotted six and a half yards of blue cloth and one of white. They were also given overcoats and felt hats. The men among the field hands received caps and the women plaid handkerchiefs known as bandannas . . . . Woolen blankets were given to the slaves when needed.

In the fall each Negro was provided with a pair of shoes of substantial quality. There was no haphazard distribution . . . each pair was ordered to fit a certain individual. To accomplish this a small cedar stick . . . was given to every slave. After measuring the length of his or her feet the slave would cut the stick accordingly and notch it to indicate the width of the feet. These sticks were sent to the factory in Charleston along with the order for the shoes. . . .

Regularly one day each week the slaves were rationed. They were given corn, sweet potatoes, rice and syrup. Each adult received four quarts of corn and one-half of this amount for each of his children. . . . Until the time of Charles Heyward, they were not given meat; this they were expected to provide for themselves. In order to do so they were allowed to raise their own hogs and were given the privilege of hunting and fishing. . . . In addition to this, most of the slaves raised poultry and often sold eggs. . . .

Sunday was always a day of rest, and frequently church services were held on the plantation by white ministers, whose salaries were supplemented and traveling expenses paid by the planters.

During the days of slavery a considerable number of slaves on the rice plantations of South Carolina were members of the Episcopal Church, as most ministers who held services for them belonged to that denomination. When the slaves were declared free . . . they very rapidly established churches of other denominations. . . .

[Poe's Criticism of Simms]

In the *Broadway Journal*, II (Oct. 4, 1845), 190–191, Poe published a review of *The Wigwam and the Cabin*, in which he says: "This is one of the most interesting numbers of the Library yet published—and decidedly the most American of the American books . . . . In a recent number of our Journal . . . we spoke of Mr. Simms as 'the best novelist which this country has, upon the whole, produced'; and this is our deliberate opinion. We take into consideration, of course, as well the amount of what he has written, as the talent he has displayed;—he is the Lopez de Vega of American writers of fiction. His merits lie among the major and his defects among the minor morals of literature. His

Mary C. Simms Oliphant et al., eds., *The Letters of William Gilmore Simms*, 5 vols. (Columbia: University of South Carolina Press, 1952–1956), II, 106, 317*n*. Copyright 1953 by the University of South Carolina Press, Columbia. Reprinted by permission of The University of South Carolina Press.

earlier works of length, such as 'The Partisan', were disfigured by many inaccuracies of style, and especially by the prevalence of the merely repulsive, where the horrible was the object—but in invention, in vigor, in movement, in the power of exciting interest, and in the artistical management of his themes, he has surpassed, we think, any of his countrymen:—that is to say, he has surpassed any of them in the aggregate of these high qualities. His best fictions . . . are 'Martin Faber' . . . 'Beauchampe'; 'Richard Hurdis'; 'Castle Dismal'; 'Helen Halsey'; and 'Murder will Out.' . . . 'Murder will Out' . . . we have no hesitation in calling it the best ghost-story we have ever read. It is . . . detailed throughout with a degree of artistic skill which has no parallel among American story-tellers since the epoch of Brockden Brown.

[J. Gordon Coogler's Famous Couplet:]

Alas! for the South, her books have grown fewer—
She never was much given to literature.

READINGS

ADDITIONAL PRINTED SOURCE MATERIALS:

Calhoun, John C. *The Works of John C. Calhoun,* ed. Richard K. Crallé.

———. *The Papers of John C. Calhoun.* Robert L. Meriwether, ed. Vol. I, 1801–1818. W. Edwin Hemphill, ed. Vol. II, December 1817–July 1818; Vol. III, 1818–1819.

Drayton, John. *A View of South Carolina, as Respects her Natural and Civil Concerns.*

J. Gordon Coogler, *Purely Original Verse* (1897), quoted in John Bartlett, *Familiar Quotations* (Boston: Little, Brown and Co., 1951), 814.

Easterby, James H., ed. *The South Carolina Rice Plantation as Revealed in the Papers of Robert F. W. Allston.*

Fraser, Charles. *Reminiscences of Charleston.*

Gregg, William. *Essays on Domestic Industry; or, An Inquiry into the Expediency of Establishing Cotton Manufactures in South Carolina . . . .*

Mills, Robert. *Statistics of South Carolina . . . .*

CORRELATED TEXTS:

Boucher, Chauncey. *The Nullification Controversy in South Carolina.*

Frechling, William W. *Prelude to Civil War: The Nullification Controversy in South Carolina, 1816–1836.*

Jervey, Theodore. *Robert Young Hayne and His Times.*

Schultz, Harold S. *Nationalism and Sectionalism in South Carolina, 1852–1860.*

Smith, Alfred Glaze, Jr. *Economic Readjustment of an Old Cotton State: South Carolina, 1820–1860.*

Snowden, Yates, ed. *History of South Carolina.* I, 524–76.

Taylor, Rosser. *Ante-Bellum South Carolina, A Social and Cultural History.*

Van Deusen, J. G. *Economic Bases of Disunion in South Carolina.*

Wallace, D. D. *History of South Carolina.* II, 352–510; III, 1–150.

———. *South Carolina: A Short History,* 346–525.

VI
CIVIL WAR AND RECONSTRUCTION

The Civil War began on a note of triumph in South Carolina, but by the end of the war and during reconstruction the state had reached the lowest point in history. In seceding from the Union, South Carolina was living up to its heritage of independence. The South Carolinians felt that they were fighting for liberty in 1861 as much as they were in 1776, but there was a great difference in the times. In 1861, the state was far more unified than it had been in 1776, and there were no "tories." The unionists of 1840 and 1850, whose counterparts might have been the whigs, had become passive secessionists by 1860.

Although South Carolina took the lead in secession, this did not mean that the state was to be foremost in the Confederacy. Despite the contribution of 60,000 officers and men to the Confederate Army, very few South Carolinians held official positions in the governments at Montgomery and Richmond.

During the first three years of the war, the interior of South Carolina was virtually free from military action, but parts of the coastal area suffered under the guns of the enemy and the fighting in and around Charleston went on for the duration. South Carolina also suffered the indignity of having Beaufort and the surrounding Sea Islands occupied by the enemy for three and one-half years. The Union blockade closed all of the coastal area except Charleston, which served as the home port for much of the blockade-running achieved by Confederate ships during the war. Early in 1865, Gen. W. T. Sherman and his Union forces, in line with his scorched-earth policy, marched into South Carolina from Georgia, and a few months later the war was over. The South Carolina troops had fought valiantly. More than a third had been killed or seriously wounded in action or had died of disease.

The war left South Carolina in desperate condition, and the coming years of reconstruction brought relief only from the ravages of military action. To the costs of war were added the losses brought about by the freeing of slaves without remuneration to their owners and by the upkeep of adventurers who poured in to enjoy the spoils of war following the conflict. To the problems of rebuilding homes and a shattered economy was added that of adjustment to a society without slavery. Neither the white people nor the freedmen were prepared for the sweeping changes which came with emancipation. The 12 years of Reconstruction government were times of chaos and uncertainty. The federally supported Republican government of "Negroes, carpetbaggers, and scalawags" was corrupt and inefficient. The reaction, in the form of the Ku Klux Klan and the "Revolution of 1876," also employed questionable methods in achieving their goals. By 1877, however, Gen. Wade Hampton had led the Democrats to a return to power and the state turned toward more stability. During the period, the U. S. government had set a precedent, which still stands, in its inhumane treatment of the "conquered."

112. An Editorial on Secession, November 3, 1860

SOUTH CAROLINA HAD BEEN TALKING OF THE POSSIBILITIES OF SECES-
SION FOR MORE THAN A DECADE, BUT IT WAS THE ELECTION OF THE
REPUBLICAN PRESIDENT, ABRAHAM LINCOLN, IN NOVEMBER, 1860, THAT
BROUGHT ON THE SECESSION CONVENTION. THE FOLLOWING EDITORIAL,
ENTITLED "WHAT SHALL SOUTH CAROLINA DO?" FROM THE CHARLES-
TON *Mercury*, INDICATES THE OPINION OF SOUTH CAROLINA LEADERS AS
THE ELECTION APPROACHED.

[R. Barnwell Rhett]

The issue before the country is the extinction of slavery. No man of
common sense, who has observed the progress of events, and who is
not prepared to surrender the institution, with the safety and independence of the South, can doubt that the time for action has come—
now or never. The Southern States are now in the crisis of their fate;
and, if we read aright the signs of the times, nothing is needed for our
deliverance, but the ball of revolution be set in motion. There is
sufficient readiness among the people to make it entirely successful.
Co-operation will follow the action of any State. The example of a
forward movement only is requisite to unite Southern States in a common cause. Under these circumstances the Legislature of South Carolina
is about to meet. It happens to assemble in advance of the legislature
of any other State. Being in session at this momentous juncture—the
Legislature of that State which is most united in the policy of freeing
the South from Black Republican domination—the eyes of the whole
country, and most especially of the resistance party of the Southern
States, is intently turned upon the conduct of this body. We have
innumerable assurances that the men of action in each and all of the
Southern States, earnestly desire South Carolina to exhibit promptitude
and decision in this conjuncture. Other states are torn and divided, to
a greater or less extent, by old party issues. South Carolina alone is not.

Charleston *Mercury* (Charleston, S.C.), November 3, 1860.

347

Any practical move would enable the people of other States to rise above their past divisions, and lock shields on the broad ground of Southern security. The course of our Legislature will either greatly stimulate and strengthen, or unnerve the resistance elements of the whole South. A Convention is the point to which their attention will be chiefly directed.

The existence of slavery is at stake. The evils of submission are too terrible for us to risk them, from vague fears of failure, or a jealous distrust of our sister Cotton States. We think, therefore, that the approaching Legislature should provide for the assembling of a Convention of the people of South Carolina, as soon as it is ascertained that Messrs. Lincoln and Hamlin will have a majority in the Electoral Colleges for President and Vice President of the United States. The only point of difficulty is as to the time when the Convention shall assemble. In our judgment, it should assemble at the earliest possible time consistent with the opportunity for co-operative action of other Southern States, which may, like ourselves, be determined not to submit to Black Republican domination at Washington. Delay is fatal, while our move will retard no willing State from co-operation. South Carolina, as a sovereign state, is bound to protect her people, but she should so act as to give the other Southern States the opportunity of joining in this policy. The Governors of Alabama, Mississippi, and Georgia can act simultaneously. With this qualification, the earliest time is the best for the following reasons:

1. Our great agricultural staples are going to market. The sooner we act, the more of these staples we will have on hand, to control the conduct of the people of the North and of foreign nations, to secure a peaceful result for our deliverance. Thousands at the North, and millions in Europe, need our cotton to keep their looms in operation. Let us act, before we have parted with our agricultural productions for the season.

2. The commercial and financial interests of the South require that we should act speedily in settling our relations towards the North. Suspense is embarrassment and loss. Decision, with separation, will speedily open new sources of wealth and prosperity, and relieve the finances of the South through the establishment of new channels. In all changes of Government, respect should be had to all classes of the people, and the least possible loss be inflicted on any.

3. The moral effect of promptitude will be immense. Delay will dispirit our friends, and inspire confidence in our enemies. The evils against which we are to provide are not the growth of yesterday. They

have been gathering head for thirty years. We have tried, again and again, to avert them by compromise and submission. Submission has failed to avert them; and wise, prompt and resolute action is our last and only course for safety.

4. Black Republican rule at Washington will not commence until the 4th of March next—four short months. Before that time all that South Carolina or the other Southern States intend to do, should be done. The settlement of our relations towards the General Government, in consequence of our measures for protection, should be completed during the existing Administration.

5. It is exceedingly important, also, that our measures should be laid as soon as possible before the present Congress. The secession of one or more States from the Union must be communicated to the President of the United States. He has done all he could to arrest the sectional madness of the North. He knows that we are wronged and endangered by Black Republican ascendancy, and he will not, we have a right to suppose, lend himself to carry out their bloody policy.

6. By communication from the President of the United States, as well as by the withdrawal from Congress of the members of the seceding States, the question of the right of a state to secede from the Union, with the question of a Force Bill, must arise in Congress for action. The Representatives from the other Southern States will most probably be forced either to continue members of a body which orders the sword drawn against the seceding states, or they must leave it. They will most probably leave it; and thus the South will be brought together by action in Congress, even though they fail to cooperate at once by their State authorities. It will not be wise to pretermit either of these instrumentalities for the union and co-action of the Southern States; but, it is our opinion, that Congress is the best place to unite them. By prompt action, and through the question of secession in Congress, the agitations which must ensue, will not only tend to unite the Southern members of Congress, but to unite and stimulate state action in the states they represent.

We conclude, therefore, by urging the Legislature about to assemble, to provide for the calling of a Convention, as soon as it is ascertained that Messrs. Lincoln and Hamlin have the majority in the Electoral Colleges for President and Vice President of the United States; and that this Convention shall assemble at the earliest day practicable, consistent with the knowledge of our course by our sister Southern States. To this end we would respectfully suggest Nov. 22nd and 23rd as the day of election, and December 15th as the time of assembling the Convention of the people of South Carolina.

113. *South Carolina Ordinance of Secession, December 20, 1860*

The Secession Convention was called by the legislature to meet on December 17, and on December 20 the Secession Ordinance was adopted. The movement toward secession met with general approval throughout the state, although a group of unionists around Greenville had uncompromising objections. The first selection is the ordinance; the second is a comment on the members and actions of the convention; and the last is a description of the reception of the Secession Ordinance by the people of Charleston.

[Ordinance of Secession]

At a Convention of the people of the State of South Carolina, begun and holden at Columbia on the seventeenth day of December, in the year of our Lord 1860, and thence continued by adjournment to Charleston and there, by divers adjournments, to the 20th day of December in the same year:

An ordinance to dissolve the union between the State of South Carolina and other states united with her under the compact entitled "The Constitution of the United States of America":

We, the people of the State of South Carolina in Convention assembled, do declare and ordain, and it is hereby declared and ordained, that the ordinance adopted by us in Convention on the twenty-third day of May, in the year of our Lord 1788, whereby the Constitution of the United States of America was ratified, and also all acts and parts of acts of the General Assembly of this State ratifying amendments of the said Constitution, are hereby repealed; and that the union now subsisting between South Carolina and the other States, under the name of the "United States of America" is hereby dissolved.

Official Records of the Union and Confederate Armies, Series I, 70 vols. in 128, for the War Department (Washington: Government Printing Office, 1880–1901), I, 110.

Done at Charleston the twentieth day of December, in the year of our Lord, 1860.

Rev. James H. Thornwell, on the Secession Convention:

That there was a cause, and an adequate cause, might be presumed from the character of the Convention which passed the Ordinance of Secession, and the perfect unanimity with which it was done. The Convention was not a collection of politicians and demagogues. It was not a conclave of defeated place-hunters, who sought to avenge their disappointment by the ruin of their country. It was a body of grave, sober and venerable men, selected from every pursuit of life, and distinguished, most of them, in their respective spheres, by every quality which can command confidence and respect. It embraced the wisdom, moderation and integrity of the bench; the learning and prudence of the bar; and the eloquence and learning of the pulpit. It contained retired planters, scholars and gentlemen, who stood aloof from the turmoil and ambition of public life, and were devoting an elegant leisure to the culture of their minds, and to quiet and unobtrusive schemes of Christian philanthropy. There were men in that convention utterly incapable of low and selfish schemes, who, in the calm serenity of their judgments, were as unmoved by the waves of popular passion and excitement, as the everlasting gravity by the billows that roll against it. There were men there who would listen to no voices but the voice of reason; and would bow to no authority but what they believed to be the authority of God. . . . They deliberated without passion, and concluded without rashness. They sat with closed doors, that the tumult of the population might not invade the sobriety of their minds. . . . That in such a body there was not a single vote against the Ordinance of Secession; that there was not only no dissent, but the assent was cordial and thoroughgoing, is a strong presumption that the measure was justified by the clearest and sternest necessities of justice and of right. That such an assembly should have inaugurated a radical revolution in all the external relations of the State, in the face of acknowledged

J. A. Leland, *A Voice from South Carolina* (Charleston: Walker, Evans & Cogswell, 1879), 21–22.

dangers, and at the risk of enormous sacrifices, and should have done it gravely, soberly, dispassionately, deliberately, and yet have done it without cause, transcends all the measures of probability. Whatever else may be said of it, it certainly must be admitted that this solemn act of South Carolina was well considered. . . .

William Plumer Jacobs on the Charleston
reaction to secession:

Scarcely had the President announced the vote unanimous before the people assembled without, sent up one universal shout of triumph and men and children ran from street to street, heralding the glad tidings. All the stores were closed, bands of soldiers were immediately parading and crowds were gathered everywhere to hear and tell the news. The Mercury extras were seized with an eagerness unparalleled in the annals of the Charleston press. At five thirty the Convention again met and proceeded in a body to the Secession [Institute] Hall to ratify the ordinance . . . . The President then read the ordinance, and when he finished it, the whole audience rose up and gave tremendous applause. One by one the delegates went up and signed the ordinance and when the last name was added, President Jamison said "I do therefore declare South Carolina to be a separate, independent commonwealth," every man, woman and child leaped up, hats flew high in the air and cheer after cheer echoed and re-echoed from floor to roof, from side to side, until exhausted it fell down in one long, loud cadence of rejoicing. It was the noblest moment of my life. Even now while I write, my blood thrills with excitement at the thought. The same scene was re-enacted in the street. Gen. Martin by the light of a street lamp read the ordinance to the crowd when it was met with similar enthusiasm. Thus ended the glorious 20th of December.

Thornwell Jacobs, ed., *Diary of William Plumer Jacobs* (Oglethorpe University, Ga.: Oglethorpe University Press, 1937), 69.

114. *Henry W. Ravenel Predicts Civil War, February 15, 1861*

FOLLOWING THE SECESSION OF SOUTH CAROLINA, SIX OTHER
SOUTHERN STATES LEFT THE UNION AND EARLY IN FEBRUARY, 1861,
THE CONFEDERATE STATES OF AMERICA WAS FORMED. PRESIDENT
JAMES BUCHANAN, WHOSE CABINET WAS PRO-SOUTH, DEPLORED SECES-
SION AS IMPOSSIBLE BUT DID NOTHING TO COERCE THE SECEDING STATES
BACK INTO THE UNION, PREFERRING TO LEAVE THE DECISION TO THE
INCOMING REPUBLICAN ADMINISTRATION. FOR SOUTH CAROLINA, AND
THE SOUTH IN GENERAL, THE PERIOD BETWEEN DECEMBER, 1860, AND
APRIL, 1861, WAS ONE OF TENSION AND SUSPENSE. SOMETHING OF THE
FEELING OF THE AVERAGE SOUTH CAROLINIAN CAN BE GLEANED FROM
THE FOLLOWING EXCERPT FROM THE JOURNAL OF HENRY W. RAVENEL,
A PROMINENT SCIENTIST.

[Henry W. Ravenel]

February 15, 1861: We are now rapidly approaching a critical period
in the complicated relations which the last two months have brought
into existence between the states of the old Confederacy. Six states
(Texas the seventh has spoken also by her convention, but has not yet
consummated the act of secession) have passed formal acts of Secession
and have met together and have formed for themselves an independent
government. They have no intention of returning to the old Union.
They will enter into war before abandoning their position of independence under a separate Confederacy. They will in a few days send commissioners to Washington and also to European powers, to demand a
recognition of their government. It is generally believed from indications
in the papers of England and France that our government will be
immediately recognized by these nations. But at Washington, there

Arney R. Childs, ed., *The Private Journal of Henry William Ravenel* (Columbia:
University of South Carolina Press, 1947), 53–54. Copyright, 1947, by the Uni-
versity of South Carolina Press, Columbia. Reprinted by permission of The
University of South Carolina Press.

is much doubt if we shall be recognized at once. The larger and stronger portion of the Republican party, as yet has shown no willingness to do so. They do not admit by any of their acts, either the right or the fact of Secession. Lincoln says the laws must be enforced in all the States and the Federal property retaken. Of course this leads to war at once if persisted in. On the other hand the eight border states, North Carolina, Virginia, Maryland, Delaware, Tennessee, Kentucky, Arkansas and Missouri have taken the strongest ground against any attempt at coercion, and have pledged themselves to resist it, and join their fortunes with the Cotton States if the attempt is made. The "Peace Conference" (as it is termed) or informal Convention now in session at Washington are endeavoring to agree upon some form of compromise or guarantee which will be acceptable to the South. So far they have been able to effect nothing. In the mean time, the day of inauguration of Lincoln is approaching, and Fort Sumter in Charleston harbor, and Fort Pickens in Pensacola Bay are held by Federal troops. As soon as our demand for recognition is refused there is but one course left, and that is to dislodge these foreign troops and take possession. They cannot be suffered to remain there a standing menace and insult on our soil. This will be the opening of a civil war, which if carried out will be one of the bloodiest the world has ever seen. . . . Every day is hurrying us onwards to the crisis which must be shortly reached, and upon which will depend the great issues at stake. In a little over two weeks, the Black Republican party come into power, and Lincoln assumes command. . . .

115. *The Call for Troops*

As secession became imminent and rumors of war were heard, the state of South Carolina made ready its own military forces. What conditions were just prior to the Secession Convention, afterwards, and through the winter of 1861 until Fort Sumter are shown in the selections following.

[Johnson Hagood]

Act to provide Military Forces:

On the 17th December 1860, in view of the probable passage of the Ordnance of Secession by the State Convention then in session, the Legislature of South Carolina passed "An Act to Provide an Armed Military Force." This act provided that whenever it shall appear that an armed force is about to be employed against the State or in opposition to its authority, the Governor be authorized to repel the same, and for that purpose to call into the service of the State such portion of the militia as he shall deem proper and to organize the same on the plan therein indicated. Three days afterward, the Convention passed the Ordinance of Secession, and the revolution which led to the establishment of the Southern Confederacy was inaugurated. Immediately after, the Convention provided for the raising of one or more corps of regulars, and for the acceptance of a regiment of six months' volunteers, both to be received into immediate service. Towards the last of December the Governor issued a call for volunteers under the legislative act, which resulted in the raising and organizing of ten regiments for twelve months' service. Under this call the militia regiments of Barnwell district (the 11th and 43rd of the old organization) assembled at Barnwell Village, and furnished, by volunteering, five companies. The regiment of Orangeburg District (15th old militia) assembled at its rendezvous, and furnished four companies; while the regiment of Colleton

Johnson Hagood, *Memoirs of the War of Secession* (Columbia: The State Company, 1910), 27–28.

District (13th old militia) assembled at Walterboro and furnished two companies;—all on the 3rd January, 1861. The Barnwell and Orangeburg companies and one of the Colleton companies being the first ten companies which responded to the call in the State were organized by the State War Department into a regiment under the name of "The First South Carolina Volunteers," and elections for field officers ordered.

[Johnson Hagood]

South Carolina's resumption of her separate sovereignty had been followed by . . . other Southern States . . . . The operations against Fort Sumter had been carried on by South Carolina unaided and were continued from her own resources. Upon application of the State authorities to the Government at Montgomery, in March, General Beauregard, a distinguished officer of the army of the Confederate States, had, however, been assigned to their direction. Now it was desired to have a considerable body of troops in reserve in and near Charleston, and it was supposed that Sumter would be reinforced . . . . Accordingly, by an order dated 8th April, several of the regiments raised under the legislative act of 1860 were ordered to rendezvous at Charleston . . . . The First Battalion arrived in the city by railroad at 10 p.m., and the Second Battalion just before day the next morning . . . .

[Johnson Hagood]

The First Regiment remained bivouacked in the sand hills near Vinegar Hill for four days. It was then moved . . . to Gadberry Hill

Johnson Hagood, *Memoirs of the War of Secession* (Columbia: The State Company, 1910), 30.

Johnson Hagood, *Memoirs of the War of Secession* (Columbia: The State Company, 1910), 34–36.

. . . . No camp equipage was received for ten or twelve days; the weather was again tempestuous and cold; the exposure, the wretched water dug from shallow pits in the sand hills, and the inefficient policing of the camps soon began to tell upon the health of the men. Much sickness ensued. We were a week on the island before the first drill could be had. The men were employed . . . endeavoring to obtain such shelter as could be improvised, even . . . constructing burrows in the sand hills, and in the difficult task of getting their rations cooked.

In ten or twelve days, however, our supply of tents, etc., began to arrive . . . . Uniforms—a short grey blouse—were distributed, drilling was diligently prosecuted, and the regiment began to assume something of discipline and acquaintance with the routine of camp duty.

. . . There was one of these batteries that deserves notice, the "Stevens," or "Iron-Clad" Battery.

It was a structure of triangular section, presenting one of its sides at a very obtuse angle to the enemy, and open to the rear. The framework was of heavy timber and the side exposed to fire was plated with common railroad iron, presenting to the hostile projectiles a sloping corrugated surface . . . . When the guns were not in the battery, the portholes were closed by curtains similarly plated and worked from the inside by a lever. It was a crude affair, but sufficient for [Major] Anderson's light, smooth bores.

116. *The New South Carolina Flag*

IN THE LATE 1850s, AS SECTIONAL FEELINGS BECAME BITTER OVER STATES' RIGHTS AND SLAVERY, SOUTH CAROLINIANS BEGAN TO USE THEIR OWN STATE FLAG MORE AND MORE TO DEMONSTRATE FORCIBLY THEIR LOYALTY TO POLITICAL PRINCIPLES OF THE SOUTH. WHEN SOUTH CAROLINA BECAME A SOVEREIGN STATE—IN THE DAYS JUST PRECEDING THE CONFEDERACY—ONE OF THE FIRST ACTIONS TAKEN BY THE STATE LEGISLATURE WAS THE ADOPTION OF A NEW FLAG. JOURNALS OF THE HOUSE OF REPRESENTATIVES AND THE SENATE FROM DECEMBER 21, 1860, THROUGH JANUARY 28, 1861, REVEAL THE DEBATE AND LEGISLATIVE PROCESSES THROUGH WHICH THE SELECTION WAS MADE. DURING THIS PERIOD, TWO DIFFERENT FLAGS WERE CHOSEN, THE FIRST ONE BEING DISPLACED BY THE PRESENT STATE FLAG. THE FOLLOWING IS A PART OF THE LEGISLATURE'S PROCEEDING.

[A.S. Salley quoting from the journal]

Mr. Moses submitted the following report: The Committee of Conference, on the part of the two Houses, appointed to determine what shall be the national flag or ensign proper to be borne by the State of South Carolina . . . beg leave to report . . . That from and after the adoption of these resolutions the national flag or ensign of South Carolina shall be blue, with a golden palmetto upright upon a white oval in the center thereof, and a white increscent in the upper flagstaff corner of the flag . . . .

[A. S. Salley]

At last South Carolina had a flag! After the many disagreements between the two Houses on that question during the preceding week,

A. S. Salley, *The Flag of the State of South Carolina,* Bulletin No. 2, S.C. Historical Commission Bulletins (Columbia: The State Printing Co., 1915), 5–14.

both Senators and Representatives must have felt pleased on that Saturday night . . . [but] there was dissatisfaction because on Monday morning the brand-new flag was altered!

Mr. Read introduced the following resolution: *Resolved,* That a message be sent to the Senate, requesting that body to consent to the alteration of the Flag, lately adopted by the General Assembly, so as to dispense with the white medallion and golden Palmetto, and in their place to insert a white Palmetto. . . . The Senate concurred, and returned a message accordingly.

This time there was no change made in the design of the flag. . . . The ironic part . . . is that as a *national* flag the ensign selected flew for only a bare seven days. On 4 February 1861 its life was cut short by the accession of South Carolina to the new Confederate States of America. . . .

The history of the palmetto flag does not end here, however. It was used as a State flag while South Carolina was in the Confederacy, as well as when she later re-joined the Union; it flies today from the State Capitol in Columbia. . . .

117. *The Attack on Fort Sumter*

THE THREE FORTS GUARDING CHARLESTON HARBOR WERE CASTLE PINCKNEY, AN OLD FORTIFICATION; FORT MOULTRIE, GARRISONED BY A SMALL NUMBER OF FEDERAL SOLDIERS; AND FORT SUMTER, UNFINISHED. PRESIDENT JAMES BUCHANAN HAD DECIDED TO LEAVE THE FORTS AS THEY WERE, TO PREVENT THE POSSIBILITY OF VIOLENCE, AND WHEN GOV. FRANCIS W. PICKENS REQUESTED THAT HE BE ALLOWED TO TAKE OVER FORT SUMTER IN DECEMBER, 1860, BUCHANAN TOLD HIM THAT HE WAS NOT PLANNING TO DISTURB THE STATUS QUO IN FAVOR OF THE U.S. GOVERNMENT, AND NEITHER WOULD HE DO SO FOR THE STATE. A FEW DAYS PREVIOUSLY, THE SECRETARY OF WAR HAD ORDERED THE U.S. COMMANDER AT FORT MOULTRIE, MAJ. ROBERT ANDERSON, TO REFRAIN FROM ANY HOSTILE ACT BUT TO HOLD THE FORTS; IF HE WERE ATTACKED, HE MIGHT "PUT HIS COMMAND IN ANY OF THEM." SUCH A STEP COULD BE TAKEN, HE WAS ORDERED, "WHENEVER YOU HAVE TANGIBLE EVIDENCE OF A DESIGN TO PROCEED TO A HOSTILE ACT." MAJOR ANDERSON TRANSPORTED HIS TROOPS FROM FORT MOULTRIE THE MILE ACROSS THE CHANNEL TO FORT SUMTER AFTER DUSK ON THE NIGHT OF DECEMBER 26, A MOVE WHICH MODERN HISTORIANS HAVE CONCLUDED WAS THE ACT THAT TRIGGERED THE CIVIL WAR. THE FIRST SELECTION IS W. H. GIBBES'S ACCOUNT OF THE FIRST SHOT; THE SECOND, AN ACCOUNT OF THE BATTLE BY ABNER DOUBLEDAY, A UNION OFFICER INSIDE FORT SUMTER; AND THE THIRD CONCERNS THE ARRIVAL AT THE STATE CAPITAL OF THE NEWS OF THE FIRING ON FORT SUMTER.

Lieutenant Gibbes and Fort Sumter

[J. P. Thomas]

At the beginning of hostilities Lieutenant [Wade Hampton] Gibbes was stationed under Captain Geo. S. James at Fort Johnson on James Island.

Yearbook of the Association of the Graduates of the United States Military Academy, 1904, p. 100 ff.

There have been conflicting statements as to who fired the first gun upon the memorable occasion of the bombardment of Fort Sumter, and I insert Major Gibbes' own statement of his part in the affair:

Columbia, S. C., April 2, 1902

Col. John P. Thomas.

Dear Sir—At your request I will undertake again to relate the incident as it occurred, of the firing of the first gun of the war of '61–'65, at Fort Sumter, in Charleston Harbor. The post at Fort Johnson was garrisoned by one company of Confederate States artillery, commanded by Captain George B. James, W. H. Gibbes, First Lieutenant; H. L. Farley, Second Lieutenant; and Theo Hayne, Third Lieutenant. On the night of April 11, 1861, the post was visited by General Stephen D. Lee and General Wigfall and General Chester . . . with orders to Captain James to open fire upon the fort at daylight the next morning. There were two batteries, each of two 10-inch mortars, one in the sandhills, some one hundred yards or more from the beach, and one directly on the beach, the first under my immediate command, and the second commanded by Lieutenant Farley, at which Captain James stationed himself. My orders were to fire a shell, to burst high up in the air, as a signal, after which signal to commence a general bombardment and to blow up a house which was inconveniently near the battery. The first shell, fired at 4:30 a. m., was immediately followed by the blowing up of the dwelling, or, rather, its attempt, and the firing of a shell aimed so as to fall into the fort. Lieutenant Meade told the writer, when the fort was surrendered, that the second shell fell into the parade ground of the fort.

So, the facts are as stated; the first shell was fired by Captain James' battery, and, incidentally, by me as his First Lieutenant.

Respectfully,

W. H. Gibbes

Our orders were from Beauregard and not through Gen. Ripley.

[Major Gibbes] is corroborated by Mr. D. A. Thomas, of Gaffney, South Carolina, who was on Morris Island at the time, who writes: "I do know that 'who fired the first gun' was a subject much talked of for some days after Major Anderson surrendered. At that time and place I only heard that Lieutenant Wade Hampton Gibbes fired the first gun at Sumter; none disputed it; all conceded it; and I have always believed, and do now believe that he did it."

Also, Major J. J. Lucas, of Society Hill, South Carolina, in writing a historical sketch for Camp Hampton, Confederate Veterans, states:

"When it became apparent that the Government at Washington meant subjugation, the Confederate Government directed General Beauregard to capture Fort Sumter. Accordingly General Beauregard ordered Captain Geo. B. James to fire the signal gun at 4:30 a.m. on the 12th of April 1861. This gun was fired by Lieutenant Wade Hampton Gibbes, afterwards Major of Artillery in the Army of Northern Virginia."

My understanding has always been that Major Gibbes pulled the lanyard of this gun himself, while his immediately surrounding subalterns pulled those of the mine and the shotted gun, which he had sighted in advance. . . ."

[Abner Doubleday's account of the battle:]

As soon as the outline of our fort could be distinguished, the enemy carried out their program. It had been arranged, as a special compliment to the venerable Edmund Ruffin, who might almost be called the father of secession, that he should fire the first shot against us. . . . Almost immediately afterward, a ball from Cummings Point lodged in the magazine wall, and by the sound seemed to bury itself in the masonry about a foot from my head . . . . In a moment, the firing burst forth in one continuous roar, and large patches of both the exterior and interior masonry began to crumble and fall in all directions. . . . Nineteen batteries were now hammering at us, and the balls and shells from the ten-inch columbiads, accompanied by shells from the thirteen-inch mortars which constantly bombarded us, made us feel as if the war had commenced in earnest. . . .

Our firing now became regular, and was answered from the rebel guns which encircled us on the four sides of the pentagon upon which the fort was built. . . . After three hours' firing, my men became exhausted, and Captain Seymour came, with a fresh detachment, to relieve us. . . . Part of the fleet was visible outside the bar about half-past ten A.M. It exchanged salutes with us, but did not attempt to enter the harbor, or take part in the battle. In fact, it would have had considerable difficulty

Abner Doubleday, *Reminiscences of Forts Sumter and Moultrie in 1860–61* (New York: Harper & Bros., 1876), 143–59.

in finding the channel, as the marks and buoys had all been taken up . . . .

On the morning of the 13th . . . about 8 A.M., the officers' quarters were ignited by one of Ripley's incendiary shells, or by shot heated in the furnaces of Fort Moultrie. The fire was put out; but at 10 A.M. a mortar shell passed through the roof, and lodged in the flooring of the second story, where it burst, and started the flames afresh. . . . It became evident that the entire block, being built with wooden partitions, floors and roofing, must be consumed. . . . By 11 A.M., the conflagration was terrible and disastrous. One fifth of the fort was on fire, and the wind drove the smoke in dense masses into the angle where we had all taken refuge. It seemed impossible to escape suffocation. . . . The scene at this time was really terrific. The roaring and crackling of the flames, the dense masses of whirling smoke, the bursting of the enemy's shells, and our own, which were exploding in the burning rooms, the crashing of the shot, and the sound of masonry falling in every direction, made the fort a pandemonium. . . . About 12:48 P.M., the end of the flagstaff was shot down, and the flag fell. . . .

[Henry W. Ravenel hears the news of Fort Sumter]

Saturday, April 13, 3 P.M. The papers give us the particulars of yesterdays engagement. Gen. Beauregard sent his last message to Major Anderson at 1:30 A.M. Friday morning, stating certain conditions under which he would refrain from opening fire upon him. As Major Anderson declined the conditions, the General's aids then passed over to Fort Johnson and gave the necessary orders. Precisely at 4:30 A.M., the signal gun was fired from Fort Johnson, and immediately the firing was followed by the Cummings Point and Iron batteries of Morris Island, by Fort Moultrie and other batteries on Sullivans Island, and by the floating battery. Anderson returned no fire until a quarter before six. The cannonading was kept up all day. Fort Sumter ceased firing at

Arney R. Childs, ed., *The Private Journal of Henry William Ravenel* (Columbia: University of South Carolina Press, 1947), 62–64. Copyright, 1947, by the University of South Carolina Press, Columbia. Reprinted by permission of The University of South Carolina Press.

7 P.M., but our batteries have continued it all night. Reports to head quarters from the various batteries state that no lives have been lost, and no serious injury done to any of the works. . . .

10 P.M. We have just received intelligence by the train from Augusta that Fort Sumter has been taken! with the loss of three men killed and fifteen wounded in the fort, none on our side. It is also stated that the fort was burned, but this must be wrong as it is fire proof. We must deplore the loss of life to the poor soldiers who were mere machines in the hands of others. Their blood must rest upon the mad fanatics who have so shamelessly left them to their fate without even an attempt to succor, or relieve them. . . .

Monday, April 15. By the papers of today we get reliable accounts of what has transpired in Charleston. Major Anderson surrendered Fort Sumter about 1 P.M. on Saturday, and with his men left for New York in the steamer Isabel on Sunday morning . . . . Dispatches from Washington state that Lincoln's proclamation will be issued tomorrow, calling for a force of 75,000 men, and declaring martial law in Washington. It is confidently expected that Virginia will secede at once. . . .

118. *The Battle of Port Royal and the Invasion of Beaufort*

FROM THE START OF THE BIG BUILD-UP OF NORTHERN FORCES IT WAS KNOWN THAT A NAVY FLOTILLA WOULD SOON BE SAILING FOR SOUTH CAROLINA; AFTER MUCH PRODDING BY PRESIDENT LINCOLN, THE FLEET WAS AT LAST ON ITS WAY TO PORT ROYAL. LEADING THE AMPHIBIOUS ASSAULT WERE COMMODORE SAMUEL FRANCIS DU PONT AND BRIG. GEN. THOMAS WEST SHERMAN. THE SPRING HAD SEEN THE FAILURE OF "PEACE TALKS" IN WASHINGTON AND THE FALL OF FORT SUMTER. OCTOBER 29, 1861, THE UNION MOVED TO SEIZE THE TEMPTING PRIZE WHICH LAY BETWEEN CHARLESTON AND SAVANNAH. ON NOVEMBER 7, HILTON HEAD ISLAND WAS TAKEN AS THE NEW BASE OF OPERATIONS. ON THE EVENING OF DECEMBER 11, BRIG. GEN. ISAAC STEVENS, ACTING ON ORDERS FROM GENERAL SHERMAN, OCCUPIED THE TOWN OF BEAUFORT. WHEN WORD SPREAD THAT THE ENEMY WAS COMING, PEOPLE FLED EN MASSE, LEAVING DINNER ON THE TABLE. OF THE HASTY EXIT GENERAL THOMAS SHERMAN REMARKED: "THE EFFECT OF THIS VICTORY IS STARTLING. EVERY WHITE INHABITANT LEFT THE ISLAND. THE WEALTHY ISLANDS OF SAINT HELENA, LADIES, AND MOST OF PORT ROYAL ARE ABANDONED . . . AND THE BEAUTIFUL ESTATES OF THE PLANTERS, WITH ALL THEIR IMMENSE PROPERTY, LEFT TO THE PILLAGE OF HORDES." AFTER THESE INCIDENTS, FIGHTING OCCURRED IN AND AROUND CHARLESTON. IN THE BATTLE OF SECESSIONVILLE, JUNE 16, 1862, THE ENEMY WAS REPULSED AND, ABOUT TEN O'CLOCK IN THE EVENING, RETREATED IN GREAT CONFUSION. FOUR HUNDRED UNION SOLDIERS WERE KILLED, WOUNDED, OR TAKEN PRISONER. THEIR DEAD IN FRONT OF THE SECESSIONVILLE WORKS NUMBERED 168. REBEL CASUALTIES AMOUNTED TO 134 KILLED, WOUNDED, AND MISSING. ALMOST IMMEDIATELY AFTER THIS BATTLE, THE FIGHTING ON MORRIS ISLAND BEGAN, ONE OF THE BLOODIEST SIEGES OF THE WAR—COMPARABLE TO THE FIGHTING AT GETTYSBURG. SELECTIONS FOLLOWING CONCERN THE CAPTURE OF THE PORT ROYAL BATTERY; AND THE FIGHTING AT MORRIS ISLAND AND SECESSIONVILLE, WHICH IS SUMMARIZED.

New Year's Battle at Port Royal Ferry
[A newspaper account]

The command of this expedition, which was to destroy three batteries erected upon the main land by the rebels, before they became too powerful, was given to Brig.-Gen. Isaac J. Stevens, an officer admirably qualified for the position. . . . The regiments were the Roundheads of Pennsylvania . . . the Pennsylvania 50th . . . 8th Michigan . . . 79th New York . . . 47th New York . . , and the 48th New York Volunteers. . . .

The troops were to be supported and covered by the gunboat Pembina . . . Seneca . . . the Ottawa . . . , and the Ellen. . . .

After their defeat at Hilton Head and our occupation of Beaufort [December 5, 1861], the rebels had retired from Port Royal Island to the mainland, and naturally fearing that an advance would be made from Beaufort towards the railroad, they had constructed a battery on the mainland bank of the Coosaw river. They had also erected another battery at Boyd's Neck, opposite the junction of the Coosaw and Broad rivers. The rebels had erected another battery at Seabrook, about three miles to the west of Boyd's Neck. . . .

About a third of the distance across, the first shell had exploded with terrible effect. The ground was literally saturated with blood; the ditches on either side of the causeway partly filled; the grass dyed with it. . . . The wounded, and most of the dead had been carried off by the rebels, but our men had that morning buried three, whose graves were at the side of the road. It was the first battle-field over which I had passed, but I suppose no ordinary carnage is so terrible, or so ghastly in its effects, as the explosion of 11-inch shells. I cannot attempt to describe it.

When the Union regiments were in possession of the fort, the gunboats were signalized, and they immediately closed in, in order to cover our troops; and these at once commenced the destruction of the fort. The gun was secured, the battery levelled, some remains of camp equippage, tents, etc., were demolished, and two buildings used for military purposes

Frank Leslie's *Illustrated Newspaper* (New York), Jan. 25, 1862.

by the rebels were burned. The rebels seeing this, and evidently anticipating an advance of our force, set fire to numerous other buildings. A small force of Unionists also crossed to Seabrook, under cover of the guns of the Seneca and Ellen, and completely demolished the fortifications there, which had been deserted before our troops arrived. At night our whole force was at Port Royal Ferry, completely covered by the guns of our men-of-war.

The Rebel Troops Engaged

Brigadier-General . . . . Maxcy Gregg
Brigadier-General . . . . [John] Pope

Troops

South Carolina German Artillery, Battery A, Captain Kinapaux
South Carolina German Artillery, Battery B
″   ″   First Artillery, Col. De Sassure
″   ″   First Regiment, Col. Gregg
″   ″   Fourth Regiment, Col. Sloan
″   ″   Ninth Regiment, Col. Blanding
″   ″   Twelfth Regiment, Col. Dunovant
″   ″   Regiment, Col. J. L. Orr
″   ″   Fifteenth Regiment, Col. De Sassure

General Thomas Sherman's Official Account

Headquarters, E.C.
Port Royal, S.C., Jan. 2, 1862

Sir—As the Vanderbilt leaves tomorrow, I deem it proper to enclose to you a letter of instructions to General Stevens, commanding the 2d brigade of this division, of December 30:

The simple object of this dash was to destroy the batteries which the enemy appeared to have erected on the Coosaw river, for the obstruction of the navigation and the passage of that stream; and also to punish him for the insult in firing into the steamer Mayflower, on her recent passage through that stream, for the purpose of sounding the depth of the channel. The affair succeeded perfectly, and the enemy were driven out of their batteries, their batteries demolished, and the property found there brought away or destroyed, with little or no loss of life on our side. After the object of the movement was executed, General Stevens, agreeably to his instructions, returned to Port Royal Island. As soon as his report reaches me, it will be forwarded.

[Summary of the Battle]

The Battle of Secessionville occurred June 16, 1862, when under cover from its gunboats, the enemy commenced advancing rapidly upon the front of the battery at Secessionville. The troops had arrived within a few hundred yards of the battery before the Rebel guns could open up, because the pickets had been captured and the enemy had not been discovered. Lt. Col. Gaillard and Smith's battalions (Charleston and Pee Dee) were moved promptly into position under the orders of Col. J. C. Lamar, the heroic commander of the post, and soon drove the enemy back in confusion and great loss. Three times the enemy was repulsed and about 10 P.M. retreated, leaving their dead and wounded on the field. The loss of Northern troops amounted to "at least four hundred in killed, wounded and prisoners. The dead of the enemy in front of Secessionville works, numbered one hundred and sixty-eight, while forty-two wounded had been brought within the works. . . . The reports . . . give casualties on our side, thirty-nine killed, ninety-three wounded, and two missing. . . ."

The fighting on Morris Island began at 5 A.M., July 10, 1862, when the enemy began heavy firing from guns on Little Folley Island. Their iron-clad monitors about the same time crossed the bar. About seven that evening the enemy advanced to Oyster Point in a flotilla, containing between 2,000 and 3,000 men. Later the Yankees made a good landing in front of the Rebel batteries on the south end of Morris Island proper. About 9 P.M., Colonel Graham gave the order for the Rebels to fall back on Battery Wagner, which was accomplished under a severe flanking fire from the monitor. The Rebels had been forced to abandon their position on Morris Island because of the lack of supporting infantry and the enemy's superior number and weight of guns.

Confederate States of America: Official Reports of Battles (Richmond, Va.: 1862), 456–61; and Johnson Hagood, *Memoirs of the War of Secession* (Columbia: The State Company, 1910), 135–67.

The next day the enemy began the assault of Battery Wagner and was repulsed, with great loss of life. Two officers and 95 men were left dead in front of the works at Battery Wagner. Six officers and 113 "rank and file" were taken as prisoners. The Rebels's loss was one officer and five privates wounded.

On July 12 and 13, the enemy was busy erecting works on the middle of Morris Island, being harassed all the while by the fire from Gregg and Sumter. In turn, Gregg and Sumter were shelled by fire from four monitors, three gunboats and two mortar vessels. Realizing that the enemy could not be driven from Morris Island, General Beauregard adopted the defensive. On July 18, it became evident that the enemy was about to attempt serious operations against Wagner. The south end of Morris Island was crowded with troops and soldiers from Folly Island were being continually landed. After various moves and countermoves during the morning, at 1 P.M. the "Ironsides," five monitors, a large wooden frigate, six mortar boats, and the land batteries—mounting five guns—concentrated their fire on Battery Wagner. This continued until dark, the enemy's fire throughout the day being very rapid, and averaging 14 shots per minute. General Beauregard remarked that this was "unparalleled until this epoch of the siege in the weight of the projectiles thrown." Brigadier General Taliaferro, the commander at Wagner, estimated that there were 9,000 shot and shell thrown in and against the battery in the 11½ hours that the bombardment lasted.

It became evident that the Yankees would attack again after dark, and therefore Brig. Gen. Johnson Hagood was relieved of his command at James Island, and with the 32d Georgia Regiment was ordered to the re-enforcement of Morris Island. The attack began at 8 P.M., but the two Rebel regiments, the Charleston battalion and the Fifty-first North Carolina, drove the enemy back, with frightful slaughter. "The main body of the enemy, after vainly endeavoring to gain a position on the parapet, retreated in disorder under a destructive fire from our guns, including those of Fort Sumter. The ditch and slope of the southeastern salient was then swept with a fire of grape and musketry to prevent the enemy lodged there from retiring, and after a brief resistance they surrendered," reported General Beauregard.

The assault was terribly destructive to the enemy. The general remarked in his official report, his "loss in killed and wounded and prisoners must have been three thousand, as eight hundred bodies were buried in front of Battery Wagner next day. . . . Our loss during the bombardment was 174 killed and wounded . . . . The enemy sent in a flag of truce to arrange for the burial of the dead . . . . Brigadier-General Hagood reported that 600 of the enemy's dead in and around our works were buried by our troops and at least 200 more were by the enemy . . . ." "My recollection is that there was no flag, but a practical truce was maintained for burial purposes all day . . . the carnage impressed me more than any witnessed during the war . . . ," General Hagood said.

The enemy's force in this fighting consisted of troops from Connecticut, Pennsylvania, New Hampshire and the Fifty-fourth Massachusetts, which was a Negro regiment.

In September, Morris Island was abandoned to the enemy, with but little loss on the part of the garrison, either in men or material.

General Beauregard reported that the total loss in killed and wounded on Morris Island, from July 10 to September 7, was 641 men, adding, "It is difficult to arrive at the loss of the enemy, but judging from the slaughter in their ranks . . . it will be well to say that his casualties were in the ratio of ten to one. . . . It may be well to remark that the capture of Morris Island resulted in but a barren victory to the enemy. . . . The possession of Cummings Point placed him no nearer the city [Charleston] than he was when he held part of James Island, from whence he was driven by the Battle of Secessionville. . . ."

119. *Home Life During the War*

The pinch of the war was felt by all South Carolinians. There were shortages of supplies of almost every kind, particularly food and drink, clothing, housing, household goods, and drugs and medicines. Transportation, industry, and farming were all affected. The selections here depict some of the hardships of the war years when the battle was lost on the home-front. From *South Carolina Women in the Confederacy* are included Mrs. M. S. Williams's "Memories" of activities, a Williamsburg Resolution, and another selection in which the significance of the blockade-runners is pointed up.

[From Memories of Mrs. M. S. Williams, and Miss Lee C. Harby]

During all that time, when every woman vied with the other in work for soldiers, there were needs at home too urgent to be disregarded. These, too, had to be met, and how was not long the question. . . . We replaced our worn dresses with homespun, planning and devising checks and plaids, and intermingling colors with the skill of professional designers. . . . Our mothers' silk stockings of ante bellum days were unraveled and transformed into the prettiest of neat-fitting gloves. The writer remembers never to have been more pleased than she was by the possession of a trim pair of boots made of the tanned skins of squirrels.

Our hats, made of palmetto and rye straw, were pretty and becoming. . . . Our jackets were made of the father's old-fashioned cloaks . . . . We even made jewelry of palmetto intermingled with hair, that we might keep even with the boys, who wore palmetto cockades! . . . For our calico dresses, if we were fortunate enough to find one, we sometimes paid one hundred dollars, and for the spool of cotton thread that made it, from ten to twenty dollars. The buttons we sewed were often made from a gourd, cut into sizes required and covered with cloth . . . . On

United Daughters of the Confederacy, South Carolina Division, *South Carolina Women in the Confederacy* (Columbia: The State Co., 1903–1907), pp. 161–62.

371

children's clothes, persimmon seeds in the natural state, with two holes drilled through them, were found both neat and durable.

The things we ate and drank came in, too, for a prominent position. . . . Coffee was made of rye, wheat and sweet potatoes, chipped, dried and parched, also okra seed, etc. It was sweetened, if at all, with sorghum or honey. For tea, the leaves of blackberry vines were gathered and dried. Fruit cakes were made of dried apples, cherries, pears and plums, without any spices at all. For medicines we used roots and herbs. . . . Salt, white and pure, was obtained by digging up the earthern floors of long-used smokehouses, dripping water through this earth in hoppers, and boiling it down. . . .

Our best lights were tallow candles, but they were too scarce to be used except on special occasions. The ordinary lights were knots of pine, supported on racks of iron at the back of the chimney, to let the smoke fly up. . . .

The ladies of the plantations soon learned how to make their own toilet soaps, as well as all the coarser kinds for laundry and kitchen. A substitute for cooking soda was found by burning corncobs to ashes in a clean Dutch oven. This was put in a jar, covered with water, and allowed to stand till clear. One part of this to two parts of sour milk, mixed into cake, or the various Southern breads, made them delightfully light. . . .

Out of the berries of the mistletoe, the young girls made the daintiest of white wax for their fancy work, while from the profuse growth of myrtle was gathered, by the wagonload, the berries, from which was boiled and refined a clear, green aromatic wax, which made candles fit for the candelabra of a king. . . .

The girls learned to card and spin, and to knit socks, stockings and gloves for the men and old people at home. Every woven stocking was treasured, and when the feet were utterly worn out, the legs were carefully unraveled, their thread twisted smoothly and firm on the spinning wheel, and knitted into new stockings, or into gloves or mittens. . . .

From the waters that laved our coast, planters made their own salt, and the children soon knew how to roll and pulverize it into the fine table article to which the family were accustomed. Mustard seed was raised, and the best and purest table preparation manufactured from it . . . . Palmetto, corn shucks, and many grasses and straws were plaited and woven into pretty, graceful hats and bonnets, while for their trimmings, bits of ribbon were saved and washed and dyed, twisted and turned, and served innumerable times through all those four years.

The girls learned to fashion and sole their own bedroom and house slippers, and became adept in all the household arts, first making their own vinegar and then putting up their own pickles. The ladies manufactured wine and superintended and directed the making of syrup from cane and sorghum, using this in lieu of sugar. They soon learned all the dyewoods of the forest, and made purples, yellows, crimsons, and browns at pleasure.

A resolution adopted by the citizens of Williamsburg, August 5, 1861:

Whereas: Many of our citizens have volunteered for service for the defense of our country, and, in a good many instances, have left families in indigent circumstances; and, whereas, the war now being waged against us has for its object the subversion of our institutions and the destruction of our liberties, it becomes the imperative duty of those of us who are not bearing the heat and burden of the day to sustain those that are; and that it is not a charity but a positive duty, which we owe to these brave men, to see that the families of those who need peculiar aid do not suffer.

Therefore, resolved, that an assessment upon the taxes of citizens, except the volunteers, is a just and equal way of raising sufficient funds.

[The Blockade-Runners]

During all this time, the blockade runners came and went with almost the regularity of packet lines, and beyond the reach of the shells was

William Willis Boddie, *History of Williamsburg.* . . . (Columbia: The State Company, 1925), 368. Copyright, 1923, by William Willis Boddie. Reprinted by permission of The State-Record Company.

United Daughters of the Confederacy, South Carolina Division, *South Carolina Women in the Confederacy* (Columbia: The State Co., 1903–1907), 163.

established, in Bull Street in Charleston, the famous Bee Store, which put on sale the entire cargo of each vessel as she came in. Everything was there, and all to be had for a price in Confederate money, which was plentiful; whether millinery or groceries, it could be found in the Bee Store, for the vessels entered with their cargoes and departed with their cotton, and laughed at the fleet lying big, threatening and belligerent before the city's seagate.

Two of these blockade runners, the "Let Her Be," and the "Let Her Rip," seemed to bear a charmed life. They were endeared to the childish heart by the very imprudence of their names, while to the Chicora Company, which owned them, they were little mines of wealth, bringing, besides, many comforts and necessaries to the people who toiled and the men who fought.

120. *The Battle of Honey Hill, November 30, 1864*

As the armies of Gen. W. T. Sherman crossed Georgia and approached Savannah, federal troops in the Port Royal area, some 5,000 strong, marched inland to cut the Charleston-Savannah Railroad. Met at Honey Hill by a body of about 1,500 Confederates, consisting of South Carolina and Georgia troops, plus some cadets from The Citadel in Charleston, they were turned back with heavy losses. This was the largest pitched battle fought outside of the Charleston area in South Carolina during the entire war.

[Maj. Gen. Gustavus W. Smith on the Battle of Honey Hill]

Within five or ten minutes after these preparations had been made, the battle began by an advance piece of our artillery firing upon the enemy. Their line of battle was soon formed and from that time until dark made continuous efforts to carry our position. We had actually engaged five pieces of artillery, and it is due to the South Carolina artillerists that I should say that I have never seen pieces more skillfully employed or more gallantly served upon a difficult field of battle.

In an hour the enemy had so extended and developed their attack that it became absolutely necessary to place in front line of battle my last troops, and the Forty-Seventh Georgia Regiment, making in all about fourteen hundred muskets, and all engaged. From time to time alterations had to be made in our lines by changing the positions of regiments and companies, extending intervals, etc., to prevent being flanked; and while we could not from the dense woods accurately estimate the number of the enemy, it was clear their force largely exceeded ours, and I awaited with some anxiety the arrival of the Thirty-Second Georgia and the forces expected from North and South Carolina. . . .

I have never seen or known a battlefield upon which there was so little confusion and where every order was so cheerfully and promptly obeyed,

U. R. Brooks, *Stories of the Confederacy* (Columbia: The State Co., 1912), 301–303.

375

and where a small number of men for so long a time successfully resisted the determined and oft-repeated efforts of largely superior forces. The flight of the enemy during the night and the number of their dead left upon the field, is evidence of the nature of the attack as well as the defense. . . . During the night the enemy retired rapidly in the direction of their gunboats.

Our loss in every arm of service was eight killed and forty-three wounded. The enemy left over two hundred of their dead upon the field, and their loss in killed and wounded is believed to be upwards of one thousand.

121. *The Burning of Columbia, February 17–18, 1865*

Sherman's federal armies entered South Carolina from Georgia early in 1865 and marched over most of the coastal and central sections of the state. In addition to Columbia, Barnwell, parts of Winnsboro and Orangeburg, many homes, mills, and factories all over the state were burned. The first account following is the report of the official committee, J. P. Carroll, chairman, appointed by the state to inquire into the burning of Columbia; the second excerpt is taken from General Sherman's own account of the burning; the third is Wade Hampton's refutation of Sherman's charges.

[From Report of Official Committee to Investigate the Burning of Columbia]

By eleven o'clock A.M. (February 17) the town was in possession of the Federal Forces, the first detachment entering being the command of the officer who had received the surrender. They had scarcely marched into the town, however, before they began to break into the stores of the merchants, appropriating the contents or throwing them in the streets and destroying them. As other bodies of troops came in, the pillage grew more general, and soon the sack of the town was universal. Guards were, in general, sent to those of the citizens who applied for them, but in numerous instances they proved unable or unwilling to perform the duty assigned them. Scarcely a single household or family escaped altogether from being plundered. The streets of the town were densely filled with thousands of Federal soldiers, drinking, shouting, carousing, and robbing the defenseless inhabitants, without reprimand or check from their officers; and this state of things continued until night. In some instances guards were refused . . . . Between two and three o'clock P.M., General [W.T.] Sherman in person rode into Columbia, informed the mayor that

U. R. Brooks, *Stories of the Confederacy* (Columbia: The State Co., 1912), 333–39.

his letter had been received, and promised protection of the town. Extraordinary license was allowed to his soldiers by General Sherman. . . . An esteemed clergyman, Rev. A. Toomer Porter, testified that the same afternoon, between six and seven o'clock, General Sherman said to him: "You must know a great many ladies—go around and tell them to go to bed quietly; they will not be disturbed any more than if my army was one hundred miles off." He seemed oblivious of the fact that we had been pillaged and insulted the whole day. In one hour's time, the city was in flames.

Meanwhile, the soldiers of General Sherman had burned, that afternoon, many houses in the environs of the town, including the dwelling of General Hampton . . . . Throughout the day, the soldiers of General Sherman gave distinct and frequent notice to the citizens of the impending calamity, usually in the form of fierce and direct threats, but occasionally as if in kindly forewarning. . . . Three rockets were seen to ascend from a point in front of the mayor's dwelling. But a few minutes elapsed before fires, in swift succession broke out, and at intervals so distinct that they could not have been communicated from the one to the other. At various parts of the town, the soldiers of General Sherman, at the appearance of the rockets, declared that they were the appointed signal for a general conflagration. The fire companies, with their engines, promptly repaired to the scene of the fires, and endeavored to arrest them, but in vain. The soldiers of General Sherman, with bayonets and axes, pierced and cut the hose, disabled the engines, and prevented the citizens from extinguishing the flames. The wind was high and blew from the west. The fires spread and advanced with fearful rapidity, and soon enveloped the very heart of the town. The pillage begun upon the entrance of the hostile forces, continued without cessation or abatement, and now the town was delivered up to the accumulated horrors of sack and conflagration. The inhabitants were subjected to personal indignities and outrages. A witness, Captain W. B. Stanley, testified that, several times during the night, he saw the soldiers of General Sherman take from females bundles of clothing and provisions, open them, appropriate what they wanted, and throw the remainder into the flames. Men were violently seized, and threatened with the halter or the pistol to compel them to disclose where their gold or silver was concealed. . . .

By three o'clock A.M., . . . more than two-thirds of the town lay in ashes, comprising the most highly improved and the entire business portion. Thousands of the inhabitants, including women, young children, the aged and the sick, passed that winter night in the open air, without shelter from the bitter and piercing blasts. About the hour mentioned, . . . Rev. A. Toomer Porter, personally known to General Sherman, was at the corner of a street conversing with one of his officers on horseback, when General Sherman, in citizen's attire, walked up and accosted him. The interview is thus described: "In the bright light of the burning city, General Sherman recognized me, and remarked, 'This is a horrible sight!'; 'Yes', I replied, 'when you reflect that women and children are the victims.' He said, 'Your Governor is responsible for this.' 'How so?', I replied. 'Whoever heard,' he said, 'of an evacuated city to be left a depot of liquor for an army to occupy? I found one hundred and twenty casks of whiskey in one cellar. Your Governor, being a lawyer or a judge, refused to have it destroyed, because it was private property, and now my men have got drunk, and have got beyond my control, and this is the result!.'

"Perceiving the officer on horseback, he said, 'Captain Andrews, did I not order that this thing should be stopped?' 'Yes, General,' said the Captain, 'but the first division that came in soon got as drunk as the first regiment that occupied the town.' 'Then, sir,' said General Sherman, 'go and bring in the second division.' The officer darted off, and Sherman bade me good evening. I am sure it was not more than an hour and a half from the time that General Sherman gave his order, that the city was cleared of the destroyers."

From that time until the departure of General Sherman from Columbia (with perhaps one or two exceptions), not another dwelling in it was burned by his soldiers, and, during the succeeding days and nights of his occupation, perfect tranquility prevailed throughout the town.

That Columbia was burned by the soldiers of General Sherman; that the vast majority of the incendiaries were sober; that for hours they were seen with combustibles firing house after house, without any affectation of concealment, and without the slightest check from their officers, is established by proof, full to repletion, and wearisome from its very superfluity. . . . Although actual orders for the burning of the town may not have been given, the soldiers of General Sherman certainly believed that its destruction would not be displeasing to him.

[General Sherman on the Burning of Columbia]

Before one single public building had been fired by order, the smoldering [cotton] fires, set by Hampton's order, were rekindled by the wind, and communicated to the buildings around. About dark they began to spread, and get beyond the control of the brigade on duty within the city. The whole of Woods' division was brought in, but it was found impossible to check the flames, which, by midnight, had become unmanageable, and raged until about four A.M., when the wind subsiding, they were got under control. I was up nearly all night, and saw Generals Howard, Logan, Woods, and others, laboring to save houses and protect families thus suddenly deprived of shelter, and of bedding and wearing apparel. I disclaim on the part of my army any agency in this fire, but on the contrary, claim that we saved what of Columbia remains unconsumed. And without hesitation, I charge General Wade Hampton with having burned his own city of Columbia, not with malicious intent, or as the manifestations of a silly "Roman stoicism," but from folly and want of sense, in filling it with lint, cotton, and tinder. Our officers and men on duty worked well to extinguish the flames; but others not on duty, including the officers who had long been imprisoned there, rescued by us, may have assisted in spreading the fire after it had once begun, and may have indulged in unconcealed joy to see the ruin of the capital of South Carolina. During the eighteenth and nineteenth [of February, 1865] the arsenal, railroad depots, machine shops, foundries, and other buildings were properly destroyed by detailed working parties, and the railroad track torn up and destroyed down to Kingsville and the Wateree bridge, and up in the direction of Winnsboro. . . .

War of the Rebellion . . . Records, 70 vols. (Washington: Government Printing Office, 1880–1901), XI, 377.

Sherman's Testimony Refuted by General Hampton:

Burning Columbia

[A newspaper account]

A "mixed commission on American and British claims" is now holding its sessions in Washington, and before this tribunal will soon be brought cases involving the question of the destruction of the city of Columbia, S.C., in February, 1865. . . .

On the night of 17th February, 1865, Columbia was burned to the ground after it had been in full possession of the Federal troops for ten hours. How was it so burned? No one of the citizens who was present during that disastrous night would be at a moment's loss to answer that question, and many of them have answered it most conclusively. . . . No one there doubted or doubts to whom the guilt attaches, and it was with surprise and indignation that my fellow-citizens saw the charge in Sherman's official report, published in April, 1865, that the destruction had been caused by myself.

While serving on the staff of General Beauregard he directed me to issue an order that all cotton stored in Columbia should be placed where it could be burned, "in case of necessity, without danger of destroying buildings." This order was published in one of the city newspapers . . . and is doubtless the same to which Sherman alludes in one of his numerous communications relative to the destruction of Columbia. . . . The post commander of Columbia at that time was Major Allen J. Green . . . [who] has been kind enough to send me the following paper, which speaks for itself:

"Huntsville, Ala., December 31, 1872.

"A day or two before the evacuation I received an order from Lieut. Gen. Wade Hampton, directing me to ascertain what amount of cotton there might be in the city, either in public or private hands, and to remove the same to vacant fields or lots adjacent, in order not to endanger the town should the necessity arise for burning the same . . . . no

Baltimore Enquirer (Baltimore, Md.), June 24, 1873.

such order (to burn it) was ever received by me . . . [and] during the night previous to or on the day of evacuation, a second order was received by me from Gen. Hampton, directing me to take no further steps with regard to the cotton, as it was not deemed necessary to destroy it. And I would further state that being in charge of the post, with my immediate command on duty up to the last moment of the evacuation . . . no fires had occurred . . . ."

Allen J. Green

OTHER AFFIDAVITS

"Soon after Gen. Hampton assumed command of the cavalry . . . he told me that Gen. Beauregard had determined not to burn the cotton, as the Yankees had destroyed the railroad, and he directed me to issue an order that no cotton should be fired. This I did at once, and when I left Columbia, which I did after the entrance of the Federal troops, not one bale of cotton was burning, nor had one been fired by our troops. At that time referred to I was acting as A.A. General to General Hampton."

Rawlins Lowndes, Capt. and A.A.G.

"M. C. Butler, a major general in the late Confederate army . . . says that he commanded a division of cavalry at the evacuation of Columbia . . . That his division was the rear guard of the cavalry of Gen. Beauregard's army . . . and occupied the town for several hours after all other troops had left . . . and that no cotton was burning . . . and none would likely have been set fire without his knowledge or orders. And this deponent further says that Lieut. Gen. Wade Hampton withdrew simultaneously . . . retiring by the Winnsboro road . . . and that when this deponent reached the eastern suburbs of the city, he halted his column, and remained there in full view of the Federal column as it marched down Main Street . . . and remained there for at least two hours . . . and when he left the suburbs he could see no evidence of cotton burning . . . That Lieut. Gen. Hampton, on the morning of the evacuation and the day previous, directed him that the cotton must not be set on fire. . . .

"The . . . statement of Gen. Hampton relative to the order issued by me at Columbia, South Carolina, not to burn the cotton in that city, is perfectly true and correct. The only thing on fire at the time of the evacuation was the depot building of the South Carolina Railroad, which caught fire accidentally from the explosion of some ammunition ordered to be sent toward Charlotte, N.C."

G. T. Beauregard

"Mich. H. Berry, being sworn, deposes: I was in Columbia in February, 1865, when the city was burned. . . . The first fire I saw, which was close to me, was set on fire by soldiers wearing the uniform of United States soldiers. . . . General Hampton's troops left in the morning previous to the burning. They left fully four hours before I saw the cotton burning as before stated."

James G. Gibbes testifies: "An alarm of fire arose, caused by the burning of some cotton in Richardson street. It was set on fire by United States soldiers. . . . My father's house was burned by them after having escaped the general conflagration. It was a fire-proof building. . . . I saw them fire furniture in the house . . . starting the fire from lace curtains, etc, etc."

"The soldiers of Gen. Sherman's army burnt Columbia."

T. J. Goodwyn
[Mayor of Columbia]

. . . But as the statements . . . may not carry weight . . . let us see what is said relative to Sherman's conduct in South Carolina by Federal writers: [and others]

The first author . . . is Capt. Conyngham, who accompanied the Federal army in its march through the South. Speaking of Columbia, he says . . . "Pillaging gangs soon fired the heart of the town . . . . I trust that I shall never witness such a scene again—drunken soldiers rushing from house to house, emptying them of their valuables and then firing them. . . .

"If a house was empty this was prima facie evidence that the owners were Rebels, and all was sure to be consigned to the flames. . . . The ruined homesteads of the Palmetto State will long be remembered. The army might march safely through the darkest night, the crackling pine woods shooting up their columns of flame, and the burning houses along the way would light it on. . . . I hazard nothing in saying that three-fifths in value of the personal property of the counties we passed through were taken by Sherman's army. The graves were even ransacked. . . . Besides compelling the enemy to evacuate Charleston, we destroyed Columbia, Orangeburg and several other places."

MAJOR NICHOLS [*of Sherman's staff*]

"The actual invasion of South Carolina has begun. The well-known sight of columns of black smoke meets our gaze again; this time houses are burning. . . . History . . . will be searched in vain for a parallel to the . . . destructive effects of this invasion of the Carolinas."

WILLIAM BEVERLY NASH [*State Senator of South Carolina*]

"W. B. Nash . . . being duly sworn . . . states that Gen. Sherman, or men acting under his permission, burned the city of Columbia, and that Gen. Hampton had nothing to do with the nefarious transaction."

ROBERT SPEER

"Robert Speer [prisoner taken by Col. Wilder of Gen. Sherman's command] deposes and says that . . . during the conversation [he] had with him [General Sherman] at his headquarters Gen. Sherman distinctly stated and avowed that the destruction with which he was then visiting the citizens of Georgia would be nothing to compare with what he had in store for the State of South Carolina; that looking upon her as an aggressor, that he would 'grease that State over and burn it up,' that 'he would have her people howling after me [Gen. Sherman] for bread.' 'All he wanted was guns and men, and damned if he did not have them.' This statement can be abundantly corroborated by other witnesses.

JOHN R. NIERNSEE [*Designer of state house*]

"I was a resident of Columbia . . . and on the evening of that day I met Capt. Ritner, of the 77th Illinois regiment. I saw rockets going up . . . and asked the meaning. . . . He drew me aside . . . and said 'Major, this is the signal for the burning of your city . . . .'"

EXTRACTS FROM REPORT OF COMMITTEE OF CONGRESS
(*Upon conduct of the war*)

Letter from Gen. Halleck,
Chief-of-Staff in Washington,
to Gen. [W. T.] Sherman

"Should you capture Charleston, I hope by some accident the place may be destroyed. . . ."

[Reply from General Sherman] "I will bear in mind . . . your hint as to Charleston. . . . When I move, the 15th corps will be on the right of the right wing . . . and if you have watched the history of that corps, you will have remarked that they generally do their work up pretty well. The truth is, the whole army is burning with an insatiable desire to wreak vengeance on South Carolina. I almost tremble at her fate, but feel that she deserves all that seems to be in store for her . . . ."

COLONEL STONE [*of Sherman's staff*]

"By this time I realized how much too small my command of 2,200 men was to properly guard a city of 40,000 inhabitants, rich, almost beyond conception, in such stores as we coveted. In addition to their own—more than ordinarily found anywhere—Richmond and Charleston had sent for safe-keeping all their surplus.

"I represented to Gen. Woods, commanding the division, how inadequate my command was to the task, particularly as this was the capital of South Carolina! . . .

"Col. J. D. Palmer, commanding my regiment, the 75th Iowa, and to whom I had entrusted the charge of the most dangerous part of the city, viz: that on the river and in 'Cotton Town,' confirmed my opinion that there was a plot to burn the city by telling me several fires had started in his district; that he had succeeded in putting them out so far, but could not hold out much longer, and that in his opinion the next one would fire the city.

"The wind after sunset had increased in violence. . . . All at once fifteen or twenty flames, from as many different places along the river, shot up, and in ten minutes the fate of Columbia was settled."

122. *A South Carolina Prisoner's Diary*

Lt. William Epps, of Williamsburg, South Carolina, was captured in Virginia in 1864 and spent about a year in federal
prisons. After some months in the North, he was transferred
to a Yankee prison on Morris Island, within the Yankee lines
near Charleston, where he was under fire from Confederate
forces. This was apparently in retaliation for some northern
prisoners having been kept in a dangerous position by the Rebel
forces. The excerpt is from his Diary, which begins at Fort
Delaware.

[Lieutenant William Epps]

Fort Delaware, August 4, 1864. Low in spirits today—thinking of
Dixie, far, far away . . . .

August 11. In high spirits about being exchanged soon—it is rumored
that six hundred officers leave here in a few days for Charleston, South
Carolina . . . .

August 20. Six hundred leave today for Hilton Head.

August 24. This morning about three o'clock ran aground just off
Cape Romain Light House—about six hours before we could move.
During the delay, we planned to capture the vessel, but gunboat came
up and our victory was crushed . . . .

September 7. Today we landed on Morris Island and are now situated in tents between Batteries Wagner and Gregg with Negroes to
guard us. . . .

September 9. The Yanks are firing furiously at our Batteries. Fort
Moultrie replied, dropping shells in beautiful style in and around Wagner and Gregg, except two that exploded over our prison, three pieces
of which fell among our tents and caused a very unpleasant feeling
among the Rebs. Fortunately none of us were hurt. . . .

W. W. Boddie, *History of Williamsburg* (Columbia: The State Co., 1923),
410–26. Copyright, 1923, by William Willis Boddie. Reprinted by permission of
The State-Record Company.

September 20. Since the 9th, nothing of very great importance has occurred except our rations have been very short and generally unfit for even a dog to live upon. They consist of, for breakfast, two hard crackers and about an ounce of salt pork; dinner, half pint bean soup, two crackers, and sometimes meat; supper, one cracker and about one ounce of meat. Upon an average I think we get about five crackers and two and one-half ounces of meat per day. . . .

October 5. I have not witnessed a more pleasant feeling among the men since I have been a prisoner. A large amount of nourishment from the citizens of Charleston has just arrived and never were provisions more joyfully received. Every man has a smile upon his face . . . .

October 16. Sunday—batteries on Sullivan's Island apparently practicing at our pen or something nearby, for several fragments of shell have just fallen among the tents. . . .

November 1. Another change in rations—nearly a pound of rice, loaf bread, about four ounces of meat, a pint of good vegetable soup, and as much salt and sugar as we need. . . .

November 24. Since the 20th, our rations have been short and issued raw, viz.: crackers (cooked), beans and salt pork, sometimes grist or rice. Very little wood is furnished and that green, such as maple, sweet-gum, and short leaf pine—oak occasionally. The weather being cold and scarcely wood enough for cooking purposes, we have suffered very much from cold . . . .

December 16. Rations of meat stopped—nothing issued to us but bread and not enough of that for two meals each day. We are not allowed to buy anything whatever, neither are we allowed to receive money, clothing, provisions, or anything whatever that would add to our comfort . . . .

December 20. Corn meal and pickles instead of molasses—camp kettles to cook in. The Yanks say they are retaliating on us for some of their officers who were treated badly at Columbia, South Carolina. Some of them who made their escape from Columbia arrived here a few days ago. Some of them said they were very roughly treated while others of the same party said they were well treated. . . .

January 1, 1865. Unwell and suffering cold and hunger—ten days of rations of corn meal and pickles issued. We have not had any meat since December 16. Dogs, rats, and cats dare not show themselves in our prison—several cats have been killed and eaten among us lately. . . .

January 17. My birthday—twenty-two years of age. We are still suffering from cold and hunger. My feet have been frost bitten and pain me considerably. A great many others of my fellow prisoners are suffering in a worse condition. No fire is allowed us at night, and, during the day, only enough to cook our small rations . . . .

January 27. Our rations increased by four ounces of salt beef and four ounces of Irish potatoes per day, in addition to the meal and pickles, but still kept under retaliation. . . .

February 19. A salute of one hundred guns fired by the fleet off this harbor and thirty-eight fired from a land battery over the fall of Charleston. . . .

February 20. Full rations issued—sixteen ounces of bread stuff, half flour and half corn meal, ten ounces of meat, pork, and bacon, per day, and also some beans and soup. . . .

March 11. Sadly disappointed—instead of being exchanged, we sail north for Fort Delaware . . . .

March 24. Taken sick with pneumonia. Went to the hospital and was kindly treated by the surgeon. . . .

April 2. Salute of one hundred guns fired over the fall of Richmond. . . . April 28. Oath of allegiance to the United States offered us on condition that all who take it are to be speedily released. Of two thousand, about half have consented to take it . . . . It is rumored that General Joseph E. Johnston, Confederate States Army, has surrendered to General U. S. Grant, United States Army.

April 30. The above rumor being confirmed, a great many are making application to take the oath, feeling that our cause is entirely hopeless, that being the only chance of deliverance . . . .

May 2. Oath again presented to those who refused a few days ago. . . . thinking all hope of success is gone now, I consent to submit to the will of a victorious people to return home with a sad heart and a conquered spirit, subject to the mercy of a powerful enemy . . . .

May 22. We are waiting in suspense for our release . . . .

June 19. At seven A.M., released from prison feeling once more at liberty . . . .

July 2. [From Charleston] take the cars for Kingstree at five o'clock A.M. Arrived at Kingstree at three-thirty P.M. At four-thirty, arrived at home, found mother and family all well, once more a happy man.

123. *The Emancipated Negro*

THE TRIALS OF THE NEWLY EMANCIPATED NEGROES, AS WELL AS
THOSE OF THE WHITE POPULATION, WERE MANY, AND LIFE WAS DIFFI-
CULT IN THE IMMEDIATE POSTWAR PERIOD. THE END OF THE WAR
BROUGHT THE NEGRO FREEDOM, BUT WITH FREEDOM CAME LOSS OF HIS
FORMER SECURITY AND THE RESPONSIBILITY FOR OBTAINING JOBS, LAND,
FOOD, CLOTHING, AND EVERYTHING THAT THE SLAVE HAD FORMERLY
TAKEN FOR GRANTED. THE DIFFICULTY INVOLVED IN THIS REARRANGE-
MENT OF PERSONAL AND RACE RELATIONSHIPS CAN BE SEEN IN THE
FOLLOWING ACCOUNT TAKEN FROM H. W. RAVENEL'S JOURNAL.

[H.W. Ravenel]

May 25, 1865. My Negroes have made no change in their behavior,
and are going on as they have always hitherto done. Until I know that
they are legally free, I shall let them continue. If they become free by law,
then the whole system must be changed. If the means which I now possess of supporting the old and the young are taken away, they must then
necessarily look for their support to their own exertions. How they can
support themselves at present, I cannot see. Labor is more abundant
(from the return of so many soldiers) and food still scarce, and money
yet more scarce, and difficult to be got. I have three or four of my Negroes who are only working out for their food. If Emancipation prevails,
the Negro must become a laborer in the field, as the whites will soon
occupy all the domestic and mechanic employments . . . .

May 29. As Gen. Gillmore's order, based on Chief Justice Chase's
opinion announces the freedom of the Negroes, there is no further room
to doubt that it is the settled policy of the country. I have today formally announced to my Negroes the fact, and made such arrangements
with each as the new relation rendered necessary. Those whose whole

Arney R. Childs, ed., *The Private Journal of Henry William Ravenel* (Columbia:
University of South Carolina Press, 1947), 238–40, 244, 247–48, 252–55.
Copyright, 1947, by the University of South Carolina Press, Columbia. Reprinted
by permission of The University of South Carolina Press.

time we need, get at present clothes and food, house rent and medical attendance. The others work for themselves giving me a portion of their time on the farm in lieu of house rent. Old Amelia and her two grandchildren, I will spare the mockery of offering freedom to. I must support them as long as I have anything to give.

May 30. My Negroes all express a desire to remain with me. I am gratified at the proof of their attachment. I believe it to be real and unfeigned. For the present they will remain, but in course of time we must part, as I cannot afford to keep so many, and they cannot afford to hire for what I could give them. As they have always been faithful and attached to us, and have been raised as family servants, and have all of them been our family for several generations, there is a feeling towards them somewhat like that of a father who is about to send out his children on the world to make their way through life. Those who have brought the present change upon us are ignorant of these ties. They have charged us with cruelty. They call us man stealers, robbers, tyrants. . . . It has pleased God that we should fail in our efforts for independence, and we return to the Union under the dominion of the abolition sentiment. The experiment is now to be tried. The Negro is not only to be emancipated, but is to become a citizen with all the rights and privileges! It produces a financial, political and social revolution at the South, fearful to contemplate in its ultimate effects. Whatever the result may be, let it be known and remembered that neither the Negro slave nor his master is responsible. . . .

I pray God for the great issues at stake, that he may bless the effort and make it successful—make it a blessing and not a curse to the poor Negro . . . .

June 14. The Negroes are very foolishly leaving their former masters. Nearly every family in Aiken has lost some, many all their servants. The novelty of the situation tempts them to make use of it. Many who are well treated, and much better off than they can be by their own exertions, are going away. They all want to go to the cities, either Charleston or Augusta. The fields have no attractions. Mine are still with me, that have been living here. Lander who was at Graniteville has lost his place there and gone to look out for work, and some of the other boys are working in the neighborhood. They have all professed a desire to remain with me. There are more than I need for servants or farm hands and they will have to provide for themselves . . . .

June 18. A majority of the Negroes have left Pooshee and gone down to Dean Hall on Cooper River, where about five hundred are collected, planting rice. Thomas . . . found that the Negroes at Woodboo had planted scarcely enough to support them one month next year. There must be want and starvation next winter among the Negroes, unless they get some other means than what they are now providing for themselves, for when left to their own judgment, they have not put in a half crop. The house servants have most generally remained . . . .

June 29. I find some difficulty in "arranging terms" with my Negroes, but strange to say, the difficulty lies in the opposite direction from what they most usually do. The fact is, I believe some of the Negroes are rather sad than rejoiced at their "freedom." None have first broached the subject to me—whenever alluded to, I have not introduced it. I told them a month ago of the state of affairs—that they had the right to leave me if they wished, and thought they could better themselves—that I had no money and could not offer them wages, but would go on feeding and clothing them for their services. They all (those whom I wished to retain about us) acquiesced very readily, and expressed a wish to remain, and have appeared perfectly satisfied. I think, however, it is only justice to them to put the matter upon a different footing, and have told them today that I must arrange for some fixed amount, so that they might have something to put up for clothing, shoes, blankets, taxes, sickness, etc. The condition is so new to both of us, that we find it awkward to arrange. I have told them to consider it over and let me know what they will be willing to take, either by week or by month, either deducting lost days or not, and either paying their own doctor bills or not. All these matters have now to be considered, and they have had no experience in taking care of themselves and providing for the future.

I still believe it would have been the part of wisdom, after emancipation was determined upon, to have made it gradual, so that labor and capital could have adjusted themselves to the new condition, and no violent shock be given to the industrial resources of the country, or to the social condition of society. If the black troops were removed altogether out of the country, and the matter of arranging terms left to some discreet and wise agent who could aid and advise both Negroes and employers, there would be no difficulty. . . .

September 3. Pompey made application to me this morning to give him permission to put up a house on a piece of my farm in the hollow near the Railroad. This is in the event of my selling out and moving away. I had intended to suggest to him that he ought to make some provision for securing a home in case I sold my farm, and had determined to give him a small tract of land from my farm to build upon. He has been raised in our family and his people before him for many generations have been serving us, and I must try to provide for him out of my limited (but more ample than his) means. All my Negroes have behaved well during this trial to their fidelity, and I would like to reward them if possible. I think that the Negroes generally as a race, have withstood the temptations to lawlessness and violence which might have been expected from 3 or 4 millions suddenly passing from slavery to freedom. . . .

September 27. Peter informed me this morning of his intention to go down the country with his family in a few days. He professes great attachment to all of us, but thinks he can do better in Charleston . . . . I told him he was right to go if he could better his condition, and at the same time, I warned him against being led away by bad example with hostility to the whites. They were his best friends and he would have to look to their aid wherever he was, for the means of living. . . .

124. The Proclamation of President Andrew Johnson for the Provisional Government of South Carolina, June 30, 1865

AFTER THE SURRENDER OF THE LAST CONFEDERATE FORCES IN THE STATE, THERE WAS A PERIOD OF POLITICAL CONFUSION. GOV. A. G. MAGRATH, THE LAST CONFEDERATE GOVERNOR, WAS NOMINALLY IN OFFICE UNTIL MAY 25, 1865, WHEN HE WAS REMOVED AND TEMPORARILY IMPRISONED. ON JUNE 30, 1865, PRESIDENT JOHNSON MOVED TO RETURN THE STATE PARTLY TO CIVILIAN CONTROL BY APPOINTING BENJAMIN F. PERRY OF GREENVILLE PROVISIONAL GOVERNOR. THE FOLLOWING SELECTION IS FROM JOHNSON'S PROCLAMATION SETTING UP THE PROVISIONAL GOVERNMENT.

[President Andrew Johnson's Proclamation]

Whereas the rebellion which has been waged by a portion of the people of the United States against the properly constituted authorities of the Government thereof in the most violent and revolting form, but whose organized and armed forces have now been almost entirely overcome, has in its revolutionary progress deprived the people of the State of South Carolina of all civil government; and

Whereas it becomes necessary and proper to carry out and enforce the obligations of the United States to the people of South Carolina in securing them in the enjoyment of a republican form of government:

Now, therefore, in obedience to the high and solemn duties imposed upon me by the Constitution of the United States, and for the purpose of enabling the loyal people of the said State to organize a State government . . . I, Andrew Johnson . . . do hereby appoint Benjamin F. Perry, of South Carolina, provisional governor of the State of South Carolina, whose duty it shall be, at the earliest practicable period, to prescribe such rules and regulations as may be necessary and proper for convening a convention composed of delegates to be chosen by that por-

J. D. Richardson, *A Compilation of the Messages and Papers of the Presidents, 1789–1897,* authorized by Congress, 10 vols. (Washington: Government Printing Office), VI, 310–11.

tion of the people of said State who are loyal to the United States, and no others, for the purpose of altering or amending the constitution thereof . . . . Provided, that in any election that may be hereafter held for choosing delegates to any State convention as aforesaid no person shall be qualified as an elector or shall be eligible as a member of such convention unless he shall have previously taken and subscribed the oath of amnesty as set forth in the President's proclamation of May 29, 1865, and is a voter qualified as prescribed by the constitution and laws of the State of South Carolina in force immediately before the 17th day of November, 1860, the date of the so-called ordinance of secession; and the said convention, when convened, or the legislature that may be thereafter assembled, will prescribe the qualifications of electors and the eligibility of persons to hold office under the constitution and laws of the State—a power the people of the several States composing the Federal Union have rightfully exercised from the origin of the Government to the present time.

And I do hereby direct—

That the military commander of the department and all officers and persons in the military and naval service aid and assist the said provisional governor in carrying into effect this proclamation; and they are enjoined to abstain from in any way hindering, impeding, or discouraging the loyal people from the organization of a State government as herein authorized. . . .

The amnesty oath required for South Carolina electors in 1865:

I, —— ——, do solemnly swear (or affirm), in the presence of Almighty God, that I will henceforth faithfully support, protect, and defend the Constitution of the United States and the Union of the States thereunder, and that I will in like manner abide by and faithfully support all laws and proclamations which have been made during the existing rebellion with reference to the emancipation of slaves. So help me God.

125. Governor Perry's Speech
to the Citizens of Greenville, July 3, 1865

BENJAMIN F. PERRY HAD BEEN A STRONG UNIONIST BEFORE 1860, BUT
AFTER SECESSION HE REMAINED LOYAL TO HIS STATE AND HELD OFFICES
OF CONFEDERATE COMMISSIONER, DISTRICT ATTORNEY, AND DISTRICT
JUDGE UNDER THE SECESSION GOVERNMENT. HIS STRONG SPEECHES OF
LOYALTY TO THE UNION PRECEDING THE EVENTS OF THE 1860S PROB-
ABLY INFLUENCED PRESIDENT JOHNSON TO APPOINT HIM PROVISIONAL
GOVERNOR. IT IS ALSO POSSIBLE THAT THE TWO MAY HAVE BEEN PER-
SONALLY ACQUAINTED PRIOR TO THE WAR YEARS, WHEN ANDREW JOHN-
SON LIVED IN LAURENS FOR TWO YEARS AS AN APPRENTICED TAILOR. AT
THE TIME THAT PERRY MADE THE FOLLOWING SPEECH AT A PUBLIC
MEETING IN GREENVILLE, HE WAS STILL UNAWARE OF HIS APPOINTMENT
AND WAS SPEAKING ONLY AS A PRIVATE CITIZEN.

[Benjamin F. Perry]

This public meeting of the citizens of Greenville is one of deep
humiliation and sorrow. A cruel and bloody war has swept over the
Southern States. One hundred and fifty thousand of our bravest and
most gallant men have fallen on the fields of battle! The land is filled
with mourning widows and orphans! There is scarcely a house in which
there has not been weeping for some one lost. Three thousand millions
of dollars have been spent by the Southern States in carrying on this
war! And now we are called upon to give up four millions of slaves,
worth two thousand millions of dollars. Moveover, our country has
been ravaged and desolated! Our cities, towns and villages are
smouldering ruins! Conquering armies occupy the country. The Confederacy has fallen, and we have been deprived of all civil government and
political rights! We have neither law nor order. There is no protection
for life, liberty or property. Everywhere there is demoralization, rapine

Benjamin F. Perry, *Reminiscences of Public Men,* 2nd Series (Greenville: Shannon
& Co., 1889), 229, 239–41.

and murder! Hunger and starvation are upon us! And now we meet as a disgraced and subjugated people to petition the conquerors to restore our lost rights! Such are the bitter fruits of Secession! . . .

I cannot, and would not, Mr. Chairman, ask my fellow citizens to forget the past, in this war, so far as the North is concerned. There have been deeds of atrocity committed by the United States armies, which never can be forgotten in the Southern States. But I do entreat them to become loyal citizens and respect the national authorities of the Republic. Abandon at once and forever all notions of Secession, Nullification and Disunion, determine to live, and to teach your children to live, as true American citizens. . . . As soon as the ferment of the revolution subsides, we shall be restored to all our civil rights, and be as free and republican as we ever were. There is no reason why there should be any sectional jealousy or ill-feeling between the North and the South. They are greatly necessary to each other. Their interests are dependent, and not rival interests, and now that slavery is abolished, there will be no bone of contention between the two sections. . . .

The resolutions which I have had the honor of submitting for the adoption of this meeting, are similar in purport to those adopted at Charleston, Columbia, Abbeville, and other places. They simply express our willingness to adopt the terms of the President's proclamation and return to our allegiance. We likewise ask for the appointment of a provisional governor and the restoration of the civil authorities. There is nothing in these resolutions to which the most sensitive can object. If a man is in a loathsome dungeon there is no impropriety in asking to be released, no matter how innocent he may have been. Nor is there anything wrong in his promising to behave himself if restored to his liberty. The resolutions likewise provide for sending some one to represent the situation of the country to the President. It may have some influence on the action of the Federal Government to have a full and free conference with the President in reference to the condition, wishes and feelings of the State. It is reported that President Johnson receives kindly all suggestions which are made in reference to the reconstruction of the States.

126. *The Constitutional Convention of 1865*

IN ACCORDANCE WITH THE PRESIDENT'S PROCLAMATION, PROVISIONAL
GOVERNOR PERRY CALLED FOR THE ELECTION OF DELEGATES TO A CON-
STITUTIONAL CONVENTION. THIS CONVENTION MET IN COLUMBIA, ON
SEPTEMBER 13, 1865, AND FRAMED A NEW CONSTITUTION WHICH RECOG-
NIZED THE FREEDOM OF THE SLAVES AND OTHER CHANGES BROUGHT BY
THE WAR. THE FOLLOWING SELECTION IS GOVERNOR PERRY'S ACCOUNT
OF THE CONVENTION.

[Provisional Governor Benjamin F. Perry]

The State Convention assembled, under my Proclamation, to reform
the Constitution of South Carolina. It was composed of the ablest,
wisest and most distinguished men of South Carolina. . . . All the
judges, Chancellors, ex-Governors, United States Senators, and members
of Congress, with few exceptions, were members of the Convention.
They met with a laudable spirit to accept the situation to which the
fate of the war had reduced them, and make the most of it, which
could be devised by wisdom and patriotism. Their sole object was to
redeem and regenerate the State, restore her prosperity and increase
the future happiness of the whole. Whilst they were unwilling to extend
to the colored people, just emancipated from slavery and in profound
ignorance of all political duties and obligations, the right of suffrage,
they were determined to protect them in the enjoyment of their freedom,
and in the security of their lives, persons and property. They felt
towards them no animosity or ill-will as a race, and could not; for the
colored people, throughout the war, with few exceptions, had behaved
well, and were quiet, industrious, and loyal to their owners. I thought
as a matter of policy and justice, that the intelligent property holders
amongst the freedmen should be allowed to vote, and so stated in the
original draft of my first message to the Convention. But my friends

Benjamin F. Perry, *Reminiscences of Public Men,* 2nd Series (Greenville: Shannon
& Co., 1889), 274–77.

advised me to leave out this recommendation, as it would only produce a division in the convention, and there was no probability of its being adopted. I did, and have ever since regretted it, for if a qualified suffrage had been extended to the colored people, we might have avoided the second reconstruction and the constitutional amendment imposed by Congress. This would have relieved us from our present degraded and ruinous condition and excluded from our midst the vile carpet-bagger and mean scalawag, who have prejudiced and weaned from us the colored people. . . .

When the convention met, I submitted my message to them, in which I urged the abolition of slavery, the destruction of the Parish system, equal representation throughout the State in proportion to taxation and population on the Federal basis, the election of Governor, and Presidential electors by the people, with some minor recommendations and reforms in our State Constitution. This message was well received by the Convention, and almost every recommendation was adopted, and became part of our State Constitution . . . .

When the Convention adjourned, I sent President Johnson a copy of their proceedings, and also a copy of the new Constitution. He wrote me in reply that he was gratified with all that had been done.

127. *The Constitution of 1865*

THE CONSTITUTION OF 1865, ALTHOUGH ACKNOWLEDGING THE FREE-
DOM OF THE NEGRO, WAS STILL A CONSERVATIVE CONSTITUTION. THREE
YEARS AFTER ITS ADOPTION, IT WAS SUPERSEDED BY THE HATED RECON-
STRUCTION CONSTITUTION OF 1868. THE CONSTITUTION OF 1865 DID,
HOWEVER, HAVE SOME PROGRESSIVE POINTS;—FOR EXAMPLE, THE POPU-
LAR ELECTION OF THE GOVERNOR AND THE ABOLITION OF PROPERTY
QUALIFICATIONS FOR HOLDING OFFICE.

Constitution of 1865:

We, the people of the State of South Carolina, by our delegates in
Convention met, do ordain and establish this Constitution for the
Government of the said State;

ARTICLE I

Section 1. The Legislative authority of this State shall be vested in a
General Assembly which shall consist of a Senate and a House of
Representatives.

Section 2. The House of Representatives shall be composed of members chosen by ballot, every second year . . . .

Section 3. Each judicial district in the State shall constitute one
election district, except Charleston District, which shall be divided into
two . . . .

Section 5. The House of Representatives shall consist of one hundred
and twenty four members, to be appointed among the several election
districts of the State, according to the number of white inhabitants
contained in each, and the amount of all taxes raised by the General
Assembly, whether direct or indirect, or of whatever species, paid in
each . . . .

J. H. Wolfe, ed., *The Constitution of 1865* (Columbia: Historical Commission of
South Carolina, 1951), 1–8. Reprinted by permission of the South Carolina
Department of Archives and History.

Section 7. In assigning Representatives to the several districts, the General Assembly shall allow one Representative for every sixty second part of the whole number of white inhabitants in the State, and one Representative also for every sixty second part of the whole taxes raised by the General Assembly. . . .

Section 11. The Senate shall be composed of one member from each election district, except the election district of Charleston, to which shall be allowed two . . . .

Section 12. Upon the meeting of the first General Assembly which shall be chosen under the provisions of this Constitution, the Senators shall be divided, by lot, into two classes; the seats of the Senators of the one class to be vacated at the expiration of two years after the Monday following the general election, and of those of the other class at the expiration of four years; and the number of these classes shall be so proportioned that one half of the whole number of Senators may, as nearly as possible, continue to be chosen thereafter every second year.

Section 13. No person shall be eligible to, or take or retain, a seat in the House of Representatives, unless he is a free white man, who hath attained the age of twenty one years, hath been a citizen and resident of this State three years . . . and hath been for the last six months . . . a resident of the District which he is to represent.

Section 14. No person shall be eligible to, or take or retain, a seat in the Senate, unless he is a free white man, who hath attained the age of thirty years, hath been a citizen and resident of this State five years . . . and hath been for the last six months . . . a resident of the District which he is to represent. . . .

Section 15. Senators and members of the House of Representatives shall be chosen at a general election on the third Wednesday in October . . . and on the same day in every second year. . . .

Section 17. Each House shall judge of the elections, returns and qualifications of its own members . . . .

Section 21. Bills for raising a revenue shall originate in the House of Representatives, but may be altered, amended or rejected by the Senate; and all other bills may originate in either House, and may be amended, altered or rejected by the other.

Section 22. Every Act or Resolution having the force of law, shall relate to but one subject, and that shall be expressed in the title. . . .

Section 25. In all elections by the General Assembly, or either House thereof, the members shall vote "vivi voce" . . . .

Section 26. The members of the General Assembly, who shall meet under this Constitution, shall be entitled to receive out of the public treasury, for their expenses during their attendance . . . five dollars for each day's attendance, and twenty cents for every mile of the ordinary route of travel between the residence of the member and the Capital. . . .

Section 30. And whereas the ministers of the Gospel are, by their profession, dedicated to the service of God, and the cure of souls, and ought not to be diverted from the great duties of their functions; therefore, no minister of the Gospel . . . shall be eligible to the office of Governor, Lieutenant Governor, or to a seat in the Senate or House of Representatives.

ARTICLE II

Section 1. The Executive authority of this State shall be vested in a Chief Magistrate, who shall be styled, the Governor of the State of South Carolina.

Section 2. The Governor shall be elected by the electors duly qualified to vote for members of the House of Representatives, and shall hold his office for four years . . . but the same person shall not be Governor for two consecutive terms.

Section 3. No person shall be eligible to the office of Governor, unless he hath attained the age of thirty years, and hath been a citizen and resident of this State for the ten years next preceding the day of election. . . .

Section 5. A Lieutenant Governor shall be chosen at the same time, in the same manner, continue in office for the same period and be possessed of the same qualifications as the Governor and shall "ex officio" be President of the Senate. . . .

Section 10. The Governor shall be Commander in Chief of the Army and Navy of this State, and of the militia, except when they shall be called into the actual service of the United States.

Section 11. He shall have power to grant reprieves and pardons . . . .

Section 12. He shall take care that the laws be faithfully executed in mercy. . . .

Section 14. All officers in the Executive Department, when required by the Governor, shall give him information, in writing, upon any subject relating to the duties of their respective offices.

Section 15. The Governor shall, from time to time, give to the General Assembly information of the condition of the State, and recommend to their consideration such measures as he shall judge necessary or expedient. . . .

Section 17. He shall commission all officers of the State. . . .

Section 21. Every bill, which shall have passed the General Assembly, shall before it becomes a law, be presented to the Governor; if he approve, he shall sign it; but if not, he shall return it, with his objections, to that House in which it shall have originated, who shall enter the objections at large on their journal, and proceed to reconsider it. If, after such reconsideration, a majority of the whole . . . House shall agree to pass the bill, it shall be sent . . . to the other House, by which it shall likewise be reconsidered; and if approved by a majority of the whole representation of that other House, it shall become a law. . . .

ARTICLE III

Section 1. The Judicial power shall be vested in such superior and inferior courts of law and equity as the General Assembly shall, from time to time, direct and establish. The Judges of the Superior Courts shall be elected by the General Assembly . . . . The General Assembly shall, as soon as possible, establish for each District, in the State, an inferior court or courts to be styled "The District Court," the judge whereof shall be resident in the district . . . , shall be elected by the General Assembly for four years . . . which Court shall have jurisdiction of all civil causes wherein one or both of the parties are persons of color, and of all criminal cases wherein the accused is a person of color . . . .

ARTICLE IV

In all elections to be made by the people of this State, or of any part thereof, for civil or political offices, every person shall be entitled to vote who has the following qualifications, to wit: He shall be a free white man, who has attained the age of twenty one years, and is not a pauper . . . . He shall have resided in this State for at least two years next preceding the day of election, and for the last six months of that time in the district in which he offers to vote; Provided, however, that the General Assembly may, by requiring a registry of voters, or other suitable legislation, guard against frauds in elections . . . and may prescribe additional qualifications for voters in municipal elections.

ARTICLE V

All persons who shall be elected or appointed to any office of profit or trust, before entering on the execution thereof shall take . . . the following oath:

"I do swear (or affirm) that I am duly qualified, according to the Constitution of this State, to exercise the office to which I have been appointed and that I will to the best of my ability, discharge the duties thereof, and preserve, protect and defend the Constitution of this State and that of the United States. So help me, God."

ARTICLE VI

Section 1. The House of Representatives shall have the sole power of impeaching . . . .

Section 2. All impeachments shall be tried by the Senate. . . .

Section 3. The Governor, Lieutenant Governor, and all civil officers shall be liable to impeachment for high crimes and misdemeanors . . . , for any misbehavior in office, for corruption in procuring office, or for any act which shall degrade their official character. . . .

ARTICLE VII

Section 1. The Treasurer and the Secretary of State shall be elected by the General Assembly in the House of Representatives, shall hold their offices for four years, and shall not be eligible for the next succeeding term.

Section 2. All other officers shall be appointed as they hitherto have been, until otherwise directed by law . . . .

ARTICLE VIII

All laws of force in this State, at the adoption of this Constitution, and not repugnant thereto, shall so continue until altered or repealed by the General Assembly . . . .

ARTICLE IX

[The first ten sections of this Article are similar to those of Article IX of the Constitution of 1790.]

Section 11. The slaves in South Carolina having been emancipated by the action of the United States authorities, neither slavery nor involuntary servitude, except as a punishment for crime whereof the party shall have been duly convicted, shall ever be reestablished in this State.

ARTICLE X

The General Assembly, whenever a tax is laid upon land, shall, at the same time, impose a capitation tax, which shall not be less upon each poll than one fourth of the tax laid upon each hundred dollars worth of the assessed value of the land taxed; excepting, however, from the operation of such capitation tax all such classes of persons, as from disability or otherwise, ought, in the judgment of the General Assembly, to be exempted.

ARTICLE XI

Section 1. The business of the Treasury shall be conducted by one Treasurer who shall hold his office and reside at the seat of Government. Section 2. The Secretary of State shall hold his office and reside at the seat of government.

ARTICLE XII

Section 1. No Convention of the people shall be called, unless by the concurrence of two thirds of the whole representation in each House . . . .

Section 2. No part of this Constitution shall be altered . . . unless agreed to . . . by two thirds of the whole representation in each House of the General Assembly . . . .

128. *The Black Code of 1865*

THE EMANCIPATION OF THE SLAVES CALLED FOR CHANGES IN THE BASIC CIVIL AND CRIMINAL LAW IN SOUTH CAROLINA. IN ORDER TO EFFECT THESE CHANGES, AND TO PROTECT AS WELL AS TO CONTROL THE FREEDMEN, A SERIES OF LAWS WHICH CAME TO BE KNOWN AS "THE BLACK CODE" WERE PASSED BY THE NEWLY ELECTED LEGISLATURE IN THE FALL OF 1865. THESE LAWS, HOWEVER, WERE NEVER PUT INTO PRACTICE. ON JANUARY 1, 1866, THEY WERE DECLARED "NULL AND VOID" BY THE MILITARY CONTROLLER, GEN. DANIEL SICKLES, WHO WAS IN CHARGE OF THE DISTRICT WHICH INCLUDED NORTH AND SOUTH CAROLINA. THE LAWS WERE ATTACKED IMMEDIATELY IN THE NORTH AS AN ATTEMPT TO RE-ENSLAVE THE NEGROES. THIS ATTACK, ADDED TO THE PROPAGANDA ABROAD, MADE IT EASIER FOR THE RADICALS IN CONGRESS TO PUSH THROUGH THEIR "CONGRESSIONAL RECONSTRUCTION" PLANS. THADDEUS STEVENS, THE FATHER OF CONGRESSIONAL RECONSTRUCTION, ADVOCATED MILITARY RULE AND TERRITORIAL GOVERNMENT, STATING THAT THE "FALLEN REBELS" COULD "LEARN THE PRINCIPLES OF FREEDOM AND EAT THE FRUIT OF FOUL REBELLION." THE SELECTIONS FOLLOWING INCLUDE THE "PRELIMINARY ACT" AND THE BLACK CODE.

An Act preliminary to the Legislation
induced by the emancipation of slaves:

Whereas the Convention of this State, by the Constitution lately ratified, did recognize the emancipation of slaves and declare that "neither slavery nor involuntary servitude, except as a punishment for crime, shall ever be re-established in this State," and did direct that, for each District in the State, there should be established an Inferior Court, to be styled "The District Court, which Court shall have jurisdiction of all civil causes wherein one or both of the parties are persons

South Carolina Statutes at Large, XIII, 269–89. Two other acts passed about the same time, an "Act to Amend the Criminal Law" and an "Act to Establish District Courts," also contained clauses distinguishing the treatment of Negroes from that of white people.

of color, and of all criminal causes wherein the accused is a person of color"; therefore,

I. Be it enacted by the Senate and House of Representatives . . . that this act shall be preliminary to "An Act to establish and regulate the domestic relations of persons of color, and to amend the law in relation to paupers, vagrancy and bastardy"; and "An Act to establish District Courts," and "An Act to amend the Criminal Law," which Acts have been induced by the Constitution aforesaid; and that in reference to these Acts, the following provisions shall obtain:

II. Words importing the singular number only shall be construed to apply to several persons or things as well as one person or thing, and every word importing the masculine gender only, shall be construed to extend to a female as well as a male, where the context does not forbid such construction.

III. All free Negroes, mulattoes, and mestizoes, all freedmen and freed women, and all descendants through either sex of any of these persons, shall be known as persons of color, except that every such descendant, who may have of Caucasian blood seven-eights or more shall be deemed a white person.

IV. The Statutes and regulations concerning slaves are now inapplicable to persons of color; and although such persons are not entitled to social or political equality with white persons, they shall have the right to acquire, own and dispose of property; to make contracts; to enjoy the fruits of their labor; to sue and be sued; and to receive protection under the law in their persons and property.

V. All rights and remedies respecting persons or property, and all duties and liabilities under laws, civil and criminal, which apply to white persons, are extended to persons of color, subject to the modifications made by this Act, and the other Acts herein before mentioned.

An Act to establish and regulate the domestic relations of persons of color, and to amend the law in relation to paupers and vagrancy:

1. The relation of husband and wife amongst persons of color is established.

2. Those who now live as such are declared to be husband and wife.

3. In case of one man having two or more reputed wives, or one woman two or more reputed husbands, the man shall, by the first day of April next, select one of his reputed wives, or the woman one of her reputed husbands; and the ceremony of marriage between this man or woman, and the person so selected, shall be performed.

4. Every colored child, heretofore born, is declared to be the legitimate child of his mother, and also of his colored father, if he is acknowledged by such a father.

5. Persons of color desirous hereafter to become husband and wife, should have the contract of marriage duly solemnized. . . .

10. A husband shall not, for any cause, abandon or turn away his wife, nor a wife her husband. . . .

13. The father shall support and maintain his children under fifteen years of age, whether they be born of one of his reputed wives or any other woman . . . .

15. A child, over the age of two years, born of a colored parent, may be bound by the father, if he be living in the District, or in case of his death or absence from the District, by the mother, as an apprentice to any respectable white or colored person who is competent to make a contract; a male until he shall attain the age of twenty-one years, and a female until she shall attain the age of eighteen years. . . .

17. Colored children, between the ages mentioned, who have neither father or mother living in the District in which they are found, or whose parents are paupers, or unable to afford to them maintenance, or whose parents are not teaching them habits of industry and honesty, or are parents of notoriously bad character, or are vagrants, or have been either of them, convicted of an infamous offense, may be bound as apprentices by the District Judge, or ône of the Magistrates for the aforesaid term. . . .

22. The master or mistress shall teach the apprentice the business of husbandry, or some other useful trade or business . . . ; shall furnish him wholesome food and suitable clothing; teach him habits of industry, honesty and morality; govern him and treat him with humanity; and if there be a school within a convenient distance, where colored children are taught; shall send him to school at least six weeks in every year of his apprenticeship, after he shall be of the age of ten years . . . .

24. The master shall receive to his own use the profits of the labor of his apprentice . . . .

30. At the expiration of his term of service, the apprentice shall have the right to recover from his master a sum not exceeding sixty dollars. . . .

35. All persons of color who make contracts for service or labor, shall be known as servants, and those with whom they contract, shall be known as masters.

36. All contracts between masters and servants, for one month or more,

shall be in writing, be attested by one white witness, and be approved by the judge of the District Court, or by a Magistrate.

37. The period of service shall be expressed in the contract; but if it be not expressed, it shall be until the twenty-fifth day of December next after the commencement of the service. . . .

45. On farms, or in out-door service, the hours of labor, except on Sunday, shall be from sun-rise to sun-set, with a reasonable interval for breakfast and dinner. Servants shall rise at the dawn in the morning, feed, water and care for the animals on the farm, do the usual and needful work about the premises, prepare their meals for the day, if required by the master, and begin the farm work or other work by sunrise. The servant shall be careful of all the animals and property of his master, and especially of the animals and implements used by him, shall protect the same from injury by other persons, and shall be answerable for all property lost, destroyed or injured by his negligence, dishonesty or bad faith.

46. . . . Work at night, and outdoor work in inclement weather, shall not be exacted, unless in case of necessity. Servants shall not be kept at home on Sunday, unless to take care of the premises, or animals thereupon, or for work of daily necessity, or on unusual occasions; and in such cases, only so many shall be kept at home as are necessary for these purposes. Sunday work shall be done by the servants in turn . . . . Absentees on Sunday shall return to their homes by sun-set. . . .

48. Visitors or other persons shall not be invited or allowed by the servant to come or remain upon the premises of the master without his express permission.

49. Servants shall not be absent from the premises without the permission of the master.

50. When the servant shall depart from the service of the master without good cause, he shall forfeit the wages due to him. The servant shall obey all lawful orders of the master or his agent, and shall be honest, truthful, sober, civil and diligent in his business. The master . . . shall not be liable to pay for any additional or extraordinary services or labor of his servant, the same being necessary, unless by express agreement. . . .

57. The master shall not be bound to furnish medicine or medical assistance for his servant, without his express engagement. . . .

61. The servant may depart from the master's service for an insufficient supply of wholesome food; for an unauthorized battery upon his own person or one of his family . . . ; for invasion by the master of the

conjugal rights of the servant; or his failure to pay wages when due; and may recover wages due for services rendered to the time of his departure. . . .

65. Whenever a master discharges a servant, the servant may make immediate complaint to a District Judge or Magistrate, and whenever a servant departs from his master's service, the master may make like complaint. In either case, the District Judge or Magistrate, shall, by summons or warrant, have the parties brought before him, hear them and their witnesses, and decide as to the sufficiency of the cause of his discharge or departure. . . .

68. The rules and regulations prescribed for master and servant apply to persons in service as household servants, conferring the same rights and imposing the same duties . . . .

70. It is the duty of this class of servants to be especially civil and polite to their masters, their families and guests, and they shall receive gentle and kind treatment. . . .

72. No person of color shall pursue or practice the art, trade or business of an artisan, mechanic or shopkeeper, or any other trade, employment or business (besides that of husbandry, or that of a servant under a contract for service or labor), on his own account and for his own benefit, or in partnership with a white person, or as an agent or servant of any person, until he shall have obtained a license therefore from the Judge of the District Court; which license shall be good for one year only. This license the Judge may grant upon petition of the applicant, and upon being satisfied of his skill and fitness, and of his good moral character, and upon payment, by the applicant, to the Clerk of the District Court of one hundred dollars, if a shopkeeper or pedler, to be paid annually; and ten dollars, if a mechanic, artisan, or to engage in any other trade, also to be paid annually. . . .

75. Where, upon any farm or lands, there now are persons of color, who were formerly the slaves of the owner, lessee or occupants . . . and who are helpless, either from old age, infancy, disease or other cause; . . . it shall not be lawful for the present, or any subsequent owner, lessee, or occupant, before the first day of January, 1867, to evict or drive [them] from the houses which now are, or hereafter shall be, lawfully occupied . . . .

76. But the owner, lessee, or occupant of such farm or lands shall, nevertheless, have authority to preserve order and good conduct in the houses so occupied as aforesaid . . . .

81. When a person of color shall be unable to earn his support, and is likely to become a charge to the public, the father and grandfathers, mother and grandmothers, child and grandchild, brother and sister, of such person shall, each according to his ability, contribute monthly for the support of such poor relative, such sum as the District Judge or one of the Magistrates, upon complaint to him, shall deem necessary and proper . . . .

82. In each Judicial District . . . there shall be established a Board, to be known as the "Board of Relief of Indigent Persons of Color," which shall consist of a Chairman and not less than three, nor more than seven other members, all of whom shall be Magistrates of the District, and be selected by the District Judge . . . .

85. A District Court Fund shall be established in each District, to be composed of aids paid for the approval of contracts . . . and of instruments of apprenticeship, and for licenses granted by the District Judge, all fines, penalties and forfeitures collected under order or process from the District Court, or a Magistrate of the District, fees for appeal from the District Judge, wages of convicts, and taxes collected under the order of the Board of Relief of Indigent Persons of Color.

86. If the District Court Fund, after payment of the sums with which it is charged, on account of the salary of the Judge of the District Court, Superintendent of Convicts, Jurors and other expenses of the Court, and of convicts, shall be insufficient to support indigent persons of color, who may be proper charges on the public, the Board aforesaid shall have power to impose for that purpose, whenever it may be required, a tax of one dollar on each male person of color . . . , and fifty cents on each unmarried female person of color between the ages of eighteen and forty-five . . . .

89. It shall be the duty of every Magistrate to make diligent inquiry into the condition and wants of the colored poor within his precinct . . . .

92. The Board of Relief of Indigent Persons of Color shall determine the sum necessary for the support of each indigent person of color, who shall be deemed a proper charge on the public . . . .

96. All persons who have not some fixed and known place of abode, and some lawful and reputable employment; those who have not some visible and known means of a fair, honest and reputable livelihood . . . persons who lead idle or disorderly lives . . . , those who, not having sufficient means of support, are able to work and do not work; those who . . . do not provide a reasonable and proper maintenance for

themselves and families; . . . shall be deemed vagrants, and be liable to the punishment hereinafter prescribed.

97. Upon information, on oath, of another, or upon his own knowledge, the District Judge or a Magistrate, shall issue a warrant for the arrest of any person of color known or believed to be a vagrant, within the meaning of this Act . . . . On conviction, the defendant shall be liable to imprisonment, and to hard labor, one or both, as shall be fixed by the verdict, not exceeding twelve months.

98. The defendant, if sentenced to hard labor after conviction may . . . be hired for such wages as can be obtained for his services, to any owner or lessee of a farm, for the term of hard labor to which he was sentenced, to be hired for the same labor on the streets, public roads, or public buildings. . . .

99. These provisions concerning vagrancy shall not be construed to repeal any other Act or Acts in whole or in part consistent herewith.

129. B. F. Perry on the Refusal of Congress to Seat the Southern Delegations, 1866

ON THE BASIS OF THE STATE CONSTITUTION OF 1865, AND WITH THE APPROVAL OF PRESIDENT ANDREW JOHNSON, SOUTH CAROLINA ELECTED NEW CONGRESSMEN, BUT THE UNITED STATES CONGRESS, CONTROLLED BY THE RADICAL WING OF THE REPUBLICAN PARTY, REFUSED TO SEAT THEM OR ANY OTHERS FROM THE FORMER CONFEDERATE STATES. THIS WAS THE BEGINNING OF THE MOVEMENT TOWARD CONGRESSIONAL CONTROL OF THE RECONSTRUCTION PROGRAM. THE FOLLOWING IS THE OPINION OF BENJAMIN F. PERRY ON THE ACTION OF CONGRESS.

[Benjamin F. Perry]

The Southern people have been peculiarly unfortunate. At one time they thought it better to withdraw their members from Congress, and live separately from the North. This they desired to do peaceably and quietly. The North objected, and declared that the Union should not be dissolved. They were repeatedly told that they must lay down their arms, elect their members of Congress, and resume their position in the Union. Finally, they consented to do so. Now they are told that the Union is dissolved, and they shall not be allowed to resume their places in it! Let the North beware, lest in forging chains for the South they do not enclose themselves. This Freedmen's Bureau is an *imperium in imperio,* and now embraces the North as well as the South. . . .

The Southern States have committed grievous errors, and terrible has been their punishment—sufficient, one would suppose, to gratify the blackest hate of the most malignant revenger. There is nothing more gratifying to a noble and generous nature than mercy and forgiveness. Nor is there anything more pleasant to a mean and cowardly spirit than the gratification of its revenge and hatred. The history of man in all ages illustrates the truth of this assertion.

Benjamin F. Perry, *Biographical Sketches of Eminent American Statesmen* . . . (Philadelphia: 1887), pp. 201–203.

The great crime of the Southern States was simply a wish to live separated from the North. They did not seek to conquer and subdue the North, or to rule over the North, but only attempted to govern themselves in their own way and after their own fashion. This boon was denied them, and their country has been devastated, their towns, cities and villages laid waste, their property taken from them, and the people left bankrupted and starving. Now they humbly ask to be permitted to live quietly, peaceably and loyally in that Union, and renew their social, political and commercial relations with the North. It is to be hoped that the kind, generous and magnanimous policy adopted by the President will be pursued and carried out by the American people, and that we shall be once more, free, united, happy and prosperous. . . .

130. *A Northerner's Description of South Carolina, 1866*

Of the many Northern reporters and writers who converged on the South after the Civil War, the most objective, and descriptive, was probably the journalist Sidney Andrews. He came with a definite Northern viewpoint, but he wrote what he saw, whether or not it was favorable to the Northern cause. His relative objectivity makes the following picture of life in South Carolina in 1866 all the more valuable.

[Sidney Andrews, A Northern Newspaper Reporter]

The people of the central part of the State are poor, wretchedly poor; for the war not only swept away their stock and the material resources of their plantations, but all values—all money, stocks and bonds—and generally left nothing that can be sold for money but cotton, and only a small proportion of the landholders have any of that. Therefore there is for most of them nothing but the beginning anew of life, on the strictest personal economy and a small amount of money borrowed in the city. It would be a benefit of hundreds of millions of dollars if the North could be made to practice half the economy which poverty forces upon this people.

They are full of ignorance and prejudices, but they want peace and quiet, and seem not badly disposed toward the general government. Individuals there are who rant and rave and feed on fire as in the old days, but another war is a thing beyond the possibilities of time. So far as any fear of that is concerned, we may treat this State as we please —hold it as a conquered province or restore it at once to full communion in the sisterhood of States. The war spirit is gone, and no fury can re-enliven it.

The spirit of oppression still exists, however, and military authority cannot be withdrawn till the relation between employer and employed

Sidney Andrews, *The South Since the War* (Boston: Ticknor and Fields, 1866), 36–37, 100, 205–206.

is put upon a better basis. On the one hand, the Negro in the country districts must be made to understand what he has already been taught in the city, that freedom does not mean idleness. On the other hand, the late master should specially be made to understand that the spirit of slavery must go to the grave with the thing itself. It will not be an easy work to teach either class its chief lesson. We must have patience —patience, and faith that neither faints nor falters. . . .

I infer from all I saw and heard while in the northeastern section, that the Negroes at work in the pines are more generally contented than those on plantations anywhere in the State. There is more variety in the turpentine and rosin business than in cotton-growing; and though the work may be harder for one or two days in any given week, there are other days in which there is but little to do. . . .

The Negro's situation in other districts of the so-called low country is not so good as in those already named. From Georgetown there are many complaints that he is turbulent and "rebellious," and these are made the pretext for treating him with much severity. A gentleman from the town of that name tells me of a case in which a Negro was cruelly beaten over the head and shoulders with a large club for insisting that an examination of his contract would show that he was under no obligation to perform certain work required of him. In the upper part of Charleston district, the planters are quietly holding meetings at which they pass resolutions not to sell land to Negroes, and not to hire Negroes unless they can show a "consent paper" from their former owner.

131. *The First Reconstruction Act, March 2, 1867*

ALTHOUGH THE FOURTEENTH AMENDMENT WAS NEVER RATIFIED BY
A MAJORITY OF THE STATES IN THE UNITED STATES, THE RADICAL
REPUBLICANS, LED BY THADDEUS STEVENS, WERE ABLE TO OVERRIDE
PRESIDENT ANDREW JOHNSON'S VETO. WITH THIS POWER, CONGRESS
IN 1867 PUSHED THROUGH A SERIES OF "RECONSTRUCTION ACTS," RE-
VERSING THE TREND OF "PRESIDENTIAL RECONSTRUCTION," AND BEGIN-
NING WHAT IS KNOWN AS THE PERIOD OF "CONGRESSIONAL RECON-
STRUCTION." FOR SOUTH CAROLINA, THIS MEANT YEARS OF CORRUPT
GOVERNMENT. THE FOLLOWING ACT WAS THE FIRST OF SEVERAL WHICH
GAVE OVER THE SOUTH CAROLINA GOVERNMENT AND THAT OF THE OTHER
DEFEATED SOUTHERN STATES TO NEGROES, CARPETBAGGERS, AND
SCALAWAGS.

An Act to provide for the more efficient
government of the Rebel States:

Whereas no legal State governments or adequate protection for life
or property now exists in the rebel states of Virginia, North Carolina,
South Carolina, Georgia, Mississippi, Alabama, Louisiana, Florida,
Texas and Arkansas; and whereas it is necessary that peace and good
order should be enforced in said States until loyal and republican State
governments can be legally established: Therefore,

Be it enacted by the Senate and House of Representatives of the
United States of America in Congress assembled, That said rebel States
shall be divided into military districts and made subject to the military
authority of the United States as hereinafter prescribed, and for that
purpose, Virginia shall constitute the first district; North Carolina and
South Carolina the second district: . . .

And be it further enacted, That it shall be the duty of the President
to assign to the command of each of said districts an officer of the army,
not below the rank of brigadier general, and to detail a sufficient military

United States Statutes at Large, XIV, 428–29.

force to enable such officer to perform his duties and enforce his authority within the district to which he is assigned.

And be it further enacted, That it shall be the duty of each officer assigned as aforesaid, to protect all persons in their rights of person and property, to suppress insurrection, disorder, and violence, and to punish, or cause to be punished, all disturbers of the public peace and criminals; and to this end . . . he shall have power to organize military commissions or tribunals for that purpose, and all interference under color of State authority with the exercise of military authority under this act, shall be null and void. . . .

And be it further enacted, That when the people of any one of said rebel States shall have formed a constitution of government in conformity with the Constitution of the United States in all respects, framed by a convention of delegates elected by the male citizens of said State, twenty-one years old and upward, of whatever race, color, or previous condition, who have been resident in said State for one year previous to the day of such election, except such as may be disfranchised for participation in the rebellion or for felony at common law, and which such constitution shall provide that the elective franchise shall be enjoyed by all such persons as have the qualifications herein stated for electors of delegates, and when such constitution shall be ratified by a majority of the persons voting on the question of ratification who are qualified as electors for delegates, and when such constitution shall have been submitted to Congress for examination and approval, and Congress shall have approved the same, and when said State, by a vote of its legislature elected under said constitution shall have adopted the amendment to the Constitution of the United States, . . . known as Article Fourteen, and when said Article shall have become a part of the Constitution of the United States, said State shall be entitled to representation in Congress, and Senators and Representatives shall be admitted therefrom on their taking the oath prescribed by law, and then and thereafter the preceding sections of this act shall be inoperative in said State: Provided, That no person excluded from the privilege of holding office by the said proposed amendment to the Constitution of the United States, shall be eligible to election as a member of the convention to frame a constitution for any of said rebel States, nor shall any such person vote for members of such convention.

And be it further enacted, That, until the people of said rebel States shall be by law admitted to representation in the Congress of the United States, any civil governments which may exist therein shall be deemed provisional only, and in all respects subject to the paramount authority of the United States at any time to abolish, modify, control, or supersede the same . . . .

The oath required for voting for delegates to the Constitutional Convention of 1868:

I, _____ _____, do solemnly swear (or affirm), in the presence of Almighty God, that I am a citizen of the State of South Carolina; that I have resided in said State for _____ months next preceding this day, and now reside in the county of _____ . . . ; that I am twenty-one years old; that I have not been disfranchised for participation in any rebellion or civil war against the United States, or for felony committed against the laws of any State or of the United States; that I have never been a member of any State legislature, nor held any executive or judicial office in any State, and afterwards engaged in insurrection or rebellion against the United States, or given aid or comfort to the enemies thereof; that I have taken an oath . . . to support the Constitution of the United States, and afterwards engaged in insurrection or rebellion against the United States . . . ; that I will faithfully support the Constitution and obey the laws of the United States, and will, to the best of my ability, encourage others to do so, so help me God.

United States Statutes at Large, **XV,** 2.

132. *The Constitution of 1868*

THE DELEGATES TO THE CONVENTION TO FRAME THE NEW CONSTITU-
TION, ELECTED IN ACCORDANCE WITH THE RECONSTRUCTION ACTS, CON-
SISTED OF 48 WHITE MEN AND 76 NEGROES. ALL BUT FOUR WERE
REPUBLICANS. MEMBERS WERE ELECTED IN NOVEMBER, 1867, BY AN
ELECTORATE THAT WAS MORE THAN TWO-THIRDS NEGRO. THEY MET
IN CHARLESTON FROM JANUARY 14 TO MARCH 18, 1868, AND THE
SELECTIONS FOLLOWING ARE TAKEN FROM THE CONSTITUTION DRAWN
UP AT THAT TIME. BECAUSE THE MAJORITY OF THE DELEGATES WERE
TOTALLY UNSKILLED IN SUCH WORK, THE CONVENTION COPIED READILY
FROM NORTHERN STATE CONSTITUTIONS, PARTICULARLY NEW YORK
AND OHIO.

The Constitution of 1868:

We, the people of South Carolina, in Convention assembled, grateful
to Almighty God for this opportunity, deliberately and peaceably entering
into an explicit and solemn compact with each other, and forming a new
Constitution of civil government for ourselves and posterity, recognizing
the necessity of the protection of the people in all that pertains to their
freedom, safety and tranquillity, and imploring the direction of the
Great Legislator of the Universe, do agree upon, ordain, and establish the
following Declarations of Rights and form of government as the Constitution of the Commonwealth of South Carolina:

ARTICLE I

Section 1. All men are born free and equal, endowed by their Creator
with certain inalienable rights, among which are the rights of enjoying
and defending their lives and liberties, of acquiring, possessing and
protecting property, and of seeking and obtaining their safety and
happiness.

Francis N. Thorpe, ed., *The Federal and State Constitutions* . . . (Washington:
Government Printing Office, 1909), 3281–3305; for amendments, *see* 3305–306.

Section 2. Slavery shall never exist in this State, neither shall involuntary servitude, except as a punishment for crime, whereof the party shall have been duly convicted.

Section 3. All political power is vested in and derived from the people only; therefore they have the right, at all times, to modify their form of government in such manner as they may deem expedient, when the public good demands.

Section 4. Every citizen of this State owes paramount allegiance to the Constitution and government of the United States, and no law or ordinance of this State in contravention or subversion thereof can have any binding force.

Section 5. This State shall ever remain a member of the American Union . . . .

Section 6. The right of the people peaceably to assemble . . . shall never be abridged.

Section 7. All persons may freely speak, write and publish their sentiments on any subject, being responsible for the abuse of that right . . . .

Section 9. No person shall be deprived of the right to worship God according to the dictates of his own conscience; provided, that the liberty of conscience hereby declared shall not justify practices inconsistent with the peace and moral safety of society.

Section 10. No form of religion shall be established by law . . . .

Section 11. The right of trial by jury shall remain inviolate . . . .

Section 14. No person shall be arrested, imprisoned, despoiled or dispossessed of his property, immunities or privileges . . . but by the judgment of his peers or the law of the land. And the General Assembly shall not enact any law that shall subject any person to punishment without trial by jury . . . .

Section 17. The privilege of the writ of habeas corpus shall not be suspended . . . .

Section 27. The General Assembly ought frequently to assemble for the redress of grievances, and for making new laws, as the common good may require. . . .

Section 31. All elections shall be free and open, and every inhabitant of this Commonwealth possessing the qualifications provided for in this Constitution shall have an equal right to elect officers and be elected to fill public office.

Section 34. Representation shall be apportioned according to population . . . .

Section 36. All property subject to taxation shall be taxed in proportion to its value.

Section 41. The enumeration of rights in this Constitution shall not be construed to impair or deny others retained by the people, and all powers not herein delegated remain with the people.

ARTICLE II

Section 1. The legislative power of this State shall be vested in two distinct branches, the one to be styled the "Senate" and the other the "House of Representatives," and both together the "General Assembly of the State of South Carolina."

Section 2. The House of Representatives shall be composed of members chosen by ballot every second year . . . .

Section 3. The judicial districts shall hereafter be designated as counties and the boundaries of the several counties shall remain as they are now established . . . provided, that the General Assembly shall have the power at any time to organize new counties by changing the boundaries . . . .

Section 4. The House of Representatives shall consist of one hundred and twenty-four members, to be apportioned among the several counties according to the number of inhabitants contained in each. . . .

Section 6. In assigning representatives to the several counties, the General Assembly shall allow one representative to every one hundred and twenty-fourth part of the whole number of inhabitants in the State; provided . . . that . . . if any county shall appear not to be entitled, from its population, to a representative, such county shall, nevertheless, send one representative . . . .

Section 8. The Senate shall be composed of one member from each county, . . . except the county of Charleston, which shall be allowed two Senators.

Section 10. No person shall be eligible to a seat in the Senate or House of Representatives who at the time of his election is not a citizen of the United States; nor any one who has not been for one year next preceding his election a resident of the county whence he may be chosen; nor anyone who has been convicted of an infamous crime. Senators shall be at least twenty-five, and Representatives at least twenty-one years of age. . . .

Section 14. Each House shall judge of the election returns and qualifications of its own members . . . .

Section 15. Each House shall choose its own officers . . . .

Section 18. Bills for raising a revenue shall originate in the House of Representatives . . . .

Section 22. No money shall be drawn from the treasury but in pursuance of an appropriation made by law . . . .

Section 23. Each member of the first General Assembly shall receive six dollars per diem while in session . . . but no General Assembly shall have power to increase the compensation of its own members . . . .

Section 28. No person shall be eligible to a seat in the General Assembly whilst he holds any office of profit or trust under this State, the United States of America, or any of them . . . .

ARTICLE III

Section 1. The supreme executive authority of this State shall be vested in a chief magistrate, who shall be styled "The Governor of the State of South Carolina."

Section 2. The governor shall be elected by the electors duly qualified to vote for members of the House of Representatives, and shall hold his office for two years . . . .

Section 3. No person shall be eligible to the office of governor who denies the existence of the Supreme Being, or who at the time of such election has not attained the age of thirty years . . . .

Section 5. A lieutenant-governor shall be chosen at the same time, in the same manner, continue in office for the same period, and be possessed of the same qualifications as the governor, and shall ex officio be president of the Senate.

Section 22. Every bill or joint resolution which shall have passed the General Assembly, except on a question of adjournment, shall, before it becomes a law, be presented to the governor, and, if he approve, he shall sign it; if not, he shall return it, with his objections, to the House in which it shall have originated; which shall enter the objections at large on its journal, and proceed to reconsider it. If, after such reconsideration, two-thirds of that House shall agree to pass it, it shall be sent, together with the objections, to the other House, by which it shall be reconsidered, and, if approved by two-thirds of that House, it shall have the same effect as if it had been signed by the governor . . . . If a bill or joint resolution shall not be returned by the governor within three days after it shall have been presented to him, Sundays excepted, it shall have the same force and effect as if he had signed it, unless the General Assembly, by their adjournment, prevent its return, in which case it shall not have such force and effect unless returned within two days after their next meeting.

Section 23. There shall be elected by the qualified voters of the State a comptroller-general, a treasurer, and a secretary of state, who shall hold their offices for the term of four years, and whose duties and compensation shall be prescribed by law.

ARTICLE IV

Section 1. The judicial powers of this State shall be vested in a supreme court, in two circuit courts, to-wit, a court of common pleas, having civil jurisdiction, and a court of general sessions, with criminal jurisdiction only; in probate courts; and in justices of the peace. The General Assembly may also establish such municipal courts as may be deemed necessary.

Section 2. The supreme court shall consist of a chief justice and two associate justices, any two of whom shall constitute a quorum. They shall be elected by joint vote of the General Assembly for the term of six years . . . .

Section 9. The judges of the supreme court and circuit courts shall . . . receive a compensation for their services, to be fixed by law . . . . They shall not be allowed any fees or perquisites of office, nor shall they hold any other office . . . .

Section 12. In all cases decided by the supreme court, a concurrence of two of the judges shall be necessary to a decision . . . .

Section 15. The court of common pleas shall have exclusive jurisdiction in all cases of divorce, and exclusive original jurisdiction in all civil cases . . . .

Section 18. The court of general sessions shall have exclusive jurisdiction over all criminal cases which shall not otherwise be provided for by law. It shall sit in each county in the State at least three times in each year . . . .

Section 19. The qualified electors of each county shall elect three persons for the term of two years, who shall constitute a board of county commissioners, which shall have jurisdiction over roads, highways, ferries, bridges . . . , provided that in all cases there shall be the right of appeal to the State courts.

Section 20. A court of probate shall be established in each county, with jurisdiction in all matters testamentary and of administration, in business appertaining to minors and the allotment of dower, in cases of idiocy and lunacy and persons non compos mentis. The judge of said court shall be elected by the qualified electors of the respective counties for the term of two years.

Section 28. There shall be an attorney-general for the State, who shall perform such duties as may be prescribed by law. He shall be elected by the qualified electors of the State for the term of four years, and shall receive for his services such compensation as shall be fixed by law.

Section 29. There shall be a solicitor for each circuit, who shall reside therein, to be elected by the qualified electors of the circuit, who shall hold his office for the term of four years . . . .

Section 30. The qualified electors of each county shall elect a sheriff and a coroner for the term of four years . . . .

ARTICLE VIII

Section 1. In all election by the people the electors shall vote by ballot.

Section 2. Every male citizen of the United States, of the age of twenty-one years and upwards . . . without distinction of race, color, or former condition, who shall be a resident of this State at the time of the adoption of this Constitution, or shall thereafter reside in this State one year . . . shall be entitled to vote for all officers that are now or hereafter may be elected by the people, and upon all questions submitted to the electors at the elections: Provided, that no person shall be allowed to vote or hold office who is now or hereafter may be disqualified therefor by the Constitution of the United States, until such disqualification shall be removed by the Congress of the United States . . . .

Section 3. It shall be the duty of the General Assembly to provide from time to time for the registration of all electors . . . .

Section 7. Every person entitled to vote at any election shall be eligible to any office which now is or hereafter shall be elective by the people . . . .

Section 9. Presidential electors shall be elected by the people. . . .

Section 12. No person shall be disfranchised for felony, or other crimes committed while such person was a slave.

ARTICLE IX

Section 1. The General Assembly shall provide by law for a uniform and equal rate of assessment and taxation . . . .

Section 2. The General Assembly may provide annually for a poll tax, not to exceed one dollar on each poll, which shall be applied exclusively to the public school fund . . . .

Section 7. For the purpose of defraying extraordinary expenditures the State may contract public debts, but such debts shall be authorized by law for some single object . . . to be distinctily specified therein . . . .

Section 9. The General Assembly shall provide for the incorporation and organization of cities and towns . . . .

Section 11. An accurate statement of the receipts and expenditures of the public money shall be published . . . in such manner as may by law be directed . . . .

Section 16. No debt contracted by this State in behalf of the late rebellion, in whole or in part, shall ever be paid.

ARTICLE X

Section 1. The supervision of public instruction shall be vested in a State Superintendent of education, who shall be elected by the qualified electors of the State . . . . His powers, duties, term of office, and compensation shall be defined by the General Assembly.

Section 2. There shall be elected biennially in each county by the qualified electors thereof one school commissioner, said commissioners to constitute a State Board of Education, of which the State Superintendent shall . . . be chairman; the powers, duties and compensation of the members of said board shall be determined by law.

Section 3. The General Assembly shall, as soon as practicable after the adoption of this Constitution, provide for a liberal and uniform system of free public schools throughout the State, and shall also make provision for the division of the State into suitable school districts. There shall be kept open at least six months in each year one or more schools in each school district. . . .

Section 6. Within five years after the . . . adoption of this Constitution, it shall be the duty of the General Assembly to provide for the establishment and support of a State normal school, which shall be open to all persons who may wish to become teachers . . . .

Section 7. Educational institutions for the benefit of all the blind, deaf and dumb, and such other benevolent institutions as the public good may require, shall be established and supported by the State . . . .

Section 8. Provisions shall be made by law, as soon as practicable, for the establishment and maintenance of a State reform school for juvenile offenders.

Section 9. The General Assembly shall provide for the maintenance of the State University, and as soon as practical provide for the establishment of an agricultural college . . . .

Section 10. All the public schools, colleges and universities of this State, supported in whole or in part by the public funds, shall be free and open to all the children and youths of the State, without regard to race or color. . . .

ARTICLE XI

Section 1. Institutions for the benefit of the insane, blind, deaf and dumb, and the poor, shall always be fostered and supported by this State, and shall be subject to such regulations as the General Assembly may enact . . . .

Section 5. The respective counties of this State shall make such provision as may be determined by law for all those inhabitants who, by reason of age and infirmities or misfortunes, may have a claim upon the sympathy and aid of society . . . .

ARTICLE XII

Section 1. Corporations may be formed under general laws, but all such laws may, from time to time, be altered or repealed. . . .

ARTICLE XIII

Section 1. The militia of this State shall consist of all able-bodied male citizens of the State between the ages of eighteen and forty-five years . . . .

Section 2. The governor shall have power to call out the militia to execute the laws, repel invasion, repress insurrection, and preserve the public peace . . . .

ARTICLE XIV

Section 5. Divorces from the bonds of matrimony shall not be allowed but by the judgment of a court, as shall be prescribed by law.

Section 6. No person who denies the existence of the Supreme Being shall hold any office under this Constitution. . . .

Section 8. The real and personal property of a woman, held at the time of her marriage, or that which she may thereafter acquire . . . shall not be subject to levy and sale for her husband's debts, but shall be held as her separate property . . . .

ARTICLE XV

Section 1. Any amendment or amendments to this Constitution may be proposed in the Senate or House of Representatives. If the same be agreed to by two-thirds of the members elected to each House . . . the same shall be submitted to the qualified electors of the State at the next general election . . . and if a majority of the electors . . . shall vote in favor . . . and two-thirds of each branch of the next General Assembly shall . . . ratify the same amendment . . . the same shall become part of the Constitution . . . .

Section 3. Whenever two-thirds of the members elected to each branch of the General Assembly shall think it necessary to call a convention to revise, amend or change this Constitution, they shall recommend to the electors to vote at the next election for representatives for or against a convention; and if a majority of all the electors voting at said election shall have voted for a convention, the General Assembly shall, at their next session, provide by law for calling the same, and such convention shall consist of a number of members not less than that of the most numerous branch of the General Assembly.

133. *The Public School Laws of 1868*

THE CONSTITUTION OF 1868 CALLED ON THE LEGISLATURE TO PROVIDE
FOR A PUBLIC SCHOOL SYSTEM WHICH WAS NOT SEGREGATED AND WAS
FREE FOR ALL CHILDREN IN THE STATE. THE LEGISLATURE RESPONDED
WITH A SERIES OF LAWS THAT SET UP, ON PAPER AT LEAST, A FAIRLY
ADEQUATE ELEMENTARY SCHOOL SYSTEM. VERY LITTLE WAS DONE TO PUT
IT INTO FORCE, HOWEVER, UNTIL AFTER 1877, WHEN, THROUGH THE
LEADERSHIP OF HUGH S. THOMPSON AS SUPERINTENDENT OF EDUCATION
AND LATER AS GOVERNOR, A BEGINNING WAS MADE TOWARD A REVITALIZED
STATE SCHOOL SYSTEM. THE FOLLOWING IS A PARAPHRASE OF THE MAJOR
SCHOOL LAWS PASSED IN 1868, AS QUOTED FROM *South Carolina:
Resources and Population,* 1883.

[School Law Paraphrased]

A new State Constitution was adopted in 1868. It incorporated a system of public instruction into the organic law of the land, and provided
for the election of a State Superintendent of Education, and for subordinate officers in the different counties for the management of schools and
the improvement of teachers. Provision was made for raising necessary
school funds, and a compulsory attendance was ordered so soon as the
school session should reach six months in each year. The sources of
revenue were threefold—first, a general legislative appropriation; second,
a poll tax of one dollar on all able-bodied male citizens (with a few
exceptions) within certain specified ages; and third, a voluntary local
taxation.

The system, perfected as it had been in other States as the result of
careful study and long experience, was good enough in theory, but in
practice proved a failure, owing partly to its novelty, but chiefly to the
ignorance and dishonesty of many parties connected with its management.

State Superintendent Jillson (1868–1876) makes repeated complaints
of the diversion of school funds to other purposes, and, in his report for

South Carolina Resources and Population, S.C. Dept. of Agriculture (Charleston:
n.p., 1883), 455–58.

1876, shows an aggregate deficiency of $324,058.40. Besides this, in almost every county existed school claims in excess of estimated appropriations, thus swelling the debt to still greater proportions.

Notwithstanding the discouragement and even exasperation of friends of education in consequence of these gross frauds against the system, the number of schools and pupils all along increased, an evidence of what might be expected under better management.

In 1877, a change of government occurred, since which time the charges of dishonesty have totally ceased, and complaints of incompetency are steadily decreasing. Much of this progress is due to the zeal and ability of the Hon. Hugh S. Thompson, for six years State Superintendent. As parents, children and officials become better acquainted with their respective duties and responsibilities, the system improves in a constantly increasing ratio.

A constitutional amendment, adopted by all parties in 1876, provides for an annual levy of not less than two mills on the dollar for public schools, to be expended in the county in which it is raised, thus insuring stability to the system. The poll-tax is devoted to educational purposes, and in some localities the option of local taxation rests with the property holders.

Each county is divided into school districts, varying in number in different counties, managed by local boards of trustees, and being for the most part coterminus with the townships. Every such school district is a body politic, capable of suing and being sued, of contracting, and of holding property for school purposes.

The State Superintendent of Education is a constitutional officer, elected biennially by the people, giving a bond for $5,000 and receiving a salary of $2100. He exercises general supervision over all the public schools of the State, and is required to visit every county for the purpose of inspecting the schools, and awakening an interest in education. He is required to secure, with the aid and advice of the State Board of Examiners, uniformity of text-books and the exclusion of secular or partisan books and instruction, and to perform such other duties as may be prescribed, or become necessary. An annual report of his visits, and of the condition and requirements of the public schools, must be made by him through the Governor to the Legislature.

The State Board of Examiners consists of the Superintendent of Education and four persons, appointed biennially by the Governor. This board meets twice a year, or oftener, if deemed advisable, and is constituted an advisory body, which the Superintendent shall consult when in doubt as to his official duty. It renders final decisions upon all questions of appeal from the County Boards. It has power to adopt rules not inconsistent with the general law for the government of the schools, to prescribe standards of efficiency for teachers, to examine teachers, and grant State certificates; and also to prescribe text-books for a period of not less than five years.

At each general election a School Commissioner is chosen by the voters of each county, giving bond for $1000, and receiving a per diem allowance not exceeding $600 a year, except in the County of Charleston. He acts as the organ of communication between the State Superintendent and the local authorities. It is his duty to apportion the school fund among the several districts in his county, and according to the average attendance of pupils during the preceding year, to visit the schools and acquaint himself with their character and condition, and to make suggestions that, in his opinion, are conducive to the welfare of the system. An annual report is sent by him to the State Superintendent.

The County Board of Examiners is composed of the County School Commissioner and two persons appointed by the State Board of Examiners, to serve two years without pay. It conducts county examinations for teachers upon questions prescribed by the State Board, arranges the school districts, appoints school trustees, and acts as a tribunal in all disputes arising between trustees and teachers or patrons.

Three School Trustees for each district are appointed biennially by the County Board of Examiners. They serve two years without compensation, and are entrusted with the general management of affairs, such as the erection and location of schoolhouses, the employment and payment of teachers, the suspension or dismission of pupils, the calling of district meetings, and the visiting and supervision of schools.

Every teacher in the public schools of South Carolina must be of good moral character, and must hold a certificate of qualification issued by the State Board, the County Board, the City Board of Charleston, or the faculty of the State Normal Institute. No school commissioner or trustee shall teach in the public schools. Three grades of excellence are recognized in the issuance of certificates. The first may be renewed for three years without re-examination; the second for two years; and the third grade certificates are valid for but one year. Three Normal Institute certificates entitle the holder to a life diploma. Teachers are required to file monthly reports of enrollment and attendance, with the branches taught, upon which pay certificates are granted by the trustees, approved by the school commissioners, and paid by the county treasurer.

In every school shall be taught, as far as practicable, orthography, reading, writing, arithmetic, geography, and English grammar, history of the United States and of the State, morals and good behavior. In some schools higher instruction is also imparted. The school age is not absolutely fixed, but the school census taken in former years embraces all children between the ages of six and sixteen years.

134. *Charleston in 1868*

ALTHOUGH CHARLESTON WAS NOT AS COMPLETELY DEVASTATED BY
THE WAR AS WAS COLUMBIA, IT SUFFERED CONSIDERABLY FROM BOMBARD-
MENTS AND FROM SEVERAL LARGE FIRES. THE SLOWNESS WITH WHICH
REPAIRS AND REBUILDING WERE ACCOMPLISHED IS INDICATED BY AN
ACCOUNT OF THE CITY AS SEEN BY A BRITISH TRAVELER, DAVID MACCRAE,
IN 1868.

[David MacCrae]

Nearly three years had passed when I travelled through the country,
and yet we have seen what traces the war had left in such cities as Richmond, Petersburg and Columbia. The same spectacle met me at Charleston. Churches and homes had been battered down by heavy shot and
shell hurled into the city from Federal batteries at a distance of five miles.
Even the valley of desolation made by a great fire in 1861, through the
very heart of the city, remained unbuilt. There, after the lapse of seven
years, stood the blackened ruins of streets and houses waiting for the
coming of a better day. The bank capital in the city, which stood formerly at $15,000,000, has fallen to $500,000. The Battery Promenade,
where two or three hundred gay equipages could have been counted
before the war, was almost deserted. "People have to content themselves
now with a ten-cent ride in a street-car," said a friend. Over the country
districts the prostration was equally marked. Along the track of Sherman's army especially, the devastation was fearful—farms laid waste,
fences burned, bridges destroyed, houses left in ruins, plantations in some
cases turning into wilderness again.

The people had shared in the general wreck, and looked poverty-
stricken, careworn, and dejected. Ladies who before the war had lived in

Allan Nevins, ed., *America Through British Eyes* (New York: Oxford University
Press, 1948), pp. 346–47. Copyright 1948 by Oxford University Press, Inc. New
edition revised and enlarged. First edition 1923 *(American Social History as
Recorded by British Travellers),* copyright by Allan Nevins. Reprinted by
permission of Oxford University Press.

affluence, with black servants round them to attend to their wish, were boarding together now in half-furnished houses, cooking their own food and washing their own linen, some of them, I was told, so utterly destitute that they did not know when they finished one meal where they were to find the next . . . .

Although three years had passed since the final crash, I found the old aristocracy still in the dust, with less and less hope of ever recovering its old position. Men who had held commanding positions during the war had fallen out of sight and were filling humble situations—struggling, many of them, to earn a bare subsistence. One of the most prominent men of the Confederacy was trying to earn a living in the peanut business; a cavalry commander was keeping a boarding school. Other officers were keeping stores, editing little newspapers, acting as clerks, and even as farm laborers, in the pay of others. I remember dining with three cultured Southern gentlemen, one a general, the other, I think, a captain, and the third a lieutenant. They were all living together in a plain little wooden house, such as they would formerly have provided for their servants. Two of them were engaged in a railway office, the third was seeking for a situation, frequently, in his vain search, passing the large blinded house where he had lived in luxurious ease before the war.

The old planters, many of them, are going about with ruin written on their faces, some of them so poor that they were trying to sell a portion of their land in order to pay the tax upon the rest. One of them, who showed me much kindness, was living in a corner of a huge house which had once been the home of gaity and princely hospitality. It was all dismantled now and shut up, excepting three rooms below, where its owner was living in seclusion. Others had shut up their houses altogether and gone to live in lodgings.

135. *The Scott Administration, 1868–1872*

UNDER THE CONSTITUTION OF 1868, AND THE CONGRESSIONAL PLAN OF RECONSTRUCTION, ROBERT K. SCOTT, A CARPETBAGGER FROM OHIO, BECAME GOVERNOR OF SOUTH CAROLINA. HE SERVED FROM JULY 6, 1868, TO DECEMBER 1872, BEING REELECTED IN 1870. HIS ADMINISTRATION WAS SORRY, ALTHOUGH POSSIBLY IT WAS NOT AS BAD AS THAT OF FRANKLIN J. MOSES, JR., "THE ROBBER GOVERNOR," WHO SUCCEEDED HIM. THE FOLLOWING DESCRIPTION OF CONDITIONS UNDER SCOTT IS TAKEN FROM *The Prostrate State*, WRITTEN BY JAMES S. PIKE, A NORTHERN NEWSPAPERMAN, WHO SPENT SOME TIME IN SOUTH CAROLINA DURING RECONSTRUCTION.

[James S. Pike, Northern Newspaperman,
Reporting on Reconstruction]

The whole of the late administration, which terminated its existence in November, 1872, was a mess of rottenness, and the present administration was born of the corruptions of that; but for the exhaustion of the State, there is no good reason to believe it would steal less than its predecessor. There seems to be no hope, therefore, that the villainies of the past will be speedily uncovered. The present Governor was Speaker of the last House, and he is credited with having issued during his term in office over $400,000 of pay "certificates" which are still unredeemed and for which there is no appropriation, but which must be saddled on the tax payers sooner or later. The Blue Ridge Railroad scrip is another scandal embracing several millions of pure stealings. The case is briefly this: Some years ago a charter was obtained for a railroad across the southern end of the Blue Ridge from South Carolina into Kentucky. It was a difficult work, and the State promised its aid on certain conditions. The road was never made, and these conditions were never fulfilled, but since the restoration the State obligations were authorized to be issued. But this was not the worst of it. The sum authorized was $1,800,000. It turns out

J. S. Pike, *The Prostrate State* (D. Appleton & Co., 1874), 26–31.

that on the strength of this authority over $5,000,000 of the scrip has been issued. It was rendered available to the holders by being made receivable for taxes, and in this way has got spread abroad. The whole scheme has been for the moment frustrated by a decision of the courts that the entire transaction is fraudulent and void from the start. With $5,000,000 of this stuff afloat, which the Legislature can legalize if the members are paid enough, what hope is there that the State will escape liability for the emission?

These are sample items of the corruptions of the late government outside of the increase of the bonded debt. The iniquity laps over into this administration, for the old Speaker has been chosen Governor, and the present Legislature has chosen Patterson Senator. . . . They plunder, and glory in it. They steal, and defy you to prove it. The purchase of a senatorship is considered only a profitable trade. . . . A leading member of the last administration was told he had the credit of having robbed the State of his large fortune. "Let them prove it," was his only answer.

The narration I have given sufficiently shows how things have gone and are going in this State, but its effect would be much heightened if there were time and room for details. Here is one: The Total amount of the stationery bill of the House for the twenty years preceding 1861 averaged $400 per annum. Last year it was $16,000. . . . The whole amount of the printing bills of the State last year it is computed (for everything here has to be in part guess-work), aggregated the immense sum of $600,000.

136. *Reconstruction Legislature*

ONE OF THE BLACK POLITICAL LEADERS OF THE RECONSTRUCTION PERIOD WAS ALONZO J. RANSIER, A NATIVE OF CHARLESTON. RANSIER, WHO HAD RECEIVED SOME EDUCATION BEFORE THE WAR, EMERGED AS A LEADER AMONG HIS PEOPLE, AND SERVED HIS DISTRICT IN THE LEGISLATURE. HE WAS ALSO LIEUTENANT GOVERNOR IN 1870, AND A MEMBER OF CONGRESS (1873–1875). AFTER HIS DEFEAT, HE SERVED AS INTERNAL REVENUE COLLECTOR FOR THE SECOND DISTRICT OF SOUTH CAROLINA UNTIL 1877. THE FIRST SELECTION IS A SPEECH HE MADE IN CHARLESTON WHICH SHOWS SOME DISAPPROVAL OF HIS POLITICAL PARTY. THE SECOND IS A DESCRIPTION OF THE SOUTH CAROLINA LEGISLATURE OF 1872, WRITTEN BY THE NORTHERN REPORTER, PIKE, WHEN "BLACK RECONSTRUCTION" WAS AT ITS HEIGHT, RADICALS WERE IN COMPLETE CONTROL OF THE STATE GOVERNMENT AND CORRUPTION WAS IN FULL SWING ON ALL LEVELS.

[Alonzo J. Ransier]

All over the country the belief obtains that the situation of affairs in our State is most deplorable. No longer can it be said that these reports are traceable to Democratic sources alone. Representations of this kind have been made by good, bad and indifferent Republicans as well as Democrat; by those who look at everything through a sort of mental magnifying glass, and by others who are actuated by a variety of motives by which the country has been to some extent deceived. Representations are made against our party in a spirit of recklessness which to me is perfectly astounding. That things are not in a satisfactory condition in this State is too true; there are many things of which just complaint might be made. That it is possible, and has been so ever since the Republican party has held the ascendancy in the State to get along with lower rates of taxation by a more judicious expenditure of the public funds, and that

A.H. Gordon, *Sketches of Negro Life and History in South Carolina,* (n.p., 1929), 260-65.

we might have selected better men to fill our most important offices, cannot be denied; but neither do exaggerated representations made by our opponents, nor reckless and injudicious public speeches made by Republicans against their own party and public men, help the situation. I am in favor of a most thorough investigation of the official conduct of any and every public officer in connection with the discharge of whose duties there is anything like well-grounded suspicion; and to this effect have I spoken time and again. Nor am I lukewarm on the subject of better government in South Carolina than that which seems to be bearing heavily on all classes and conditions of society today. Still, recognizing that which I believe to be true that such is the determined opposition to the Republican party and its doctrines by our opponents that no administration of our affairs, however honest, just and economical, would satisfy any considerable portion of the Democratic masses in the State of South Carolina, and satisfied that the principles and policy of the great Republican party to which I belong is best adapted for the promotion of good government to all classes of men, our party leaders should be judicious in dealing with the situation . . . . In the spirit of this suggestion, I would ask for an advised action on the part of the Republicans throughout the State. I would ask you to calmly consider the state of affairs as they are presented to us today, and if you cannot reach those who have brought this ruin upon us through the medium of the courts instituted by us as a party, and by the officials whose duty it is to prosecute those who violate the law, then let them be forever discarded from the party. And, again, when you are called upon in your primary meetings in your county and state nominating conventions, let each man act as if, by his individual vote, he could wipe out the odium resting upon our party, and help to remove the evils that afflict us at present. Let him feel, black or white, that the country holds him responsible for the shortcomings of his party, and that it demands of him the elevation to public positions of men who are above suspicion . . . . For I say tonight . . . that Republicanism is best calculated for the welfare of the Democrats as well as Republicans. It is the government of the people made by the people and for the people and you dare not, as a Republican, trample on any right of a Democrat, or trifle with the important interest of the people, while at the same time it is your duty to prevent them from trampling upon any of yours. . . .

But we find ourselves today, as a race, passing through a crisis. The colored people in the United States, with all the grand achievements of the past ten years, are today passing through the crisis of their political history in this country. We present to the world a noble spectacle, a record unparalleled in the annals of any people similarly situated. No race has been subjected to such a scathing fire of criticism; no people have had such tremendous disadvantages to labor under. And I feel free to say, no race in a similar position could have acquitted themselves more creditably; but now, in this trying epoch of our history, we seem to forget much that we should remember, we must not trifle with our responsibilities and let slip our best opportunities to prove our fitness for government. We are charged as giving evidence in some localities of unfitness in this direction . . . . The country accepts in a great part the representations made by our opponents as to the situation of affairs in this State. It rests with you to remove every just cause of complaint, remembering that by every unworthy man you elevate to office, by every scoundrel you keep in office, you justify the public opinion in the country adverse to the well-being of the Republican party in this State, and to the fitness of the colored man for franchise . . . . And when, in the next campaign, you are called upon, as you will be, to select men for our important offices, see to it that they are men whom you can trust, men who will not deceive nor disgrace you. As to myself, I shall go against any man, be he black or white, whose past conduct in or out of office does not give us the assurance of better government, cost me what it may.

[James S. Pike, Northern Newspaper Reporter]

Yesterday, about 4 P.M., the assembled wisdom of the State . . . issued forth from the State-House. About three-quarters of the crowd belonged to the African race. They were of every hue, from the light octoroon to the deep black. They were such a looking body of men as might pour out of a market-house or a court-house at random in any Southern state. Every Negro type and physiognomy was here to be seen, from the genteel serving-man to the rough-hewn customer from the rice or cotton field. Their dress was as varied as their countenances. There was the second-hand frock-coat of infirm gentility, glossy and threadbare. There was also to be seen a total disregard of the proprieties of costume in the coarse and slouch hats of soiling labor. In some instances, rough woolen com-

J. S. Pike, *The Prostrate State* (D. Appleton & Co., 1874), 10–21.

forters embraced the neck and hid the absence of linen. Heavy brogans, and short, torn trousers, it was impossible to hide. The dusky tide flowed out into the littered and barren grounds, and, issuing through the coarse wooden fence of the inclosure, melted away into the street beyond. These were the legislators of South Carolina. . . .

A white community . . . lies prostrate in the dust, ruled over by this strange conglomerate, gathered from the ranks of its own servile population. It is the spectacle of a society suddenly turned bottom-side up. . . .

Let us approach nearer and take a closer view. We will enter the House of Representatives. Here sit one hundred and twenty-four members. Of these, twenty-three are white men, representing the remains of the old civilization. These are good-looking, substantial citizens. They are men of weight and standing in the communities they represent. They are all from the hill country. The frosts of sixty and seventy winters whiten the heads of some among them. There they sit, grim and silent . . . . They say little and do little as the days go by . . . . They feel themselves to be in some sort martyrs, bound stoically to suffer in behalf of that still great element in the State whose prostrate fortunes are becoming the sport of an unpitying Fate . . . . The dense Negro crowd they confront do the debating, the squabbling, the law-making, and create all the clamor and disorder of the body. These twenty-three white men are but the observers, the enforced auditors of the dull and clumsy, imitation of a deliberative body, whose appearance in their present capacity is at once a wonder and a shame to modern civilization.

Deducting the twenty-three members referred to, who comprise the entire strength of the opposition, we find one hundred and one remaining. Of this one hundred and one, ninety-four are colored, and seven are their white allies . . . . As things stand, the body is almost literally a Black Parliament, and it is the only one on the face of the earth which is the representative of a white constituency . . . . The Speaker is black, the Clerk is black, the door-keepers are black, the little pages are black, the Chairman of the Ways and Means [Committee] is black, and the chaplain is coal-black. At some of the desks sit colored men whose types it would be hard to find outside of the Congo. . . .

One of the first things that strikes a casual observer in this Negro assembly is the fluence of debate, if the endless chatter that goes on there can be dignified with this term. The leading topics of discussion are well understood by the members, as they are of a practical character, and appeal directly to the personal interests of every legislator, as well as to those of his constituents. When an appropriation bill is up to raise money to catch and punish the Ku-Klux, they know exactly what it means. They feel it in their bones. So, too, the educational measures. The free school comes right home to them; then the business of arming and drilling the black militia: they are eager on this point. Sambo can talk on these topics and those of a kindred character, and their endless ramifications, day in and day out. There is no end to his gush and babble. . . .

The Speaker orders a member whom he has discovered to be particularly unruly to take his seat. The member obeys, and with the same motion that he sits down, throws his feet onto his desk, hiding himself from the Speaker by the soles of his boots . . . . After a few experiences of this sort, the Speaker threatens, in a laugh, to call "the gemman" to order. This is considered a capital joke, and a loud guffaw follows . . . . Seven years ago these men were raising corn and cotton under the whip of the overseer. Today they are raising points of order and questions of privilege. They find they can raise one as well as the other. . . .

137. *The Election of 1872*

IN THE 1872 ELECTION, THE RADICAL REPUBLICANS NOMINATED FRANK-
LIN J. MOSES, JR., FOR GOVERNOR. HE WAS A SCALAWAG, AND SO TIED IN
WITH THE CORRUPT ELEMENTS OF THE REPUBLICAN PARTY THAT A
MINORITY WITHDREW AND NOMINATED REUBEN TOMLINSON FOR GOV-
ERNOR. MOSES WON BY A LARGE MAJORITY, WHEN MOST OF THE WHITE
POPULATION ABSTAINED FROM VOTING. IN THE CONGRESSIONAL RACE, B. F.
PERRY WAS A CANDIDATE, AND AT FIRST IT WAS THOUGHT THAT HE HAD
BEEN ELECTED. HIS COMMENTS ON THE ELECTION ARE USED HERE.

Benjamin F. Perry on the election of 1872:

I do regret, lament and deplore the success of the Radical party
throughout the State, in the recent election for Congress and State officers. It seems to indicate that there is to be no change in the present
corrupt, oppressive and infamously rotten State Government, or hope of
representation for the white people of South Carolina in the Congress of
the United States. Sixty thousand voters, representing nearly 300,000
persons, owning, in a great measure, all the property of the State, agricultural, commercial and manufacturing, and comprising in the same
ratio all the intelligence, education, virtue and patriotism of the State,
are without the semblance of representation in a government purporting
to be republican.

The State Government has, confessedly, fallen into the hands of rogues,
swindlers and corrupt men, who have openly plundered the public treasury, robbed the people, forged State bonds, increased the indebtedness of
the State $27,000,000 in four years, levied and collected intolerable taxes,
and enriched themselves by the most bare-faced bribery and corruption,
as well as by arrant roguery and plunder. And yet the result of the recent
election shows that these rogues, swindlers and robbers are to be reinstated in authority for two years to come, with carte blanche to rob, steal
and plunder ad libitum.

Benjamin F. Perry, *Biographical Sketches of Eminent American Statesmen* . . .
(Philadelphia: 1887), 214–15.

It is sad and melancholy to think that the honest, patriotic and virtuous white people of South Carolina are in some measure responsible for this horrible and appalling condition of public affairs. In many counties they did not turn out to vote on the day of election. Can human weakness and human apathy exceed this? The Negro, carpetbaggers and scalawags turned out, almost to a man . . . . I know that the Negroes are banded together, as a race, under the lead of vile carpetbaggers and infamous scalawags, who would as quickly sell their God for thirty pieces of silver as they have betrayed their race and country for office, promotion and the hope of stealing, swindling and plundering.

138. *The Disputed Election of 1876*

BY 1876, THE WHITE CITIZENS OF SOUTH CAROLINA, DETERMINED TO
WREST CONTROL OF THE STATE GOVERNMENT FROM THE BLACK REPUBLI-
CANS, NAMED WADE HAMPTON AS THEIR DEMOCRATIC CANDIDATE. THE
RESULT OF THE ELECTION WAS DISPUTED, BOTH HAMPTON AND THE
INCUMBENT, DANIEL CHAMBERLAIN, CLAIMING VICTORY. LIKEWISE, IN
THE NATIONAL ELECTION FOR THE PRESIDENCY, THERE WAS A DISPUTE
INVOLVING CANDIDATES TILDEN AND RUTHERFORD B. HAYES. HAYES
FINALLY WON THE NOMINATION, WITH SOUTH CAROLINA'S HELP. AFTER
DUAL GOVERNMENT HAD BEEN IN EFFECT IN SOUTH CAROLINA FOR ABOUT
FOUR MONTHS (CHAMBERLAIN AND HIS GOVERNMENT MEETING IN THE
CAPITOL, AND HAMPTON AND HIS LEGISLATURE SITTING IN CAROLINA
HALL), CHAMBERLAIN WAS FORCED TO WITHDRAW UPON PRESIDENT
HAYES'S OFFICIAL ORDER THAT FEDERAL TROOPS VACATE THE STATE.
HAMPTON'S ACCESSION MARKED THE END OF RECONSTRUCTION IN SOUTH
CAROLINA. THE FIRST SELECTION IS AN ACCOUNT OF THE DISPUTE; THE
SECOND IS CHAMBERLAIN'S LETTER TO A FRIEND.

[John A. Leland]

The nomination of Gen. Wade Hampton for Governor sent a thrill like
electricity through the State, and revived hopes, long drooping and well
nigh dead. The mere possibility of having this favorite son of the State at
the head of affairs, stirred the hearts of all her people, and awakened
emotions of patriotism long deemed crushed out.

Hampton, himself, seemed inspired for the occasion. Busily occupied
in efforts to recover something from the ruins of his once magnificent
estates, he at once threw aside all private matters, and boldly entered
upon a campaign unequaled in the annals of Republics. All the State
officers were arrayed against him, with their "election machinery"
arranged and perfected through a whole decade of unbroken success. The

John A. Leland, *A Voice from South Carolina* (Charleston: Walker, Evans &
Cogswell, 1879), 160–74.

Radical State census called for more than 30,000 majority of colored votes. The administration at Washington was ready and anxious to furnish all the resources of the army and navy to uphold this nondescript government, in order to secure the electoral vote of the State, in the exceedingly close contest, then going on, for President of the United States . . . .

Within sight of these everlasting hills, which look down upon the memorable battle-fields of "Cowpens" and "King's Mountain," he first raised his clarion voice for Redemption and Home Rule. An enthusiasm was at once enkindled, which drew out unprecedented crowds to his first appointment. It was feared that this unanimity would be confined to that section of the State—always Democratic, and comparatively exempt from the heel of the oppressor. But as Hampton approached the middle country, the crowds became even greater, and the enthusiasm reached delirium. Each county had one or more of its "Hampton Days," and each of these "days" vied with its predecessor, not only in numbers, but in decorations and pageantry. . . .

But where was Chamberlain all this while? Invitation after invitation has appeared in the papers, calling upon him to meet Hampton at some of these places most convenient to him, but he clung to his Executive hole in Columbia, sending forth his meshes, spiderlike, all over the State, to entrap a hated people.

To thwart the growing enthusiasm, he naturally looked to the bayonet, which had placed him where he was, and still retained him there. He was most ardently desirous to have martial law proclaimed, but that was in the power of the President, and from the course of the Federal canvass, then going on, the President himself would have to plead a strong case . . . . He next thought of striking at the "chivalry" of the State by calling for the disbanding and disarming of all the rifle clubs, and by volunteer military organizations throughout the State. By specious representations made to Washington, he did induce the President to issue a Proclamation to that effect. . . .

The election came on, at last, and Chamberlain had his United States soldiers and marshals distributed throughout the State, to his entire satisfaction. But to the surprise of friend and foe, Wade Hampton had a clear majority of over twelve hundred votes! In the strong Radical precincts in Charleston, Colleton and Beaufort Counties, such untold frauds had been practiced that the most sanguine had begun to despair of success; and when it was found that the election was safe, in spite of all these frauds, "the people rejoiced with exceeding great joy." But the shout of triumph soon subsided, when that omnipotent Radical "Returning Board" was summoned to "canvass the votes." By the simple device of "counting out" the two counties of Laurens and Edgefield, which had gone Democratic by large majorities, it was attempted to reverse the result, and "count in" Chamberlain and his crew. . . .

The Time for the convening of the Legislature now drew nigh, and all eyes were turned to Columbia to see which party would secure the supremacy. The same vote which had made Hampton Governor, secured a majority of the House of Representatives. There were senators enough holding over to give that body to the Radicals by a small majority.

A short time before the day of meeting, Chamberlain had procured an order from President Grant to have a company of United States infantry quartered in the State House. This was effected at midnight, and the next morning, the citizens found access to the halls of their fathers debarred by armed sentinels wearing the United States uniform, and posted at every door!

On the day of the meeting of the Legislature . . . the officer in command announced that only those bearing certificates from the Returning Board would be admitted. The excitement became intense until Hampton himself appeared on the steps. He had just been refused admittance, but was as calm as a summer's morning. He only uttered a few words, to the effect that the handful of United States soldiers before them represented a power it would be madness to resist. That he felt that place was not a proper one for him, and, therefore, that he was going to his office. His advice was, for all who felt as he did, to follow him down the street. As he advanced to the gate, the whole crowd silently melted away into a solemn procession, following his lead. His Excellency's "office" was a unit of two rooms, over one of the stores on Main Street.

The members elect had all been admitted into their hall, excepting the two delegations from Laurens and Edgefield. The Radical members were sworn in, and, although without a quorum, proceeded to organize by the election of Mackey of Charleston, as Speaker. The Democratic members then withdrew to "Carolina Hall," and organized the true House of Representatives, by electing Gen. Wallace of Union, as their Speaker. There were several defections from the Mackey to the Wallace House, which soon secured the Constitutional quorum, beyond all cavil. . . .

Not long after this, Chamberlain was "inaugurated" before a constitutional Senate, and usurping House; Hampton also took the oath of office, in the open air, and in presence of the constitutional House, a minority of the Senate, and a large concourse of distinguished citizens. Soon after this, the whole Legislature, real and fictitious, adjourned sine die.

Hampton, after his inauguration, made a demand on Chamberlain for the executive office, papers, etc., but as Chamberlain had this office, as well as his private residence, strictly guarded by U.S. troops, he sent back a peremptory refusal. . . .

Soon after this came the "counting in" of President Hayes, and his inauguration . . . , but those United States bayonets were still in the State House at Columbia, and Chamberlain was still daily riding to and from the Executive Office in his closed carriage. After weeks of suspense had run into months, to the surprise of everybody, Hampton and Chamberlain were both invited to personal interviews with the President, and at the same time. What passed at these interviews, which were separate, are State secrets, but what the public could ascertain was cheering enough to the friends of Hampton . . . .

Not long after . . . there was issued from the War Department an order for the Unites States Infantry, then in charge of the State House, by noon of a certain day to march out, and resume their old quarters at the garrison post. This was all—but it was all we wanted. That little paper of some ten lines, ordering about two dozen United States enlisted men to march about half a mile, produced a mighty revolution, as peaceful as it was complete, and changed the status of our ancient commonwealth for all time to come! . . . The whole monstrous fabric of radicalism which the usurpers proudly thought securely pinned together by bayonets, for this generation at least, in a moment came toppling about their ears. . . .

A second demand from Hampton now promptly brought about the humiliating surrender of Executive office, archives, etc., and Chamberlain was soon after wholly absorbed in boxing up his elegant household furniture, for the steamer in Charleston. A day or two afterwards, he followed these boxes himself . . . .

[Governor Chamberlain explains his defeat
in a letter to William Lloyd Garrison, June 11, 1877]

Your prophecy is fulfilled, and I am not only overthrown, but as a consequence I am now a citizen of New York. It seems to be a remarkable experience, indeed, though I hope I do not egotistically exaggerate it, for I am sure it will soon be forgotten by most men in the press and hurry of new events. Why I write this line now and send it to Boston when I know you are in Europe, is because I feel like putting on record my main reflections on my experiences of the last three years . . . .

First, then, my defeat was inevitable under the circumstances of time and place which surrounded me. I mean here exactly that the uneducated Negro was too weak, no matter what his numbers, to cope with the whites.

We had lost, too, the sympathy of the North, in some large measure, though we never deserved it so certainly as in 1876 in South Carolina. The Presidential contest also endangered us and doubtless defeated us. The hope of electing Tilden incited our opponents, and the greed of office led the defeated Republicans under Hayes to sell us out. There was just as distinct a bargain to do this at Washington as ever existed, which was not signed and sealed on paper. And the South is not to be blamed for it, if anybody is; but rather those leaders like Evarts who could never see their Constitutional obligations towards the South until the offices were slipping away from their party.

So the end came, but not as you expected. . . .

Walter Allen, *Governor Chamberlain's Administration in South Carolina* (New York: G. P. Putnam's Sons, 1888), 504.

139. *Chamberlain's Thoughts on the "Frightful Experiment"*

NO ONE WAS MORE CAPABLE OF RENDERING A VERDICT ON RECON-
STRUCTION IN SOUTH CAROLINA THAN THE CARPET BAG EX-GOVERNOR,
DANIEL CHAMBERLAIN. CHAMBERLAIN, KNOWN AS A "REFORM REPUBLI-
CAN," HAD BEEN AN OFFICER IN A NEGRO REGIMENT AND HAD SERVED AS
ATTORNEY GENERAL OF SOUTH CAROLINA BEFORE HIS ELEVATION TO THE
GOVERNORSHIP. THE STATE WAS ALREADY BANKRUPT WHEN HE CAME
INTO THE OFFICE—A CONDITION TO WHICH HE HAD CONTRIBUTED HEAV-
ILY AS A GUIDING SPIRIT OF THE "PRINTING RING." DURING HIS TENURE
AS GOVERNOR, HOWEVER, CHAMBERLAIN SEEMED TO EXPERIENCE A
CHANGE OF HEART. HE SOUGHT DURING HIS ADMINISTRATION TO STEM
THE CORRUPTION WITHIN THE STATE GOVERNMENT, AND WAS INSTRU-
MENTAL IN REFORMING THE TAX SYSTEM. IN HIS LATER CONTEST FOR THE
GOVERNORSHIP WITH WADE HAMPTON, DESPITE HIS HAVING WON MANY
OF THE WHITE PEOPLE TO HIS SIDE HE WAS NO MATCH FOR THE HERO.
LONG AFTER HE RETURNED NORTH, CHAMBERLAIN WROTE THE ARTICLE
WHICH FOLLOWS. IN IT, HE SUMMARILY LAYS THE ILLS OF RECONSTRUC-
TION AT THE DOOR OF THADDEUS STEVENS AND OTHER LAWMAKERS
IN WASHINGTON, MOST OF WHOM—HE CHARGED—WERE INTERESTED
CHIEFLY IN ONE THING: THE NEGRO VOTE FOR THE REPUBLICAN PARTY.
CHAMBERLAIN'S ARTICLE GIVES A PICTURE OF SOUTH CAROLINA ECO-
NOMICALLY AND POLITICALLY AT THE END OF RECONSTRUCTION, AND IT
INCLUDES SOME ADVICE FOR THE FUTURE, ABOUT WHICH HE WROTE WITH
ASTONISHING VISION. CHAMBERLAIN, WHO WAS A DISTINGUISHED GRAD-
UATE OF YALE, A FORMER HARVARD LAW STUDENT AND PRACTICING ATTOR-
NEY, PRACTICED LAW IN NEW YORK AFTER HE WAS REMOVED BY
PRESIDENTIAL ORDER FROM THE SOUTH CAROLINA GOVERNORSHIP. LATER,
HE RETURNED TO HIS NATIVE STATE OF MASSACHUSETTS, AND DIED IN
1907 IN CHARLOTTESVILLE, VIRGINIA.

RECONSTRUCTION IN SOUTH CAROLINA

[Ex-governor of South Carolina, Daniel H. Chamberlain, writing in
The Atlantic Monthly on what he terms "The Frightful Experiment"]

The Civil War of 1861–65 (the term is used here for convenience,
though it lacks perfect accuracy) was conducted in substantial or reasonable accordance with the settled rules of war; and at its close there was
a large measure of liberal feeling on the part of the North toward the
South, notwithstanding the murder of Mr. Lincoln. This feeling viewed
the struggle as one in which both sides were sincere and patriotic (the
word is used of design, but in its high and broad meaning), in which
both sides were equally brave and devoted; as well as one which had
come to pass quite naturally, from causes which were far deeper than
politics or even than slavery. While the victorious section was enjoying
the first or early sense of success, sentiments of liberality, of concord,
readiness to look forward to better relations, not backward to old quarrels, statesmanlike plans or suggestions of reunion, and restoration of old
associations, widely prevailed.

Two main causes now came into operation to disturb this tendency
and course of feeling and events. The first of these was the existence at
the North, on the part of a strenuous, ardent, vigorous minority, of a
deep-seated, long-maturing, highly-developed distrust of the South;
a sentiment resting partly on moral antagonism to slavery, but chiefly
on a feeling of dread or hatred of those who had brought on a destructive, and worst of all, a causeless or unnecessary war. Not all of those
who belonged to this class are to be described so mildly. Some, it may be
said, if not many, were really moved by an unreasoning antipathy
toward those whom they had so long denounced as slaveholders and
rebels. Slavery abolished and rebellion subdued, their occupation was
gone; and still they could not adjust themselves to a new order of
things.

The other great cause of reaction from the friendly and conciliatory
spirit which was the first result of the victory for the Union was the
conduct of the South itself. Beaten in arms and impoverished, stripped of

The Atlantic Monthly (April, 1901), 473–84.

slavery, the white South found solace, or saw relief, if not recompense, in harsh treatment of the emancipated negroes, in laws, in business, and in social relations. The effect of this folly was decisive at the North. But added to this was the fatuous course of President [Andrew] Johnson, to whom the South, not unnaturally, gave warm support.

Out of these adverse conditions came reconstruction. Its inception and development into policy and law were not the results or dictates of sober judgment of what was best; least of all were they inspired by statesmanlike forecast, or the teachings of philosophy or history. The writer has recently turned over anew the congressional discussions, in 1866 and 1867, of reconstruction, the South, and especially the negro question, some large part of which he heard at first-hand. It is, for by far the greater part, melancholy reading,—shocking in its crudeness and disregard of facts and actualities, amazing for the confident levity of tone on the part of the leading advocates of the reconstruction acts of 1867, and for its narrowly partisan spirit. Confidence here rose easily into prophecy, and the country was assured of a peaceful, prosperous South, with negro loyalty forever at the helm. The white South was helpless. The black South was equal to all the needs of the hour: ignorant, to be sure, but loyal; inexperienced, but, with the ballot as its teacher and inspiration, capable of assuring good government. Hardly anywhere else in recorded debates can be found so surprising a revelation of the blindness of partisan zeal as these discussions disclose. But it may now be clear to all, as it was then clear to some, that underneath all the avowed motives and all the open arguments lay a deeper cause than all others,—the will and determination to secure party ascendency and control at the South and in the nation through the negro vote. If this is a hard saying, let any one now ask himself, or ask the public, if it is possibly credible that the reconstruction acts would have been passed if the negro vote had been believed to be Democratic.

True views of the situation—views sound, enlightened, and statesmanlike—were not wanting even then. Mr. Lincoln had presented such views; but above all other men in the whole land, Governor Andrew, of Massachusetts, in his farewell address to the Massachusetts legislature, January 2, 1866, discussed with elaboration the Southern situation, and urged views and suggested policies which will mark him always in our annals, at least with the highest minds, as a true, prescient, and lofty statesman, versed in the past and able to prejudge the future. His valedictory address is veritably prophetic,—as prophetic as it is politic and practical. With this great word resounding through the country, the last excuse for reconstruction as actually fixed upon is swept away; for it could no longer be held, as it had been said by the more timid or doubtful, that the whole business was a groping in the dark, without light or leading. Sentiment carried the day, sentiment of the lower kind,—hate, revenge, greed, lust of power.

It is, however, necessary at this point to be just. Not all who bore part in fixing the terms of reconstruction were ignorable or ignorant. Among them were many unselfish doctrinaries, humanitarians, and idealists of fine type. Among them, too, were men who ranked as statesmen, who in other fields had well earned the name, but who now were overborne or overpersuaded. Back of all these, however, were the party leaders, who moved on, driving the reluctant, crushing and ostracizing the doubtful, brutally riding down those who dared to oppose.

Governor Andrew's argument and policy may be briefly stated. Three great, flashing apothegms summarize it; (1) Prosecute peace as vigorously as we have prosecuted war. (2) Inflict no humiliation, require no humiliation, of the South. (3) Enlist the sympathy and services of "the natural leaders" of the South in the work of reconstruction. To the oft-repeated dictum that those who had ruled the South so long and rigorously—its natural leaders—could not be trusted with this work, Andrew pointed out, with prophetic insight, that these men, if not accepted as friends, would resume their leadership as enemies. Such a vision of the future, such a clear annunciation of truth and fact, fell on blind and impatient or angry minds. The most radical of ante-bellum and war Republicans, the greatest of all our war governors, was struck from the list of party leaders, and reconstruction proceeded apace on other lines and under other leaders. The writer recalls almost numberless interviews on reconstruction with Republican leaders at Washington, especially in the winter of 1866–67, and the summer and fall of the latter year, and particularly with the late Oliver P. Morton. Mr. Morton shared to some large degree with Mr. Thaddeus Stevens the leadership in this enterprise. Against the two combined, no policy could gain even consideration. With Mr. Stevens no argument was possible. His mind was fixed, proof against facts or reason that suggested other views. Mere personal self-respect limited the writer's intercourse with him to one brief conversation. Not one of these leaders had seen the South, or studied it at first-hand. Not one of them professed or cared to know more. They had made up their minds once for all, and they wished only to push on with their predetermined policy. The one descriptive feature, the one overshadowing item, of their policy was, as has been said, negro suffrage, loyalty under a black skin at the helm,—a policy which, like other historical policies of "Thorough," like the policy of Strafford and Laud, whence the fitting word has come, brooked no opposition or delay, and halted for no arguments or obstacles whilst these leaders led. The personal knowledge of the writer warrants him in stating that eyes were never blinder to facts, minds never more ruthlessly set upon a policy, than were Stevens and Morton on putting the white South under the heel of the black South. Again it is necessary to say that not all eminent Republican leaders shared these sentiments, though they acquiesced in the policy. Mr. Sumner, it shall be said, did not, and, strange perhaps to add, Mr. Blaine did not; but both submitted, and even advocated the acts of 1867.

Reconstruction thus conceived, thus developed, thus expounded, was put to test in South Carolina in the winter of 1867–68. Passed, as these acts were, in lofty disregard of the feelings or interest of the whites of the South, the first crucial test they met was of course the attitude of those who were thus disregarded. The first force or element to be reckoned with was the element left out of the account. The property, the education and intelligence, the experience in self-government and public affairs, in this state, were of course wholly with its white population. Numbers alone were with the rest. The first registration of voters in South Carolina under the reconstruction acts, in October, 1867, gave a total of 125,328 persons eligible to vote, of whom 46,346 were whites, and 78,082 were blacks or colored, or a ratio of about 3 to 5. Upon the question of holding a constitutional convention, the first question prescribed by the acts for decision, the total vote in November, 1867, was 71,807,—130 whites and 68,876 colored voting pro, and 2801 contra. Of the members of the convention, 34 were whites and 63 colored. It did not contain one Democrat or one white man who had had high standing in the state previously. By this convention a constitution was framed, made up entirely of excerpts from other state constitutions, but yet a fairly good constitution in all its most important provisions. It continued in force, with a few rather unimportant changes, until 1897. State officers, under this constitution, and a legislature were elected in April, 1868, and the new government went into operation in July, 1868. In the first legislature under reconstruction, the Senate, numbering 33 members, contained 9 colored and 24 whites, of whom 7 only were Democrats. The House of Representatives numbered 124, of whom 48 were whites and 76 colored, only 14 being Democrats. The whole legislature was thus composed of 72 whites and

85 colored, with a total of 21 Democrats to 136 Republicans, or a ratio of nearly 3 to 20.

Truth here requires it to be said that the abstention of the whites from cooperation at this stage of reconstruction was voluntary and willful. The election for members of the convention went by default so far as they were concerned. They might, by voting solidly, and by the use of cajolery and flattery, such as they later did use, or by grosser arts, from which at last they did not shrink, have won an influential if not a controlling voice. All this is clear and certain; but the fact only shows the recklessness with which the sponsors of reconstruction went ahead. Such abnegation of lifelong sentiments or prejudices, such absolute reversal of themselves, as such a line of conduct required, was possible; but decent statesmanship does not build on possibilities. The question should have been, not, Is such conduct on the part of the whites possible? but, Is it to be expected? No man can say less than that it was to the last degree improbable; it would hardly be too much to say it was morally impossible. Alone of all prominent men in the state, Wade Hampton in 1868 publicly advised cooperation with the negroes in elections, but his advice passed unheeded.

But it is not true that Stevens or Morton counted on such cooperation of the whites, or cared for it. It was an after-thought to claim it; a retort to those who uttered reproaches as the scheme of reconstruction gradually showed its vanity and impossibility. It cannot be too confidently asserted that from 1867 to 1872 nothing would have been more unwelcome to the leaders of reconstruction at Washington than the knowledge that the whites of South Carolina were gaining influence over the blacks, or were helping to make laws, or were holding office. The writer knows his ground here; and there is available written evidence in abundance to avouch all his statements and opinions,—evidence, too, which will sometime be given to the world.

No view of the situation in South Carolina in these years would be accurate or complete which did not call to mind the peculiar political or party condition of the white or Democratic population. For fully ten years, if not twenty, prior to 1850, Mr. Calhoun's immense personality, strenuous leadership, and unquestionably representative views and policies dominated the state,—dominated it to the complete efface-ment and disappearance of all other leaders or leadership. This influence projected itself forward, and controlled the thought of the state until 1860, as truly as in the lifetime of Calhoun. American political history, for its first century, will record no other insistance of individual supremacy over a high-spirited, ambitious, politics-loving community such as the career of Calhoun presents. Nor was his influence in the smallest degree factitious or adventitious. It was simply the result of the application of a stern will, prodigious industry, sleepless but not selfish ambition, and the very highest order of ability to the leadership of a political cause. Calhoun led South Carolina till the outbreak of the war, if not through the war. At the close of the war and at the date of the reconstruction acts, new leadership in political thought and action was necessary; but South Carolina then had no leaders. Not only had she no trained party or political leaders; she had no men of single commanding influence. The most influential men of the state were the heroes of the war, who, though many of them able and public-spirited, were none of them greatly experienced in public affairs. The state had its full share of able men, an especially able bar, great numbers of planters and business men who had the old-time training in politics, but no man who could to any great degree mould public opinion or control party action. This fact—and it is referred to here only as a fact—was significant of much. In consequence, the Democratic or white party merely drifted, rudderless and at haphazard, from 1867 to 1874, the critical years of reconstruction.

Here, as at all points in this paper, the writer intends to speak with moderation of spirit and entire frankness. He thinks he can do justice to all parties and persons who took active part in reconstruction, though himself an actor, at times somewhat prominent. It will be for others to judge whether he has succeeded, as he has tried to do, in laying aside prejudices or feelings naturally developed by his activity in these scenes, so that he can see the men and events of those days objectively and disinterestedly.

It is now plain to all that reconstruction under the acts of 1867 was, at any rate, a frightful experiment, which never could have given a real statesman who learned or knew the facts the smallest hope of success. Government, self-government, the care of common public interests by the people themselves, is not so easy or simple a task as not to require a modicum of experience as well as a modicum of mental and moral character. In the mass of 78,000 colored voters in South Carolina in 1867, what elements or forces could have existed that made for good government? Ought it not to have been as clear then as it is now that good government, or even tolerable administration, could not be had from such an aggregation of ignorance and inexperience and incapacity? Is it not, has it not always been, as true in government as in physics, ex nihilo nihil fit?

Added to this obvious discouragement and impossibility in South Carolina was the fact that these 78,000 colored voters were distinctly and of design pitted against 46,000 whites, who held all the property, education, and public experience of the state. It is not less than shocking to think of such odds, such inevitable disaster. Yet it was deliberately planned and eagerly welcomed at Washington, and calmly accepted by the party throughout the country. What Republican voice was heard against it?

But the cup of adverse conditions was not yet full. To this feast of reconstruction, this dance of reunion, rushed hundreds, even thousands, of white and colored men from the North, who had almost as little experience of public affairs as the negroes of the South; and it must be added that, as a class, they were not morally the equals of the negroes of the South. The story at this point is threadbare; but it must be again said in this review that the Northern adventurers at once sprang to the front, and kept to the front from 1867 to 1874. To them the negro deferred with a natural docility. He felt that they represented the powers at Washington, as they often did, and his obedience was easily secured and held. Are Stevens and Morton and their applauding supporters chargeable with countenancing these men? Not by express, direct terms; but they are justly chargeable with opening the doors to them, and not casting them off when their true character was perfectly known. So ingrained was the disregard of Southern Democrats in all affairs that concerned the political control at the South, so inflexible was the determination of officials and leaders at Washington to keep the heel on the neck, that hardly one high Republican authority could be appealed to for discountenance of the class referred to. To this tide of folly, and worse, President Grant persistently yielded; while one noble exception must be noted, the gallant and true Benjamin H. Bristow, of Kentucky, as Solicitor-General, Attorney-General, and Secretary of the Treasury.

The quick, sure result was of course misgovernment. Let a few statistics tell the tale. Before the war, the average expense of the annual session of the legislature in South Carolina did not exceed $20,000. For the six years following reconstruction the average annual expense was over $320,000, the expense of the session of 1871 alone being $617,000. The total legislative expenses for the six years were $2,339,000.

The average annual cost of public printing in Massachusetts for the last ten years has been $131,000; for the year 1899 it was $139,000, and this included much costly printing never dreamed of in South Carolina in those days. In reconstructed South Carolina the cost of public printing for the first six years was $1,104,000,—an annual average of $184,000, the cost for the single year 1871–72 being $348,000.

The total public debt of South Carolina at the beginning of reconstruction was less than $1,000,000. At the end of the year 1872, five years later, the direct public debt amounted to over $17,500,000. For all this increase the state had not a single public improvement of any sort to show; and of this debt over $5,950,000 had been formally repudiated by the party and the men who had created the debt, and received and handled its proceeds.

Prior to reconstruction, contingent funds were absolutely unknown in South Carolina; a contingent fund, as known under reconstruction, being a sum of money which a public officer is allowed to draw and expend without accountability. During the first six years of reconstruction the contingent funds in South Carolina amounted to $376,000.

These are pecuniary results, but they tell a moral tale. No such results could be possible except where public and private virtue was well-nigh extinct; nor could they exist alone. In fact, they were only one salient effect or phase of a wide reign of corruption and general misrule. Public offices were objects of vulgar, commonplace bargain and sale. Justice in the lower and higher courts was bought and sold; or rather, those who sat in the seats nominally of justice made traffic of their judicial powers. State militia on a vast scale was organized and equipped in 1870 and 1871 solely from the negroes, arms and legal organization being denied the White Democrats. No branch of the public service escaped the pollution. One typical and concrete example must suffice here. In the counties of South Carolina there is a school commissioner whose powers and duties cover the choice of all teachers of the public schools, their examination for employment or promotion, the issue of warrants for installments of their salary, and, in general, all the powers and duties usually devolved on the highest school officer in a given area of territory. In one of the counties of South Carolina, during the years 1874 and 1875, the school commissioner was a negro of the deepest hue and most pronounced type, who could neither read nor write even his own name; and his name appeared always on official documents in another's handwriting, with the legend "his X mark." He was as corrupt, too, as he was ignorant. Now, what course a county in Massachusetts or other Northern state would take under such an infliction the writer does not venture to say. He is only certain no Northern community would stand it. The people of this county, one morning, found their chief school officer dead in the highway from a gunshot. Such incidents must lead, will lead, in any intelligent community, to deeds of violence. The famous and infamous Ku-Klux Klan of 1870 was an organized attempt to overawe and drive from office Republican state officers, and especially negroes. It was brutal and murderous to the last degree, being from first to last in the hands almost exclusively of the lower stratum of the white population. Yet it was symptomatic of a dreadful disease,—the gangrene of incapacity, dishonesty, and corruption in public office. No excuse can be framed for its outrages, but its causes were plain. Any observer who cared to see could see that it flourished where corruption and incapacity had climbed into power, and withered where the reverse was the case.

Gradually, under the spur of public wrongs and misrule, political party remedies began to be used by the Democrats,—a word practically synonymous with whites, as Republican was with negroes,—and in 1872 a Democrat canvass was made for state officers. In 1874 the Democrats united with a section of disaffected Republicans in a canvass, in which the Republican candidate for governor received 80,000 votes, and the Democratic candidate 68,000. Still no great or preeminent leader of the Democratic party forces had appeared. In 1874, under the stress of fear of consequences, symptoms of which were then clear, the Republican party, by some of its leaders, and some part of its rank and file, undertook a somewhat systematic effort for "reform within the party." For the next two years the struggle went determinedly on, with varying success. Two facts or incidents will illustrate the flow and ebb of reform here. Early in 1875, a notorious, corrupt negro, who had long led the negroes in one of the strongest Republican sections of the state, put himself up as a candidate for judge of the chief [Charleston] circuit of the state. The reform forces barely succeeded in defeating him. Other conflicts from time to time arose, and it was only by a close union of the Democrats in the legislature, and the free and constant use of the executive power of veto, that the reform party was saved from overthrow and rout—no less than nineteen vetoes being given to leading legislative measures by the governor in a single session. When the legislature assembled for the session of 1875–76, the reform and anti-reform forces were nearly equally matched; the former including all the Democratic members of the legislature, who were in turn heartily backed by the Democratic party of the state.

A decisive test of strength soon came. As the event of this test marks accurately the turning point in the fortunes of reconstruction in South Carolina under the congressional plan of 1867, the story must be here told with care and some degree of fullness. December 15, 1875, occurred an election by the legislature of six circuit or nisi prius judges for the several circuits into which the state was then divided. On the night preceding the election a secret caucus of the negro members of the legislature was held, instigated, organized, and led by the most adroit as well as the ablest negro in the state, one Robert B. Elliott, formerly of Boston. At this caucus, an oath was sworn by every member to support all nominations made by the caucus for the judgeships. The caucus proceeded to make nominations, choosing for the two most important circuits—Charleston and Sumter—a negro, Whipper, and a white man, F. J. Moses. Not till the legislature was ready to meet on the following day did the fact of this caucus become known. Every man nominated was elected. The storm now broke over the heads of the conspirators in fury. The laugh which for a long time greeted remonstrance died away, and men asked one another what could be done. The governor at once took his stand, undoubtedly a novel and extreme stand; but, like all decent men who saw the situation at first-hand, he probably felt that sometimes in politics, as in other things, "new occasions teach new duties." He publicly announced his determination to refuse to issue commissions to Whipper and Moses. The wrath of the conspirators rose high, but the white citizens strongly backed the executive, and no commissions were ever issued. The sequel was that, after much loud boasting of their courage on the part of Whipper and Moses, they quailed, like the craven cowards they were, before the determination of the people, and never took another step to enforce their claim to office.

At this precise point came the parting of ways between the governor and his Republican supporters, on the one hand, and his white Democratic supporters, on the other hand, in their common reform struggle. It seems dramatic, almost tragic, that, in a matter of so much importance to South Carolina, hearts equally earnest and honest, as we may now believe, and minds equally free and clear, saw in the same event, and that event a signal triumph over the powers of misrule by the allied forces of the reformers, totally different meanings and significance. To the Republican reformers it seemed a splendid vindication of their policy and belief,—that all that was needed was a union of the forces of intelligence and honesty against the common enemy; to the Democratic reformers, on the other hand, it seemed a final and crowning proof that the forces of misrule were too strong to be overcome by ordinary, peaceful methods. Less cannot be said here than that, as is usual, there was truth in both views. There were, no doubt, many searchings of heart in the ranks of each division of the reformers. One eminent and devoted reformer, who felt compelled to go with the Democrats, has left on record an expression of his feelings, in quoting the words of Sir William Waller to his friend and antagonist in the English Civil War of 1640: "That great God who is the searcher of my heart knows with what a sad sense I go upon this service, and with what a perfect hatred I detest this war without an enemy. . . . But we are both upon the stage, and must act such parts as are assigned us in this tragedy." It was the feeling of many before the contest had opened or passed to the stage of hard fighting.

Pause must be made here long enough to set before an uninformed reader the array of forces for this contest, so significant to South Carolina, and so characteristic and illustrative of the inevitable results of reconstruction on the lines of 1867. It has been remarked that South Carolina had no great leader or leaders after Mr. Calhoun. This was true until 1876, but not later. Great new occasions usually bring leaders. At the head of the Democratic forces in South Carolina, in June, 1876, appeared General Wade Hampton, known only, one might say, till then, except locally, as a distinguished Confederate cavalry officer. He had led the life of a planter on a large scale, and possessed well-developed powers and habits of command. Totally unlike Calhoun, Hampton's strength of leadership lay, not in intellectual or oratorical superiority, but in high and forceful character, perfect courage, and real devotion to what he conceived to be the welfare of South Carolina. Not even Calhoun's leadership was at any time more absolute, unquestioned, and enthusiastic than Hampton's in 1876; and it was justly so from the Democratic point of view, for he was unselfish, resolute, level-headed, and determined. He was for the hour a true "natural leader"; and he led with consummate mingled prudence and aggressiveness.

The progress of the canvass developed, as must have been apprehended by all who saw or studied the situation, not only into violence of words and manner, but into breaches of the peace, interference with public meetings called by one party, and latterly into wide-spread riots. The chapter need not be retold. The concealments of the canvass on these points have long been remitted, with the occasion which called for them. It is not now denied, but admitted and claimed, by the successful party, that the canvass was systematically conducted with the view to find occasions to apply force and violence. The occasions came, and the methods adopted had their perfect work. The result is known, but must be stated here for historical purposes purely. By a system of violence and coercion ranging through all possible grades, from urgent persuasion to mob violence and plentiful murders, the election was won by the Democrats. The historian here is no longer compelled to spell out his verdict from a wide induction of facts; he need only accept the assertions, even the vaunts, of many of the leading figures in the canvass since the canvass was closed.

Is there anything to be said by way of verdict upon the whole passage? Yes; plainly this, at least,—that the drama or tragedy lay potentially, from the first, in the reconstruction policy of Morton and Stevens. The latent fire there concealed was blown to flame by the conduct of affairs in South Carolina under the inspiration, if not direction, of Republican leaders at Washington. No proper or serious efforts were ever made there to ward off or prevent the conflict. Till October, 1876, no doubt seemed to enter the minds of Republican politicians that the brute force of numbers would win, as it had won. Cries of distress, shouts of encouragement, promises of reward for the party in South Carolina, now burdened the mails and kept telegraph wires hot. Managers of the Republican national canvass vied with one another in the extravagance of hopes and promises sent to South Carolina. But the forces aroused by ten years of vassalage of white to black, and eight years of corruption and plunder and misrule, moved on to their end till the end was fully reached.

It has often been asked, Could not the end—freedom from negro domination and its consequent misrule—have been reached by other more lawful and more peaceful methods? Into speculations of this kind it is not worth while to venture. One thing may be said with confidence, —the whites of South Carolina in 1876 believed no other methods or means would avail. Their course was guided by this belief. Mr. Hallam declares that "nothing is more necessary, in reaching historical conclusions, than knowledge of the motives avowed and apparently effective in the minds of the parties to controversies." The vowed motives of the whites in the struggle of 1876 are fully recorded. Are there any evidences that these motives were simulated or affected? The policy adopted and carried does not discredit the existence and force of these motives. The campaign of 1876 was conducted as if it were a life-or-death combat.

Finally, the more serious, most serious, question has often been raised:

conceding the wrongs suffered and the hopelessness of relief by other methods, was this campaign warranted? Different answers will be given by different moralists and casuists. To the writer, the question does not seem of first or great importance. What is certain is that a people of force, pride, and intelligence, driven, as the white people of South Carolina believed they were in 1876, to choose between violence and lawlessness for a time, and misrule for all time, will infallibly choose the former.

The overthrow of Republican or negro rule in South Carolina in 1876 was root-and-branch work. The fabric so long and laboriously built up fell in a day. Where was fancied to be strength was found only weakness. The vauntings were turned to cringings of terror. Poltroons and per-jurers made haste to confess; robbers came forward to disgorge, intent only on personal safety; and the world saw an old phenomenon repeated, —the essential and ineradicable cowardice and servility of conscious wrongdoers. The avalanche caught the innocent with the guilty, the patriot and reformer with the corruptionist, the bribe-giver and bribe-taker. It could not be otherwise; it has never been otherwise in such convulsions.

The historian who studies this crowning event of reconstruction in South Carolina will be sure to meet or to raise the question, Why did Republican reformers there adhere to the Republican party in 1876? The answer to this is easy. They were, most of them, trained in another school than South Carolina. Resort to violence and bloodshed was not in their list of possible remedies for political wrongs or abuses. They were ready to risk or to lose their own lives in a contest for good government; they were not ready to take the lives or shed the blood of others for any political cause not involving actual physical self-defense.

A close or interested student of reconstruction will doubtless ask, In the light of retrospect and the disillusionment of later events, does it seem that good government could have been reached in South Carolina by a continuance of the union of a part—the reforming part—of the Republican party and the whole body of Democrats in the state? Speculation and reflection have been and will be expended on this question, for to some degree it touches a vital moral point. It has already been said that on this question the two wings—Republican and Democratic—of the reformers of 1874–76 held opposite opinions. It must be conceded that, unfortunately but inevitably, into the decision of the question in 1876 purely party considerations entered strongly. It would be vain for either side to deny it. Republican reformers were party men; so were Democratic reformers. Personal ambitions, also, played their usual part—a large one. Instigations to a strict Republican party contest came freely from Washington. On the other hand, Mr. Tilden, who was made to bear in those days so heavy a load of responsibility for everything amiss in the eyes of his party opponents, was specially charged—a charge still current among the uninformed or the victims of ancient party prejudices—with influencing the Democratic party in South Carolina in this crisis to enter on a party canvass on the lines of violence and fraud. The writer thinks he now knows the charge to be unfounded; that, on the contrary, if Mr. Tilden's influence was felt at all, it was in the direction of a canvass for state officers and the legislature on non-partisan lines, and in any event a peaceful and lawful canvass. If there is any interest still attaching to the writer's own view, he is quite ready now to say that he feels sure there was no possibility of securing permanent good government in South Carolina through Republican influences. If the canvass of 1876 had resulted in the success of the Republican party, that party could not, for want of materials, even when aided by the Democratic minority, have given pure or competent administration. The vast preponderance of ignorance and incapacity in that party, aside from downright dishonesty, made it impossible. An experienced or observant eye can see the causes. The canvass on purely party lines in 1876 necessarily threw Republican reformers and Republican rascals again into friendly contact and alliance. Success would have given redoubled power to leaders who had been temporarily discredited or set aside; the flood gates of misrule would have been reopened; and, as was said by one of the leaders of reform when Whipper and Moses were elected judges, "a terrible crevasse of misgovernment and public debauchery" would have again opened. The real truth is, hard as it may be to accept it, that the elements put in combination by the reconstruction scheme of Stevens and Morton were irretrievably bad, and could never have resulted, except temporarily or in desperate moments, in government fit to be endured. As Macaulay's old Puritan sang in after years of Naseby, so may now sing a veteran survivor of reconstruction in South Carolina:—

> "Oh! evil was the root, and bitter was the fruit,
> And crimson was the juice of the vintage that we trod."

There is an important inquiry still to be noticed and answered: How did the victors use their victory? The just answers seems to be, "Not altogether well," but emphatically, "As well as could have been expected,"—as well as the lot and nature of humanity probably permit. Some unfair, unjust, merely angry blows were struck after the victory was won. For the rest, forbearance and oblivion were the rule. Good government, the avowed aim, was fully secured. Economy succeeded extravagance; judicial integrity and ability succeeded profligacy and ignorance on the bench; all the conditions of public welfare were restored.

Of secondary results, it is hardly necessary to this review and picture of reconstruction in South Carolina to speak; but it would be an impressive warning for other like cases if it were added that the methods of 1876 have left scars and wounds which generations of time cannot efface or heal. The appeal for the truth of this remark may be safely made to the most ardent defender of those methods. The price of what was gained in 1876 will long remain unliquidated. No part of it can ever be remitted. The laws of human society, not written in statute books, proclaim that wrong and wrong methods are self-propagating. Long before Shakespeare told it, it was true, even from the foundation of the moral order:—

> "We but teach
> Bloody instructions, which, being taught, return
> To plague the inventor; this even-handed justice
> Commends the ingredients of our poison'd chalice
> To our own lips."

Every present citizen of South Carolina knows, and those who are truthful and frank will confess, that the ballot debauched in 1876 remains debauched; the violence taught then remains now, if not in the same, in other forms; the defiance of law learned then in what was called a good cause survives in the horrid orgies and degradation of lynchings.

The chapter of recent events covered by this paper is made up largely of the record of mistakes and crimes followed by the sure, unvarying retributions which all history teaches are the early or late result of evil courses in nations and states as well as in individuals. To whom, humanly speaking, are these woes and wastes chargeable? The answer must be, to those who devised and put in operation the congressional scheme of reconstruction,—to their unspeakable folly, their blind party greed, their insensate attempt to reverse the laws which control human society.

The designed plan of this paper does not extend to any discussion of the always grave topic of the condition and prospects of the negro race in South Carolina and the South. It has abundantly appeared in what has already been written that that race was used as the tool of heartless partisan leaders. As in all such cases, the tool was cast aside when its use was ended. Who can look on the picture,—the negro enslaved by physical chains for some two centuries and a half, then bodily lifted into freedom by other hands than his own, next mercilessly exploited for the benefit of a political party, and heartlessly abandoned when the scheme had failed,—what heart of stone, we say, would not be touched by these undeserved miseries, these woeful misfortunes, of the negro of the United States?

What had the negro to show after 1876 for his sufferings? Merely the paper right to vote,—a right which he had no earthly power or capacity to use or to defend; while, with smug faces, with hypocritic sighs and upturned eyeballs, the soi-disant philanthropists and charitymongers of the North looked on the negro from afar, giving him only an occasional charge to still stand by the grand old party that had set him free! To all who feel a real solicitude for the welfare of the Southern negro, it ought to be said that the conditions of his welfare lie in reversing at all points the spirit and policy of reconstruction which brought on him this Iliad of woes. Philanthropy without wisdom is always dangerous. Disregard of actual conditions is never wise. The negro depends for his welfare, not on the North, but on the South; not on strangers, however friendly or sympathetic or generous in bestowing bounty, but on his white neighbors and employers. Whatever can be done to promote good relations between him and his actual neighbors will be well done; whatever is done which tends otherwise will be ill done. By industry and thrift the negro can secure all he needs, both of livelihood and of education; whatever is given him gratuitously promotes idleness and unthrift. With all emphasis let it be said and known—and the writer's knowledge confirms the saying, as will like knowledge acquired by any honest and clear-sighted person—that the negro at the South is not, in the mass or individually, the proper object of charity.

And of his education let a word be said. Education is, no one disputes or doubts, essential to the welfare of a free or self-governing community. The negro in his present situation is not an exception to the rule. But what sort of education does he need? Primarily, and in nine hundred and ninety-nine cases out of one thousand, he does not need, in any proper sense of the words, literary, scientific, or what we call the higher educa-tion. It is not too much to say that, up to this time, a great amount of money and effort has been worse than wasted on such education, or attempts at such education, of the negro. To an appreciable extent, it has been a positive evil to him. Give him, or rather stimulate him to provide for himself, education suited to his condition: to wit, abundant training in the three R's; and after that, skill in handicraft, in simple manual labor of all kinds, which it is his lot to do—lot fixed not by us, but by powers above us. If there be aspiring spirits in the race, capable of better things, this is the soil from which they may rise, rather than from hotbeds or forcing grounds,—the so-called negro colleges and universities now existing in the South. Beyond this, let the negro be taught, early and late, in schools and everywhere, thrift, pecuniary prudence and foresight, the duty, the foremost duty, of getting homes, property, land, or whatever constitutes wealth in his community. Above all things, let him be taught that his so-called rights depend on himself alone. Tell him, compel him by iteration to know, that no race or people has ever yet long had freedom unless it was won and kept by itself; won and kept by courage, by intelligence, by vigilance, by prudence. Having done this, let Northern purses be closed; let sympathy and bounty be bestowed, if anywhere, upon far less favored toilers nearer home, and leave the negro to work out his own welfare, unhelped and unhindered. If these simple methods are adopted and rigorously observed, the negro problem at our South will tend toward solution, and the flood of ills flowing from reconstruction as imposed from without will at last be stayed; and they can be stayed in no other ways. Constitutional limits of aid by legislation have already been reached and overpassed. Rights, to be secure, must, in the last resort, rest on stronger supports than constitutions, statutes, or enrolled parchments. Self-government under constitutions presupposes a firm determination, and mental, moral and physical capacity, ready and equal to the defense of rights. Neither the negro nor the white man can have them on other terms.

READINGS

ADDITIONAL PRINTED SOURCE MATERIALS:

Allen, Walter. *Governor Chamberlain's Administration in South Carolina.*

Chesnut, Mary Boykin. *A Diary from Dixie.*

Fleming, W. L., ed. *A Documentary History of Reconstruction.*

Hagood, Johnson. *Memoirs of the War of Secession.*

Leland, John A. *A Voice from South Carolina* . . . .

May, John Amasa, and Joan Reynolds Faunt. *South Carolina Secedes.*

Pike, James S. *The Prostrate State* . . . .

Pringle, Mrs. E. W. A. *Chronicles of Chicora Wood.*

Reynolds, John S. *Reconstruction in South Carolina.*

The State Newspaper. *The Burning of Columbia.*

CORRELATED TEXTS:

Cauthen, Charles E. *South Carolina Goes to War, 1860–1865.*

Channing, Steven A.: *Crisis of Fear: Secession in South Carolina.*

Johnson, Guion Griffis. *A Social History of the Sea Islands* . . . , 154–215.

Kibler, Lillian. *The Life of Benjamin F. Perry.*

Rose, Willie Lee. *Rehearsal for Reconstruction: The Port Royal Experiment.*

Simkins, Francis B. *South Carolina During Reconstruction.*

Simms, William Gilmore. *Sack and Destruction of the City of Columbia, S.C.,* ed. with notes, A. S. Salley.

Snowden, Yates, ed. *History of South Carolina,* II.

Wallace, D. D. *History of South Carolina.* III, 151–321.

———. *South Carolina: A Short History,* 525–606.

VII
THE STATE IN THE NEW SOUTH

After Reconstruction, South Carolina took its place as a state in the South and strove to rise from defeat and regain its former position in the nation. In the new South, South Carolina was no longer the leader. Other states had thrown off Reconstruction earlier and were advancing more rapidly. In industry, education, and political leadership, South Carolina lagged behind.

Within the state, the population of 1,000,000 in 1880 was 60 percent Negro and 40 percent white. By 1910, the ratio, due to the migration of Negroes, had become 55 percent Negro and 45 percent white, and by 1920, 52 percent Negro and 48 percent white. Today the races are more evenly balanced, with the white people holding a majority.

After 1877, the minority of white people were firmly in the political saddle, although until 1895 Negroes played a small role in state politics (until the 1954 Supreme Court decision). A few Negro legislators from Low Country counties and one or two Negro congressman were elected.

Among the white population, the Democratic party reigned supreme, but the leadership of the party changed sharply in the year 1890. Before that date, the old-guard Democrats, the "Bourbons," who had been instrumental in bringing about the end of Reconstruction, were in power under Gen. Wade Hampton and his successors. But in 1890 a new political power came forward. This was brought about through the leadership of Benjamin Ryan Tillman (1847–1918) and as a result of the economic distress of the 1880s, which saw over 900,000 acres of land forfeited for taxes. Tillman launched the "Farmers' Movement," which soon merged into the "Tillman Movement"; eventually—backed by the hundreds of small farmers—Tillman became virtually a political dictator.

Prior to 1860, under the parish system, which gave a few hundred farmers of the Low Country the same representation as thousands in the Up Country, the small farmer had been a political nobody. During

467

the white supremacy struggle in the 1870s, the white farmer had been courted assiduously, since his votes were needed, and he tasted political power. Within the next decade, the farmers organized their forces, stormed the political strongholds of the Bourbons, and put "Pitchfork Ben" Tillman in the governor's chair.

Their demands were many, including a state agricultural college, agricultural experimental farms, state control of the railroads, and the disenfranchisement of the Negro. Nearly all of these demands were realized in the 1890s and were made permanent by the Constitution of 1895. That constitution conferred suffrage on all men who were able to read and write the constitution or, failing that, who paid taxes on $300 worth of property. This provision stood until the South Carolina legislature passed a law (now outlawed by the Voting Rights Act) that voters must have at least an eighth-grade education. The 1895 constitution also forbade mixed marriages, a provision which has been upset by the 1967 Supreme Court ruling; and the mingling of races, a section deleted as a result of the Supreme Court ruling against Clarendon County in 1954. Divorce, disallowed by the 1895 Constitution, is now common practice in South Carolina.

Economically and socially, from 1895 on the state experienced slow, gradual progress until the 1920s. Schools were improved under the laws adopted in 1868, and after the High School Act of 1908 they began to approach adequacy. New state colleges at Clemson, Rock Hill, and Orangeburg and several private colleges were founded during this period to help round out the educational system.

Industry, largely textiles, was established, and the mill village became a common sight, particularly in the Piedmont. In agriculture, cotton remained the dominant crop, with tobacco replacing rice as the second staple.

By the early twentieth century, Clemson and its experimental farms were paving the way for new crops, diversified farming, and improved stock strains. At the end of the first World War, the state was still predominantly agricultural, and economically it was far behind most of the nation. A new era was trying to dawn, but it never seemed to arrive.

140. *Some South Carolina Towns in 1883*

THE HALF CENTURY BETWEEN 1826 AND 1883 SAW MANY CHANGES IN SOUTH CAROLINA'S TOWNS. SOME DECLINED IN POPULATION AND IMPORTANCE; OTHERS IMPROVED; AND A FEW NEW TOWNS EMERGED. THROUGH THE WHOLE PERIOD CHARLESTON REMAINED THE METROPOLIS OF THE STATE. COLUMBIA, FACED WITH LACK OF INDUSTRY AND THE GREAT FIRE OF 1865, WAS A POOR SECOND IN SIZE, ALTHOUGH IT WAS IMPORTANT POLITICALLY. THE FOLLOWING ARE REPORTS ON SOME OF THE IMPORTANT TOWNS OF SOUTH CAROLINA.

[The Department of Agriculture's Report on South Carolina Towns]

AIKEN

Aiken . . . was settled in 1833, when the South Carolina Railroad, then the longest in the world, was built. The first settlers were persons from the lower country in search of a healthy and invigorating climate during summer. Since then it has become a famous health resort for those from Northern latitudes seeking a warm dry winter air and sunshine . . . . In addition to numerous excellent boarding houses, the Highland Park Hotel, open during the spring and winter months for Northern visitors, is one of the largest and in many respects one of the best hotels in the South. There is a private bank in the town. The population in 1880 was 1817. The streets of Aiken are wide. The sidewalks are raised and covered with clay. This clay, resting on a bed of deep sand, is kept well drained, and forms a smooth, hard, elastic surface. A broad drive of the same material has been similarly constructed from the Highland Park Hotel to the freight depot, three-quarters of a mile, at a cost of $600. It forms an excellent roadway, over which even heavily laden cotton wagons are in the habit of moving at a trot. . . .

ANDERSON

Anderson . . . is on the Columbia, Greenville and Blue Ridge railroad, and is the terminus of the Savannah River Valley railroad, which is being built. The population in 1860 was 625, in 1870, 1432, and in 1880, 1850, and it has increased much since. There are two hotels,

South Carolina Resources and Population, S.C. Dept. of Agriculture (Charleston: n.p., 1883), 686–715.

three halls for public entertainment owned by private individuals . . . .
The whites have five churches—Presbyterian, Baptist, Methodist, Episcopal and Catholic; colored persons, two churches—Baptist and Methodist. There are three public and a number of private schools, and two weekly newspapers. Stores rent for from $100 to $600 per year. Personal property is estimated at $350,000; real estate, $4,000,000. The town tax is seventy cents on the $100; no town debt. . . . About 20,000 bales of cotton are shipped annually to Charleston, Philadelphia and New York.

CHERAW

Cheraw, at the junction of the Cheraw and Darlington Railroad with the railroad to Salisbury, N.C., is one mile from the head of navigation on the Great Pee Dee river. There is a population of 1000 within the corporate limits, and about the same number on the outskirts of the town. In 1825 the population was 1200 and 20,000 bales of cotton were shipped by steamboat on the Pee Dee river from this point; in 1840 the population was 400; in 1860, it was 960. It is regularly laid off. The streets are one hundred feet wide and have an aggregate length of fifteen miles; three lines of handsome full grown shade trees, one on each side, and one in the middle, render them delightful drives and walks. A handsome two-story town hall has the upper story occupied as a Masonic lodge, the lower story is supplied with seats and scenery, and is used for public entertainments (charges, including licenses and lights, five to ten dollars). There is a skating rink, and the river, several streams and two beautiful lakes nearby afford good fishing. There is a race-course near the town. There is a Methodist, Baptist, Presbyterian, Episcopal and Catholic church for the whites . . . . There are also several churches for the colored population. Stores rent for $100 to $400 per annum, and dwelling houses about the same. The real estate is estimated at $500,000 and the personal property at $250,000. Taxes are restricted by the town charter to one-half of one per cent, and it has been found necessary to call for only half of this amount. Personal property is not taxed, except for bar rooms. There is no town debt. . . . There is a tannery, a tin-ware, a wagon, and a fertilizer manufactory in the town, besides two steam grist mills, and gins, and one steam saw mill . . . . Cheraw is one of the oldest settlements in the State, and has been long noted for the wealth and culture of its citizens.

FLORENCE

Florence, on the Columbia and Wilmington railroad, and at the terminus of the Northeastern and the Cheraw and Darlington railroads, had a population in 1866 of 600, and in 1880, of 1940; now estimated at 2500. There are fourteen miles of streets, constructed at a cost of $75.00 per mile. There are two hotels, a two-story town hall, costing $5,000, seven churches . . . and four schools. Dwellings rent from $7.00 to $17.00 a month, and stores from $15.00 to $40.00 a month. Excellent bricks are burned in the vicinity, and lumber is abundant and cheap. The town taxes are one-half of one per cent on property and there is a town debt of $3,000, at seven per cent interest, for the purchase of a steam fire engine. About 4,000 bales of cotton are shipped annually. The Florence Times is published weekly. There is a carriage factory, four steam and two water gins and grist mills, three steam saw mills, and the railroad shops located here employ about 150 hands.

GEORGETOWN

Georgetown covers an area a mile square. In 1820, the population was 2000; in 1840, it was 1500 . . . ; in 1860, it was 1720 . . . ; and in 1880 it was 2557. It is regularly laid out and has fourteen miles of streets paved with stone, brick or wood. Transportation through the streets is performed by drays or carts, at fifteen cents a load. Buggies and carriages may be hired at $2.50 to $4.00 a day. Wells and cisterns afford an abundant supply of water. Four main drains, with a number of lateral drains, empty into Sampit river, and constitute an excellent system of drainage. There are three boarding houses; charges, from $1.00 to $2.00 a day for transient boarders. The court house, jail, and market house are of brick, and were erected at a cost of $50,000. The hall of the Winyaw Indigo Society is also of brick; it is two stories and cost $18,000. The lower story is used as a school, the upper story has a library, and is used as a public hall; fees for exhibitions, $5.00. There are five churches, three for whites, Episcopal, Methodist, and Baptist, and two for the colored population, Methodist and Baptist. They have an aggregate seating capacity of over three thousand, and cost about $30,000. The pupils of the Winyaw Indigo Society school are prepared to enter West Point and the colleges and universities of the United States. There are two public schools, one white and one colored, and, in addition, a number of private schools . . . . The choicest game, fish and oysters are abundant and cheap. Beef and mutton sell at ten to twelve cents a pound; eggs, twelve to fifteen cents per dozen; fowls, twenty to twenty-five cents. . . . The total value of all property, real and personal, is stated at $800,000, and the annual taxes are about $7,000. The town has no debt.

175 sail of vessels, of from 50 to 500 tons burthen, and drawing six to thirteen feet of water, cross Georgetown bar annually. There is regular communication with Charleston and Cheraw by steamboat . . . . There are three saw mills . . . , a shingle mill . . . , and a large rice-pounding mill has recently been established. The direct shipment of this grain to Northern ports is increasing. Other manufactures are the preparation of naval stores, and of corn in various forms . . . . The average wages paid to laborers is 25 to 75¢ a day, and for skilled labor, $1 to $2 a day.

GREENVILLE

Greenville . . . long noted for the salubrity of its climate and the beauty of its situation . . . is located on Reedy river, at the junction of the Columbia and Greenville railroad with the Atlanta and Charlotte Air Line railroad. In 1820, the population was 500; in 1840, 850; in 1860, 1518; and in 1880, it was 6160. A careful enumeration by the Interstate Directory Company, in 1883, shows the population to be 8355. It appeared that on the same date there were in course of erection 16 residences, seven stores, one warehouse, one stable, one large church, and a musical conservatory three stores high, and including 21 rooms.

It [Greenville] has an elevation of 1050 feet above the sea level. It has 600 yards of brick pavement. There are two miles of street railway in the town. Reedy river, with two falls of over thirty feet each, traverses the town, which has in addition twenty-five street cisterns, capacity, fifteen thousand gallons each. Rock culverts and drains, with side drains of terra cotta, make a good system of drainage and sewerage. There are six hotels and three livery stables in the town. The handsome brick court house cost $25,000, and an opera hall, costing $15,000, has seven hundred seats. . . . There are ten churches, with a seating capacity of three hundred to one thousand each . . . . There are two colleges, a military institute, a public school, and a number of private schools . . . . The value of real and personal property is stated at $2,500,000 . . . . The taxes are six and a half mills on the dollar, yielding $11,500 per annum. There is a debt of $55,000 . . . . 40,000 bales of cotton . . . have been shipped in one year to New York, Baltimore, Philadelphia and yarn to the value of $200,000, to Boston. . . .

Besides the Huguenot and Camperdown cotton mills, there is a carriage factory, a furniture factory, an iron foundry, a cotton seed oil mill, a mattress factory, three saddle and harness shops, a flour mill, a terra cotta factory, three brick yards, and a mill turning out pearl grits. There are three printing offices, two newspapers and a religious paper. The town is lighted with gas; the mills have electric lights.

SPARTANBURG

Spartanburg . . . is situated at the junction of the Spartanburg, Union and Columbia Railroad, and the Spartanburg and Asheville railroad, with the Atlanta and Charlotte Air Line railroad. The population in 1820 was 800; in 1840, 1000; in 1860, 1216; and in 1880 it was 3253. It has an elevation above sea level of 787 feet. Besides the court house and jail, there is an opera house costing $11,000, and three large and handsome brick hotels, one of which has 100 rooms. There are four churches for the whites and three for colored persons. The Wofford College here is under the direction of the Methodist church. There is also a male seminary, a female seminary, six public and private schools, and an orphan house. The National Bank has a paid in capital of $100,000; surplus, $30,000. Property is valued at $1,250,000. There is a city debt of $150,000 for subscription to railroads, and $20,000 for macadamizing the streets. 25,000 to 30,000 bales of cotton are shipped annually to New York and Charleston. . . . The town is lighted with gas.

SUMTER

Sumterville, on the Columbia and Wilmington railroad, near the headwaters of the Wynee river, was founded in 1800. It occupies a level site on sandy soil, three-fourths of a mile in each direction from the court house square as a centre. There is an intendant and four wardens, with a chief of police, an assistant and three regular policemen. There are ten miles of streets, with elevated sidewalks of rammed clay. Besides a fine court house building, there is a music hall fitted for public amusements . . . . There are five churches for the whites: Episcopal, Methodist, Baptist, Presbyterian and Catholic. The colored population have three churches: two Methodist and one Baptist. The educational establishments are the Sumter Institute, the St. Joseph's Academy (Catholic), the Sumter public school for whites, cost $1200, pupils 200; the Lincoln public school, colored, cost $1200, pupils 250; and several private schools. Stores rent from $12.50 to $60.00 a month; dwelling houses from $5.00 to $20.00. The town taxes are four-tenths per cent on real, and two-tenths per cent on personal property, realizing on the assessments about $2000 per annum. The indebtedness of the town is $12,000 for the music hall, and fire engines . . . . About 12,000 bales of cotton are shipped annually. The yearly sales are estimated at: provisions, $250,000; dry goods, $200,000; hard ware, $150,000; miscellaneous, $100,000. The Bellemonte cotton factory, recently erected, is in successful operation. There are three weekly newspapers and the town is growing rapidly.

YORK

Yorkville . . . is on the Chester and Lenoir narrow-gauge railway . . . . In 1840 the population was 600; in 1860, 1360; and in 1880, 1339. There are ten miles of streets paved at a cost of 25¢ to $1 per yard . . . . The court house is a venerable and handsome building, costing originally $8,000. The King's Mountain Military Academy and the Female Academy are fine buildings, costing about $20,000 each. There are several other schools, and a newspaper. The churches are the Episcopal, Methodist, Presbyterian, Baptist and Associate Reformed. Building materials are chiefly stone and brick from the vicinity. Taxes are four mills on the dollar, two of which go to pay the balance due on paving the streets, which is nearly paid up. Six to ten thousand bales of cotton are shipped to New York annually.

COLUMBIA

Columbia . . . is two miles square, regularly laid out in streets 100 and 150 feet in width, most of them planted with beautiful shade trees. The streets aggregate 60 miles in length, and are neatly kept. The roadways of the main thoroughfares are macadamized, the sidewalks paved. They are maintained, including lamps, at a cost of $8,000 annually. Facilities for transportation of all kinds are ample and cheap. Natural springs, issuing from a valley between the town and river, afford an ample supply of excellent water, which is raised one hundred and twenty feet by steampower, for use at the rate of one million gallons a day. The soil is porous, and its elevation above the river offers every facility for thorough drainage. There are eight hotels and first-class boarding houses, with moderate charges, and the place is much frequented by invalids from the North during winter.

The public buildings are the State House, built of enormous blocks of granite, quarried in the vicinity, and to cost $5,000,000 when completed. The U.S. Courthouse and Postoffice [now City Hall] is built of Fairfield granite, which at a distance might be mistaken for marble. The large and extensive fire-proof buildings of the Insane Asylum; the numerous buildings of the State University, and those of the Presbyterian Theological Seminary; a large and handsome City Hall and Opera House (800 seats; rent and license fee $40 a night); the Court House and Penitentiary, with some fine blocks of business houses, etc., . . . cost in excess of $6,000,000.

Columbia is noted for the beauty of its public and private grounds, and for its beautiful flower gardens. Sydney Park covers twenty acres, furnishing attractive promenades. The Agricultural Society of the State has extensive fair grounds, with numerous buildings, and during fair week in November, as many as twenty thousand persons assemble here from all parts of the State. There are two handsome cemeteries. There are fourteen churches; three free and fifteen private schools. Stores rent from $20.00 to $50.00 a month, dwellings from $50.00 to $500.00 per annum. The assessed value of real and personal property is $3,000,000, and the estimated true value is given at $5,000,000. The taxes aggregate $45,000 yearly, of which $33,000 are levied on property and $12,000 come from licenses. The city debt, incurred for permanent improvements, water works, streets, etc., aggregates $850,000. The receipts of cotton in Columbia . . . in 1883 . . . will overrun 40,000 bales for the whole year, not counting large amounts purchased by factors here from points more or less distant on the railroads, and shipped thence directly . . . .

The manufacturing establishments of Columbia, as stated in the Tenth U.S. Census, include 52 establishments, employing 293 hands. This statement does not include the products of the manufacture of gas, nor of quarrying, or the statistics of establishments owned and operated by the railroad companies and by the State. . . . A cotton seed oil mill is being erected, and when the work on the canal, which is being done by the State, is completed, and power for several large factories furnished, Columbia will be a manufacturing centre of considerable importance.

The population in 1820 was 4,000, and it was about the same in 1840. In 1860, it was 8052, and in 1880, 10,036. . . . The growth which set in in the 1850's was much increased during the war, to be swept off during the single night which Sherman occupied the town, by the great fire which destroyed it almost completely. During Reconstruction an unhealthy growth was stimulated by the corrupt politicians who congregated here. This has passed away, and the city has entered a promising period of normal and substantial progress.

141. *The Farmers' Convention of 1886*

THE AFTERMATH OF WAR AND RECONSTRUCTION BROUGHT A DECLINE
IN THE NUMBER OF PLANTATIONS. MANY WERE IN THE HANDS OF
ABSENTEE OWNERS, WHO ACQUIRED THEM AS A RESULT OF FORECLOSURES
OR AT U.S. GOVERNMENT TAX SALES. THERE WAS ALSO A GREAT INCREASE
IN THE NUMBER OF SMALL FARMS, WITH SMALL ACREAGE BEING BROKEN
OFF FROM THE PLANTATIONS AND SOLD TO FORMER TENANTS. OWNERS
AND OPERATORS OF THE SMALL FARMS FELT THAT THE STATE GOVERN-
MENT WAS NOT BEING OPERATED TO THEIR BENEFIT, AND IN THE EARLY
1880S THEY BEGAN TO ORGANIZE THEMSELVES INTO ASSOCIATIONS. AT
FIRST THE ASSOCIATIONS WERE FOR AGRICULTURAL IMPROVEMENTS, BUT
SOON THEY BECAME POLITICALLY INVOLVED. THE RESOLUTIONS ADOPTED
AT A MEETING OF THE STATEWIDE "FARMERS' CONVENTION" OF 1886
GIVE AN INDICATION OF THEIR AIMS AND DEMANDS.

[J.A. Chapman Writes of Farmers and their Activities]

A farmers' convention met in Columbia, April 29, 1886 . . . . The
convention was to a large extent composed of practical farmers. A few
of the professions were represented, and several members of the Legislature were present as delegates. The leader of the convention was B. R.
Tillman.

Resolutions were adopted stating that, in the year 1862, Congress had
appropriated certain land scrip, the proceeds of the sale of which should
be a fund, the interest of which should be used to sustain an agricultural
and mechanical college, for the education of the industrial classes in
each state accepting the donation; that South Carolina had accepted
the fund, but had failed to carry out in good faith the conditions; that
the agricultural interests were languishing, and in need of an institution
to furnish practical and scientific training at less cost than could be
obtained. The Legislature was urged to establish a real agricultural and

J. A. Chapman, *School History of South Carolina* (Newberry: Newberry
Publishing Co., 1893), 214–15.

mechanical college like that of Mississippi or Michigan, and that the control of this college be given to the Board of Agriculture, and that experimental stations be established at such college, to be under the control of its faculty, and that Congress be asked to pass the Hatch Bill appropriating $15,000 annually to each State for this purpose, and that the senators and congressmen from this State be asked to secure its passage by all right means. A protest was also made against this money's being received by the present trustees of the South Carolina College, as, in the opinion of the convention the agricultural annex to the South Carolina College was a failure. The convention also recommended that the Board of Agriculture, instead of being chosen by the Legislature, be elected by a farmers' convention, composed of delegates from each county agricultural society, to meet annually in November at Columbia for the purpose, and that this convention take into consideration all matters of legislation pertaining to agricultural interests, and to make such recommendations to the Legislature about the same as they might deem proper. To obtain funds to sustain the agricultural college, the convention recommended that the privilege tax on the sale of fertilizers be doubled. With this privilege tax and the land script fund it was thought that the college could be supported. It was further recommended that more rigid inspection of fertilizers be made to secure the needed protection to the farmers against fraud; that the Citadel Academy, as a military school be abolished, and that so much of the money now appropriated to its use, as shall be needed, be given to the South Carolina College, so as to make it a first-class college for the training of youth; that the State owes it to her daughters to provide an institution for their liberal and practical education, and that such a school be opened at the Citadel in place of the Military Institute, and that it be liberally supported by the State; that a constitutional convention be called at the earliest practicable day; that the lien law be repealed; that the judicial tenure of office be during good behavior; that taxation can be lessened by abolishing all useless offices; that a large per cent of property is not returned for taxation; that property returned is not assessed at its true value; that the law ought to be so amended as to correct the evils thus complained of, and bring a more full and complete return of personal property, and more correct valuation of all property.

142. *The Earthquake of 1886*

THE HISTORY OF CHARLESTON IS FILLED WITH DISASTERS—FIRES, STORMS, HURRICANES, AND EPIDEMICS—BUT NOTHING STRUCK WITH THE FORCE OF THE GREAT EARTHQUAKE OF 1886. ONE OF AMERICA'S WORST DISASTERS, THE QUAKE ATTRACTED INTERNATIONAL ATTENTION, INCLUDING OFFERS OF FINANCIAL AID FROM MANY COUNTRIES AND A TELEGRAM FROM QUEEN VICTORIA OF ENGLAND. THE LOSS OF LIFE WAS COMPARATIVELY SMALL, BUT THE FINANCIAL LOSS WAS INESTIMABLE. BUILDINGS IN CHARLESTON TODAY BEAR THE IRON RODS WHICH WERE USED TO REPAIR AND SUPPORT THOSE NOT TOTALLY DESTROYED. "OLD-TIMERS" WHO RECALL THE EARTHQUAKE SAY THAT IT WAS ALSO FELT IN COLUMBIA, AS WELL AS IN THE AREAS BETWEEN THE TWO CITIES, AND THAT ENTREPRE- NEURS BOTTLED THE COLORED SANDS LEFT IN FISSURES AND SOLD THEM TO THE PUBLIC. THE FOLLOWING OFFICIAL REPORT WAS PUBLISHED IN THE *Charleston Yearbook*, 1886.

[Official Report on the Charleston Earthquake]

When the bells of St. Michael's Church, in Charleston, chimed the third quarter after nine o'clock on the evening of Tuesday, August 31, 1886, their familiar tones spoke peace and peace alone . . . . There was no whispered warning in the well known sounds, or in any subdued voice of the night, to hint of the fearful calamity so near at hand . . . . It was upon such a scene of calm and silence that the shock of the great earth- quake fell, with the suddenness of a thunderbolt launched from the starlit skies; with the might of ten thousand thunderbolts falling together; with a force so far surpassing all other forces known to men, that no similitude can be truly found for it. . . . Within seven minutes after the last stroke of the chime, and while its echoes seemed yet to linger in listening ears, Charleston was in ruins. And the wreck had been accomplished in one minute and the last of the seven. Millions of dollars worth of prop- erty, the accumulation of nearly two centuries, had been destroyed in the

Charleston Yearbook (1886), 347–59.

time a child would take to crush a frail toy. Every home in the city had been broken or shattered—and beneath the ruins lay the lifeless or bruised and bleeding bodies of men, women and children, who had been stricken down in the midst of such security as may be felt by him who reads these lines at any remote distance of time or space. . . .

After the storm the sunshine brings light and rest and gladness in its train. The earthquake was followed by hours of darkness, relieved only by the glare of burning ruins. The morning sun lit up a scene of devastation such as had never before greeted the eyes of the weary watchers, revealing to them the extent of the danger through which they had passed, and to which they were momentarily exposed anew . . . . The first shock occurred at about nine minutes of ten . . . . The second shock, which was but a faint and brief echo of the first, occurred eight minutes later.

Soon after it had passed, the writer started homeward . . . . St. Michael's steeple towered high and white through the gloom, seemingly uninjured. The Station-house, a massive brick building across the street, had lost its parapet and the roof of the portico, which had fallen in a mass—killing a woman whose body then lay under the wreck. A little farther on, the portico of the Hibernian Hall, a handsome building in the Grecian style, had crashed to the ground carrying down the massive pillars with it. All the way up Meeting Street . . . the ground was piled with debris, from the tops of the walls on either side. In passing the Charleston Hotel . . . the third shock was felt, about ten minutes after the second, and of course caused the greatest alarm . . . . At Marion Square . . . a great crowd had already collected, as even the borders of the extensive plaza could not be reached by the nearest buildings in event of their fall, and the number of fugitives was momentarily increased by new arrivals pouring in from every side. From this crowd, composed of men, women and children of both races, arose incessant cries and lamentations, while over the motley, half-clad assemblage was shed the lurid light of the conflagration that had broken out a hundred yards beyond the square immediately after the first shock, and now enveloped several buildings in flames. In three other quarters of the town, at the same time, similar large fires were observed . . . .

Exaggerated rumors as to the number of the killed spread throughout the city soon after the shock, causing needless pain to many who, though spared the sight of the scenes of suffering and death . . . yet feared for the safety of relatives and friends of whom no tidings could be heard.

The long, anxious watch between midnight and day was not less trying than the shock itself. . . .

The rising sun on Wednesday morning looked on empty and broken homes and on streets encumbered with continuous lines or heaped masses of ruins, amidst which the wearied and shelterless citizens gathered together in little groups, or picked their way from place to place wondering at the extent of the damage inflicted everywhere and with renewed thankfulness in view of the perils escaped. No one was prepared for the scene that was presented by daylight. Every house was in worse condition than had been suspected. Some were utter wrecks, and many others were but little better off. For the first time, the magnitude of the disaster began to be somewhat appreciated. . . .

The number of killed, as shown by the official records, was 27; whites, 7; colored, 20. The number of wounded has never been ascertained. The total number of deaths attributed to injuries, cold and exposure was 83, which is not believed to cover the actual deaths from those causes . . . . The records of the City Assessor's office show that the damages caused by the earthquake were officially estimated, during the following week, at about $5,000,000. . . . A Board of Inspectors . . . reported that they had inspected 6956 buildings; that 90 per cent of the brick buildings were injured more or less, while frame buildings suffered from falling chimneys, cracked plastering, and injured foundations; that . . . the whole number of buildings adjudged unsafe and ordered to be pulled down was 102. Some of these were preserved by wholesale repairs, while others . . . proved to be wrecks on closer examination and were demolished by the owners . . . . The work of reconstruction was continued for months, and at the end of the year, and after, unsightly piles of debris were still encountered in out-of-the-way places where they did not interfere with public or private convenience.

143. *The Shell Manifesto, January 23, 1890*

As the election of 1890 approached, followers of B. R. Tillman determined that they would control the Democratic party in the state and that they would elect their candidate as Governor of South Carolina. The following statement of their position and their program was purportedly written by W. G. Shell, president of the Farmers' Association, but was actually prepared by Tillman.

Mr. W. G. Shell, of Laurens . . . requests the
News and Courier to publish the following address:

To the Democracy of South Carolina: For four years the Democratic party in the State has been deeply agitated, and efforts have been made at the primaries and conventions to secure retrenchments and reforms, and a recognition of the needs and rights of the masses. The first Farmer's Convention met in April, 1886. Another in November of the same year perfected a permanent organization under the name of the "Farmers' Association of South Carolina." This Association representing the reform element in the party, has held two annual sessions since, and at each of these four conventions, largely attended by representative farmers from nearly all of the counties, the demands of the people for greater economy in the Government, greater efficiency in its officials, and a fuller recognition of the necessity for cheaper and more practical education have been pressed upon the attention of our Legislature.

In each of the two last Democratic State Conventions the "Farmers' Movement" has had a large following and we only failed of controlling the Convention of 1888 by a small vote—less than twenty-five—and that, too, in the face of the active opposition of nearly every trained politician in the State. We claim that we have always had a majority of the people on our side, and have only failed by reason of the superior political tactics of our opponents and our lack of organization. . . .

The News and Courier (Charleston, S.C.), Jan. 23, 1890.

The executive committee of the Farmers' Association did not deem it worthwhile to hold any convention last November, but we have watched closely every move of the enemies of economy—the enemies of true Jeffersonian Democracy—and we think the time has come to show the people what it is they need and how to accomplish their desires. We will draw up the indictment against these who have been and are still governing our State, because it is at once the cause of and justification of the course we intend to pursue.

South Carolina has never had a real republican government. Since the days of the "Lords Proprietors" it has been an aristocracy under the forms of democracy, and whenever a champion of the people has attempted to show them their rights and advocated these rights, an aristocratic oligarchy has bought him with an office, or failing in that, turned loose the floodgates of misrepresentation and slander in order to destroy his influence.

The peculiar situation now existing in the State, requiring the united efforts of every true white man to preserve white supremacy and our very civilization even has intensified and tended to make permanent the conditions which existed before the war. Fear of a division among us and consequent return of a Negro rule has kept the people quiet, and they have submitted to many grievances imposed by the ruling faction because they dreaded to risk such a division.

The Farmers' Movement has been hampered and retarded in its work by this condition of the public mind, but we have shown our fealty to race by submitting to the edicts of the party, and we intend, as heretofore, to make our fight inside the party lines, feeling that truth and justice must finally prevail. The results of the agitation thus far are altogether encouraging. Inch by inch and step by step true Democracy—the rule of the people—has won its way. We have carried all the outposts. Only two strongholds remain to be taken, and with the issues fairly made up and plainly put to the people we have no fear of the result. The House of Representatives has been carried twice, and at last held after a desperate struggle.

The advocates of reform and economy are no longer sneered at as "three for a quarter" statesmen. They pass measures of economy which four years ago would have excited only derision, and with the Farmers' Movement to strengthen their backbone have withstood the cajolery, threats, and impotent rage of the old "ring bosses." The Senate is now the main reliance of the enemies of retrenchment and reform, who oppose giving the people their rights. The Senate is the stronghold of

"existing institutions" and the main dependence of those who are antago-
nistic to all progress. As we captured the House we can capture the
Senate; but we must control the Democratic State Convention before we
can hope to make economy popular in Columbia, or be assured of no
more pocket vetoes.

The General Assembly is largely influenced by the idea and policy of
the State officers, and we must elect those before we can say the Farmers'
Movement has accomplished its mission. It is true that we have wrenched
from the aristocratic coterie who were educated at, and sought to
monopolize everything for, the South Carolina College, the right to control the land script and Hatch fund and a part of the privilege tax on
fertilizers for one year, and we have $40,000 with which to commence
building a separate agricultural college, where the sons of poor farmers
can get a practical education at small expense.

But we dare not relax our efforts or rely upon the loud professions of
our opponents as to their willingness now to build and equip this
agricultural school. . . .

All the cry about "existing institutions" which must remain inviolate
shows that the ring—The South Carolina University, Citadel, Agricultural Bureau, Columbia Club, Greenville building ring—intend in the
future, as in the past, to get all they can, and keep all they get. These
pets of the aristocracy and its nurseries are only hoping that the people
will again sink into their accustomed apathy. . . .

To the zeal and extravagance of this aristocratic oligarchy, whose sins
we are pointing out, in promising higher education for every class except
farmers, while it neglects the free schools which are the only chance for
an education to thousands of poor children, whose fathers bore the brunt
in the struggle for our redemption in 1876. To the continued recurrence
of horrible lynchings—which we can but attribute to bad laws and their
inefficient administration. To the impotence of justice to punish criminals
who have money. To the failure to call a constitutional convention that
we may have an organic law framed by South Carolinians for South
Carolinians and suited to our wants, thereby lessening the burdens of
taxation and giving us better government.

Fellow Democrats, do not all these things cry out for a change? Is it
not opportune, when there is no national election, for the common people
who redeemed the State from Radical rule to take charge of it? Can we
afford to leave it longer in the hands of those who, wedded to ante
bellum ideas, but possessing little of ante bellum patriotism and honor,

are running it in the interest of a few families and for the benefit of a
selfish ring of politicians? As real Democrats and white men, those who
here renew our pledge to make the fight inside the Democratic party and
abide the result, we call upon every true Carolinian, of all classes and
callings, to help us purify and reform the Democratic party and give us
a government of the people, by the people and for the people.

144. *The State Liquor Dispensary Law of 1892 and the "Whiskey Rebellion"*

No subject has been discussed more in South Carolina history than liquor and its control. The newly powerful "Tillmanites," and the state as a whole, were sharply divided over the question of liquor manufacture and sales. One faction wanted complete prohibition and another full freedom in making, selling, and consuming alcoholic beverages, or at least with only a small amount of government supervision. As a poor compromise between two extremes, Governor Tillman advocated, and pushed through the legislature, the State Liquor Dispensary Law, which put South Carolina into the liquor business and gave the state control of the manufacture and sale of the beverage. The selections following show that the Dispensary Act was a poor compromise. The first is Chapman's note on the passage of the act; the second is Governor Tillman's defense of it.

[J.A. Chapman]

The passage of the Dispensary Law of 1892:

A very important measure was the passage, at the session of 1892, of an act known as the Dispensary Law. By this law the sale of all liquors of an alcoholic or intoxicating nature, by private persons, is strictly forbidden in the limits of the State. The right to import and sell is reserved to the State, and, for the purpose of selling, dispensaries are established at the incorporated towns, whenever and wherever a majority of the freehold voters may desire it. This law went into operation July 1, 1893. The State has long had control of liquors through the operation of the license laws. A separate box was placed at the polls in the election of 1892 to test the sentiment of the people on the question of prohibition. A majority of those voting in this separate box voted for prohibition, but the total

J. A. Chapman, *School History of South Carolina* (Newberry: Newberry Publishing Co., 1893), 232–33.

vote for prohibition was a minority of the white vote of the State. When the Legislature met, it was found to be impossible, or thought to be inexpedient, to enact a prohibitory law, and the Dispensary Law was passed as a compromise measure.

Governor Tillman defends the Dispensary Law:

1st. The element of personal profit is destroyed, thereby removing the incentive to increase the sales.

2nd. A pure article is guaranteed, as it is subject to chemical analysis.

3rd. Treating is stopped, as the bottles are not opened on the premises.

4th. The consumer obtains honest measure of standard strength.

5th. Liquor is sold only in the day time—this under a regulation of the Board, and not under the law.

6th. The concomitants of ice, sugar, lemons, etc., being removed, there is not the same inclination to drink remaining; and the closing of the saloons, especially at night, and the prohibition of the sale of liquor by the drink destroy the enticements and seductions which have caused so many men and boys to be led astray and enter on the downward course.

7th. Liquor is sold only for cash, and there is no longer "chalking up" for daily drinks against pay-day. The working man buys his bottle of whiskey Saturday night and carries the rest of his wages home.

8th. Gambling dens, pool rooms, and lewd houses, which have hitherto been run almost invariably in connection with the saloons, which were thus a stimulus to vice, separated from the sale of liquor, have had their patronage reduced to a minimum, and there must necessarily be a decrease of crime.

9th. The local whiskey rings, which have been the curse of every municipality in the State, and have always controlled municipal elections, have been torn up root and branch, and the influence of the barkeeper as a political manipulator is absolutely destroyed. The police, removed from the control of these debauching elements, will enforce the law against evil doing with more vigor, and a higher tone and greater purity in governmental affairs must result.

Quoted in John E. Eubanks, *Ben Tillman's Baby* (Augusta, Ga.: n.p., 1950), 79–80. Reprinted by permission of J. Evans Eubanks

145. *The Constitution of 1895*

THE CROWNING ACHIEVEMENT OF THE "TILLMANITES" WAS THE ADOP-
TION OF THE CONSTITUTION OF 1895. THE CONSTITUTION OF 1868, PASSED
UNDER THE RECONSTRUCTION GOVERNMENT, HAD LONG DISSATISFIED, BUT
FEAR OF FEDERAL ACTION, AND FACTIONALISM IN STATE POLITICS, PRE-
VENTED AN EARLIER CHANGE. THE CONSTITUTION OF 1895 REMOVED THE
NEGRO FROM STATE POLITICS AND FROM SOCIAL STATUS, BUT IT EMBODIED
PROGRESSIVE FEATURES. THE FIRST SELECTION GIVES A CONTEMPORARY
DISCUSSION OF THE CONVENTION AND ITS WORK. THE SECOND CONTAINS
SOME EXCERPTS FROM THE CONSTITUTION, BRINGING OUT THE MAJOR
DIFFERENCES BETWEEN IT AND THE 1868 CONSTITUTION. THE THIRD IS A
DEFENSE OF THE CONVENTION.

[Historian D. D. Wallace on the convention of 1895]

There were two subjects that occupied the Convention of 1895, either
of which should give national interest to its proceedings. The first of these
was the suffrage question; the second was the State control of the liquor
traffic. Since 1868, the people of South Carolina had been living under
a constitution formed in that year by the Republicans and modeled after
the constitution of New York. This constitution, known as "The Radical
Rag," proved a very satisfactory instrument of government, having required amendment in only a few particulars. But for the Tillman movement in 1890 and that ever present factor in Southern life, the Negro,
South Carolina would for years have required no new organic law. Intel-
ligently to comprehend the late Convention we must begin with 1876,
when the united white people overthrew the Negro and carpetbag government that had for eight years misgoverned, robbed, and disgraced the
State. From this year dates the present political epoch in South Carolina,
namely, the epoch of white unity in the face of a two-thirds Negro
majority in population. An important era in South Carolina politics,

D. D. Wallace, "The South Carolina Constitutional Convention of 1895,"
Sewanee Review, IV (1895–1896), 348–60.

though not of a kind or importance to be called an epoch, was instituted in 1890 by the consummation of what had until then been known as the Farmers' Movement, but which has since under the leadership of B. R. Tillman borne that other name so much better suited to political purposes, "Reform." The gist of "Reform" was the cry that the government had been monopolized by a class called by demagogues and ignorant outsiders "The Bourbons" . . . and that the common people should now take the administration into their own hands. The cry was to abrogate government by rings and conventions and assert government by the people through primaries, etc. . . .

The fear of Negro domination having grown less with time, the arraying of the farmers against other classes became a possibility, under constant protestations that any division among the white people was deprecated. The Reformers obtained complete control of the Democratic machinery at a blow in 1890, and in four years and less were treating their political opponents in the Democracy like a different party, as the Conservatives were in turn treating them. The Conservatives have an idea that they are the only people in South Carolina who are in any wise fit to rule, and the supremacy of the Tillmanites is a thorn in the flesh to them. . . . To them, the Tillmanite is not a fellow citizen, a victorious political opponent; he is a usurper. . . . Things had come to such a pass in 1892 that some of the Conservatives hinted that it might be a service to the State to get the Negroes to vote with them and so defeat the Tillmanites. This was only a hint, but in 1894 many thought seriously of it . . . . Therefore it was necessary [for the Tillmanites] to take time by the forelock, and disfranchise the Negro before the next election. Accordingly we have the South Carolina Constitutional Convention of 1895, which was more the outcome of sociological questions than of purely political ones.

In its membership the Convention was composed of white Democrats, excepting six Negro Republicans from the low country. By parties, they stood, Tillmanites or Reformers, 111; Anti-Tillmanites, or Conservatives, 43; Republicans, 6. . . . In their speeches on the suffrage several of the Negro delegates well made good the claim of their race to being natural orators. But they were speaking in vain; the Negro's political record from 1868 to 1876 would rise overwhelmingly like a whole army of Banquo's ghosts and would not at all down. Yet the Negro delegates were treated as respectfully and as kindly as they would allow. . . . The Convention met September 10, and after an eleven days', a three days', and a six days' recess, adjourned on December 4. Although many politicians were among them, it was not a body of politicians . . . . The Convention seemed to be a body of patriots, which by the dignity, fairness, and excellence of its deliberations commanded the respect of every South Carolinian.

The motive for calling the Convention was, as we have seen, to effect such a revision of the suffrage laws as would make any appeal to the Negro or any chance of Negro domination an impossibility. The interest of South Carolinians centred on this and it was this that chiefly attracted outside attention. "The Mississippi plan or something better" was all that was in sight or ever had any chance of success. The essence of this plan as originated in the present constitution of Mississippi is that the registration officer is allowed to refuse registration to illiterate voters whom he judges unable to understand any clause of the constitution he may read to them, and to accord the right to those whom he judges able to understand. The object is of course to disfranchise the ignorant Negro, while retaining the illiterate white vote, and in this the scheme has not failed. Such in general was the plan which the South Carolina Convention of 1895 adopted; but it also introduced important and palliating modifications. In the first place, the understanding clause by which the illiterate voter is placed at the discretion of the registration officer to be disfranchised if the officer chooses, for race or party reasons, presents a perpetual opportunity for fraud; whereas in the South Carolina plan this understanding clause is to remain in effect for only two years. The illiterate are entitled to vote regardless of their educational status if they can prove that they have paid taxes on three hundred dollars worth of property. A roll of the voters registered before January 1, 1898, is to be kept, and all whose names are on it are entitled to vote for the rest of their lives without more ado. It is presumed that any white man will be able to "understand" the clauses read to him, so that the promise not to disfranchise any white man will be kept, and, as was earnestly urged in the debate, the suffrage is insured to every illiterate Confederate soldier. After January 1, 1898, the understanding clause is done away with, and to vote one must be able to read and write or present proof of having paid taxes on three hundred dollars worth of property. Such is the South Carolina suffrage law, under which it is hoped to put Negro control of the State beyond possibility and still preserve the suffrage for the illiterate whites of the present generation . . . .

Passing now to the important subject of education, we find that the Convention accepted the principle that common schools are the true basis of the State's educational system and that the State owes its aid to the great masses of the people who desire to obtain primary education rather than to those desiring college education, who are presumably better able to help themselves. . . . No mixing of races is allowed in any schools. . . . A motion to have the State furnish free books to the common school scholars met with no favor . . . .

In inserting in the Constitution the provision that the Legislature shall never allow any municipality, county or township to license the sale of liquor, a great safeguard was secured for the peace of the community and the happiness of the home. State control of everything connected with the traffic is inalienably retained, together with the present regulations prohibiting selling by drinks or after dark . . . .

It seems to be the general opinion of the people that they have a good Constitution. Opportunity for ratification at the polls could not be given for fear of a grand rally of the Negroes to save their rights of suffrage. But the white people seem satisfied, and the political apathy of the Negroes is undisturbed. The bitterest political enemies have worked hand in hand for a common object; the fiercest opposition papers have had to change from jibes to commendations . . . . If these things are not miraculous, they are at least marvellous, and South Carolina is the better for them.

[The provisions of the Constitution of 1895
referring to suffrage and the Negro]

Article II, Section 3: Every male citizen of this State and of the United States twenty-one years of age and upwards, not laboring under the disabilities named in this Constitution and possessing the qualification required by it, shall be an elector.

The qualifications for suffrage shall be as follows:

Section 4: Residence in the State for two years, in the county for one year, in the polling precinct in which the elector offers to vote for four months . . . .

Registration, which shall provide for the enrollment of every elector once in ten years, and also an enrollment during each and every year of every elector not previously registered under the provisions of this Article.

Constitution . . . of the State of South Carolina, 1895, pp. 39–41, 49, 116.

Up to January 1st, 1898, all male persons of voting age applying for registration who can read any section in this Constitution submitted to them by the registration, or understand and explain it when read to them by the registration officer, shall be entitled to register and become electors. A separate record of all persons registered before January 1st, 1898, sworn to by the registration officer, shall be filed [,] one copy with the Clerk of Court and one in the office of the Secretary of State, on or before February 1st, 1898, and such persons shall remain during life qualified electors unless disqualified by the other provisions of this Article. The certificate of the Clerk of Court or Secretary of State shall be sufficient evidence to establish the right of said citizens to any subsequent registration and the franchise under the limitations herein imposed.

Any person who shall apply for registration after January 1st, 1898, if otherwise qualified, shall be registered: Provided, that he can both read and write any Section of this Constitution submitted to him by the registration officer, or can show that he owns, and has paid all taxes collectible during the previous year on, property assessed at three hundred dollars ($300) or more.

Managers of election shall require of every elector offering to vote at any election, before allowing him to vote, proof of the payment thirty days before any election of any poll tax then due and payable . . . .

Section 6: The following persons are disqualified from being registered or voting: First. Persons convicted of burglary, arson, obtaining goods or money under false pretenses, perjury, forgery, robbery, bribery, adultery, bigamy, wife-beating, house-breaking, receiving stolen-goods, breach of trust with fraudulent intent, fornication, sodomy, incest, assault with intent to ravish, miscegenation, larceny, or crime against the election laws: Provided, that the pardon of the Governor shall remove such disqualifications. Second. Persons who are idiots, insane, paupers supported at the public expense, and persons confined in any public prison. . . .

Article III, Section 33: The marriage of a white person with a Negro or mulatto, or person who shall have one-eighth or more of Negro blood, shall be unlawful and void. . . .

Article XI, Section 7: Separate schools shall be provided for children of the white and colored races, and no child of either race shall ever be permitted to attend a school provided for children of the other race. . . .

[George D. Tillman on the Constitutional Convention of 1895]

Mr. President, we can all hope a great deal from the Constitution we have adopted. It is not such an instrument as we would have made if we had been a free people. We are not a free people. We have not been since the war. I fear it will be some time before we can call ourselves free. I have had that fact very painfully impressed upon me for several years. If we were free, instead of having Negro suffrage, we would have Negro slaves. Instead of having the United States government, we would have the Confederate States government. Instead of paying $3,000,000 pension tribute, we would be receiving it. Instead of having many things that we have, we would have other and better things. But to the extent that we are permitted to govern ourselves and pay pension tribute to our conquerors, we have framed as good an organic law, take it as a whole, as the wisdom and patriotism of the State could have desired. . . .

The Republicans realize that the Negro question is a secondary question now . . . . Besides, the Republicans, when they choose to exercise it, without passing any laws, can exercise great power over the South—admitting or excluding her Representatives or Senators. They will be put to the test whether they will be willing to shut the doors of Congress to the South Carolina Representatives in the present Congress . . . . They are divided themselves on the silver question. The East is not solid for silver. The West has a large majority of silver, and today the only two principles left to the Democratic Party in South Carolina are enmity to Cleveland and friendship to free silver, and the silver Senators will not permit any legislation on the Negro question, and the Courts have recently shown that they are not eager to punish South Carolina. So we can reasonably hope to have some peace and quiet for a few years at least. . . .

It must be a source of great gratification to every member here and to their constituents at home to see with what unanimity, with what courteousness, and yet with what independence of action their representatives in this body have made the Constitution which we have just ratified. It is a rainbow of hope that the State may hereafter be united, as in the past, as one man. . . . I have an abiding faith in the Anglo-Saxon race, as there never has been a considerable number of them together anywhere that they did not dominate any race with which they came in contact; and whatever may happen, I have faith that they will rule.

Journal of the Constitutional Convention of the State of South Carolina, 1895, pp. 731–34.

146. *Agriculture*

THE PERIOD FROM 1880 TO 1920 SAW A DECLINE IN THE PRODUCTION
OF RICE, A LARGE INCREASE IN TOBACCO GROWING, AND THE CONTINUED
DOMINANCE OF COTTON. SMALLER FARMS, SHARE CROPPING, TENANT
FARMING, AND THE EXTENSIVE USE OF FERTILIZERS WERE OTHER DEVEL-
OPMENTS, ALONG WITH SOME MINOR IMPROVEMENTS IN STOCK RAISING
AND TRUCK FARMING. SOUTH CAROLINA REMAINED A PREDOMINANTLY
AGRICULTURAL STATE UNTIL WELL AFTER THE TWENTIETH CENTURY HAD
BEGUN. THE *South Carolina Handbook* INDICATES THE AGRICULTURAL
PROGRESS IN THE STATE TO THAT DATE.

[Department of Agriculture report]

Agriculture has not developed with the phenomenal rapidity of the
cotton manufacturing industry, but in the last few years there has been a
general and substantial revival of interest, and the trucking branch of the
industry has developed with remarkable speed. The immediate future is
full of promise. . . .

The tendency has been for two decades for the farmer's son to leave
the farm for the city, and for the farmer to turn his farm over to Negro
renters, tenants and share croppers. This has gone on until the agricultural industry, particularly during the period of rapid development of
cotton manufacturing, has been left almost entirely to the inferior race
. . . . The people in the cities became so numerous and the people on
the farms so few that there was created a great demand for vegetable,
fruit, poultry, dairy and other diversified agricultural products at excellent prices, and soon some were returning to the farms. . . .

In the last decade or so, very much more attention has been paid in
South Carolina to agricultural education than for many years preceding.
The establishment of Clemson College . . . has stimulated the young
men of the State engaging in agriculture to the employment of better

Handbook of South Carolina: Resources, Institutions and Industries of the State,
Dept. of Agriculture (Columbia: The State Company, 1907; rev. ed., 1908),
236–51, 290, 305, 330, 340.

methods looking to larger yields per acre . . . . The College in addition to the education of the young men in scientific agriculture, has been conducting State and county farmers' institutes, and an institute train has been sent on several occasions on a tour over the State, carrying the exhibit of agricultural products and a corps of scientists giving lectures to such farmers as come to the school on wheels . . . . During the summer vacation from 1000 to 1500 farmers assemble annually at the College for the study of agricultural and industrial problems . . . . The State also maintains a State college for Negroes, in which the Negro youth are trained in practical agriculture, carpentering, and such callings.

It is particularly noteworthy that the most conspicuous increases in agricultural lines have been in live stock, horses, mules, hogs, etc., while most material increases are shown in the matter of the growing of cereal crops. . . .

In 1850 the average sized farm was 541 acres; in the succeeding decade it dropped to 488; in 1870 it had come down to 233; and in 1880 to 143. It is now less than 90 acres, and the tendency is to still smaller and more diversified and better cultivated farms. . . . In South Carolina cotton continues the ranking crop, both in acreage and value; the 1907 acreage being 2,463,000, which, if the average price of 10 cents is obtained, will bring the farmers in over $56,500,000. Corn comes second, with a value of product of about $18,000,000. Then come wheat and hay in the order named. . . .

The value of farm products in South Carolina, which was nearly $42,000,000 in 1870, fell greatly during the period of Reconstruction. In 1890 the figures went back to $51,337,985, and in 1900, $68,266,912. In 1905 the value was $76,721,786, an increase of 10.8 percent, and in 1906 the value was about $83,000,000, according to figures available.

The farmers of the State are spending approximately $5,000,000 a year for fertilizers, and considerably over $6,000,000 for labor. At last . . . the people of the State are paying more attention to the raising of home supplies, and saving thousands upon thousands of dollars they have been since the war spending for such products with Western producers, as well as for freight. . . .

The development of the trucking industry in South Carolina has been one of the most conspicuous of all the developments in the State in recent years. This industry has heretofore been confined to practically five counties—Charleston, Colleton, Beaufort, Horry and Berkeley. In 1889 the acreage in truck in these counties amounted to only 2103; in 1900 . . . to 4928.

While rice growing is not so general today, it is still more or less profitable and it still commands the highest price for this article in the markets of the world. The competition that has sprung up in the Southwest, however, since the Civil War, greatly reducing the cost of production of rice, has injured the industry in this State, and at this time special efforts are being made by the State Department of Agriculture to find some means of reducing the cost of production of Carolina rice on the coast, with a view to the re-establishment of the industry . . . . In 1900 there were 77,657 acres planted in rice in the State, while in 1906 there were only 19,036 acres in rice. . . .

The tenth United States census, published in 1880, contains no mention of South Carolina as a tobacco-growing state. This was not a quarter of a century ago, and the tobacco crop of this State in 1904 aggregated about 26,000,000 pounds . . . . In . . . 1890, South Carolina ranked 19th in the procession of tobacco-growing states, while . . . ten years later South Carolina ranked 9th out of 42 tobacco-growing states . . . . The tobacco counties are Florence, Darlington, Williamsburg and Marion, with a little in Horry and Clarendon. . . .

South Carolina is the fourth largest sweet potato producing State in the Union . . . . Sweet potatoes are grown on some 80,000 farms in the State and some 50,000 acres are devoted to this crop. The annual yield is about $3\frac{1}{2}$ million bushels. . . .

South Carolina's total rural population is 1,169,060 (1900), and of this, 697,963 persons are Negroes—a percentage of 59.7. The percentage of the Negro population living in the country districts is 89.2 . . . . Negroes were operating—that is as owners, renters, tenants or croppers—in 1900, 85,361 farms in the State, representing an acreage of 3,791,510, with 60 per cent of it improved . . . . Of this number of farms, 15,503 were operated by their owners, and 66,231 by tenants. The vast majority of these farms were between 10 and 50 acres. The vast majority showed value of product between $50 and $500 per annum. Nearly 70,000 of these farms were devoted almost exclusively to cotton. . . . Under the system that has grown up between the Civil War and 1900, 55 per cent of the farms are being operated by Negroes. . . . In 1900 there were 155,355 farms in the State, of which 60,471 were operated by owners, 57,046 by cash tenants, and 37,838 by share tenants.

147. Education

The half-century following the war saw the foundation laid for the present-day educational system of the state. The school laws of 1868 were strengthened; the High School Act of 1907 placed secondary education on a state-supported basis; and several public and private colleges were founded to round out a system of higher education. Thomas G. Clemson, son-in-law of John C. Calhoun, was instrumental in the founding of Clemson University; excerpts from his will are given here. Following are accounts of the founding of Winthrop College and the State Negro College at Orangeburg and a discussion of the High School Act of 1907.

The Will of Thomas G. Clemson, November 6, 1886:

Feeling a great sympathy for the farmers of this State, and the difficulties with which they have had to contend in their efforts to establish the business of agriculture upon a prosperous basis, and believing that there can be no permanent improvement in agriculture without a knowledge of those sciences which pertain particularly thereto, I have determined to devote the bulk of my property to the establishment of an agricultural college upon the Fort Hill place.

This institution, I desire, to be under the management and control of a board of trustees, a part of whom are hereinafter appointed, and to be modeled after the Agricultural College of Mississippi as far as practicable.

My purpose is to establish an agricultural college which will afford useful information to the farmers and mechanics, therefore it should afford thorough instruction in agriculture and the natural sciences connected therewith—it should combine, if practicable, physical and intellectual education, and should be a high seminary of learning in which the

A. G. Holmes, *Thomas Green Clemson* (Richmond: Garrett and Massie, Inc., 1937), 193–97. Copyright, 1937, By Garrett & Massie, Inc., Richmond, Va. Reprinted by permission of Garrett and Massie, Inc.

graduate of the common schools can commence, pursue and finish the course of studies terminating in thorough theoretic and practical instruction in those sciences and arts which bear directly upon agriculture, but I desire to state plainly that I wish the trustees of said institution to have full authority and power to regulate all matters pertaining to said institution—to fix the course of studies, to make rules for the government of the same, and to change them, as in their judgment, experience may prove necessary, but to always bear in mind that the benefits therein sought to be bestowed are intended to benefit agricultural and mechanical industries. I trust that I do not exaggerate the importance of such an institution for developing the material resources of the State by affording to its youth the advantages of scientific culture, and that I do not overrate the intelligence of the legislature of South Carolina, ever distinguished for liberality, in assuming that such appropriations will be made as will be necessary to supplement the fund resulting from the bequest herein made.

Item I. I therefore give and devise to my executor, hereinafter named, the aforesaid Fort Hill place, where I now reside, formerly the home of my father in law, John C. Calhoun, consisting of eight hundred and fourteen acres, more or less, in trust, that whenever the State of South Carolina may accept said property as a donation from me, for the purpose of thereupon founding an agricultural college in accordance with the views I have hereinbefore expressed, (of which the Chief Justice of South Carolina shall be the judge), then my executor shall execute a deed of the said property to the said State, and turn over to the same all property hereinafter given as an endowment of said institution to be held as such by the said State so long as it, in good faith, devotes said property to the purposes of the donation; provided, however, that this acceptance by the State shall be signified and a practical carrying-out be commenced within three years from the date of the probate of this will. During this term of three years or as much thereof as may elapse before the acceptance or refusal of this donation, my executor shall invest the net produce of the land and other property; such invested fund awaiting the action of the Legislature, and to form a part of the endowment of the college or school hereinafter provided for, should the donation not be accepted by the State . . . .

The founding of Winthrop College:

For nearly one hundred years the State of South Carolina had made liberal provision for the higher education of her sons. But up to 1891 her daughters were neglected, except that a small annual appropriation was made by the Legislature for the support of one pupil from each county in the Winthrop Training School for Teachers at Columbia. This school was organized November 15, 1886, under the auspices of the Board of City School Commissioners of Columbia.

D. B. Johnson, LL.D., the superintendent of the city schools, was largely instrumental in the establishment of this school. For many years an annual appropriation was made by the Peabody Board, which gave substantial aid to this most laudable enterprise.

The name Winthrop was given in honor of Hon. Robert C. Winthrop, who as President of the Board of Trustees of the Peabody Educational Fund, has done so much for the cause of education in the South. To Mr. Winthrop and Hon. J. L. M. Curry, the general agent of this fund, is due much of the success of this school. But to no man, however, is more credit and honor due than to Dr. D. B. Johnson, who has thrown his whole soul and untiring energy into the cause. In 1890 Gov. Benjamin R. Tillman, in his inaugural address, recommended the appointment of a commission to ascertain and report upon the advisability of establishing a normal and industrial school for women by the State. Upon a favorable report by the commission, composed of Prof. D. B. Johnson, Miss Mary Yeargin and Miss Hannah Hemphill, the Act incorporating "The Winthrop Normal and Industrial College of South Carolina for the Education of White Girls" was passed December, 1891. The Board of Trustees located the College at Rock Hill, S.C., and began the erection of suitable buildings in 1892, which were completed and occupied in 1894. From the very beginning this College took deep root in the hearts of the people, meeting with the unanimous approval of the men and women of all classes, conditions and ideas, without regard to differences in politics or religion. The city of Rock Hill was most generous in contributing to secure this College, giving $60,000 in money and other property valued at $40,000–$100,000 in all.

Handbook of South Carolina: Resources, Institutions and Industries of The State, Dept. of Agriculture (Columbia: The State Company, 1907; rev. ed., 1908), 184–85.

This school has grown from a school of two teachers, nineteen pupils, and one room, in 1886, to a great school of forty-seven officers and teachers, five hundred students, and a plant costing $300,000 in 1906. It is now a State institution and receives an annual appropriation for its expenses. The State maintains one hundred and twenty-four scholarships in it, worth each $100 and free tuition, leaving only four dollars to be raised by the beneficiary for college expenses for the entire session of nine months. Winthrop College is emphasizing teacher-training and industrial work in accordance with its charter.

The founding of the State Negro College:

At the session of the Legislature of South Carolina for 1896, the Colored Normal, Industrial, Agricultural and Mechanical College was established for the education of the Negro youth of this State. From 1869 to 1896 the College of Agriculture and Mechanics' Institute, for colored students, had been conducted in connection with Claflin College, but supported by the State.

It was decided to locate this institution at Orangeburg, because: (1) The State owned a tract of land unsurpassed in strength of productiveness and fertility, especially adapted to mixed husbandry and rotation of crops. (2) There was already here an industrial plant which could not be duplicated at the same cost, well established and thoroughly equipped for instruction in all the mechanical and industrial arts. (3) There was also a herd of registered dairy cattle, the equal of any in the State. (4) Orangeburg is a healthful locality, situated in the geographical center of the Black Belt of South Carolina, and a railroad center.

Bradham Hall, an imposing structure, three and one-half stories high, 62 by 126 feet, containing dormitories and class rooms, in convenience of arrangement, symmetry, beauty and comfort, is the equal of any building for like purposes in the South. The new dining hall, 36 by 75, is the handsomest dining room owned by any college in the State. There is also a new college building, Morrill Hall, recently completed, 90 by 154 feet,

Handbook of South Carolina: Resources, Institutions and Industries of the State, Dept. of Agriculture (Columbia: The State Company, 1907; rev. ed., 1908), 217–18.

containing chapel, library, reading room, laboratory, two literary auditories, gymnasium, commercial departments, class rooms, and fifty sleeping rooms, heated by steam, with water works on each floor. The College campus consists of about eight acres, with the main and industrial buildings occupying a beautiful, elevated site. A farm of 130 acres is adjacent to the campus, upon which have been erected dairy, barn and stables.

The Industrial Hall, just erected, is a large two-story building, made of brick, every one of which was laid by student labor. It is to be devoted entirely to the industrial arts, and is the equal of any building of a like nature anywhere. Its dimensions are 120 by 90 feet, and it contains the following departments: Woodworking, Ironworking, Mechanical and Architectural Drawing, Spinning Room, Tailor Shop, Shoe Making, Harness Making, Painting, and Masonry. In addition, there are in operation College Normal, Normal and Preparatory, Model School, Musical, Art, Industrial, Mechanical, Trained Nursing, Agricultural, Engineering, and Military Departments.

The Normal Course gives the graduate the Degree of Licentiate of Instruction upon its completion, and also the privilege of teaching in the public schools of the State without examination. It is the best industrial plant for Negro education south of Hampton Institute. The State intends to bring the best education easily within the reach of colored people of limited means. The school stands for the best education of the hand, head and heart of the Negro race.

The High School Act of 1907:

The War . . . and the consequent demoralization and poverty of the people swept out of existence the private academies so long the pride of the state as preparatory schools. It took a number of years for the public schools to become either popular or efficient. The revenue for the support of the common schools was inadequate, but by 1880 a few cities and towns were levying a special supplementary school tax. Now nearly every town of five hundred population is levying this supplementary tax. The

Handbook of South Carolina: Resources, Institutions and Industries of the State, Dept. of Agriculture (Columbia: The State Company, 1907; rev. ed., 1908), 222–23.

larger towns added high school grades to their public schools, and for nearly twenty years these higher grades have furnished the greater part of the high school facilities in the State. In many places a tuition fee has been charged in the high school department in order to maintain it. In most instances these high schools are not adequately equipped as to teaching force or apparatus, consequently their courses of study are short and narrow. In the villages and rural communities the high school work has been of a very irregular and uncertain character. One year a school may offer fairly good high school training; the next year, owing to a change of teachers, the same school may offer no real high school work.

Through the efforts of the State Board of Education, the Association of City Superintendents, the State Teachers' Association, and a few earnest legislators, a high school law was enacted in February, 1907. This law looks toward the establishment of secondary schools under State aid, and State supervision. At present the State appropriation is small— $50,000 annually, but it is to be used to supplement and encourage local effort. No high school can receive from the State more than fifty per cent of its own income, nor can it receive more than $1200 aid. Each high school receiving State aid must employ not fewer than two teachers, nor have fewer than twenty-five high school pupils. The courses of study and the details of management are left to the local high school boards; only the inspection and classification of these schools are given to the State Board of Education.

Under this law a county, a township, or aggregation of townships, an aggregation of school districts, or an incorporated town of not more than one thousand inhabitants can establish a high school and receive State aid. Since this is the first direct attempt on the part of the State to foster secondary schools, a defective law was to be expected. However, the defects are within easy remedy.

Fifty-eight high schools are in operation under this Act at this time, December 1, 1907. Nearly all these schools will be established either by several rural school districts combining to form a high school district, and levying a high school tax, or by the union of a larger town with some adjoining rural districts.

The high school movement means the enlarging of high schools already in operation, by lengthening and broadening the courses of study; the establishing of schools where none exist; the employment of more competent teachers; the improvement of the common schools; the raising of college entrance requirements and college standards; and the bettering of agricultural and other industrial conditions.

148. *Industry*

AFTER 1880, THE PIEDMONT AREA OF THE STATE WAS THE SCENE OF
CONSIDERABLE ACTIVITY IN TEXTILE MANUFACTURING, ALTHOUGH OTHER
TYPES OF INDUSTRY WERE STILL LACKING. THE LOWER PART OF THE
STATE, OUTSIDE OF CHARLESTON, HAD ALMOST NO INDUSTRY. THE FOL-
LOWING INCLUDE A BRIEF SKETCH OF THE SHORT-LIVED PHOSPHATE
INDUSTRY, A SUMMARY OF THE TEXTILE INDUSTRY UP TO 1907, AND
ANOTHER THAT BRINGS THE STORY UP TO 1919.

[F.B. Van Horn]

Until 1867 all phosphatic material for fertilizer manufacture was
imported, but the discovery in that year of phosphate rock near Charleston marked the great beginning of the fertilizer industry in the United
States. The Charleston Mining and Manufacturing Company, backed by
northern capital, was organized for the exploitation of the South Carolina phosphate rock. The formation of this company was directly due to
the efforts of Professor Francis Holmes and Dr. N. A. Pratt, who had
been among the first to recognize fully the value of the phosphate
deposits around Charleston. Professor Holmes was President, and R.
Pratt, chemist and superintendent of the company. From this time the
industry developed rapidly, and in 1870 there were thirteen companies in
South Carolina engaged in mining the rock and manufacturing it into
fertilizers.

There are two classes of phosphate rock in South Carolina, classified
according to their mode of occurrence as land rock and river rock. The
land rock consists of so-called pebble rock, which is in fact a solid mass
from which the calcium carbonate has been leached out and partly
replaced by phosphate; thus cavities are left which connect and penetrate
through the rock, giving it the appearance of being made up of separate

J. A. C. Chandler et al., eds., *The South in the Building of the Nation,* 13 vols.
(Richmond: The Southern Historical Publication Society, 1909–1913), VI,
213–14.

pebbles. The river rock is so called because it is mined from the river channels. It consists essentially of water-rounded fragments of the land rock. The land rock runs about 58 per cent tricalcium phosphate and the river rock about 55 per cent.

Until 1888, South Carolina enjoyed a monopoly of the phosphate industry of the United States. In that year Florida came forward as a phosphate producer, and in 1894 its production surpassed that of South Carolina. . . . In 1892 phosphate was discovered in Tennessee, and in 1899 this state went ahead of South Carolina in production . . . . Between 1867 and 1908, South Carolina produced 12,138,454 long tons of phosphate, valued at $54,211,153, but in recent years the competition from other states has caused the production in South Carolina to steadily decrease . . . .

The growth of the textile industry, 1870–1907:

It was not . . . until about 1884–1885 that the cotton mill industry of the State began its remarkable development. The next census (1890) was a surprising revelation, showing that in ten years the number of mills had more than doubled, the number of spindles more than quadrupled, and that the amount of cotton consumed was very little short of four times as great. The progress of the industry since 1890 is even more wonderful, the number of mills having increased from 34 to 138, the number of spindles from 332,784 to 2,479,521, or 645%, and the number of bales consumed from 133,342 to 587,126, or 340%. The per cent of the State's crop consumed increased from 17.8 in 1890 to 63.4 in 1902–1903.

More substantial and real, but without such large percentages of increase, has been the development for the half-decade between 1900 and 1905—109.7% in capital against 252.4% for the period between 1890 and 1900, and 301.3% for the decade between 1880 and 1890, with proportionate increase in the number of wage-earners, cost of materials used and value of products . . . . The number of establishments increased from 80 in 1900 to 127 in 1905, while the capital increased $43,078,483,

Handbook of South Carolina: Resources, Institutions and Industries of the State, Dept. of Agriculture (Columbia: The State Company, 1907; rev. ed., 1908), 435–36.

or 109.7%; the number of wage-earners 7070 or 23.4%; the wages paid, $2,634,849 or 52%; and the value of the products, $19,713,725, or 66.3%. The number of producing spindles was 1,431,349 in 1900 and 2,864,092 in 1905, an increase of slightly more than 100%. The number of looms also showed a large gain, the increase being from 42,663 to 72,702, or 70.4% . . . . In the manufacture of cotton in the United States, measured by value of products and number of producing spindles, South Carolina held second rank at the census of 1905. . . .

The capital invested, which amounted to $1,337,000 in 1870, was $82,337,429 in 1905. During this period of thirty-five years the number of wage earners increased from 1123 to 37,271 and the value of the products from $1,529,937 to $49,437,644 . . . . In 1870 the cotton mills were operated entirely by water power, a total of 955 horse power being reported at that census, while at the census of 1905 a total of 156,117 horse power was reported, composed of steam, 96,842; electric, 29,707; and water, 29,568 . . . . In 1900 there were 8110 children under sixteen years of age working in the cotton mill plants . . . , while in 1907, owing in part to the operation of the child labor law, and in part to the general desire of manufacturers not to employ children when possible, the number had increased to 8121, only eleven more than the small number of mills had employed seven years before.

[Yates Snowden]

The state's industry in 1919:

South Carolina was upon a firm basis industrially in 1919. There was no phenomenal bulge in the production or prices, but a steady increase and a very considerable increase in wages. When we consider what a truly wonder year 1918 was, we may well be grateful that there was no recession in 1919. But, even after the armistice, even during the drab days when industry the world over was paralyzed by strikes and labor agitations, everything moved smoothly forward in South Carolina. . . .

Yates Snowden, ed., *History of South Carolina,* 5 vols. (Chicago: The Lewis Publishing Co., 1920), II, 1178–79, compiled from Annual Report of the State Department of Agriculture, Commerce and Industries, for 1919.

While traditionally and fundamentally an agricultural State, South Carolina has the unique distinction of being first in the South and second in the Union in the extent of textile manufacturing industry. The relative importance of this industry to the life of the State is observed when I say that the value of the product of the textiles is, in round numbers, $210,-000,000, while the total value of all manufactured products, including textiles, is but $355,200,000. There are 81,800 persons employed in industry in this State, while in textiles alone there are 51,400.

In the late months of 1914 it seemed that the textile industry in this State, as well as the crushing of cotton seed, the manufacture of lumber and the making of commercial fertilizers, was adrift on a sea of chaos. None of us likes to look back upon those times of disorder and discouragement, but for the sake of comparison it is permitted that we do, to realize how much better is the situation of the State today with regard to the future. There is now no feeling of helplessness, and the people of South Carolina have their destiny in their hands. . . .

The first effect of the European war upon our finances, our agriculture and our industries was bad, as was to be expected . . . . The warring countries were clamoring for the constituent elements necessary for the conduct and prolongation of the war, and it appeared that the textile industry might receive a blow which would set it back half a century. But the industry was saved. After months of anxiety and careful business management the textile manufacturers have come through and at last have come into the realization of a prosperity long merited and long deferred. The paralysis of our industries was temporary and our great system has begun to function in a tremendous manner and will continue to do so. . . .

In 1919, $201,237,320 was invested in industry in South Carolina to produce goods to the value of $355,181,322, while $58,519,003 was paid as wages to 81,807 employees. The amount of horsepower consumed, steam, water and electric, was 197,087, to operate 4,947,644 spindles and 115,130 looms, and consume 837,152 bales of cotton in the textile industry alone. The average number of working days in all industry was 252, and in the textile industry, 296.

149. *Trade and Transportation Around the Turn of the Century*

ONCE THE RAILROADS WERE REPAIRED FOLLOWING THE CIVIL WAR,
MOST OF SOUTH CAROLINA'S EXPORTS WENT OUT THROUGH RAIL SHIP-
MENTS. BUT AROUND THE TURN OF THE CENTURY MOVEMENTS WERE
BEGUN TO REVITALIZE SHIPPING THROUGH THE PORT OF CHARLESTON AND
TO LURE DIRECT EUROPEAN TRADE. WITH THE ADVENT OF THE AUTOMO-
BILE, THERE WAS ALSO A NEED FOR BETTER TRANSPORTATION. THIS RE-
SULTED IN THE "GOOD ROADS" PROGRAM. THE FOLLOWING SELECTIONS
DESCRIBE ACTIVITIES CONCERNING THE SEAPORT, THE ROADS, THE
RAILROADS, AND THE WATER AVENUES.

[Department of Agriculture report]

Since the war nothing had been accomplished in the way of putting
Charleston in touch with foreign markets until the efforts of the State
Department of Agriculture, Commerce and Immigration brought an
initial ship into Charleston harbor in 1906 . . . . As this is written, it
looks as if the port of Charleston is soon to be opened as a result of the
efforts . . . by the people of the city . . . and the railroad interests
involved.

The port of Charleston has a commanding geographical location, the
best on this continent, perhaps, and this is said with no reference to
South America, Porto Rico, Cuba, the other islands of the West Indies,
of Panama, in relation to which she is premier. Take the great group of
rail gateway points, for instance. She is nearer by rail than from New
York or Norfolk to Kansas City, St. Louis, Louisville and Memphis; and
almost 65 miles nearer to Cincinnati than is New York. She lacks only a
few miles of being as near as either of these ports to Chicago—the air
line distance being about the same. She is 146 miles nearer to St. Louis
than is New York, and 385 miles nearer Memphis. Again, Charleston is

Handbook of South Carolina: Resources, Institutions and Industries of the State,
Dept. of Agriculture (Columbia: The State Company, 1907; rev. ed., 1908),
488–94.

125 miles nearer the center of Population of the United States than New York. . . .

The export business of Charleston has dwindled most deplorably since 1890, while the import business has been increasing. . . . In 1890, domestic exports totalled $13,788,751, while imports reached only $661,-285 in value. In 1906, on the other hand, exports were only $661,285 in value, while imports rose to $2,751,482.

The "Good Roads" movement:

Nothing aids more in the development of the agricultural industry of a commonwealth than good roads. South Carolina has ever been a pioneer in the matter of good roads . . . . But subsequent to the Civil War little in this direction was done until the year 1895, when the introduction of the rural mail delivery system made speedier transportation in the outlying country districts desirable. The real agitation, however, began about the summer of 1888, when the sand-clay treatment—since so generally adopted and so successfully used as to become the object-lesson system for other portions of the United States—was suggested by Charles C. Wilson. The State abolished its old county government system and in 1895 adopted the new system permitting the use of short term convicts in the construction of roads, the convicts working in conjunction with free labor. Such a provision was naturally viewed with apprehension, and in Richland County, in the latter part of 1895, pushed vigorously by F. H. Hyatt and others, the new system was put in practice. By private subscriptions, supplementing county work, an experimental road was built out of Columbia on the "Winnsboro Road" about three miles. This experiment really started the work off in South Carolina, and by January, 1899, the sand-clay road scheme was being put into practical and successful operation in several counties . . . . The first builded of these roads lasted for about five years, practically without repairs. A State Good Roads Association was formed in 1898, the influence of which has been most effective.

Handbook of South Carolina: Resources, Institutions and Industries of the State, Dept. of Agriculture (Columbia: The State Company, 1907; rev. ed., 1908), 322–36.

Very recently there has been a general agitation in favor of a statute requiring the use of broad tires, and broad-tired wagons have been voluntarily brought into use by many farmers in many sections, but the legal requirement has not yet been made. The sand-clay roads are now built regularly at a cost varying from $150 to $300 per mile; the annual cost of repairs is about $10 per mile. Many of these roads, particularly those leading out of the chief centers of population, are exceptionally fitted for automobiling, and the horseless carriage is often passed in a fifteen or twenty mile journey at this time; its use is daily becoming more general. . . .

In 1904 there were 41,830 miles of public roads in the State of South Carolina. Of this mileage, 69 miles were surfaced with stone, 179 with gravel, 1575 miles with sand-clay mixtures, and 55 miles with shells, making in all 1878 miles of improved road. It will be seen from these figures that 4.5 per cent of the roads have been improved . . . .

The county or township boards of commissioners of the various counties or townships may cause a road tax to be levied of not to exceed one mill on all taxable property in any county or township . . . . In counties where the contract system of working the roads is adopted, the county or township boards may authorize a special annual levy not to exceed one mill on all taxable property. . . . All able-bodied male persons between certain ages—which vary in the different counties—unless by law exempt, are required to perform or cause to be performed annually not less than two nor more than ten days' labor upon the public roads. . . . In lieu of such labor a commutation tax of not less than $1 nor more than $3 may be paid by the person so liable . . . . Since 1904 the Legislature has authorized the county commissioners to fix the number of days the taxpayers are required to work on the roads and the rate at which this labor may be commuted in cash. . . .

Railroad service in the state:

Today South Carolina has as fine railroad facilities as any State in the Union, with the Capital City as a hub, and lines radiating in every direc-

Handbook of South Carolina: Resources, Institutions and Industries of the State, Dept. of Agriculture (Columbia: The State Company, 1907; rev. ed., 1908), 503–504.

tion. Through the State pass the North-to-South main line of the three great railway systems connecting Washington with Florida, the Southern, the Atlantic Coast Line, and the Seaboard Air Line. Each has numerous branch lines. The Southern has more of its mileage in South Carolina than in any other Southern State. The passenger rate is 3¢ per mile, but is soon to be voluntarily reduced. The mileage of the railroads in this State in 1882 was 1600. Since that time it has grown until today it is 3207. In 1821 the cost of transportation of freight per ton per mile was 17.22 cents; in 1882 it had fallen to 2.7 cents per ton per mile.

The tale of our State's progress is told in a few simple comparisons. The total gross earnings from railroad transportation in 1833 was $160,-907.51. Seventy years later there was earned in the State $11,785,946.52. In 1833 there were 136 miles of road in the State with wood track; in 1903 there were 3064 miles of steel track. The largest engine then weighed four and a half tons and ran under its load capacity of 18 tons at the rate of ten miles per hour. Engines of today weigh 80 tons, run from seventy to eighty miles per hour with a load of 3000 tons.

There is scarcely a section of this State today that is remote from railroad transportation. There are many places, however, that are paying the railroads a higher rate for freight than they should, simply because they have not availed themselves, under modern conditions of ship building and operation, of the navigable streams at their doors, and put steamboat lines into operation, thus applying competitive rates automatically, as it were. At this time, however, this is being realized, and one interior point after another is seizing the opportunity.

At this time also there is . . . a general awakening to the immense value of the opening and operation of the inland waterways on the coast, and the Federal Government is taking an active and substantial interest. Improvements are now in progress that mean a great deal to the future commerce of this State, the railroads and inland waterway lines of course operating in conjunction with the service on the several river courses with the several ports. . . .

Conspicuous and of vast importance in railroad transportation has been the advent of the electric railway. Beginning about 1896, as a development of the street railways with cars drawn by horses, which were introduced first in Charleston about 1870, the construction of such municipal interurban lines progressed so rapidly that by 1905 about $3,000,000 of capital was invested in such lines and there were in daily operation about 158 cars moving over 129 miles of trackage. Noteworthy accomplishments have been the building of the interurban lines between Aiken and Augusta, and between Anderson and Belton. The service is rapid and continuous and is of incalculable value. Charleston, Columbia, Spartanburg, Greenville and Anderson all have fine electric city and suburban lines, and a number of other towns are arranging to construct systems. There is contemplated, also, a network of long-distance electric lines to connect the principal cities and towns of the State. . . .

150. *The Newspapers*

FOLLOWING THE DEATH OF THE *Mercury,* WHICH HAD PROCLAIMED
AND INSTIGATED SECESSION, THE VOICE OF SOUTH CAROLINA WAS
ASSUMED BY *The News and Courier.* THE PAPER MADE GREAT STRIDES
UNDER THE LEADERSHIP OF CAPTAIN F. W. DAWSON, ALTHOUGH HE WAS
VIEWED WITH SUSPICION BY SOME OF THE CONFEDERATE LEADERS. ON
FEBRUARY 18, 1891, A NEW JOURNAL, *The State,* MADE ITS APPEARANCE
IN SOUTH CAROLINA. ITS EDITOR AND MANAGER, N. G. GONZALES, WAS
A MAN WHO HAD ALREADY ACHIEVED CONSIDERABLE FAME AS A COR-
RESPONDENT FOR THE CHARLESTON NEWSPAPER. FOLLOWING ARE THE
STATED PURPOSE OF THE NEW PAPER AND COMMENTS FROM CONTEM-
PORARIES.

[N.G. Gonzales]

In the dawn of this new day, with the lifting of the shadows and the
coming of the eastern tints of promise, certain men, loving their State,
reverencing the nobleness of her past and watchful of her future, send
out to their brethren, far and near, this messenger, which, with loyal
pride in the land of their birth, they name THE STATE.

A frail and modest bark it may be to bear so proud a name, but it
is freighted with good intent and high resolve, and bears at the fore
as symbols of inspiration and hope, the noble emblems and brave
mottoes of South Carolina.

Out into an illimitable sea of human thought, and energy, and
passion, toward a far horizon concealing the mysteries of the days to
come which no eye of man can pierce; out to the angry buffetings of
storms and the stagnant solitudes of calms, the ship of THE STATE fares
forth. . . .

Theirs is a venturesome voyage, no doubt, and one upon which timid
spirits would not embark; but it is a mission of duty, and honor, and
right, and there is no coward in the crew.

The State Newspaper (Columbia, S.C.), Feb. 18, 1891. This was the date of the
first issue of the newspaper established by the Gonzales brothers.

So the anchor is up, and the charts are scanned, and with fair white sails filled and fearless colors floating, THE STATE, prow-pointed by the needle of Truth, clears the haven of Faith, and is in the wide ocean of endeavor.

May her helm prove steady and her timbers stout!

[Editorial in *The News and Courier*]

"THE STATE"

The State newspaper made its first appearance on Wednesday. It will be published every day in the year and semi-weekly by The State Publishing Company at Columbia, and starts out with good prospects of an eventful though prosperous career.

Mr. N. G. Gonzales, for ten years connected with The News and Courier as Washington and Columbia correspondent, is the editor . . . . He is an accomplished writer and will doubtless make his mark in the wider field of journalism . . . . He promises that The State will be a Democratic paper, an independent paper, a fair paper, a State paper, a progressive paper . . . .

The initial number of our new contemporary is very creditable. We need not say that we are sincere in our wishes that it may be attended by all . . . the good fortune . . . .

The State, Columbia's new daily, made its appearance yesterday.

The first issue is an execptionally bright and newsy one. The telegraphic service is excellent, and the local and state news well covered.

The State is a six-column quarto of very neat appearance . . . . The subscription price is $8.50.

The News and Courier (Charleston, S.C.), Feb. 19, 1891.

The World (New York, N. Y.), Feb. 19, 1891.

READINGS

ADDITIONAL PRINTED SOURCE MATERIALS:

Ball, W. W. *The State That Forgot: South Carolina's Surrender to Democracy.*

Kohn, August. *The Cotton Mills of South Carolina.*

Potwin, Marjorie A. *Cotton Mill People of the Piedmont.*

South Carolina. Dept. of Agriculture. *Handbook of South Carolina. South Carolina: Resources and Population,* 1883.

CORRELATED TEXTS:

Chapman, John A. *School History of South Carolina,* 214–15.

Cooper, William J. *The Conservative Regime: South Carolina, 1877–1890.*

Eubanks, John Evans. *Ben Tillman's Baby* . . . .

Lander, Ernest McPherson, Jr. *A History of South Carolina, 1865–1960.*

Simkins, Francis B. *Pitchfork Ben Tillman.*

————. *The Tillman Movement in South Carolina.*

Snowden, Yates, ed. *History of South Carolina.* II, 863–1189.

Wallace, D. D. *History of South Carolina,* III.

————. *South Carolina: A Short History,* 607–74.

VIII

THE END OF THE NINETEENTH CENTURY AND INTO THE 1960s

At the close of the nineteenth century, South Carolina had not recovered from the effects of the Civil War and Reconstruction. Northern capital had been brought in to help raise the South industrially, but there was no "gold rush," and in 1900 less than 4 percent of the state's population was engaged in manufacturing. Seventy percent was still occupied with agriculture. Among the tycoons interested in putting new capital to work in the South after the crash of 1893 was J. P. Morgan, the father of the idea to revive, reorganize, and consolidate the railroads and other industries. The result was that the South was still in peonage to the North, a hold that was not loosened until well after World War II.

The people, who had become weary and wary of professional politicians, pushed the candidacy of Duncan Clinch Heyward, a Colleton rice grower, for the governorship of South Carolina. Heyward administered his office with dignity and with progressive ideas.

The end of World War I found South Carolina more politically united than it had been in years. As politics on the national and local levels tended to be less belligerent, the people and the state government turned toward solving some of their economic and social problems. More and better schools, better health facilities, housing, scientific farming, and improved industry were some of the issues occupying leaders of South Carolina. Migration had reduced the percentage of Negroes in the population, so that by 1925 the white people were in a majority. The Negroes who remained were more conscious of their position, more interested in education, and more clamorous for equal rights and equal public facilities. Race relations were very good and the two races began to work together for the common good.

From 1921, South Carolina's agricultural economy was in a state of

515

depression. The price of cotton fell to five cents per pound, and, although other crops were expanded, the total picture was one of gloom for almost two decades.

Industry—particularly textiles—increased during the 1920s, and with industry came organized labor, and some inevitable strikes. Conditions in the mills and mill villages improved gradually, with shorter hours, better working conditions, and more pay per hour.

When the Great Depression struck in 1929, South Carolina was plunged into a time of economic stagnation which seemed to defy all efforts to end it. There were many foreclosures on homes and farm lands, but the misery was endured in the South Carolinians' stoic way until the "prosperity is just around the corner" slogan proved to be at least partially true.

In the Democratic victory of 1932 the state contributed its share of votes. In the ensuing New Deal, the people of the state became accustomed to the WPA and all of the other agencies and aids which were formulated to get the economy moving again. Slowly, conditions improved in the late 1930s; but only with the beginning of World War II did the depression situation ease. In the meantime, government had become big business. County, state, and federal government employed larger and larger numbers of South Carolinians to carry on the increased governmental functions. At the same time as the people of the state profited from state and federal aid, they began contributing more and more in taxes.

World War II was a mixed blessing for South Carolina. Thousands of the state's youths went into the armed forces. Thousands also left for work elsewhere in war industries. In return, the armed services brought men and women to government installations within South Carolina.

For the farmer the war meant increased demand for his products and increased income. At the same time, there was a scarcity of labor and more government controls.

After the war, new industry flooded the state, and by 1950 agriculture was—for the first time—only one part of the economy.

The Negro citizen climbed to a new position of respect and to new heights, with increased rights, including enfranchisement, and higher education. Now that he was assimilated into the mainstream, he ac-

cepted his new responsibility with dignity and made notable contributions to society.

As a whole, life for everyone was better. Diversified farming, increasing industry, better trade and transportation facilities, improved schools, hospitals, public services, greater emphasis on the arts, education, and good race relations helped make the situation the best in a hundred years.

There was still improvement to be made: More education for all, a higher per capita income, and increased services, but at last South Carolina and the people were equal to the tasks before them. The future stretched out bright and wholesome.

151. *Life in South Carolina between 1865 and 1914*

THE END OF THE NINETEENTH CENTURY AND THE BEGINNING OF THE TWENTIETH BROUGHT LITTLE CHANGE IN THE LIFE OF SOUTH CARO- LINIANS. MOST OF THE CHANGES HAD COME WITH THE CIVIL WAR AND THE ABOLITION OF SLAVERY. THE FOLLOWING SELECTIONS, DEPICTING LIFE IN SEVERAL PARTS OF SOUTH CAROLINA, ILLUSTRATE THE FACT THAT, TO A GREAT EXTENT, THINGS WERE GOING ON IN ROUTINE FASHION AT THE TURN OF THE CENTURY.

[Ben Robertson]

Life on an Up Country farm:

The Civil War gave the slaves their freedom, but the Southern white folks lost the war, so for thirty years after the surrender we all had to work like slaves in our country—the white and the black. All that we had left after Appomattox, besides ourselves, was the land with its sunshine. Also we had cotton, and we knew how to graze cows and fatten pigs, and we happened to like hominy for breakfast, and turnip greens and cornbread for dinner. Being poor was not so hard for us as it would have been for many people. . . .

We had practically no money at all . . . so we stayed at home, and worked in the fields, and sat on the piazzas and talked, and we fished and trapped rabbits and went to all-day singings and to old Confederate reunions at the Courthouse. We were told to limit our wants, to enjoy what we had, to do without, and although we did have a hard time, we did not suffer greatly. Our folks were soldiers, and by nature they were stoics, and they would have made us eat all the food we took on our plates if we had been as rich even as Croesus. We were simple; always the home was the center of our life. . . .

We lived in our plain big houses about as the tenants lived in their plain three-room houses, and as the colored people lived in their houses. All of us wore home-spun clothes and hobnail shoes. Nor was there much social difference between us and our white tenants in those days. Tenants came to the front doors of our houses and we called them "mister" if they were not kin to us, and drove with them to the same church, and we attended the same one-room country school. All of us came from the same stock . . . . All of us had the same sort of pride, and we were all spontaneous, religious, philosophical, romantic, emotional, and occasionally murdersome—tough as nails and set in our ways. We were Democrats; we were Baptists. We liked to visit, to plant cotton, to sit and stare at the stars. All of us knew what we wanted. We set the same measure for a life.

Until 1914 we bought very little from stores other than cloth and shoes and black pepper and salt and sugar and rice, and even for these commodities we did not often pay cash—we swapped eggs and ham for shoes and sugar. We had houses to live in, rough clothes to wear, abundant victuals to eat, and no matter what happened to the price of cotton, we never worried about starving or about sleeping in a ditch. We had everything except money. . . .

Our wagon was hitched to cotton's star, where it had been hitched for a hundred years . . . . The truth is we liked to grow cotton. It is a beautiful crop to cultivate and gather . . . . We can plant it in April, plow and hoe it, work hard in the fields until August and then lay the crop by and go off to camp meetings and all-day singings and fish fries. We need work but six months in a year in a cotton culture. Diversified agriculture calls for a twelve-month working season, and it would do us good to work for twelve months—we admit that. Still, it would interfere with a lot of hunting and fishing and going to church. We have turned down dairying in our country, principally because a man is never free from a cow. Cotton gives you freedom. It does not perish, either, like melons or like an acre of lettuce . . . . Cotton with us is almost human . . . . Sometimes I think a Southerner's idea of heaven is a fine cotton-growing country with the price of cotton pegged at ten cents a pound. I will amend that: heaven is a fine cotton-growing country with the price of cotton pegged at twenty cents a pound. . . .

[Mrs. Pringle]

Life on a Low Country rice plantation:

March 30, 1903: I live at Cherokee [Plantation] alone . . . two miles from any white person. With my horses, my dogs, my books, and piano, my life has been a very full one. There are always sick people to be tended and old people to be helped and I have excellent servants.

My renters here, nearly all own their farms and live on them, coming here to their work every day in their ox-wagons or buggies; for the first thing a Negro does when he makes a good crop is to buy a pair of oxen, which he can do for $30, and the next good crop he buys a horse and buggy.

The purchase of Cherokee does more credit to my heart than head, and it is doubtful if I shall ever pay off the mortgage. I have lost two entire crops by freshet, and the land is now under water for the third time this winter, and, though I have rented 125 acres, it is very uncertain if I can get the half of that in. March is the month when all the rice-field ploughing should be done. The earliest rice is planted generally at the end of March, then through April, and one week in May. Last season I only got in fifty acres of rent rice and ten of wages; for in the same way the freshet was over the rice land all winter, and when it went off, there was only time to prepare that much. The renters made very fine crops—30, 40 and 45 bushels to the acre, while the wages fields made only 17 . . . . The seed rice I had paid $1.35 a bushel for and planted two and one-half bushels to each acre; the cost of cultivating and harvesting it is $15 the acre, so that makes $17.37 which it cost to produce seventeen bushels of rice, which sold at 80¢ a bushel, $13.60. . . .

Just after the war there was a splendid body of workers on this plantation, and every one in the neighborhood was eager to get some of the hands from here. My father gave prizes for the best workers in the different processes, and they felt a great pride in being the prize ploughman or ditcher or hoe hand of the year; but now, alas, poor things, they have been so confused and muddled by the mistaken ideas

Mrs. E. W. A. Pringle, *A Woman Rice Planter* (New York: Macmillan Co., 1914), 5–38.

and standards held out to them that they have no pride in honest work, no pride in anything but to wear fine clothes and get ahead of the man who employs them to do a job.

It is very hard for me to say this; I have labored so among them to try to elevate their ideals, to make them bring up their children to be honest and diligent, to make them still feel that honest, good work is something to be proud of. Even last year I would not have said this, but, alas, I have to say it now. I have just come in from the corn-field, where two women have been paid for cutting down the corn-stalks, so that there will be nothing to interfere with the plough. They have only broken off the tops of the stalks, leaving about eighteen inches of stout corn-stalks all through the field. I shall have to send someone else to do the work and pay once more. . . .

June 1, 1903: Yesterday, I went down to give out the seed rice to be clayed for planting today. I keep the key to the seed-rice left, though Marcus has all the others. I took one hand up into the upper barn while Marcus stayed below, having two barrels half filled with clay and then filled with water and well stirred until it is about the consistency of molasses. In the loft my man measured out thirty-five bushels of rice, turning the tub into a spout leading to the barn below, where young men brought the clay water in piggins from the barrel and poured it over the rice, while young girls, with bare feet and skirts well tied up, danced and shuffled the rice about with their feet until the whole mass was thoroughly clayed, singing, joking and displaying their graceful activity to the best advantage. It is a pretty sight. When it is completely covered with clay, the rice is shoveled into a pyramid and left to soak until the next morning, when it is measured out into sacks, one and one-fourth bushels to each half acre. Two pairs of the stoutest oxen on the plantation are harnessed to the rice-drills, and they lumber along slowly but surely, and by twelve o'clock the field of fourteen acres is nearly planted.

It is literally casting one's bread on the waters, for as soon as the seed is in the ground the trunk door is lifted and the water creeps slowly up and up until it is about three inches deep on the land. That is why the claying is necessary; it makes the grain adhere to the earth, otherwise it would float. . . .

Near the bridge two Negro women are fishing, with great strings of fish beside them. The streams are full of Virginia perch, bream and trout; you have only to drop your line in with a wriggling worm at the end, and keep silent, and you have a fine sport. Then the men set their canes securely into the bank just before dark and leave them, and almost invariably they find a fish ready for breakfast in the morning. There is a saying that one cannot starve in this country, and it is true.

As I drove down I saw little children with buckets and piggins picking blackberries; such big, sweet berries, covering acres of old fields which were once planted in corn. As I walked down the bank I found a "cooter" [terrapin] which had come out of the river to lay eggs. My excellent Chloe will make a delicious soup from it, or, still better, bake it in the shell. All winter we have quantities of English ducks in the rice fields, and partridges and snipe on the upland, and in the woods wild turkeys and deer, so that if there is a sportsman in the family, one can live royally with no expense. . . .

October 1, 1903: Another gorgeous autumn day . . . . The cowpeas were picked today, and they are bearing finely, and the people know how to pick them; it is not like the cotton. One woman who never can pick more than twenty pounds of cotton had seventy pounds of peas, and Eva had ninety pounds. I feel much better satisfied with the day's work than usual. I got the hay which had been dried put into the barn, which is much better than stacking it, when no one knows how . . . . One of the renters came up and paid his money quite voluntarily, which is so unusual that it put me in good spirits for the day. . . .

October 3: I am making a suit of white flannel woven from the wool of my own sheep . . . .

October 8: The harvest has come and with it real harvest weather —crisp, cool, clear; and the bowed heads of the golden grain flow in the sunshine. The hurricane which was reported as wandering around last week frightened me terribly, but after waiting Monday, Tuesday and Wednesday for it to materialize, I had to cut on Thursday, for the rice was full ripe, and though we have had some light showers, there has been no serious bad weather. Today the hands are "toting" rice into the flats.

You see a stack of rice approaching, and as it makes its way across the plank which bridges the big ditch, you perceive a pair of legs or a skirt, as the case may be, peeping from beneath. Men, women, and children all carry, what look like immense loads, on their heads, apparently without effort. This is the gayest week of the year. Thursday the field was cut down by the hands with small reap hooks, the long golden heads being carefully laid on the tall stubble to dry until the next day, when it was tied into sheaves, which the Negroes do very skillfully with a wisp of the rice itself. Saturday it was stacked in small cocks to dry through Sunday, and today it is being loaded into the flats, having had every advantage of weather . . . . Flats are one of the heavy expenses on a rice plantation—large flat-bottomed boats from twenty to eighty feet long and from ten to twelve feet wide, propelled in the most primitive way by poles and steered by one huge oar at the stern. They can be loaded up very high if the rice is properly stowed. . . .

October 16: I have threshed the May rice, and it has turned out very well, considering the hard time it had for two months after it was planted. My wages field made twenty-five bushels to the acre, and the hands nearly the same, only a little less, but it is good rice, and weighs forty-six pounds to the bushel; and as I hear of every one complaining of very light rice, I am thankful it is so good. I have an offer of $1.05 for my rice in the rough, and I am going to take it, though I shall miss the cracked rice and the flour which we get when the rice is milled, and the rice will have to be bagged up and sewed, which is a great deal of work . . . .

[August Kohn]

Life in a mill village:

When the operatives go to the cotton mills they do not generally take very much with them. Of course, some who go there are more prosperous than others, but a great many . . . have but little, because they have been accustomed to but little in their primitive mountain homes. It does not take them very long to get accustomed to modern things, including the phonograph and organ, when they get to the mill community because the soliciting agents are exceedingly active in their efforts to get the new-comers interested in the ins and outs of the installment business. When the operative arrives at the mill village, he is turned over to what is known as the outside man, who assigns him with his family to the best available house. If there be any choice as to houses, it is given to those who have been at the mills longest, and from what I could gather, the desirability of the home is very largely based

August Kohn, *The Cotton Mills of South Carolina,* reprinted in *Handbook of South Carolina: Resources, Institutions and Industries of the State,* Dept. of Agriculture (Columbia: The State Company, 1907; rev. ed., 1908), 438–44.

upon its nearness to the cotton mill, since the early start which has to be made in the day's work is about the worst phase of the mill work. In this State the cotton mills all own their dwellings and provide homes for their operatives at nominal rental. The idea is to build the homes adjacent to the cotton mills, to have the operatives lose as little time as possible in getting to and from their work . . . . All the operatives' dwellings . . . are of wood, as are most of the homes in South Carolina . . . . The homes that are provided are very generally the same throughout the mill districts, only that some of the houses are kept in better repair and look fresher and cleaner, but as a rule the desire of the owners is to keep the houses in as good repair as possible, and they do not stint themselves in spending money on their villages if it can accomplish any good. The rent is generally by the room, and varies in the various villages, running all the way from nothing to $1 per room per month . . . . The general style of the house is familiar to most people living in this State, and the types are generally what are known as three, four and six room cottages. They are tightly built, have ample windows, and doors, have a ten foot ceiling, are generally weather-boarded and ceiled with wood on the inside, and there is no occasion for crowding, each of the houses generally occupying a lot covering fully one-quarter of an acre, and if there is any desire for more room it can be gotten . . . .

I found that there is a very general disposition and desire on the part of the cotton mill owners to give their operatives garden plots, in the hope that they will cultivate both vegetable and flower gardens . . . . At a number of cotton mills . . . prizes are offered for the best gardens, and some of these gardens are really attractive. . . .

The statute law of South Carolina . . . says that no child, unless there are special circumstances necessitating work, should be employed who is not 12 years of age . . . . With this statute on the books, it may as well be admitted that there are a great many other children working in the cotton mills without certificate . . . . Children under 12 are in the mills, and a great many of them are there, but there are not thousands upon thousands, as some agitators would have people believe . . . .

A number of mill companies during the last few years have been erecting at their own expense, in their villages, club houses, hospitals, swimming pools, and handsome school and church buildings. The most expensive of these cost $25,000; another cost $18,500. In the various South Carolina mills there are, perhaps, fifty such mill buildings for the operatives, paid for entirely by the companies at a cost of from

$5,000 to $10,000 each. There are now between ten and fifteen salaried welfare workers (not including school teachers and ministers), with salaries from $500 to $1000 each, in South Carolina mill villages paid entirely by the companies . . . .

[J.A. Rice]

Negro life on a plantation:

Through a crack in the fence I could see beyond the intervening cotton patch into another world. Around their quarters Negro children played, darting into sight and out among the ancient oaks, or sitting underneath the cabins, coaxing from their nests with whirling twigs the doddlebugs—little grey insects that made their home in the dust. The cabins stood high up off the ground, to keep them cool in summer and dry in winter. The oldest were built of pine logs chinked with clay, but often the clay had fallen out and on a cold winter's night the passerby could see ribbons of light broken by chair and Negro legs crowded close around the fire. When the logs of one had rotted and the roof of white oak shingles could not be patched again, another took its place, built this time of different materials and in a different way, breaking into the row and standing out at first harsh in its newness. Two by fours and rough dressed pine were cheap and nails could now be bought at the general store, no longer hammered out by hand but machine made. But with age these cabins began to take on an unexpected beauty, as sun and rain painted them grey, mottled with the yellow of pine knots and streaked with brick red and black from resin and rusting nails.

The quarters stretched in a thin line squeezed between grove behind and cotton field in front. . . . Here in the narrow space the men and women lay or sat in spots of sun, and talked and dozed—this was the slack time of the year and they could be as lazy as they pleased—the men in groups and the women in twos . . . . Some of the women moved slowly between cabin and woodpile and washpot, calling to one another, scolding the children, and breaking into piercing cackles.

J. A. Rice, *I Came Out of the Eighteenth Century* (New York: Harper & Bros., 1942), 34–36.

Irresponsibility, easeful death-in-life, made its lazy bid. All the Negroes on the place—field hands who sat contented at the bottom of the social scale, and house servants—were descendants of slaves. A few still lived who had moved from one world to another when they were already old and accustomed to their lot. Slow of speech and action, they and their children, and their children's children, clung to the rights and privileges of slavery and shunned the burden imposed by their new freedom. They stumbled about laughing in half darkness, slyly choosing whatever was to their advantage in their old life or their new. If treated as slaves, they became instantly, sometimes aggressively, free; if treated as free, they retreated into slavery . . . .

The sanctions of slavery were gone—no one on the plantation was allowed to punish them, however great the provocation—and no effective new sanctions had come to take their place, for they did not want much money, the white man's sanction. I can remember the time when, if they were paid at the rate of fifty cents a day, they worked six days; if a dollar a day, they worked three. All they wanted was three dollars a week . . . . They were sometimes dismissed, but that was no great hardship, because most of their wants were satisfied much as they had been under slavery. They had shelter—eviction was unknown on my grandmother's place—and if food got scarce they could beg or borrow (the same thing) corn from their more opulent fellows, and there were rabbits and 'coons and 'possum—they all had dogs. They might resort to theft—chickens were a real temptation— but this more obscure form of borrowing was rare, not exactly within the code . . . . They might even go so far as to take another job on a plantation, an extreme expression of disapproval of the treatment they had received, but this was frowned upon by their families and neighbors as being a breach of loyalty. . . .

Their whole life was an easy community. A Negro was seldom seen alone. If he was, he was asleep. They swarmed in and out of each other's cabins, went to church in groups, worked when they could together—at corn shucking, cane grinding, cotton chopping, hog killing —whenever they were paid by the day. Even during cotton picking time, when each was paid according to the amount he brought in at night, they bunched together in the late afternoon in one part of the field and sang. . . .

152. *The Charleston Exposition of 1901–1902*

THOUGHTS OF REVITALIZING INDUSTRY WERE PARAMOUNT IN 1900, AND CHARLESTON WAS PARTICULARLY ANXIOUS TO REFORGE THE OLD LINK OF TRADE BETWEEN SOUTH CAROLINA AND THE WEST INDIES WHICH HAD DOMINATED ITS PORT AND CULTURE THROUGHOUT COLONIAL AND ANTEBELLUM DAYS. TO AWAKEN THE STATE TO THE CITY AND THE PORT'S VALUE, AND THE NATION TO THE IMPORTANCE OF SOUTH CAROLINA, CHARLESTON LEADERS PLANNED THE SOUTH CAROLINA AND WEST INDIAN EXPOSITION. THE HUGE FAIR WAS HELD IN CHARLESTON FROM DECEMBER 1, 1901, TO MAY 31, 1902. THE EXPOSITION WAS SYMPTOMATIC OF THE LONGING FOR THE "GOOD OLD DAYS," AND THE FAIR DID CALL ATTENTION TO THE INDUSTRY AND AGRICULTURE OF THE STATE, TO THE POTENTIALITIES OF CHARLESTON AS A MAJOR SEAPORT, AND TO THE POSSIBILITIES OF RENEWING DIRECT TRADE. FROM THE POINT OF VIEW OF VISITORS, THE EXPOSITION WAS A SUCCESS, BUT MATERIAL IMPROVEMENT IN CHARLESTON'S SEAGOING TRADE DID NOT RESULT. A DESCRIPTION OF THE EXPOSITION FOLLOWS.

[Magazine report on the Charleston Exposition]

The South Carolina and West Indian Exposition which opened on December 1 at Charleston is really the first typically Southern Fair . . . . The people of South Carolina and more especially of Charleston have in this enterprise two general objects in view besides the specific purpose of stimulating the trade and progress of their own city . . . : To exhibit before the world the achievements of Southern industry and art, and to demonstrate the great and important future of the trade with the West Indies and Spanish America.

Although it was as late as January, 1901, that the General Assembly of South Carolina appropriated $50,000 for the State exhibit . . . the entire exposition was in a much more complete condition on opening day than is the rule with such institutions. In general, the South Caro-

Review of Reviews, XXV (1902), 58–61.

linians, under the energetic leadership of Capt. F. W. Wagener, President of the exposition committee, have shown the most notable enterprise, ingenuity, and good taste in availing themselves of their natural advantages for making an attractive and imposing exposition with the comparatively small amount of money at their disposal . . . .

The site of the exposition is a tract of 160 acres situated as regards the city of Charleston just about as if it lay along upper Riverside Drive, were Manhattan substituted for the neck upon which Charleston is built . . . . The exposition grounds are extremely fortunate in location . . . . Only two and one half miles from the business section of the city, they can be reached easily by private conveyance, electric or steam cars, and their frontage on the water enables ocean going vessels to unload right on the exposition premises. . . .

A beautiful park was already awaiting the exposition makers on the famous old Lowndes estate, now owned by Capt. Wagener. . . . The exposition has fourteen principal buildings and all are now completed. . . . The central figure is appropriately the Cotton Palace, 360 feet long, 160 feet wide, and covering 50,000 square feet. These figures will show that the enterprise is on no small scale. The architecture of the main buildings is throughout more or less true Spanish renaissance. The color is ivory, with the roofs simulating the red tile of the Spanish American type. The material of the buildings is Carolina pine with iron strengthening, the whole covered with the usual "staff" composition.

As one looks down the Plaza, the Liberal Arts building is on the right of the Cotton Palace, and to the left, the Agricultural building. At the northern end of the Plaza is the auditorium with a seating capacity of 4000 and at the entrance are the Administration building, and the Minerals and Forestry edifice. The great Plaza itself is 1200 feet long and 900 feet wide, while the general effect of spaciousness and the impressiveness of the building masses on the sides have been increased by the construction of a sunken garden below sloping green terraces in the center of the space. This pleasant court, lined with majestic palmettoes will, over and above the aesthetic use, add greatly to the comfort of seeing the exhibits in the buildings about it.

There is a Midway, of course, and a race track and a livestock exhibit . . . . The attendance has promised to be very good; there were 20,000 people present on opening day.

153. *The Arrival of the* Wittekind, *November, 1906*

TWO MOTIVES LED TO THE ARRIVAL OF THE NORTH GERMAN LLOYD
STEAMSHIP *Wittekind* AT THE PORT OF CHARLESTON ON NOVEMBER 4,
1906. THE FIRST WAS THE DESIRE FOR DIRECT TRADE BETWEEN CHARLES-
TON AND NORTH EUROPEAN PORTS; THE SECOND WAS THE HOPE THAT
EUROPEAN IMMIGRANTS WOULD COME TO WORK IN THE FIELDS AND
FACTORIES OF SOUTH CAROLINA. IN NEITHER WAS THERE MUCH SUC-
CESS. THE *Wittekind* MADE ONLY ONE OTHER VOYAGE, AND ONLY A FEW
MORE IMMIGRANTS ARRIVED. BUT THE *Wittekind's* VISIT IN 1906 REPRE-
SENTED A STRONG ATTEMPT ON THE PART OF CHARLESTON AND SOUTH
CAROLINA TO COMPETE WITH NORTHERN PORTS FOR TRADE AND WORKERS.

[*Arrival of the* Wittekind, *as reported
in the* Charleston Yearbook]

On the morning of Sunday, November 4, 1906, the steamship
'Wittekind' of the North German Lloyd Steamship Company, Capt. C.
Von Bardeleben, out of Bremen Thursday afternoon, October 18, came
into the port of Charleston with 26 cabin passengers and 450 in the
steerage, immigrants from Europe under the personal guidance of E. J.
Watson, Commissioner of Agriculture, Commerce and Immigration of
the State of South Carolina, by whose efforts in Europe they had been
attracted to South Carolina and the facilities for their direct passage to
this State supplied.

The vessel brought a freight cargo of 4000 tons of kainit and other
fertilizer material, valued at $56,000 consigned to the Virginia-Caro-
lina Chemical Company.

The arrival of the 'Wittekind' at Charleston marked the first successful
undertaking to promote direct immigration from Europe to the South
Atlantic section of the United States in half a century, and was the

Charleston Yearbook (1906), reprinted in a *Handbook of South Carolina:
Resources, Institutions and Industries of the State,* Dept. of Agriculture
(Columbia: The State Company, 1907; rev. ed., 1908), 520–21.

immediate result of the effort of South Carolina to supply, through a State agency, the pressing necessities of a white industrial population to develop its resources and increase its productiveness. Commissioner Watson had been laboring for two years to attract settlers to South Carolina to supply the demand for labor in the fields and in the factories, meeting with only indifferent success in his solicitations in other sections of the United States, and through the channels of immigration at the Northern ports of entry, and, after a careful study of all the conditions, he had determined to seek the establishment of a line of ships plying directly between a European port and Charleston to bring immigrants to the State. To this end he was especially moved by the solicitations of the cotton manufacturing interests of the State, whose mills were hampered seriously in their operations by a scarcity of labor.

The conditions in South Carolina prevailed generally throughout the South and the necessity for supplementing the population with desirable aliens had appeared to the people of the whole section, but South Carolina was the first of the States to carry the idea into action. The availability of Charleston as a port of entry for immigrants was a large factor in the determination to make the experiment and in its successful undertaking. . . .

The 'Wittekind' sailed from Charleston on her return voyage to Bremen on Saturday, November 24, [1906,] at 2:30 o'clock in the afternoon. She had a cargo of 10,349 bales of cotton.

154. *First Establishment of the Building and Loan Associations*

LACK OF CAPITAL HAD LONG BEEN A SERIOUS DETERRENT TO THE EXPANSION OF BUSINESS AND INDUSTRY IN SOUTH CAROLINA. TO ENCOURAGE SUCH GROWTH—AS WELL AS TO INDUCE THRIFT—DANIEL AUGUSTUS TOMPKINS, AN EDGEFIELD NATIVE, THEN A CHARLOTTE, NORTH CAROLINA, INDUSTRIALIST, TURNED HIS MIND TO THE PROBLEM. AFTER CAREFUL STUDY, HE DECIDED THAT THE BEST WAY TO ACHIEVE THIS GOAL WAS THROUGH BUILDING AND LOAN ASSOCIATIONS. FURTHER, HE FELT THAT, THROUGH SAVING WITH BUILDING AND LOAN ASSOCIATIONS, WORKMEN WOULD EVENTUALLY ACQUIRE HOMES. FIRST HE DEVOTED HIMSELF TO ESTABLISHING AN ASSOCIATION IN HIS HOME TOWN. THE FOLLOWING IS AN ANNOUNCEMENT OF THE EDGEFIELD BUILDING AND LOAN ASSOCIATION.

[Announcement of the Edgefield Building and Loan Association]

HOME MONEY FOR HOME PEOPLE

The Edgefield Building & Loan Association has money to loan its members. It invites working people to become members. It is a savings institution as well as the working man's bank. While some kind of property is required in all cases to make a loan perfectly safe, yet the real basis of credit is the borrower's labor—his willingness to work and the known fact that he is an energetic worker. . . .

The working man may be a carpenter, lawyer, farmer, merchant, spinner, bricklayer, doctor, weaver, or any other working man who is energetic and active and earns wages, fees, or other compensations as the result of his labor.

The association will require all its members to pay exactly as they agree to pay. . . . The association can arrange for farmers to repay loans in annual installments in three payments in the fall. . . . Me-

George Taylor Winston, *A Builder of the New South* (Garden City: Doubleday, 1920), 329–43.

chanics working for wages by the week or month. The payments are made suitable to all classes of working people. . . .

This is a local or home institution. It is to be managed at home and all the money will be loaned at home. None can be loaned outside of Edgefield County. Instead of sending away to borrow money from land loan companies or from foreign building and loan associations, with a lot of discounts, this home institution will accumulate the savings of home people and loan these accumulations to home people.

The home building and loan association has been successful in all parts of the United States. . . .

155. *The Water Powers of South Carolina*

FEW STATES IN THE UNION ARE MORE FORTUNATE THAN SOUTH
CAROLINA IN ABUNDANCE OF WATER POWER. IN 1910, AUGUST KOHN
MADE A SURVEY OF DEVELOPED POWERS. HE INCLUDED A REPORT ON
PICKENS AND OCONEE COUNTIES, AND HIS COMMENTS ON THE HEAD-
WATERS OF THE SAVANNAH RIVER ARE NOTEWORTHY IN VIEW OF DUKE
POWER COMPANY'S KEOWEE-TOXAWAY PROJECT.

[August Kohn]

DEVELOPED WATER POWERS

It will be interesting at this juncture to give a summary of the larger
water power developments in this State, that is, those that are actually
and daily in operation. The plants given below are entirely industrial
developments, and it is altogether safe to figure at least 25,000–horse
power development belonging to the smaller industries, such as grist and
roller mills, but of which there is no itemized summary available:

Name of Plant and Location	Horse power developed.
Anderson Water, Light and Power Co., Anderson, S.C.	6,000
Apalache Mills, Arlington, S.C.	1,500
Batesville Cotton Mills, Batesville, S.C.	150
Aiken Manufacturing Company, Bath, S.C.	1,200
Belton Power Company, Belton, S.C.	4,000
Hermitage Cotton Mills, Camden, S.C.	500
Norris Cotton Mills, Cateechee, S.C.	650
Cherokee Falls Manufacturing Company, Cherokee Falls, S.C.	1,100
Clifton Manufacturing Company, Clifton (two plants)	3,000
Carolina Light and Power Company, Aiken, S.C.	850
Columbia E. S. L. and P. Co., Columbia, S.C.	10,000

August Kohn, *Water Powers of South Carolina* (Columbia: The State
Company, 1910), 40–42.

Enoree Manufacturing Company, Enoree, S.C.	1,200
Fairmount Mills, Fairmount, S.C.	275
Fingerville Manufacturing Company, Fingerville, S.C.	250
Electric Manufacturing and Power Co., Gaston Shoals, S.C.	10,000
Graniteville Manufacturing Company, Graniteville, S.C.	1,000
Greenville-Carolina Power Company, Greenville, S.C. (Southern Power)	3,000
North, S.C., Municipal, Edisto, S.C.	150
Langley Manufacturing Company, Langley, S.C.	1,500
Reedy River Power Company, Laurens, S.C.	2,000
Lockhart Mills, Lockhart, S.C.	3,500
Courtenay Manufacturing Company, Newry, S.C.	1,000
Pacolet Manufacturing Company (1&2), Pacolet, S.C.	2,500
Pelham Mills, Pelham, S.C.	600
Pelzer Manufacturing Company, Pelzer (two plants)	5,500
Piedmont Manufacturing Company, Piedmont, S.C.	3,000
Reedy River Manufacturing Company, Reedy River	500
Southern Power Company, Rock Hill (Catawba plant)	8,500
Southern Power Company, Great Falls	42,000
Southern Power Company, Ninety-nine Islands	25,000
Southern Power Co. (Rocky Creek), Catawba River	30,000
Tucapau Mills, Tucapau (two plants)	2,500
Union-Buffalo Mills, Union-Neal's Shoals	6,000
Ware Shoals Manufacturing Company, Ware Shoals	6,000
Whitney Manufacturing Company, Whitney	1,000
Savannah River Power Company, Gregg Shoals	2,800
Enoree Power Company (Mr. Groce), Enoree River	3,000

In the establishment of any industrial enterprise there are a number of essential considerations. Sixty-five years ago William Gregg contended that a cotton mill would pay anywhere in South Carolina, with proper management, but made an especial plea for ample capital. He argued that the great majority of failures in cotton mills in this State at that time were on account of being undercapitalized and not having the necessary money with which to build and operate.

In considering the water development of this State, one recognizes that, although there has been a great advance in this direction, particularly within the last ten years, there is likely to be very much more growth, and those who are now developing water power for sale are anxious to have others in the field, because there seems to be a demand for practically unlimited power if offered at proper prices. . . .

A great many water power developments in this day are not under-taken because the promoters have not sold the power to be developed. Of course, it is much safer to sell power before undertaking such a development, but . . . the sale of power under such conditions involves a sacrifice in the price. The Southern Power Company, for instance, invested three million dollars in its plants before it sold its securities and it had its power stations completed before it made contracts for power. True, this was because it had the immense wealth of the Dukes behind it, but the way of the Dukes is the successful way to do business. . . .

. . . In a general way it might be said that power sells at from $12.50 per horse power per annum, where used in larger quantities, for an average of ten or eleven hours per day, to $25 per horse power per annum, also on large contracts. These rates apply, of course, only to large consumers, such as cotton mills, paper pulp crushers and others, who might use 1,000 or more horse power per annum. . . .

Just by way of illustration, I have an interesting report from Pickens County, dealing with the powers of Oconee and Pickens.

Both Pickens and Oconee counties are well supplied with water power. . . . The sites are varied in character, those in the lower section being of comparatively low heads, while those in the upper section rival the high heads of the Pacific slope. The principal rivers are the Saluda, Keowee and the Chattooga, with their tributaries.

The Saluda River . . . has one power plant in operation, developing several thousand horse power. On the headwaters of the river are several good powers of a few hundred horse-power each.

The Chattooga River . . . has considerable power. . . .

The Keowee River and tributaries . . . has by far the greatest amount of power. . . .

Twelve-mile River . . . has two plants in operation. . . . Just above Cateechee the river has a fall of 300 feet in three miles. . . .

Estatoe Creek has a fall of about 300 feet in two and one half miles with room for storage. . . .

On the Keowee . . . there are two good heads available of 40 feet each. Also one capable of a head of 100 feet. This is by far the best all 'round site in the county. The river at this place being only a few feet wide, firm rock bottom and mountain rising precipitously on both sides, with the finest rock in abundance. This is the best storage reservoir in this section. It would cover a bottom five miles long and one-half mile wide with a 60-foot dam. A higher dam would practically cover no more area, as the mountains rise on all sides at about 50 degrees. About 7,000 horse-power could be developed there.

The Toxaway and Horsepasture Rivers have considerable fall, but very little storage capacity.

The Whitewater River has practically 2,000 feet fall in four miles. The lower fall being in South Carolina has 800 feet fall in a few hundred yards, with the shoal included about 1,000 feet, and has excellent storage room. It will develop about 8,000 horse-power. Within sight is the upper falls in North Carolina, only one and one-half miles away. The foot of the shoal is in South Carolina, but the main fall is in North Carolina. It will develop in storage about 8,000 horse-power.

Only two miles to the east are the two falls of the Thompson River, a tributary of the Whitewater. They have about 2,000 feet fall, the lower one being in South Carolina. . . .

Ninety-five per cent of the headwaters of the Chattooga and Keowee Rivers have a forested watershed. The rainfall is the greatest in the United States, being from 70 to 84 inches per annum.

Of the storage reservoirs projected on the headwaters of the Savannah [River] by the Government several are in these counties, viz:

	Drainage Area. Square Miles.
Keowee River	270
Little River	90
Twelve-Mile River	160
Twenty-Three-Mile Creek	150
Conneross Creek	80
Tugaloo River	260
Chattooga River	120

On the Toxaway and Horsepasture, in North Carolina, there are several lakes which serve to hold the flood waters in check and help regulate the flow lower down. . . .

156. *State Politics and "Tommy" Wilson*

A RENEWAL OF INTEREST IN NATIONAL POLITICS WAS EXPERIENCED BY SOUTH CAROLINIANS WHEN WOODROW WILSON BEGAN HIS CAMPAIGN FOR THE PRESIDENCY. "TOMMIE" WAS A HOMETOWN BOY TO COLUMBIANS, AND THE WHOLE STATE CLAIMED HIM BECAUSE HE HAD LIVED IN THE CAPITAL CITY AS A YOUTH. HIS FATHER HAD BEEN A MEMBER OF THE FACULTY OF THE COLUMBIA THEOLOGICAL SEMINARY, AND RELATIVES WERE STILL LIVING IN COLUMBIA. WHEN WORD CAME THAT WILSON HAD BEEN ELECTED PRESIDENT, THE CITIZENS WERE ELATED. HOPES ROSE THAT SOUTH CAROLINIANS WOULD AGAIN PLAY A LEADING ROLE IN NATIONAL AFFAIRS. FEW COULD RECALL THE LAST TIME A DEMOCRAT HAD BEEN IN THE WHITE HOUSE, AND NOT SINCE ANDREW JACKSON HAD THERE BEEN A PRESIDENT AS CLOSE TO SOUTH CAROLINA AS WILSON. THE SAME HOUSE IN WHICH WILSON HAD LIVED—NOW ONE OF COLUMBIA'S TOURIST ATTRACTIONS—WAS OFFERED AS THE "WINTER CAPITAL." OTHER TIES WERE WITH THE FIRST PRESBYTERIAN CHURCH, WHERE WILSON HAD WORSHIPPED, AND WHERE HIS PARENTS AND OTHER RELATIVES ARE BURIED. THE FOLLOWING NEWS STORIES SHOW THE REACTION TO WILSON'S ELECTION.

[Excitement over Wilson's election described in *The State*]

When it was announced that "Tommy" Wilson was elected president of the United States most of the people in Columbia went wild. "Tommy is president," said an old schoolmate who now calls him "Woodrow Wilson," . . . and after that the bell in the city hall and after that the bell at central fire station jangled out the news and the people celebrated accordingly. The city clock was agitated by City Councilman Stieglitz and the button for the fire bell was touched by the delicate hands of Chief May.

It was a great night for Wilson. The youngest inhabitant could not remember when a Democrat was the leading man of the nation and

The State Newspaper (Columbia, S.C.), Nov. 5, 1912.

the oldest inhabitant had to think a while before he could recall the dates for the second term of Grover Cleveland. There were bitter arguments over the telephone as to the vote cast in 1884, in 1896 and in other years too numerous to mention. It was not the fault of the telephone. Almost any telephone can transmit a message. But several hundred people in Columbia who knew Woodrow Wilson when he was "Tommy Wilson," and several hundred others who met him here on his visit . . . about fourteen months ago, when he addressed the South Carolina Press Association, wanted to celebrate and the local telegraph offices were deluged with telegrams for him, and some wanted to call him over the long-distance phone. This is just to show what Columbia's spirit will do. Everybody was public-spirited last night . . . .

[*The State* Newspaper]

AUNT OF "TOMMY" LIKED THE RESULT

The aunt of the nation's president-elect usually answers her own door bell, for when it rings she always expects a friend and she evidently wishes to be personal and immediate. But yesterday . . . she waited for her daughter to usher in the inevitable callers. There is nothing formal about the little Columbia woman whom Woodrow Wilson calls "Aunt Felie," and whom Columbians who are not kin to her know as Mrs. James Woodrow. She has been a Columbian almost all of her life and she has lived quietly and serenely behind the thick red brick walls of her home on Sumter and Washington Streets and the high wooden fence of her own lovely garden. . . .

No attempt, in fact, was made to repress the natural feeling of joy at the great victory of her nephew. Her eyes were bright and her cheeks flushed in spite of the fact that she had been up late that night before. . . .

It seems that Mrs. Woodrow was not quick to accept the great news. She and her daughter, in the midst of a small family group, watched the election returns from a private room at the YMCA. From time to

The State Newspaper (Columbia, S.C.), Nov. 5, 1912. *See also* Nov. 6 and 9, 1912, for further comment on Wilson.

time she was urged to wire her congratulations to "Tommy" at Princeton, but again and again she refused, feeling that it might be premature, and it was not until yesterday morning that she felt perfectly safe in sending over the wire: "Hear latest [stop] congratulations on your election."

[*The State*]

CHARLESTON GLAD OVER ELECTION

Keen satisfaction is taken in Charleston in results of the election of Woodrow Wilson and there was sufficient interest in the outcome to keep many people up last night . . . that they must assure themselves of the results.

Today, the election of Woodrow Wilson and Marshall was the chief topic of conversation. Every body talked politics.

[*The State*]

COLUMBIA LIKELY WILSON'S CHOICE

[Washington date-line] Columbia, S.C. was the recipient of a vast deal of widely distributed publicity this morning—and publicity of the sort that does not hurt.

The special correspondents at Princeton, of New York, Philadelphia, Baltimore and Washington papers conveyed to their journals the distinct impression that Columbia's offer to be the winter capital of the United States was favorably received by the President-elect and in headlines in those papers this morning Columbia is referred to as the probable winter capital. *The Washington Post* and the *New York Sun* give especial prominence to the visit of the Columbia delegation.

The State Newspaper (Columbia, S.C.), Nov. 6, 1912.

The State Newspaper (Columbia, S.C.), Nov. 6, 1912.

157. *Charleston in 1915*

CHARLESTON, HAVING ALWAYS BEEN ONE OF AMERICA'S "FIRST" CITIES, HAS BEEN DESCRIBED BY A NUMBER OF PEOPLE—SOME VISITORS AND SOME NATIVES—THROUGH THE YEARS. THE FOLLOWING IS SIGNIFICANT FOR TWO REASONS, FIRST BECAUSE OF ITS AUTHOR, WILLIAM DEAN HOWELLS, AND SECOND BECAUSE OF THE DATE OF ITS PUBLICATION. THE YANKEE AUTHOR WAS, ON THE WHOLE, SYMPATHETIC; AND, UNLIKE HIS PREDE-CESSORS AFTER 1865, DID NOT SEEK TO BE EITHER PATRONIZING OR CRITI-CAL. ALTHOUGH THE CIVIL WAR HAD NOT BEEN FORGOTTEN IN 1915, THE PASSAGE OF TIME HAD DULLED SECTIONAL BITTERNESS. HOWELLS COULD ENJOY A VISIT TO THE PICTURESQUE AND HISTORIC TOWN WITHOUT RAISING THE GHOST OF FORT SUMTER.

[William Dean Howells]

When the weather cleared at Charleston and the sun came out, the mocking birds came out with it on the Battery. The flowers seemed never to have been in, but were only waiting to be recognized in the gardens that flanked the houses facing across the space of palmettos and live-oaks and columns and statues and busts, and burly Parrot guns glowering east-ward and southward over the sea-walls. The flowers were there to attest the habitual softness of the Charleston winter, but experience . . . had taught me that flowers are not to be trusted in these matters. Still, I am not saying that the Charleston winter is not mild, and as for the Charles-ton spring, what I saw and felt of it was divine, especially on the Battery.

It is a city imagined from a civic consciousness quite as intense as that of any of the famed cities of the world, say such as Boston, and it built most of its stateliest dwellings on the Battery. All the old houses that front upon it are stately; on the South modern houses have intruded themselves in some of the gardened spaces; but on the East Battery the line is yet unbroken. I should not know quite how to justify them in making me

W. D. Howells, "In Charleston," *Harper's Monthly* CXXXI (1915), 747–57.

540

think of a line of Venetian palaces, but that was what they did, and the sense of something Venetian in them recurred to me throughout our ten days. Perhaps it was the sea and the sky that conspired to trick my fancy; certainly it was not the spacious gardens beside the spacious houses, nor the make of the houses, though their size, if not their shape, flattered my fond notion. Without being exactly of one pattern, they were of one general type which I found continually repeated throughout the city. A certain rather narrow breadth of stone or brick or wood abuts on the street, and as wide a space of veranda, colonnaded and rising in two or even three stories, looks southward or westward over a more or less ample garden-ground. The street door opens into the house, or perhaps into the veranda, or perhaps you enter by the gate from the garden where the blossoms of our summer paint the April air, and the magnolia shines and sparkles over the coarse-turfed lawn. . . .

Charleston is a city of some seventy thousand people, black and white, and it covers, I should say, about as much space as Manhattan, rashly judging from what seemed our night-long drive from the railroad station to the hotel on our arrival. Probably, also, the city's extent is an illusion arising from the indefinite repetition of such houses and gardens in every quarter. There are certain distinct business thoroughfares, long, very long, stretching out in shops mostly low; but people who built their dwellings in the old time seem to have built them wherever they liked, unhampered by any dictate of fashion . . . . I have a feeling that the streets, whatever make they were of, were better kept than the streets of Northern towns, which have not known the impulse to purge and live cleanly given by Colonel Waring to New York. Certainly they looked neater than the streets of such a typical New England town as Portsmouth, but how they were kept so I cannot tell. The old tradition of the turkey-buzzard as the scavenger of Charleston dwindled, in my observance, to a solitary bird of the species in the street beside the Old Market. . . .

Every city has its temperament, and in most things, Charleston is like no other city that I know, but there were moments in her long, long streets of rather small shops which recalled the High streets of English towns. There were even moments when London loomed upon the consciousness, and in breaths of the sea air one was aware of Folkstone. But these were very fleeting illusions, and the place reserved its own strong identity, derived from a history very strenuous in many epochs. I do not know how well the commercial life of the port survives, and I am rather ashamed of having tried so little to know. In the waters widening from the Batteries, South and East, vessels of not a very dominant type lay in the offing or slowly smoked across it. But the walk along the ancient wharves which I took one rather over-warm afternoon did not persuade me of a prospering traffic. The aging warehouses had been visited by many fires which left tumbled walls and tangled pipes and wires in gaps of blackened ruin. The footways were broken, and the coarse grass sprouted between the cobblestones of the wheelways. The freight-cars on many railroad tracks shut me from the piers, and there might have been fleets of commerce lying at them, for all I could see, but I doubt if there were. . . .

You must constantly take account of the galleries and the gardens if you are to sense Charleston aright. The galleries give the city its peculiar grace, and the gardens its noble extent . . . . The car on Meeting Street (such an acceptable name!) took us by the beautiful old church of St. Michael's, and into a grouping of other churches, with their graveyards so old and so still beside them in the heart of the city. If you are very worthy or very fortunate it will be the Saturday before Easter Sunday when you stray into St. Michael's and find the ladies of the parish trimming the interior with sprays and flowers, and one of these may show you the more notable among the wall tablets which you have brought the liking for from English churches. St. Michael's is of a very sisterly likeness to St. Philip's Church in the architectural charm derived from their mother architecture of the Georgian churches of the Strand. These two Charleston churches seem to me more beautiful than any of the Strand churches; and St. Philip's is especially fine with the wide curve of open space before it . . . . But we went for our own Easter service to the perpendicular Gothic of the Unitarian church which keeps the social eminence enjoyed by that sect in Charleston almost from the time of the break with the elder faith in Boston. . . .

Society as we saw it a little in Charleston had the informal charm of the vast cousinship which results in a strongly localized community where people of various origins intermarry and meet one another in constant ease and intimacy. It is the charm of all aristocracies, and I suppose Charleston is and always has been an aristocracy; a commercial aristocracy to be sure; but Venice was a commercial aristocracy. . . . The very diversity of their origin in Charleston contributes to the picturesqueness of the aspect which its society wears to the strangers. Here for once in the human story, the victims of oppression did not suffer for their wrongs even in their pride; the Huguenots who fled from France found not merely refuge in Columbia, but instant worldly honor. Their abounding names are of the first in Charleston; the very names of the streets testify to their equal value in the community proud to welcome them . . . . I like to think it was their qualification of the English ideal which has tended to give the Charlestonians their gentle manners. But if I am altogether mistaken in this, I like these manners better than our brusque Northern ways. I like a place where the very ticket-seller makes the question of a Pullman section an affair of social courtesy, and the telegraph-operator stays with my despatch in his hand to invoke my conjectures of the weather. In a world where tomorrow so often galls . . . it is pleasant to draw breath awhile where the present keeps a leisured pace . . . and mid-April, such as we left in Charleston, promises to stay through the year.

158. *A Final Tribute to Benjamin Ryan Tillman, December 15, 1918*

AFTER HIS STORMY BUT SUCCESSFUL CAREER AS GOVERNOR OF SOUTH CAROLINA, B. R. TILLMAN BECAME A UNITED STATES SENATOR IN 1896, REMAINING IN OFFICE UNTIL HIS DEATH IN 1918. IN THE SENATE HE CONTINUED TO BE A CONTROVERSIAL FIGURE, BUT DURING HIS LATER YEARS, ESPECIALLY DURING WORLD WAR I, HIS VALUABLE SERVICES TO HIS STATE AND NATION WERE RECOGNIZED EVEN BY HIS ENEMIES. THE FOLLOWING EXCERPTS, PAID IN TRIBUTE TO HIS FELLOW CAROLINIAN, ARE TAKEN FROM THE *Memorial Address* BY JAMES F. BYRNES, THEN A MEMBER OF THE HOUSE OF REPRESENTATIVES.

[Excerpts from Byrnes's address:]

He knew little of parliamentary law and cared less. The truth is that Tillman had no regard for any kind of law. In his consideration of a proposition there was but one question, "Is it just?" If he became convinced that the object sought to be accomplished was a just and righteous one, he was impatient of any interference by any law, rule, or regulation.

With this indifference to law, and with the absolute power that he wielded while governor, the salvation of the people was, that Tillman acted always from impulse, and Tillman's impulses were always good.

It is impossible here to refer to his many achievements in the Senate . . . . During the control of the Senate by the Republicans, Tillman was placed in charge of the railroad-rate bill, and his successful handling of it won the commendation of his colleagues. His exposure of the frauds of the armor-plate manufacturers finally led to the construction by the Government of its own armor-plate plant. He established the Charleston Navy Yard and has consistently labored for its development. As chairman of the Naval Affairs Committee he devoted his time and talents to the development of the Navy, and he lived to see his efforts rewarded by the demonstration of naval efficiency in the world war that has won the plaudits of the Nation. . . .

U.S. Congress, *Benjamin Ryan Tillman, Memorial Address* (Washington: Government Printing Office, 1919), 91–95.

Tillman's service in the Senate quickly made him a national figure and he was in great demand as a public speaker. It was Champ Clark, Speaker of the House, who first suggested to a Chautauqua organization that Tillman should be induced to go upon the lecture platform. They succeeded in inducing him to go upon a lecture tour, and thirty days after he started the president of the organization advised Mr. Clark that Tillman was the best drawing card they had. While he had several lectures, his lecture upon the race problem attracted most attention. Through this lecture he undoubtedly presented to the people of the North more clearly than did any other man the view of the South upon this question. But while rendering his section a service, the fatigue of the travel, after an arduous session, weakened him physically and contributed to his physical break-down. He was stricken with paralysis. From this stroke he recovered, and while he did not regain his former strength, he continued his active service in the Senate until three days before his death on July third of this year. . . .

As I learned to know him I wondered how, even in the heat of political contests, his enemies misjudged him as they did. I saw his finer qualities, his love of truth, and his hatred of hypocrisy; his love of his fellow man and his sympathy for the down-trodden and the unfortunate; his chivalrous respect for women and his love of children. I learned, too, of his simple but firm faith in a Supreme Being, and to-day, as I recall how in daily life he practiced religion, I have an abiding confidence that a just and merciful God has granted to him that eternal rest to which a life of service justly entitles him . . . .

The years of his public life he had crowded to the utmost with service to the people of South Carolina, and I make bold to say that when the history of this period is written, the historian of the future, freed from the prejudice engendered by political contests, will say not only that he was "a Carolinian and a patriot," but he will say that Benjamin Ryan Tillman was the greatest man that South Carolina has produced.

159. *Governor Manning's Report on His Administration, 1919*

DURING WORLD WAR I, SOUTH CAROLINA'S GOVERNOR WAS RICHARD I. MANNING, WHO MIGHT BE TERMED A "CONSERVATIVE." DESPITE THE ENERGIES SPENT IN THE PROSECUTION OF THE WAR, CONSIDERABLE PROGRESS, PARTICULARLY IN SOCIAL LEGISLATION, WAS MADE IN THE STATE. GOVERNOR MANNING, IN HIS LAST ADDRESS BEFORE THE STATE LEGISLATURE, DEPLORED SOUTH CAROLINA'S POSITION AS FORTY-SEVENTH IN THE NATION IN EDUCATION. HE EMPHASIZED THE NEED FOR A STATEWIDE SCHOOL-ATTENDANCE LAW AND ADVOCATED A MODERN AND EFFECTIVE SYSTEM OF HIGHWAYS. MANNING'S REPORT ON HIS ADMINISTRATION, DELIVERED ON JANUARY 15, 1919, CAME SHORTLY BEFORE HE RETIRED FROM OFFICE.

[Governor Richard I. Manning]

When I assumed the office of governor four years ago, you will recall the fact that the party rules and the laws governing primary elections were loose and were conspicuous by lack of safeguards which would guarantee to every man qualified to vote the right to vote once, but only once, in an election. Now the party rules have been strengthened, and the laws governing primary elections have been tightened. As far back as 1894, I introduced in the Legislature a bill to provide the Australian ballot system. The Australian ballot system has now been enacted into law, and has been found a safeguard and guaranty for the free and untrammeled expression of the popular will.

Four years ago, the law was a by-word and reproach. The verdicts of juries and the sentences of the courts had been ruthlessly set aside; barrooms were in operation in violation of the law; gambling was openly practiced, and the race track crowd had free swing to operate as they pleased. Other lawless and immoral acts were committed without concealment, and without punishment. Those conditions had so much

Yates Snowden, ed., *History of South Carolina,* 5 vols. (Chicago: The Lewis Publishing Co., 1920), II, 1081–87.

encouragement that they were regarded as almost irremediable. Criminals claimed a vested interest in crime, and regarded themselves as secure from punishment. Violations of law were committed with the certain knowledge that pardons would be forthcoming. During the four year period preceding the beginning of my first administration one thousand seven hundred and eight pardons and paroles were granted, an average of more than one convicted criminal a day released upon society.

In my campaign I promised the people of South Carolina to correct these evils. I put my hand on the situation, relentlessly and without discrimination. Today the situation is changed; good citizens respect and criminals fear the law, and there is no longer any one community that can be held up as an example of lawlessness. Grand juries, from the force of public opinion, now bring in true bills, and petty juries bring in verdicts of guilty where guilt exists. Certain local authorities which formerly flagrantly violated the law now faithfully and efficiently support the law. Public sentiment is healthy, and this public spirit has strengthened our courts and the hands of officers of the law.

Throughout the State I advocated local option compulsory school attendance. The opposition to compulsory attendance was vigorous. I believed then that such a law would be the opening wedge for a State-wide compulsory attendance law, and public sentiment would demand increased school facilities until such a law would become a necessity. The Legislature enacted the local option compulsory attendance law, and it has been put into operation in 630, or one-third, of the school districts of the State. It has been demonstrated that it is practicable and workable. It has therefore achieved its purpose, and has blazed the way for an expansion of that principle, so that today there is an insistent and strong demand for a State-wide compulsory law.

A distinct advance has been made in legislation affecting education. Placing the insurance of school houses under the sinking fund commission has meant a great saving. Provision for a supervisor of mill schools has proven of distinct benefit. There has been a large growth in the number of school districts which have levied local taxes, and today eight-ninths, or 1659 school districts, have voted local taxes for school purposes. Night schools were inaugurated in 1915. The act of the General Assembly providing for longer terms required a term of seven months, where the local levy was as much as eight mills, and 25 pupils attend a school. This was marked progress. Notwithstanding war conditions and the scarcity of labor, enrollment and average attendance have been maintained. There has been an increase of about 20 per cent in the salaries of teachers, especially the women teachers, and the State appropriation for education during 1918 is more than double the appropriation for 1914.

The Highway Commission was created in 1917, with the idea of giving to the State a comprehensive and scientific system of roads. The Commission has not been able to accomplish what was desired, because of the inadequacies of the law under which it operates, but a valuable start has been made which promises well for the future.

In 1915 the age limit for child labor in South Carolina was, upon my recommendation, raised to fourteen years; and again in 1916 the Legislature, acting upon my recommendation, very wisely raised the limit to sixteen years. This is of the greatest importance since it affects the whole fabric of our social and economic life. . . .

In 1916 the debt of the State was refunded at the rate of four per cent instead of four and one-half per cent, as in the former issue. The saving in interest resulting from the reduction in the rate, and retiring a part of the principle of the State debt, will be $35,754.75 annually. The refunded bonds have not the tax deduction feature as did the old Brown bonds, and this has added to the taxable property of the State a million and a half dollars which before escaped taxation and which will increase the revenues of the State about $30,000 annually, making a total saving each year of over $66,000.

The credit of the State stands high, as is attested by the fact that money for the current expenses of the State government has been borrowed at a lower rate of interest than other States have obtained. In one year money for this purpose was borrowed at two per cent. . . .

The National Guard of South Carolina played a part in the Great War in Europe which has established for all time a record for that organization. In the Thirtieth and the Forty-Second Divisions, South Carolinians played a conspicuous part by their courage, daring and effectiveness as fighters, and when the history of this war is written these two divisions will be placed in history among the immortals.

Under the act of the Legislature and by authority of the War Department, sixteen companies of State reserve militia have been organized in South Carolina since the National Guard has been absorbed into the National Army, the Federal Government furnishing arms and ammunition and certain equipment, and the State supplying such additional equipment as is necessary. . . .

South Carolina remains almost at the foot of the ladder in point of illiteracy—the forty-seventh state in the Union. The one State which by its position saves South Carolina from being at the very bottom—Louisiana—is already taking serious and far-reaching steps to climb to a higher plane. This blot must be removed from the fair name of our State, and South Carolina must no longer occupy this degraded position. She must in education and efficiency be fully abreast of her sister states . . . . The amount given by the people of South Carolina for humanitarian and relief purposes during the War is almost four times the amount appropriated for educational purposes by the State during the past four years. . . .

Automobiles and heavy trucks have multiplied. This heavy traffic has cut up our roads and now they are a disgrace. A makeshift system of road work will no longer suffice. South Carolina must adopt a modern practical and effective system of highways. The civilization of the State can not progress without good roads.

The time has come to stop and take an accounting. Can we, the people of South Carolina who have raised nearly a hundred millions of dollars for the War, do the things which lie before us in the broad path of duty? There are to my mind but two essentials—the vision and the willingness to go forward. Such a program as our vision of a better State outlines will require as a primary and fundamental means the expenditure of more money than the State has heretofore appropriated for education, highways, public health, humanitarian causes and other purposes, and larger and adequate appropriations mean an increased taxation.

South Carolina's per capita tax is $2.05, the lowest of any State in the Union save one, and this is just one cent lower. Our assessments are low. We can well afford to increase our taxes in order to advance and go forward with the march of an enlightened world and a civilization which has been made secure by the sacrifices of millions of heroic and unselfish men who were not afraid even to die for their ideals. If there be those who would oppose these forward measures which our awakened public conscience dictates because of higher taxation, they are, I hope, that small minority who have failed, perhaps, to grasp the meaning of the new Americanism, which is closely allied with Christianity. May God give us the wisdom and courage for these tasks.

160. *South Carolina Becomes a "White" State, 1925*

FROM 1820 TO 1920 THE U.S. CENSUSES SHOWED THAT A MAJORITY OF THE POPULATION OF SOUTH CAROLINA WAS NEGRO. THIS HAD LITTLE EFFECT ON THE POLITICAL CONTROL OF THE STATE EXCEPT DURING THE RECONSTRUCTION PERIOD, WHEN THE REPUBLICAN PARTY WAS SWEPT INTO POWER. THE SWITCH TO A WHITE MAJORITY IN THE STATE IS DESCRIBED IN THE FOLLOWING SELECTION.

[Department of Agriculture report]

Change from Negro to white majority in the population of South Carolina has been the most important if not the most interesting event in the State's history in the last twenty-five years. The Bureau of the Census estimated the population of the State July 1, 1925, at 1,804,000 —893,000 colored and 910,000 white. . . .

The Negro majority in proportion to whites has been rapidly diminishing since 1900. In that year the Negroes were 782,321 and the whites 557,807, the Negro majority being 224,514. In 1910, it was 156,682, but by 1920, when the whites were 818,538, and the Negroes 864,719, it had dropped to 46,181. The Census Bureau's estimate for July, 1925, was that the number of whites exceeded that of Negroes by 15,200. . . .

In the first ten years of the present century, the percentage of increase, as shown by the thirteenth census, was 21.8% for whites and 6.8% for Negroes. In the second, as shown by the census for 1920, it was 20.5% for whites and 3.5 for Negroes. In these sharply contrasting percentages for the twenty years, migration of Negroes was not the commanding factor—indeed, it was scarcely important. Considerable Negro migration from South Carolina did not begin until after the census of 1920, general infestation of South Carolina cotton fields by boll weevils not having taken place until 1922. That, and the coincident in time with it, strong demand for unskilled labor in the North, caused Negroes to leave South

Handbook of South Carolina, 1927, Dept. of Agriculture (Columbia: The State Co., 1927), 20–23.

Carolina farms in numbers for two or three years, though for the last two years the number has been smaller.

The departure of Negroes upon the arrival of the weevils was not in an economic sense calamitous. For the most part they left lands which they had rented and which had not had skillful tillage. These lands were worn and usually had been yielding meager support to the colored labor that occupied them as renters or sharecroppers. The damage done by the weevil so reduced the cotton crop on them that the family support vanished. Those sharecroppers who had not the endorsement of solvent landlords could no longer obtain credit upon which to make a crop. Thus the lands abandoned were those which had long been barely productive enough to support their occupants scantily. . . .

In 1920, the number of white people operating farms in South Carolina was 83,683 compared with 82,186 according to the farm census of 1925. The colored farmers numbered 109,010 in 1920 and 90,581 in 1925. Thus, in the five years the white farmers held their own, decreasing only 447, as compared with 18,429 colored farmers who, when the weevils came, sought other fields and kinds of employment.

South Carolina is a rural state. In 1925, 911,885 persons were living on farms, of whom 529,292 were colored and 382,593 were white . . . . Of the people in the incorporated towns and cities, 117,300 are white and 74,100 are Negroes. . . .

The existence of a Negro majority for more than a full century in South Carolina, fifty-five years of it after slave emancipation, has had political, social and economic results, depressing in character, which can hardly be measured. Only one other state has had a Negro majority. Hardly does one risk exaggeration in saying that a great, if not the greater, part of the troubles that the commonwealth has endured is explained by it. Despite the census bureau's estimate of 1925, placing the white majority at 16,200, made with no consideration of the unusual migration since 1920, one hazards the opinion that this majority will appear close to 75,000 or 100,000 in 1930.

This means a new freedom for South Carolina. It is the removal of a vague but always present shadow. South Carolina at last has become a white state. . . .

161. *The State of the State in the 1920s and Early 1930s*

ECONOMIC CONDITIONS DID NOT IMPROVE IN THE LATE 1920S OR IN THE
EARLY 1930S, AS W. W. BALL POINTS OUT IN THE FIRST EXCERPT HERE.
THIS IS FOLLOWED BY AN ACCOUNT OF THE JOYS OF FARMING IN THE
COASTAL AREA. THE LAST SELECTION IS "DEPRESSION."

[William Watts Ball on South Carolina in 1932]

The South Carolinians of 1932 are the children and grandchildren of
those of 1890, but they pursue different ways and their South Carolina
is a different State.

The South Carolina of the "Tillman years" had 1,151,149 inhabitants
of whom 77,033 lived in cities and towns, but in 1930, 371,080 of 1,738,-
765 were urban. The percentage of rural farm population is now 52.6,
including the Negro farmers. Outside of the towns of more than 2500
inhabitants are now 296,029 whites, of whom are the majority of the
textile workers, in unincorporated villages, the keepers of filling stations
and little stores that bead the paved highways, and the dwellers in the
suburbs of all the towns rapidly expanding in widening circles.

These white country people not engaged in farming together with the
white townspeople are 528,670, and they are 113,590 more than the
white farming population of 415,080, implying a voting majority of at
least 50,000 over the farmers in a Democratic primary.

A repetition of the Tillman or Farmers' Movement campaign would
be a hopeless enterprise, and it has come to pass that the landowning
farmers are seeking coalition with the real-estate owners, corporations and
private citizens, in towns and cities, against whom Captain Tillman's . . .
guidance they made political war forty-two years ago.

In these decades white illiteracy has been lowered from 21.9 to 5.2%.
Negro illiteracy is 26.9%. The population in the cotton-mill villages
(some of them are within the cities) in 1890 was about 13,000, the textile
voters about 2500, but these villages now contain 170,000 inhabitants and

W. W. Ball, *The State That Forgot: South Carolina's Surrender to Democracy*
(Indianapolis: Bobbs-Merrill Co., 1932), 275–80, 289. Reprinted by permission
of William Watts Ball, Jr.

their voters, white men and women, are 60,000 to 65,000. In the primaries they are formidable, for often they vote with a degree of concentration for a candidate who has specialized in cultivating and flattering them. Of the same blood and origin that other South Carolinians are, two or three generations at most from the farms or the mountains, there has grown rapidly among them huddled in their villages a pathetic aloofness toward the rest of the population, and of this some of the politicians make the most with skill and assiduity. These politicians are not labor agitators, they have little understanding of labor's problems, they are careful to give no offense to other classes, they do not encourage trade unions, they join the popular fraternal orders and call the mill people by their first names. That suffices. . . .

The momentous change in South Carolina has been from a black to a white majority in population. In 1890 the Negroes were 688,934, the whites 462,008; the Negro majority was 226,926. In 1930, the whites were 944,080 and their majority over the 793,681 Negroes were 150,399. The fear of the division of the whites in the Tillman year had reason in the fact of a Negro majority of adult males of 30,292; now the white women and men who could legally qualify to vote outnumber the Negroes 444,364 to 222,518; they are two to one, and there could be no need for a Red Shirt campaign to save white supremacy. The fear lingers were the Negroes to form the voting habit, most of them would be controlled by depraved white politicians, and there is substance in that . . . .

The State needs more white people . . . Nordics, Latins, Slavs, and if they should bring with them new religions, Roman Catholic, Jewish, Greek Orthodox, as well as Protestant, so much the better.

We South Carolinians have been so insulated in ignorance that a horrible crust of vanity and self-righteousness has encased us, and anything that pierces it will help though it brings pain. The politicians boast of the State's "homogeneous and Anglo-Saxon" population. That is what ails it. For two centuries the blood has been stagnant.

A judgment formed upon surface aspects would be that South Carolina has made great strides in the four decades [since 1890]. The holders of diplomas from colleges and high schools have multiplied; in the average rural county the college graduates could be counted by dozens in 1890; now they are thousands, and the common-school plant is respectable in appearance and dimensions. In the last ten years an excellent system of hard roads, not completed or paid for yet, has come into being and motor and gasoline sales taxes are carrying the burden of it. In any direction one may ride smoothly quite through South Carolina. . . . Electric power installations are numerous, some of them huge, and the whole state is a factory site. Albeit only 10,400,000 acres of the 19,500,000 are described by the census as "land in farms" (which does not mean that nearly so much is under cultivation) and most of the lands have been stripped of their original forest, the state looks vastly better to the casual observer than it did forty years ago. . . .

In South Carolina, as in other Southern states, the Republican organization is no more than a contrivance to choose delegates to national conventions and distribute federal patronage when the Washington administration is Republican. The fewer the Republican voters the more convenient is the division of the offices. The sham which is the party would not exist were there no delegates to be sent to national conventions. . . . These Republicans are looked upon by the Democrats as lucky fellows to whom a foreign government is paying off small debts, and they are not disliked. Besides, the Republican Administrations have been scrupulous to choose Federal judges of the best material available.

The Democratic party is without a creed, except white solidarity, and without a code beyond mechanical rules necessary for the running of the machine.

At present, government in South Carolina is a failure. It has reduced the State to a point at which the hateful word, bankruptcy, is openly spoken . . . . Every political sign visible is that in the Republic, South Carolina is a dead thing, harmless perhaps except to itself. Its desire to lead is gone. It contains tens of thousands of good people, brave enough in time of trial . . . , but it has in some strange manner lost its memory, and is sundered from its past . . . . The lasting victory was won in 1868 by the Carpetbaggers, the Scalawags, and the Negroes, when, under the guns of an army of occupation, they gave the State democracy, foreign to its nature. There is no recovery.

[James Henry Rice, Jr.]

Farming in Coastal Carolina:

For producing corn cheaply the coast is supreme. There is also the advantage of planting it after truck, when the soil is in superb condition.

James Henry Rice, Jr., *Glories of the Carolina Coast* (Columbia: The R. L. Bryan Co., 1925), 19–28. Copyright, 1925, by The R.L. Bryan Co. Reprinted by permission of The R.L. Bryan Company.

Discarding extravagant claims, while it is true that yields after truck are small, due to inferior cultivation, demonstrations show they can always be made large.

The coast is supreme likewise in producing forage crops, from cow peas to clover, and it has no rival in growing winter vegetables for shipment to metropolitan markets. Their quality is universally recognized when the crops are properly grown.

Fall oats and wheat yield heavily, though spring oats usually fail. Spillman and other world authorities, who have given thought to the subject, concluded that the coast possesses advantages over all the country in growing live stock, hogs, sheep and cattle. Permanent pastures are easily made and silos easily filled. Five acres will pack a silo capable of keeping 30 cows fat all winter. Most crops are abundant. Some of our big live oaks will yield 100 bushels of acorns. Pine, beech, chinquapin and haws are great yielders of mast. Berries, wild fruits and roots exist in profusion. Mild winters make housing superfluous. Poultry, like live stock, thrives with proper attention.

If a man stick to the coast with the determination to make a home and stay there he will in due time have his portion of the blessings of God.

Most deplorably, spectacular operations, like phosphate mining and an occasional flush profit from truck and lumbering, have deluded too many into the notion that fortunes may be picked up . . . . The wealth of ante bellum days did not come easy but was won through generations of labor and hard thinking.

BEAUTY OF THE LAND

Artists tell us that man craves beauty in his heart. The azaleas and camellia japonicas underneath the live oaks at Magnolia Gardens have appealed to the world's heart. More than one literary artist has said that no description of them can be adequate. Not far away to the west is another garden, Middleton, of a different type and neither has anything to fear from critics. [A third world-famous garden in Charleston is Cypress, owned by the City of Charleston.]

From colonial times lovely gardens have been a feature of the coast. General Pinckney had one in the heart of Charleston. Thomas Rhett Smith, enamored of the royal gardens at Versailles, had them reproduced in miniature on Chee-Ha, a detail of which was a ten acre rosary, just outside his study window, tended by a French gardener. Bluffton, Beaufort, McClellanville and Georgetown all possess beauty spots. Beaufort has been termed the most beautiful town on the Atlantic—true enough, except that it is not on the Atlantic but on the Beaufort River. The panorama of its harbor is one of the sights of North America. Were it in California or Florida it would be as well known as the Riviera.

Picturesqueness and variety, which characterize the lower coast, reach perfection at Bluffton on the River May, lauded by all travelers from Ribault down. All the country, indeed, from North Edisto to Savannah, exhibits the same richness and variety in its flora, the same opulence in fauna, . . . but, at Bluffton, the live oaks are uniformly larger and more symmetrical in the unfolding of their mighty crowns. The limbspread is enormous, one limb measuring recently eighty-four feet, two inches.

Bluffton is the "Appleboro," made famous in the novels of Marie Conway Oemler.

Over the May River, towering above sheer forest and marsh and gleaming white in sun or moon, rises the mansion of Col. R. T. Wilson, fitly called "Palmetto Lodge." Around it extends its lordly acres, twenty-six thousand in all, more than twice the size of old time baronies. . . . Adjoining it is the Vanderbilt place, itself large and commodious, with lovely grounds. Under the roots of a cedar, gnarled and old, standing just above the bluff as you enter the grounds, are broken slabs from a tomb, said to mark the resting place of Pendarvis, the pirate, slain by the son of a man he murdered.

Two miles below Bluffton is Hunting Island, now called Palmetto Beach, the favorite collecting ground of Mellichamp, through whose labors it is known to the world, for Mellichamp belongs to the nobility of science . . . and is known and honored by every biologist in the world. . . . He is buried at old St. Luke's, five miles away in the forest.

. . . Palmetto Beach has become a summer fishing camp and a winter playground for northern people. The site is of singular beauty, with the May winding around it and other islands looming with billowy growth over the marshes. A few miles east the May turns into Calibogue Sound and passes out to sea between Hilton Head and Daufuskie islands.

Bluffton retains enough flavor of old days to let one know he is within the pale, surrounded by the purple-born, who, through storm and stress, war and misfortune, have clung tenaciously to their birthright. Only on Edisto and along the Pon Pon does one get so fragrant an aroma of our "Golden Prime."

A summer trip along one of the coastal rivers will show the giant yuccas in flower and the magnolia, "the royal woman of the Southern wood," with its creamy white blossoms laid on shining green leaves; the cypresses clad in vivid green and "lilies" floating on still waters, while the wampee shows forth its blossoms—everywhere bloom run riot. On the uplands tall brooding pines sway in the wind and murmur things unutterable. Huge wood ibises stalk along the shore; redwings chatter and quarrel; rails cry in the reeds; coots and gallinules patter over the lily pads; the bald eagle soars, often a speck, in the empyrean, while coppices are snow white with egrets; and nonpareils cling to grass stalks, eating seeds. All is life, life omnipresent—bird and beast, insect and flower, reptile and fish. What sane man could call so fruitful a region poor? It is opulent, prodigal, with a lure no soul may resist.

To know the coast is to love it—love it even in its vast silent spaces, as in the solitude where Cape Romain Light warns marines of the treacherous reefs, off the mouth of Santee, a region so wild that you can readily believe yourself in Asia or Africa.

In variety lies the charm of the coast. No description of one part can apply to another. The May River at Bluffton is not more different from the broad Waccamaw, than are the picturesque homes on James Island or Edisto from the windswept wastes of North Island or the sand dunes of Pawley. There is a change for each mile, often many changes to the mile. . . .

[David Duncan Wallace]

"DEPRESSION"

Before the boll weevil made his inroads here, South Carolina profited by the good price of cotton caused by his cutting of the crop in the Southwest. Though amply forewarned by the steady spread of the weevil, almost all farmers continued to stick to cotton on account of a climate whose droughts it alone is suited to endure, the absence of markets for other products, and the ignorance . . . of any other crop. . . .

The long agricultural depression beginning in 1921, following a period in which farmers and thousands whose prosperity was dependent on theirs had contracted debts based upon inflated values of land and produce, inevitably led to widespread distress and even bankruptcy. Between January 1, 1921, and February 28, 1933, 34 National and 273 State banks in South Carolina closed their doors. There had been in 1919, 78 National banks, and in 1920, 387 State banks.

David Duncan Wallace, *The History of South Carolina,* 4 vols. (New York: American Historical Society, 1934), III, 479. Reprinted by permission of Robert Marsden Wallace.

162. *South Carolina in 1947: A Northern Viewpoint*

THOSE WRITING ABOUT SOUTH CAROLINA NORMALLY SPEND MORE TIME
IN THE STATE THAN DID JOHN GUNTHER, AUTHOR OF THE SELECTION
FOLLOWING, WHOSE THOUGHTS ARE INTERESTING THOUGH SOMEWHAT
BIASED AND NOT ENTIRELY ACCURATE. AS A REPLY TO AND A REFUTATION
OF HIS STATEMENTS, THE *South Carolina Magazine* RAN A FEATURE
ENTITLED, "INSIDE JOHN GUNTHER" IN THE AUGUST, 1947, ISSUE. THE
SELECTION FOLLOWING COMES FROM THE 1951 REVISED EDITION OF GUN-
THER'S BOOK. IN THE 1947 EDITION, GUNTHER MENTIONED THAT SENA-
TOR OLIN D. JOHNSTON WAS ONCE A MILL HAND AND THAT THE
GOVERNOR, J. STROM THURMOND, WAS A LIBERAL. HE NOTED THAT
SOUTH CAROLINA HAD RECENTLY REPEALED ITS ELECTION LAWS AND THAT
THE "PRETENSE WAS PUT FORWARD THAT THE PRIMARY IS PURELY AN
AFFAIR OF THE DEMOCRATIC PARTY, WITH WHICH THE STATE HAS
NOTHING TO DO . . . ."

[John Gunther]

South Carolina is one of the poorest of American states, and probably
the balkiest. Like its big sister to the north, it has pronounced section-
alisms; the chief division is between the "low country" . . . and the
"uplands"; one might also mention a third region, the sand hills above
tidewater, where poor folk called "sandlappers" live. These segmentations
arise out of history as well as geography. . . .

The first colonists thought of themselves . . . not so much as inhabiting the southern tip of America, but the northernmost tip of the West
Indies—and West Indian influence is still distinct in Charleston. . . .

The low country people and upland people are still at loggerheads.
One reason is poor communications; nobody will understand this until he

John Gunther, *INSIDE U.S.A.* (New York: Harper & Bros., 1951). Abridg-
ment of pp. 792–797 from INSIDE U.S.A., Revised Edition, by John Gunther.
Copyright, 1946, 1947, 1951 by John Gunther. Copyright, 1947, by The Curtis
Publishing Company. Reprinted by permission of Harper & Row, Publishers.

tries, by rail, to cross the inland area. Charleston . . . dominated everything until half century ago; Columbia was made the capital to satisfy the hinterland. The uplands . . . make a kind of "crossroads society" and are spotted with industry to an extent, for instance in textile towns like Greenville and Spartanburg . . . ; Spartanburg is the home of James F. Byrnes, among other things. The "lintheads," as the mill workers are called, are among the most poverty blanched and backward folk in America. There were 38,931 homes in South Carolina without a toilet or privy in 1947.

South Carolina lucklessly had one economic factor after another shot from under her. Turpentine and the trade in ship's stores declined when sail gave way to steam. Indigo . . . was killed by the advent of aniline dyes. Then rice, after a time, could not compete against the "highland" rice of Arkansas or Texas, where harvesting was possible by machinery; cultivation in South Carolina had to be done under water, by hand, as in Japan. Finally, Sea Island . . . cotton was mostly destroyed by the boll weevil thirty years ago and subsequent techniques in spinning made this variety of cotton less valuable. . . .

Perhaps I am sounding too dour a note. South Carolina, for all its poverty and ill luck, has a certain somber and shadowy magnificence . . . . CHARLESTON . . . is a gem; it is also a kind of mummy, like Savannah. I heard one unkind friend nickname it "Death on the Atlantic," and call it "a perfect example of what the South must never be again." Be this as it may, it belongs in that eclectic category of American "sights" not to be missed, like the Taos Pueblo and Niagara Falls. Once it was the fourth biggest city in America, and probably the most brilliantly sophisticated; today much of its polish has worn off, though it still retains a cardinal quality of grace. . . .

The town keeps up a considerable intellectual and social life. Of course it has never heard of Minneapolis or Akron, and is just coming to recognize Atlanta; but it has a good art gallery and a theater. It contains one of the best clubs in the country, the oldest St. Andrews Society outside Scotland, and the oldest surviving home of Scottish Rites Masonry. . . .

South Carolina is a white supremacy state par excellence . . . . Nevertheless South Carolina has a curious eruptive quality. The Negro community is self-conscious and adult, and South Carolina is the only state in which Negroes have, in effect, sought to establish their own political party . . . . The background of this cannot be appreciated easily without cognizance of the fact that the state for many years had a Negro majority. . . .

In 1950 Governor Thurmond, leader of the Dixiecrats, was beaten for the Senate by Olin D. Johnston . . . and the renowned James F. Byrnes returned to political life at the age of seventy-one as governor . . . . Byrnes's inaugural speech shocked many; he reassured his white supremacy followers that segregation would be maintained in the schools no matter what. . . .

163. *Strom Thurmond, as Governor, Reports on 1947–1948*

J. STROM THURMOND WAS ELECTED GOVERNOR OF SOUTH CAROLINA IN 1946 AND SERVED UNTIL JANUARY, 1951. IN NOVEMBER, 1948, HE WAS A CANDIDATE FOR PRESIDENT OF THE UNITED STATES ON THE "STATES' RIGHTS PARTY" (OR "DIXIECRAT") TICKET. THURMOND AND HIS CAMPAIGN PARTNER, FIELDING WRIGHT OF MISSISSIPPI, RECEIVED 39 ELECTORAL VOTES. THE FOLLOWING SELECTION IS FROM HIS REPORT TO THE PEOPLE OF SOUTH CAROLINA ON THE FIRST TWO YEARS OF HIS ADMINISTRATION AS GOVERNOR.

[Strom Thurmond's report while governor]

The State of South Carolina, like other states of the South, has made many progressive strides during the past year. Our people are nearer to economic security and social well-being than they have ever been. Never before have they been so united in their determination to bring about the industrial and agricultural developments, the educational growth, the public health improvements, and the sound governmental reforms that are needed for their happiness and prosperity . . . .

The first two years of my administration as Governor has been dominated by the conviction that a sound, honest, progressive and efficient government can provide the best possible impetus for the development of our State and its resources. . . .

In the implementation of this policy, the General Assembly has made provision for a broad reorganization program, and for continued support of the promotional activities of our Research, Planning and Development Board. In addition, this policy has been further supported by educational and agricultural legislation designed to prepare South Carolina for the balanced economy which is our aim.

The reorganization of the executive branch of the State government is being studied by a State Reorganizational commission authorized by the 1948 General Assembly. This group will prepare proposed legislation to

The Charlotte Observer (Charlotte, N.C.), Feb. 8, 1949.

streamline and co-ordinate the 109 separate agencies now overburdening our system. I am confident that the commission will find the means to eliminate duplication and useless activities of the government to promote efficiency.

A Joint Committee on Reorganization of the General Assembly, also authorized last year, has already submitted its report, and legislators are now studying its proposals to modernize the operation of the Legislature. . . .

A Commission on Revision of the 1895 Constitution, appointed in 1948, has begun the work of modernizing the Constitution and eliminating outmoded sections for later submission to the people. . . .

A Constitutional amendment was passed to restrict the Governor's present power of pardon and parole, leaving only the commutation of death sentences directly in the hands of the Governor . . . .

An increase in funds was made possible for the public school system, so that approximately $750,000 more will be spent this fiscal year. . . . The General Assembly also appropriated an additional fund of $1,714,000 for the present fiscal year for teachers' salaries to take care of those who have qualified for higher ratings. South Carolina's plans for participation in the plan for regional schools, developed by the Southern Governors' conference, was approved.

A State Agricultural Marketing Commission was created to acquire sites and construct wholesale farmers' markets thereon, in order to insure our farmers better prices for their products. Provision was made for the expenditure of $9,000,000 a year for three years on our farm-to-market road system, a program of vital importance to our rural areas . . . .

With so many important reforms under way, the 88th General Assembly which convened January 11, 1949, has an equally great opportunity to render service of historic importance to South Carolina. Among the measures which I recommended to the legislators in my annual message on January 12 were the following:

1. Ratification of the amendment restricting the Governor's pardoning power to commutation of death sentences.

2. Educational improvements, including: increased pay and restored sick leave for teachers; increased aid for school bus transportation, and school plant building aid; full support for the Regional Education plan; and co-ordination of our college system to eliminate duplication and inefficiency.

3. A number of improvements designed to improve the situation of our farmers, including: an animal disease prevention program; modernized

insecticide laws; a cotton seed analysis laboratory; research projects in marketing and processing.

4. A broad labor program, including: a wage and hour law; health safeguards in industry; upward revision of workmen's compensation, and downward revision of insurance rates; and a labor welfare committee to study revision of our labor statutes.

5. Continued support of the industrial development program of our Research, Planning and Development Board.

6. A comprehensive program for conservation of our natural resources, including soil, forests, power, seaports, state parks, and wild-life. Depletion of natural resources is today one of our most serious problems.

7. Four improvements in the interest of public welfare, including: increased public assistance; improved child welfare legislation; provision for inspection of custodial institutions; and an industrial school for Negro girls.

8. A broad program of mental rehabilitation, including: increased aid to the State Hospital; a clinic for the treatment of alcoholics; a training school for feeble-minded Negroes; a detention clinic for treatment of sex criminals.

9. Further measures for the continued better control of the liquor industry.

10. Approval of the proposed $5,000,000 state penitentiary to replace the present outmoded and inadequate plant.

11. A State Bureau of Investigation which would convert the present Constabulary into a modern crime and detection organization.

12. A central purchasing agency for all State departments and institutions, which would save hundreds of thousands of dollars annually.

13. Elimination of the unwieldly and costly system whereby the General Assembly spends so much time enacting local legislation and passing county supply acts . . . .

14. Establishment of a merit system for state employees to promote efficiency in government.

15. Modernization of our general election laws to include a secret ballot, permanent registration, removal of the poll tax as a pre-requisite for voting, and strengthening of voting qualifications. . . .

South Carolina's effort to raise the economic level of her people is inextricably bound up with the task of solving our educational problems. Our economic development is inevitably dependent upon equipping our people, both white and colored, to become productive citizens and carry their per capita share of the load. Higher income follows better education. Our State struggles under health, welfare, and educational burdens of nearly 2,000,000 people, only 60 per cent of whom contribute substantially to our economic production and the payment of tax burdens. The productive potential of our colored people is perhaps our largest undeveloped economic resource as a State. Increased purchasing power and greater production are needed if we are to raise our economic standards. Education is the means whereby we can most quickly equip our colored citizens to make their maximum contribution to the State's total economy . . . .

In the field of economic development, we have made remarkable gains in a short time . . . . Our farm cash income, which now rests on a broader production base, reached approximately $411,000,000 in 1948 . . . . During 1948, industrial plants began production in South Carolina which represented a total of $93,000,000 and which employ 13,000 persons . . . . Our pay rolls now exceed a billion dollars annually . . . . According to the last census, South Carolina ranks first in the percentage of white population who are four-year college graduates. . . .

It is clear that the eyes of the industrial world are turning southward. Our lower living costs, our great natural resources, and our energetic, friendly homogenous people are combining to attract industry. In addition, we are now on the verge of enjoying the fruits of a decade's work to break down the unfair differentials of other years.

South Carolina is striving for leadership in the growing effort to create for the beautiful Southland a new era of economic well-being and social progress.

164. *The Coming of the H-Bomb Project, 1950*

AFTER WORLD WAR II, THE ATOMIC ENERGY COMMISSION DECIDED TO
BUILD A PRODUCTION PLANT BY THE SAVANNAH RIVER, BETWEEN AIKEN
AND ALLENDALE, IN THE VICINITY OF ELLENTON AND BARNWELL. AL-
THOUGH IN LATER YEARS FACILITIES OF THE "BOMB" PLANT WERE TO BE
CUT BACK, AT THE TIME OF THE ANNOUNCEMENT THERE WAS MUCH
SPECULATION ABOUT WHAT IT WOULD MEAN. MANY WERE AFRAID OF THE
PLANT ITSELF; OTHERS SPECULATED WHAT IT WOULD MEAN IN TERMS OF
DOLLARS; AND HUNDREDS REALIZED SUDDENLY THAT THEY WOULD BE
UPROOTED FROM THEIR HOMES. THE FIRST SELECTION IS THE INITIAL
ANNOUNCEMENT OF THE PROJECT, THE FIRST WORD FOR MANY SOUTH
CAROLINIANS OF THE COMING OF THE PROJECT; THE SECOND EXCERPT
SPEAKS OF THE EFFECTS OF THE H-BOMB PLANT ON SOUTH CAROLINA.

[Newspaper story]

The United States Atomic Energy Commission announced Tuesday
(November 28) that its new production plants to be designed, built and
operated by the E. I. du Pont de Nemours Company of Wilmington,
Delaware, will be located in Aiken and Barnwell counties, South Carolina, near the Savannah River. About 250,000 acres will be acquired for
the site. Exact boundaries remain to be determined. The new site will be
known as the Savannah River Plant.

As was noted by the President last July in asking Congress to appropriate $260,000,000 to start construction, these additional plants, like the
existing facilities, will provide materials which can be used either for
weapons or for fuels potentially useful for power purposes. The Commission emphasized, however, that the operations at the Savannah River
Plant will not involve the manufacture of atomic weapons. The site was
chosen . . . after a four-month study of more than 100 sites by . . . Du
Pont and AEC engineers with the assistance of other federal agencies
. . . . The following factors were of major importance in determining
the site:

Barnwell People-Sentinel (Barnwell, S.C.), Nov. 30, 1950.

1. Military considerations including vulnerability to attack.

2. Operating requirements of the facilities themselves, the details of which cannot be disclosed for reasons of national security.

3. Accessibility to population centers to avoid establishing a new government community such as those at Oak Ridge, Los Alamos, and Richland.

4. Public health and safety considerations involving the location and adequacy of the site.

Acquisition of the land will be undertaken by the Corps of Engineers. The specific boundaries of the site will be announced later after completion of detailed engineering studies . . . . To make way for the plants and the surrounding security and safety zone, it will be necessary for about 1500 families to relocate in the next 18 months. The Federal-State agricultural agencies are organizing to give help to the families who must relocate. . . . In addition, the Commission and Du Pont will proceed within a short time to obtain rights of way for railroad spurs, roads and other facilities necessary for large-scale construction activities.

The site is located in Aiken and Barnwell counties, about 15 air miles south of Aiken, South Carolina, and about 20 air miles southeast of Augusta, Georgia. It is expected that the construction force will reach approximately 8000 during the first six months of construction which will be started early in 1951.

The new AEC plant, while having a primary military purpose at this time, will add to the nation's capacity for producing fuels which someday will be needed to utilize atomic energy for useful power. If the new facilities are not needed for defense, they can produce fuel for industry. The new facilities will be of advanced design and their operation will provide the commission with further information and understanding that will speed the progress of the national atomic energy program both for military and civilian purposes . . . .

Barnwell County residents . . . were completely stunned by the announcement. Visualizing the magnitude of the plant was impossible, particularly when one read the announcement that $260,000,000 had been appropriated for its construction. It was also impossible for the local people to realize that the towns of Snelling, Dunbarton and Ellenton would be completely wiped off the map and that an area including some 250,000 acres would be necessary to house the project and to provide the security area . . . . The potential growth of the town of Barnwell, which is the nearest town to the site, is unbelievable. The construction job will have some 8000 employees in the first six months and double that number in 12 months.

[Morgan Fitts]

The H-Bomb Plant Fifteen Months Later, In March, 1952

When Uncle Sam puts the finger on the spot for making the world's mightiest weapon of war, what happens to the spot? The answer comes from people who have had to move families, homes, jobs, and even their cemeteries to make way for H-Bomb on the Savannah—the government's 202,000-acre Hydrogen bomb plant.

Their stories are sometimes tragic, sometimes comic. Some folks are joyous with sudden new wealth, others have come on sudden hard times. There's greed, ambition and crime. There's a lot of what you would expect when a great new technical city—with its easy money, easy virtue, and thousands of new workers to house and care for—is suddenly rolled out on top of a drowsy Southern farm area.

One of the biggest headaches is housing, both for those whose homes have been uprooted and for the thousands of workers who are pouring in. A woman in nearby Augusta, Ga., had a garage apartment for rent, so she put an ad in the paper. She was aroused by a phone call at 2:30 the next morning. It was from a man who had waited up to get the paper as it came off the press . . . . That's the way housing is around here. Prices of farm land and lots in and around Aiken, also on the bomb plant fringe, jumped 50 to 75 per cent. Costs of three- to five-bed-room houses zoomed more than 30 per cent.

Most of the people of Ellenton and the other three villages in the plant area were well paid by the government for their property. But the boomtown price of new homes and land nearby, plus the expense of pulling up roots and putting them down elsewhere, have left some families worse off financially than they were before. About 80 families in Ellenton have had their houses put on wheels and moved outside the plant area. This hasn't always worked out too well. One house crashed through a bridge, and inexperienced movers damaged others . . . .

The uprooted people of Dunbarton, Meyers Mill, and Snelling—as well as from the farmlands nearby—are flooding into towns and villages outside the vast plant site. With them have come thousands of construc-

Morgan Fitts, in *The Anderson Independent* (Anderson, S.C.), Mar. 28, 1952.

tion workers. Jackson, for instance, previously had only 300 people. Now nobody's sure just how many people it has, but there are too many. And the nervous village fathers expect an eventual population of 10,000. The wheels of government have ground slowly in providing housing which it was known would be needed . . . . Only in the last few months has a start been made on trailer camps and low-cost housing projects . . . .

Some of the old guard Southerners deplore the influx of Northerners as another Yankee invasion of their homeland. What they feel is in peril this time is their leisurely, friendly way of life. On the other hand, the Big Boom is welcomed by many of the younger people in this area of South Carolina . . . .

There's still another aspect of the situation which is causing concern. What happens when the bubble bursts? The number of workers required to build the 250 permanent plant buildings, 66 miles of railroads, and 105 miles of roads, will hit a peak of about 45,000 this September. Then the hordes of tin-hatted construction gangs will mount their trailers and battered autos and move on. After construction is completed sometime in 1955, a regular plant force of only about 7000 will be required.

165. *Charleston Greets the New Year, January 1, 1953*

GAY OLD CHARLESTON HAD ANOTHER BIRTHDAY IN 1953, AND THE CELEBRATION, WHILE NOT A MOMENTOUS ONE, DOES HAVE THE MAKINGS OF HISTORY IN IT. THE GREAT AND HISTORIC CITY IS SHOWN AS IT PAUSED ON THE THRESHOLD OF ANOTHER YEAR.

[Richard D. Bullock]

A roaring Charleston shrieked welcome last night to her 272nd New Year. St. Michael's great bell, in keeping with the church's ancient by-law, led the clamor at 11:50 p. m., tolling the old year out in solemn strokes. At midnight the lighter bells chimed in to ring the changes for 1953.

But the venerable bells were soon drowned in a flood of sound as ships in the harbor roared deep-throated response, factories of the North Area piped shrill greetings, and the less majestic rattles, tin horns, and noise-makers of thousands of revelers joined in celebration. Hundreds of private parties livened usually quiet streets in the city's residential sections, while larger gatherings kept orchestras blaring in local hotels, clubs and night spots.

Today is just another working day for stevedores at Charleston's state-owned docks. The Italian freighter "Alceo" is discharging chrome ore at the Ordnance Dock, while the Swiss "Calanda" and the American "Steel Executive" unload Egyptian cotton at North Charleston terminals.

Other Charlestonians with responsibilities today are the Hibernians, enjoined by their constitution to meet at noon for their traditional dinner of hoppin' john and oratory.

Getting off to an earlier start this morning will be a celebration of the 89th Emancipation Day by the city's Negro community. The group's parade will move at 11 a.m. in President Street to Line, east to King, south to Calhoun, east to Alexander, north to America, to Hampsted Square, to Aiken, and to Cooper Street.

Richard D. Bullock in *The News and Courier* (Charleston, S.C.), Jan. 1, 1953.

A celebration will follow at the Jerusalem Baptist Church at Cooper and American Streets, led by the Rev. Charles A. Cherry, pastor of Central Baptist Church.

The entrance of 1953 last midnight wasn't riotous in all its parts. Worshippers at watchnight services throughout the city prayed the New Year might bring peace to the world and safety to themselves and loved ones.

166. *Agriculture from 1925 to 1963*

THE DROP IN FARM LANDS AND THE CHANGE IN AGRICULTURAL PRODUCTS AS WELL AS FARM METHODS WAS THE STORY FROM THE 1920s TO THE 1960s. AFTER WORLD WAR II, AGRICULTURE WAS A CLOSE SECOND TO INDUSTRY IN THE STATE. THERE WAS PROGRESS IN SELECTIVE CROP GROWING, PARTICULARLY IN TOBACCO, TRUCK, AND FRUITS. THE FOLLOWING SELECTIONS CONCERN THE GENERAL AGRICULTURAL PICTURE IN THE STATE IN 1925, IN 1940, IN 1952, AND IN 1963.

[1925]. [Department of Agriculture report]

The 1925 census of Agriculture showed 172,767 farmers in South Carolina, of whom 82,186 were white and 90,581 were colored. White owners were 41,601; colored 18,368; white tenants, 40,251; colored 72,179. The percentage of tenancy was 65.1. About 76,000 farmers lived on improved roads, and 96,000 on unimproved. The total acreage in farms was 10,638,900—54.5 per cent of total area of the State. The farm acreage was divided into crop lands, 5,035,956; pasture land, 1,637,431; woodland, 2,562,000; all other land in farms, 1,403,507. The average acreage per farm was 61.6, but crops were harvested from only 25 acres per farm . . . .

Cotton holds the first place in acreage, with about 45 per cent; corn the second with around 30 per cent. These two occupy from two-thirds to three-fourths of the crop land. It is sometimes said that cotton is "King," that the South is a "one-crop section." It is plain that these statements are disproved by the crop acreage; nor do they apply to the crop values, for out of a total of $159,597,291 in South Carolina in 1924, cotton lint produced $88,509,130—about 55 per cent only . . . . The State has two great cash crops—cotton and tobacco; five grain crops, corn, wheat, oats, rye, rice; four legumes that yield both hay and grain, cowpeas, soy beans, velvet beans, peanuts; two for sirup, sorghum and sugar cane. Both white and sweet potatoes are planted in every county, with a total value for the State of over $12,000,000. . . .

Handbook of South Carolina, 1927, 102–107, 138–43, 177–84, 192–94.

While most of the commercial trucking—in watermelons, lettuce, tomatoes, snap beans, asparagus, green peas, cucumbers and spinach—is carried on in the coast region proper, certain vegetables are grown in large quantities in market gardens for sale to the people in nearby cities, as in Anderson, Greenville, Spartanburg, Lexington, and Charleston. Canneries are beginning to exert an influence in some counties, as in Union, Sumter, and Clarendon. . . . Throughout the State, plums, dewberries, blackberries, muscadine grapes, and walnuts grow wild. These wild varieties are much improved by attention, and many orchards have improved varieties. Pecans and figs also grow well in every county; the fig is rarely damaged seriously by the winter . . . . In 1924, the State produced 600,000 bushels of apples, 912,000 bushels of peaches, 114,000 bushels of pears, and 1,210,000 quarts of strawberries for commercial use. . . .

The average yield of tobacco for the State is about 70,000,000 pounds and the selling price is approximately 20 cents a pound. The average yield per acre is about 740 pounds. . . .

There is in South Carolina less than one milk cow to the farm, upon the average. This means short milk rations even for the farm family . . . . There are not half as many hogs, not half as many cattle and just a twentieth as many sheep in South Carolina in 1925 as there were 75 years ago! Yet the people number a million and three-quarters now to 668,000 then . . . .

A state-wide agricultural policy is summed up in three suggestions: cultivated crops on good land only; more grass and cattle on the poorer cleared land; systematic reforestation throughout the State.

[J. Roy Jones]

[Diversification of farm products, 1940]

Diversification is today the theme of agricultural leaders in South Carolina. More fruits and vegetables for home consumption and the

J. Roy Jones, "Diversification of Farm Products," *South Carolina Magazine*, III (Spring, 1940), 8–9. Reprinted by permission of J. Roy Jones.

possibilities of the surplus going into organized trade channels to bolster the annual income should follow. The days of depending on one cash crop, have apparently passed into history . . . .

Cotton is still the leading cash crop, but each year its supremacy is being contested. Adaptable to the soil and climate of this section, cotton reigned longer than the two great cash crops, which have been the foundation of our agricultural existence through the years. First it was indigo, then rice and for a hundred years or more, cotton. The decline of cotton has been due, mainly, to the loss of export markets. Before we realized that foreign competition was definitely to stay in the field of cotton cultivation, the United States had built such surpluses that curtailment of production was not only advisable but necessary. . . .

The coming of cotton mills to the South and especially South Carolina insured that this State would have a market for the cotton crop. During the first years of their operation, mill consumption of Carolina cotton was limited. This was due to lack of type of lint cotton needed. After many years of persistent studies by farmers, seed breeders and agricultural leaders, South Carolina is today producing the major portion of its cotton adaptable to the large number of cotton mills within the State. . . .

It has been most gratifying to watch the attitude of the farmers in changing to other crops. The enthusiasm and alacrity with which they have grasped . . . new ideas have gone a long way to forestall a calamity which it is only logical to think, would befall any farming section when the main cash income crop was impaired.

Fruit crops of commercial importance are chiefly peaches, apples, pears, grapes, strawberries, dewberries, pecans and figs. Peaches, the most important fruit crop . . . during the past ten years [have] increased over 350,000 bushels annually and it is expected over a million new trees should come into production the next four to five years. . . .

Increased raising of livestock has become a definite factor in diversification. During the past several years the production of cattle and hogs has shown a very decided increase. Along with this increase there has been a concerted action on the part of the farmers to better the type and breed of both cattle and hogs. Where formerly scrub livestock roamed bare fields, it is now a gratifying sight to see purebred livestock in well organized pastures.

Dairy cattle have not shown any decided increase in numbers, but tremendous improvement in stock. This is evidenced by the increased

milk production per cow from 275 gallons in 1919 to 411 gallons in
1938. South Carolina produced in 1938, 15,000,000 gallons of milk
less than necessary local total consumption. . . .

[Agriculture in 1952]

Recent years have seen definite trends towards fewer but larger and
more valuable farms, buildings and equipment. Better farms with new
and greater conveniences, electric power, radios, home freezers and
refrigerators, telephones, good roads, better churches and schools are
to be found over the entire state. Tall gawky television antennae sprout
from the tops of rural as well as urban homes . . . . Today the number
of farms has been reduced to 139,365 with an average size of 85.2 acres.
The number of very large farms has greatly increased. Industrial
expansion in South Carolina and defense plants over the nation have
syphoned off much of the farm population until today good farm labor
is comparatively scarce and high priced. Stepped-up production for war
purposes during World War II has stimulated production of farm
products, and at better prices. Hostilities in Korea have kept the tempo
high.

Twenty years ago 65% of the farms were operated by tenants, but
now the tenancy rate has dropped to 45%. More Negroes than white
people have left the farms. Even in ten years, the use of electricity on
the farm has shown great improvement. The 1940 Agricultural census
shows electricity was used by slightly over 28,000 farm homes and a
more recent count, in 1949, lists more than 95,000 farm homes with
electricity. Telephones on the farm have increased in ten years from
4267 in 1939 to 11,901 in 1949.

Farmers owned 63,653 automobiles in 1939 and 81,579 in 1949; 7392
farms had motor trucks ten years ago and the latest published estimate
places trucks on 25,433 farms; ten years ago, there were only 4285
South Carolina farms using tractors while at the present time more
than 25,000 farms use this power machinery. Horse and mule numbers
have dwindled as tractors and other machinery have increased on the
farm. In the 1930 census, South Carolina farms had over 30,000 horses
and about 189,000 mules; in 1950, there were 25,000 horses and
147,000 mules.

Equally as significant is the trend in crops and livestock production.
Spectacular increases in per acreage production has occurred in corn,

The Palmetto State, S.C. Dept. of Education (Columbia: n.p., 1952), 42–45.

where it has been practically doubled. Practically the same size cotton crop is produced on fewer acres than formerly. South Carolina farmers accomplished the remarkable feat in 1951 of producing an average yield of 394 pounds of lint cotton per acre, an all time high for the State . . . . Another record high in 1951 was the per acre production of 1345 pounds of flue-cured tobacco . . . . Tobacco is sold by auction and fifty-two sales warehouses located in eleven market centers operated in 1951.

The total volume of 21 staple and 13 commercial truck crops produced in 1951 had a farm value of $381,973,000. South Carolina farmers continued to ship more fresh peaches to market than any other state.

Irish potatoes led the list of 1951 truck crops with a value of $2,250,000, followed in order by watermelons, $1,982,000; snap beans, $1,515,000; and cucumbers, $1,474,000. Other truck crops produced in commercial quantities were asparagus, cantaloupes, lettuce, green peas, strawberries and tomatoes. The production of beef, dairy products and hogs have all taken on new impetus in recent years. Improved pastures where "year round" grazing is made possible, better disease control measures, the introduction of artificial insemination and the greatly increased "know how" of farmers have all contributed to the march of progress in South Carolina agriculture.

Approximately one million hogs were raised in South Carolina in 1951 and the increase in beef cattle will probably run about 20% over recent years. Poultry and poultry products, especially in the production of broilers and turkeys, have increased until they now account for a cash income exceeding twenty million dollars. It has been estimated that over fifteen million dollars is invested in incubators and hatchery equipment. Turkey production is estimated as exceeding a million birds a year.

The establishment of a million dollar State Farmers Market near Columbia is a highlight in agricultural developments in recent years. A similar market has been established at Greenville; there is a pecan auction market at Orangeburg; and livestock markets are located in many sections of the state. Meat packing plants, canneries, feed mills, freezer locker plants, and many other facilities are located so as to aid farmers in marketing their produce.

[South Carolina's Agriculture, 1963]

Agriculture in South Carolina is a big business and even though some think it is "on the way out" our economy is still basically dependent on the successes and failures of agriculture.

During the past decade farming costs have increased quite noticeably. This increase in farming costs has forced many small or marginal farmers out of the business of farming. Farmers caught in this cost-price squeeze have sold their farms to neighbors who were more financially able to manage farms. This has caused the number of farms in the state to decrease which in turn has brought about an increase in the average size. In 1945 there were 147,745 farms, average size being 74.6 acres, as compared to 78,162 farms with an average size of 117 acres in 1959. In 1959 average value per farm was $14,461 as compared to a value of $2,982 in 1945.

The value of production of South Carolina field crops, fruits and vegetables in 1962 is estimated at $302,153,000. These crops were harvested from 2,563,000 acres in 1962. Cattle, hogs, sheep, milk cows, chickens and turkeys on South Carolina farms as of January 1, 1963, were valued at $76,040,000. Because of the decrease in number of mules as work animals in the state, surveys are not now conducted as to their value. Government payments (not loans) to farmers during 1962 amounted to $21,400,000. Forest products sold by farmers in 1959 were valued at $24,831,000 and the value of these products, together with their manufactured by-products, was $386,000,000.

Until recent years, cotton had the reputation of being the most important cash crop to South Carolina farmers and was known as "King Cotton." During the past few years, tobacco has come into its own and dethroned cotton as the big money crop. The production of cotton in 1962 is valued at $84,127,000 as compared to tobacco's valuation of $112,913,000 for the same year.

South Carolina is the number two peach producing state in the nation. During 1962 there were 7,000,000 bushels of peaches produced in the state for a value of $13,838,000. Each year, just before peach season, peach festivals are held in several communities through the state. Tobacco and watermelon festivals are also celebrated in the major tobacco and watermelon areas of the state. Animal raising contributes highly to the assets of agriculture in this state. Cattle and hogs are

Handbook of South Carolina, 1963, Dept. of Agriculture (Columbia: n.p., 1963), 131–32.

raised as a source of meat. Sheep are raised primarily as a source of wool. Horses are raised for pleasure riding, racing and other sports purposes. Mules are still used as work animals on some farms. Milk cows furnish milk to the dairy industry. Chickens and turkeys furnish both eggs and meat for consumption by South Carolina's population.

The standard of living in most of South Carolina's rural areas was very low not too many years ago. However, there has been such an improvement during the past few years that rural living now is as comfortable as living in the city. There are paved roads to practically all rural areas. Conveniences found in city homes such as the telephone, television, freezers and running water are now found in almost every rural home in the state. Churches and modern up-to-date schools are found in all rural communities.

During the past decade a large number of new industries have located in rural areas throughout the state. Some of the industries utilize the farmer's products, such as peaches for canning and grapes for processing into grape juice and wine. These industries have proven to be a great asset to the economy of the communities in which they locate.

167. *Education through 1963*

THE SOUTH CAROLINA SCHOOL SYSTEM IN 1920 WAS VASTLY DIF-
FERENT FROM THAT OF MID-CENTURY. PROGRESS WAS MADE IN THE
1930s AND 1940s. FROM 1954, THE SEGREGATION-INTEGRATION PROBLEM
DOMINATED THE EDUCATIONAL SCENE. IN THE EARLY PART OF THE
TWENTIETH CENTURY THERE WERE HUNDREDS OF ONE-TEACHER SCHOOLS,
HUNDREDS OF UNCONSOLIDATED SCHOOL DISTRICTS, NUMBERS OF POORLY
PREPARED TEACHERS, ALMOST NO STATE AID, AND LITTLE TRANSPORTATION.
THE NEGRO SCHOOLS PARTICULARLY SUFFERED FROM LACK OF FUNDS
AND TRAILED FAR BEHIND THE OTHER SCHOOLS IN EVERYTHING EXCEPT
THE NUMBER OF ELEMENTARY PUPILS. NO NEGRO PUPIL, HOWEVER,
WAS DENIED THE CHANCE TO GO TO SCHOOL. AFTER THE SUPREME
COURT DECISION OF 1954—POPULARLY KNOWN AS THE "CLARENDON
CASE"—MORE AND MORE NEGROES BEGAN TO TAKE AN INTEREST IN
GETTING AN EDUCATION. BY 1964, ALTHOUGH ONLY A TOKEN NUMBER
OF NEGRO CHILDREN WERE ENROLLED IN FORMERLY ALL-WHITE SCHOOLS,
THERE WAS THE BEGINNING OF A MOVEMENT TO PROVIDE QUALITY
EDUCATION FOR ALL OF THE STATE'S CHILDREN. BETTER SCHOOLS WERE
PROVIDED FOR WHITE AND NEGRO CHILDREN, AND THE NUMBER OF
SCHOOL DISTRICTS WAS GREATLY REDUCED. ONE-TEACHER SCHOOLS
DISAPPEARED, STANDARDS FOR TEACHERS WERE RAISED, CERTIFICATION
WAS REQUIRED, THE SALARIES OF TEACHERS WERE EQUALIZED ACCORDING
TO TRAINING AND CERTIFICATION, AND THE EDUCATIONAL PROGRAM WAS
IMPROVED IN EVERY WAY. THE FOLLOWING SELECTIONS EVIDENCE THIS
PROGRESS IN EDUCATION.

[A summary of public educational
facilities in the state in 1922:]

The status of our public schools during the last twelve months may
be told briefly in a few significant figures. During the year substantial
progress has been made in spite of deflation, the ravages of the boll
weevil, business depression, and the postponement and noncollection of

Annual Report, S.C. Dept. of Education (Columbia: n.p., 1922), 11–37.

taxes . . . . School revenues for the year amounted to $10,562,761, a loss of $267,532 from the high-water mark of the preceding twelve months. Under the law, the school funds are derived from five sources —the district poll tax, the three-mill Constitutional county tax, direct State appropriations, special or extra county appropriations, and local district taxes voted by resident community electors . . . .

Expenditures fell from $10,029,444.55 in 1921 to $9,517,968.21 in 1922 . . . . This loss was due almost altogether to a slackening in schoolhouse construction. . . . This temporary lull by no means indicates that our schoolhouse needs have been met. Scores of districts are planning new buildings or are enlarging existing buildings. The program for new high schools alone will require at least four million dollars whenever it can be undertaken. The aggregate of teachers' salaries was $6,402,407.93, the highest on record. However, this was due to an enlarged teaching corps rather than to higher pay for the individual teacher. . . . For the year the per capita cost was $36.10 for whites; $4.17 for Negroes. . . .

The General Assembly of 1922 made eleven specific appropriations to aid public education . . . . The amount derived from the State Treasury was supplemented by Federal aid for vocational training under the Smith-Hughes Act as follows: for agriculture, $37,958.89; for trade, industry and home economics, $4,934.97; and for teacher training, $15,993.88. . . . 1059 of the 1993 districts in the State participated in the appropriation of $295,000 to encourage consolidated and graded schools in country districts. The Law is helping fifty-three per cent of the school districts of the State. It has done more to standardize and promote rural education than any other act of recent years. . . .

For the whites the year's work has been done in 2286 schools, employing 7239 teachers, for an enrollment of 235,535, with an average attendance of 171,742 during a session of 140 days . . . . During the year the number of schools was reduced by nineteen. This tendency is now so well established that it has almost become a regular and characteristic feature of the State Superintendent's report. It may be explained in the one word "consolidation" . . . . The country district maintaining two separate schools is now a rare exception . . . . Partly through population growth and partly through consolidation the number of one-teacher schools has dropped to 840—36% . . . . The old slogan "More schools and better schools" has been changed to "Fewer schools but better schools" . . . . The enrollment of white pupils was the largest on record . . . .

For the Negroes there were 2493 schools with 3755 teachers, for an enrollment of 243,774, and an average attendance of 174,143 during an average session of 77 days. In this connection one ought to remember that 51.4% of the State's population is colored, according to the census of 1920. Among the Negro schools are 2040 with one teacher, 292 with two teachers, 73 with three teachers, and 88 with more than three teachers. These one-teacher Negro schools explain South Carolina's illiteracy. The State Board of Education has approved fourteen colored high schools for State aid. The Rosenwald fund is helping to provide a number of fine new schoolhouses. The Jeanes supervisors are bringing valuable assistance in industrial and in primary methods. The problem is most difficult, but unselfish constructive forces are gradually working out its solution. The Negro can now secure anything in South Carolina except social and political equality.

Four years ago the Statewide Compulsory Education Law was passed. Two years ago this Law was revised and rewritten. It has proved a great stimulus and incentive to school attendance, and at the same time has added thousands of pupils to the enrollment lists. . . .

As soon as the State is able to meet the cost, free text-books ought to be provided for all public schools. The expense of introduction would require perhaps a Statewide text-book levy of 3 mills. Maintenance would require not less than one mill yearly. The question ought to have careful consideration.

The "6-0-1 Law" of 1924:

An act to provide for the payment of salaries of school teachers in all schools in South Carolina and to appropriate funds to meet same.

Section 1. Be it enacted by the General Assembly of the State of South Carolina: The General Assembly shall make sufficient appropriation to pay the salaries of all school teachers in the public schools of the State for six months, according to the schedule outlined below; Provided, however, that no school in any school district shall continue open for a longer period of time than that fixed by the Board of Trustees in the district where such school is located.

General School Law of South Carolina, 1929, pp. 78–83.

Section 2. To meet the amount provided for in Section 1 . . . there is hereby levied upon all taxable property of each county of this State four (4) mills and in addition thereto the constitutional three mill tax in each school district, which levy of four (4) mills and the constitutional three mill tax shall be supplemented by an appropriation from the State in order to provide for the payment of the salaries for the six months term, as provided for in Section 1; Provided, that each district or county shall be required to provide a sufficient amount to continue for one additional month its school or schools, in order to participate in the revenues provided by this Act.

Section 3. That in any accredited high school applying for support under this Act, the schedule of teachers' salaries to be paid from regular or special funds shall be as follows: The Principal of an accredited high school shall be paid during the first year not more than One Hundred and Thirty ($130.00) dollars per month; any principal returning to the same may be paid during the second year an additional stipend of Five Dollars per month, and during the third year a further stipend of Five dollars per month. An assistant teacher in the high school grades of an accredited high school shall be paid during the first year not more than One Hundred ($100.00) Dollars per month; any assistant teacher returning to the same school may be paid during the second year an additional stipend of Five Dollars per month, and during the third year a further stipend of Five Dollars per month. An assistant teacher in the elementary grades of an accredited high school holding a first grade certificate shall be paid not more than Ninety ($90.00) Dollars a month; an assistant teacher holding a second grade certificate shall be paid not more than Seventy-five ($75.00) Dollars per month, and an assistant teacher holding a third grade certificate shall be paid not more than Sixty ($60.00) Dollars per month. Any assistant teacher in the elementary grades of an accredited high school returning to the same school may be paid during the second year an additional stipend of Five Dollars per month, and during the third year, a further stipend of Five Dollars per month. A superintendent, a supervisor, or a principal of any school with more than ten teachers in all the grades shall receive the same remuneration as the principal of an accredited high school . . . .

Section 5. That in any school the local district Board of Trustees may run the school for a period of time longer than six months and may, within its discretion, pay salaries in excess of the schedule outlined in Sections 4 and 5 of this Act, but such excess salaries must be paid out of the funds of the district or county in which such school is situated. In no case shall the salaries paid by the State be in excess of those paid by the county or local district.

Section 6. That any accredited high school receiving benefits from this Act shall comply with the following minimum enrollment and average monthly attendance requirements in the high school grades: A high school with two teachers employed in the high school grades shall enroll twenty-five pupils and maintain an average monthly attendance of eighteen pupils in the high school department; a high school with three teachers employed in the high school grades shall enroll fifty pupils and maintain an average monthly attendance of thirty-five pupils in the high school department; a high school with four teachers . . . shall enroll seventy-five pupils and maintain an average monthly attendance of fifty pupils in the high school department . . . . An additional teacher in the high school grades shall be allowed for every twenty-five pupils enrolled; provided, the total average monthly attendance is seventy per centum of the total enrollment in the high school department . . . .

Section 10. That the State Board of Education shall define an accredited high school and shall have the authority to prescribe all such regulations in the premises as may not be inconsistent with this Act and the General School Law. . . .

Section 12. No part or provision in this Act shall be so construed as to interfere with the issuance of bonds or the voting of special tax levies by any local school district. . . .

[The educational picture in 1949:]

Total expenditure for public schools continued to increase in 1948–1949 over previous years. Increases over 1947–1948 . . . amounted to $8,378,135 . . . making the total expenditures $59,049,258 for 1948–1949 . . . . 2038 school busses carried a total of 116,129 children to school daily out of a total enrollment of 478,103. 16,342 teachers in 3359 schools received an average of $1,795 each in salary. There were

Annual Report, S.C. Dept. of Education (Columbia: n.p., 1949), 23–24, 76, 87.

still 979 one-teacher schools in operation and 960 with two teachers each . . . . There were 1284 white and 2075 Negro schools . . . .

Of the total school expenditures for the year, $29,899,690.18 came from the State, $22,715,042.00 came from local taxes, and $6,305,092.64 came from the Federal government. Other miscellaneous funds came from such sources as the General Education Board and the Veterans' Administration. State aid for teachers' salaries total $24,713,328.29 . . . .

Near the close of the 1949 session of the General Assembly, a Joint Resolution was passed directing the county boards of education to appoint committees to study school district organization and propose a plan for each county for reorganization of present school districts into larger administrative units . . . . In 1920 there were 1895 school districts; in 1949, 1631 . . . .

During the school year, 1540 schools in South Carolina participated in the national school lunch program. Of this number 957 were white and 583 Negro. Federal aid amounted to $1,548,402.07 in cash and $2,050,911.00 in commodities. School children paid a total of $3,129,628.67. School districts provided a total of $165,457.11 for program operations and equipment . . . .

In 1948–1949 there were 297 accredited white schools, 76 accredited Negro high schools and 10 accredited white junior high schools . . . . The year was the first in which all high schools . . . had a full twelfth grade class . . . . 77,370 students were enrolled in white accredited high schools, including 36,852 boys and 40,518 girls. In the Negro accredited high schools, there were 9,002 boys and 13,622 girls for a total of 22,624. 8172 high school diplomas were issued to white students and 2084 to Negroes of whom 806 white and 229 Negro went on to college. . . .

[*The News and Courier*]

THE CLARENDON SCHOOL CASE

While the United States Supreme Court meditates on the Clarendon school case, forces of great importance are churning beneath the

The News and Courier, Dec. 27, 1952.

surface. South Carolina is going ahead on the assumption that the Supreme Court will uphold the law as now recognized. That means continued separation of white and Negro pupils in the school.

By "going ahead" is meant construction of new school buildings, chiefly to bring Negro schools into "equality" with the white ones. In fact, some white people are beginning to object that schools for their children will be unequal to the Negro schools.

In Clarendon County, where the suit now pending in the Supreme Court started, the effort to equalize public schools has created Negro facilities superior to those for whites. And a curious situation has been noted there. Many—in our opinion, most—of the Negroes do not want to send their children to school with the white pupils. Some of those who brought suit did not have mingling the races in mind when they signed the petition on which the suit is based . . . . One of the plaintiffs has said: "Before I'll let my children go to school with white children I'll take them out of school and teach them what little I know myself." . . .

All the Negroes wanted was better schools. These they are getting. The white people are becoming dissatisfied. They are resentful toward the Negroes. We believe none but a tiny militant group in either race wants mixed schools. So what if the Supreme Court should outlaw separation? Will the federal government force whites and Negroes to go to school together against their will? How will that be carried out? What steps has South Carolina taken to meet an adverse decision?

So far as we can discover, only one step has been taken. That was the approval by the voters in the November 4 election of a proposed constitutional amendment to free the state of the requirement that it operate public schools. *The News and Courier* favors that amendment. But if the Supreme Court outlaws separate schools for the races, the result will still be chaos. There is no other word to describe what will happen.

If the Supreme Court upholds the present doctrine of "separate but equal," a rash of new suits probably will break out. In other school districts, Negro plaintiffs will be found who will sign petitions for "better schools and buses." The State will be defending legal actions on every hand, and building new schools for Negroes everywhere.

What is being taught in these expensive new houses? That is a question we have not seen explored. Are Negro pupils being taught how to live in this new age? Or are they learning by rote subjects which have no meaning to them? *The News and Courier* has heard of chemistry classes with no laboratory equipment; of geometry and trigonometry being taught children in rural regions who could scarcely add and multiply; of physics and French and other college preparatory courses in areas where hygiene and basic English would be more in order.

[U.S. Supreme Court decision, May 17, 1954, concerning school integration.]

These cases came to us from the States of Kansas, South Carolina, Virginia and Delaware. They are premised on different facts and different local conditions, but a common legal question justifies their consideration together in this consolidated opinion.

In each of the cases, minors of the Negro race, through their legal representatives, seek the aid of the courts in obtaining admission to the public schools of their community on a nonsegregated basis. In each instance, they had been denied admission to schools attended by white children under laws requiring or permitting segregation according to race.

This segregation was alleged to deprive the plaintiffs of the equal protection of the laws under the Fourteenth Amendment. In each of the cases other than the Delaware case, a three-judge Federal District Court denied relief to the plaintiffs on the so-called "Separate but Equal" doctrine announced by this court in Plessy v. Ferguson, 163 U.S. 537.

Under that doctrine, equality of treatment is accorded when the races are provided substantially equal facilities, even though these facilities be separate . . . . The plaintiffs contend that segregated public schools are not "equal" and cannot be made "equal," and that, hence, they are deprived of the equal protection of the laws. Because of the obvious importance of the question presented, the Court took jurisdiction. Argument was heard in the 1952 term, and re-argument was heard this term on certain questions propounded by the Court. . . .

In the first cases in this Court construing the Fourteenth Amendment, decided shortly after its adoption, the court interpreted it as proscribing all state-imposed discriminations against the Negro race.

The doctrine of "Separate but Equal" did not make its appearance in this court until 1896 in the case of Plessy v. Ferguson, supra, involving not education but transportation. . . .

We come then to the question presented: Does segregation of children in public schools solely on the basis of race, even though the physical

U.S. Supreme Court Reports, 347 U.S. 483 (Brown v. Board of Education).

facilities and other tangible factors may be equal, deprive the children of the minority group of equal educational opportunities? We believe that it does. . . .

The effect of this separation on their educational opportunities was well stated by a finding in the Kansas case by a court which nevertheless felt compelled to rule against the Negro plaintiffs:

"Segregation of white and colored children in public schools has a detrimental effect upon the colored children. The impact is greater when it has the sanction of the law; for the policy of separating the races is usually interpreted as denoting the inferiority of the Negro group.

"A sense of inferiority affects the motivation of a child to learn. Segregation with the sanction of law, therefore, has a tendency to retard the educational and mental development of Negro children and to deprive them of some of the benefits they would receive in a racially integrated system."

Whatever may have been the extent of psychological knowledge at the time of Plessy v. Ferguson, this finding is amply supported by modern authority. Any language in Plessy v. Ferguson contrary to this finding is rejected.

We conclude that in the field of public education the doctrine of "Separate but Equal" has no place. Separate educational facilities are inherently unequal. Therefore, we hold that the plaintiffs and others similarly situated for whom the actions have been brought are, by reason of the segregation complained of, deprived of the equal protection of the laws guaranteed by the Fourteenth Amendment. . . .

[Governor George Bell Timmerman, Jr., on the Supreme Court segregation decision, January 11, 1956]

A major problem still before us is the preservation of public schools acceptable to the people of our state. The problem is foremost in the minds of our people. I am confident it is foremost in the mind of each of you. There have been many suggestions for preserving our separate but equal school facilities, including the doctrine of interposition.

Two principles distinguish our form of government and provide it with stability and greatness. Both are essential to protect our form of government. Both are essential to preserve the rights of the states and the

George Bell Timmerman, Jr., "Second Annual Message to the South Carolina General Assembly, January 11, 1956." From a script kindly supplied by the speaker to the editors.

people. One is the historic balance between the authority delegated to the federal government and the power reserved to the states and the people. It is expressed in the Tenth Amendment to the Constitution . . . . Nowhere does the Constitution delegate to the central government the power to control public schools.

The other principle is the process of amendment expressed in Article V of the Constitution which forbids any change in the basic law without the approval of the states. The Supreme Court has flagrantly violated both of these principles. It has undertaken to upset the balance between federal authority and state sovereignty. It has weakened the stability of the written Constitution.

If the opinion is accepted, it will have established a precedent for destroying the greatest system of government ever established. In striking down the separate but equal doctrine, the Court has not only usurped the authority of Congress to propose changes in the fundamental law, but it has also usurped the sovereignty of the states to approve changes in the Constitution.

It is unlikely that all of the members of the Supreme Court could have been ignorant of what they were doing. In their opinion, they confessed that they would not interpret the Constitution according to its meaning when it was adopted, or in the light of how it had been interpreted by the Court . . . . No document can be interpreted truthfully except in the light of what it meant when it was written. For the purposes of judicial interpretation, consideration of previous court decisions is also essential to a correct interpretation. Rather than resting their opinion upon established law, the present members of the Supreme Court based their opinion upon writings on sociology and psychology.

It must be remembered that the Congress has the authority to curb the Court and restore Constitutional government. Among many things, the National Senate must exercise greater care in confirming appointments to our federal courts. An active constitutional bloc could soon force any President to give more consideration to judicial qualifications and less consideration to politics. In this way, a great service would be rendered our nation.

Throughout this crisis, we have pursued a policy of working within the framework of the law, resorting to lawful means to preserve an acceptable system of public schools. Your attitude has been one of intelligent restraint and commendable action. It is in sharp contrast to the attitude of those who seek to destroy our schools.

Last year, the sovereignty of our State was interposed between the central government and local trustees when you wrote into the law that no funds appropriated for school purposes shall be used for any school from which or to which any pupil may be assigned by the order of any Court. This year our schools are operating in peace and in conformity with the pattern of racial separation which has made for that peace.

Not one child has sought to gain admittance to a school for the children of the other race. Many Negro parents living in Washington and other cities to the north of us are leaving their children with relatives in our State so that their children can enjoy the benefit of a Southern climate in segregated public schools.

Nevertheless, no one can offer a magic solution to the threats that continue to face us. It is imperative that we continue to consider with great care each move that we shall undertake . . . .

[Governor James F. Byrnes on school integration, 1957]

. . . Following the War Between the States with its devastation, particularly during the period of occupation by federal troops, our poverty had made it impossible for us to provide for the Negro children, or . . . the white children, adequate public schools. Our principal revenue came from real property. While in the cities there were improved schools, schools of the rural areas for both races were not equal to schools of the cities. In later years in some cities there were Negro schools equal to those provided for white children, but that was not true in rural areas and in many cities.

When I urged a bond issue and a sales tax for the purpose of equalizing school facilities, the people were magnificent in their response. Of the first $75 million dollars of bonds issued, 70% was allotted for Negro schools even though the Negro school population was only 40% of enrollment. As a result of that educational revolution, we can say that in every school district in the state there is a good high school for Negroes. In fact, in many instances they are better than the schools for white students because they are modern. There are also adequate elementary schools.

The second factor contributing to our peaceful relations is the splendid attitude of the real Negro leaders in this state. We can be sure that in every community there are some Negroes, as well as whites, who are

James F. Byrnes, "Politics Has No Place in Education," a speech delivered before "Industry Appreciation Celebration," Bennettsville, S.C., Sept. 27, 1957. From a script kindly supplied by the speaker to the editors.

natural disturbers of the peace. From outside the state will come some Negro men and women who will try to arouse ill feeling in our colored neighbors in an effort to foment strife. But to the everlasting credit of the sane, sensible Negroes, to this day they have successfully resisted these efforts.

They could have pointed out that their schools are better than they could have dreamed of having; they are satisfied with their colored teachers and do not want to force their children into schools where they are not wanted. They know that when integration occurs, there will cease to be education for either the white or colored child. They know that the only result of the efforts to integrate the races in the schools is to destroy all that has been done by men and women of both races to promote better relations between the races during the last half-century.

What is happening today in some states of the South is a tragedy. It is a tragedy that in communities where a few years ago the two races enjoyed the best of neighborly relations, blood should now be shed in racial conflicts. The cause of that tragedy is the decision of the Supreme Court. In the United States Constitution there is nothing about segregated schools. The Supreme Court had so decided in eight different cases over a period of seventy-five years, but nine men on the Supreme Court reversed those decisions, ignored the Constitution and declared that Negro children could not be denied the right to sit by white children in school without suffering an inferiority complex. That is a cruel indictment of the Negro race that was acquiring pride of race.

The Supreme Court based its decision, not on law, but on the writings of some sociologists who were declared by the United States House of Representatives Un-American Committee and by the Department of Justice to have subversive connections . . . .

Race feeling is not confined to the South . . . . It is useless to deny the existence of feeling resulting from pride of race. It exists . . . . Such feeling cannot be erased over night. It requires time and patience. When the Supreme Court went to legislating, it moved too far, too fast . . . .

When integration is attempted in rural areas in many Southern States, conditions will be worse than in Little Rock . . . .

The people of the South deplore violence. It helps no cause. The United States government has the military power to enforce the orders of its courts. The people do not speak or think of resisting the armed forces but they know the armed might of the United States government cannot change the minds and hearts of the people. Whenever the tanks and guns are removed, there will remain the same determination on the part of the white people to resort to every legal means to prevent the mixing of the races . . . .

In this State, we have a law providing that if a student, by order of any court, state or federal, is assigned to a school different from that to which he has been assigned by state school officials, then all appropriations shall cease for the school to which he is assigned, and the school from which he comes. If in violation of all law, the federal government shall seek by orders of federal courts and military force to require legislators to vote appropriations for public schools [,] that will be the end of our liberties. If the Supreme Court and the federal executives shall destroy the public school system, I repeat what I have heretofore said, that the white people of the South who have respect and genuine affection for their colored neighbors, will do all in their power to see to it that colored children are not denied an education, in spite of the political activities of reckless reformers . . . .

Notwithstanding the political gloom that now surrounds us, the South may be restored to its place in the councils of the Nation if its leaders, forgetting all political differences, will now begin to organize for a United South, selecting as leaders only stout-hearted men, who just before the election will not surrender to false promises, either for a vice-presidential nomination or a judicial appointment . . . . But if you organize and let the people know the Southern states are not in the bag for either political party, we may have some chance of securing written pledges that will assure some respect for the United States Constitution and some respect for local governments.

[W. D. Workman, Jr., on "The Dark Multitude"]

It might be logical to assume the Supreme Court was thinking in terms of national averages when it said "separate educational facilities are inherently unequal." Since the nation-wide ratio of Negroes to whites is approximately one in ten, then let's try that formula for size on a Southern state—say, South Carolina.

A major obstacle to the application of that formula to South Carolina immediately arises because the state has roughly forty per cent Negroes

William D. Workman, Jr., *The Case for the South* (New York: Devin-Adair Co., 1960), 148–50. Copyright © 1960 by William D. Workman, Jr. Reprinted by permission of William D. Workman, Jr.

to its total population instead of the ten per cent which characterizes the nation as a whole. Negroes could not possibly achieve the advantages inherent in exposure to a ninety per cent white population unless some drastic action be taken, either importing more whites, or exporting some of the state's surplus blacks.

The state conceivably, and with all propriety, could call on its Northern neighbors to supplement their denunciation with deeds, and could ask that enough surplus whites (those in excess of ninety per cent of the population) be sent into South Carolina so that the proper ratio could be attained. It might be that some of the nation's leading figures in executive, judicial, and legislative posts would take advantage of the opportunity to have their own presently-segregated children enjoy the fruits of integration by journeying to South Carolina.

On the other hand, the state might work toward the transplanting of excess South Carolina Negroes (there were about 693,000 over and above the ten per cent quota on the basis of the 1950 census), into non-Southern states which fall below their Negro quotas. The possibilities here are wide and varied, but as an example, South Carolina could send about 529,000 Negroes into the State of California, where they might be welcomed by Chief Justice [Earl] Warren and Vice President [Richard] Nixon as harbingers of the happier days which would come with an increase of California's Negro population to the ten per cent national average.

That would still leave South Carolina with a surplus of some 164,000 Negroes, but they could be absorbed easily by the State of Minnesota (home of Sen. Hubert Humphrey). Minnesota, incidentally, needs 281,-000 more Negroes to bring its colored percentage up from less than one-and-a-half per cent to the average ten per cent ratio. Minnesotans would have to recruit Negroes from additional Southern states in addition to drawing from South Carolina.

Meanwhile, back in South Carolina, the public school administrators might then find their way out of the dilemma which now confronts them. Consider their present plight for a moment:

If they integrate on the basis of current population distribution, they will put twenty-seven white children into a class with three Negro children in the schools of upstate Pickens county. At the same time, they could put only three white children with twenty-seven Negro students in the Summerton District schools of Clarendon County . . . .

Of course, it would be difficult to re-distribute the white and Negro youngsters so that all would profit by the same degree of exposure to each other, but by that time, perhaps the New York City experiment in racial re-shuffling will have produced some effective recipe for boiling all schoolrooms down to a common stew.

Some difficulty might arise if scattered whites and Negroes sought to insist on some imagined right to select their own place of residence and school of attendance, but the Supreme Court certainly would tolerate no assertion of any such fancied privilege as that of choosing one's associates. But while awaiting the Court-directed millenium, do Southerners begin to export Negroes or import whites in order to conform to the national standard?

[E.M. Lander, Jr.]

Strangely, in the 1946 election little attention was focused on the race issue. Only John D. Long of the 11 gubernatorial hopefuls vigorously expressed an extreme racist viewpoint . . . . Long, however, did voice the dominating issue in South Carolina politics. Race has been, is, and will be in the forseeable future the issue that dwarfs all others in the state. It is responsible for the absence of genuine two-party politics in the state. Moreover, the race issue has become intensified since 1941 due to Supreme Court anti-segregation decisions and civil rights battles in Congress.

In the congressional struggle, Southern leaders have repeatedly blocked most features of the civil rights bills, but the South has no way to check the Court. As matters stood, South Carolina whites grumblingly accepted the federal judiciary's doctrine of equality until May, 1954. At that time the Supreme Court handed down its South-shaking Clarendon County decision. . . .

The Court did not, however, order immediate enforcement of its decree.

Ernest McPherson Lander, Jr., *A History of South Carolina, 1865–1960* (Chapel Hill: University of North Carolina Press, 1960), 72–73. Copyright © 1960 by University of North Carolina Press. Copyright © 1970 by University of South Carolina Press. First edition published 1960 by the University of North Carolina Press, Chapel Hill, N.C. Second edition published 1970 by the University of South Carolina Press, Columbia, S.C. Reprinted by permission.

After the stunning decision some religious and civic leaders urged caution and moderation. Several newspapers followed the same line, intimating that eventual integration might be achieved. . . .

[Superintendent of Education reports on state school progress, 1963]

The statistical phase of this report, shows that consistent improvements are made from year to year. For example, the public school enrollment for the year closing was 643,086, while ten years ago in 1952–53 the schools enrolled 525,011 pupils. The number of students awarded high school diplomas during the 1962–63 school year was 24,310 compared to 13,984 in 1952–53.

Much has been said and is being said about the holding power of the schools. The record shows that the white eighth grade enrollment for the year closing was 33,760 or 90.5% of the first grade enrollment eight years before, and the Negro, 63.2%. Ten years ago the white grade enrollment was only 64.6% of the first grade enrollment eight years before, and the Negro enrollment, 30.8%. This gives us more than 100% increases in the Negro holding power and approximately 50% for the white schools. . . .

The Legislature from year to year has appropriated for public education such additional funds as it felt that it could justifiably. In 1962 an across-the-board raise was provided for all state aid teachers, and in 1963 a three million dollar raise for merit pay was recommended by Governor [Donald] Russell and passed by the Legislature. The total appropriation for 1962–63 for public education amounted to $78,395,758, compared to $41,114,009 in 1952–53. This indicates South Carolina's efforts to meet increased costs in education. . . .

Governor Russell has put public education as his Number One need for the total improvement and advancement of South Carolina, and his leadership should mean much to the State during the coming years. . . .

The need for trained technical workers to man the industrial plants now in South Carolina and new ones opening has been met in a general way by technical training centers financed by the state with the local citizenry providing the buildings. . . .

The Legislature in 1963 ratified the constitutional amendment which was voted by the people in 1962 changing the organization of the State Board of Education. Formerly consisting of seven members appointed by the Governor, a fifteen-man State Board will take office January 1, 1964,

Annual Report, State Superintendent of Education (Columbia: n.p., 1963), 13–16.

consisting of one member from each judicial circuit appointed by the legislative delegations from the judicial circuits. The new Board will face many problems but will probably be the means of better coordination among all of the Commissions that deal with some phase of public education. . . .

The status of school integration in South Carolina in 1963:

Charleston became the state's first and only desegregated school district on Sept. 3, when 11 Negro children began classes with whites in four high schools.

At the same time 15 Negro Catholics, taking advantage of a special order by Bishop Francis E. Reh, head of the South Carolina Diocese, attended formerly all-white parochial schools in the sea-port city.

Although Charleston historically has been a center of opposition to Negro movements, the desegregation took place with even less fanfare than that which attended the entrance of Harvey B. Gantt [the first Negro to enroll in a South Carolina college] to Clemson College last January.

When Gantt, a Charleston native incidentally, broke the state's college color line, he was heavily guarded by state troopers who virtually sealed off the upcountry campus to head off possible violence.

Only one or two city policemen—mostly crossing guards—were in evidence at each school on Aug. 30, when the Negroes enrolled, and on Sept. 3, when classes began.

Charleston Mayor J. Palmer Gaillard said, however, that other police units were poised and could have been on the scene in minutes had trouble arisen . . . .

A leader in the summer-long protest marches against Charleston businesses said he has received dozens of anonymous telephone calls because of his NAACP activities and because his daughter is one of the 11 students entering white schools.

"I don't worry about it," he said. "If someone is going to blow you up, he won't be giving you advance notice."

Southern School News (Sept., 1963), 1.

[Report from *Southern School News*]

Fall term registration saw the number of Negroes attending state-supported colleges with whites jump from one to six. Four were admitted without having to resort to court action.

The Negroes enrolled at three different campuses—Clemson in the northwest mountains, the University of South Carolina's main campus in mid-state Columbia, and its branch at Beaufort.

As was the case when Harvey B. Gantt broke the color line in this state last January when he entered Clemson, there was no trouble, no violence. . . .

The University, working with law enforcement officials, carefully laid plans for the entrance of the three Negroes at the main Columbia campus, where most of the school's 7,000-plus students attend classes.

Students were bluntly warned that no demonstrations or acts of violence by them would be permitted. Pool arrangements were required of the news media representatives covering registration. The Negroes' registration went off without a hitch and was virtually ignored by other students, who themselves were busy registering for classes . . . .

[On Technical Education]

The accomplishments of South Carolina's new technical education program, which was opened to Negro applicants almost from its inception, were praised . . . during a session of the State House Ways and Means Committee.

The accolade came during the appearance of O. Stanley Smith, chairman of the State Technical Education Commission. . . .

Smith noted that 3,468 people had been placed in better paying (by

Southern School News (Oct., 1963), 16.

Southern School News (Jan., 1964), 8.

an average of $9 per week) jobs as of September, 1963—or before the majority of the modern centers were opened in major South Carolina cities. This, he said, accounted for additional personal income of $1.5 million.

Smith was asked about the policy of admitting Negroes. He said that, since the physical facilities for the centers are financed primarily out of local funds, there is no statewide policy in regard to Negroes and local centers are free to adopt their own admission rules. In other words, he added, the admission policy is based strictly on qualifications.

He admitted that "several" are desegregated. This was the first public statement on this. . . .

168. *Government*

THROUGHOUT ITS HISTORY, SOUTH CAROLINA HAS HAD A CENTRALIZED FORM OF GOVERNMENT, WITH THE PROVINCIAL OR STATE GOVERNMENT BEING SUPREME OVER LOCAL GOVERNMENTAL UNITS. THIS HAS WORKED FAIRLY WELL OVER THE YEARS, BUT THERE HAS BEEN A GROWING TENDENCY IN THE TWENTIETH CENTURY, ESPECIALLY FOLLOWING THE DEPRESSION AND THE DAYS OF THE NEW DEAL, TO OPPOSE "LEGISLATIVE GOVERNMENT" AND TO MOVE TOWARD MORE AUTONOMY FOR THE COUNTY AND CITY GOVERNMENTS. THE FOLLOWING INCLUDE NOTES ON THE FORM OF GOVERNMENT IN 1927; AN OUTSIDE LOOK AT GOVERNOR OLIN D. JOHNSTON'S DIFFICULTIES WITH THE HIGHWAY COMMISSION IN 1935 (IN WHICH THE GOVERNOR'S ARGUMENT WITH THE DEPARTMENT REPRESENTED EFFORTS OF A WEAK EXECUTIVE POSITION OVER A POOR STATE TO COERCE A STRONG, ALMOST AUTONOMOUS HIGHWAY COMMISSIONER WHO HAD POWERFUL FINANCIAL BACKING); A CRITICISM (IN 1947) OF THE LEGISLATIVE GOVERNMENTAL SYSTEM FROM A RELATIVELY OBJECTIVE VIEWPOINT; AND AN ACCOUNT OF SENATOR STROM THURMOND'S "WRITE-IN" ELECTION IN 1954. AT THE TIME, THURMOND WAS A DEMOCRAT; LATER HE BECAME A REPUBLICAN. HOWEVER, THURMOND, WHO WAS MORE OF AN INDEPENDENT IN HIS BELIEFS AND ACTIONS, REALLY BEGAN THE SWING TO A TWO-PARTY SYSTEM IN THE STATE WITH HIS "DIXIECRAT" MOVEMENT. INDIRECT RESULTS OF THAT MOVEMENT COULD WELL HAVE BEEN THE SHOWING THE STATE MADE FOR PRESIDENT EISENHOWER IN 1952, WHEN THE INDEPENDENTS DIVIDED THE REPUBLICAN VOTE, GIVING ADLAI STEVENSON A PLURALITY, AND IN 1964, WHEN SOUTH CAROLINA WENT FOR BARRY GOLDWATER, REPUBLICAN CANDIDATE FOR PRESIDENT.

[From *Handbook of South Carolina*]

A just and impartial government. [South Carolina government in 1927]

The government of South Carolina . . . has three branches, executive, legislative and judicial. The governor and most of the elective state offi-

Handbook of South Carolina, 1927, 17–19. The first governor to serve a four-year term was John G. Richards (1927–1931).

cers, by the recent amendment to the Constitution, serve four years. The governor is ineligible to succeed himself. He has the veto power, subject to reversal by two-thirds majority in each house of the legislature, called the "General Assembly."

The House of Representatives has . . . 124 members apportioned to the 46 counties according to population. The Senate [in 1927] is composed of 46 members, one for each county, one-half of whom are elected every two years. They serve four years, while representatives serve two years.

The Supreme Court, or court of appeals, has five members elected for ten year terms and is presided over by the chief justice. The State is divided into fourteen judicial circuits with a circuit judge resident in each and serving four years. These judges preside over the courts of common pleas and general sessions by rotation in the fourteen circuits. By custom, rarely broken, a judge in South Carolina serves during life of good behavior. Supreme court and circuit judges are elected by the General Assembly and one of them is seldom defeated for re-election. Not in fifty years, since the end of the Reconstruction period, has any scandal attached to the judiciary in South Carolina . . . . It was never said to be subject to the influence of private or corporate interest, and it is notable for impartial administration of justice without respect to wealth, race, or political affiliations.

To be a voter in South Carolina a man or woman must be 21 years old and must have lived in the State two years, in the county one year and in the voting precinct four months. The voter must obtain a certificate of registration, which is conditioned on showing that he or she is able to read and write any section of the State constitution or has paid taxes the preceding year on property assessed at $300 or more. The suffrage has been based since 1896 on this alternative educational and property qualification. South Carolina has never had the so-called "grandfather clause."

While the Republican party the last third of a century has not nominated State and county tickets, and the public officers have been virtually chosen in Democratic primaries, there is no discrimination against Republicans or members of other parties. . . .

South Carolina has seven Congressional districts. The First includes Berkeley, Charleston, Clarendon, Colleton and Dorchester. The Second includes Aiken, Allendale, Bamberg, Barnwell, Beaufort, Edgefield, Hampton, Jasper, and Saluda. The Third comprises Abbeville, Anderson, Greenwood, McCormick, Newberry, Oconee, and Pickens. The Fourth is made up of Greenville, Laurens, Spartanburg and Union. The Fifth includes Cherokee, Chester, Chesterfield, Fairfield, Kershaw, Lancaster, and York. The Sixth is made up of Georgetown, Horry, Darlington, Dillon, Florence, Marion, Marlboro, and Williamsburg, while the Seventh embraces the counties of Calhoun, Lee, Lexington, Orangeburg, Richland, and Sumter.

[D.D. Wallace]

Governor Olin D. Johnston and the Highway Commission.

Governor Johnston's opposition to what he, like many others, denounced as "the Highway ring," was inflamed by his personal antipathy to Benjamin M. Sawyer, the executive head of the department. Failing to persuade the legislature to oust the commission of fourteen members appointed by previous Governors for staggered terms, Governor Johnston declared several commissioners removed and, on October 28, 1935, proclaimed the commission in rebellion, insurrection, and insurgency, declared martial law over the department, and occupied it with troops. The Supreme Court ruled that only the Governor could decide when "rebellion" or "insurrection" existed, but declared illegal his removal of the commissioners, forbade the persons to whom he had handed over the department to exercise any function, and took possession of all funds of the department until the lawful commissioners should be in unhindered control. Governor Johnston defended his coup, and his order that automobile plates should be sold for $3.00 instead of the legally prescribed rates, as sanctioned by the people in voting for him on his promise to conquer the commission and oust Sawyer; he ignored the fact that thousands voted for him only to avoid a third term for his opponent and erstwhile chieftain Blease. To a special session of the legislature he complained that he had been opposed by "aristocrats" who sneered at his "having lint in his hair" as once "a cotton mill boy." The House voted

108 to 3 and the Senate 39 to 3 for the restoration of constitutional civil authority. It was finally agreed that the Governor would withdraw the troops and sign an act placing the department for sixty days under control of two expert employees of the old commission and an advisory committee of three State officials. The Governor's two months' possession of the records of the department failed to discover the slightest irregularity.

The original commission, reinstated by the Supreme Court, functioned until May, 1936, when the General Assembly revamped the department over the Governor's veto, by giving to the legislature instead of the Governor the selection of the commission, and temporarily transferred from the Governor to the State Treasurer the duty of signing road bonds. . . .

[V.O. Key]

Legislative government in South Carolina, in the 1940s:

South Carolina politics cannot be understood by analysis of gubernatorial politics alone. Its government is, as its politicians are wont to say, "legislative government." South Carolina's chief executive has limited power. He controls the State constabulary. He has power of appointment to State office except many of the really important State agencies. He can grant pardons, send messages to the legislature, and exercise the power of veto, yet he has the narrowest sort of power of direction of State administration.

The legislature has grasped firm control of the critical sectors of State administration. The chairman of the senate finance committee and the chairman of the house ways and means committee, with the Governor as a minority of one, compose the State budget commission. The State highway commission, often a bone of contention in South Carolina politics, consists of fourteen members, one from each judicial circuit elected by the legislative delegations from the circuit. The public service commission, the utility regulatory agency, consists of seven members elected by the

V. O. Key, *Southern Politics* (New York: A. A. Knopf, 1949), 150–52. Copyright 1949 by Alfred A. Knopf, Inc. Reprinted by permission of Alfred A. Knopf, Inc.

legislature. Not only does the legislature choose the chiefs of some of the more important state agencies; now and again individual legislators hold these posts by election of their colleagues. In other instances, the Governor or the responsible commission appoints them to such places. . . .

The legislature not only controls the strategic points of State administration. County legislative delegations constitute the real governing bodies of their respective counties. County-delegation autonomy in local legislation is, of course, not peculiar to South Carolina, but the scope of local legislation is unusually broad. The legislature, in fact the local delegation, makes county appropriations and fixes the local tax levy or it enacts the county "supply bill," as the process is called in South Carolina. By its power to appropriate county funds the legislative delegation, of course, controls county government. It goes further usually and becomes associated directly or indirectly with the designation of appointive county officials. County boards of welfare, for example, are appointed by the State department upon the recommendation of a majority of the county legislative delegation. . . .

The legislative delegation, in effect, makes most of the important local governmental decisions and usually the senator from the county becomes its first-ranking politician. His position is often symbolized in bills authorizing the legislative delegation to take action between legislative sessions. The decision—on such matters as transfers among appropriation items—must be taken by the senator and a majority of the house members. All of which gives the senator the final say on such questions. The power and position of the legislative delegation in local government have reached such a point that a proposal has been made to authorize it to enact county laws between sessions of the legislature.

Such is the formal allocation of governmental powers in South Carolina: a weak executive, a legislature that takes a hand in the management of administrative departments, and a legislature whose county delegations, with the senator as the kingpin, in effect, govern their respective counties.

Senator Strom Thurmond's write-in election, 1954.

For the first time in history, a man whose name was not printed on the ballot is going to take a seat in the United States Senate.

Reprinted from *U.S. News and World Report*. Copyright 1954. *U.S. News & World Report*, Inc. (Nov. 19, 1954), 49–52. Reprinted by permission of *U.S. News & World Report*.

Strom Thurmond is becoming the new Democratic Senator from South Carolina because 150,000 voters in the State wrote his name on their ballots in the November 2 election. This gave him a majority of almost 60,000 votes over Edgar A. Brown, whose name had been put on the ballot by the Democratic State Committee . . . .

The election marked a full-scale rebellion by voters who had been convinced that the State Democratic Executive Committee was preventing them from having a free voice in the choice of a Senator for a full six-year term . . . .

The write-in, itself, was hedged about by technicalities. The vote could not be cast by attaching a sticker bearing the name "Strom Thurmond" at the proper place on the ballot. Each voter had to find the right place on the ballot and write in "Strom Thurmond" in such a way as to make it clear that this was the man for whom he wanted to vote. Under a ruling of the State Attorney General, the name did not have to be spelled correctly. But it did have to be written in the proper place . . . .

What happened in South Carolina was this: On September 1, Senator Burnet R. Maybank died. He already had been renominated in the Democratic primary for another term. This meant that he would have been re-elected if he had lived.

Two days after the death of the Senator, the State Democratic Executive Committee met and ruled that, under the State Law, there was not enough time to hold a special primary and nominate another candidate to take the place of Senator Maybank on the ticket. In this situation the Committee designated Mr. Brown as the nominee of the party. This, ordinarily, would have assured his election for a six-year term.

Behind the scenes there were clashing ambitions and tugging factions. The names of both Mr. [James F.] Byrnes and Mr. Thurmond were injected into the discussions that circled about the Committee meeting, if they did not enter the meeting itself . . . .

The controlling group in the State Committee took the position that the nomination should not go to either of the men [Byrnes and Thurmond] who had led the effort to give the State's electoral vote to the Republican candidate for President [General Dwight Eisenhower] in 1952. And so Mr. Byrnes and Mr. Thurmond were passed over . . . .

The net result of the voting is that Mr. Thurmond got about three times as many votes by means of the write-in as were cast for Senator in the 1950 mid-term election . . . .

South Carolina wound up by sending to the Senate for the Democrats a man who has been at the front of two rebellions against the national party. But this does not mean that Mr. Thurmond plans to be a professional rebel in the Senate. He says that he considers himself a Democrat and that he plans to vote and caucus with the Democrats in Washington. On legislation, however, he expects to vote his own views and not necessarily those of the party . . . .

Strom Thurmond . . . gave this sketch of his views to a member of the Board of Editors of "U.S. News and World Report":

Q. Do you think South Carolina will drop back into its old Democratic groove in future presidential elections?

A. I think this, that the other States of the nation can just mark this down: That South Carolina is not in the bag for any party in the future.

Q. In general, do you expect to go along with other Southern Democrats voting in the Senate?

A. I expect to vote with the Democrats in organizing the Senate. I expect to caucus with the Democrats. On matters coming before the Senate, I expect to vote my own convictions. I expect to vote for what I think is in the best interest of the people in my State and country. I hope that the policies of the national party will be along that line. But I do not expect to be a rubber stamp.

Q. Would you describe yourself personally as an independent or a Democrat?

A. I am a Democrat—A South Carolina Democrat—one who believes in the principles of the South Carolina Democratic Party—one who has been faithful to the principles of the Democratic Party of South Carolina.

169. *Industry*

Probably the most remarkable phase of South Carolina's recent history has been its industrial growth. From a rather slow movement in the 1920s and the 1930s, the development of manufacturing in the state went forward in tremendous strides in the 1940s, until by mid-century industry was pushing agriculture very closely as the most important factor in South Carolina's economy. The following selections give a general picture of industry in the state in the 1920s; a description of the vast Santee-Cooper project; an optimistic report of 1950; a general discussion of textile progress by Governor James F. Byrnes in 1952; and an account of industry in 1962.

South Carolina industry in the 1920s:

South Carolina stands as the first cotton-cloth producing State in the United States. For a small, until recently unimportant, industrial State, this is a remarkable record. More operating looms, with greater cloth production, are here than in other states with slightly more, but not so active spindles. . . . In 1925, South Carolina had 5,321,264 spindles and 125,732 looms. For comparison, the figures for 1900 were 1,693,649 and 42,663, respectively. . . . The next nearest number of looms in a Southern state to South Carolina is in North Carolina, with 83,564, but North Carolina is about ten per cent richer in spindles. . . . In 1925, 220 textile mills in South Carolina employed 70,068 employees to produce products valued at $195,027,756. Again in comparison, the figures for the same items in 1900 were 115; 30,201; and $29,723,919. . . .

What do South Carolina cotton mills make? Practically every and any textile of which cotton is the important ingredient. There was a time when yarns, print cloths, sheetings, shirtings, and ginghams were the chief products. These were the backbone of the industry and basis of the development. As the years went by the grade of goods became finer and

Handbook of South Carolina, 1927, pp. 45, 50, 57–62, 69, 71, 73, 77, 84–86.

604

the products more diversified. Print cloth, sheeting, shirtings, drills and osnaburgs are still largely produced, but side by side with the sheeting are being made the sheerest and most beautiful veils and lawns and daintiest handkerchiefs. One successful manufacturer in the Piedmont has given this list of products in his immediate group, and daily some of these products are going into the world's marts: Bedspreads, pillow tubing, shade cloth, automobile fabrics, dress goods, pajama checks, jeans, sateens, print cloths, wide and narrow sheeting, bandage cloth, tobacco cloth, drills, gingham, voiles, lawns, crepes, tissue ginghams, poplins, suitings, airplane cloth, casket cloth, and plush. . . .

The mills set out to spin the cotton growing around them—in 1925 they consumed 1,027,458 bales—for many mills of today stand in the cotton fields of yesterday, but their consumption has gone ahead of the production. The five outstanding developments in recent years in South Carolina may be thus listed: 1. Modernizing of homes and equipment; 2. Trend to finer goods and specialties; 3. Development and use of hydro-electric power; 4. Independence of exacting commission houses; and 4. The development of bleacheries, finishing plants and diversification to plush mills, worsted plants, and the like . . . .

The law of South Carolina prohibits persons under 14 years old working in textile plants, and it is strictly and vigorously enforced by frequent inspections and personal observation . . . .

Among other industries in South Carolina, the cottonseed oil plants in 1924 crushed 222,735 tons of seed out of the year's crop of 357,000 tons, valued at $13,160,000. The number of mills operating was 46, employing 1593 people, and operating on an average of 146 days during the year. In 1922, the lumber industry in the State employed 18,000 men and produced more than 850 million board feet ranking South Carolina twelfth in the nation in lumber production. Many related industries could be developed around the lumber industry, including the making of veneers, creosoted timbers, and furniture . . . . In 1924, $3,444,366 worth of mineral products were produced in the State, largely in stone and clay products. South Carolina is rich in mineral products and this industry has much room for expansion . . . .

Seventeen large complete sulphuric acid and fertilizer manufacturing plants, six large acidulating and fertilizer manufacturing plants, and 53 registered mixing plants were operating in South Carolina in 1926. These produced approximately 800,000 tons of fertilizer, valued at more than $24,000,000 . . . . Charleston, the home of the industry was until quite recently the largest manufacturing point of commercial fertilizers in the world, but recently has been outstripped by Baltimore. The port of Charleston receives and handles more fertilizer and fertilizer materials than any port in the country . . . .

The commercial canning industry in South Carolina ranks rather low except as to oysters, clams and shrimps. Enough cases of these three products are packed each year to make South Carolina of some importance in the fish-canning trade. The yearly pack of fruits and vegetables is small compared to that of some of the larger canning states, although it has steadily increased during the past five years . . . .

South Carolina ranks sixth among the States . . . in the amount of developed water power . . . . Including smaller plants in the various sections of the state, there are 58 waterpower plants in South Carolina, with a total capacity of 514,428 horsepower. . . . They employ 2285 persons and produced electricity valued at $10,072,940 in 1925 . . . from plants valued at over $63,000,000. . . .

[John A. Zeigler]

The Santee-Cooper project:

The South Carolina of tomorrow will necessarily follow the development of essential electric power. Organized efforts to build the industrial and agricultural wealth of the State have definitely proven that electric power must, and will, lead the way. Thus it is that the outstanding development in South Carolina in recent years has been the creation of the huge Santee-Cooper power development.

Utilizing Carolina's greatest watershed, including the Catawba, Broad, Wateree, Pacolet, Saluda, Enoree, Tyger, Congaree and other great rivers that converge into the Santee, the project is assured of continuous operation. Like a great funnel, the Santee supplies a daily average of more than twelve billion gallons of water producing water. Here, at the Santee-Cooper project, the power is set to work transforming nature's storehouse of undeveloped resources, with which the Carolinas abound, into new wealth, finished products, and services, for the benefit of the nation.

John A. Zeigler, "The Santee-Cooper Project," *South Carolina Magazine*, VIII (March, 1945), 36–38. Reprinted by permission of Mrs. Virginia E. Zeigler.

For the first time in the history of the State we are developing adequate power in the coastal regions in close proximity to our harbor and shipping facilities. This development means much to South Carolina. It is rapidly becoming the motivating force of inevitable industrial expansion which is being felt not only in the tide-water regions, but throughout the State. Already new industries are pointing the way to other newcomers, as they recognize and advertise the unusual advantages which South Carolina offers. They are finding an abundance of steady power at reasonable rates which encourages low production costs and facilitates successful competition. . . .

Since the first delivery of power on February 17, 1942, to the Pittsburgh Metallurgical Company of Charleston, this plant has since been in round-the-clock operation manufacturing. . . . Santee-Cooper power is also being used by an aluminum plant . . . now in operation at Harleyville, S.C.

The latest large plant to be attracted to the Santee-Cooper area is the Santee-Gair Paper Mill, which will be located on Lake Marion . . . . This $12,000,000 plant will manufacture corrugated board which it will make into shipping boxes . . . . The Santee-Gair Paper Mill will use the deep waterway extending from the site of their plant to the port of Charleston for the transport of much of their finished product. The two other large paper mills in the Santee-Cooper area are also seeking docking sites for the water portage of pulp wood to their plants at Georgetown and Charleston.

Santee-Cooper's contribution to inland navigation begins with a 12-feet-depth near Fort Motte, extends southward 46 miles across Lake Marion to the seven-mile-long diversion canal, then 12 miles across Lake Moultrie to the single 60 by 180 foot lock that will lower the crafts 75 feet to the tailrace canal below. From thence they can travel 14 miles to deep water on the Cooper River at Strawberry Landing and then southward 36 miles to Charleston. Thus 105 miles is open to water travel. This waterway will be extended to Columbia according to postwar plans of the U.S. Army Engineering Corps who have approved a 10-foot channel in the Congaree River to the capital . . . .

Although most of Santee-Cooper's 70,000,000 KWH out-put per year is now being sold to war industries and to private power companies serving the war effort, a considerable portion of this power will be re-captured for sale to new permanent industries in the post-war adjustment period. A sizeable block of power is also being reserved for the Rural

Electric Cooperatives who plan as soon as materials are available to build transmission lines to the source of this low-cost electricity.

To sum it all up briefly, Santee-Cooper's low-cost electricity has already attracted four huge industries; health conditions have been immeasurably improved; 105 miles of inland waterway between Charleston and Fort Motte have been completed; the project helped solve the unemployment problem; millions of dollars were put into circulation; a wildlife paradise created; county, school and municipal taxes have been paid; all debts met promptly out of the revenue; and we enter the third year of operations under the soundest possible business management.

South Carolina industry in step with a New South, 1950:

The coming of the Celanese corporation's huge plant to Rock Hill late in 1945 was of great and often over-looked significance in the State's remarkable industrial growth since the end of World War II. There had been the beginnings of an industrial movement to South Carolina even before Pearl Harbor, but during the war years it had slowed, except for the establishment of a few war-time operations and a great expansion around the Charleston Navy Yard . . . . Even the most optimistic of the State's industrial boosters would have hesitated to predict the flood of new industries that have entered the State since the War.

For since January 1, 1945, industry has spent or allocated around $500,000,000 for new construction and expansion in the State with strong indications that the growth will continue. And a considerable part of this growth can probably be laid to the decision of Celanese officials to choose the State for their newest plant. Their decision focused the attention of other industrialists on the State and once they had studied the State and the advantages it had to offer many of them made their own decisions to set up operations here.

Another industrial giant that studied the South Carolina prospect and found it pleasing was Du Pont, whose huge Orlon plant at Camden will be in operation before the end of the year. There are many others,

South Carolina Magazine, XIII (March, 1950), 7, 23–24. Reprinted by permission of *South Carolina Magazine.*

including Stevens which is constructing its rayon finishing mill near Cheraw; Deering-Milliken, whose plant near Pendleton is considered one of the finest textile mills in the world; Textron, which has ten plants in the State; and woolen manufacturers, who are following other fiber and fabric industries south. And particularly pleasing to South Carolinians has been the expansion of great local operations such as the Springs and Self mills, which are expanding and continuing to expand.

There must be a reason for the attractions South Carolina offers out-of-state industries and there is no man better qualified to explain them than L. W. Bishop, director of the state research, planning and development board. This board was created by the General Assembly in 1945, and since that time has won the support and approval of political leaders, businessmen and citizens for the job it has done, as well as the praise of industrialists for the help and cooperation it has given. R. M. Cooper was the board's first director . . . .

Mr. Bishop says that the State has been particularly fortunate in its postwar industrial development, with its progress diversified and built upon solid foundations . . . . Despite the new industries that have come into the State, the greatest diversification has been within the textile industry itself, still the industrial giant of the State. Not too many years ago the great part of the State's textile production consisted of coarse fabrics, usually cheap and low grade. But the new and modern plants are producing the finest fibers and fabrics, suited for all uses.

One of the major attractions to new industry has been the abundant supply of ambitious, capable and cooperative employees. In some instances industrialists considering the State have wondered whether sufficient and suitable labor would be available. In every case they have been more than satisfied. Management and labor have worked as a team in South Carolina and the loss of time from strikes has been almost non-existent. During 1949, the loss of man hours by reason of industrial dispute in manufacturing enterprises amounted to one ten-thousandth of one per cent of the total man hours worked, the best record in the nation . . . .

The State's development, particularly in textiles, is shown by census figures which reveal an increase of 369.3 per cent in the value added by manufacturing between 1939 and 1947, leading all states except New Mexico . . . . The State's mills accounted for 10.4% of the nation's textile products in 1947 . . . and 41% of all cotton woven goods produced in the country in 1949 . . . . The development of the chemical industry has also featured recent progress, with the value added by manufacture of chemicals totalling $16,600,000 in 1948. The stone, clay and glass industry, while not a major factor in the State's economic development, has shown a gratifying growth, with a value added of $11,600,000.

Lumber and allied products have also played a leading part in recent developments with the value added by manufacture in 1947 reported as $59,400,000. The value added for paper and allied products the same year was $36,900,000 . . . .

Closely tied in with the State's industrial growth has been the remarkable development of the port of Charleston, where tonnage figures have doubled since the pre-war years. In 1948 a total of well over 4,000,000 tons was handled at the port. During the fiscal year 1948–1949 imports and exports valued at $79,000,000 moved through the port, an increase of 51% over the previous fiscal year. Just ten years ago the total value of imports and exports was only $13,194,000 . . . . Much of the credit for the port's development goes to the South Carolina State Ports Authority which has encouraged not only shipping, but industrial development.

So from every economic angle, South Carolina faces the second half of the century with faith in its sound economic foundations and confidence in what the future may hold.

Governor Byrnes describes recent
textile progress, May 17, 1952:

South Carolina has shown tremendous industrial progress during the past decade and especially in textiles during the post-war period. . . . The last figures quoted to me by our Research, Planning and Development Board graphically demonstrate what has been accomplished in this brief period. . . .

In 1941 the textile industry in South Carolina employed 102,342 persons in the plants of the State. But in 1951 the larger and still expanding textile industry provided jobs for 130,838 people. All industries, including the textile industry, provided jobs for 145,889 persons in 1941. That year the average income for the man or woman employed in an industrial plant in South Carolina was only $813.12. But in 1951 the total industrial

Charlotte Observer, May 17, 1952.

employment of the State reached 183,596. And the average wage earner in the plants of South Carolina was receiving an annual income of $2,483.40 from industrial employment.

While the industrial employment generally was rising slightly more than 25 per cent in that 10-year period, the wages earned by the employees was increasing approximately 300 per cent. Wages in textile plants rose nearly 400 per cent during that time. That shows how the industrial worker in this State benefited during the past decade as industry itself progressed.

In the textile industry alone the value of the annual product increased from $382,753,951 to $1,608,984,643 between 1941 and 1951. . . . From 1950 to 1951 the capital investments in manufacturing plants rose from $775,304,036 to $867,285,102, an increase of $102,502,071. These figures apply to the 1795 industrial plants operating in South Carolina during 1951. . . . Since January, 1951, seventy-five new and existing industries have announced the investment of $141,600,000 in South Carolina. These investments will provide new jobs for our people and give them increased incomes, with greater purchasing power.

Industry and manufacturing

South Carolina's industrial growth in recent years has attracted nationwide attention. Its percentage growth in this field has been at, or near, the top of all states since World War II.

During the past few years, our state has enjoyed its greatest industrial progress in its history. All-important diversification of industry—an admittedly new phenomenon in South Carolina's economy—has become solid fact out of optimistic theory. Such growth has resulted in appreciable increases in per capita income of the state's citizens.

In the four years from 1959–1962, more than $200 million was committed each year for new and expanded plants in South Carolina. In 1961, the total value of new and expanded industry had reached a record $217,677,000. Facilities for the manufacture of such items as glass, related products, and metal products accounted for a large portion of total industrial growth.

Handbook of South Carolina, 1963, 63–65.

Particularly outstanding is the rapid growth of metalworking. Of all industrial plants built in South Carolina in 1961, every fifth one was a metalworking operation, a dramatic example of South Carolina's shift from an agricultural to an industrially-oriented economy.

In the early 1960's some giants of the metalworking industry have located large operations in the state, where over 300 metalworking companies are already successfully operating. Six new plants have been announced at Spartanburg, Belton, Woodruff, Cayce, Clemson, and Edgefield, while six others are being built in Spartanburg, Charleston, Columbia, Greer, Bennettsville, and Georgetown.

Today's South Carolinians are working on new exciting projects which will culminate in fulfillment of the age-old adventure dream, exploration of outer space. Products being manufactured here and now are being used as vital components in programs of the National Aeronautics and Space Administration, as well as in privately sponsored programs such as Telestar. In addition, the state's industry and technology are being used in long-range missile fields. At least a dozen firms now operating in South Carolina have contributed varying portions of their production to nuclear and space projects.

Electric capacitor production constitutes the most astronomical rise of all. In 1950, this form of manufacture was unknown to the Palmetto State. In 1962, the state was the nation's leader in the field. . . . In 1962 five capacitor plants were located over the state in Walhalla, Columbia, Myrtle Beach, Florence and Darlington. These factories employ about 3,860 South Carolinians.

South Carolina has for years been the nation's consistent leader in spinning activity and the average number of spindle hours in operation. In 1954, for the first time, the state forged ahead of North Carolina in the number of spindles in place, and still holds that position.

Large gains have also been made in the garment industry. Several companies have combined operations from raw cotton to spinning, weaving, finishing, cutting, and sewing. South Carolina is also a leader in bleaching and finishing.

The forest products industry—including pulp and paper, lumber, veneer, furniture, poles, etc.—ranks next to textiles in total manufacturing goods, with plants fairly evenly distributed over the state. Large pulp and paper mills are at Georgetown, Charleston, Catawba, Hartsville, and Rock Hill. South Carolina's rich forest areas yield many valuable forest products. An extensive program of reforestation, forest fire protection, and forest management assistance helps to maintain and to increase the supply of forest products for these important industries.

Adding to South Carolina's growing diversity of industries are such products as glass, furniture, plastics, fishing equipment, sewing machines, and many others.

During the 1950's the Atomic Energy Commission constructed a plant near Aiken at an estimated cost of $1.5 billion, bringing the state's postwar industrial development to over $2.5 billion. Approximately 145,000 new jobs resulted from this industrial activity.

Recently the Carolinas-Virginia Nuclear Power Associates built a nuclear power station at Parr, in Fairfield County, at a cost of $29 million. The reactor, with its furnace heated by 2,000 pellets of slightly enriched uranium-235, is situated adjacent to the South Carolina Electric and Gas plant at Parr. There atomic energy will be converted into an estimated 19,000 kilowatts of electricity. . . .

A growing industry in South Carolina is that created by the increasing number of tourists visiting the state's parks, mountains, beaches, gardens, and historic spots each year. An official estimate placed the income for this business at over $200 million in 1962.

170. *Rural Electrification in South Carolina*

No single thing within the past half-century has had greater impact on the lives of rural South Carolinians than the passage of the Rural Electric Cooperative Act [173] in 1939, under the leadership of Governor Burnet R. Maybank. Just over 30 years ago, the first lights were turned on in the rural areas of South Carolina through electric cooperatives, and thousands who had never experienced the benefits that electricity could bring were able to enjoy for the first time modern appliances and other conveniences. Despite the pleas of rural people all over America for electricity, their words were unheeded because investor-owned utilities saw little, if any, profit in stringing electric lines through sparsely populated areas. President Franklin D. Roosevelt created the Rural Electric Administration by executive order; and people formed their own cooperatives to bring electricity into their areas. The following selections describe the birth of the REA at President Roosevelt's cottage at Warm Springs, Ga., where he was recuperating from an attack of polio; the cooperatives in South Carolina, and their comparison of service and cost with private utilities serving the state.

[President Roosevelt on Creation of the REA]

There was only one discordant note in that first stay of mine at Warm Springs. When the first-of-the-month bill came in for electric light for my little cottage, I found that the charge was eighteen cents a kilowatt hour . . . . That started my long study of public utility charges for electric current and the whole subject of getting electricity into farm homes . . . so it can be said that a little cottage at Warm Springs, Georgia, was the birthplace of the Rural Electrification Administration.

Clyde T. Ellis, *A Giant Step* (New York: Random House, 1966), 34. Reprinted by permission of Random House.

South Carolina Association of Electric
Cooperatives, *Report,* 1966, 1968

LET THERE BE LIGHT

A half-century ago, rural Americans had no idea that electricity would come to them along the sparsely settled countryside and into isolated back roads. But people began to get a vision of the advantages of the miracles of electricity and what it could add to their living. Then, in 1935, the Rural Electrification Administration was created by men who saw in the future a new way of life for rural people.

The Rural Electrification Administration was created to serve as a lending agency. Commercial power companies were given first claim on borrowing these funds, but they did not take the money, and refused to serve in rural areas. This money may still be borrowed by commercial power companies and municipalities at the same rate of interest charged to electric cooperatives . . . but only if the borrower agrees to supply persons who do not have central station service.

Even after passage of the Act, there was little progress in the nation or in South Carolina. Then the rural people came to realize that they must do the job themselves. With the help of the County agents, Agriculture teachers, and other rural leaders, these "country folk" began to organize Rural Electric Cooperatives.

With their Co-ops incorporated, the rural residents were able to apply for loans to electrify the countryside.

The loans were secured by mortgages on the property of the borrower, to be paid with interest. The REA, not owning one foot of line, served only as the banker, with a banker's interest in the value and use of the loans.

The Cooperatives are owned and paid for by the rural people who receive electric service from it. Incorporated under the laws of the State of South Carolina, they operate for service, not for profit.

The Co-ops operate under a Board of Trustees, made up of people elected by the Co-op member-users. The non-salaried trustees perform their duties as a community service to their neighbors.

Today there are 22 rural electric cooperative systems in South Carolina, which are made up of 21 distribution cooperatives and one generation and transmission cooperative, and about 97% of the homes and businesses are receiving adequate, dependable, low-cost electricity. Co-ops in South Carolina serve 80% of these rural customers to their satisfaction.

South Carolina Co-ops operate in the rural areas from the palmettoes on the coast to the Blue Ridge mountains, in every county except Greenwood.

Electric Co-ops . . . serve more than 164,000 rural homes and businesses, or about one-fourth of the population of the State.

In 1966, Co-ops had a gross income of $19 million, and a payroll of $4,716,000 for 800 employees.

Electric Co-ops have removed much of the toil and drudgery of rural life. Today electricity, with its labor-saving devices, its entertainment gadgets, and its economy make rural life the equal of urban living.

But the rural family is not the only one to benefit from rural electric power. For every dollar spent by the Co-ops for electric facilities, Co-op members spend an average of $5.00 for wiring, electrical appliances and equipment.

They are a $100 million investment, exclusive of steamplant ($27 million), and transmission ($21 million).

This means that in South Carolina more than $500 million in new and taxable wealth has been created as a direct result of the existence of Rural Electric Cooperatives. This is what Main Street merchants have sold in the rural areas.

Electric cooperatives in South Carolina [1966–1967] serve an average of four and one-half consumers per mile, and revenue for these consumers averages $529 per mile per year. This is in contrast with 25.5 consumers per mile of line served by the commercial power companies whose revenue averages $7,122 per mile of line per year.

The locally owned, locally controlled, locally managed Co-ops in South Carolina are: Aiken, Aiken; Berkeley, Moncks Corner; Black River, Sumter; Blue Ridge, Pickens; Broad River, Gaffney; Coastal, Walterboro; Edisto, Bamberg; Fairfield, Winnsboro; Horry, Conway; Laurens, Laurens; Little River, Abbeville; Lynches River, Pageland; Marlboro, Bennettsville; Mid-Carolina, Lexington; Newberry, Newberry; Palmetto, Ridgeland; Pee Dee, Darlington; Salkehatchie, Barnwell; Santee, Kingstree; Tri-County, St. Matthews; and York, York.

The Generating and Transmission Cooperative is Central Electric Power Cooperative, Inc., Cayce.

[South Carolina Public Service Commission]

Miles of Line and Income of Power Suppliers Serving in South Carolina

Name	Miles of line	Income in South Carolina	Customers Served
Carolina Power and Light Co.	4,739	$ 20,359,559	91,180
Duke Power Company	8,483	69,718,704	211,355
South Carolina Electric & Gas Co.	7,549	57,861,728	226,705
Totals	20,771	*$147,939,991	529,240

*Users Avg. Persons, 25.479; $7,122 per mile per year

21 Electric Co-ops	36,295	**$ 19,199,755	164,137

**Users Avg. Persons, 4.5; $528.99 per mile per year

The Rural Electrification Program in South Carolina

At the time the Rural Electrification Administration was created on May 11, 1935, only 3,796 farms in South Carolina, or 2.3 per cent, were

89th *Annual Report,* 1966–67, S. C. Public Service Commission.

Report, U.S. Dept. of Agriculture, Rural Electrification Administration, Jan., 1960.

receiving central station electric service. . . . 94.5 per cent of all farms recorded in the 1954 Census were being served by June 30, 1959. REA borrowers serve about 67.0 percent of these electrified farms.

The first REA electrification loan in South Carolina was approved in September of 1935. The first REA-financed line was placed in operation on July 24, 1937, by the Greenwood County Rural Electric System of Greenwood.

Up to January 1, 1960, the beginning of REA's 25th year, the agency had approved a total of $85,580,210 in loans to 28 electric borrowers in the State, of which 26 are cooperatives. The loans were made to enable the borrowers to construct 35,407 miles of line and other electric facilities to serve 156,461 consumers.

Loan funds actually advanced to these borrowers amounted to $75,687,205 by January 1, 1960. With the help of this financing, the locally owned and managed systems had already placed 33,315 miles of line in operation and were serving 138,077 farm and other rural outlets. The average monthly consumption of electricity by these consumers had increased 104 kilowatt-hours in 1950, to 251 kwh in 1958.

REA electric borrowers in South Carolina have repaid $14,300,054 on the principal of their government loans. In addition, they have paid $8,728,417 in interest and $2,194,206 ahead of schedule. As of January 1, 1960, no borrower in the State was overdue in its loan payments.

[R. M. Jeffries on Rural Cooperatives]

We can today ascribe the real beginning of widespread rural electrification to the time of the inauguration of President Roosevelt in 1933. Prior to that time in thickly settled communities the private power companies had extended their lines but the development of rural electrification was hampered partly by regulatory rules, partly by expensive standards of construction which were then prevalent and partly by the fact that the power companies had to see enough revenue available to make a profit with which to pay dividends. The early lines built by the rural electric cooperatives were far less expensive than the prevailing standards but were sufficient for the purpose of carrying power for lights and household appliances to thousands of farm homes that had never had the opportunity to have the benefits of such services.

R. M. Jeffries, "Rural Utilities," a speech delivered at the Ruritan National Convention, Asheville, N.C., Jan. 29, 1952. From a script kindly supplied by the speaker.

Regardless of what may be said today about the New Deal, rural America will have to give President Franklin D. Roosevelt large credit for its marvelous progress during the last 18 years in securing the blessings of electricity. You will recall that the first appropriation was emergency money provided by executive order of the President, but the Congress soon saw the benefits to the national economy of the extension of this necessary utility to farm people and has almost unanimously and without regard to party lines supported the program from the time of its inception. Rural electrification is here to stay.

Of course rural electrification had its opponents in the very beginning as well as now. Opposition stems largely from private power companies. Their argument is that such things are socialistic in nature. This argument of course fails when we realize that the Rural Electrification Administration plan today is that the facilities are owned by the people whom they serve. All funds advanced by the National Rural Electrification Administration are in the nature of loans and are being paid back 100 percent. There is no better illustration of the value of free enterprise than that found in the rural electrification cooperatives today.

Private power companies have likewise fought publicly owned power whether it be municipal, state or national. The Santee-Cooper Hydroelectric and Navigation System is owned completely by the State of South Carolina and its people, but from its very inception during the legislative fights in 1933 and 1934 down practically to the present time all accomplishments and expansions have occurred over the opposition of the private power companies.

Of course from the standpoint of the management of the private power companies their opposition, whether sensible or not, may be expected because, after all, the private power company's idea is not one of free enterprise even though it may be termed private enterprise. There is a big difference between the two things. Free enterprise is the underlying philosophy of the people of America. Its most distinguishing characteristic is competition. The private power companies in their doctrine of private enterprise have asked for and obtained monopolies. Familiar methods of such monopolistic enterprises are to fight competition and to allege that public power is socialistic. The people should own all monopolies because monopolies do not promote the general welfare—to promote the general welfare is not socialistic. Public power is no more socialistic than the mail service or the public schools or many other facilities afforded by the Government. Briefly, public power believes in competition while private power believes in monopoly. Public power offers cheap power for the development of domestic, commercial and industrial pursuits while private power naturally charges higher for its product in order to maintain more expensive overheads and to pay dividends.

There are only about two businesses to which the Government will guarantee reasonable returns on invested capital. These are the private power and telephone companies which insist that they cannot have competition and that they must be allowed by regulatory commissions to charge rates for their commodities sufficient to pay reasonable returns on invested capital . . . . For capital invested in your store, your farm, your mill, your profession, you are not guaranteed a fair return but you must earn it by your brain and your constant activity. . . .

The record of the rural electric cooperatives throughout the Nation is most astounding. . . .

June 30, 1951, South Carolina had 139,364 farms, with 106,473 electrified, a percentage of 76.4 electrified and 23.6 unelectrified. . . .

In spite of the tremendous accomplishments to date in the cause of rural electrification, we are really just beginning this important work. The Electrical World . . . in its issue of December 3, 1951, gives a report predicting that the farmers will use during the next 5 years double the amount of electrical energy now being used and that there is a farm market for electrical goods of approximately one-half billion dollars. . . .

As the Manager of a rather large publicly owned power development, it is my belief that the farm load from a utility standpoint offers the best promises of growth of any type of electric load now visible. The uses of electricity are being extended almost daily, and things that were electrically considered phenomenal even a year or two ago are now becoming obselete and giving way to greater improvements.

. . . The use of this type of power on the farm is expanding even greater than in other lines of activity. Forced-air drying . . . was first applied to forage crops but it is now being extended to the processing of root crops of all kinds. Research is now far advanced for the use of high frequency and supersonic energy for pest control and for processing and preserving human and animal food on the farms . . . . At first in rural electrification, emphasis of course was on home lighting. Now the successful farmer lights the farmstead. Well-equipped farms now contain shops having drill presses, grinders, shapers, lathes, saw and other tools propelled by electricity. Electrical welding is becoming common on the better farms. The usual estimates of the number of uses of electricity on the farm is a figure of over 200 practical applications of this fine form of energy. Administrator Claud Wickard of the Rural Electrification Administration stated recently that these uses would total over 400 but when we consider that there are 30 or 40 common uses of comparatively cheap equipment available to the farmers we can begin to perceive what a great boon this will be at a time when farm labor has migrated to urban areas or when the use of hand labor on the farm has become too expensive for production. . . .

All of this means that those engaged in supplying electrical energy and facilities for rural electrification must see to it that the lines are extended to reach all farmers just as quickly as possible and that all existing lines are enlarged to carry the load that farm life requires in order that the farmers . . . may stay abreast of everything progressive. . . .

The accompanying utility to electrification is that of the telephone, without which farmers often fail to make profits by lack of knowledge of markets, etc., and families are deprived of easy means of communication with their neighbors. We . . . have had the blessings of telephones for so long until we could not conceive of what it is to be without them . . . . Our complete dependence upon the use of this utility should be sufficient to enable us to do everything we can to promote its extension to the farmers of America.

One of the greatest tragedies sustained by rural life is the fact that today, from a national standpoint, there is a smaller number of telephones in farm homes than there was thirty years ago. In 1920, there were in the United States 2,498,493 farm telephones . . . . In 1950, the United States Census Report showed that only 2,059,474 farms enjoyed telephone service.

In South Carolina in 1920 there were 10,943 telephones, or 5.7 per cent of the farms; in 1950, on farms there were 11,901 telephones, or 8.5 per cent of the 139,364 farms . . . a gain of about 3%.

Again, the trouble is partly the profit incentive that must actuate our private telephone companies. It stands to reason that such companies would greatly prefer to do business in closely settled towns and cities than to have to run and maintain lines through miles of rural areas with only a few customers to each mile.

. . . Failure of our farmers to be afforded telephone service has caused the National Government to make available through Rural Electrification Administration funds with which to finance rural telephone systems. These loans are so arranged that private telephone companies can secure funds for extensions of telephones into farm areas, but rural telephone cooperatives are also financed and many of these are forming . . . . The loans for rural telephones were not authorized by the Congress until October, 1949. By the end of 1951, REA had approved 146 telephone loan allocations. . . .

We can all agree that the way to restore American country life is to give farmers all of the conveniences and utilities possessed by residents of cities. The tremendous growth of rural electrification demonstrates that utilities can be rapidly supplied to farming peoples . . . .

Let us believe that the worst is over with rural life in America. Let us cherish everything that can be done to extend utilities to farming people. Then, with our economy in perfect balance we may go down through the centuries sustained by the prosperity and the happiness of a united people.

171. *Social Services*

THE LAST THREE DECADES HAVE SEEN THE COOPERATION OF STATE, FEDERAL AND LOCAL AGENCIES IN CONCERN FOR THE PUBLIC'S WELFARE. THE CONSIDERABLE EXPANSION OF THE FUNCTIONS OF THE STATE BOARD OF HEALTH AND THE ESTABLISHMENT OF THE DEPARTMENT OF PUBLIC WELFARE IN 1937 ILLUSTRATE THE PROGRESS OF SOCIAL AGENCIES IN SOUTH CAROLINA. INCLUDED HERE ARE NOTES ON HEALTH SERVICES IN THE 1920s; AN ACCOUNT OF THE ORGANIZATION OF THE STATE BOARD OF HEALTH IN 1940; SOME EXCERPTS FROM THE PUBLIC WELFARE ACT OF 1937; AND A REPORT ON A TYPICAL YEAR OF PUBLIC ASSISTANCE SERVICES (1948). THE SOUTH CAROLINA DIVORCE ACT WHICH BECAME LAW IN 1949 AND A CENSUS REPORT FOR 1960 ARE ALSO ADDED.

Health services in the 1920s:

The State Board of Health is now one of the most important departments of State government. . . . Its duty is to prevent diseases among the people as far as it is possible to do so. It is at present carrying out many lines of work toward that end. Control work has been concentrated in a few diseases, and some of them have shown a remarkable decrease in prevalency. In 1916 the death rate in South Carolina from tuberculosis reached 145.9 per 100,000 population. In 1925 that rate had been reduced to 93.8, showing a decrease of 52.1 per cent per 100,000 population, these figures being based on reports of the United States bureau of vital statistics.

The division of tuberculosis cares for a number of victims of the disease, limited by facilities provided by the State, in the hospital at State Park. The number of beds for whites and Negroes is 138 and the children's building, nearing completion, will take care of 150 . . . .

In 1916 deaths from malaria reached 39 per 100,000, and in 1925 that rate had dropped to 10.1 . . . . The prevalence of malaria has been reduced almost unbelievably due to concentrated work of the

Handbook of South Carolina, 1927, 234–37.

department of malaria control of the State board of health, co-operating with the malaria division of the United States public health service. Drainage of malaria areas has played an important part in the reduction.

In 1916 typhoid took its toll of 34.1 deaths per 100,000 population. In 1925 this rate was 26.8. Seven hundred and twenty-nine persons died from pellagra in South Carolina in 1916; in 1925, 435. The total death rate from all causes in South Carolina in 1916 was 13.8 per thousand population. With a great increase in population since 1916, making the control of disease more difficult, the death rate in 1925 had dropped to 12.2 per 1000.

Even more pronounced has been the reduction of infant mortality; that is, the deaths of infants under one year of age. In 1919, when the first records were kept, the death rate totaled 113 to every 1000 births. This revelation inspired concerted endeavor to bring such a death rate to a minimum. Steadily the rate was decreased until in 1925, the low mark of 91.8 deaths per thousand births was reached, favorably comparing with that of any state.

One of the most difficult problems is the health education of the Negro. The Negro death rate in 1925 was 14.9 per 1000, considerably less than for previous years, but much work in public health remains to be done among the Negroes. Toward this end South Carolina State Board of Health is working. Negro tubercular patients are now being cared for. Midwifery classes are a part of the routine work of the bureau of public health nursing. Literature treating of health subjects is generously distributed. . . .

The death rate among whites of the State for 1925 was 9.5 per 1000 population. It is among the white people that the State Board of Health has worked primarily since its organization, and with splendid results. The death rate has been seen to drop year after year until at present the white people of South Carolina are among the healthiest in America.

South Carolina maintains seven institutions, besides the hospital for tuberculosis patients heretofore mentioned, for sick persons and youthful delinquents. The oldest of these is the South Carolina State Hospital, Columbia . . . which cares for the mentally diseased. . . . Other charitable institutions of the State are The South Carolina Industrial School for Boys, at Florence; The South Carolina Industrial School for Girls, at Columbia; The State Reformatory for Boys (Negro), at Columbia; The State Training School at Clinton; the John De La Howe School at McCormick; and the Confederate Soldiers' Home, at Columbia. In addition, the Confederate Home School, at Charleston; the Association for the Blind, at Columbia; and the Fairwold Industrial School for Negro girls, near Columbia, receive some assistance from the State.

The State Board of Health in 1940:

The State Board of Health is charged with the responsibility of promoting and protecting the public health, and it has been given almost unlimited power by virtue of its authority to make rules and regulations which have the force of law. There are times, especially during epidemics, when that power has to be exercised for the best interest of the State, but such times are exceptions rather than rules.

The function of the State Board of Health is to teach by demonstration and actual service and not by force. Every activity sponsored or carried on by the State Board of Health is primarily concerned with teaching the individual and the general public the basic principles of public health, and in order that all services . . . might be taken directly to the people in their own homes and communities, especially those in the rural areas where the practice of preventive medicine has been so sadly neglected, a County Health Department has been established in every county.

The County Health Officer, the public health nurse, and the sanitarian are . . . the front line soldiers of the State Board of Health. Their duties are to stand guard against the approach of disease and ill-health and to promote in every . . . way better health conditions in the county to which they are assigned. Their chief concerns are (1) environmental sanitation; (2) control of communicable diseases; (3) maternal and child health; (4) school hygiene; and (5) public health education.

The County Health Officer is the administrative head of a County Health Department. As a physician with special training in public health, he is qualified to appraise the health conditions of his county and to plan and supervise a health program fitted to its needs. He supervises the activities of the personnel of his department; consults with other physicians in his district; lectures to professional and lay groups;

South Carolina State Board of Health (1941).

conducts clinics; makes investigations, inspections and examinations; and performs other related duties. He is directly responsible to the State Health Officer for the conduct of his department.

The Public Health Nurse, under the direction of the County Health Officer, assists in analyzing health problems and related social problems . . . ; gets in touch with prospective mothers and sees that they have all types of prenatal care . . . ; assists in securing complete birth registration . . . ; participates in formulating and developing a health education program based on the needs of the pupils . . . ; encourages periodic health examinations . . . ; promotes the complete reporting of reportable diseases; helps under medical direction to secure specific immunization of all infants and pre-school children, and of other age groups as needed . . . ; and assists in finding tuberculosis cases and contacts, and securing medical examination and supervision for them.

The Sanitary Inspector . . . devotes his efforts towards environmental control. His activities in relation to specific phases of the public health program include: assisting in securing safe water and milk supplies . . . ; assists in securing safe and sanitary conditions in public schools, and in teaching children the principles of healthy living; inspects all restaurants, roadside stands, and other public eating places, dairies, canneries, packing plants, meat markets, etc; and assists in securing proper sanitation of barber shops, beauty parlors, railroad stations, bus terminals, theatres, churches, construction camps . . . and other places as prescribed by regulations of the State Board of Health. . . .

The central headquarters of the State Board of Health is organized along lines to best serve the State and its people. There are the Divisions of Administration, Rural Sanitation, Preventable Diseases, Maternal and Child Welfare, Dental Health, Industrial Health, Venereal Disease Control, Crippled Children, and Cancer Control; plus the Bureau of Vital Statistics, and the Hygienic Laboratory. In addition, the South Carolina Sanitorium is operated as an agency of the State Board of Health, with supervision and control being vested in the Sanitorium Committee.

The Board of Health, through the Sanitorium, also operates a Mobile Unit or a traveling Tuberculosis Clinic. The clinic physician, with his X-ray technician, is available to all Counties, by appointment made through the County Health Departments. During the fiscal year 1939–1940 this Traveling Clinic visited thirty-nine counties and held eighty-three clinics; 2395 physical examinations were made and 3278 x-rays were processed. . . .

Since 1936, through the aid of Federal funds, all activities of the State Board of Health have been increased. The organization as a whole has grown tremendously, and now employs approximately 400 persons.

The South Carolina Public Welfare Act, 1937:

Section 1. There is hereby created a State Department of Public Welfare hereinafter referred to as the State Department with such subordinate divisions as may now or hereafter be created or authorized by law, which shall operate under the South Carolina Board of Public Welfare, the members of which shall be elected by the General Assembly and shall consist of a Chairman elected from the State at large for a term of four (4) years . . . and one Commissioner elected from each Congressional district . . . . In case of any vacancy by death, resignation or otherwise in the office of Chairman or Commissioner from any district, the Governor shall appoint a successor to serve only for the unexpired term.

Section 2. The State Department shall supervise and administer the public welfare activities and functions of the State as provided in this Act or as subsequently authorized by law, and is authorized to act as the agent of the State and to cooperate with any Federal agency for the purpose of carrying out matters of mutual concern and to administer any Federal funds granted the State in the furtherance of the duties now or hereafter imposed upon the Department by law. The Department shall study the various social problems confronting the State, inquiring into their causes and possible cures, making such surveys, gathering such statistics, and formulating such recommended public policies in connection thereto as may be in the interest of the State, and make such information available in published form.

The Department shall have the authority to adopt all necessary rules and regulations and formulate policies and methods of administration when not otherwise fixed by law, to carry out effectively the activities and responsibilities regulated to it. . . .

South Carolina Public Welfare Act, 1–15.

Section 7. There is hereby created in each county of the State a County Department of Public Welfare . . . , and in each County a County Board of Public Welfare . . . to be composed of three members, who shall be appointed by the State Board or the State Director upon the recommendation of a majority, including the Senator, of the County Legislative Delegation . . . .

Section 8. The respective County Boards shall act as the representatives of the State Department in administering such welfare activities within the county as are provided in this and subsequent Acts or as directed and required by the said State Department when not otherwise provided for by law. Each of the County Boards shall see that all laws are enforced for the protection and welfare of minors, the removal of moral menaces to the young, and to safeguard and to promote the health, education and general welfare of minors . . . .

Section 15. Applications for assistance under the provisions of this Act shall be made . . . in accordance with the manner and form prescribed by the State Department. An investigation shall be made by the County Department, as provided by this Act, or as required by the State Department . . . .

Section 16. Upon the completion of its investigation the County Department shall decide whether the applicant is eligible for assistance under the provisions of this Act, and to determine the amount of such assistance and the date on which such assistance shall begin . . . . The County Department shall make a decision which shall be binding and be complied with until such decision is modified or vacated. The County Department shall certify its decision to the State Department and shall also notify the applicant of its decision in writing. Assistance, if granted, shall be paid monthly . . . .

Section 30. Old age assistance shall be paid under this Act to any person who shall comply with the requirements of this Act and who has attained the age of sixty-five years, is a citizen of the United States and has been a resident of the State of South Carolina for at least five years . . . and has no income or has income which . . . is inadequate to provide a reasonable subsistence; provided, however, that where an applicant for assistance has an income of $240.00 or more annually, no assistance shall be granted. . . .

Section 34. For the purpose set forth herein, the term "dependent" child means a child under the age of sixteen years who has been deprived of parental support or care by reason of the death, continued absence trom home, or physical or mental incapacity of a parent. . . .

Section 38. In granting aid for dependent children the amount granted shall not exceed $15.00 per month for one child in any home, nor $10.00 for each additional child in the same home. . . .

Section 40. The State Department shall grant assistance in the form of money payments to blind persons in need. . . .

Section 50. To assist the respective counties of the State in rendering assistance to other handicapped and unfortunate persons in need and to prevent suffering, distress, and need among persons not otherwise provided for in this Act, there is hereby appropriated from the General Funds . . . the sum of $200,000 and a similar amount for each succeeding year, which shall constitute a Fund to match county expenditures for general relief. . . .

Section 61. The State Department shall have the authority to make investigations into the administration and affairs of any institution or agency, public or private, in this State concerned with the care, custody or training of persons or the handling of problems of delinquency, dependency or defectiveness. . . .

A typical year's record in public assistance, 1948–1949:

From many standpoints the fiscal year 1948–1949 has been one of the best in the history of the Department of Public Welfare. Certainly, the recipients of public assistance have fared better than in any previous year. This was made possible through the generosity of the State Legislature, which provided additional funds for all public assistance categories, and by a change in the formula used by the Federal Government in matching State appropriations . . . . These increased contributions along with the increased State appropriations made it possible for the Department to give for the first time in its history a maximum award of $45.00 per month to recipients of old age assistance and aid to the blind. It was also possible to increase the percentage of unmet need provided to 100% in these categories. Children in need of assistance were not so fortunate, but it was possible for the Department to increase the percentage of need provided from 45% to 75%. This

Twelfth Annual Report, 1949, S.C. State Dept. of Public Welfare, 15–16.

resulted in an average monthly increase of assistance received of about $3.00 per child. Although there was some increase in the appropriation for general assistance, the Department was not able to increase the percentage of need given handicapped people because of the large number of cases added to the pay roll during the preceding year. No Federal contribution is available in this category.

In addition to the improved financial lot of public assistance recipients, they have benefitted perhaps to a greater degree than ever before from numerous services provided through county staff members. The Department has never limited its responsibilities to the giving of assistance only . . . ; any recipient has available at all times the skilled and sympathetic attention of his worker.

Although there has been some leveling off in the rate of applications received as related to the years just following the end of the war, there has been a steady increase in the actual number received in the categories of old age assistance and aid to dependent children . . . . The recession in business activities which occurred during the year undoubtedly had its effect. Many aged people prefer to work as long as they can get a job, but they are the first to lose out when it becomes necessary for industry to retrench. The ability of relatives to assist is also affected by employment opportunities. Many children bereft of the support of a father are supported by their mother through employment, but here again a woman is among the first to be laid off when business becomes slack. Then, too, it must be remembered that the proportion of aged people to total population is increasing every year and the great majority of them have been unable to lay aside anything for retirement. Family life is still suffering from the aftermath of the war years. Many homes continue to be broken up through desertion, separation, and divorce. The Department, through aid to dependent children or foster home placements, is frequently able to ameliorate at least to some degree the hard lot of children so tragically affected by the break-up of their homes . . . .

Given below are some comparative statistics for the years 1947–1948 and 1948–1949:

On June 30, 1948, 45,112 cases in the State were receiving public assistance with 69,169 individuals represented. On June 30, 1949, the number of cases was 51,756 with 80,575 individuals represented. The average award in June, 1948, was $20.41; in June, 1949, $25.58.

In June, 1948, old age assistance was received by 33,456 persons with awards averaging $19.81; a year later recipients numbered 37,674 with awards averaging $24.70.

Aid to the needy blind was given to 1311 persons in June, 1948, the average award being $20.26; the figures for June, 1949, were 1408 persons receiving awards averaging $28.73.

In June, 1948, 6149 households including 17,302 children were receiving aid to dependent children, the average award being $27.00 per household, or $9.60 per child; the number of households receiving aid to dependent children in June, 1949, was 7690 with 21,914 children, the average award being $35.51 per household or $12.46 per child.

During June, 1948, 4196 individuals received general assistance from State and local funds with an average of $15.62 as compared to 4984 individuals with an average of $17.03 in June, 1949. In June, 1948, 3824 individuals received general assistance from State funds only as compared to 4511 in June, 1949. In June, 1948, 372 individuals received general assistance from local funds as compared to 473 in June, 1949.

The South Carolina Divorce Act of 1949:

Section 1. Actions for divorce from the bonds of matrimony shall in all cases be only in the equity jurisdiction of the Court of Common Pleas.

Section 2. No divorce from the bonds of matrimony shall be granted except upon one or more of the following grounds, to wit:

1. Adultery;
2. Desertion for a period of one year;
3. Physical cruelty;
4. Habitual drunkenness.

Section 3. In order to institute an action for divorce from the bonds of matrimony, the plaintiff must have resided in the State of South Carolina at least one year prior to the commencement of the action.

Section 4. Actions for divorce from the bonds of matrimony shall be tried in the county in which the defendant resides at the time of the commencement of the action, or in the county where the plaintiff resides if the defendant is a non-resident or after due diligence cannot

Sumner, The South Carolina Divorce Act of 1949, 3 *South Carolina Law Quarterly,* 253–303 (1951). Reprinted by permission of the *South Carolina Law Quarterly.*

be found, or in the county in which the parties last resided as husband and wife. . . .

Section 5. In all cases referred to a Master or Special Referee, such Master or Special Referee, shall summon the party or parties within the jurisdiction of the court before him, and it shall be the duty of such officer to make an earnest effort to bring about a reconciliation between the parties to such cause. . . .

Section 8. In every action for divorce from the bonds of matrimony, the wife, whether she be plaintiff or defendant, may in her complaint or answer or by petition pray for the allowance to her of alimony and suit money, and for the allowance of such alimony and suit money . . . . if such claim shall appear well founded, the court shall allow a reasonable sum therefor. . . .

Section 10. In any action for divorce from the bonds of matrimony, the court shall have the power at any stage of the cause, or from time to time after final judgment, to make such orders touching the care, custody and maintenance of the children of the marriage; and what, if any, security shall be given for the same, as from the circumstances of the parties and the nature of the case and the best spiritual as well as other interests of the children may be fit, equitable and just. . . .

Section 13. If it shall appear, to the satisfaction of the Court, that the parties to said divorce proceedings colluded or that the act complained of was done with the knowledge or assent of the plaintiff for the purpose of obtaining a divorce, then the Court shall not grant such divorce. . . .

Section 15. The Court may, upon granting of final judgment, allow a wife to resume her maiden name or the name of any former husband.

Section 16. Any married person shall, for the purpose of maintaining or defending any action of divorce and settlement of property rights arising thereunder, be deemed of age. . . .

Population:

The population of South Carolina, according to the 1960 census, was 2,382,594, an increase of 265,567 or 12.5% as compared with 1950. The

Handbook of South Carolina, 1963, p. 70.

average density of population for the state as a whole was 78.7 persons per square mile. The density varies between 18.5 persons per square mile in Jasper County and 267.5 in Richland County.

In 1960 the urban population amounted to 981,386 or 41.2% of the total; the rural nonfarm, 1,050,054 or 44.1% and the rural farm 351,154 or 14.7%. The 1960 census shows South Carolina had 1,550,632 white people and 831,962 nonwhite people. Between 1950 and 1960 the white population increased by 257,227 and the nonwhite by 8,340. About 45% of the white people and 34% of the nonwhite people are living in urban areas. . . .

The median grades of school completed by the people 25 years old and over in 1960 was 7.6 years.

172. *Religion*

Although there has been no such great religious revivals in the twentieth century as there were in the 1730s and in the 1740s when Church Acts were enacted, or even a great humanitarian movement as in the 1830s and in the 1840s, there has been a steady growth of organized religion. During the first part of the twentieth century, too, at least two great evangelists came to South Carolina to lead converts to Christianity: Billy Sunday and Billy Graham. In the numbers of churches and in members, in ministers trained to preach the gospel, and in new methods for reaching the people, the first half of the century was significant. The following summarizes the religious development.

[Austin Adkinson]

Organized religion in South Carolina expanded far and fast in many fields during the twentieth century's first fifty years. Gains in membership, scope of activities, and contributions reflect church progress. Membership in major Christian churches, for example, has increased proportionately much more than the State's population.

Churches in South Carolina counted about 252,000 members in 1900 and more than 655,000 last year. The State's population, meanwhile, climbed from 1,340,316 in 1900 to an estimated 2,200,000 in 1950. All but one of the denominations checked had seen their membership at least double during the fifty years. Baptists led numerically in 1900, as in 1949. The State Baptist Convention had 122,471 church members enrolled in 1900 and 352,063 last year. South Carolina Baptists had 1003 churches in 1900 and 1267 in 1948.

Methodists, Presbyterians, Lutherans, Associate Reformed Presbyterians, Episcopalians and Roman Catholics, in that order, compromise the other major religious groups in South Carolina.

Austin Adkinson, "Churches of South Carolina," *Charlotte Observer,* Jan. 9, 1951.

Sunday School growth was also proportionately larger. The 1238 Baptist Sunday Schools of 1948 had 256,121 students, compared with 53,146 in 731 Sunday Schools of 40 years ago. Indicating the rate of membership growth is the 6316 converts baptized in 1908, and 15,902 baptized in 1948. Women's Missionary Union membership climbed from 7185 to 69,251; Baptist Training Union membership to 58,357. State Baptists maintained two senior colleges and four academies in 1908 with total enrollment of 1175. Now they have one senior college (Furman University) and two Junior colleges with a total of 1949 students.

The Baptist denomination contributed $1,987,602 for missions (including Christian Education and benevolences) and $7,426,435 for local church work in 1948. Total contributions in 1908 were $511,982. Baptists have added a hospital at Columbia and established the Baptist Foundation of South Carolina, also at Columbia, in the 40 years. They still maintain the Connie Maxwell Orphanage at Greenwood and publish the Baptist Courier at Greenville, as they did in 1908.

South Carolina Methodists divided into two conferences in 1914, but those merged again in 1948 to reform the South Carolina Methodist conference. Membership climbed from 74,729 in 1900 to 167,803 in 1948. Eighty-nine local preachers served congregations of 50 years ago; now there are nearly 400. The 710 Methodist Sunday Schools represent an increase of only 5 over the 1900 figure. But enrollment has soared from 41,996 to 107,329; the number of officers and teachers from 4853 to 8949. State Methodists contributed $17,000 for presiding elders, $121,000 for preacher salaries, and $1583 for bishops in 1900; in 1948, they gave $66,675 for presiding elders (or district superintendents), $857,380 for preachers and $12,634 for bishops.

The 737 church buildings owned by the Methodist Church in 1900 were valued at $977,000; its 182 parsonages at $247,000; and other church property at $60,000. That is hardly a drop in the church's financial bucket today. A handsome new four-story center in Columbia is valued at $240,000 alone. Columbia College for Women is worth $700,000, conservatively. Wofford College for men at Spartanburg has resources of about $2,287,500. The denomination has recently set aside about $750,000 to build a new Epworth Orphanage plant in Columbia. In addition, Methodists financed such varied activities as the Wesley Foundation, a hospital fund, homes for retired preachers, and benevolent work.

Wofford's enrollment was 182 in 1900, counting 56 in the fitting school. It now has 668 students, and 40 instructors. Columbia College students filled "to capacity" its one downtown building in 1900, church records state, without giving enrollment. Now the 371 girls live on a spacious building-studded campus in a residential area. Epworth cares for 260 children now, compared with 112 in 1900. The Church took over, operated and relinquished Lander College at Greenwood during the 50 years.

Two new Presbyteries—Congaree and Piedmont—were added by the Synod of South Carolina Presbyterian Church, U.S., in the 50 years. The six with which the Synod began the century were Bethel, Charleston, Enoree, Harmony, Pee Dee and South Carolina. In these six there were 271 churches, 134 ministers, 930 ruling elders, 853 deacons, 20,123 church communing members, and 11,529 Sunday School pupils. Total contributions to all benevolences were $33,768; to pastors' salaries $71,026.

Last year the Synod had 292 churches, 193 ministers, 1792 ruling elders, 2174 deacons, 45,589 communing members, and 37,526 Sunday School pupils. In addition, the denomination maintained 57 outposts, preaching points and chapels. Gifts for benevolences amounted to $793,-818 from April, 1948, to March, 1949. Pastors' salaries totaled $455,190. Presbyterian College at Clinton in 1900 had a small faculty and student body, and a graduating class of eight. Last year it had 34 faculty members, 508 students, 17 buildings valued at $963,000 and an endowment of $473,272. The Synod of Georgia now shares in supporting the school.

Thornwell Orphanage, also at Clinton, cared for 200 children in 1900. Now jointly supported by the Synods of South Carolina, Georgia and Florida, it has 295 children, 54 staff members, 31 buildings valued at $724,750 and an endowment of $463,982. The South Carolina Synod also helps support Columbia Theological Seminary at Decatur, Georgia, and Queens College at Charlotte, N.C.

The Evangelical Lutheran Synod of South Carolina saw its confirmed membership more than triple—from 8712 to 28,212—in the century's first half. Sunday School enrollment rose from 5524 to 18,342. Thirty-four Lutheran ministers served 68 churches in 1900, while 104 ministers have 122 churches now. Members contributed on benevolence (for the work of the church at large or outside the local congregation) $2922 in 1900 and $248,142 in 1949. Value of church property was estimated at $268,000 in 1900; today the estimate is $2,820,923.

Newberry College, founded in 1865 by the State Lutheran Synod, had 175 students and operated on a $6847 budget with practically no endowment funds 50 years ago. Now it has 565 students, the current year's expenses are $293,927, and the college has a $250,000 endowment. Value of the plant is more than $500,000. The college was maintained solely by the state Synod in 1900. Now it gets its support from the Georgia-Alabama and Florida Synods also. The Lutheran Theological Seminary, at Mt. Pleasant in 1900, was moved to Columbia in 1912. Now owned and supported by the Synods of Virginia, North and South Carolina, Georgia-Alabama, Florida and Mississippi, it has 42 students and two main buildings. The South Carolina Synod founded it in 1830. In 1911 the State Synod established the Lowman Home for Aged and Helpless at White Rock, near Columbia. Other southern Synods now help support it. The home had four residents in its first year, has 92 now in five buildings, and assets of $233,251.

The General Synod of the Associate Reformed Presbyterian Church had the same number of ministers—104—in 1900 and 1948. But in the same period membership more than doubled, from 11,344 to 25,799. Pastors' salaries jumped from $34,771 to $240,207. The Synod's 143 congregations last year represented an increase of 11 for the period. Sunday School enrollment climbed steadily from 9059 to 17,831. Women's Missionary Societies gained in membership from 1757 to 4886; Young People's Societies from 2353 to 3242. Members' total contributions totaled $1,040,475 last year, compared with $66,140 in 1900. The average contribution was $41.00, compared with $5.83 in 1900. Value of Church property increased from $264,300 to $3,387,250.

The church supports Erskine College at Due West, which is valued at more than $1,000,000. This includes $400,947 in endowment funds and the plant and equipment, worth approximately $645,000. Erskine has 35 faculty members, 442 students and a graduating class of 79 this year. This compares with a faculty of seven, an enrollment of 104, and 22 graduating seniors in 1900. The 1900 endowment was $86,768; college income and receipts $8480. Last year income and receipts totaled $314,075.

The Episcopal Diocese of South Carolina included the entire State in 1900. It then had 93 parishes and missions, 11,195 baptized members and 6610 communicants. Now there are the Diocese of South Carolina with headquarters at Charleston, and the Diocese of Upper South Carolina, centered at Columbia. Together they have 127 parishes and missions, 24,389 baptized members and 18,834 communicants. The Church supports Porter Military Academy at Charleston, homes for women at Charleston, orphanages at Charleston and York, and the Voorhees School and Junior College (for Negroes) at Denmark. The two dioceses also are part owners of the University of the South at Sewanee, Tennessee.

The Roman Catholic Diocese of Charleston, taking in the entire State, has nearly doubled its membership since 1900. Then there were 8500 members attending 29 churches. Now there are 15,165 members and 70 churches in South Carolina.

173. *Trade and Transportation*

The automobile was well known before 1920, but it was not until after this date that South Carolina developed a statewide system of paved roads that made automobile and truck transportation convenient and profitable. Other notable developments in trade and transportation included the redevelopment of Charleston as a major port, the commercial use of the waterway system, the increasing movement of passengers and freight by bus and truck, and the growth of air traffic. More and more of South Carolina's exports came to be finished goods rather than raw materials, and less of the imports were foods and necessities that could be produced at home. The following selections include an account of the highway building program of the 1920s, a discussion of the Port of Charleston and its effect on the state's trade, and a picture of postwar developments in transportation.

The state's highways in the 1920s:

South Carolinians and their visitors may travel over good roads from almost any point in the State to almost any other on almost any day of the year. The job that the State highway department has immediately on hand, and on which it is making rapid progress, is to eliminate the three almosts from this statement. We are already sufficiently out of the mud that the department can devote some of its attention to the beautification of the highways, which is beginning to be urged from all quarters.

Less than ten years ago, motorists traveling over South Carolina's roads were too busy with picking their way between holes and ruts to indulge in lamentations over landscapes marred by advertising signs. Today they are practically unanimous in commending a recent order of the chief highway commissioner requiring all advertising signs to be moved back

Handbook of South Carolina, 1927, pp. 196–201.

at least 50 feet from the center line of the state roads. . . . The roads of the state highway system are marked and numbered so that a stranger may generally find his way without difficulty. The numbering system is keyed to the department's road condition map, which is issued and distributed monthly. Up-to-date copies of this map can be seen or secured at filling stations throughout the State . . . .

As of December 31, 1925, there were 4951 miles of roads in the State highway system, of which 303 miles were hard surface, 3253 were of earth or gravel improved surfacing, and 1395 miles were unimproved . . . . The work completed during 1925 consisted of 420.5 miles of road at a cost of $4,219,650.23 and 78 bridges at a cost of $1,012,442.28 . . . . Work was carried on in 45 counties and has included 190 projects, of which 160 were road . . . and 30 bridge projects. Roads under State maintenance average 3765 miles for the year at a total cost of $1,650,867, making an average of $379.66 per mile per year. The average cost for paved roads was $291.77 and unpaved roads $385.05 per mile.

New construction is constantly on the increase. The "Pay-As-You-Go" highway act turns over to the highway department the revenue from the motor vehicle license fees and from a 5-cent per gallon tax on gasoline sales. These revenues will amount to somewhat less than $5,000,000 for 1926, and are estimated to increase at the rate of about 10 per cent per year. The State's apportionment of federal aid is in the neighborhood of $1,100,000. After paying for maintenance and betterment, the remainder of the department's revenue is available for construction. In 1926, the department's construction fund, with federal aid, amounts to approximately $3,500,000. The counties are advancing an aggregate amount almost equal to this under reimbursement agreements with the department; so that the total construction expenditures on State highways for 1926 will be some $7,000,000. Since the passage of the "Pay-As-You-Go" act, March 21, 1924, the expenditures for new roads and bridges have been (to September 1, 1926), $13,500,000. There have been 960 miles of road constructed and 38,200 lineal feet of standard bridges built.

The recently constructed bridges include several of national significance. For example, the Santee river crossing on Interstate Highway Number 17 (State Highway Number 41) is 4 miles in length, cost $750,-000 and has opened the way into Charleston for thousands of Eastern tourists. The Ashley River bridge at Charleston, which cost $1,250,000, lets in traffic from the south. These two are among the major highway bridges that have been built in America. . . . The Santee, which until recently had no crossing point from Columbia to the sea, is being bridged at two additional points and the Great Peedee bridge between Georgetown and Conway is just now being completed.

Already Interstate Highway 29 (State Highway 8) has been paved or given a bituminous surfacing from Blacksburg, through Gaffney, Spartanburg and Greenville to Anderson, except for a section between Spartanburg and Greer now under construction. On Interstate Highway 1 (State Highway 50) a relatively small proportion has been paved; and, on account of the excellent quality of the local materials out of which it is constructed, paving is not urgent. . . .

In general, the paving projects contemplated at present for the other main interstate highways are confined to heavy traffic sections that have not already been paved in the vicinity of the cities and towns. They are all being planned to avoid interference with the use of the present roads as far as possible.

[Louise Jones DuBose]

The South Carolina Ports Authority to 1947:

Rock Hill to Rotterdam, Greenville to Guatemala, Spartanburg to Shanghai, Columbia to Cape Town, Charleston to China—that's how the goods will go! South Carolina textiles are already being shipped to South Africa, and lumber to the Netherlands—all from the Port of Charleston. An impractical dream that seemed almost impossible of realization ten and twenty years ago is now becoming a hard business fact.

For the State of South Carolina is now actively launched on a program to revive the waterborne commerce of her seaports which made her one of the leading maritime states of the country a century ago. At Charleston, South Carolina's principal port, the State has taken over the operation of shipping facilities which will enable the products of her fields and factories—the cotton, the lumber, the textiles—to flow into world trade across the seven seas. . . .

A saving of many dollars a ton on textiles shipped from South Carolina mills out of the Port of Charleston has been calculated, and cotton goods

Louise Jones DuBose, "From Plant to Port," *South Carolina Magazine,* X (April, 1947), 6–7. Reprinted by permission of Mrs. Louise Jones DuBose.

can be sold 1 to 1½¢ per yard cheaper in foreign lands because of the saving on freight charges . . . it cost the shipper less to send the goods from the Piedmont straight through South Carolina to the coast, than to send them hundreds of miles northward to ports there.

The story of how the shipping facilities finally came to be owned by the State is one of persistent optimism on the part of a few South Carolinians who were determined that the harbors once more take their place as important points in world commerce. In was in 1942 that the State Ports Authority was set up after preliminary work had been started by Cotesworth P. Means, then State Senator from Charleston. In May, 1941, Mr. Means introduced a resolution in the Senate "creating a committee to investigate the causes of the shrinkage of waterborne commerce through the Port of Charleston and to recommend legislative action." The committee . . . recommended that the authority be set up and an act was passed creating it in May, 1942.

That legislative action was the outcome of many years of planning, however. The North Charleston Terminals were constructed for use during the First World War, but were not completed before that conflict was over. Then, for two years the warehouses were used for surplus material of the army quartermaster organization. For the next fifteen years they were little used, and upkeep was at a minimum. A private Charleston concern leased them, and then the Ports Utilities Commission of Charleston took them over. In the 1930's the West Virginia Pulp and Paper Company established its plant in Charleston and through the efforts of James F. Byrnes, then United States Senator, the terminal property was transferred to the City of Charleston, by an act of Congress. Shortly afterward, it was leased to the paper company, and a five million dollar mill was erected on a part of the terminal property, where some of the warehouses were renovated to be used by the concern. Just before that time, World War II began, and it was necessary for the United States government to take over the terminal for a port of embarkation. Millions of dollars were spent in restoring the docks and warehouses which, at the present time, are some of the most modern and thoroughly equipped installations of the sort in the world. They are valued at $20,000,000. In 1945 the port was deactivated.

Then the State Ports Authority began active efforts to have the terminals taken over by the State. Finally, in the latter part of March, 1947, after President Truman had released the installations officially, the State of South Carolina began operating all public shipping facilities in the Port of Charleston. . . . In addition to the Port of Charleston, the

Georgetown and Beaufort Harbors are to be improved to permit ocean going vessels fuller access there. Besides the terminals at North Charleston, three piers in Charleston were transferred to the State by the City of Charleston. They are the quay type dock at Columbus Street, the Union pier and Adger's Wharf. A thirteen mile belt line waterfront railroad is also part of the equipment now at the disposal of shippers. . . .

In the few months since the Authority assumed control, two lines have been secured for regular sailings. They are the American–South African Lines of New York, and the DeLaRama Steamship Company. . . . Textiles from South Carolina and lumber form the chief export products at the present time. . . . Nowadays, the warehouses shelter thousands of bales of grey goods and finished cloth from the South Carolina mills, bound for the African ports of Cape Town, Beira, Durban, Johannesburg, or Port Elizabeth. From the docks eighteen to twenty million feet of lumber have been shipped to the Netherlands during the past year . . . . There is a special plant at North Charleston for repacking textiles and other articles that come in cartons from the manufacturing centers. They must be either compressed and baled or boxed up in wooden crates. Incidentally, these crates are purchased from South Carolina plants and thus open an additional manufacturing interest.

[T.J. Tobias]

South Carolina's seaports of Charleston, Georgetown and Port Royal set new records last year in the value of exports and imports, according to figures released by the U.S. Department of Commerce. . . . At the Charleston docks ships from the seven seas discharge and load cargo of all kinds bound to and from all parts of the world. Mahogany logs from the steamy jungles of Costa Rica are unloaded for Carolina furniture makers. Textiles from the Piedmont are headed for the Philippines. Chrome ore from Turkish mines tumbles into gondola cars on the pier to be made into hard steel for the defense program. Thousand pound hogsheads of flue-cured tobacco from South Carolina's Pee Dee will soon go up in smoke in the pipes of Englishmen in London. Huge rolls of kraft

T. J. Tobias, "The Story of South Carolina's Ports," *South Carolina Magazine,* XVI (July, 1952), 16–17, 31. Reprinted by permission of Thomas J. Tobias.

paper from the Palmetto State's mills will be used in a few weeks to wrap packages in stores in Paris. The aroma of Brazilian coffee is wafted over the waterfront as the savory bags swing onto the dock. Scotch whiskey, Canadian newsprint, Cuban sugar, Central American bananas, Australian wool, Chilean nitrate, and French perfume . . . the parade of products down the two way street of world trade is endless. . . .

The 1951 banner year saw the value of cargo bound for foreign ports soar to $110,400,000, nearly twice the total of $57,700,000 reported for the South Carolina customs district for 1950. Also reflecting a brisk 1951 import year was the commodity value total of $55,400,000, showing a 48.8 per cent increase over the $38,000,000 worth of goods brought from foreign countries the year before.

Charleston's leadership of the South Atlantic in cargo value reflects the renaissance of the State's chief port under the development program of the South Carolina State Ports Authority begun after the close of World War II. It's been called "one of the greatest comebacks in shipping history." For Charleston, Georgetown and Port Royal, once great centers of world trade a century and more ago, had literally "dried up" as commercial seaports through neglect. . . . Now South Carolina's ports not only serve the State, but through them funnel exports and imports to and from the entire Southeast, and also the rich manufacturing Middle West, which is a logical territory served by the ports because of favorable freight rates. . . .

Transportation at mid-century:

South Carolina roadbuilding was slow moving until fairly recent years . . . . In fact, the present highway system has come about largely in the last three decades, and has doubled since 1940. The original State highway system, as designated in 1920, included only 3046 miles. The ensuing tremendous growth in terms of mileage resulted from a periodic transfer of roads from county jurisdiction to the State. In 1946, when it became apparent that the State system had been expanded to encompass a great many miles of purely local roads, the General Assembly authorized the

"Transportation in South Carolina," *South Carolina Magazine*, XVI (Aug., 1952), 6–9, 20–22. Reprinted by permission of the *South Carolina Magazine*.

Highway Department to classify State highways according to primary and secondary routes.

The primary system was to consist of a system of principal State highways not to exceed 10,000 miles, connecting centers of population as determined by the State highway commission; the secondary system to include all other roads in the State highway system. On May 30, 1952, the State highway system embraced 22,907 miles of roads, of which 8824 were in the primary system and the remainder in the secondary system. A total of 14,321 miles of the roads are paved, 8622 in the primary system and 5699 in the secondary. The South Carolina highway system now represents an investment of $285,000,000. . . .

The first air transportation offered in the United States was between Detroit, Chicago, and Cleveland in 1926. Soon thereafter in 1928 the first scheduled air service to South Carolina was inaugurated in Spartanburg when Pitcairn Aviation stopped there once daily with mail on their route between New York and Atlanta. Passenger service was first offered in the State to Greenville on August 20, 1930, by Eastern Air Transport, Inc., with one trip daily between New York and Atlanta. This service was given as an adjunct to air mail service which was the primary purpose of the air transportation at that time. The type of plane and the facilities of that day bears little resemblance to the luxurious air liner of today with its modernized and uniform type of equipment . . . . The growth and development of air transportation since 1926 has been phenomenal. South Carolina is today being served by five scheduled air carriers in eight cities with over five thousand scheduled stops each year. The South Carolinian of today can, within hours, arrange for scheduled air transportation to any part of the world. For example, one can fly in a modern forty passenger deluxe liner from Columbia to either New York or Miami in three hours. . . .

Industry in South Carolina is also making use of air transportation. Executives, salesmen, and other personnel . . . are using the aircraft in the pursuit of their business traveling to points in South Carolina and all over the world. In increasing numbers, these businesses own and operate their own aircraft . . . . One . . . textile manufacturing firm owns and operates three aircraft, employing ten crewmen with an annual investment of $500,000. . . .

Soon after the invention and development of the automobile, buses replaced the inter-urban carriage of that day and the taxi replaced the one-horse hack. Similarly the light airplane of today has taken its place in the air transportation picture as a commercial carrier of passengers, replacing in many instances surface transportation normally done by automobile, bus or railroad. Light aircraft seating from two to five passengers are offering an air-taxi service to the traveler from or to almost any point in South Carolina . . . .

Heading the list of the State's transportation agencies is the extensive rail network which criss-crosses the State in every direction. More than 3300 miles of railroads bring the benefits and advantages of rail transportation to every section. The major portion of the rail mileage is operated by three companies—Seaboard Air Line Railroad, Southern Railway, and Atlantic Coast Line Railroad. But there are also smaller companies, such as the Piedmont and Northern Railway, Lancaster and Chester Railroad, Clinchfield Railroad, and Columbia, Newberry and Laurens Railroad, to name a few, which form important links in the State's rail system.

Modern in every sense of the word, and determined to remain that way, the railroads have spent huge sums in recent years for the improvement of their plants. Large expenditures have been made for new diesel-electric locomotives and new rolling stock. . . . Moreover, South Carolina railroads have been active in developing the potentials of the State. Through their efforts, coordinated with those of other agencies, many new industrial and agricultural enterprises have been located here. This is a continuing activity of the rail lines, and they maintain special staffs of qualified industrial and agricultural development experts whose full time is devoted to seeking out sound opportunities for still further development in those fields. The progressive outlook and long-term planning of the railroads give assurance that they will continue their important role in working for the industrial growth of South Carolina—and that the transportation needs of the State will be met adequately, efficiently and at low cost.

Transportation improvements in the 1950s:

The end of World War II marked the beginning of an extensive rural road improvement program in South Carolina. In 1946, all roads falling

Handbook of South Carolina, 1963, pp. 65–70.

under state jurisdiction were classified according to importance into the primary and secondary system . . . . Early in the 1950's, the General Assembly established a special program for financing secondary road construction. Since that time, secondary road construction has progressed at the rate of about 1,000 miles per year. Meanwhile, primary system highways have been greatly improved, always keeping within the 10,000 mile limit. Emphasis has been placed upon widening and reconstruction of both bridges and roads to bring them up to standards required for today's heavy traffic.

The interstate system, construction of which began in 1956, constitutes a third segment of the overall state highway system. This system, planned nationally to include about 41,000 miles, will total approximately 678 miles in South Carolina when completed. . . .

Having constructed and improved the highway system, the state must spend additional millions of dollars annually to maintain the highways in safe travel condition. Maintenance and highway resurfacing costs each year average more than $14 million, and total expenditures for these purposes continue to rise as additional miles are completed or added to the system. . . .

A major key to the success of the highway program in South Carolina has been that most highway user revenues—that is motor fuel taxes and vehicle license fees have been used for highway improvements. Without such a plan the state would have lagged seriously in its road program, with resulting lags in the overall economy. . . .

Four airlines operating from some 30 municipal airports adjacent to South Carolina's larger cities furnish through, or connecting, air service to major cities of the United States. Turbo-jets fly into and out of Charleston, Columbia and the joint Greenville-Spartanburg airport, while air-taxi service is available in several major cities. The Charleston Airport, a 'port of entry' for over-seas flights as well as a military base, ranks as one of the ten busiest in the United States. Air express and freight service are available over all four commercial airlines operating in the state. There are more than 500 private planes licensed in the state, operating from some 100 airports, including municipal and privately owned airstrips and those operated by the South Carolina Aeronautics Commission.

South Carolina is served by three major lines which operate luxury trains through the state. . . . These three major railroads together with several smaller lines operate nearly 4,000 miles of track and make rail transportation available to most of the communities in the state.

Numerous motor bus lines operating over more than 27,000 miles of hard surfaced highways in South Carolina make available bus passenger service to nearly every community in the State. Hundreds of motor truck operators furnish motor freight service throughout the state. . . .

READINGS

ADDITIONAL PRINTED SOURCE MATERIALS:

Andrews, Columbus. *Administrative County Government in South Carolina.*

Ball, W. W. *The State That Forgot* . . . .

Coleman, J. K. *State Administration in South Carolina.*

Kohn, August. *The Cotton Mills of South Carolina.*

———. *Water Powers of South Carolina.*

Potwin, Marjorie A. *Cotton Mill People of the Piedmont.*

Rice, James Henry, Jr. *Glories of the Carolina Coast.*

Robertson, Ben. *Red Hills and Cotton.*

Sherrill, George R., and Robert H. Stoudemire. *Municipal Government in South Carolina* . . . .

South Carolina. Dept. of Agriculture. *Handbook of South Carolina,* 1907, 1927, and 1963.

CORRELATED TEXTS:

Lander, Ernest McPherson, Jr. *A History of South Carolina, 1865–1960,* pp. 35–245.

Wallace, D. D. *History of South Carolina.* III, 336–494.

———. *South Carolina: A Short History,* 614–700.

BIBLIOGRAPHY

Alderman, Edwin Anderson, et al., eds. *Library of Southern Literature.* 16 vols. New Orleans: The Martin and Hoyt Co., 1908–1913.

Allen, Walter. *Governor Chamberlain's Administration in South Carolina.* New York: G.P. Putnam's Sons, 1888.

American Husbandry; containing an account of the soil, climate, production and agriculture of the British colonies in North America and the West Indies. 2 vols. London: 1775.

Andrews, Columbus. *Administrative County Government in South Carolina.* Chapel Hill: University of North Carolina Press, 1933.

Andrews, Sidney. *The South Since the War, as Shown by Fourteen Weeks of Travel and Observation in Georgia and the Carolinas.* Boston: Ticknor and Fields, 1866.

Archdale, John. *A New Description of That Fertile and Pleasant Province of Carolina, with a Brief Account of Its Discovery, Settling, and the Government Thereof to This Time.* London, 1707. (Reprinted in A.S. Salley, ed., *Narratives of Early Carolina,* 277–312.)

Ashe, Thomas. *The Present State of Affairs in Carolina.* London, 1706. (Reprinted in A.S. Salley, ed., *Narratives of Early Carolina,* 265–76.)

Ball, W.W. *The State That Forgot: South Carolina's Surrender to Democracy.* Indianapolis: Bobbs–Merrill Co., 1932.

Bartlett, John. *Familiar Quotations.* Boston: Little, Brown and Co., 1951.

Boddie, William W. *History of Williamsburg: Something About the People of Williamsburg County, South Carolina, from the First Settlement by Europeans About 1705 Until 1923.* Columbia: The State Co., 1923.

Boucher, Chauncey. *The Nullification Controversy in South Carolina.* Chicago: University of Chicago Press, 1916.

Brooks, Ulysses R., ed. *Stories of the Confederacy.* Columbia: The State Co., 1912.

649

Brown, Richard M. *The South Carolina Regulators*. Cambridge: Belknap Press of Harvard University Press, 1963.

Byrnes, James F. "Politics Has No Place in Education," a speech delivered before "Industry Appreciation Celebration," Bennettsville, S.C., Sept. 27, 1957. From a script kindly supplied by the speaker to the editors.

Carolina; or, A Description of the Present State of That Country, and the Natural Excellencies Thereof . . . . London, 1682. (Written by T.A., supposedly Thomas Ashe; reprinted in A.S. Salley, ed., *Narratives of Early Carolina*, 135–60.)

Carroll, B.R., ed. *Historical Collections of South Carolina* . . . . 2 vols. New York: Harper, 1836.

Cauthen, Charles E. *South Carolina Goes to War, 1860–1865*. Chapel Hill: University of North Carolina Press, 1950.

Chandler, J.A.C., et al., eds. *The South in the Building of the Nation*. 13 vols. Richmond: The Southern Historical Publication Society, 1909–1913.

Channing, Steven A. *Crisis of Fear: Secession in South Carolina*. New York: Simon & Schuster, 1970.

Chapman, John A. *School History of South Carolina*. Newberry: Newberry Publishing Co., 1893.

Charleston Yearbook, 1883, 1886, 1906. Charleston: Walker, Evans & Cogswell Co.

Chesnut, Mary B. *A Diary from Dixie*. New York: D. Appleton and Company, 1905.

Childs, Arney R., ed. *The Private Journal of Henry William Ravenel, 1859–1887*. Columbia: University of South Carolina Press, 1947.

Coleman, J.K. *State Administration in South Carolina*. Columbia University Publications: Studies in history, economics and public law, no. 406. New York: Columbia University, 1935.

Collections of the Historical Society of South Carolina. 5 vols. William Ellis Jones, 1856–1897. Vol. V, called the "Shaftesbury Papers," is particularly valuable for the early days of South Carolina.

Confederate States of America: Official Reports of Battles. Richmond, 1862.

Cook, Harvey T. *The Life and Legacy of David Rogerson Williams.* New York, 1916.

Cooper, William J. *The Conservative Regime: South Carolina, 1877–1890.* Baltimore: Johns Hopkins University Press, 1968.

Crallé, Richard K., ed. *The Works of John C. Calhoun.* 6 vols. New York: D. Appleton and Co., 1854–1856.

Crane, Verner. *The Southern Frontier.* Durham: Duke University Press, 1928.

Dalcho, Frederick. *An Historical Account of the Protestant Episcopal Church in South Carolina, from the First Settlement of the Province to the War of the Revolution.* Charleston: E. Thayer, 1820.

Defoe, Daniel. *Party Tyrrany, or, An Occasional Bill in Miniature as Now Practiced in Carolina.* London, 1705. (An account of the church controversy brought by the Church Act of 1704, reprinted in A.S. Salley, ed., *Narratives of Early Carolina,* 219–64.)

Doubleday, Abner. *Reminiscences of Forts Sumter and Moultrie in 1860–61.* New York: Harper & Bros., 1876.

Draper, Lyman C. *Kings Mountain and Its Heroes* . . . . Cincinnati: P.G. Thompson, 1881.

Drayton, John. *A View of South Carolina, as Respects Her Natural and Civil Concerns.* Charleston, 1802.

———. *Memoirs of the American Revolution* . . . . 2 vols. Charleston: A.E. Miller, 1821.

Easterby, James H., ed. *The South Carolina Rice Plantation as Revealed in the Papers of Robert F.W. Allston.* Chicago: University of Chicago Press, 1945.

Ellis, Clyde T. *A Giant Step.* New York: Random House, 1966.

Emery, Edwin. *The Press and America,* 2nd. ed. Englewood Cliffs: Prentice–Hall, Inc., 1962.

Eubanks, John Evans. *Ben Tillman's Baby: The Dispensary System of South Carolina, 1892–1915.* Augusta, Ga., 1950.

Fleming, W.L., ed. *Documents relating to Reconstruction.* Morganton, W. Va. n.p., n.d.

Force, Peter, comp. *American Archives . . . .* Fourth Series, 6 vols. Vol. VI, Washington: M. St. Clarke and Peter Force, 1837–1853.

———. *American Archives . . . .* Fifth Series, 3 vols. Vol. I, Washington: M. St. Clair Clarke and Peter Force, 1848–1853.

Fraser, Charles. *Reminiscences of Charleston.* Charleston, 1854.

Freehling, William W. *Prelude to Civil War: The Nullification Controversy in South Carolina, 1816–1836.* New York: Harper, 1966.

Gibbes, Robert W. *Documentary History of the American Revolution, . . . Chiefly in South Carolina.* Rev. ed. 3 vols. New York: D. Appleton & Co., 1855.

Glenn, James. *A Description of South Carolina, Containing Many Curious and Interesting Particulars Relating to the Civil, Natural and Commercial History of That Colony.* London, 1761. (Reprinted in B.R. Carroll, ed., *Historical Collections of South Carolina,* and in Chapman J. Milling, *Colonial South Carolina: Two Contemporary Descriptions by James Glen and George Milligen–Johnston.*)

Gordon, A.H. *Sketches of Negro Life and History in South Carolina.* Industrial College, Ga., 1929.

Graham, James. *The Life of General Daniel Morgan of the Virginia Line . . . .* New York: Derby and Jackson, 1858.

Gregg, Alexander. *History of the Old Cheraws . . . .* New York: Richardson and Co., 1867.

Gregg, William. *Essays on Domestic Industry, Or, an Enquiry into the Expediency of Establishing Cotton Manufacturing in South Carolina.* Charleston, 1845. (Reprinted by the Graniteville Co., Graniteville, S.C., 1945.)

Gunther, John. *INSIDE U.S.A.* New York: Harper & Bros., 1947. Rev. ed., 1951.

Hagood, Johnson. *Memoirs of the War of Secession*. Columbia: The State Co., 1910.

Hakluyt, Richard. *The Principal Navigations, Voyages, Traffiques and Discoveries of the English Nation* . . . . 8 vols. London: Dent, 1926.

Hemphill, W. Edwin, ed. *The Papers of John C. Calhoun*, Vols. II, III, IV. Columbia: University of South Carolina Press, 1964–1969.

Hewat, Alexander. *An Historical Account of the Rise and Progress of the Colonies of South Carolina and Georgia*. 2 vols. London, 1779. (Reprinted in B.R. Carroll, ed., *Historical Collections of South Carolina*.)

Heyward, Duncan Clinch. *Seed from Madagascar*. Chapel Hill: University of North Carolina Press, 1937.

Hilton, William. *A Relation of a Discovery Lately Made on the Coast of Florida* . . . . London, 1664. (Reprinted in A.S. Salley, ed., *Narratives of Early Carolina*.)

Hodge, F.W., ed. *Spanish Explorers in the Southern United States, 1528–1543*. New York, 1907.

Holmes, A.G. and G.R. Sherrill. *Thomas Green Clemson*. Richmond: Garrett and Massie, Inc., 1937.

Horry, Peter and Mason Weems. *Life of General Francis Marion*. Philadelphia: Joseph Allen, 1809.

Humble Address of . . . *Lords Spiritual and Temporal* . . . *presented to Her Majesty on Wednesday the Thirteenth day of March, 1705, relating to the Province of Carolina* . . . . London: Printed by Charles Bill. 3 pp.

Jacobs, Thornwell, ed. *Diary of William Plumer Jacobs*. Oglethorpe University, Ga.: Oglethorpe University Press, 1937.

Jameson, J. Franklin, gen. ed. *Original Narratives of Early American History*. New York: Charles Scribner's Sons, 1907.

Jeffries, R.M. "Rural Utilities," a speech delivered at the Ruritan National Convention, Asheville, N.C., Jan. 29, 1952. From a script kindly supplied by the speaker to the editors.

Jervey, Theodore. *Robert Young Hayne and His Times.* New York: Macmillan Co., 1909.

Johnson, Guion Griffis. *A Social History of the Sea Islands . . . .* Chapel Hill: University of North Carolina Press, 1930.

Journal of the Constitutional Convention of the State of South Carolina, 1895, ed. by Francis M. Hutson. Printed for the Historical Commission of South Carolina. Columbia: State Commercial Printing Co., 1946.

Kennedy, Lionel H. and Thomas Parker. *An Official Report of the Trials of Sundry Negroes Charged with an Attempt to Raise an Insurrection in the State of South Carolina . . . Prepared and Published at the request of the Court.* Charleston, 1822.

Key, V.O. *Southern Politics in State and Nation.* New York: Alfred A. Knopf, 1949.

Kibler, Lillian. *The Life of Benjamin F. Perry.* Durham: Duke University Press, 1946.

Klingberg, Frank J., ed. *Carolina Chronicle, 1665–1717.* Berkeley: University of California Press, 1956.

———. *Carolina Chronicle: the Papers of Commissary Gideon Johnston, 1707–1716.* Berkeley: University of Carolina Press, 1946.

Knight, Edgar W., ed. *A Documentary History of the Education in the South Before 1850.* 5 vols. Chapel Hill: University of North Carolina Press, 1949–1952.

Kohn, August. *The Cotton Mills of South Carolina.* Charleston, 1907.

———. *Water Powers of South Carolina.* Columbia: The State Co., 1910.

Kohn, David, comp. *Internal Improvement in South Carolina, 1817–1828.* Washington, 1938.

Lander, Ernest McPherson, Jr. *A History of South Carolina, 1865–1960.* Columbia: University of South Carolina Press, 1970.

Laudonnière, René. *A Notable Historie Containing Four Voyages Made by Certain French Captains into Florida . . . .* London, 1598.

(The original appeared in French in 1586; long excerpts from the translation are included in Yates Snowden, ed., *History of South Carolina*, I, 5–30.)

Lee, Henry. *Memoirs of the War in the Southern Department of the United States* . . . . 2 vols. Philadelphia: Bradford & Inskeep, 1812.

Leland, John. *A Voice from South Carolina; Twelve Chapters Before Hampton; Two Chapters After Hampton, with a Journal of a Reputed Ku-Klux.* Charleston, 1879.

Lewis, Theodore, ed. "The Narratives of the Expedition of Hernando De Soto By the Gentleman of Elvas," in *Spanish Explorers in the Southern United States, 1528–1543.* New York: Charles Scribner's Sons, 1907.

McCrady, Edward. *The History of South Carolina Under the Proprietary Government, 1670–1719.* New York: Macmillan Co., 1897.

————. *South Carolina Under the Proprietary Government.* New York: Macmillan Co., 1897.

————. *South Carolina Under the Royal Government.* New York: Macmillan Co., 1899.

————. *The History of South Carolina in the Revolution, 1775–1783.* 2 vols. New York: Macmillan Co., 1901–1902.

McDowell, W.L., Jr., ed. *Journals of the Commissioners of the Indian Trade, Sept. 20, 1710–Aug. 29, 1718.* South Carolina Archives Publications: No. 1 of the Series, *The Colonial Records of South Carolina* [The Indian Books]. Columbia: S.C. Archives Dept., 1956.

————. *Documents Relating to Indian Affairs, 1750–1754.* South Carolina Archives Publications: No. 2 of the Series, *The Colonial Records of South Carolina* [The Indian Books]. Columbia: S.C. Archives Dept., 1958.

————. *Documents Relating to Indian Affairs, 1754–1765.* South Carolina Department of Archives and History Publications: No. 3 of the Series, *The Colonial Records of South Carolina* [The Indian Books]. Columbia, S.C.: University of South Carolina Press, 1970.

May, John Amasa and Joan Reynolds Faunt. *South Carolina Secedes.* Columbia: University of South Carolina Press, 1960.

Meriwether, R.L. *The Expansion of South Carolina.* Kingsport, 1940.

————, ed. *The Papers of John C. Calhoun,* Vol. I. Columbia: University of South Carolina Press, 1959.

Milligen-Johnston, George. *A Short Description of the Province of South Carolina . . . .* London, 1770.

Mills, Robert. *Statistics of South Carolina . . . .* Charleston: Hurlburt and Lloyd, 1826.

Moultrie, William. *Memoirs of the American Revolution.* 2 vols. New York: D. Longworth, 1802.

————. *Diary,* in *Charleston Yearbook,* 1884.

Nevins, Allan, ed. *America Through British Eyes.* New York: Oxford University Press, 1948.

Niles, Hezekiah, ed. *Principles and Acts of the Revolution in America . . . .* Baltimore, 1822.

North Carolina. *The Colonial Records of North Carolina,* ed. W.L. Saunders. 10 vols. Raleigh, 1886–1890. (Much South Carolina material is included, especially in Vol. 1.)

Official Records of the Union and Confederate Armies, see under U.S. Government.

Oldmixon, John. *The British Empire in America.* 2 vols. London, 1708. (South Carolina material is included in A.S. Salley, ed., *Narratives of Early Carolina,* 313–74.)

Oliphant, Mary C. Simms, et al., eds. *The Letters of William Gilmore Simms.* 5 vols. Columbia: University of South Carolina Press, 1952–1956.

Parrington, Vernon L. *The Romantic Revolution in America, 1800–1860,* in *Main Currents in American Thought.* 2 vols. New York: Harcourt, Brace & World, Inc., Harvest Book, 1927.

Perry, Benjamin F. *Biographical Sketches of Eminent American States-men, with Speeches, Addresses and Letters.* Philadelphia: Ferree Press, 1887.

―――. *Reminiscences of Public Men, with Speeches and Addresses.* Greenville: Shannon & Co., 1889.

Pike, James S. *The Prostrate State, South Carolina under Negro Government.* New York: D. Appleton & Co., 1874.

Potwin, Marjorie A. *Cotton Mill People of the Piedmont.* New York: Columbia University Press, 1927.

Pringle, Mrs. E.W.A. *Chronicles of Chicora Wood.* New York: Charles Scribner's Sons, 1922.

―――. *A Woman Rice Planter.* New York: Macmillan Co., 1914.

Purry, Peter. *Proposals by Mr. Peter Purry, of Newfchatel for Encourage-ment of Such Swiss Protestants as Should Agree to Accompany Him to Carolina to Settle . . . .* (Originally in French, about 1730; translation reprinted in B.R. Carroll, ed., *Historical Collections of South Carolina,* II, 121–40.)

Ramsay, David. *History of South Carolina, from Its First Settlement in 1670 to the Year 1808 . . . .* Charleston: David Longworth for the author, 1809.

―――. *History of the Revolution of South Carolina from a British Colony to an Independent State . . . .* 2 vols. Trenton: Isaac Collins, 1785.

Randolph, Edward. *Letter of Edward Randolph to the Board of Trade, 1699.* (Reprinted in A.S. Salley, ed., *Narratives of Early Carolina.*)

Ravenel, Mrs. Harriott Horry (Rutledge). *Eliza Pinckney.* New York: Charles Scribner's Sons, 1902.

Reynolds, John S. *Reconstruction in South Carolina.* Columbia, 1905.

Rice, J.A. *I Came Out of the Eighteenth Century.* New York: Harper & Bros., 1942.

Rice, James Henry, Jr. *Glories of the Carolina Coast.* Columbia: The R.L. Bryan Co., 1925.

Richardson, J.D.A. *A Compilation of the Messages and Papers of the Presidents*. Prepared Under the Direction of the Joint Committee on Printing, of the House and Senate. Pursuant to an Act of the Fifty-Second Congress of the United States. (With Additions and Encyclopedic Index by Private Enterprise.) 10 vols. New York: Bureau of National Literature, Inc., 1897. (Vol. VI, 310–11, contains interesting South Carolina material.)

Rivers, William J. *A Sketch of the History of South Carolina to the Close of the Proprietary Government by the Revolution of 1719 . . . .* Charleston: McCarter and Co., 1856.

Robertson, Ben. *Red Hills and Cotton*. Columbia: University of South Carolina Press, 1960. (Originally published in New York, 1942.)

Rose, Willie Lee. *Rehearsal for Reconstruction: The Port Royal Experiment*. Indianapolis: Bobbs-Merrill, 1964.

Salley, A.S., ed. *Commissions and Instructions from the Lords Proprietors of Carolina to Public Officials of South Carolina, 1685–1715*, for the South Carolina Historical Commission. Columbia: The State Co., 1916.

———. *Documents Relating to the History of South Carolina During the Revolutionary War*, for the South Carolina Historical Commission. Columbia: The State Co., 1908.

———.*The Flag of the State of South Carolina*. Bulletin No. 2, South Carolina Historical Commission Bulletins. Columbia: The State Co., 1915.

———. *Journal of the Commissioners of the Indian Trade in South Carolina, 1710–1715*, for the South Carolina Historical Commission. Columbia: The State Co., 1926.

———. *Narratives of Early Carolina, 1650–1708*. New York: Charles Scribner's Sons, 1911.

Sandford, Robert. *A Relation of a Voyage on the Coast of the Province of Carolina, 1666*. (Not printed contemporaneously; included in A.S. Salley, ed., *Narratives of Early Carolina*, 75–108.)

Saunders, William L., ed. *The Colonial Records of North Carolina*. 10 vols. Raleigh: P.M. Hale, State Printer, 1886–1890.

Schultz, Harold S. *Nationalism and Sectionalism in South Carolina, 1852–1860.* Durham: Duke University Press, 1950.

Sherrill, George and Robert H. Stoudemire. *Municipal Government in South Carolina: A Study in Public Administration.* Columbia: University of South Carolina Press, 1950.

Shipp, Albert M. *The History of Methodism in South Carolina.* Nashville: Southern Methodist Publishing House, 1883.

Simkins, Francis Butler. *Pitchfork Ben Tillman.* Baton Rouge: Louisiana State University Press, 1944.

———. *The South Old and New: A History 1820–1947.* New York: Alfred A. Knopf, 1951.

———, ed. *The Tillman Movement in South Carolina.* Durham: Duke University Press, 1926.

Simms, William Gilmore. *Sack and Destruction of the City of Columbia, S.C.,* ed. with notes by A.S. Salley. Oglethorpe University Georgia: Oglethorpe University Press, 1937.

Sims, Harry Marion, ed. *The Story of My Life, by J. Marion Sims (1813–1883.)* New York: D. Appleton & Co., 1889.

Singer, Charles G. *South Carolina in the Confederation.* Philadelphia: University of Pennsylvania, 1941.

Smith, Alfred Glaze, Jr. *Economic Readjustment of an Old Cotton State: South Carolina, 1820–1860.* Columbia: University of South Carolina Press, 1958.

Snowden, Yates, ed. *History of South Carolina.* 5 vols. Chicago: Lewis Publishing Co., 1920.

South Carolina. *Acts and Joint Resolutions of the General Assembly of the State of South Carolina* (1966). Columbia, 1967.

———. Association of Electric Cooperatives. *Report* (1966, 1968.)

———. *Code of South Carolina Laws, from its Founding through 1838.* 10 vols. Thomas Cooper, ed., Vols. I–V; David T. McCord, ed., vols. VI–X. Columbia, 1836–1840.

————. *Commons House of Assembly, Committee to Inquire into the Causes of the Failure of the Expedition to St. Augustine, Report.* (Included in B. R. Carroll, ed. *Historical Collections of South Carolina,* II, 357–59).

————. *Council Journals, Sept. 27, 1671, and Oct. 26, 1671,* in William J. Rivers, *Sketch of the History of South Carolina,* 372–74.

————. *Council Journal, Oct. 5, 1767,* in Alexander Gregg, *History of the Old Cheraws,* 135.

————. Dept. of Agriculture. *Handbook of South Carolina: Resources, Institutions and Industries of the State,* 1883, 1907, 1927, 1963.

————. Dept. of Education. *Annual Report of the State Superintendent of Education.* Columbia, 1922, 1949, 1963.

————. Dept. of Education. *The Palmetto State.* Columbia, 1952.

————. Dept. of Education. Education Survey Committee. *The Public Schools* of South Carolina. Nashville, 1948.

————. Dept. of Public Welfare. *Report,* 1920. *Public Welfare Act,* 1937. *Twelfth Annual Report,* 1949.

————. *General School Law of South Carolina* (1929).

————. Historical Society. *Collections of the Historical Society of South Carolina.* 5 vols. Richmond: William Ellis Jones, 1856–1897.

————. Laws. *Statutes at Large.* (Vols. I–X, *see Code of Laws.*)

————. *Statutes at Large,* XIII.

————. *Journal of the South Carolina Assembly,* in Hezekiah Niles, ed., *Principles and Acts of the Revolution in America.* Baltimore: 1822.

————. Public Service Commission, State of South Carolina, *Eighty-ninth Annual Report of Public Service Commission, 1966–1967.* Columbia, 1967.

————. State Board of Health. *Report,* 1941.

The State Newspaper. Ed. William D. Workman, Jr.; researcher, Eugene B. Sloan, *The Burning of Columbia.* Columbia, 1967.

Tarleton, Banastre. *History of the Campaigns of 1780 and 1781 in the Southern Province of North America*. London: T. Cadell, 1787.

Taylor, Rosser. *Antebellum South Carolina: A Social and Cultural History*. Chapel Hill: University of North Carolina Press, 1942.

Thorpe, Francis M., ed. *The Federal and State Constitutions, Colonial Charters and Other Organic Laws*. 7 vols. Washington: Government Printing Office, 1909.

Timmerman, George Bell, Jr. "Second Annual Message to the South Carolina General Assembly," January 11, 1956. From a script kindly supplied by the speaker to the editors.

United Daughters of the Confederacy, South Carolina Division. *South Carolina Women in the Confederacy*. Columbia: The State Co., 1903–1907.

United States. The Congress, *Benjamin Ryan Tillman, Memorial Addresses*. Washington: Government Printing Office, 1919.

————. Dept. of Agriculture. *REA Report,* January, 1960.

————. *Public Statutes at Large of the United States,* IV, XIV, XV.

————. Supreme Court Reports. 347 U.S. 483, *Brown v. Board of Education*.

————. War Dept. Records of Union and Confederate Armies. *Official Records of the Union and Confederate Armies, Series I, 70 v. in 128*. For the War Department. Washington: Government Printing Office, 1880–1901.

Van Deusen, J.G. *Economic Bases of Disunion in South Carolina*. New York: Columbia University Press; London, 1928.

Wallace, David Duncan. *The History of South Carolina*. 4 vols. New York: American Historical Society, Inc., 1934.

————. *The Life of Henry Laurens*. New York: G.P. Putnam's Sons, 1915.

————. *South Carolina: A Short History, 1520–1948*. Columbia: University of South Carolina Press, 1961.

————. *The South Carolina Constitution of 1895.* Columbia: Bureau of Publications, University of South Carolina, 1927.

Walsh, Walter Richard, ed. *The Writings of Christopher Gadsden, 1746–1805.* Columbia: University of South Carolina Press, 1966.

Whitefield, George. *Journal,* in Yates Snowden, ed., *History of South Carolina.*

Williams, George Croft. *A Social Interpretation of South Carolina.* Columbia: University of South Carolina Press, 1946.

Wilson, Samuel. *An Account of the Province of Carolina . . . .* London, 1682. (Reprinted in A.S. Salley, ed., *Narratives of Early Carolina.*)

Winston, George Taylor. *A Builder of the New South.* Garden City, N.J.: Doubleday, 1920.

Wolfe, John Harold. *Jeffersonian Democracy in South Carolina.* Chapel Hill: University of North Carolina Press, 1940.

————, ed. *The Constitution of 1865.* Columbia: Historical Commission of South Carolina, 1951.

Woodmason, Charles. *The Carolina Backcountry on the Eve of the American Revolution . . . .* ed. with introduction by Richard Hooker. Published for the Institute of Early American History and Culture at Williamsburg, Virginia. Chapel Hill: University of North Carolina Press, 1953.

Workman, William D., Jr. *The Case for the South.* New York: Devin-Adair Co., 1960.

Yearbook of the Association of the Graduates of the United States Military Academy (1904).

Yonge, Francis. *A Narrative of the Proceedings of the People of South Carolina in the Year 1719.* London, 1726. (Reprinted in B.R. Carroll, ed., *Historical Collections of South Carolina,* II, 141–92.)

ARTICLES AND PERIODICALS

Anderson Independent (Anderson, S. C.), March 28, 1952, Morgan Fitz, "The H-Bomb Plant Fifteen Months Later, in March 1952."

Atlantic Monthly, The (April, 1901), Daniel Chamberlain, "Reconstruction in South Carolina."

Baltimore Enquirer (Baltimore, Md.), June 24, 1873, Wade Hampton, "Burning Columbia."

Barnwell People-Sentinel (Barnwell, S. C.), November 30, 1950, "U. S. Atomic Energy Commission Announces Savannah River Plant."

Charleston Mercury (Charleston, S. C.), November 3, 1860, editorial, "What Shall South Carolina Do?"

Charleston Morning Post (Charleston, S. C.), May 1, 1786, "The New Capital at Columbia."

Charlotte Observer, The (Charlotte, N. C.), Feb. 8, 1949, "Strom Thurmond's Report to the People."
May 17, 1952, "Governor Byrnes Describes Recent Textile Progress."
Jan. 9, 1951, Austin Adkinson, "Churches of South Carolina."

Columbia Telescope (Columbia, S. C.), March 16, 1816, quoted in H. T. Cook, pp. 203–4, "David R. Williams's Enterprise."

Congressional Globe (Washington, D. C.), XIX (1850), Part I, 451–5, B. F. Perry's Speech to the S. C. House of Representatives, Dec. 11, 1850.

Daily News and Herald (Savannah, Ga.), June 27, 1866, "South Carolina Railroads."

Frank Leslie's *Illustrated Newspaper* (New York), Jan. 25, 1862, "Gen. Sherman's Official Account."

Harper's Monthly, CXXXI (1915), William Dean Howells, "In Charleston."

Historical Magazine of the Protestant Episcopal Church (Austin, Tex.), XIV (1945), "The Rev. Thomas Morritt to the Society for the Propagation of the Gospel."

Messenger, The (Pendleton, S. C.), Sept. 22, 1836, Letter from John C. Calhoun.

News and Courier, The (Charleston, S. C.), Jan. 23, 1890, article on the "Shell Manifesto."

Feb. 19, 1891, a comment on the new Columbia newspaper, *The State*.
Dec. 27, 1952, "The Clarendon School Case."
Jan. 1, 1953, "Charleston Greets the New Year."

Review of Reviews, XXV (1902), "Charleston Exposition."

Sewanee Review, IV (1895–1896), D. D. Wallace, "The South Carolina Constitutional Convention of 1895."

South Carolina Gazette (Charleston, S. C.), May 10, 1735, "The Death of Governor Robert Johnson."
July 7–14, 1739, "Inducement to Settlers."
July 27–Aug. 3, 1767, "Regulator Troubles."
Sept. 2, 1768, "Letter from Gentleman at Peedee to Friend in Town."
June 4, 1774, Opening of School at St. Thomas's Parish.
Oct. 19–31, 1765, "Liberty and No Stamp Act."

South Carolina Historical and Genealogical Magazine, LII (1951), "A Frenchman Visits Charleston in 1777."
L (1949), Thomas Thompson to the Rev. Dr. Humphreys, Secretary of the Society for the Propagation of the Gospel.
XLI (Jan. 1940), List of Men who gathered under the Liberty Tree.
XLIX (1948), "Impressions of Charleston."
LI (1950), Autobiography of William James Grayson.
LII (1951), Letter from Preston Brooks to his brother, J. H. Brooks.
XLVIII (1957), Autobiography of William J. Grayson.

South Carolina Law Quarterly, III (March, 1951), "The South Carolina Divorce Act of 1949."

South Carolina Magazine, III (Spring, 1940), J. Roy Jones, "Diversification of Farm Products."
VIII (March, 1945), John A. Zeigler, "The Santee-Cooper Project."
XIII (March, 1950), "Carolina Industry in Step with a New South, 1950."
X (April, 1947), Louise Jones DuBose, "From Plant to Port."
XVI (July, 1952), T. J. Tobias, "The Story of South Carolina's Ports."

Southern Chronicle (Columbia, S. C.), Oct. 15, 1845, Announcement of Limestone, a female academy.

Southern History Association *Publications,* VI (Nov., 1902), W. H. Wills, "A Sulky Ride in 1837."

Southern School News, The, (Nashville, Tenn.), Sept. 1963, "The Status of School Integration in South Carolina in 1963."

State, The (Columbia, S. C.), Feb. 18, 1891, editorial announcing stated purpose of new newspaper, *The State.*
Nov. 5, 1912, "Election of 'Tommy' Wilson."
Nov. 6, 1912, "Aunt of 'Tommy' Liked Result."
Nov. 6, 1912, "Charleston Glad Over Election."
Nov. 6, 1912, "Columbia Likely Wilson's Choice."

U.S. News and World Report (Nov. 19, 1954), "Senator Strom Thurmond's Write-in Election, 1954."

Virginia Gazette. Nov. 18, 1780, quoted in Draper, L.C., *Kings Mountain . . .,* "Colonel William Campbell's Official Report to the Continental Congress."

World, The (New York), Feb. 19, 1891, announcement of *The State.*

INDEX